ISBN 978-1-5279-0811-6
PIBN 10913119

# 1 MONTH OF
# FREE
# READING

at

## www.ForgottenBooks.com

By purchasing this book you are eligible for one month membership to ForgottenBooks.com, giving you unlimited access to our entire collection of over 1,000,000 titles via our web site and mobile apps.

To claim your free month visit:
www.forgottenbooks.com/free913119

7

(For complete index to entire record of six volumes, see end
of this volume.)

---

UNITED STATES OF AMERICA

v.

MOTION PICTURE PATENTS CO. ET AL.

---

RECORD—VOLUME VI.

---

**TESTIMONY OF WITNESSES FOR THE DEFENDANTS.**

---

INDEX TO VOLUME VI.

PAGE

BRYLAWSKI, AARON:

Direct Examination ..................... 3239–3246
Cross Examination ..................... 3246–3248
Redirect Examination ................... 3248

KENNEDY, JEREMIAH J.:

Direct Examination ..................... 3156–3206
Cross Examination ..................... 3206–3238
Redirect Examination ................... 3238

LUBIN, SIEGMUND:

(For Direct Examination see Vol. V, p. 3045.)
Cross Examination ..................... 3081–3089
Redirect Examination ................... 3089
Recross Examination ................... 3089–3090

PAGE

MARVIN, HARRY N.:

(For Direct Examination see Vol. III, p. 1246.)
Direct Examination, Continued............ 3252–3278
Cross Examination ..................... 3278–3397
Redirect Examination .................. 3307–3308
Redirect Examination .................. 3315–3324
Recross Examination ................... 3308–3313
Recross Examination ................... 3324


MATTHEWS, ANNA S.:

(For Direct Examination see Vol. V, pp.
   2913, 3019.)
Cross Examination ..................... 3147–3154
Redirect Examination .................. 3154–3155


SPOOR, GEORGE K.:

(For Direct Examination see Vol. V, p. 2986.)
Cross Examination ..................... 3052–3069
Redirect Examination .................. 3069
Recross Examination ................... 3069–3070


TALMADGE, ARTHUR E.:

Direct Examination .................... 3250–3252
Cross Examination ..................... 3252


WATERS, PERCIVAL L.:

(For Direct Examination see Vol. V, p. 2961.)
Cross Examination ..................... 3072–3080
Redirect Examination .................. 3080
Redirect Examination .................. 3081
Recross Examination ................... 3080–3081

# PETITIONER'S EVIDENCE IN REBUTTAL.

## (Pages 3328-3425.)

BEACH, FREDERICK C.:                              PAGE

Direct Examination ..................... 3328–3332
Cross Examination ...................... 3332–3335
Redirect Examination ................... 3335–3337
Recross Examination .................... 3337–3339

BRICK, ALFRED D.:

Direct Examination ..................... 3418
Cross Examination ...................... 3419–3420
Redirect Examination ................... 3420

BRULATOUR, JULES E.:

Direct Examination ..................... 3420
Cross Examination ...................... 3421–3422
Redirect Examination ................... 3422–3423
Redirect Examination ................... 3423
Redirect Examination ................... 3425
Recross Examination .................... 3423
Recross Examination .................... 3423–3425

STREYCKMANS, HECTOR J. (recalled):

Direct Examination ..................... 3347–3363

SWAAB, LEWIS M. (recalled):

Direct Examination ..................... 3363–3364

WEISS, ALFRED:

Direct Examination ..................... 3364–3368
Cross Examination ...................... 3379–3384
Redirect Examination ................... 3384–3385
Redirect Examination ................... 3386–3387
Recross Examination .................... 3385–3386
Recross Examination .................... 3387–3391

## DEFENDANTS' EVIDENCE IN SURREBUTTAL.
### (Pages 3427-3434.)

HENRY, THOMAS YARROW:                          PAGE

    Direct Examination ..................... 3431–3433


WRIGHT, WILLIAM:

    Direct Examination ..................... 3427–3428
    Cross Examination ..................... 3428–3430
    Redirect Examination ................... 3430
    Redirect Examination .................. 3431
    Recross Examination ................... 3430–3431


DEFENDANTS' EVIDENCE IN SURREBUTTAL ....... 3427–3434


PETITIONER'S EVIDENCE IN REBUTTAL .......... 3328–3425


STIPULATION re Defendants' Exhibit No. 164,
    being Docket Entries of Dyer & Dyer, etc... 3092


STIPULATION as to Custody of Defendants' Ex-
    hibits Nos. 174 to 183, inclusive ........... 3313


STIPULATION as to Letters Patent, Defendants'
    Exhibits Nos. 185 to 201, inclusive......... 3326


STIPULATION as to Return of Exhibits ........ 3424


STIPULATION Waiving Signatures of Witnesses.. 3435


STIPULATION as to Certification of Record ...... 3435

PETITIONER'S EXHIBITS.

VOLUME VI.

(This list includes only exhibits introduced at hearings reported in this volume.)

Exhibit 220.  Replevin Suits Instituted by Manufacturers Licensed by Motion Picture Patents Co., from March 11, 1909, to Jan. 6, 1913.................  3341
(See also Vol. I, p. 389; Vol. II, p. 1217.)

"    264.  Skipped.

"    265.  Skipped.

"    266.  Skipped.

"    267.  Opinion of Judge Coxe in the Case of The Goodwin Film & Camera Co. v. Eastman Kodak Co., United States Circuit Court of Appeals, Second Circuit .........................  3294

"    268.  Book entitled "Motion Pictures, How They Are Made and Worked," by Frederick A. Talbot, published in 1912 ...........................  3330

"    269.  For identification.  Munn & Company's Catalogue of Scientific and Technical Books for 1914.............  3336

"    270.  Book entitled "Romance of Modern Photography," by Charles R. Gibson, F.R.S.E. ...................  3337

  PAGE

Exhibit 271. Article by George Kleine in Show
               World, March 7, 1908, entitled
               "Kleine Talks—Biograph Company
               Denies Validity of Patents".......  3347
               (See also Govt.'s Ex. 263, Vol. V,
               p. 2509.)

  "      272. Article by George Kleine in Show
               World, April 4, 1909, entitled
               "Kleine Disputes Validity of Edison
               Patents" ........................  3357

  "      273. Opinion of Circuit Court of Appeals,
               Second Circuit, March 18, 1911, in
               Case of Motion Picture Patents Co.
               v. Yankee Film Co., and M. P. P. Co.
               v. William Steiner (187 Fed., 1017)  3369

  "      274. Testimony given by Harry N. Marvin
               in Case of Greater New York Film
               Rental Co. v. Biograph Co. and Gen-
               eral Film Co., in the District Court
               of the United States, Southern Dis-
               trict of New York, Sept. 9, 1913..  3370

  "      275. Testimony given by Frank L. Dyer in
               Case of Greater New York Film
               Rental Co. v. Biograph Co. and Gen-
               eral Film Co., in the District Court
               of the United States, Southern Dis-
               trict of New York, Oct. 23, 1913....  3376

  "      275a. Suits brought under the Latham Pat-
               ent No. 707,934, by Motion Picture
               Patents Co., between June 14, 1909,
               and July 15, 1911...............  3391

  "      276. Suits brought under the Pross Patent
               No. 722,382, by Motion Picture Pat-
               ents Co., between June 14, 1909, and
               July 15, 1911 ..................  3392

PAGE

Exhibit 277. Opinion of the Circuit Court of Ap-
peals, Second Circuit, in case of
Motion Picture Patents Co. v. The
Independent Moving Picture Com-
pany of America (200 Fed., 411),
Aug. 10, 1912, on the Latham Patent
No. 707,934 ...................... 3393

"       278. Strip of Negative Motion Picture Film  3418

"       279. Strip of Positive Motion Picture Film  3418

DEFENDANTS' EXHIBITS.

VOLUME VI.

(This list includes only exhibits introduced at hearings
reported in this volume.)

Exhibit 164. Docket Entries of Dyer & Dyer, Gifford
& Bull, and Kerr, Page & Cooper *re*
various suits by Edison on Letters
Patent No. 589,168, and Reissue
Patents Nos. 12,037, 12,038 and
12,192, brought between 1897 and
1909 .......................... 3093

"       165. Contract between Theatre Film Supply
Co., Birmingham, Ala., and General
Film Co., dated Aug. 23, 1910...... 3170

"       166. Letter, General Film Co. to Theatre
Film Supply Co., March 21, 1912... 3184

"       167. Letter, Theatre Film Supply Co. to J.
J. Kennedy on Letterhead of South-
ern Amusement & Supply Co., Aug.
21, 1911 ........................ 3186

PAGE

Exhibit 168. Letter, J. J. Kennedy to A. R. Boone, President, Theatre Film Supply Co., Aug. 26, 1911.................... 3188

" 169. Letter, Theatre Film Supply Co. to J. J. Kennedy, Aug. 31, 1911........ 3189

" 170. Letter, Theatre Film Supply Co. to J. J. Kennedy, Sept. 9, 1911......... 3190

" 171. Letter, J. J. Kennedy to Theatre Film Supply Co., Dec. 29, 1910......... 3191

172. Statement of cost of Branches of General Film Co., as per balance sheet of December 30, 1911. (See, also, Petitioner's Exhibit 62, Vol. I, p. 190.) ......................... 3200

" 173. Skipped.

" 174. Motion Picture Camera, known as the Warwick Camera ............... 3261

" 175. Projecting Machine, known as the Power Projecting Machine ....... 3261

" 176. Negative Motion Picture Film ...... 3261

" 177. Positive Motion Picture Film ....... 3262

" 178. Defendants' Illustrative Apparatus.... 3263

" 179. Photographs, marked 1 to 7, showing Defendants' Illustrative Apparaus; Defendants' Exhibit 178 ......... 3266

PAGE

Exhibit 180.  Chart explanatory of Photograph No.
1, Defendants' Exhibit 179........  3266

"        181.  Chart explanatory of Photograph No.
2, Defendants' Exhibit 179.........  3267

"        182.  Chart explanatory of Photograph No.
5, Defendants' Exhibit 179........  3268

"        183.  Chart explanatory of Photograph No.
7, Defendants' Exhibit 179........  3269

"        184.  List of Suits brought on Camera Patent No. 12,037 after the Assignment
of that Patent to Motion Picture
Patents Co. ....................  3270

"        184a. Motion Picture Scenario, etc., from
Evening Sun, March 30, 1914......  3316

"        185.  Edison Reissue Patent No. 12,037,
dated Sept. 30, 1902.............  3326

"        186.  Edison Reissue Patent No. 13,329,
dated Dec. 5, 1911...............  3326

"        187.  Edison Reissue Patent No. 12,192,
dated Jan. 12, 1904.............  3326

"        188.  Smith Patent No. 673,329, dated April
30, 1901 ......................  3326

"        189.  Smith Patent No. 744,251, dated Nov.
17, 1903 ......................  3326

"        190.  Smith Patent No. 770,937, dated Sept.
27, 1904 ......................  3326

"        191.  Smith Patent No. 771,280, dated Oct.
4, 1904 ......................  3326

PAGE

Exhibit 192. Ellwood Patent No. 785,205, dated
March 21, 1905................... 3326

" 193. Smith Patent No. 785,237, dated March
21, 1905 ...................... 3326

" 194. Armat atent No. 578,185, dated March
2, 1897 ...................... 3326

" 195. Armat Patent No. 580,749, dated April
13, 1897 ...................... 3326

" 196. Jenkins and Armat Patent No. 586,-
953, dated July 20, 1897.......... 3326

" 197. Steward and Frost Patent No. 588,916,
dated Aug. 24, 1897............. 3326

" 198. Casler Patent No. 629,063, dated July
18, 1889 ...................... 3326

" 199. Armat Patent No. 673,992, dated May
14, 1901 ...................... 3326

" 200. Latham Patent No. 707,934, dated
Aug. 26, 1902.................. 3326

" 201. Pross Patent No. 722,382, dated March
10, 1903 ...................... 3326

" 202. Last page of paper wrapper of Book
entitled "Moving Pictures," by Frederick A. Talbot, advertising the
Books entitled "Railway Conquest
of the World" and "Steamship Conquest of the World," by the same
author ........................ 3338

" 203. For identification. Statement of Business done by the Alfred Weiss
Branch of the General Film Co. for
the week ended July 11, 1910...... 3382

PAGE

Exhibit 204. For identification. Statement of Business done by the Alfred Weiss Branch of the General Film Co. for Week ended July 16, 1910......... 3383

"      205. For identification. Statement of Business done by the Alfred Weiss Branch of the General Film Co. for Week ended July 23, 1910........ 3383

"      206. For identification. Statement of Business done by the Alfred Weiss Branch of the General Film Co. for Week ended July 30, 1910........ 3384

"      207. For identification. Statement of Business done by the Alfred Weiss Branch of the General Film Co. for Week ended Aug. 10, 1910........ 3389

"      208. For identification. Statement of Business done by the Alfred Weiss Branch of the General Film Co. for Week ended Aug. 13, 1910........ 3390

"      209. For identification. Statement of Business done by the Alfred Weiss Branch of the General Film Co. for Week ended Aug. 20, 1910........ 3390

"      210. For identification. Statement of Business done by the Alfred Weiss Branch of the General Film Co. for Week ended Aug. 27, 1910........ 3390

"      211. For identification. Statement of Business done by the Alfred Weiss Branch of the General Film Co. for Week ended Sept. 3, 1910......... 3391

PAGE

Exhibit 212. For identification. Statement of Business done by the Alfred Weiss Branch of the General Film Co. for Week ended Sept. 10, 1910........ 3391

" 213. Statement showing Receipts and Expenses of the Alfred Weiss Branch of the General Film Co. for Week ended July 9, 1910, and for the nine succeeding weeks ............... 3433

" 214. Article Published in Harper's Weekly June 13, 1891, page 446, entitled "Edison Kinetograph, by George Parsons Lathrop" ............... 3434

## Volume VI.

1

# DISTRICT COURT OF THE UNITED STATES

### FOR THE EASTERN DISTRICT OF PENNSYLVANIA.

| | |
|---|---|
| UNITED STATES OF AMERICA,<br>Petitioner,<br><br>*v.*<br><br>MOTION PICTURE PATENTS CO. and others.<br>Defendants. | No. 889.<br>Sept. Sess., 1912. |

2

NEW YORK CITY, March 12, 1914.

The hearings were resumed pursuant to adjournment on this March 12, 1914, at 10:30 o'clock A. M., at Room 159, Manhattan Hotel, New York City.

Present on behalf of the Petitioner, Hon. EDWIN P. GROSVENOR, Special Assistant to the Attorney General.

JOSEPH R. DARLING, Esq., Special Agent.

CHARLES F. KINGSLEY, Esq., GEORGE R. WILLIS, Esq., and FRED R. WILLIAMS, Esq., appearing for Motion Picture Patents Company, Biograph Company, Jeremiah J. Kennedy, Harry N. Marvin, Armat Moving Picture Company, Melies Manufacturing Co. and Gaston Melies.

J. H. CALDWELL, Esq., and H. K. STOCKTON, Esq., appearing for William Pelzer, General Film Company, Thomas A. Edison, Inc., Kalem Company, Inc., Pathe Freres, Frank L. Dyer, Samuel Long and J. A. Berst.

HENRY MELVILLE, Esq., attorney for George Kleine, Essanay Film Manufacturing Company, Selig Polyscope, George K. Spoor and W. N. Selig.

JAMES J. ALLEN, Esq., appearing for Vitagraph Company of America, and Albert E. Smith.

3

4

1       Thereupon GEORGE K. SPOOR, resumed the stand for cross examination.

Cross examination by Mr. GROSVENOR:

Q. Mr. Spoor, what was your first connection with the business of entertaining the public? A. Why, I conducted an exhibition business of moving pictures, that is, I furnished what is known as a complete service to the larger vaudeville theatres through the Middle West and the West as part of the vaudeville programs under contract, from 2   week to week.

Q. You furnished the entertainers? A. No, no.

Q. Or did you furnish the entertainment? A. I furnished the entertainment.

Q. You, in your own person, furnished the entertainment? A. Oh, pardon me, no, sir, I am not guilty.

Q. What were you, manager for others? A. I don't believe I got your question quite right. May I have the question read first?

3       The last five questions and answers were read to the witness.

The Witness: Does that not answer it?

By Mr. GROSVENOR:

Q. Were you one of the incorporators of the General Film Company? A. Yes, sir.

Q. I wish you would look at the answers you gave on your direct examination at page 2996. A. All right.

Q. I refer to: "Q. So far as you were concerned, 4   was it your purpose in organizing, or assisting to organize the General Film Company, to acquire all of the licensed exchanges in the United States? A. No, not at all, sir. Q. Did you hear any of your associates in that organization express any such purpose or intention? A. No, sir, I never did hear anything of the kind." Is there anything you wish to add to those answers? A. No, sir.

Q. Do you wish to change those answers in any way? A. No, sir.

Q. I show you Petitioner's Exhibit No. 78, printed in

Volume 1, at page 251, being a letter addressed by J. J. [1]
Kennedy, President of the General Film Company, dated
January 23rd, 1912, to Mr. William Pelzer, Secretary of
the General Film Company. Please read that exhibit? A.
Yes, sir, I have read it.

Q. Was Mr. J. J. Kennedy, who signed that letter, the
President of the General Film Company? A. Yes, sir.

Q. And was he the officer of the company who had in
charge the buying of the various rental exchanges? A. Mr.
Kennedy purchased the rental exchanges, yes, sir.

Q. He was the officer of the General Film Company who
had in charge that matter for the company? A. Yes, sir. [2]

Q. I read to you the beginning of that letter: "Dear
Sir: Some time before the General Film Company
was organized, an estimate of the value of the business of
exchanges leasing licensed motion pictures, was made by
men familiar with the manufacture of motion pictures, and
also with the business of exchanges. According to this estimate, the value of said business was $3,468,847." Did you
help to make up that estimate? A. No, sir.

Q. You knew about its having been made? A. I knew
nothing about it, sir. [3]

Q. I ask you to read Petitioner's Exhibit No. 80, printed
in Volume 1 of the record, page 265, being a copy of the
minutes of a meeting of the Board of Directors of the General Film Company held October 11th, 1910? A. I have
read it.

Q. These minutes report as present, "Messrs. Kennedy,
Berst, Dyer, Kleine, Long, Lubin, Selig, Smith, Spoor, and
Pelzer, Secretary." Each of the persons so named was a
Director or officer or principal owner in one of the manu-
facturing companies licensed by the Patents Company? A.
I think so. [4]

Q. Leaving out Mr. Pelzer, Secretary, and considering
the names of the others, you may state whether or not any
one of the licensed companies was represented by more
than one person on the Board of Directors of the General
Film Company on the date stated in the minutes, namely,
October 11th, 1910? A. There was but one of each there.

Q. The nine persons named, Kennedy, Berst, Dyer, Kleine,
Long, Lubin, Selig, Smith, and Spoor were all Directors of
the General Film Company A. Yes sir.

1    Q. Did any one go on the Board of Directors of the General Film Company when it was organized who was not an officer, Director, or principal owner of one of the companies licensed by the Motion Picture Patents Company? A. I think not. I would not be sure as to that, though.

Q. Can you recall any one that was not connected with a licensed company? A. I don't recall any one.

Q. Did any one of the licensed companies have more than one representative on the Board of Directors of the General Film Company? A. No, sir.

Q. And each of the licensed companies had one representative on that Board? A. Yes, sir.

2

Q. These minutes continue: "Mr. Kennedy reported on behalf of the Executive Committee that the Company had purchased 39 exchanges, and made the following detailed report of conditions as of October 10, 1910:

"Number of licensed exchanges in entire country, including Yale Company of St. Louis, 59; owned by General Film Company, 39; not owned by General Film Company, 20; percentage of exchanges owned by General Film Company, 66 per cent.; percentage of business of entire country controlled by General Film Company, based on reels, 71 per cent." You may state how long the General Film Company had been doing business at the time of this meeting, namely, October 11th, 1910? A. I should say, six months.

3

Q. When the General Film Company was organized was it a consolidation of a number of existing exchanges, or is it the fact that all the exchanges acquired by it were acquired after its organization? A. They were acquired after its organization.

Q. Then the 39 exchanges named here as owned by the General Film Company had all been acquired in a period of six months? A. Yes, sir, I would say so.

4

Q. The minutes continue:

|  | Stock. | Cash. |
| --- | --- | --- |
| "Payments authorized for Exchanges owned Oct. 10th... | $591,400 | $1,483,200 |
| Prices—actual—including interest amounting to $90,500 | 535,900 | 1,369,600 |
| Saving .................. | 55,500 | 113,600 |
| Combined saving .......... |  | 169,100 |

1

Please state when the payments named there and stated to be authorized for exchanges owned October 10th, were authorized? A. I don't know of any authorization.

Q. What does that phrase mean, then, in the minutes, being the minutes of a meeting at which you are reported by the minutes to have been present, "Payments authorized for exchanges owned October 10th"?

Mr. CALDWELL: Objected to, as calling for the witness' interpretation of the minutes.

2

The Witness: I don't know what it means.

By Mr. GROSVENOR:

Q. Do you have any recollection of such authority being conferred on Mr. Kennedy, or the Executive Committee by the Board of Directors? A. No, I do not. In a number of instances Mr. Kennedy was authorized or a payment for an exchange was authorized after it had been bought. It was authorized afterwards in several instances, as I remember.

Q. Now, this table which I have read to you compares actual payments with payments authorized, and points out the saving? A. I never knew of any authorization for payments of that kind.

3

Q. Do you recall any discussion at this meeting after Mr. Kennedy had made this report, as stated in the minutes, on behalf of the Executive Committee? A. I don't think there was any discussion of any length, or of any great importance. I think it was merely listened to. I remember of hearing something of some figures, and it passed out of my mind very quickly.

Q. But you do recall the fact that those figures were read to the meeting? A. There were some figures read. I presume those, they might have been those, or some others; something of that kind.

4

Q. You remember something of that kind, that is, something relating to the acquisition of the exchange, and the number of exchanges acquired by the General Film Company? A. Yes, sir.

Q. This continues: "Total payments authorized for all exchanges in entire country, Stock $988,800, Cash $2,480,-000." Does that sentence refresh your recollection as to

authorization being conferred on the Executive Committee?
A. No, I don't remember anything of any authorization, no,
sir.

Q. Can you explain in any way how such a statement appeared in the minutes of the meeting of the Directors of the
General Film Company of this date?

> Mr. Caldwell: Objected to, as calling for the
> opinion of the witness as to the acts of the Secretary
> in recording the minutes, and as to what he meant
> by it.
> Mr. Grosvenor: I answer that objection by stating that Mr. Pelzer has already been examined about
> this matter, and several others present at the meeting, without any explanation being given, and it therefore seems proper to examine this witness, who was
> present, about it.  .
> Mr. Caldwell: That does not necessarily open the
> door to call for this witness' opinion for anything
> contained in the minutes, or for an explanation by him
> of the minutes.

The Witness: No, I cannot explain it.

By Mr. Grosvenor:

Q. These minutes use the phrase, "Payments authorized
for all Exchanges in entire country." Do you recall any
discussion on the subject of how much it would cost to acquire all the exchanges in the entire country? A. I do not,
no, sir.

Q. And you do not recall the estimate which Mr. Kennedy stated in his letter to Pelzer, to which I have called
your attention, being Petitioner's Exhibit No. 78, in Volume
1, at page 251, as an estimate made "some time before the
General Film Company was organized?" A. No, sir, I never
heard of it.

Q. Mr. Spoor, I direct your attention to the fact that
the figure given in Mr. Kennedy's letter as the value of
the entire business in the country, according to estimate
made some time before the General Film Company was
organized, was $3,468,847. I also direct your attention
to the fact that the minutes of this meeting of October

11th, 1910, state that the total payments authorized for all exchanges in entire country in stock and in cash was $3,468,800. Does this correspondence between the figure given in the estimate and the figure given in the authorization refresh your recollection as to any such authorization having been given? A. I don't remember anything of any authorization.

Q. Does it refresh your recollection in any manner as to such an estimate having been made before the General Film Company was organized? A. I know of no such estimate.

Q. I direct your attention, Mr. Spoor, to Petitioner's Exhibit No. 83, being the minutes of a meeting of the Board of Directors, held January 16th, 1911, printed in Volume 1, page 278. A. I have read it.

Q. These minutes state that there were present, Messrs. Kennedy, Berst, Dyer, Kleine, Long, Lubin, Selig, Spoor and Pelzer, Secretary; also Messrs Blackton, Marvin, Paul Melies and Rock. The nine individuals first named were the Directors of the General Film Company? A. Yes, sir.

Q. And the persons named as also being present, Blackton, Marvin, Paul Melies and Rock, were connected with some of the licensed manufacturers? A. Yes, sir.

Q. Mr. Marvin was one of the officers at that time, of the Motion Picture Patents Company? A. Yes, sir.

Q. He was the President? A. He was one of the officers.

Q. Either the President or the Vice-President? A. Yes, sir.

Q. These minutes use this phrase, page 279, folio 1, Volume 1: "Original estimate of value of exchanges not bought but still licensed, $351,300, cash, and stock $140,100." Do you know when that original estimate referred to in the minutes was made? A. I do not, no, sir.

Q. Did you ever see such an estimate? A. No, sir, I know nothing of any estimate.

Q. A number of the licenses of exchanges were cancelled in the year 1910, is that not the fact, by the Patents Company? A. Yes, sir, there were some licenses cancelled, but I don't know that there were any more than in 1909. They were cancelled right along.

Q. Mr. Albert Smith, of the Vitagraph Company, has testified that he was present at various meetings of the

1   licensed manufacturers in 1909, and also in 1910 and 1911, at which was considered, from time to time, the subject of cancelling the licenses of various rental exchanges. Do you recall attending any such meetings? A. Yes, sir.

Q. He has also testified that after this subject had been discussed by the manufacturers, they made recommendations from time to time to the Motion Picture Patents Company. Is your recollection in accord with his, on that point? A. In a number of instances, perhaps.

Q. Is it not a fact that one representative of each of the licensed manufacturers attended the meetings to which 2  I have referred? A. Generally.

Q. Do you have any recollection of any discussion being had at this meeting of the Directors of the General Film Company, January 16th, 1911, referred to in these minutes, on this "Original Estimate of Value of Exchanges not Bought but Still Licensed?" A. No, I have no recollection of any, sir.

Q. Are you able to explain how that term came into the minutes? A. No, I do not know.

Q. Is there any competition to-day between the li-3  censed manufacturers in respect to the prices at which they lease their output to the General Film Company? A. I think the price is the same, except for special features, or something of that kind.

Q. That is, it is so much per foot? A. Yes, sir.

Q. And that price per foot is the same for each of the licensed manufacturers? A. As far as I know.

Q. You testified that at the time the General Film Company was organized, you had a rental exchange in Chicago, did you not? A. Yes, sir.

Q. Which you subsequently sold to the General Film 4  Company? A. Yes, sir.

Q. Did you have any interest in the exhibiting end of the business at that time? A. I had several theatres in north Michigan, Calumet, and Hancock, Michigan, Ishpeming, and Negaunee, four or five, I had up in that country, and one in Chicago, the Columbia Theatre, on North Clark Street.

Q. Do you still retain your interests in the exhibiting end of the business? A. No, sir.

Q. Do you own any theatres to-day? A. There is one

of them left in Laurium, Michigan. I disposed of one in
Hancock, Michigan, about eight months ago.

Q. On direct examination, you referred to the meeting
of December 8th, 1908. That was the meeting at which
each of the manufacturers signed the license agreements
with the Patents Company? A. Yes, sir.

Q. And at that meeting the license agreement was read
to the assembled manufacturers before it was executed? A.
Yes, sir.

Q. And after it had been read and discussed by the
various manufacturers, each of them signed one of those
agreements? A. Yes, sir, I think so.

Q. You also testified, on direct examination, in regard
to the meeting in January, 1909. That was the time the
exchange agreements were submitted to the exchange men
who had gathered here in New York City? A. I probably
attended that meeting, yes, sir.

Q. You lived in Chicago at that time? A. Yes, sir.

Q. And you had come East with the other manufacturers, in order to be present in New York when that
subject was presented to the exchange men? A. I don't
believe I knew that that was something that would come
up at the meeting. I came on in the regular way to the
meeting.

Q. What meeting did you come to attend in the regular
way? A. Well, all of them. I never had any advance information as to what was going to be done or come up at
any meeting.

Q. Now, what was that a meeting of? I refer to the
meeting in January, 1909? A. After I came on here to
New York I might have gone down to the Edison office,
or it might be there was a meeting of the licensees down
there. That is probably the only thing I had in mind. In
1909?

Q. January, 1909, yes. A. There was a meeting of some
film men, some film exchange men, at the Imperial Hotel,
I think.

Q. That was in January, 1909? A. I won't be sure as
to the date, but there was a meeting there. Yes, in 1909.

Q. And that was the meeting at which they considered
this subject of having license exchange agreements between

1  the Patents Company and the rental exchanges? A. I was not at the meeting, but I understood they did, yes.

Q. You were in New York at the time? A. Yes, sir, I was in New York.

Q. That was a very important development in the motion picture business, was it not? A. Yes, it was.

Q. And you came on to be present in New York with the other manufacturers when the matter was brought up? A. Yes, I was here.

Q. Many exchange men had gathered from all parts of the country in order to be present at that meeting? A.
2  There was a number of exchange men here, yes, sir.

Q. And after the proposed license agreements were submitted to the exchange men, was there not considerable talk and comment among the exchange men and the motion picture men on that subject?

Mr. CALDWELL: Objected to, the witness having already stated that he was not present at the meeting.

3  The Witness: I was not at the meeting, sir.

Mr. GROSVENOR: Read the question to the witness, please.

The question was repeated by the Examiner to the witness as follows:

"Q. And after the proposed license agreements were submitted to the exchange men, was there not considerable talk and comment among the exchange men and the motion picture men on that subject?"

Mr. GROSVENOR: I refer, not necessarily to the
4  meeting, but in the business was there a great deal of talk about this change in the methods of doing business?

The Witness: Yes, sir, there was.

By Mr. GROSVENOR:

Q. And when you were in New York at that time did you not talk with exchange men about this proposed change in the method of doing business? A. Very few, yes, sir.

1

Q. Was that not the subject that was uppermost in the minds of motion picture men at that time? A. Yes; yes, sir.

Q. Now, it was at that time that you say you went to Jack's with Kleine and Selig, and met Mr. Swanson there? A. It was late that night.

Q. And didn't you and Swanson, and Kleine and Selig, talk about this new development in the motion picture business, that is, this new method of doing business with the exchange men? A. We must have talked something concerning it. We must have said something, because it was in the air.

2

Q. You must have had a talk about it because it was a subject that was uppermost in the minds of you all at that time? A. Yes, sir, I should say so, that we made some reference to it, but not to any great length.

Q. You referred on direct examination to the condition of Mr. Swanson when he was at the Republican Club with you three gentlemen on that evening. What time was it when you and Mr. Swanson parted on that occasion? A. Why, I think Mr. Swanson went to his room, I should say, maybe three o'clock.

Q. Three o'clock in the morning? A. Yes, sir, I would say so.

3

Q. You four Chicago gentlemen, Mr. Kleine, Mr. Selig, yourself, and Mr. Swanson, had been together a large part of that night and early morning? A. No, that was not correct. We had not been together. We went into Jack's place. Mr. Selig and Mr. Kleine and myself, quite late, I should say after one o'clock, and Mr. Swanson was there with a number of film exchange men, there must have been fifteen or twenty of them, and they had their table piled full of wine, and everything you could think of. They were there, and Mr. Kleine, Mr. Selig and myself, because we know these men, we spoke to the various men, but did not join their table, but went over and sat down at another table across the way—they couldn't get any more tables in there—and Mr. Swanson came over there and spoke to us, and we could not get rid of him. He stuck like glue. We didn't want him.

4

Q. What did he want to talk to you about? A. I don't know.

Q. Was it not a fact that he was trying to talk to you

1  about this new license exchange agreement? A. Well, I wonder why he didn't talk about it then?

Q. I am asking you was that not the subject he was discussing? A. No, sir, he was not.

Q. What was your condition at the time you described Mr. Swanson's condition on page 3003? A. My condition?

Q. Yes. A. Why, I was perfectly all right. I don't drink except moderately, and very moderately.

Q. You had taken some drinks that night? A. Oh, I might have had one or two drinks, but not any more; I am strong for water, and always have been.

2  Q. Did you have any drinks at Jack's? A. That is where I had them.

Q. What were you doing before you went to Jack's? A. I think we had been over around the Knickerbocker, and may be over in the Astor.

Q. Then, after you went back to the Republican Club did you have some drinks there? A. Had some water.

Q. What is that? A. I had some water.

Q. Did you have anything but water? A. Nothing but water.

3  Q. Now, Mr. Caldwell read to you on page 3002 a question and answer addressed to Mr. Swanson on direct examination as follows:

" 'Q. Was anything said about patents during this conversation at the Republican Club? A. They went over the ground, of course, that they had accumulated all the available patents on projecting machines, and on cameras, and on films, that it was possible to get, and, that they had formed that into a holding company to be known as the Motion Picture Patents Company; that they had made arrangements with the Eastman Kodak Company to get the exclusive use of

4  the Eastman stock, and that a competitor would have but very little chance entering the field, owing to the fact that they had all the patents on the various apparatus, and particularly the Eastman stock, the Eastman raw stock.' What truth, if any, is there in that statement of Swanson's? A. I don't know that there is any truth in it." Mr. Spoor, is it not a fact that the Motion Picture Patents Company did enter into an arrangement with the Eastman Kodak Company providing that the Eastman Company should not sup-

ply raw film to manufacturers not licensed by the Patents 1
Company?

Mr. CALDWELL: Objected to, as calling for the witness' interpretation of a written contract which is already in evidence, and not proper cross examination.

Mr. GROSVENOR: He said there was not any truth in Swanson's statement, and I am asking him now if it was not the fact—

Mr. CALDWELL: You are asking him about the contents of that contract.

Mr. GROSVENOR: Read him the question, Mr. Examiner.

The question was read to the witness by the Examiner as follows:

"Q. Now, Mr. Caldwell read to you on page 3002 a question and answer addressed to Mr. Swanson on direct examination as follows: 'Q. Was anything said about patents during this conversation at the Republican Club? A. They went over the ground, of course, that they had accumulated all the available patents on projecting machines, and on cameras, and on films, that it was possible to get, and, that they had formed that into a holding company to be known as the Motion Picture Patents Company; that they had made arrangements with the Eastman Kodak Company to get the exclusive use of the Eastman raw stock, and that a competitor would have but very little chance entering the field, owing to the fact that they had all the patents on the various apparatus, and, particularly, the Eastman stock, the Eastman raw stock. What truth, if any, is there in that statement of Swanson's? A. I don't know that there is any truth in it.' Mr. Spoor, is it not a fact that the Motion Picture Patents Company did enter into an arrangement with the Eastman Kodak Company providing that the Eastman Company should not supply raw film to manufacturers not licensed by the Patents Company?"

The Witness: It is a fact that later we learned of that, but I don't believe that I knew anything of it at that particular time that Mr. Swanson speaks of.

1    By Mr. Grosvenor:

Q. Don't you know that during the period of the Edison licensees practically a similar arrangement had been completed with the Eastman Company? A. I don't recall that; no, sir. I don't know that I ever knew that. The Biograph Company was getting film from Eastman.

Q. When you stated on direct examination, "I don't know that there is any truth in it," what you mean to say is, you don't know anything about that subject? A. What I mean to say is I don't know that there is any truth in the fact that
2    Mr. Swanson said that we stated, I, or Mr. Kleine or Mr. Selig, stated all that to him.

Q. You do not mean to deny the fact that there was an arrangement between the Patents Company and the Eastman Kodak Company preventing the Eastman Kodak Company from selling to manufacturers not licensed by the Patents Company? A. There was some kind of an arrangement, yes, sir, but at that time you speak of, that night that you are referring to Mr. Swanson, I don't believe we knew anything of it at that time. I don't believe we had any information at that time that the Eastman Company would not sell them
3    film.

Q. You had signed your contract with the Patents Company before this meeting with Swanson, had you not? A. I won't be sure of that without looking to or referring to some papers.

Q. Didn't you sign the contract with the Patents Company in December, 1908? A. Yes, sir, we did; that is right.

Q. And you did sign the contract with the Patents Company before this meeting in New York City with Swanson? A. Yes, sir.

4    Q. Don't you know that that contract that you signed with the Patents Company in December, 1908, provided that an agreement should be entered into with the manufacturer of raw film preventing that manufacturer of raw film from supplying film to anybody except the licensed manufacturers?

Mr. Caldwell: Objected to as stating, and incorrectly stating, the legal effect of a written instrument which is in evidence.

Mr. Kingsley: Objected to, on the ground that it is not proper cross examination, and it does not tend

to discredit the witness' answer with respect to the ¹
alleged conversation with William H. Swanson, and
that it does not tend to substantiate the statement
which William H. Swanson made.

The Witness: I do not recall that it was in the license
agreement, and my impression was it was something I learned
of later. I don't believe I ever read that license agreement
after that.

By Mr. GROSVENOR:
                                                        2
Q. You were fresher about the contents of that license
agreement in January, 1909, than you are today?

Mr. KINGSLEY: Objected to, as immaterial, and
not proper cross examination.

The Witness: I might have been, and I ought to have
been.

By Mr. GROSVENOR:
                                                        3
Q. You knew that that agreement provided that such an
arrangement should be entered into, that is, preventing the
sale of raw film to the manufacturers not licensed?

Mr. CALDWELL: Objected to, on the ground that
the license agreement with the Motion Picture Patents Company does not contain any such provision.

The Witness: I must have known it.

By Mr. GROSVENOR:                                       4

Q. Now, does that reflection on the contents of the
license agreement refresh your recollection as to this subject having been discussed between you and Swanson, and
Selig, and Kleine, on this night in January? A. No, it
does not. I don't think we discussed with Mr. Swanson
very much of anything.

Q. You testified on direct examination that there had
been a meeting on the day of this talk with Swanson, and

1    that there was another meeting the next day.  Did you go
to the meeting the next day?  A. No, sir.

Q. Did you go to either of the meetings at the Imperial?
A. No, sir, I did not.

Q. Well, then, how do you know at which of these meetings the license exchange agreement had been submitted to
the rental exchange men?

Mr. CALDWELL: Objected to, on the ground that
the witness has not made any such statement in his
direct examination that he did know.

2

The Witness: I didn't know that they had been.  I
heard it on the street.

Mr. GROSVENOR: What was the meeting on the
second day about?

The Witness: I don't know.  I was not present at that
meeting.

3            Mr. CALDWELL: Objected to, on the ground that
the witness stated that he did not attend the meeting.

Mr. KINGSLEY: Objected to, on the ground that
the question calls for hearsay testimony.

Mr. GROSVENOR: The witness on direct examination testified as to the first meeting in order to refute
some of the testimony of Mr. Swanson, and this is
proper on cross examination.

Mr. MELVILLE: I object to that statement as
being an incorrect statement of what the witness
testified to, and I refer to the record.

4            Mr. GROSVENOR: Counsel has evidently not read
the record.  I direct your attention to page 3007, Vol.
V, of your direct examination: "Q. Do you recall
whether the night that Swanson spent at the Republican Club, to which reference has just been had,
was the night preceding the convention of the F. S.
A. at the Imperial Hotel?  A. No, there had been
a convention during that day, and they were going to,
I guess, have another meeting the next morning, of

some kind, but they had had their convention that
very day."

Mr. CALDWELL: That does not justify the question propounded to this witness as to what transpired
at that meeting.

Mr. GROSVENOR: It is his direct testimony as to
what transpired. He calls it a "convention," and
gives the direct implication there that the agreement
had been submitted before this meeting with Mr.
Swanson.

Mr. CALDWELL: Not at all.

Mr. GROSVENOR: In contradiction of the testimony of Swanson.

By Mr. GROSVENOR:

Q. Now, witness, I direct your attention to the reading
of the testimony given by you on direct examination, at
page 3007, Vol. V: "Q. Do you recall whether the night that
Swanson spent at the Republican Club, to which reference
has just been had, was the night preceding the convention
of the F. S. A. at the Imperial Hotel? A. No, there had
been a convention during that day, and they were going
to, I guess, have another meeting the next morning, of
some kind, but they had had their convention that very
day." Do you know when the license exchange agreement
was submitted to the exchange men? A. No, I do not.

Q. Had you been down to the hotel? A. Not at the
meeting.

Q. Had you been down to the Imperial Hotel? A. I was
in there in the early evening after their meeting the first
day, in the office, or out in the lobby, for a few minutes.

Q. You had been, then, to the Imperial Hotel, during
the day of the convention?

Mr. KINGSLEY: Objected to, on the ground that
the witness has already answered he was there in
the evening after the convention.

The Witness: I had been there in the early evening.

By Mr. GROSVENOR:

Q. That is, before dinner? A. Just before dinner.

1    Q. And the convention was in the afternoon? A. I believe it was.

Q. Did you meet some of the manufacturers down there? A. I think Mr. Selig was with me. If he was not, I met him there.

Q. Did you meet any of the other manufacturers there? A. I think I saw Mr. Long there for a few minutes.

Q. Did you meet any of the others? A. I don't recall any more.

Q. You met quite a number of exchange men whom you
2  knew? A. Well, five or six. I saw five or six I knew, there. I remember distinctly of talking with one of them from Ohio.

Q. What was the Western Committee? A. The Western Committee was not an official committee. Out in the West, in Chicago, and in the vicinity, the exhibitors and exchange men were not—well, they were in a very disturbed condition out there. They didn't know what, or they didn't seem to interpret their exchange license agreements just right, and they were in conflict all the time, and naturally, they would run to either Mr. Selig's office, or to my office,
3  or to Mr. Kleine's—more to Mr. Selig's and to Mr. Kleine's offices than to mine, because I was out of the way, situated to the North, for some suggestions, or some help of some kind, wanted to straighten some disputes, or something that was irritating them, and the Patents Company asked Mr. Selig and Mr. Kleine and myself to act on such matters as would come up out there, in the way of helping to straighten them out.

Q. You sat as sort of judges as to whether or not the terms of the exchange licenses had been violated? A. Well, I would not say "judges." I mean in an advisory way.

4    Q. Arbitrators would be the better word? A. I don't know as I would say that.

Q. Those were the matters you had before you principally, were they not? A. Well, such as they were. I was called upon but very few times to take any part in anything or to help out. It was not of any consequence, the Western Committee; they didn't have much to do after all.

Q. Who asked you to be on that committee? A. I think it was the Patents Company.

Q. Well, who of the Patents Company? A. Mr. Kennedy, I think.

Q. He later became the President of the General Film Company? A. Yes, sir. It might have been Mr. Marvin. I am not sure as to that.

Redirect examination by Mr. CALDWELL:

Q. Have you seen Mr. William N. Selig, lately? A. Yes, sir; last Friday afternoon.

Q. Do you know whether or not he entered the hospital in Chicago, for treatment? A. He is at the hospital every day. He is under the treatment of Doctor Freund.

Q. Did he tell you whether his condition would be such that he could come on here to testify in this case? A. He said that he hoped he could, but he couldn't very well get away now.

Recross examination by Mr. GROSVENOR:

Q. Is Mr. Selig confined to the hospital, or does he go about? A. He goes about, goes there every day.

Q. He simply visits the hospital once in a while? A. No, he is there every day.

Q. He does not stay there, he goes there for treatment? A. No, he is not confined there, if that is what you mean.

Q. How long has he been going to the hospital? A. Oh, for a long time.

Q. What do you mean by a "long time?" A. From last five or six weeks, that I know of.

Q. And in the meantime, he has attended to his business, and is going to his office daily? A. He is very little at his office. Some days he is not there at all, and some days he is there for only an hour or half an hour in the evening and then goes home in his car, and he is at home.

Mr. GROSVENOR: If Mr. Selig is unable to come on to New York to attend these hearings as it is apparent he would be able to attend a hearing in Chicago, if we should go on there, I am perfectly willing, as counsel for the Government, to have a hearing in Chicago, to examine Mr. Selig, if you feel that he is a necessary witness. I do not wish this to be any opportunity for defendants to urge later that Mr. Selig cannot come here, and to urge that as a ground for getting an extension of time.

Mr. CALDWELL: That is not my purpose in asking these questions. The record shows that in opposition to the motion of the petitioner before Judge McPherson to limit our time to take testimony, I stated to the Court, as one of the reasons why I thought further time should be extended, that it was my purpose to examine Mr. Selig, and that Mr. Selig was about to enter a hospital, and it would probably be necessary for him to have an operation. Now, my only purpose in asking these questions is that the record might show that if we did not call Mr. Selig it would be on this ground. It is not for the purpose of laying foundation for an application for a further adjournment.

Mr. GROSVENOR: Well, if counsel for the defendants would like to have Mr. Selig testify, it is apparent that he is now able to testify if we have a hearing in Chicago, and I am quite willing to go to Chicago at any time between now and April 1st, and have such meeting, if you advise me.

Mr. CALDWELL: I would not say that it is quite apparent that Mr. Selig would be able to testify in Chicago, but we may avail ourselves of Mr. Grosvenor's offer to take his testimony there, if his condition will permit.

Whereupon, at 12:20 o'clock P. M., on this March 12th, 1914, the hearings were adjourned until 10:30 o'clock A. M., March 13th, 1914, to be resumed at Room 159, Manhattan Hotel, New York City.

1

IN THE

# DISTRICT COURT OF THE UNITED STATES

FOR THE EASTERN DISTRICT OF PENNSYLVANIA.

UNITED STATES OF AMERICA,
Petitioner,

*v.*

No. 889.

Sept. Sess., 1912.

MOTION PICTURE PATENTS CO. and others.
Defendants.

2

NEW YORK CITY, March 13th, 1914.

The hearings were resumed pursuant to adjournment, at 10:30 o'clock A. M., March 13, 1914, at Room 159, Manhattan Hotel, New York City.

Present on behalf of the Petitioner, Hon. EDWIN P. GROSVENOR, Special Assistant to the Attorney General.

JOSEPH R. DARLING, Esq., Special Agent.

3

CHARLES F. KINGSLEY, Esq., GEORGE R. WILLIS, Esq., and FRED R. WILLIAMS, Esq., appearing for Motion Picture Patents Company, Biograph Company, Jeremiah J. Kennedy, Harry N. Marvin, Armat Moving Picture Company, Melies Manufacturing Co. and Gaston Melies.

J. H. CALDWELL, Esq., and H. K. STOCKTON, Esq., appearing for William Pelzer, General Film Company, Thomas A. Edison, Inc., Kalem Company, Inc., Pathe Freres, Frank L. Dyer, Samuel Long and J. A. Berst.

4

HENRY MELVILLE, Esq., attorney for George Kleine, Essanay Film Manufacturing Company, Selig Polyscope, George K. Spoor and W. N. Selig.

JAMES J. ALLEN, Esq., appearing for Vitagraph Company of America, and Albert E. Smith.

Hon. R. O. MOON, appearing for Lubin Manufacturing Company, and Siegmund Lubin.

1      Thereupon, PERCIVAL L. WATERS resumed the stand
for cross examination.

Cross examination by Mr. GROSVENOR:

Q. Mr. Waters, you are to-day the General Manager of
the General Film Company? A. Yes.

Q. As such, your immediate superior is J. J. Kennedy,
the President of the General Film Company? A. Yes.

Q. At the time of these interviews with Mr. Fox and Mr.
Rosenbluh, respecting which you have testified on direct
2  examination, you were the General Manager of the General
Film Company? A. Yes.

Q. And at that time, also, your immediate superior was
Mr. J. J. Kennedy, the President of the Company? A. Yes.

Q. Did you before testifying, read the testimony given
by Mr. Fox when he was examined as a witness in this case
on behalf of the petitioner? A. Not immediately before, but
some time before.

Q. Before testifying in this case you did read the evidence given by Mr. Fox? A. Yes.

Q. And also the evidence given by Mr. Rosenbluh? A.
3  Yes.

Q. As I understand your direct examination, you did not
deny that on the dates stated by Mr. Fox, or about the time
stated by him, there were such conversations as he described,
that is to say, there were meetings between you and Mr. Fox
and Mr. Kennedy, or between you and Mr. Rosenbluh? A.
Yes, sir.

Q. The difference between you goes to the nature of
the conversation, and not to the fact that there was an
interview? A. There is no question about the interviews.

Q. That is, you are agreed that there were interviews?
4  A. Positive.

Q. You are also agreed that the principal subject under
discussion at these interviews, was the matter of the sale of
Mr. Fox's business, namely, the business of the Greater New
York Film Rental Company, to the General Film Company?
A. It developed into the principal subject.

Q. I am not asking you whether it developed into the
principal subject, but, as a matter of fact, the principal subject discussed at these interviews was the matter of the sale

of the business of the Greater New York Film Rental Company to the General Film Company? A. Yes.

Q. You made some references on your direct examination to some account between the General Film Company, and the Greater New York Film Rental Company. That was an account for money due from your company to his company, was it not? A. I have not made any reference to any account between the Greater New York Film Rental Company and the General Film Company.

Q. You referred in your direct examination to some account you said you talked to Mr. Fox about? A. A personal account.

Q. In that transaction, or account, whatever money was owed was not owed by Mr. Fox, was it? A. It was owed by me to Mr. Fox's company.

Q. Do you generally telephone to people that may be in the position of creditors to you and ask them to come to see you at your office about it, or is it more customary for you to go to their offices to see them about it? A. There was a question involved as to whether the money was really due.

Q. Well, can you answer that question more specifically?

Mr. KINGSLEY: I object to the question, on the ground that it assumes a custom with respect to dealings, and is not warranted by anything said by the witness in his direct testimony.

The Witness: Yes, I can give the details of the transaction.

By Mr. GROSVENOR:

Q. I didn't ask you for the details. Any way, Mr. Waters, you know, don't you, that the discussion as to that account was only incidental, and that the main subjects discussed at these conversations was the sale of the Greater New York Film Rental Company to the General Film Company? A. I have not said anything to indicate that.

Q. I am not asking you whether you have said anything to indicate it. I am asking you as to the fact. Is it not true that whatever discussion there was about such an account was only incidental— A. No.

Q. —to the principal subject matter discussed? A. No.

1

Q. And you mean to say that when you owe somebody money, or, there is a question about your owing somebody money, you telephone for that man to come to your office?

Mr. KINGSLEY: I object to the question, as being a grossly unfair characterization of anything the witness has stated in his direct examination, and also as immaterial, irrelevant and incompetent, and I object to it as not being proper cross examination.

Mr. GROSVENOR: Read the question, please.

2

The question was read by the Examiner as follows:

"Q. And you mean to say that when you owe somebody money, or there is a question about your owing somebody money, you telephone for that man to come to your office?"

The Witness: Always, in a similar case.

By Mr. GROSVENOR:

Q. When was it that you sold out your own company to the General Film Company? A. Some time in 1910, I don't

3

recall just the date of the contract.

Q. You were one of the earliest exchanges to sell to the General Film Company? A. I think so.

Q. It was understood before you sold that you were to become an officer of the General Film Company? A. I never have been an officer of the General Film Company.

Q. It was understood before you sold that you were to become an employe of the General Film Company? A. It never was mentioned.

Q. The subject had not been discussed? A. No.

Q. How soon after the sale did you become an employe?

4

A. I think the matter of the sale was first brought up in April, or the first of May, and I became the General Manager of the Company in June, as well as I remember.

Q. The actual sale of the business of your former company did not take place until September, or October, 1910? A. It was consummated then.

Q. Then you did become an employe of the General Film Company before the sale of your business to the General Film Company had been consummated? A. No, the sale was made, but the date of the contract was afterwards

changed, due to the fact that the business was not in shape
to be readily turned over to the General Film Company.

Q. And the business was not turned over until October?
A. I don't recall, but some time in September, or October.

Q. Then you did become an employe of the General Film
Company before your former business had actually been
turned over to the General Film Company? A. Yes, sir.

Q. Mr. Kingsley read to you certain questions and answers of Mr. Fox given on his direct examination, and on
page 2964, Vol. V, you were asked this question: "Q. At the
time he called upon you at your office in September, 1911,
did you say to him on that occasion, either in terms, or in
substance: 'Fox, I have sent for you, and my object in sending for you is to tell you that in my opinion this would be
the very best time to sell your plant to the General Film
Company, as you are no doubt aware that we have all the
business now? A. No.'" At the time of this interview with
Mr. Fox was there any one of the formerly so-called licensed
rental exchanges which was any longer doing business in
the films of the licensed manufacturers, except the Greater
New York Film Rental Company? A. That I am not sure
of.

Q. Isn't it true that at the time of this meeting between
you and Mr. Fox, the Greater New York Film Rental Company was the only surviving licensed rental exchange? A
That I do not know.

Q. Can you at this moment recall any licensed rental
exchange that was doing business at that time other than
the Greater New York Film Rental Company, and your-
selves? A. No, I cannot remember the conditions at that
time.

Q. On your direct examination, then, by your denial of
the statement of Mr. Fox that this remark was made at that
interview, you did not mean to testify that it was not true
that the General Film Company had all the business at that
time?

> Mr. KINGSLEY: I object to the question, on the
> ground that the witness' answer upon direct examina-
> tion speaks for itself, the original statement addressed
> to him being with respect to an alleged statement
> that Fox said the witness had made to him, and he

1       was denying the conversation itself. The question
did not refer to any facts that might have been discussed in the alleged and fictitious conversation.

The Witness: I couldn't follow the question. You will
have to repeat it.

By Mr. GROSVENOR:

Q. On the same page (2964, Vol. V) this question is addressed to you by Mr. Kingsley: "Q. Did you tell him that
2   he had been in business for a good long time, and that everybody else was out? A. No." Isn't it true that everybody
else was out except the Greater New York Film Rental Company? A. That I can't say, positively.

Q. Can you name any licensed exchange which was not
out at that time? A. I can't say that there was any, either
in or out.

Q. Was not the Greater New York Film Rental Company
the last of the licensed exchanges? A. Yes.

Q. To survive? A. Yes.

Q. Then there was some time in 1911 at which time the
3   Greater New York Film Rental Company was the only survivor? A. I won't say positively in 1911.

Q. That was true in December of 1911 or the early part
of 1912? A. I think so.

Q. It is probable, then, is it not, that it is the fact that
at the time of this interview the Greater New York Film
Rental Company was the only survivor? A. I won't say
that.

Mr. KINGSLEY: Objected to, on the ground that it
calls for a conclusion of the witness.
4

By Mr. GROSVENOR:

Q. I understand your direct examination to be, that
after you had talked with Mr. Fox for some time about
the sale of his business you called up Mr. Kennedy? A.
After talking with Mr. Fox a short time I called up Mr.
Kennedy.

Q. And what did you tell Mr. Kennedy? A. I told
Mr. Kennedy that Mr. Fox was there, and had said something relative to the sale of his exchange to the General

Film Company, and asked him if he wished to take up
the matter with Mr. Fox.

Q. And what did Mr. Kennedy say? A. He said if Mr.
Fox wanted to talk business he would be very glad to meet
him.

Q. What else happened that afternoon? A. Mr. Kennedy came to the office, No. 200 Fifth Avenue, and met
Mr. Fox.

Q. And the matter they discussed was the sale of
the business? A. The sale of the Greater New York Film
Rental Company.

Q. You say that you did not, on that day, call Mr.
Kennedy the "big chief," as testified to by Mr. Fox? A.
Positively no.

Q. As a matter of fact, whether Mr. Kennedy was so
termed on that day or not, he was in fact the big chief?

> Mr. KINGSLEY: Objected to, as calling for a con-
> clusion of the witness, and as being a grossly im-
> proper question.

The Witness: Not to my knowledge.

By Mr. GROSVENOR:

Q. Was he not the man who had in charge the purchasing of the various rental exchanges? A. Yes.

Q. Who else for the General Film Company took part
in the matter of purchasing exchanges? A. I really don't
know. I never participated in the purchasing of an exchange.

Q. Did you or not from time to time introduce rental
exchange men to Mr. Kennedy, who came there on the
subject of selling their business? A. I don't think so.

Q. A number of the witnesses produced by the defendants here from various parts of the country have testified
that they did meet you, and that you did go in with
them to meet Mr. Kennedy, on the subject of purchasing
their several exchanges. Your recollection is to the contrary? A. No, I think they came here for that specific
purpose, and that possibly preliminary arrangements had
been made with them. I probably acted as just simply introducing them to Mr. Kennedy, as a personal matter.

1
Q. Did you introduce them to anybody except Mr. Kennedy, on this general subject?

> Mr. KINGSLEY: I object to the question, because the witness has answered that he introduced them as a personal matter.

The Witness: I have introduced exchange men to a good many of the manufacturers and officers of the General Film Company.

2
> Mr. GROSVENOR: Repeat the question to him.
> The question was read to the witness by the Examiner as follows:
> "Q. Did you introduce them to anybody except Mr. Kennedy, on this general subject"?

The Witness: I don't recall introducing anybody to Mr. Kennedy on this particular subject.

By Mr. GROSVENOR:

3
Q. Giving the term its ordinary significance, is it not true, Mr. Waters, that Mr. Kennedy was the big chief on this general matter of purchasing exchanges? A. I don't just get that term "big chief." I have only heard it referred to in connection with Indians and Tammany Hall.

Q. You are unable to understand what the term could mean, then? A. In connection with Mr. Kennedy, or any officer of the company, yes.

Q. Now, you deny on your direct examination, page 2967, Vol. V, having enumerated the several offices which Mr. Kennedy held at that time, and which Mr. Fox testified you did enumerate. Whether or not those offices were enumerated, it is true that Mr. Kennedy was at that time the President of the General Film Company, was he not? A. Yes.

Q. And the President of the Biograph Company? A. I think so.

Q. And connected with some other company? A. A good many other companies, I believe.

Q. And connected with the Motion Picture Patents Company? A. Yes, sir.

Q. On page 2970, Vol. V, you testified, in response to a question: "Mr. Fox said that he didn't understand why Mr. Kennedy would let a few thousand dollars stand in the way of the deal. He says, 'I would accept a hundred thousand dollars for the exchange.' I told him as well as I knew Mr. Kennedy, I took it for granted he would not trade, but if he wanted me to mention a hundred thousand dollars to Mr. Kennedy, I would." What did you mean by that sentence, given by you on your direct examination, "I told him, as well as I knew Mr. Kennedy, I took it for granted he would not trade, but if he wanted me to mention a hundred thousand dollars to Mr. Kennedy, I would?" A. I had understood that Mr. Kennedy had prices set for the exchanges, and offered the one price, and would not trade, or, that is, he would not vary the price.

Q. Your understanding was, there was a general schedule of prices for each exchange, which schedule Mr. Kennedy followed? A. Yes.

Q. Do you recall that the two last survivors of the so-called licensed exchanges were an independent exchange, doing business in the West, and the Greater New York Film Rental Company? A. I don't just get that.

Mr. GROSVENOR: Read the question, please.

The question was read by the Examiner as follows:

"Q. Do you recall that the two last survivors of the so-called licensed exchanges were an independent exchange doing business in the West, and the Greater New York Film Rental Company?"

The Witness: No, I don't recall that.

By Mr. GROSVENOR:

Q. Has your employment as General Manager of the General Film Company been continuous, since 1910, up to the present time? A. No.

Q. With what company were you connected when you left the General Film Company? A. Some months after leaving the General Film Company I was connected with the Kinetograph Company.

1    Q. Who was the President of that company? A. Mr. Kennedy.

Q. Was he your immediate superior in that company? A. No, we were both officers of the company.

Q. As President of the company he had supervision over the management of your end of the business? A. Not necessarily.

Q. Did you leave the Kinetograph Company with Mr. Kennedy? A. Neither one of us has ever left the Kinetograph Company.

2    Q. What happened to it? A. We discontinued the distribution of films. The corporation still exists.

Redirect examination by Mr. KINGSLEY:

Q. Mr. Waters, will you tell us who it was used the term "big chief," if it was used in your conversation with Mr. Fox and to whom the term "big chief" in reality referred? A. Mr. Fox used the term, and it referred to the late Mr. T. D. Sullivan.

Q. And by that, do you mean the gentleman who was popularly known as "Big Tim Sullivan"? A. Yes.

3    Q. You told Mr. Grosvenor that the term "big chief" was one which you heard in connection with politicians. Was "Big Tim Sullivan" a Tammany politician? A. To the best of my recollection, yes.

Q. Was the Kinetograph Company a licensed exchange? A. Yes, sir.

Q. Did the Kinetograph Company conduct spirited competition with the General Film Company? A. Yes, very spirited.

Q. Did it conduct competition with the Greater New York Film Rental Company? A. It did.

4

Recross examination by Mr. GROSVENOR:

Q. Why is the Kinetograph Company no longer doing business? A. We decided to close out the rental end of it. We thought it advantageous to do so.

Q. Did you make any money while you were in business? A. Not very much.

Q. Did you lose considerable money, and I mean by

"you," did the company lose considerable money? A. Why, it lost some.

Q. It didn't make any money, then? A. That I am not prepared to say. I am not conversant with the books right off hand, and have not gone over them for some months.

Q. Don't you know that the company was a failure, and that it did not make any money at all? A. No, I don't know that. I won't admit that the company was a failure.

Q. Can you state that the company made any money? A. No, I cannot.

Q. You don't know one way or the other? A. Not exactly, no.

Q. But you do know the company is not doing business now? A. Yes.

Q. Did it ever pay any dividends? A. No.

Q. On direct examination you stated that Mr. Fox said that he controlled the business of the Greater New York Film Rental Company? A. He said he practically controlled it.

Redirect examination by Mr. KINGSLEY:

Q. How long was the Kinetograph Company doing business? A. I can't recall just how long.

Q. Several months? A. Several months, yes.

Q. And during that period were you spending money in developing your business and acquiring customers? A. A great deal.

Thereupon, SIEGMUND LUBIN, resumed the stand for cross examination:

Cross examination by Mr. GROSVENOR:

Q. Mr. Lubin, since you testified several days ago, have you refreshed your recollection as to dates by an examination of any of the papers or records in this case? A. No, I don't know the dates. You can help me along with the dates, if you will do it, as you have everything down here.

Q. You testified rather generally, as to a number of occurrences without fixing them as to time. Have you done

1    anything since you testified on direct examination in order
to enable you to testify more definitely as to those transactions? A. I don't think so. When it comes down to asking me for the dates, you have positively got all the dates
here, but I was speaking in testifying of when Edison won
the suit, and lost it and when he won it again. You have
got the dates here, and if you tell me it is the true date.

Q. You testified on your direct examination, that you
left this country? A. Yes, sir.

Q. And had to go to Europe? A. Yes, sir, owing to the
fact that Edison got the injunction.

2    Q. You are now referring to the injunction that Edison
got in the lowest Court in 1901 or 1902 against the Biograph
Company? A. That is right.

Q. And that decision was reversed a year or two later
by the Circuit Court of Appeals in this District? A. That
is right, and I came back.

Q. You came back? A. Yes, sir, I came back.

Q. And that all happened five or six years before the
Patents Company was organized? A. It did. Then after
a while, I would say after a little while, then Edison won
3    again the suit against the Biograph; and now what could I
do? I must take out a license to be in existence. I cannot
take the whole factory away again. I lost everything I had
that time, and I was forced to go away from this country.

Q. Are you a Director of the General Film Company?
A. I am.

Q. Have you been a Director of the General Film Company ever since it was organized? A. I have.

Q. As a Director on the Board of the General Film Company you represent the interests of the Lubin Company? A.
I do.

4    Q. Each one of the other Directors on the Board of the
General Film Company represents one of the other so-called
licensed manufacturers? A. I suppose so.

Q. Is there any one a Director on the Board of the
General Film Company who is not one of the licensed importers, or an important officer or stockholder in a licensed
manufacturer? A. Yes.

Q. Who is that? A. One man which represents Kleine,
I don't know what he is by Kleine, but he is a Director, and
he represents Kleine.

Q. Kleine is a licensed importer? A. Yes, sir.

Q. Now, is there anybody on the Board of Directors of the General Film Company who is not a licensed manufacturer or a licensed importer? A. I don't know.

Q. You don't know of anyone? A. I don't know that there is.

Q. You testified something on direct examination about the condition in the rental exchange business, and the formation of the General Film Company. What was the purpose in forming the General Film Company? A. The General Film Company? We had so many customers which did not pay us their bills. They didn't pay us the money when we gave them goods, and in some cases, for instance, to New York, when I came there, five men then proprietors of it, and I could not get anything on even thousands and thousands of dollars, but I lose; I could not get my money— I could not get money. I could not get my money from the licenses from them people before the General Film Company was started.

Q. Didn't some of the licensed exchanges pay their bills? A. The licensed? They were all complaining they could not make it pay.

Q. Didn't some of the licensed exchanges pay their bills? A. I think some didn't, quite many didn't.

Q. Well, did some of them pay their bills? A. Some paid positively. You can't lose everything, and you can't stay there without money.

Q. Well, then, what was the purpose in forming the General Film Company? A. In the way it was explained to me, for the betterment of the business to start with, and they asked me if I would like to sell out, and I said, "Gentlemen, I am willing to sell out," and then I cashed the rental business in which I had; I had one rental business in Norfolk, and it didn't pay, and I cashed it in. It was a loss to me—a great loss to me, as the customers, I could not watch them so close. People on one street would show the same films, all customers alike, the same program, and that had great effect. One man done business, and the other didn't, and the other was able to pay, and the other was not able to pay, and we thought this was a business that we will give them a program like the whole world does it, in England, and all over. The same as you go today to the bureau for actors, you go there and get to the theatre, and they come

1 in and give you a program; the man gives you the actors,
and in this way we thought we would be able to run business.

Q. That is, the idea of you people in forming the General
Film Company was to do all of this rental exchange business that had been done by the other exchanges, many of
which did not pay their bills? A. Didn't pay their bills.
That is No. 1, and when I sold my business the majority of
people which had rented films from the manufacturers, they
went to New York, they wanted to sell out. We had no
intention of buying them all out, no such intention at all.
2 That was not our idea. We had no such intention, but the
people came there and said, "Well, I would like to sell out,"
and what was done in this was in the other offices. I don't
know. I was not there when the places were sold. I know
they passed through Philadelphia, and said, "Mr. Lubin, I
would like to sell out," and I said, "I have nothing to do
with it," that they would have to go over there, and they
asked me what I think about it, and I myself I thought we
would not be able to pay the people—I didn't, as the business was in such condition it was almost impossible to be in
existence.

3 Q. Will you please look at Petitioner's Exhibit No. 78,
Volume 1, page 251, being a letter signed by J. J. Kennedy,
President of the General Film Company, addressed to Mr.
William Pelzer, Secretary, dated January 23rd, 1912? A.
This letter was sent from who, from Kennedy to Pelzer?
Well, I don't know anything at all about that, and I have no
knowledge of what correspondence he got. I have no busi-
ness with him.

Q. I asked you to read the letter. Have you read it? A.
I have.

Q. This letter states: "Some time before the Gen-
4 eral Film Company was organized an estimate of the
value of the business of exchanges leasing licensed motion
pictures, was made by men familiar with the manufacture
of motion pictures and also with the business of exchanges.
According to this estimate, the value of said business was
$3,468,847." Did you see such an estimate before the Gen-
eral Film Company was organized? A. You have got the
name, who is that man's name, Mr. So and So—

Q. Now, for the purpose of getting your mind clear on the
subject I will read it to you again: "Some time before the

General Film Company was organized an estimate of the value of the business of exchanges leasing licensed motion pictures, was made by men familiar—" A. I want to ask one question. You tell me that this letter was sent to Mr. Pelzer?

Q. By Mr. Kennedy? A. Why, no, I have no knowledge about things from another man.

Q. I am not asking you about the letter. Kindly concentrate your attention on what I am reading now, Mr. Lubin. A. Yes.

Q. This letter states: "Some time before the General Film Company was organized an estimate of the value of the business of exchanges leasing licensed motion pictures, was made by men familiar with the manufacture of motion pictures and also with the business of exchanges. According to this estimate, the value of said business was $3,468,847." Now, my question is, did you see any such estimate of the value of the business of the licensed exchanges prior to the formation of the General Film Company? A. I have no knowledge at all whatever of it; never heard about it, don't know whether it was three millions or fifty millions; I don't know anything at all about it.

Q. Mr. Kennedy was the President of the General Film Company? A. Yes, sir, he was.

Q. From the start? A. Yes, sir, from the first. At the first of the General Film Company, he was from the start, the President.

Q. Was he the officer who had principal charge of buying the various rental exchanges? A. I think he was the man. I never knew what he paid to the people, never was there in such transactions, never had them.

Q. Will you kindly direct your attention to Petitioner's Exhibit No. 80, being the minutes of a regular meeting of the Board of Directors of the General Film Company, held at No. 10 Fifth Avenue, New York City, October 11th, 1910, at 4 P. M. Kindly read that exhibit. A. I have read it.

Q. The minutes of this meeting report you as having been present. Does the reading of these minutes refresh your recollection as to your having been present at the meeting referred to in the minutes? A. When it says so, I was there. One thing I don't understand here is he saying, "Business of the entire country controlled by

1    the General Film Company, based on reels, 71%." Now,
when he says in this letter "71%," is what he means only
control of the General Film licensed? There was another
two hundred per cent. independent also in existence. When
he says "71%," what does he mean by that?

Q. If you will kindly wait until I address my question
to you, we will get along.

Mr. KINGSLEY: If you would enlighten the witness, you could get the information you seek.

2    The Witness: He speaks about the whole country—

By Mr. GROSVENOR:

Q. This exhibit states (Volume 1, page 266, folio 3):
"Payments authorized for exchanges owned October 10th,
stock, $591,400, cash, $1,483,200." Do you recall when the
authority was given to pay those amounts? A. I don't recall, but I see something here that I don't like, which I
don't understand in here. It is in this paper, "the number in entire country," what is he talking about? He is
talking through his hat, and it is impossible. At that time
3    there were so many others, I believe, independent, a couple
of hundred. He only speaks now, in this statement here,
of the licensed manufacturers, but there are unlicensed
manufacturers.

Q. If you will look at it, and particularly in folio 3,
you will see this statement— A. Yes.

Q. "Total payments authorized for all exchanges in entire country, stock, $988,800?" A. Nine hundred and—

Q. "Nine hundred eighty-eight thousand eight hundred
dollars stock, and cash, $2,480,000." Please state when the
authority was given to pay those sums for all the licensed
4    exchanges? A. I don't know anything at all about it. I
don't know anything about it at all. It never was brought
before me, so I cannot tell you, I don't remember.

Q. This purports to be the minutes of the meeting at
which you were present. Do you recall Mr. Kennedy making this report? A. I didn't watch it so closely. I don't
remember, gentlemen, only in this statement he is talking
through his hat when he says it requires so much. It
would require ten times that amount of money to buy the
rental business. He is speaking here about the General
Film Company people which had the licensed.

Q. Now, when was the authority given to pay that much for all the licensed exchanges? A. I don't know. I cannot tell you. Mr. Kennedy will have to attend to this business. I don't know anything about it. I never was present when one single rental exchange company was sold, never was there, and so I cannot tell you.

Q. If you will now turn back to the other exhibit, at page 252, you will see that Mr. Kennedy states, in his letter to Mr. Pelzer— A. The letter states what you say. I don't know what correspondence he had with that man; I don't know. I have nothing to do with that letter. I don't read Pelzer's letters, I don't write him, so I can't tell you anything about his letter business—about anything that was told by letters.

Q. If you will look at the top of page 252, you will see that Mr. Kennedy states that the estimate made of the value of the business— A. He wrote it—

Q. Wait till I get my question—before the General Film Company was formed, was $3,468,847— A. He wrote to Pelzer that letter? He wrote to Pelzer that letter, or did he bring it up there?

Q. Then look at Exhibit No. 78? A. Yes, sir. Which is the letter of Mr. Kennedy to who?

Q. To Pelzer. A. I have no knowledge about it; he never showed me the letter.

Q. Wait a moment, and let me finish my question, and we will get along faster. A. Yes.

Q. Dated January 23rd, 1912? A. Yes.

Q. Now, Mr. Kennedy states that before the General Film Company was organized, an estimate of the value of the business of exchanges leasing licensed motion pictures was made, and he says the value of such business was $3,-468,847. Now, then, if you will turn back— A. He wrote Pelzer the letter. He never showed me that letter.

Q. Now, if you will turn back to Exhibit No. 80, you will see that he states that the total payments authorized for all exchanges in entire country, in stock and in cash, amounts to $3,468,800. A. Yes.

Q. Now, does the comparison made between the figure stated by Mr. Kennedy to have been an estimate made before the General Film Company was organized, with the figure given in these minutes, refresh your recollection as to there having been such an estimate made? A. I don't

1  know what correspondence he has got with Mr. Pelzer. Mr. Pelzer and Mr. Kennedy may have had conversations between themselves. I don't remember anything at all about that thing.

Q. Can you explain how that report got into the minutes? A. I don't know. He wrote him a letter. You must have the letter he wrote. He can explain it.

Q. I am not asking you about the letter. I am asking you about the minutes of the meeting of the Directors, at which you were present? A. To my knowledge, I honestly don't remember anything like that—that was never brought

2  before us. To my knowledge, such a thing never was brought before us that I remember of.

Q. Do you recall the meeting in December, 1908, at which you signed the license agreement with the Patents Company? A. Was I there?

Q. Yes. A. Whether I was there?

Q. I say do you recall the meeting at which you signed the license agreement on December 18th, 1908, with the Patents Company? A. That is the Patents Company. That is, the first time I signed it with the Edison people, before the Patents Company was in existence.

3  Q. Do you recall the meeting in the latter part of December, 1908, at which all the manufacturers signed the agreement with the Patents Company? A. I don't know if all signed on the same day; may be some signed it the next day. I know when I signed it the paper must have been there, when I signed it.

Q. Is it a fact that a number of manufacturers signed it on the same day after they had had the meeting and had had the contracts read, and in the presence of all of them? A. I don't know if all signed it the same day or not. They

4  signed it later, or some did, I can't remember.

Q. How many signed it the same day you signed it? A. I cannot remember the number.

Q. Didn't the most of them sign it at the same time you did? A. Yes, sir, some did.

Q. The most of them? A. Yes, sir.

Q. And didn't all of them sign it then? A. I don't remember. I would not say something I am not sure of.

Q. Can you name any one that signed it afterwards? A.

I cannot say that they all signed it; I don't remember exactly how many were there.

Q. Are you in litigation with this Mr. Swaab that you referred to on direct examination? A. Have I what?

Q. Do you have any lawsuit with Mr. Swaab? A. I think there is a lawsuit for some films which was taken over here at some time.

Q. And these films were taken at the time that his rental exchange was taken possession of, when his license was cancelled?

Mr. Kingsley: I object to the question.

The Witness: I don't know, I can't tell you. I don't know anything further.

By Mr. Grosvenor:

Q. But you do know that you and he have a lawsuit? A. Yes, sir, we have, I think so.

Q. Is this the same Swaab who got a verdict of twenty thousand dollars by a jury in Philadelphia against the Vitagraph Company, two or three days ago? A. It is the same Swaab, I think so.

Q. And that suit against the Vitagraph Company related to the same matter that your suit with Swaab relates to? A. I don't know. In my suit he only got fifteen hundred dollars, or twelve hundred dollars.

Redirect examination by Mr. Kingsley:

Q. Your suit was reversed by the higher Court? A. Yes, sir.

Q. Is Mr. Berst a Director and officer of the General Film Company? A. Now?

Q. Yes, at the present? A. Yes, sir.

Q. Is he connected with any manufacturer at all, at present? A. No, sir.

Recross examination by Mr. Grosvenor:

Q. What position does Mr. Berst have with the General Film Company? A. He is Secretary.

1      Q. Has he been a Director of the General Film Company ever since it was organized?  A. He represented Pathe at the time, and I think he was a Director.

Q. He represented Pathe?  A. Yes, sir, at that time.

Q. And he left Pathe two or three months ago?  A. I don't know how long.

Q. It was very recently?  A. Yes, sir, a couple of months ago.

Whereupon, at 12:10 o'clock on this March 13th, 1914, the hearings were adjourned until 10:30 o'clock, A. M., March 2  17th, 1914, to be resumed at Room 159, Manhattan Hotel, New York City.

3

4

IN THE

# DISTRICT COURT OF THE UNITED STATES

## FOR THE EASTERN DISTRICT OF PENNSYLVANIA.

UNITED STATES OF AMERICA,
Petitioner,

*v.*

MOTION PICTURE PATENTS CO. and others,
Defendants.

No. 889.
Sept. Sess., 1912.

2

NEW YORK CITY, March 17, 1914.

The hearings were resumed pursuant to adjournment at 10:30 o'clock A. M., March 17, 1914, at Room 159, Manhattan Hotel, New York City.

Present on behalf of the Petitioner, Hon EDWIN P. GROSVENOR, Special Assistant to the Attorney General.

3

JOSEPH R. DARLING, Esq., Special Agent.

CHARLES F. KINGSLEY, Esq., GEORGE R. WILLIS, Esq., and FRED R. WILLIAMS, Esq., appearing for Motion Picture Patents Company, Biograph Company, Jeremiah J. Kennedy, Harry N. Marvin, Armat Moving Picture Company, Melies Manufacturing Co. and Gaston Melies.

J. H. CALDWELL, Esq., and H. K. STOCKTON, Esq., appearing for William Pelzer, General Film Company, Thomas A. Edison, Inc., Kalem Company, Inc., Pathe Freres, Frank L. Dyer, Samuel Long and J. A. Berst.

4

HENRY MELVILLE, Esq., attorney for George Kleine, Essanay Film Manufacturing Company, Selig Polyscope, George K. Spoor and W. N. Selig.

JAMES J. ALLEN, Esq., appearing for Vitagraph Company of America, and Albert E. Smith.

Mr. KINGSLEY: I offer in evidence copies of the entries from the office dockets of Dyer & Dyer, Gifford

& Bull, and Kerr, Page & Cooper, counsel for complainants and defendants in the various suits on Edison Patent No. 589,168, and re-issue patents 12,037, 12,038, and 12,192, brought between 1897 and 1909, also copies of the entries in said docket books relating to suits on re-issue patent No. 12,192, which were brought by the Edison Manufacturing Company against the various individuals, firms or corporations to the number of thirty, in the Northern District of Illinois, Eastern Division; five in the Northern District of Ohio, Eastern Division; three in the Eastern District of Missouri; and three in the Eastern District of Wisconsin.

## STIPULATION OF COUNSEL.

IT IS STIPULATED AND AGREED that the exhibit offered by Mr. Kingsley, which is marked Defendant's Exhibit No. 164, and is printed immediately below this stipulation, is a copy of all the docket entries entered in the usual course of business on the books of Dyer & Dyer, Gifford & Bull and Kerr, Page & Cooper, counsel for complainants and defendants in all suits on Edison Patent No. 589,168 and re-issue patents No. 12,037, 12,038 and 12,192, brought between 1897 and 1909, except that where an entry appeared in the docket books twice by reason of being entered once in the books of counsel for complainants and once in the books of counsel for defendants, such entry has been copied only once in said Defendant's Exhibit No. 164, and except that in addition to the suits named in said Defendant's Exhibit No. 164, suits on the re-issue patent 12,192, were brought by the Edison Manufacturing Company against various individuals, firms or corporations, between March 16, 1908, and April 25, 1908, thirty of such suits having been brought in the Northern District of Illinois, Eastern Division, three in the Eastern District of Missouri, and three in the Eastern District of Wisconsin, and that in none of said last mentioned suits was anything done after the filing of the answer therein until the suits were dismissed by consent and without costs in the month of March or April, 1909.

Defendants' Exhibit No. 164, offered above, is re-  1
ceived in evidence and is as follows:

**Defendants' Exhibit No. 164.   E. H.**

(*Docket of Dyer & Dyer.*)

U. S. CIRCUIT COURT,

SOUTHERN DISTRICT OF NEW YORK.

On Patent 589,168

2

THOMAS A. EDISON,

*vs.*

CHARLES H. WEBSTER individually and as   In Equity.
a member of the INTERNATIONAL FILM   No. 6,796.
COMPANY; and EDWARD KUHN individ-
ually and as a member of the INTERNA-
TIONAL FILM COMPANY.

RICHARD N. DYER, Complainant's Solicitor.   3
GEORGE COOK, Defendant's Solicitor.

1897
Dec.   7   Bill filed and subpœna issued.
1898
Jan.   3   Defts. appear by George Cook.
Feb.   3            do.
       17   Answer filed.
Mch.   7   Replication filed.
April 11   Decree for Complainant, consented to by parties,
               signed by Lacombe, J. and entered.   4
Aug.  10   Injunction issued.

(*Docket of Dyer & Dyer.*)

## U. S. CIRCUIT COURT,

### SOUTHERN DISTRICT OF NEW YORK.

On Patent 589,168

| | |
|---|---|
| THOMAS A. EDISON,<br><br>*vs.*<br><br>MAGUIRE & BANCUS, LIMITED; JOSEPH D. BANCUS, individually and as President of said M. & B. Ltd.; FRANK Z. MAGUIRE, individually and as Vice-President and Managing Director of said M. & B. Ltd., and WILLIAM M. PAYTON, Jr., individually and as Secretary of said M. & B. Ltd. | In Equity.<br>No. 6,798. |

RICHARD N. DYER, Complainant's Solicitor.
HENRY B. GAILEY, Defendant's Solicitor.

1897
Dec. 7   Bill filed and subpœna issued.
1898
Jan. 3   Defts. appear by Henry B. Gailey
Feb. 2   "    time to answer extended to Feb. 17, 1898
Feb. 10   "    "    "    "    March 1/98
Mch. 1   "    "    "    "    "    8/98
    7    "    15/98
    14    ' 25/98
1900
June 19   Consent Decree
    "    22   Injunction issued
    "    25   Injunction filed p. s. on all defts., June 25/1900
        Maguire & Bancus, Ltd., J. D. Bancus, Henry
        J. Mayer, Walter B. Home.)

(*Docket of Dyer & Dyer.*)          1

## U. S. CIRCUIT COURT,

EASTERN DIST. OF PENNA.

On Patent 589,168

| | |
|---|---|
| THOMAS A. EDISON, *vs.* SIEGMUND LUBIN. | In Equity. No. 50, October Session, 1897. |

1898
Jan.  10  Bill filed and subpœna issued
Feb.   7  Deft's appearance entered by Strawbridge & Taylor
Mch.   2  Time for defendant to plead extended to Mar 20/98
      29  Answer filed
April 13  Amendment to answer consented to by Complainant's counsel April 12, 1898.   filed.
May    2  Filed replication in usual form
June  11  Subpœna served on Lubin to certify before Sam'l          3
          Bell on June 14/98
  "   13  Taking of testimony before Sam'l Bell postponed
          to June 16/98
  "   16  Opened *prima facie* testy at Philadelphia and adjourned indefinitely.
1903
June   2  Bill dismissed without prejudice on motion **of C.**
          Bradford Fraley for Complainant.

*(Docket of Dyer & Dyer.)*

## UNITED STATES CIRCUIT COURT,

### NORTHERN DISTRICT OF ILLINOIS.

On Patent 589,168

THOMAS A. EDISON,

*vs.*

EDWARD A. AMET.

> RICHARD N. DYER, Complainant's Solicitor (Poole
> & Brown, Resident Solicitors)
> MUNDAY, EVARTS & ADCOCK, Defendant's Solicitors.

1898

Jan. 10    Bill filed and subpœna issued (Bill sent to Poole
       & Brown 1/8/98 for filing).
       Appearance entered for Defendant.
       Stipulation extending Deft's time to plead till
       Apr. 4.

(*Docket of Dyer & Dyer.*)    1

## U. S. CIRCUIT COURT,

### Southern District of New York.

On Patent 589,168

Thomas A. Edison,

*v.*

Eden Musee American Company (Ltd.), a corporation, and Richard G. Holl-
man, individually, and as President of said company.    2

Richard N. Dyer, Complainant's Solicitor.

1898
Feb.    7 Bill filed and subpœna issued.
       8 Subpœna served on Hollman.

3

4

(*Docket of Dyer & Dyer.*)

## UNITED STATES CIRCUIT COURT,

### SOUTHERN DISTRICT OF NEW YORK.

On Patent 589,168.

THOMAS A. EDISON,

*v.*

2   THE VERISCOPE COMPANY, DANIEL A. STUART, individually, and as President of the company, and FRANK C. MEEHAN individually and as Secretary of the company.

Equity Docket No. 6857.

RICHARD N. DYER, Complainant's Solicitor.
Defendants' Solicitors, NATHAN, LEVENTRITT, & PERHAM, 27 William St.

1898

3  Feb. 19   Bill filed and three subpœnas issued.

  19   Subpœnas personally served on Deft. Co. and on Stuart; Meehan not found.

April 4   Appearance entered for defendant by Leventritt & Nathan.

April 26   Time to file and serve the answer extended to June 6/98.

June 6   Time to file and serve the answer extended to June 8/98.

June 7   Answer filed—received copy from Defts. Sol. June 18/98.

4  July 2   Replication filed.

1899

Jan. 19   Consent order entered substitution Nathan, Leventritt & Perham as Sol's for defendants.

(*Docket of Dyer & Dyer.*)     1

## UNITED STATES CIRCUIT COURT,

SOUTHERN DISTRICT OF NEW YORK.

On Patent 589,168

THOMAS A. EDISON,

*v.*

MARC KLAW and ABRAHAM ERLANGER, individually and as members of the firm of KLAW and ERLANGER, and W. W. FREEMAN.

Equity No. 6,853.     2

RICHARD N. DYER, Complainant's Solicitor.
MITCHELL S. ERLANGER, Defendants' Solicitor (66 B'way).

1898.
Feb. 15 Bill filed and subpœnas issued.
    15 Subpœnas served on Messrs. Erlanger and Free-    3
        man.
    16 Subpœna served on Mr. Klaw.
Mch. 7 Appearance entered for defendants.
April 2 Time to plead extended ten days, to Apr. 14, 1898.
April 20 Discontinuance entered.

4

DEFENDANTS' EXHIBIT NO. 164.

(*Docket of Dyer & Dyer.*)

## UNITED STATES CIRCUIT COURT,

SOUTHERN DISTRICT OF NEW YORK.

On Patent 589,168

|  |  |
|---|---|
| THOMAS A. EDISON, | |
| *v.* | In Equity 6877. |
| AUGUSTIN C. DALY. | |

RICHARD N. DYER, Complainant's Solicitor.

1898

Mch. 14  Bill filed, subpœna issued.

15  Subpœna served.  Service of subpœna admitted by Warren G. Foster, Sol'r.

April 20  Discontinuance entered.

*(Docket of Dyer & Dyer.)*

## UNITED STATES CIRCUIT COURT,

### SOUTHERN DISTRICT OF NEW YORK.

On Patent 589,168

| | |
|---|---|
| THOMAS A. EDISON, | |
| *v.* | In Equity. No. 6883. |
| WALTER S. ISAACS. | |

Complainant's Solicitor, RICHARD N. DYER.
Defendant's Solicitor, E. A. ISAACS.

1898.

Mch. 22  Bill filed and subpœna issued.

  23  Subpœna personally served.

May 31  Defendant's time to answer extended to June 15/98.

June  6  Defendant's time to answer extended to June 22/98.

  25  Consent Decree.

  29  Injunction issued and handed to Marshal for service—Marshal's return June 30.

1

(*Docket of Dyer & Dyer.*)
U. S. CIRCUIT COURT,
SOUTHERN DISTRICT OF NEW YORK.

On Patent 589,168

THOMAS A. EDISON,
*v.*

AMERICAN MUTOSCOPE COMPANY and BEN-
JAMIN F. KEITH.

In Equity.
No. 6928.

2

Complainant's Solicitor, RICHARD N. DYER.
Defendant's Solicitor, JOHN T. EASTON, Counsel,
KERR, CURTIS & PAGE (For Company only).

1898

May 13   Bill and praecipe filed.
     14   Subpœna put in Marshal's hands.
          Appearance entered by John T. Easton for Amer-
          ican Mutoscope Co.
June 27   Deft. A. M. Co's time to answer extended to July
          15, 1898.

3

July 15   Answer filed.
  "  29   Replication filed.
Aug. 12   *Prima facie* proofs opened.
Sept. 21    "      "      "    closed.
1899
Mch.  6   Amendment to answer filed.
          Defendants' proofs opened.
            "          "     closed.

1900
Aug. 29   Complainant's rebuttal testimony opened.

4

Sept. 19    "          "          "    closed.
Dec. 15   Original testimony and exhibits filed.
  "  18   Argued by R. N. Dyer, F. P. Fish, closing argu-
          ment of Mr. Fish printed.
1901
July 15   Opinion by J. Wheeler, granting decree.
  "  19   Served defendants' solicitor with copy of proposed
          interlocutory decree to be presented before J.
          Wheeler. Wednesday, July 24/01, at 10 A. M.
  "  25   Interlocutory decree presented to J. Wheeler for
          signature—also defendant's motion to stay in-
          junction pending appeal.

"   25   Decree signed.                                          1
    26        filed.
"   27   Opinion by J. Wheeler—deft's motion granted,
            subject to certain conditions.
"   29   Served by deft's. with copy of Assgt. of errors, ci-
            tation and Petition on Appeal to C. C. A.
Aug.  2  Served copy of notice, affidavit and proposed order
            under J. Wheeler's memorandum, filed July
            27/01, noticed for Aug. 6, at 10 A. M.
"    6   Memorandum for complainant filed with J.
            Wheeler.                                             2
"    6   Argued by R. N. Dyer at Brattleboro, Vt.
"    6   Order signed by J. Wheeler.
"    8   Order filed and certified copy served upon deft.,
            American Mutoscope Co.
"    8   Injunction issued.
     9        "         served and filed.
         Printed record on appeal filed.
Oct.  21  Briefs on behalf of Defendant-Appellant filed.
"    31  "      "      "      "      " Complainant-Appellee
                      "        and served on Defendant-Appel-
            lant's attorneys.                                    3
Nov.  7 & 8  Appeal argued before Judges Wallace, La-
            combe and Townsend by F. P. Fish, Esq. and
            R. N. Dyer, Esq. for Complainant-Appellee.

   1902
Mch. 10  Opinion of Circuit Court of Appeals (written by
            Judge Wallace) reversing decree of Circuit
            Court and instructiong the Circuit Court to dis-
            miss bill of complaint with costs.
         Order entered directing the turning over to defend-
            ant's solicitors of bond filed for costs on appeal
            and bond filed on staying injunction of Circuit   4
            Court.
         Bonds given to Mr. Kerr of Kerr, Page & Cooper.
Mch. 31  Stipulation that either party might withdraw
            model exhibits filed in their behalf without notice.
April    Costs taxed by Clerk of U. S. Circuit Court.
"    14  Defendant's counsel served notice of appeal from
            Clerk's taxation of costs together with affidavit
            in support of motion. Hearing set for April 18,
            1902.

1    1902

"    18    Hearing of taxation of costs postponed to April 25, 1902 by consent.

"    25    Hearing on taxation of costs postponed to May 2, 1902, by consent.

May    1    Notice of application for writ of certiorari to be presented May 19th, 1902 before U. S. Supreme Court served on defendant's attorneys. Petition for writ, brief in support thereof, certified copy of transcript of record in U. S. C. C. A. and $25 as deposit for Clerk's fees forwarded to J. H. McKenney, Clerk U. S. Supreme Court, Washington, D. C.

2

"    2    Defendant's motion of appeal from taxation of costs argued by Mr. Edmonds on behalf of Compl't, and brief filed.

"    3    Received copy of defendant's brief on costs matter.

"    3    Received copy of defendant's brief on costs matter.

"    5    Opinion of Lacombe, J. on question of costs allowing part and disallowing remainder served with notice fixing May 9th, 1902 for settlement of decree.

3

"    9    Motion on settlement of decree argued and decree submitted by Defendant's counsel. Order staying execution and affidavit in support thereof filed by Compl't's counsel.

"    14    Decision of Lacombe, J. allowing Complainant to stay execution on filing security for costs within five days from May 15, 1902, judgment however to be entered.

"    16    Bond filed with Defendant's attorneys and order submitted to Lacombe, J. staying execution.

4    "    19    Petition for writ of certiorari submitted to U. S. Supreme Court by Philip Mauro, Esq.

June    2    Petition for writ of certiorari denied by U. S. Supreme Court.

"    5    Costs amounting to $2618.65 paid and satisfaction piece received from Complainant's attorneys.

Satisfaction piece filed and order filed discharging bond filed by National Surety Co. for costs.

Bond returned to National Surety Company and cancelled.

(*Docket of Dyer & Dyer.*)

## U. S. CIRCUIT COURT,

SOUTHERN DISTRICT OF NEW YORK,

On Patent 589,168.

| | |
|---|---|
| THOMAS A. EDISON,<br><br>*vs.*<br><br>J. STUART BLACKTON and ALBERT E. SMITH, individually and as co-partners trading under name and style of "COMMERCIAL ADVERTISING BUREAU" and AMERICAN VITAGRAPH COMPANY. | In Equity.<br>No. 6991. |

Complainant's Sol'r RICHARD N. DYER.
Deft's Sol'r.

1898.

July 12  Bill filed and subpœna issued and served.

Aug.  4  Consent decree.

"  10  Injunction issued.

Oct.  28  "  served and filed with Marshal's return.

1900.

Feb.  5  Copy of above injunction served on Wm. T. Rock, p. s. Feb. 5, 1900.

Mar.  24  Copy of above injunction served on G. S. W. Arthur, p. s. Mch. 24/1900.

Mar.  26  Served summons on J. Stuart Blackton to appear before J. A. Shields on Mch. 27, 1900, at 2:30 o'clock.

"  27  J. Stuart Blackton examined before the Master.

"  28  Albert E. Smith  "  "  "  "

"  29  Served summons on Wm. T. Rock to appear before J. A. Shields on Mch. 30, 1900, at 2:30 P. M.

"  30  Wm. T. Rock examined before the Master.

Apr.  9  Served summons on Walter Arthur to appear before J. A. Shields Apr. 10, 1900, at 2:30 P. M.

"  10  Examination of Arthur extended to Apr. 11, 1900, at 2:30 P. M.

"  11  Walter Arthur examined before the Master.

1  "  11  Served with copy of order to show cause, return-
              able Apr. 13/00.
   "  12  Stipulation extending the return on the order to
              show cause to Apr. 20, 1900.
   "  20  Hearing before J. Lacombe.
   "  24  Motion denied—endorsed on cover of order to
              show cause.
       1900.
   Apr. 25  Presented order.
   "  25  Order entered—denying motion to vacate the
              interlocutory decrees.
2  "  27  Order served; admission of service by Wm. R.
              Baird, Atty. for Dfts.
   May  1  Served papers re motion to punish for contempt
              admission of service by Wm. R. Baird, attor-
              ney for defendants, returnable May 4, 1900.
   May  2  Note of issue filed putting case on calendar for
              May 4, 1900.
   "   4  Hearing postponed to May 11, 1900.
   "  11    "       "     "  "  18, 1900.
   "  18    "       "     "  "  25, 1900.
3  "  25    "       "     "  June  8, 1900.
   June  8  Argued by S. O. Edmonds.
   Aug.  3  Opinion by J. Lacombe.  Motion denied without
              prejudice.
   Aug. 18  Served defendants with notice of motion to with-
              draw former motion and to punish for con-
              tempt.  Admission of service by C. G. Coe, for
              deft. Rock.
   "  18  Note of issue filed, putting case on calendar for
              Aug. 20/00.
   "  20  Hearing on motion postponed to Sept. 18/00.
4  Sep. 10  Hearing on motion indefinitely postponed and
              motion stricken from calendar, subject to re-
              newal per stipulation.

(*Docket of Dyer & Dyer.*)

## U. S. CIRCUIT COURT,

### Southern District of New York.

On Patent 589,168.

| | |
|---|---|
| Thomas A. Edison,<br><br>*v.*<br><br>Eberhard Schneider. | In Equity.<br>No. 7125. |

## 2

Complainant's Solicitor, Richard N. Dyer; S. O. Edmonds, of Counsel.

Defendant's Solicitor:

**1898.**

Dec. 21  Bill filed and subpœna issued.

"   21  Subpœna filed; served Dec. 21 on Deft's wife.

**1899.**

Mar.  4  Entered Rule taking bill *pro con.*

April  6  Filed notice of motion for Inter. Decree, Apr. 7/89.

"   8  Filed and entered interlocutory decree.

"   14  Preliminary injunction issued—served Apr. 15 and on Lowell Mason April 17.

"   17  Preliminary injunction filed with Marshal's return.

May  29  Served notice and motion papers on deft. for attachment for violation of Injunction.

"   31  Motion papers filed.

"   31  Note of issue filed placing motion on calendar for June 2.

June  6  Motion postponed to June 9.

   9  Motion postponed to June 17.

"   17  Motion heard.

"   29  "Attachment may issue," J. Lacombe's memo. on motion filed.

1  July  8  Filed and entered order for attachment (with stay).

"  14  Served Lowell Mason with copy of order at 1:10 o'clock P. M.

24  Served Eberhard Schneider with copy of order at 5:40 o'clock P. M.

1900

Jan.  23  Issued attachment on films at Dewey Theatre. Executed same day.

23  Filed undertaking on attachment.

2

26  Issued summons to Schneider and Wisniewiki to appear before the Master, returnable Monday, January 29, 1900.

Feb.  1  Order to show cause signed by Lacombe, J.

2  Served Schneider and Wisniewiki with copies of order and affidavits.

2  Filed order to show cause and affidavits.

6  Note of issue filed, placing order to show cause on calendar for Feb. 9.

9  Hearing on order to show cause postponed to Feb. 16th.

3

15  Received copies of affidavits of Schneider and Wisniewiki.

16  Argued contempt proceedings before Lacombe, J. Schneider and Wisniewiki found guilty and fined. Opinion by Lacombe, J. '

April 17  Presented order for settlement.

24  Order entered; S. fined $50; W. 20. Films seized; ordered destroyed.

25  Order served. Admission of service by Chas. E. Poucher, Atty. for Defts.

25  Films seized at Dewey Theatre; destroyed in

4  presence of S. O. Edmonds.

25  Bond $500 to Marshal and bond $250 to Clerk withdrawn and delivered to National Surety Co. for cancellation.

1902.

April 12  Stipulation and order exempting claims 1, 2, 3 and 5 of the patent from the operation of the injunction.

(*Docket of Dyer & Dyer.*)                    1

## U. S. CIRCUIT COURT,

SOUTHERN DISTRICT OF NEW YORK.

On Patent 589,168

THOMAS A. EDISON,

v.

GEORGE HUBER.

In Equity.
No. 7225.

2

Complainant's Solicitors, DYER, EDMONDS & DYER;
S. O. EDMONDS, of Counsel.

Defendant's Solicitors, STRALEY, HASBROUCH &
SCHLOEDER, 280 Broadway.

1899.

| | | |
|---|---|---|
| April | 28 | Bill and præcipe filed and subpœna issued. |
| | 29 | Subpœna filed—p. s. April 28. |
| June | 5 | Appearance entered for defendant. |
| | 30 | Defendant's time to answer extended to and including July 10/99. |
| July | 14 | Filed and entered decree. |
| | 22 | Injunction issued. |
| | 24 | Injunction filed, p. s. 7/22/99. |

3

4

1

(*Docket of Dyer & Dyer.*)

U. S. CIRCUIT COURT,

S. D. N. Y.

On Patent 589,168.

THOMAS A. EDISON,

*vs.*

FREDERICK M. PRESCOTT.

In Equity.
No. 7276.

Complainant's Sol'r, DYER, EDMONDS & DYER; S.
O. EDMONDS of Counsel.
Def't's Sol'r.

1899.

June 19    Bill filed and subpœna issued, returnable Aug.
rule day.

"    20    Filed subpœna p. s. on defendant.

3    Aug.    7    Appearance entered for defendant by

Sept.    4    Answer filed.

Oct.    2    Replication filed.

4

*(Docket of Dyer & Dyer.)*

## U. S. CIRCUIT COURT,

NORTHERN DISTRICT OF ILLINOIS—NORTHERN DIVISION.

On Patent 589,168

| | |
|---|---|
| THOMAS A. EDISON,<br><br>*vs.*<br><br>SEARS, ROEBUCK and CO., a corporation organized and existing under the laws of the State of Illinois, and having a place of business in the City of Chicago, in said State. | In Equity. |

2

Complainant's Sol'r, ISHAM, LINCOLN & BEALE, 718 The Temple, Chicago, (DYER, EDMONDS & DYER, of Counsel).

Defendants' Solicitor, Messrs. OFFIELD, TOWLE & LINTHICUM.

**1900.**

April 27   Bill forwarded to Messrs. Isham, Lincoln & Beale.   3

"      30   Bill filed and subpœna issued.

Subpœna filed p. s.

Appearance entered for defts. by Messrs. Offield, Towle & Linthicum.

July    2   Answer filed.

"     30   Replication forwarded.

Aug.   6      "        filed.

Oct.   23   Stipulation extending time for taking *prima facie* proofs until Jan. rule day.

**1901.**

| | | | | | | |
|---|---|---|---|---|---|---|
| Jan. 3 | do. | do. | until | March Rule day. | | |
| Feb. 25 | do. | do. | " | June | " " | |
| June 3 | do. | do. | " | Aug. | " " | |
| Aug. 5 | do. | do. | " | Oct. | " " | |
| Oct. 7 | do. | do. | " | Jan. | " " | 1902 |
| Dec. 27 | do. | do. | " | Apr. | " " | 1902 |

4

**1902.**

May 12   Order entered dismissing bill at complainant's costs without prejudice (reciting that costs have been paid) and discharging bond filed as security for costs.

1

*(Docket of Dyer & Dyer.)*

## U. S. CIRCUIT COURT,

SOUTHERN DISTRICT OF NEW YORK.

On Patent 589,168

THOMAS A. EDISON,

*vs.*

2    THE ENTERPRISE OPTICAL MANUFACTURING   In Equity.
Co. and WILLIAM J. FRY individually   No. 7522.
and as Manager, trading under the name
and style of ENTERTAINMENT SUPPLY
Co.

1900.

May 31   Bill filed and subpœna issued. Returnable 1st
Monday of July.

July   2   Appearance entered for defendants by P. J. Adams,
3           175 Duane Street, City.

"   18   Served with copies of defendants' motion papers
for order setting aside and quashing service of
the subpœna on defendants.

"   23   Motion postponed to August 20th, 1900.

Aug. 20    "    argued by S. O. Edmonds.

"   25   Served with copies of defendants' replying affidavits.

"   29   Motion granted as to The Enterprise Optical Mfg.
Co.

Sept. 26   Order entered.

4

*(Docket of Dyer & Dyer.)*        1

## U. S. CIRCUIT COURT,

SOUTHERN DISTRICT OF NEW YORK.

On Patent 589,168

| | |
|---|---|
| THOMAS A. EDISON,<br><br>*vs.*<br><br>AMERICAN VITAGRAPH COMPANY and WAL-<br>TER ARTHUR individually and as General<br>Manager of said Company. | In Equity.<br>No. 7597. |

Complainant's Sol'r, DYER, EDMONDS & DYER.
Defendants' Solicitor, WILLIAM R. BAIRD.

1900.

Sep. 13  Bill filed and subpœna issued; returnable 1st
          Monday of November.
"    13  Subpœna filed p. s. on all defendants 9/13/00.
"    17  Appearance entered for defendants, by Wm. R.
          Baird.
"    17  Filed and entered consent decree.
"    18  Injunction issued.
"    18  Injunction filed p. s. on defendants.

1

*(Docket of Dyer & Dyer.)*

## U. S. CIRCUIT COURT,

SOUTHERN DISTRICT OF NEW YORK.

On Patent 589,168

THOMAS A. EDISON,

        *vs.*

2       WILLIAM T. ROCK.

       In Equity.
       No. 7599.

Complainant's Solicitors, DYER, EDMONDS & DYER.
Defendant's Solicitor, CHARLES S. COE, 5 Beekman
   St., City.

1900

Sept. 13  Bill filed and subpœna issued. Returnable 1st
        Monday of November
Sept. 13  Subpœna filed p. s. on defendant 9/13/00
3  "  14  Appearance entered for defendant
   "  17  Filed and entered consent decree
   "  18  Injunction issued
   "  18  Injunction filed p. s. on defendant

4

(*Docket of Dyer & Dyer.*)

## U. S. CIRCUIT COURT,

SOUTHERN DISTRICT OF NEW YORK.

On Patent 589,168

|  |  |
|---|---|
| THOMAS A. EDISON,<br><br>*vs.*<br><br>THE "FARMER" DUNN MOVING PICTURE MACHINE COMPANY and ELIAS B. DUNN individually and as President of said company. | In Equity.<br>No. 7650. |

Complainant's Solicitors, DYER, EDMONDS & DYER.
Defendant's Solicitors, BOARDMAN, PLATT & SOLEY,
N. Y. City.

**1900**

Nov. 15   Bill filed and subpœna issued; returnable 1st Monday of January, 1901

Nov. 16   Subpœna filed p. s. on defendants Nov. 15, 1900

**1901**

Jan.   7   Appearance filed and entered for defendants

"   29   Stipulation extending time to file answer to March rule day

Mch.   4   Answer filed

April   1   Replication filed

July   1   Time for taking *prima facie* proofs extended to Sept. rule day

Sept.   2   Time for taking *prima facie* proofs extended to Nov. rule day

Oct.   26   Time for taking *prima facie* proofs extended to Feb. rule day /02

**1902**

Feb.   1   Time for taking *prima facie* proofs extended to May rule day /02

*(Docket of Dyer & Dyer.)*

## U. S. CIRCUIT COURT,

### Northern District of Illinois—Northern Division.

On Patent 589,168

|  |  |
|---|---|
| Thomas A. Edison,<br><br>*vs.*<br><br>William N. Selig. | In Equity.<br>No. 25,761. |

Complainant's Solicitors, Isham, Lincoln & Beale, Chicago, Illinois. (Dyer, Edmonds & Dyer, of Counsel.)

Defendant's Solicitors, Banning and Banning, 1303 Marquette Bldg., Chicago.

**1900**

Dec. 3    Bill of complaint forwarded to Isham, Lincoln & Beale

Dec. 5    Bill filed and subpœna issued

**1901**

Jan. 7    Appearance entered for defendant

Feb. 5    Answer filed

" 25    Replication forwarded

Mch. 2    "    filed

June 3    Stipulation extending time for taking *prima facie* proofs until Aug. rule day

Aug. 5    Stipulation extending time for taking *prima facie* proofs indefinitely

**1902**

May 12    Order entered dismissing bill at complainant's costs without prejudice (reciting that costs have been paid) and discharging the bond filed as security.

*(Docket of Dyer & Dyer.)*

## U. S. CIRCUIT COURT,

NORTHERN DISTRICT OF ILLINOIS—NORTHERN DIVISION.

On Patent 589,168

THOMAS A. EDISON,

*vs.*

STEREOPTICAN and FILM EXCHANGE and
WILLIAM B. MOORE individually and as
Treasurer and Manager of said Company.

In Equity.
Gen'l No. 25,809.

Complainant's Solrs., ISHAM, LINCOLN & BEALE
(Dyer, Edmonds & Dyer, of Counsel.)
Defendants' Sol'r, CHARLES T. BROWN.

1901

Jan. 31  Bill of complaint forwarded to Isham, Lincoln &
Beale

Feb. 5  Bill filed; subpœna issued
Subpœna served and filed p. s. on defendants

Mch. 4  Appearance entered for defendants, by Chas. T,
Brown

"  30  Answer filed

May 2  Replication forwarded

"  6  "  filed

Aug. 5  Stipulation extending time for taking *prima facie*
proofs until November rule day

Oct. 26  Stipulation extending time for taking *prima facie*
proofs until February rule day, 1902

1902

Feb 6  Wrote Isham, Lincoln & Beale to either secure
extension of time or dismissal of suit "without prejudice"

10  Isham, Lincoln & Beale appeared before Judge
Kohlsaat on opposition to dismiss complaint.
Affidavit of W. B. Moore for defendants and
affidavit of Richard N. Dyer for complainant,

1

submitted. Judge Kohlsaat extended the time for taking proofs on condition that all proofs for both parties be taken before May rule day, otherwise action to be dismissed

May 12  Order entered dismissing bill at complainant's costs without prejudice (reciting that costs have been paid) and discharging the bond filed as security.

2

3

4

(*Docket of Dyer & Dyer.*)

## U. S. CIRCUIT COURT,

Northern District of Illinois—Northern Division.

On Patent 589,168

Thomas A. Edison,

*vs.*

Edward D. Otis and N. M. Kent individually and as co-partners trading under the firm name and style of Chicago Projecting Company.

In Equity.
No. 25,996.

2

Complainant's Solicitor, Isham, Lincoln & Beale (Dyer, Edmonds & Dyer, of Counsel).
Defendant's Counsel, Banning and Banning.

**1901.**

Sep. 14 Forwarded bill of complaint to Isham, Lincoln & Beale for filing.

" 16 Bill filed and subpœna issued, returnable October rule day. Subpœna served on Otis (not served on Kent).

Oct. 7 Appearance for Otis by Banning & Banning.

" 19 Answer for Otis filed.

" 26 Replication forwarded to Isham, Lincoln & Beale for filing.

**1902.**

Feb. 1 Stipulation extending times to take *prima facie* testimony until May rule day.

Sep. 16 Order signed by Judge Kohlsaat and entered, providing for dismissing bill without prejudice and without costs and discharging bond for costs.

" 18 Copy of order discharging bond filed with National Surety Co.

Nov. 4 Isham, Lincoln & Beale have credited to our account $7.45, being refund to them by Clerk of balance deposited for costs unexpended.

3

4

1

(*Docket of Dyer & Dyer.*)

## U. S. CIRCUIT COURT,

NORTHERN DISTRICT OF ILLINOIS—NORTHERN DIVISION.

On Patent 589,168.

THOMAS A. EDISON,

*vs.*

2  THE ENTERPRISE OPTICAL MFG. CO. and FRANK MCMILLAN, individually and as President and Manager of said Company.

In Equity. No. 25,994.

Complainant's Solicitors, ISHAM, LINCOLN & BEALE; DYER, EDMONDS & DYER, Of Counsel.
Defendants' Counsel, BANNING and BANNING.

1901.

Sept. 14   Bill filed and subpœna issued returnable October rule day.
3
Subpœna served on McMillan as individual and for Company.

Deposited $25 with Clerk for costs.

Oct.    7   Appearance for defendants by Banning & Banning.

"    19   Answer filed.

"    26   Replication forwarded to Isham, Lincoln & Beale for filing.

1902.

Feb.   1   Stipulation extending times to take *prima facie*
4
testimony until May rule day.

Sept. 16   Order signed by Judge Kohlsaat and entered providing for dismissal of bill without prejudice and without costs and discharging bond for costs.

"    18   Copy of order discharging bond filed with National Surety Co.

Nov.   4   Isham, Lincoln & Beale have credited to our %
$7.45, being unexpended balance of deposit for costs received by them from Clerk.

(*Docket of Dyer & Dyer.*)

## U. S. CIRCUIT COURT,

SOUTHERN DISTRICT OF NEW YORK.

On Edison Reissue 12,037.

THOMAS A. EDISON,
     Complainant,

    *vs.*

AMERICAN MUTOSCOPE & BIOGRAPH COM-
PANY,
      Defendant.

In Equity.
No. 8289.

Complainant's Sol'r, RICHARD N. DYER.
Defendant's Sol'r, KERR, PAGE & COOPER.

1902.

Nov. 7 Bill filed and subpœna issued and served, returnable December rule day, 1902.

Dec. 1 Appearance of Kerr, Page & Cooper entered for
defendant.

1903.

Jan. 5 Answer filed.

Feb. 2 Replication filed.

July 27 Compl't *prima facie* proofs opened pursuant to
notice served July 23, 1903.

    Complainant's *prima facie* proofs closed subject
to motion to be brought by defendant's counsel
to compel witness to answer.

    Motion to compel witness to answer served by
defendant's counsel setting hearing for Sep.
23, 1903.

Sept. 23 Motion argued before Lacombe, J., by D. W. Cooper for the motion and J. R. Taylor opposed.
Motion granted.

" 24 Order entered giving complainant 20 days to produce witness for further cross-examination.

Oct. 13 Cross-examination of F. L. Dyer continued and
completed and *prima facie* proofs closed.

    Papers turned over to J. Edgar Bull as counsel.

1

*(The following entries from the docket of Gifford & Bull.)*

Oct. 27 Deft's testimony commenced. Witness Wm. Main. Adjourned to Oct. 28.

" 28 Deft's testimony continued. Witness Wm. Main. Adjourned to Oct. 29.

" 29 Deft's testimony continued. Witness Wm. Main. Adjourned to Oct. 30.

" 30 Deft's testimony continued. Witness Wm. Main. Adjourned to Oct. 31.

2

" 31 Deft's testimony continued. Witness Wm. Main. Adjourned to Nov. 2.

Nov. 2 Deft's testimony continued. Witness Wm. Main. Adjourned to Nov. 4.

Nov. 4 Deft's testimony continued. Witness Wm. Main. Adjourned to Nov. 5.

5 Deft's testimony continued. Witness Wm. Main. Adjourned to Nov. 10.

10 Adjourned to Nov. 14, 1903.

14 Deft's testimony continued. Witness Wm. Main. Direct exam. closed.

3 Dec. Received notice and papers on motion to limit time.

28 Above motion withdrawn.

29 R. N. Dyer consented to substitution of G & B as solrs. and counsel for complt.

1904

Jan. 4 Above consent filed.

May 19 Cross examination of Prof. Main commenced.

20 Cross examination of Prof. Main continued.

Aug. 2 Cross examination of Prof. Main continued.

3 Cross examination of Prof. Main closed.

4 1905.

May 3 Complainant's testimony in rebuttal, witness F. N. Waterman.

June 7 Complainant's testimony in rebuttal witness F. N. Waterman, continued.

8 Complainant's testimony in rebuttal, witness F. N. Waterman, continued.

9 Complainant's testimony in rebuttal, witness F. N. Waterman, continued.

10 Complainant's testimony in rebuttal, witness F. N. Waterman, continued.

15 Complainant's testimony in rebuttal, witness F. N. Waterman, continued.   1

16 Complainant's testimony in rebuttal, witness F. N. Waterman, continued.

19 Complainant's testimony in rebuttal, witness F. N. Waterman, continued.

Complainant Rests.

Oct.   2 Notice of Final Hearing Served on Kerr, Page & Cooper.

  2 Note of Issue filed, placing cause on Oct. 1905 Cal.

1906.   2

Jan.   8 Stipulation that copies of patents & publications may be used in lieu of originals.

24-25 Argument before J. Ray.

1906

Mch. 26 Opinion of Ray dismissing bill.

April 18 Decree dismissing bill.

May   7 Appeal allowed. Citation ret. June 5/06.

May   9 Appeal papers served on Kerr, Page & Cooper, and filed with Clerk.

June     Transcripts received.   3

Dec. 26 Briefs for Complt. filed.

1907

Feb.1&4 Argument in C. C. A.

Mch.   5 Decree reversed.

Mch. 19 Mandate received.

23 Notice settlement and entry of order on Mandate & Decree served.

23 Decree approved as to form by Kerr, P. & C.

25 Decree signed & Mandate sent down to C. C.

27 Injunction issued and served. (151 Fed., 767).

*(Following entries from docket of Kerr, Page & Cooper.)*   4

1908

Mch.   6 Received notice of commencing accounting proceedings, returnable on March 11th, 1908, before John A. Shields, Master.

  6 By agreement with opposing counsel, proceedings before Master adjourned to March 17th, 1908, at 11 a. m.

17 Counsel met before Master, who ordered defend-

1

ant to file a statement with him on March 31st, 1908, showing all negatives taken in the "Warwick" camera from September 30, 1902, to March 27, 1907; name of subject of each negative; length of film of each negative; number of positive prints of each negative made; names of parties to whom prints were sold; cost of production; cost of material, etc.

1908

31   Counsel met before Master. Defendant's time within which to furnish data required by Master's order enlarged to April 14th, 1908. Defendant filed a partial statement showing list of infringing films, but did not disclose the names of parties to whom the infringing films were sold.

April 4   Mailed copy of brief in opposition to Master's order that defendant disclose the names of customers to whom infringing films were sold to Master and served copy on complainant's counsel.

21   Received copy of reply brief for complaint that was sent to Master today.

14   Counsel met before Master. Defendant's time for filing list data called for by Master's order enlarged for one week.

20   Furnished additional installment of list of films taken in infringing camera.

21   Counsel met before Master. Defendant's time for filing list further enlarged to April 28th, 1908.

28   Counsel met before Master and defendant's time for filing list showing infringing business further enlarged to May 5, 1908.

May   5   Counsel met before Master. Defendant's time for filing completed statement further enlarged to May 12th, 1908. Master presented his opinion at this hearing which directs defendant to furnish a list showing length of each film, etc., but not the names of customers.

12   Counsel met before Master. Proceedings adjourned to May 19th, 1908.

May 26   Furnished last installment of report to complainant's counsel.

*(Docket of Dyer & Dyer.)*          1

## U. S. CIRCUIT COURT,

### SOUTHERN DISTRICT OF NEW YORK.

On Patent 12,038

THOMAS A. EDISON,
                    Complainant,

*vs.*                                   In Equity.
                                        No. 8290.          2
AMERICAN MUTOSCOPE & BIOGRAPH COM-
          PANY,
                    Defendant.

Complainant's Sol'r, RICHARD N. DYER.
Defendant's Sol'r, KERR, PAGE & COOPER.

1902.
Nov.   7   Bill filed and subpœna issued and served, return-
           able Dec. rule day 1902.
Dec.   1   Appearance of Kerr, Page & Cooper entered for          3
           defendant.
1903.
Jan.   5   Demurrer filed.
 "    15   Notice and motion to strike from files demurrer
           filed by defendant, and served on defendant's
           solicitor.
           Note of issue on motion filed.  Hearing set for
           Jan. 23, 1903.
 "    23   Motion argued before Lacombe, J.  R. M. Dyer
           for motion, D. W. Cooper opposed.          4
 "    27   Brief on motion filed by defendant and memo. in
           reply by complainant.
Mch.  26   Motion denied (Lacombe, J.), no opinion.
April  6   Demurrer set down for argument by Complain-
           ant's counsel.
Oct.  12   Motion served by defendant's counsel for an order
           setting demurrer on calendar for next term of
           Court, beginning Oct. 20, 1903.

1    "    16    Order entered by consent setting demurrer for hearing for term commencing Dec. 7, 1903.

Papers turned over to J. Edgar Bull as Counsel.

*(Following entries from docket of Gifford & Bull)*

Dec.   7    Call of calendar adjourned to Dec. 14, 1903.

   "    17    Demurrer argued before Judge Hazel by Mr. Bull.

   "    19    Our reply brief mailed to Judge.

   "    22    Deft's brief in reply rec'd.

   "    "    Our reply to Deft's reply mailed.

2    "    29    R. N. Dyer consented to substitution of G & B as solrs. and counsel for complt.

1904.

Jan.   4    Above consent filed.

     8    Demurrer overruled. Deft. must file answer in 30 days.

Order discontinuing suit with costs signed — —.

3

4

1

*(Docket of Dyer & Dyer.)*

## U. S. CIRCUIT COURT,

EASTERN DISTRICT OF PENNA.

On Edison Reissue 12,037.

THOMAS A. EDISON,
               Complainant,

        *vs.*

SIEGMUND LUBIN,
               Defendant.

In Equity. No. 24.
October Session,
1902.

2

Complainant's Sol'r, RICHARD N. DYER.
Defendant's Sol'r, CHARLES N. BUTLER, 1001
    Chestnut St., Philadelphia.

1902.

Nov. 6   Bill filed and subpœna issued and served; return-
        able Dec. rule day.

3

Dec. 1   Appearance by Charles N. Butler, Esq., entered.
1903.

Jan. 5   Answer filed.

Feb. 2   Replication filed.

Mch. 23   Notice of taking testimony served on defendant's
        Solicitor for Friday, March 27th, 1903, at 11
        A. M.

" 27   Opened *prima facie* proofs (joint record with suit
        on patent 12,038 Reissue).

July 15   *Prima facie* case closed.
        Papers turned over to J. Edgar Bull as counsel.  4

        *(Following entries from docket of Gifford & Bull)*

Sept. 23   Served notice of motion for order for limiting
        deft's time.

Nov. 16   Motion to limit time argued. Granted.

" 17   Order entered limiting deft's time to Jan. 15, 1904.

Dec. 29   R. N. Dyer signed consent substituting G & B as
        solrs and counsel for complt.

1      1904.

Jan.  2  Above consent sent to clerk at Phil. with instruc-
             tions to enter and file.
  "    2  Consented to order amending answer.
  "    4  Consent to substitution filed.
  "    8  Consented to order extending deft's time to take
             testy until Feb. 15, 1904.
Feb. 10  Consented to order extending deft's time to take
             testy until Mar. 15, 1904.
  "   10  Deft's testy commenced.  Witness C. F. Jenkins.
2  Mch.  8  Notice of taking testy at Phila. on Mar. 11/04
             rec'd.
  "   11  Testimony for deft. continued.  Witness C. F.
             Jenkins Adj. Mar. 12.
  "   12  Testimony for deft. continued.  Witness C. F.
             Jenkins and J. J. Fraley.
  "   15  Deft's time extended to Apr. 15, 1904.
April 15  Deft's time extended to May  15, 1904.
May  15    "    "    "    "  June  "    "
June 15    "    "    "    "  July  "    "
       1909.
3  Mch. 29  Order entered by consent dismissing bill.

4

*(Docket of Dyer & Dyer.)*        1

## U. S. CIRCUIT COURT,

Eastern District of Penna.

On Reissue Patent 12,038.

| | |
|---|---|
| Thomas A. Edison,<br>Complainant,<br><br>*v.*<br><br>Siegmund Lubin,<br>Defendant. | In Equity. No. 25,<br>October Session,<br>19        2 |

Complainant's Solicitor, Richard N. Dyer.

Defendant's Solicitor, Charles N. Butler, 1001 Chestnut St., Philadelphia, Pa.

1902

Nov.   6   Bill filed and subpœna issued and served, returnable Dec. rule day 1902.

Dec.   1   Appearance of Charles N. Butler entered.        3

1903

Jan.   5   Answer filed.

Feb.   2   Replication filed.

Mch.  23   Notice of taking testimony served on defendant's Solicitor for Friday, March 27, 1903, 11 A. M.

27   Opened prima facie proofs (Joint record with suit on reissue 12,037).

July  15   *Prima facie* case closed.

Papers turned over to J. Edgar Bull as Counsel.

*(The following entries from docket of Gifford &*   4
*Bull.)*

Sept. 23   Served notice of motion for order limiting deft's time.

Nov.  16   Motion to limit deft's time argued and granted.

17   Order entered limiting deft's time Jan. 15, 1904.

Dec.  29   Dyer signed consent substituting G & B as solrs. and counsel for complt.

3130

1904
Jan.    2   Consent mailed to Clerk at Phil., with instruc-
                tions to enter & file.
        2   Consented to amendment to answer.
        4   Consent to substitution filed.
        8   Consented to order extending deft's time to take
                testy. until Feb. 15.
    1909
Mch.  29   Dismissed by consent.

2

3

4

(*Docket of Dyer & Dyer.*)     1

## U. S. CIRCUIT COURT,

NORTHERN DISTRICT OF ILLINOIS—NORTHERN DIVISION.

On Edison Reissue 12,037.

THOMAS A. EDISON,
Complainant,

*v.*

SELIG POLYSCOPE COMPANY,
Defendant.

In Equity.

2

Complainant's Solicitors, ISHAM, LINCOLN & BEALE (R. N. DYER, of Counsel).

Defendant's Solicitors, BANNING & BANNING, Chicago, Ill.

**1902**

Nov. 7 Bill filed and subpœna issued, returnable Dec. rule day 1902; Bond of National Surety Co. for costs in the sum of $250 filed.     3

Dec. 1 Appearance of Banning & Banning entered for defendant.

**1903**

Jan. 5 Answer filed.

Feb. 2 Replication filed.

April 12 Served notice of opening *prima facie* proofs on defendant's solicitors for April 30, 1903.

June 11 Complainant's *prima facie* proofs opened (joint record with suit on patent 12,038).

July 10 Complainant's *prima facie* proofs closed.     4

Papers turned over to J. Edgar Bull as Counsel.

(*The following entries from docket of Gifford & Bull.*)

Dec. 29 Dyrenforth, Dyrenforth and Lee substituted as solrs. for complt.

30 Notice of motion for order limiting deft's time served.

Hearing of motion Jan. 4, 1904.

1

    1904

May 25    Stipulated and agreed as follows: Printed copies of all testy. in N. Y. case to be used in this case. Deft. to close its testy. on question of infringement in 60 days. This cause shall not be brought on for final hearing until after decision in N. Y. Case. Complt. may at any time move for preliminary injunction.

June 27    Rec'd notice of taking testy. for deft. on July 7, 1904.

2 July    7    Defendant's testimony on question of infringement commenced. Witnesses W. N. Selig and O. W. Bond.

     Cross examination of both witnesses waived by complt's counsel.

     Deft's proof closed.

    1906

Dec. 17    Time for closing proofs extended to 1st Monday in March by court.

    1907

Feb.    Stipulation extending time to close proofs to 1st

3          Monday in July.

April 19    Notice of motion for preliminary inj. & mo. papers sent to Dyrenforth.

May    7    Motion argued.

Oct.    24    Motion for injunction granted.

Nov.    1    Injunction order entered and injunction served.

4

*(Docket of Dyer & Dyer.)*     1

## U. S. CIRCUIT COURT,

NORTHERN DISTRICT OF ILLINOIS, NORTHERN DIVISION.

On Patent Reissue 12,038.

THOMAS A. EDISON,
                   Complainant,

        *v.*                                    In Equity.

SELIG POLYSCOPE COMPANY,                              2
                   Defendant.

Complainant's Solicitor, ISHAM, LINCOLN & BEALE
   (R. N. DYER, of Counsel).
Defendant's Solicitor, BANNING & BANNING.

1902

Nov.   7   Bill filed and subpœna issued, returnable Dec.
           rule day 1902.
           Bond of National Surety Co. for costs in the sum
           of $250 filed.

Dec.   1   Appearance of Banning & Banning entered for de-    3
           fendant.

1903

Jan.   5   Answer filed.

Feb.   2   Replication filed.

April 12   Served notice of opening *prima facie* proofs on de-
           fendant's solicitors for April 30th.

June 11   Complainant's *prima facie* proofs opened (joint
           record with suit on reissue patent 12,037—)

July  10   Complainant's *prima facie* proofs closed.
           Papers turned over to J. Edgar Bull as Counsel.     4
           *(The following entries from docket of Gifford &
           Bull.)*

Dec.  29   Dyrenforth and Dyrenforth and Lee substituted
           as solrs for complt.

 "    30   Notice of motion for order limiting deft's time
           served.
           Hearing of motion Jan. 4, 1904.
           Stipulation signed discontinuing suit without
           costs.
           Order entered

1

(*Docket of Kerr, Page & Cooper.*)

## UNITED STATES CIRCUIT COURT,

### SOUTHERN DISTRICT OF NEW YORK.

| | |
|---|---|
| THOMAS A. EDISON, <br><br> *v.* <br><br> WILLIAM PALEY and WILLIAM F. STEINER. | In Equity. No. 8911. <br><br> Suit on Edison Reissue Patent No. 12,192. |

2

1904
Nov. 23   Bill filed and subpœna issued.
1905
Jan.   2   Appearance for defts. entered by Herman Herst, Jr.
Feb.   6   Stipulated that defts. may have until March Rule Day to file answer.
Mch.   6   Stipulation signed extending defts. time to answer to March 25.

3   "   25   Answer filed.
May.   1   Replication filed.
There is an oral agreement between counsel that the disposition of this suit shall depend upon the outcome of the suit of Edison *v.* Eberhardt Schneider, on the same patent as is here sued on, and which has been made a test case.

1913
Mch.   3   On the call of the calendar this suit was dismissed for lack of prosecution.

4

(*Docket of Kerr, Page & Cooper.*)

## UNITED STATES CIRCUIT COURT,

### SOUTHERN DISTRICT OF NEW YORK.

|  |  |
|---|---|
| THOMAS A. EDISON,<br><br>*v.*<br><br>COMPANIE GENERALE DE PHONOGRAPHES CINEMATOGRAPHES, ET APPARIELS DE PRECISION and J. A. BERST, doing business under the name PATHE CINEMATOGRAPH COMPANY. | In Equity, No. 8,912.<br><br>Suit on Edison Reissue Patent No. 12,192. |

1904

Nov. 23   Bill filed and subpœna issued.

1905

Jan.   2   Appearance for defts. entered by Herman Herst, Jr.

Feb.   6   Stipulated that defts. may have until March Rule day to file answer.

Mch.   6   Stipulation signed extending defts. time to answer to March 25.

"   25   Answer filed.

May   1   Replication filed.

There is an oral agreement between counsel that the disposition of this suit shall depend upon the outcome of the suit of Edison *v.* Eberhardt Schneider, on the same patent as is here sued on, and which has been made a test case.

1913

Feb. 27   Order signed and entered dismissing bill of complaint.

(*Docket of Kerr, Page & Cooper.*)

## UNITED STATES CIRCUIT COURT,

### SOUTHERN DISTRICT OF NEW YORK.

| | |
|---|---|
| THOMAS A. EDISON,<br><br>*vs.*<br><br>GEORGE MELIES & GASTON MELIES, doing business under the name Gaston Melies. | In Equity, No. 8,913.<br><br>Suit on Edison Reissue Patent No. 12,192. |

1904.
Nov. 23   Bill filed and subpœnas issued.
1905.
Jan.   2   Appearance for defts. entered by Herman Herst, Jr.
Feb.   6   Stipulated that defts. may have until March Rule day to file answer.
Mch.   5   Stipulation signed extending defts. time to answer to March 25.
"     25   Answer filed.
May   1   Replication filed.
          There is an oral understanding between counsel that the disposition of this suit will depend upon the outcome of the suit of Edison *vs.* Eberhardt Schneider, on the same patent as is here sued on, and which has been made a test case.
1913.
Feb. 27   Order signed and entered dismissing bill of complaint.

*(Docket of Kerr, Page & Cooper.)*        1

## UNITED STATES CIRCUIT COURT,

### SOUTHERN DISTRICT OF NEW YORK.

THOMAS A. EDISON,

*vs.*

EBERHARDT SCHNEIDER, doing business as American Cinematograph Co. and German-American Cinematograph and Film Co.

> In Equity,
> No. 8,914.
> Suit on Edison
> Reissue Patent
> No. 12,192.        2

1904.

Nov. 23   Bill filed and subpœna issued.

1905.

Jan.   2   Appearance for deft. entered by Herman Herst, Jr.

Feb.   6   Stipulated that deft. may have until March Rule Day to file Answer.

Mch.   6   Answer filed.        3

April   3   Replication filed.

July   3, 5   Met by agreement and deposition of Henry W. Carter, for complainant, taken.

Nov.   2, 3, 4   Met pursuant to agreement and examination of William Main, for Defendant, begun. Further proceedings adjourned to November 10th, 1905.

"   10, 11   Examination of Prof. Main continued and adjourned to date to be agreed upon.

Dec.   11, 14   Met pursuant to agreement and examination of Prof. Main continued and adjourned to meet   4 on notice.

1906.

Feb.   2, 6   Met pursuant to agreement. Examination of Prof. Main continued and concluded.

Feb.   6   Parties stipulated on record that if Thomas A. Edison, C. H. Kayser, F. P. Ott and J. F. Randolph were called as witnesses in this case they would testify as they did in the case of Edison *vs.* American Mutoscope & Biograph Co. Defendant's case closed.

1908.

May   1   Served notice of motion on complainant's solicitor, by mail, for an order placing case on calendar for final hearing at the April, 1908, Term, returnable on Friday, May 8th, 1908.

"   1   Filed note of issue of motion to place case on calendar of April Term.

"   6   Served copy of affidavit that defendant will present to Court at argument of motion to place case on calendar for final hearing on complainant's counsel, Mr. Bull.

"   8   Argument of motion to place case on calendar for present term of court postponed for one week, complainant's counsel to serve their reply papers on us one day before argument.

"   15   Received copy of complainant's papers on motion.

"   16   Motion argued before Judge Ward. Decision reserved.

"   19   Memorandum filed stating that if the Edison Mfg. Co. (assignee of complainant) will file a stipulation within two days after service of order that it will file a supplemental bill the motion is denied; otherwise it will be granted.

"   20   Order, in conformity with Court's memorandum, signed and entered and a copy thereof served on complainant's counsel.

"   21   Received copy of stipulation that Edison Co. *will* file herein an original bill of complaint in the nature of a supplemental bill. A copy of this stipulation was filed in the clerk's office.

"   21   Wrote to Mr. Bull objecting to form of stipulation.

"   22   Received copy of stipulation that Edison Co. will *apply* for leave to file a supplemental bill. The original copy of this stipulation was filed in the office of the clerk.

1913.

Feb.   27   Order entered dismissing bill of complaint.

(*Docket of Kerr, Page & Cooper.*)                    1

## UNITED STATES CIRCUIT COURT,

### SOUTHERN DISTRICT OF NEW YORK.

THOMAS A. EDISON,

*vs.*

AMERICAN VITAGRAPH COMPANY, WILLIAM
T. ROCK, J. STUART BLACKTON and
ALBERT E. SMITH.

In Equity, No.
9,035.

Suit on Edison
Reissued Cam-
era Patent No.
12,037.                    2

1905
Mch. 13  Bill of complaint filed, subpœna issued and served.
April 3  Appearance for defts. entered by K., P. & C.
"      4  Amendment to bill of complaint filed.
May    2  Answer filed.
June   5  Replication filed.
      1907
Mch. 28  Order entered substituting Gifford & Bull as solici-  3
              tors for complainant, in place of Frank L. Dyer.
      1913
Feb. 25  Order entered dismissing bill of complaint.

4

(*Docket of Kerr, Page & Cooper.*)

## UNITED STATES CIRCUIT COURT,

### SOUTHERN DISTRICT OF NEW YORK.

| | |
|---|---|
| THOMAS A. EDISON,<br><br>*vs.*<br><br>AMERICAN VITAGRAPH COMPANY, WILLIAM T. ROCK, J. STUART BLACKTON and ALBERT E. SMITH. | In Equity, No. 9,034. Suit on Edison Reissued Film Patent No. 12,192. |

1905

Mar. 13  Bill of complaint filed, subpœna issued and served.

April 3  Appearance for defendants entered by K., P. & C.

"    4  Amendment to bill of complaint filed.

May 2  Answer filed.

June 5  Replication filed.

There is an oral agreement between counsel that the disposition of this suit shall depend upon the outcome of the suit of Edison vs. Eberhardt Schneider, on the same patent as is here sued on, and which has been made a test case.

1907

Mch. 28  Order entered substituting Gifford & Bull as solicitors for complainant in place of Frank L. Dyer.

1913

Feb. 25  Order entered dismissing bill of complaint.

*(Docket of Kerr, Page & Cooper.)*

## UNITED STATES CIRCUIT COURT,

NORTHERN DISTRICT OF ILLINOIS—EASTERN DIV.

EDISON MANUFACTURING COMPANY,

vs.

KLEINE OPTICAL COMPANY.

Suit based on Edison reissue No. 12,192, Film.

1908

Mch.  6  Bill of complaint filed, appearance for complainant entered by Offield, Towle & Linthicum and subpœna issued

Mch.  6  Subpœna served on Mr. Kleine.

"  7  Appearance for defendant entered by Rector, Hibben & Davis.

April 6  Filed defendant's answer.

"  24  On defendant's application court issued an order to show cause why an order of court should not be entered prohibiting complainant from bringing further suits against defendant's users until this suit, as a test, shall have been disposed of, returnable on April 28th, 1908.

April 24  Served copies of order to show cause and petition to restrain complainant from bringing additional suits on complainant's solicitors at Chicago.

April 28  Argument of petition postponed until May 11th, 1908; complainant, in the meantime, to bring no new suits.

May  4  Replication filed.

"  11  Petition presented and court entered an order stating that it took the matter of injunction under advisement and that the 90 days' time for taking testimony was apportioned by giving each side 45 days thereof; this was upon the agreement of the Edison Company's attorneys that no more suits will be brought without leave of court and no advertisements of suits made.

May  21  Counsel met pursuant to agreement at complain-
          ant's counsel's office at Orange, N. J.  Counsel
          stipulated that the suit brought against George
          Kleine may be considered as consolidated with
          this one, that uncertified copies of patents may
          be used, that the capacity of complainant is as
          alleged, etc.  Testimony of George F. Scull
          taken.  *Prima facie* case closed.

May 25-29

June. 1-5 Taking of defendant's proofs begun.  Direct tes-
          timony of Prof. William Main taken and pro-
          ceedings adjourned to June 9th when Prof.
          Main will be cross-examined.

June 9-12
   15-19  Cross-examination of Prof. Main begun, continued
          and concluded.

June 19   Testimony of George H. Stockbridge taken.

"  20-22  Testimony of Harry N. Marvin taken.  Further
          proceedings adjourned to June 25th, 1908.

June 25   Testimony of defendant's witness Arthur E.
          Johnstone taken.  Further proceedings ad-
          journed subject to notice.

July   3  Counsel met pursuant to agreement at defendant's
          counsel's office.  Testimony of Joseph Mason
          and William Main (recalled) taken.  Further
          proceedings adjourned to July 6, 1908.

July 6-7-8 Testimony of defendant's witness Herman Casler
          taken.  DEFENDANT'S CASE CLOSED.

   1909
Mch. 17   Signed stipulation dismissing bill of complaint
          without costs.

Mch. 23   Order signed and entered dismissing bill of com-
          plaint.

*(Docket of Kerr, Page & Cooper.)*     1

## U. S. CIRCUIT COURT,

### NORTHERN DISTRICT OF ILLINOIS—EASTERN DIVISION.

| | |
|---|---|
| EDISON MANUFACTURING COMPANY,<br><br>*v.*<br><br>GEORGE KLEINE. | In Equity, No.<br>Suit on Edison<br>Reissued Patent<br>No. 12,192, for a<br>Film. |

2

1908

Mch.  6  Bill of complaint filed, appearance for complain-
         ant, entered by Offield, Towle & Linthicum and
         subpœna issued.

      6  Subpœna served on Mr. Kleine.

      7  Appearance for defendant entered by Rector,
         Hibben & Davis.

April  6  Filed defendant's answer.

May    4  Replication filed.

1909                                                         3

Mch. 17  Signed stipulation dismissing bill of complaint
         without costs.

      23  Order signed and entered dismissing bill of com-
          plaint.

4

(*Docket of Kerr, Page & Cooper.*)

## U. S. CIRCUIT COURT,

### SOUTHERN DISTRICT OF NEW YORK.

EDISON MANUFACTURING COMPANY,

*v.*

HENRY LORSCH, HUGO SUSSFELD, EDMOND SUSSFELD and EDWIN LORSCH, doing business under the firm name and style of Sussfeld, Lorsch & Company.

In Equity, No. 168. Suit based on Edison Reissued Patent No. 12,192.

1908

Mch. 16   Bill of complaint filed, appearance for complainant entered by Gifford & Bull, and subpœnas issued, returnable on Rule Day of April, 1908.

April 6   Entered appearance of K., P. & C. on behalf of defendants.

May 4   Filed defendant's answer.

June 1   Replication filed.

1909

Mch. 30   Signed stipulation directing dismissal of bill of complaint without costs to either party.

April 1   Order dismissing bill of complaint signed and entered.

*(Docket of Kerr, Page & Cooper.)*      1

## U. S. CIRCUIT COURT,

SOUTHERN DISTRICT OF NEW YORK.

| | |
|---|---|
| EDISON MANUFACTURING COMPANY | In Equity, No. 169. |
| *v.* | Suit based on Edison Reissued |
| AMERICAN MUTOSCOPE AND BIOGRAPH COMPANY. | Patent No. 12,192. |

2

1908

Mch. 16  Bill of complaint filed, appearance for complainant entered by Gifford & Bull, and subpœna issued, returnable on Rule Day of April, 1908.

April  6  Entered appearance of K., P. & C. on behalf of defendant.

May  4  Answer filed.

June  1  Replication filed.

June  1  Served notice of motion, also supporting affidavit, on complainant's solicitors for an order apportioning times for taking proofs, returnable on June 19, 1908.

3

June  1  Filed note of issue placing motion to apportion times for taking proofs on calendar for June 19, 1908.

June 19  Court signed an order directing that proofs be closed by Sept. 19, 1908, that complainant have forty-five days for taking its proofs and defendant likewise to have forty-five days for taking its proofs.

4

June 19  Served copy of order apportioning time for taking proofs on complainant's solicitors.

June 30  July 1-3, 6, 8-11, 13, 14. Counsel met at the office of F. L. Dyer at Orange, and the taking of complainant's *prima facie* proofs were begun and concluded. Greenleaf Whittier Pickard witness.

1    July
22, 23    Counsel met at our offices and taking of defendant's proofs begun. Harry N. Marvin, witness. Further proceedings adjourned subject to notice.

1909

Mch. 30    Signed stipulation directing dismissal of bill of complaint without costs to either party.

April 1    Order dismissing bill of complaint signed and entered.

2

3

4

Thereupon, ANNA S. MATTHEWS, resumed the stand 1
for cross examination.

Cross examination by Mr. GROSVENOR:

Q. Miss Matthews, what are the duties of this Information Division of the Motion Picture Patents Company, of which you are Supervisor? A. The principal duties relate to the records regarding motion picture theatres in the United States.

Q. You are referring to the preparation of the tables, respecting which you testified on direct examination? A. 2 Yes.

Q. What other records does the Information Division maintain? A. It maintains geographical records, according to the theatres in the different States. Then we have records according to the addressograph plates, for mailing lists.

Q. Do you have any other records? Do you keep any other records? A. We keep records of the licensed exhibitors and of the independent exhibitors.

Q. These records, which are now referred to, are records which are kept separate and distinct from these other 3 tables, respecting which you testified on direct examination? A. Yes, sir, they are kept weekly, and changes are made weekly in the records.

Q. What other records do you keep? A. I don't just get what you mean by "what other records."

Q. What other records, if any, does your Information Bureau maintain or keep from day to day, or from week to week? A. I think that is about all. Service records of the active and closed theatres.

Q. How do you ascertain the names of the licensed theatres? Who furnishes those names? A. The exchanges 4 report their customers; the licensed exchanges report their customers.

Q. That is, each branch of the General Film Company sends in to you the names of its customers? A. Yes.

Q. And that has been the practice all the time that you have been the supervisor of this Information Division? A. Yes, sir.

Q. Before the General Film Company was organized

1 you received the lists of the customers from the licensed exchanges? A. Yes, sir.

Q. What do you do with these reports after you get them? A. Well, we enter them in our records, transcribe the information that the exchange gives on exhibitors' index cards, which show the service reported that each exhibitor uses.

Q. Who uses these tables that are made up? A. Anybody in the office that needs to refer to them.

Q. They are used, then, for general reference use, by the officers of the company? A. Yes, sir.

2 Q. And they have been so used during the time that you have been the Supervisor of the Information Division? A. Yes, sir.

Q. That is to say, these records are frequently consulted by the officers of the company? A. When occasion arises they consult them.

Q. Does the Information Division receive any reports from the General Film Company's branches, from time to time, other than these lists of customers? A. You mean regarding other theatres?

3 Q. Yes. A. Well, we send out asking them for information regarding theatres in their city at each checking period. Otherwise they do not give us information.

Q. What information does the General Film Company give you, then? A. They furnish us with the names of their customers, and the service they formerly used, if they have any record of it.

Q. That is to say, if a branch of the General Film Company gets a new customer, it advises you from what company that customer was taking service? A. No.

Q. Before the customer came to them? A. No, not what 4 company. They just say whether they used independent service, or whether they were closed, or whether the theatre was a new theatre.

Q. What other reports, if any, does the General Film Company send to your bureau? A. Those are the only reports we get.

Q. Do they send you any information as to the amount of business they are doing? A. Not to our department.

Q. You would not know as to that, whether your company, the Patents Company, receives such reports from

the General Film Company? A. No, not other than the
reports I have mentioned.

Q. That is to say, you don't know anything about anything except the reports you have mentioned? A. Yes, sir.

Q. That is what you mean to say? A. Yes, sir.

Q. Your bureau does not concern itself with the amount
of business done by the Patents Company, or anybody at
all? A. Only regarding the motion picture theatres.

Q. You concern yourself only regarding the motion picture theatres? A. Yes, sir.

Q. You gave some testimony on direct examination
respecting the territory of Mr. Brandon. How do you
know what his territory is as branch manager of the General Film Company? A. I have no knowledge of the territory, but just know what territory Mr. Brandon stated
was his territory.

Q. Did you read Mr. Brandon's examination? A. Yes,
sir.

Q. Didn't you notice that in his examination he testified
that in certain parts of his territory, or of the territory
reached by his branch, other branches of the General Film
Company did business? A. Yes, sir.

Q. How did you distinguish or draw a line between his
territory and the territory of the other branches? A. Well,
he said what his territory was, and in preparing the statement I took his testimony.

Q. You have got, then, no more accurate limits on his
territory than those given by him in his examination? A.
No.

Q. On pages 2933-2934, Vol. V, Miss Matthews, you gave
certain answers purporting to disclose the number of new
theatres on hand at various dates. How did you arrive at
those figures? A. In checking with the return postal lists of
the various checkings mentioned, if there were any theatres
listed thereon which did not appear upon our records, we as-
signed a new number to it, a new unlicensed number for our
records, and placed it in our files, and from this checking we
procured from the dates mentioned October, 1910, to January, 1911, approximately eighteen hundred and twenty-five
theatres from the postal checking, and also, from printed
information sheets which we sent out to the various theatres.

Q. You have not subtracted from that number of eighteen

1  hundred and twenty-five, the number of theatres that went out of business? A. No.

Q. As a matter of fact there were, on October 31st, 1910, 9,480 theatres according to Defendants' Exhibit No. 154, page 3026, Vol. V? A. Yes, sir.

Q. And on January 30th, 1911, there were 10,090 theatres as shown by Defendants' Exhibit No. 155, at page 3232? A. Yes.

Q. Witness, please look at Defendants' Exhibit No. 155, page 3028, which shows the total number of theatres on 2  January 30th, 1911, as 10,090, and compare that with Defendants' Exhibit No. 154, which shows the total number of theatres October 31st, 1910, of 9,480. This gives an increase on the January estimate of six hundred and ten theatres. Please explain the apparent discrepancy between those figures "610" and the figures given by you on page 2933 of your direct examination, where you stated: "Q. How many new theatres did you get from the checking of October, 1910? A. I cannot give the exact figures procured from that one checking, but including that checking, and the time intervening between that and the January, 1911, checking, we procured approximately eighteen hundred and twenty-five. 3  Q. How many new theatres, approximately, did you get from the checking of January, 1911? A. Approximately four hundred and forty-five."

Mr. Kingsley: I object to the question on the ground that it does not fairly present the statements made in the exhibits and in the witness' answer which appears at page 2933, the witness having stated that she could not give the exact figures procured from the checking of October, 1910, but could give figures in4  cluding that checking and also the time intervening between that checking and the checking of January, 1911.

The Witness: The only difference I can state is that a number of the theatres in the meantime had closed, and other new theatres were opened.

Mr. Grosvenor: My question is this: How did you get that figure given on page 2933, namely, "1825" theatres?

The Witness: Eighteen hundred twenty-five theatres?    1

> Mr. KINGSLEY: I ask counsel to read it cor-
> rectly—1825 new theatres.
> Mr. GROSVENOR: What I want you to do is to give
> a clear explanation of that answer given by you on
> direct examination. I do not understand it, and that
> is what I am trying to ask you to explain?

The Witness: The 1825 theatres were procured within
that time, the time stated, of which the Patents Company had no record.    2

> Mr. KINGSLEY: No previous record?

The Witness: No previous record.

By Mr. GROSVENOR:

Q. You do not mean to imply, then, that there were
eighteen hundred and twenty-five new theatres that sprung
up in that period of three months? A. No, I did not mean
to imply that.    3

Q. You mean that you got that number of additional
names in that period for your books? A. Yes, sir.

Q. Then, please explain why that new or enlarged number, 1825, of new names, does not appear on your exhibit for
January, 1911? A. Why, in January, 1911? It was the
Winter following, and several of the Summer theatres might
have been closed.

Q. In any event, the number of theatres shown on your
list in January, 1911, is only six hundred and ten more, or
larger than the number shown on your books for October
30th, 1910? A. I presume the theatres were closed.    4

Q. Please answer my question, Miss Matthews. Isn't it
a fact that only six hundred and ten more theatres are shown
on your books for January, 1911, than were shown in October, 1910? A. Yes, 610 active theatres.

Q. And your explanation is that there were in that interval twelve hundred theatres closed? Is that your explanation that you give for the apparent vanishing of the balance
of the eighteen hundred and twenty-five theatres named on
your direct examination? A. Yes—no—no.

1     Q. Why does not that number, 1825, appear in your list
for January, 1911, if they were new theatres discovered by
you? A. The 1825 new theatres, or approximately that, were
included in the October checking as active theatres.

Q. The most of them were included in the October, 1910,
checking? A. Yes, sir, as active theatres.

Q. Why, then, are they put down in your direct examination as being new theatres, which I understand you discovered between your October and January accounting?

2          Mr. Kingsley: I object to the question, on the
ground that the answer of the witness states that these
new theatres were discovered during the October accounting, and subsequently added on to the January
accounting.

The Witness: Not including the January accounting, but
to the January accounting.

          Mr. Kingsley: I object to the question, on the
ground that the answer of the witness, at page 2933,
3        Vol. V, is as follows: "I cannot give the exact number
procured from that one checking (meaning the checking of October, 1910), but including that checking, and
the time intervening between that and the January,
1911, checking, we procured approximately 1825." I
also object to the question on the ground that it is a
misstatement of the witness' statement occurring at
page 2933, as the reading of the question and answer
will disclose.

          Mr. Grosvenor: If counsel will read my last ques-
tions he will see that they do not refer only to that
4        question on page 2933, but also to other questions and
answers given today.

          Mr. Kingsley: I have heard all of your ques-
tions, and I respectfully submit for the record that
they are not fairly deducible from the witness' testimony, or from the exhibits she has submitted.

          Mr. Grosvenor: Please repeat my last question
to the witness.

The question was read to the witness by the Examiner, as follows:

"Q. Why, then, are they put down in your direct 1
examination as being new theatres, which, I understand, you discovered between your October and January accounting?"

The Witness: It says including that checking and the
time intervening between that and the January, 1911, checking.

Mr. KINGSLEY: You mean, Miss Matthews, that
this number, 1825, was obtained from the October
checking and the time intervening up to the January
checking?                                                   2

The Witness: Including the October checking and the
time intervening.

By Mr. GROSVENOR:

Q. Now, let us get at it again. This is the only question
I want: Whatever was meant by the answer on page 2933,
which I did not understand—this is the fact, is it not, 1825
new theatres were not discovered in that period from October to January, 1911? A. They were from our records.     3

Q. They were what? They were discovered or were not?
A. They were put on our records.

Q. Let me see if this is what you mean: Between the
October, 1910, checking, and the January, 1911, checking,
eighteen hundred and twenty-five new names were added to
your books? A. No, sir.

Q. Well, when were the 1825 new names added to your
books? A. Approximately between October 1st, 1910, and
January 1st, 1911.

Q. Referring to Defendants' Exhibit No. 154, at page
3026, produced by you, in the last column there are fol-    4
lowing many of the figures minus signs. That minus sign
in each case indicates that the number after which the
minus sign appears represents the excess of licensed theatres
over the unlicensed theatres in the State opposite which
the number is placed? A. Yes, sir.

Q. And the same thing is true of Defendants' Exhibits
Nos. 155, 156, 157 and 158? A. Yes, sir.

Q. On the other hand, where there is no minus sign, but

1 the number is given without any sign following it in the last column, that means that the number of unlicensed theatres exceeds the number of licensed theatres by the number represented by the figure in the State opposite which the number appears? A. Yes, sir.

Q. And the same thing is true in Defendants' Exhibits Nos. 159, 160, 161, 162 and 163? A. Yes, sir.

Re-examination by Mr. KINGSLEY:

Q. Miss Matthews, in your department, do you keep a
2 list of the theatres which are made up in the form of addressograph plates? A. Yes, sir.

Q. And is that one of the lists to which you referred in your testimony? A. Yes, sir, it would be the same as the geographical file.

Q. When you checked the number of theatres in the United States you sent information sheets to the various exchanges, did you not? A. Yes.

Q. And the reports which you received from the General Film Company were in response to postals and blanks which you had forwarded to the various exchanges and the
3 branches? .A. Yes, sir, requesting information regarding the theatres.

Q. When you made up the totals which appear in Defendants' Exhibits Nos. 154, 155, 156, 157, 158, 159, 160, 161, 162 and 163, did you add all the new theatres reported which were available for those various tables, and subtract the theatres which had either closed or gone out of business? A. Yes, sir.

Q. So that if you obtained eighteen hundred and twenty-five new theatres, which you added to a new list, pursuant to that checking, you would also subtract from that same
4 list the names of all theatres which had closed or had gone out of business of which you were informed? A. Yes, sir.

Mr. GROSVENOR: And the number, 1825, was arrived at before you had deducted the number of theatres that had gone out of business?

The Witness: No.

Re-examination by Mr. KINGSLEY:  1

Q. Much stress has been laid upon the number "1825" which occurs in your answer at page 2933, Vol. V. Will you tell us briefly how you obtained that number, 1825 theatres? A. These figures were obtained from the October, 1910, checking of new theatres not appearing upon the Motion Picture Patents Company's records, and also from the printed theatre information sheets which we sent out to the various exhibitors. Part of the 1825 theatres were included in the October checking, and the others were not.  2

Q. And does the number approximately, 1825, represent the new theatres obtained by the checking of October, 1910, plus the checking which went on continuously up to January, 1911? A. Yes, sir.

Whereupon at 11:30 o'clock A. M., March 17th, 1914, a recess was taken until 3 o'clock P. M., March 17th, 1914, the hearing to be resumed at Room 159, Manhattan Hotel, New York City.

3

4

1                              NEW YORK CITY, March 17th, 1914.

The hearing was resumed pursuant to adjournment, at
3 o'clock P. M.

Appearances—the same as at the morning session.

JEREMIAH J. KENNEDY, a witness produced on behalf of the defendants, being first duly sworn by the Examiner, deposed as follows:

Direct examination by Mr. KINGSLEY:
2

Q. Where do you live, Mr. Kennedy?  A. At 529 Second
Street, Brooklyn.

Q. How long have you been connected with the Biograph
Company?  A. Since the Summer of 1907.

Q. Have you been an officer of the Motion Picture Patents Company at any time?  A. I have been Treasurer since
its formation, and also Director.

Q. Do you recall the formation of the Motion Picture
Patents Company?  A. I do, very distinctly.

Q. Does the Motion Picture Patents Company have any
3  interest in or any investments in theatres?  A. It has not,
and never had, and never contemplated having any.

Q. Have you been an officer of the General Film Company
at any time?  A. I was President and Director from its
incorporation until about May 27th, 1912, that is, from April
18th, 1910.

Q. Are you an officer of the General Film Company at
present?  A. I have been President since January 20th of
this year.

Q. Does the General Film Company have any interest in
or any investments in theatres?  A. Never had any and
4  never contemplated having any during my connection with it.

Q. Do you recall the time when various producers of motion pictures became Edison licensees?  A. I do not know
the exact date on which they became licensees, but I remember approximately the time and what occurred immediately prior thereto.

Q. You do remember, however, that a number of the producers of motion pictures became licensees under the Edison
patents?  A. Yes.  I never saw their licenses, but I was
reliably informed that they had become licensees.

Q. Did the Biograph Company become an Edison licensee at that time? A. It did not.

Q. Why did the Biograph Company fail or refuse to become an Edison licensee? A. For various reasons, among them being the reason that the Edison Company refused to allow it any consideration for the patents which it held, and for the further reason that the Biograph Company felt that it was entitled to some such consideration in the way of lesser royalty for a license under the Edison patent.

Q. Did the Biograph Company or Armat companies manufacture or sell projecting machines? A. Never during my connection with them.

Q. Who owned the stock of the Motion Picture Patents Company at the time of its organization? A. The Edison Company and the Biograph Company.

Q. In what proportions did the Edison Company and the Biograph Company own the stock of the Motion Picture Patents Company? A. Each had an equal stock holding.

Q. Who owns the stock now? A. The same parties, or their successors.

Q. In the same proportions? A. In the same proportions. .

Q. Did any of the other producers of motion pictures aside from the Edison Company and the Biograph Company have any stock or any financial interest whatever in the Motion Picture Patents Company? A. None of them had any interest directly or indirectly, or any say in the management of the business or affairs of the company. Their relations with the Motion Picture Patents Company were solely those of licensees to licensor.

Q. Do you recall the market situation in 1908, prior to the formation of the Motion Picture Patents Company, when certain producers of motion pictures were operating under the Edison patents, and the Biograph Company and George Kleine were operating without licenses under the Edison patents? A. I do.

Q. Did the Biograph Company cut the prices of motion pictures during the year 1908, prior to the formation of the Motion Picture Patents Company? A. No, it increased its prices on account of the increasing cost of the productions.

Q. Was there competition among the licensed producers of motion pictures after the formation of the Motion Picture

1  Patents Company? A. The competition was as keen and active, if not more so, than before.

Q. Is there such competition at present? A. There is a greater competition today than before, not only as to quality, but also as to price.

Q. In what respect is this competition evident at present? A. On the shorter subjects, the competition is—and by shorter subjects, I mean one-reel subjects—the competition is almost entirely, if not entirely, a competition of quality, each producer endeavoring to produce a quality of motion pictures superior to his competitors. On the longer subjects, the competition is not only as to quality, but also as to price, for these longer subjects frequently could not be leased at three times the minimum price named in the license agreement, without suffering serious loss.

Q. Do you remember the occasion on December 18th, 1908, when the licensed producers of motion pictures met to discuss and sign the license agreements with the Motion Picture Patents Company? A. Did you say in 1908?

Q. December 18th, 1908. A. I do; very clearly.

Q. Were you present on that occasion? A. I was.

3  Q. Do you remember that one J. J. Lodge, who was a witness in this action, was present on that occasion? A. He was. I did not know who he was at the time, but I learned his identity afterwards.

Q. Did you have any conversation with the witness Lodge, relative to forming a rental exchange in which the licensed producers of motion pictures should be stockholders? A. I did not.

Q. Did you have any conversation with anyone else on December 18th, 1908, relative to the possibility of forming a rental exchange which licensed producers of motion pictures should own and operate? A. I did not, and had no such idea for a long time afterwards.

Q. Did you hear any conversation between Lodge and any of the other persons then present, as to the possibility of forming a rental exchange to be owned by licensed producers of motion pictures? A. No such conversation took place within my hearing.

Q. Did you hear any conversation between any of the other persons there, relative to the possibility of forming a rental exchange to be owned by the licensed producers of motion pictures? A. There was no such conversation.

Q. Did anyone state in your hearing that a portion of the royalties collected by the Motion Picture Patents Company would be used to form a gigantic fund for litigation? A. No one ever made such a suggestion. Such an idea was never considered.

Q. Were you, subsequent to December 18th, 1908, and during the early months of 1909, present at any meeting or gathering of producers of licensed motion pictures at which the witness Lodge was also present? A. I was not, according to the best of my recollection. I have no record of being present at such meeting, either.

Q. Were you present at any meeting of the licensed producers of motion pictures after the 1st of January, 1909, at which the witness Lodge was present, where there was any discussion whatever, relative to the possibility of forming a rental exchange which should be owned by the licensed producers, and operated by them? A. I was not, and I never heard the idea advanced, until I suggested it myself, about a year after December 18th, 1908.

Q. About what time was it that you made this suggestion or discussed the proposition? A. I told the guests who were present at a dinner on or about December 18th, 1909, that in my opinion, they would eventually provide a reliable and impartially conducted source of supply for the exhibitors.

Q. What were the reasons that caused you to believe that such an exchange should be organized? A. The many abuses and evils that existed in the business at that time, and during the whole time, prior to that time that I was connected with the business, and which evils and abuses were the subject of many complaints to the Biograph Company, and to the Motion Picture Patents Company, by exhibitors and exchanges.

Q. Did the Motion Picture Patents Company own any interest whatever in the General Film Company? A. It never had any interest, and no provision was ever made for its having any interest. The relations of the two companies were solely those of licensor and licensee. In fact, the management of the General Film Company was always more or less hostile to the Patents Company. By management, in this case, I am referring to the Board of Directors.

Q. Will you specify what, in your judgment, were the

1   principal reasons for forming the General Film Company?
A. Well, the conditions which led up to the experiment of
the General Film Company were many, and as I have said
before, covered the whole period of my connection with
the motion picture business.

A few of the reasons were the fact that many exchanges
used the motion pictures which they handled as a lever
or a power to force unfair business conditions, or to crush
or to control exhibitors by forcing, in some cases, the exhibitors to pay them a part of their receipts or profits. In
2   other cases, exhibitors were threatened with extinction
if they did not take service from exchanges. In other
cases exchanges owned theatres which they supplied—
to which they gave the preference in the supply of
motion pictures. The number of exchanges throughout
the country, which were interested in, or which owned
or controlled theatres, was such as to enable other
exchanges to force exhibitors to deal with them, to submit
to unfair treatment under threat of establishing similar
competition by opening theatres in competition with the
exhibitors whom they threatened.

3   In many cases, the exchanges were financially irresponsi-
ble. All the producers had suffered large losses through
failure of the exchanges to pay their bills, in fact, it was
common understanding in the business that sooner or later
the last two or three weeks' bill of each exchange would
be a loss. This and other abuses resulted in numerous complaints to the producers and to the Motion Picture Patents
Company, and a request for some relief or protection in
some form. Many of the exhibitors suggested as a protection, the adoption of a price schedule. Others suggested
a classification of motion pictures. Other suggestions were
4   made with the object of compelling exchanges to live up
to their agreements with the theatres. Other suggestions
were made with a view to obtaining protection from the
crushing power of certain combinations that had been made,
notably, those at Rochester, New York, New York City and
Chicago, which combinations had for their object the preventing of any of their members from serving or agreeing
to serve a customer supplied by another member except at
an advance of ten per cent. or more over the preceding price.
In many cases exhibitors were paying all they could pay

for their service, and were not able to go to other exchanges  1
and obtain even other service at a higher price. Such exhibitors were obliged to accept just what the exchange
gave them, and were unable to make any change, for the
reason that none of the other exchanges would serve them
except at a higher price. These companies had also deposits
to be forfeited in the event of their violating any of the
conditions agreed upon, and also had by-laws or agreements
which provided for fines or other punishment for violation.

Many exhibitors appealed for protection from these conditions. The question of the price never appeared to be an
important question. Most of the exhibitors whom I have  2
met were willing to pay a higher price, and stated that they
could afford to pay a higher price for a good reliable film
service, for a supply of motion pictures which they could advertise. For protection against exchanges conniving with
their competitors to break up their programs whenever they
did advertise subjects. That was another abuse which had
become very common.

Now, one great demand of the exhibitor seemed to be a
reliable and impartial supply of motion pictures, the motion
pictures which were necessary for the existence of his busi-  3
ness, and after serious consideration had been given by the
different producers at different times to these conditions,
which were ruinous not only to the exhibitor, but also to the
exchanges as well as the producers, resulted in my making
the suggestion that as the exhibitor wanted only a reliable
and proper supply of motion pictures, the logical thing to do
was to experiment with the providing of such a supply. If
that was found to be the proper solution, that would end it;
if not, they would have to look further.

Q. Did the majority of the licensed producers of motion
pictures express an opinion in conversation with you, as to  4
whether the General Film Company would be profitable or
unprofitable to them? A. Yes. They were very much
opposed to it, claiming it could not possibly earn enough to
pay its expenses, that their business was likely to be seriously injured by antagonism on the part of exchanges.

Q. Have you already sufficiently indicated what it was intended to accomplish by the formation and operation of the
General Film Company? A. Well, the object was very
simple. It was to provide a means whereby the exhibitor

could obtain a reliable and impartial supply of motion pictures. The intention was to try this experiment in localities where these abuses were greatest, with a view of putting the exhibitor in a position to protect himself.

Q. When did the General Film Company go into the exchange business? A. It opened its first exchange on or about June 6th, 1910.

Q. Did the General Film Company engage in a fair competition with existing exchanges? A. It did, unquestionably.

Q. Was there any price-cutting? A. There was not. In fact, that was one of the evils which the business had always been subject to and which it had never been free from. I refer to the period prior to the General Film Company becoming a factor in the exchange business.

Q. At the time of the organization of the General Film Company, did any of the licensed producers own rental exchanges? A. Yes. Several.

Q. What was their position with regard to the formation of the General Film Company? Did they favor or oppose the proposition? A. They, with possibly one or two exceptions, opposed it. The others would not agree to sell to the General Film Company their stocks of motion pictures and auxiliaries until after they saw whether or not the experiment was likely to be able to take care of itself in the way of income. Two of the owners of such exchanges advised other exchanges—or the owners of other exchanges—to be very cautious with their dealing with the General Film Company.

Mr. GROSVENOR: I object to this statement as hearsay, and I move to strike it out.

The Witness: For the reason that the General Film Company would very probably be a failure, and they might not get any price at which they agreed to sell. Those were the Vitagraph Company and Spoor. They did not deliver their exchanges or sell their exchanges or their exchange property to the General Film Company, until a later date. Mr. Lubin at first refused to sell or deliver the property of his exchange but afterwards did deliver it at an earlier date than either the Vitagraph Company or Mr. Spoor.

By Mr. KINGSLEY:                                              1

Q. Were prices to exhibitors increased by the General
Film Company? A. The average price was slightly less
than formerly, although the prices were readjusted so as to
be more uniform for the same class of service. We found
that in many instances exchanges were favoring theatres by
charging them a price which was so low as to involve a very
serious loss, and such loss was made up by unjustifiably
higher prices charged to other exhibitors whom they were
able to control by threats or otherwise.

Q. Would you say that the prices charged by the General   2
Film Company to exhibitors after this equalization, were
higher or lower, on the average? A. Lower.

Q. Do you recall an occasion when you had some negotiations with one William Fox, a witness in this action, relative to the possible sale of the motion pictures, stock and
equipment, of the Greater New York Film Rental Company?
A. I do.

Q. On the occasion of your conversation with William
Fox, did you say to him in terms or in substance, that you
had laid out a schedule of how much would be paid exchanges
by the General Film Company? A. I did not.          3

Q. On the occasion of your conversation with William
Fox, relative to the possible sale of the motion pictures, stock
and equipment of the Greater New York Film Rental Company, did you say to him, either in terms or in substance, that
such a schedule existed, and that the schedule permitted
you to pay him $89,000? A. I did not. Such a sum was not
mentioned, furthermore.

Q. Do you recall that at the time you were negotiating
with William Fox for the sale of the motion pictures, stock
and equipment of the Greater New York Film Rental Company, that after you had agreed with him upon terms, you   4
called up Mr. Marvin with regard to suspension of cancellation of Fox's license? A. That was at a later date, yes.

Q. Did you say to Mr. Marvin on the occasion in question, either in terms or in substance, that you did not want
such a situation as in the case of Marcus Loew? A. I never
made such a statement or request.

Q. Did you say to Fox on the occasion when you had
agreed with him as to the purchase of the motion pictures,
stock and equipment of the Greater New York Film Rental

1 Company, either in terms or in substance: "Well, this is the finish of my work; this is the end of what I set out to do?" A. I did not. I could not have understood what he meant by such a remark. At least, I want to modify that **if I may.**

Q. You may. A. There would be no sense in such a remark.

Q. Why did you call up Mr. Marvin with regard to the suspension of the cancellation after you had agreed with Fox as to the purchase of the motion pictures, stock and 2 equipment of his exchange? A. At the earnest solicitation of Mr. Fox, and I said to Mr. Marvin just what Mr. Fox requested me to say.

Q. And that was? A. That was a request, if possible, to have the license restored for the purpose of saving Mr. Fox's face.

Q. Did you say to Fox on the occasion of this negotiation, either in terms or in substance, that the General Film Company had to have the field? A. I did not.

Q. Did you, on the occasion of your first interview with Fox, take figures relative to prices of motion pictures, stock 3 and equipment of his exchange, from your pocket, and on a second interview, part of the figures from your pocket, and part from the safe? A. No, I never had any figures in my pocket.

Q. Did you say to him you had to be careful regarding the keeping of these figures ? A. No, I don't know what figures he would refer to. I never made such a statement.

Q. Did you tell Fox on the occasion of your negotiations with him, either in terms or in substance, that the General Film Company had no right to buy the Greater New York plant if it did not have a license? A. No. Such a 4 statement would have been untrue.

Q. Did the General Film Company, as a matter of fact, ever buy the license of a rental exchange? A. No, it did not.

Q. Was there competition between the General Film Company and the Greater New York Film Rental Company in the local field? A. There must have been the usual competition between exchanges, but no particular competition.

Q. Was any special effort made on the part of the Gen-

eral Film Company to induce the customers of the Greater
New York Film Rental Company to leave it? A. No. We
paid no attention whatever to the Greater New York's customers, or to the customers of any other exchange.

Q. Do you recall negotiations between the General Film
Company and Lewis Swaab, of Philadelphia, relative to the
sale of motion pictures, stock and equipment of his exchange? A. Very clearly.

Q. How far did those negotiations progress? A. They
progressed to the point of having agreed upon a price and
time for the delivery of the property, the conditions in that
respect being rather unusual.

Q. In what respect were they unusual? A. They were
unusual in respect of the time of delivery, which was to be
not less than two months from the time at which the conference was held. We had no one available to receive or
take possession of, or work the property, and part of the
conditions under which we agreed to purchase was in view
of our not being able to receive or handle the property, but
Mr. Swaab should remain in charge of it for two months,
until we could find someone to assign to the care and
operation of it.

Q. Was the negotiation consummated? A. No, I terminated the negotiations as President of the company.

Q. Under what conditions? A. I entered into them re-
luctantly. One of the conditions under which we purchased, was that Mr. Swaab should remain in charge of
the property for at least two months at a merely nominal
salary, and that such services should be included as a
part of what we purchased, and be included in the price
we agreed to pay. The compensation was fixed at $50
a week. There was another condition, the other condition
being that a number of contracts between the owners of
exchanges who sold property to the General Film Company
and that company, remained to be drawn, and I refused
to give the contract between Mr. Swaab and the General
Film Company precedence over the others who had closed
their negotiations before he had. Therefore, Mr. Swaab
was informed that it might be several weeks before his contract would be ready, but it would be ready before the
expiration of the two months. Immediately on Mr. Swaab's
return to Philadelphia, he communicated with the General

1   Film Company, through Mr. Waters, and stated that in agreeing to accept $50 a week compensation, he had over-looked the fact that he had an automobile, that he did not see how he could live and operate an automobile on a com-pensation of $50 a week. He further, after a few days, be-came very insistent in his demands for his contract. He in-dicated by the tone of his communications a dissatisfaction, or not a complete satisfaction with the terms of his sale, although I stipulated at the beginning of our negotiations that he must not accept—stipulated that we would conduct

2   our negotiations subject to the condition that he would not agree to accept any price which was not entirely satisfac-tory. Being in doubt as to whether Mr. Swaab was satis-fied or not, prompted me to terminate the negotiations and cancel the entire transaction. I may say that Mr. Swaab had no communication with the General Film Company prior to his coming to the office and insisting upon our negotiating with him for the purchase of the exchange property which he had.

Q. Do you recall having negotiated on behalf of the General Film Company for the purchase of the motion

3   pictures, stock and equipment of the Lake Shore Film & Supply Company's exchange, located at Cleveland, Ohio, with one Emanuel Mandelbaum, a witness in this case? A. Yes, I conducted the negotiations with Mr. Mandelbaum.

Q. Will you give us, briefly, the history of those nego-tiations? A. Mr. Mandelbaum called at the office one afternoon without any appointment having been made in advance, and requested that we consider the purchase of the motion pictures and other exchange property which the Lake Shore Company owned. I explained to Mr. Mandel-baum that we were not very well equipped to take on any

4   more business at that time, but on his insisting, we pro-ceeded with the negotiations, subject to the condition that if they were concluded, Mr. Mandelbaum would remain in charge of the exchange and manage the property for us. The question of price was next discussed, and Mr. Mandel-baum had estimated that he should receive $75,000 for the entire property. He stated that he computed that on the basis of his earnings capitalized at ten per cent., or on a ten per cent. basis. I showed him that that was entirely unreasonable, for the reason that the permanence of the

moving picture business was considered very doubtful by a
great many, and that to pay him any price on the basis that
he assumed, would mean that we would be guaranteeing the
existence of the business forever.  We parted, and he called
the following day and attempted to renew his negotiations,
and I refused to have any further dealings with him.  On
the following day Mr. Gilligham and Mr. Gleichman of
the National-Vaudette Exchange of Detroit, called, and
after brief negotiations, agreed to sell their exchange property to the General Film Company.  Mr. Mandelbaum was
interested in the National-Vaudette as a stockholder, but
I had no knowledge of that at the time.  At Mr. Gilligham's request, he informing me that Mr. Mandelbaum
was still in town, although I did not know it, and the request of Mr. Waters, the general manager of the General
Film Company, to whom Mr. Mandelbaum had telephoned,
I agreed to meet him again.  He requested that the General Film Company make an offer on the property which he
offered to sell.  I showed him that the greatest value of
the property which he had, to the General Film Company,
would be, including 90 per cent. of the last week's film
bill, and all the merchandise which he claimed to have,
approximately $59,000.  He stated that he thought that was
a very reasonable price, that the former basis of computing
values was entirely wrong, that he would accept it there
before we would have any opportunity to change our minds.
Mr. Mandelbaum returned to Cleveland.  In a few days we
received clippings from the newspapers showing that he
had been interviewed, and his remarks indicated that he
was not entirely satisfied with the price that he accepted,
and which he stated was entirely satisfactory to him, and
as we always refused to do business on any basis except
mutual satisfaction of both parties, I notified him that
the negotiations were ended.  There were also other reasons
which were—which we could not confirm, which were entirely matters of rumor—but which had some bearing upon
it, such as the disposition of property which was included
in the price we agreed to pay.

Q. Do you recall that one J. M. Ensor, representing
the Colorado Film Exchange, called upon you at your
office in New York in reference to the possible sale of his
motion pictures, stock and equipment?  A. Yes.  A man

1   named Ensor called at the company's office at 10 Fifth
Avenue.

Q. Do you recall the interview? A. I do.

Q. Will you tell us about it, briefly? A. Mr. Ensor
called and stated that he controlled the Colorado Film Exchange, that he desired to enter into an arrangement with
the General Film Company for the control of that entire territory between them, the General Film Company and the
Colorado Company, to become secret partners. He suggested the elimination of all other exchanges. He showed,
2   or he stated, that tremendous prices could be charged for
the service under those conditions, because all the other
exchanges were too remote to compete, and the difference in
transportation alone would afford an enormous profit. I
informed him the General Film Company would not engage
in any such project or relation. He called again with a
suggestion that the General Film Company make him a
proposition for his motion pictures and other exchange property. I informed him that we were unable to do so for the
reason that it was our impression that no one could give a
clear title to the property, this objection being based upon
3   the fact that it had peddled stock all over that section of
the country in which it was located, and that a certain doctor, whose name I don't remember, claimed to hold the controlling interest, although Mr. Ensor claimed that he had
never paid for his stock. At the same time, there was litigation threatened, all of which was explained to Mr. Ensor,
as our reason for not wanting to continue negotiations. Mr.
Ensor stated before departing that he regretted that we
were not obliged to operate our own branches. He understood we had acquired or were about to acquire the exchange
property of George Kleine and possibly the property of Mr.
4   Buckwalter; that if we went out there to manage that property ourselves, he would meet us at the station and give us
a very warm and unhealthy reception, but that we were too
foxy for that sort of thing; we would probably send some
poor hired man out there that everybody would be too sorry
for to interfere with. With that, he departed. He called the
next day and stated that he would have to have something
to show for the expenses of his trip to the East and asked
as a favor if we would give him an idea of the amount that
we would be likely to value his exchange at, his exchange

property. I told him approximately, without making any 1 calculation, subject to the condition that he retire if I did so, and not return.

Q. Did you say to J. M. Ensor on that occasion, either on the first or the second interview, "I want you to know, by God, that I am a bad one?" A. I never used such language to Ensor or to anyone else, or any language that could be possibly twisted to such a meaning.

Q. Did you say to Ensor, on the occasion of either of these interviews, either in terms or in substance, "Whenever I make an offer or proposition one time, I won't be 2 responsible for the outcome if it ain't accepted?" A. Never made any such statement to anyone.

Q. Do you recall the purchase of the motion pictures, stock and equipment of the Theatre Film Supply Company of Birmingham, Alabama, from Acton R. Boone? A. I do. We purchased it late one afternoon. I remember the circumstances clearly.

Q. Was the contract which you made with Mr. Boone, carried out? A. It was.

Q. Was the contract which the General Film Company made on that occasion with Mr. Boone, typical of the other 3 contracts made with other exchanges? A. It was. All contracts, as far as possible, contained exactly the same conditions, so as to show no favoritism.

Q. Have you a copy of that contract with you? A. I have the original. I can get you a copy of it.

Mr. KINGSLEY: I offer it in evidence.

The paper offered is received in evidence and is marked "Defendants' Exhibit No. 165," and the same is as follows:

4

**Defendants' Exhibit No. 165.**

CONTRACT

---

THEATRE FILM SUPPLY COMPANY

AND

GENERAL FILM COMPANY.

---

2             AUGUST, 1910.

THIS AGREEMENT, made and entered into this twenty-third day of August, in the year Nineteen Hundred and Ten, by and between the THEATRE FILM SUPPLY COMPANY, a corporation organized and existing under the laws of the State of Alabama, and having an office in the City of Birmingham, State of Alabama, and hereinafter referred to as the party of the first part, and the GENERAL FILM COMPANY, a corporation organized and existing under the laws of the State of Maine, and having 3 an office at No. 10 Fifth Avenue, in the Borough of Manhattan, City of New York, State of New York, and hereinafter referred to as the party of the second part,

WITNESSETH:

WHEREAS, the Motion Picture Patents Company, having an office at No. 80 Fifth Avenue, in the Borough of Manhattan, City of New York, State of New York, has licensed the Biograph Company, of New York City, the Edison Manufacturing Company, of Orange, N. J., the Essanay Film Manufacturing Company, of Chicago, Ill., 4 the Kalem Company, of New York City, George Kleine, of Chicago, Ill., the Lubin Manufacturing Company, of Philadelphia, Pa., Pathe Freres, of New York City, the Selig Polyscope Company, of Chicago, Ill., the Vitagraph Company of America, of New York City, and Gaston Melies, of New York City, to manufacture or import motion pictures under Letters Patent that are owned by said Motion Picture Patents Company; and

WHEREAS, said Motion Picture Patents Company has licensed exhibitors of motion pictures to exhibit li-

censed motion pictures on projecting machines that are 1
used under Letters Patent owned by said Motion Picture
Patents Company; and

WHEREAS, said Motion Picture Patents Company has
granted licenses to the party of the first part and to
the party of the second part, to lease licensed motion pictures from the manufacturers and importers thereof, and
to sub-lease such licensed motion pictures to exhibitors
licensed by the said Motion Picture Patents Company to exhibit licensed motion pictures; and

WHEREAS, the party of the first part and the party
of the second part are separately engaged in the busi- 2
ness (hereinafter referred to as the "business aforesaid")
of leasing licensed motion pictures from the manufacturers and importers thereof, and of sub-leasing such licensed motion pictures to exhibitors licensed by said Motion Picture Patents Company to exhibit them; buying,
selling and renting motion picture projecting machines,
stereopticons, stereopticon views and slides, and phonographic records; buying and selling parts of motion picture projecting machines and stereopticons, electric light
carbons, admission tickets, and similar equipment and sup- 3
plies required by exhibitors of motion pictures; and re-
pairing motion picture projecting machines and stereopticons; and

WHEREAS, the party of the first part represents that
it is engaged in the business aforesaid, at No. 2104 First
Avenue, in the City of Birmingham, State of Alabama;
that it is the sole and exclusive owner of all the right,
title and interest in and to the business aforesaid in which
it is engaged at the place mentioned, and in and to all the
property that collectively forms the equipment and stock
of motion pictures and merchandise of said business ex- 4
cepting motion pictures leased by it from the licensed
manufacturers and importers thereof, which motion pictures are held by it as lessee and are hereinafter referred
to as "leased motion pictures;" that its business is the
business generally known and referred to as the "Theatre
Film Exchange of Birmingham;" and that none of the
property aforesaid is mortgaged, hypothecated or in use as
collateral security for loans, debts or claims; and

WHEREAS, the party of the first part desires to sell

1  the foregoing property so owned by it and all its right, title
and interest in and to all said leased motion pictures held
by it as aforesaid, together with certain additions hereinafter noted which may hereafter be made thereto, subject
to the condition that the purchaser accepts an assignment
of all agreements and rights under which the party of the
first part acts as agent or jobber for manufacturers of or
dealers in motion picture projecting machines and apparatus and supplies for exhibitors of motion pictures, and
subject to the further condition that the purchaser agrees
to accept an assignment of the lease under which the party
2  of the first part occupies the premises in which the party
of the first part transacts its business aforesaid at the
place hereinbefore mentioned, and agrees to protect the
party of the first part from any loss or damages and cost
of defending law-suits that may result from failure of the
party of the second part to comply with any or all of the
requirements of such agreements, rights and lease; and

WHEREAS, the party of the second part relying upon
and induced by the foregoing representations of the party
of the first part desires to purchase the foregoing property
3  and the right, title and interest of the party of the first
part in and to the leased motion pictures aforesaid, together with the additions thereto hereinafter noted, and is
willing to accept assignments of the agreements, rights and
lease aforesaid, and to protect the party of the first part
from the aforesaid loss, damages and cost of defending law-
suits;

NOW, THEREFORE, in consideration of the sum of
One Dollar paid by each of the parties hereto to the other,
the receipt of which is hereby acknowledged, and in further
consideration of the mutual covenants and agreements
4  hereinafter set forth, the party of the first part and the
party of the second part agree with each other as follows:

FIRST: The party of the first part agrees to sell to
the party of the second part, all its right title and interest in and to all leased motion pictures, wherever located, held by it as lessee as aforesaid, now and during the
period ending at eight o'clock in the forenoon of the sixth
day of September, 1910, and the entire right, title and interest in and to all other motion pictures of every age and
make and all other property, wherever located,—including

motion picture projecting machines, stereopticons, auxiliaries and attachments for motion picture projecting machines and stereopticons, parts of motion picture projecting machines, stereopticons and auxiliaries, slides of songs, announcements, views and advertisements, posters, electric light carbons, admission tickets, phonographic records, fixtures, furniture, and equipment of every description, both fixed and portable, including safes, vaults, typewriters, reels, rewinders, film boxes, film cases, repair shop equipment, small tools and instruments, horses, wagons, automobiles, stationery, and materials and supplies of every sort,—now and during the period aforesaid collectively forming, with said leased and other motion pictures, the equipment and stock of motion pictures and merchandise of the business aforesaid in which the party of the first part is engaged at the place aforesaid; said equipment and stock of motion pictures and merchandise being hereinafter referred to as the "property aforesaid," while the interest therein which the party of the first part agrees herein to sell to the party of the second part is hereinafter referred to as the "right, title and interest aforesaid."

SECOND: The party of the first part further agrees that the right, title and interest aforesaid in the property aforesaid shall pass to the party of the second part at eight o'clock in the forenoon of the sixth day of September, 1910, and the party of the first part further agrees to deliver at the same time to the party of the second part, at the hereinbefore mentioned place of business of the party of the first part, all leased motion pictures that the manufacturers and importers thereof leased to the party of the first part between January 1, 1909, and the fifth day of September, 1910, all motion pictures held by it otherwise than as lessee, and all of the other property aforesaid, with the exception of such leased motion pictures as the party of the first part returned to the manufacturers and importers thereof, under the terms of said Motion Picture Patents Company's license to the party of the first part; leased motion pictures destroyed by fire, lost in transportation or by theft, and reported to the licensed manufacturers and importers thereof, in conformity with the requirements of said license; such motion pictures as the party of the first part has at that time sub-leased to ex-

1  hibitors in the regular course of business; such motion picture projecting machines, stereopticons and slides as the party of the first part has at that time rented to exhibitors, and such motion pictures, motion picture projecting machines, stereopticons and slides as are in the possession of express and other transportation companies, in transit in the regular course of the business of the party of the first part.

THIRD: The party of the first part further agrees to assign to the party of the second part, on or before the fifteenth day of November, 1910, all agreements and rights

2  under which the party of the first part acts as agent or jobber for manufacturers of motion picture projecting machines, and apparatus and supplies for exhibitors of motion pictures, and to assign to the party of the second part, between the sixth day of September, 1910, and the fifteenth day of November, 1910, the lease under which the party of the first part occupies the premises in which it transacts its business aforesaid at the place hereinbefore mentioned, and all rights of renewal of said lease, subject to the conditions that such assignment of agreements, rights and

3  lease shall be considered to have been made at eight o'clock in the forenoon of the sixth day of September, 1910, and that the rights and obligations of the party of the second part thereunder shall be considered to have commenced at eight o'clock in the forenoon of the fifth day of September, 1910.

FOURTH: The party of the first part further agrees that it will promptly, when requested so to do by the party of the second part, execute any and all papers, and do and perform any and all acts, that the party of the second part may deem necessary or expedient to vest the right, title

4  and interest aforesaid in and to the property aforesaid, as well as the right, title and interest of the party of the first part in, to and under the agreements, rights and lease aforesaid, in the party of the second part.

FIFTH: The party of the first part further agrees to prepare at its own cost, and to deliver personally or mail to the party of the second part at its office at No. 10 Fifth Avenue, New York City, on or before the fifteenth day of November, 1910, a correct inventory of all the property aforesaid in which the party of the first part herein agrees

to sell the right, title and interest aforesaid to the party ¹
of the second part, and in which the party of the second
part will, at eight o'clock in the forenoon of the sixth day
of September, 1910, acquire such right, title and interest
aforesaid, under the terms of this agreement, including all
of such property as is in the possession of exhibitors and
transportation companies in the regular course of the aforesaid business of the party of the first part.

SIXTH: The party of the first part further agrees
that if errors or omissions of property should be found by
the party of the second part in the aforesaid inventory, it
will furnish to the party of the second part such additional ²
inventories and information as the latter may demand for
the correction of such errors, the supplying of such omissions and for the locating and obtaining possession of
property so omitted.

SEVENTH: The party of the first part further agrees
that the property aforesaid in which the party of the first
part herein agrees to sell the right, title and interest aforesaid to the party of the second part, and in which the party
of the second part will, at eight o'clock in the forenoon
of the sixth day of September, 1910, acquire such right, ³
title and interest under the terms of this agreement, shall
include all of the property which collectively formed the
equipment and stock of motion pictures and merchandise
of the aforesaid business of the party of the first part on
the first day of March, 1910, wherever located, and all
additions to said equipment and stock of motion pictures
and merchandise between the date last named and eight
o'clock in the forenoon of the fifth day of September, 1910,
with the following exceptions: (1st) new motion picture
projecting machines, new stereopticans, new auxiliaries and
attachments for motion picture projecting machines and ⁴
stereopticons, new parts of motion picture projecting machines and stereopticons, new slides of songs, announcements, views and advertisements, electric light carbons,
admission tickets, new phonographic records, and supplies
for exhibitors of motion pictures, which were sold by the
party of the first part as new merchandise, and shipped to
the buyers thereof, before eight o'clock in the forenoon of
the fifth day of September, 1910, the party of the first
part, however, expressly agreeing that all such articles of
merchandise as have been rented to any exhibitor or used

1  in connection with the exhibition of motion pictures at
any time shall not be included in this exception or considered to be new merchandise; and (2nd) such leased
motion pictures as the party of the first part returned to
the licensed manufacturers and importers thereof under
the terms of said Motion Picture Patents Company's license to the party of the first part, and leased motion pictures destroyed by fire, lost in transportation or by theft,
and reported to the licensed manufacturers and importers
thereof, in conformity with the requirements of said license.

2  EIGHTH: The party of the first part further agrees
that all the records and books of account of its aforesaid
business, with the exception of its cash book, journal,
ledger, capital stock book and minute book, shall be considered to be a part of the aforesaid equipment of its business, for a period of four (4) months from and after
eight o'clock in the forenoon of the fifth day of September,
1910, subject to the condition that the party of the first
part and the party of the second part shall have joint
possession and use of said records and books during said
period of four (4) months, and that all right of the party
3  of the second part to have joint possession of or to use
said records and books shall terminate when said period
of four (4) months expires.

NINTH: The party of the first part further agrees
to promptly pay all bills and settle all claims of the manufacturers and importers of licensed motion pictures, for
motion pictures leased by them to the party of the first
part, and which the party of the first part is permitted,
under the terms of its license from the Motion Picture Patents Company, to sub-lease to licensed exhibitors before
eight o'clock in the forenoon of the fifth day of September,
4  1910; to promptly pay all bills and settle all claims of
manufacturers and dealers in projecting machines, stereopticons and other property, included in the aforesaid
equipment and stock of motion pictures and merchandise;
and to protect the party of the second part from loss resulting from the failure of the party of the first part to
pay any bill or bills or settle any claim or claims which
in any way affect adversely the right, title or interest aforesaid which the party of the second part acquires, under the
terms of this agreement, from the party of the first part in
the property aforesaid.

TENTH: The party of the second part agrees to buy
from the party of the first part the right, title and interest aforesaid in the property aforesaid; and the party
of the second part further agrees that all said right, title
and interest shall pass from the party of the first part to
the party of the second part, at eight o'clock in the forenoon of the sixth day of September, 1910.

ELEVENTH: The party of the second part further
agrees to receive from the party of the first part, at eight
o'clock in the forenoon of the sixth day of September, 1910,
at the hereinbefore mentioned place of business of the
party of the first part, all of the property aforesaid which
the party of the first part hereinbefore agrees to deliver
to the party of the second part at that time.

TWELFTH: The party of the second part further
agrees to accept from the party of the first part, assignments of all agreements, rights and lease, under which the
party of the first part acts as agent or jobber and occupies the premises hereinbefore mentioned in which it transacts its business aforesaid; and the party of the second part
further agrees to sign and execute such agreements, instruments in writing and leases as are necessary to transfer
to the party of the second part, the rights and obligations
of the party of the first part as agent, jobber, and lessee of
said premises, from and after eight o'clock in the forenoon
of the fifth day of September, 1910.

THIRTEENTH: The party of the second part further
agrees that rebates on licensed motion pictures leased by
the party of the first part and released by the manufacturers and importers thereof before eight o'clock in the
forenoon of the fifth day of September, 1910, unpaid bal-
ances on new motion picture projecting machines and auxiliaries that were sold by the party of the first part, bills
receivable, accounts receivable, and money earned by the
party of the first part, postage stamps, cash in hand, and
remittances in transit to the party of the first part, are
not included in the right, title and interest aforesaid which
the party of the first part hereinbefore agrees to sell to the
party of the second part.

FOURTEENTH: The party of the second part further agrees to return to the manufacturers and importers
of licensed motion pictures, for or in the name of the party
of the first part, all the leased motion pictures that the

1  Motion Picture Patents Company's license to the party
of the first part requires the party of the first part to return to said manufacturers and importers, after the fifth
day of September, 1910.

FIFTEENTH: The party of the first part and the
party of the second part mutually agree that all motion
pictures, motion picture projecting machines, stereopticons
and slides, and any of the other property aforesaid, which
are in the possession of exhibitors and in transit to or
from exhibitors, in the regular course of the business of the
party of the first part, at eight o'clock in the forenoon of

2  the sixth day of September, 1910, shall be considered to
have been delivered at that time by the party of the first
part to the party of the second part, as a part of the property aforesaid at the hereinbefore mentioned place of business of the party of the first part.

SIXTEENTH: The party of the second part further
agrees to pay to the party of the first part, in full payment
for all the right, title and interest aforesaid in the property aforesaid, the sums of money and other considerations hereinafter mentioned, subject to the terms and con-

3  ditions under which the party of the second part hereinafter agrees to make such payments of money and other
considerations.

a.   The party of the second part agrees to pay to the
party of the first part, the sum of TWELVE THOUSAND,
FIVE HUNDRED (12,500.) DOLLARS, in lawful money
of the United States of America, which sum shall be paid
in twenty (20) equal installments, the amount of each installment being SIX HUNDRED AND TWENTY-FIVE
(625.) DOLLARS.

The first and second installments shall be paid to the

4  party of the first part, on or before the tenth day of November, 1910, and in addition, interest at the rate of five
(5) per cent. per annum on the sum of Twelve Thousand,
Five Hundred (12,500.) Dollars, from the fifth day of
September, 1910, to the tenth day of November, 1910; the
third installment shall be paid on the first day of January, 1911, and in addition, interest at the rate of five (5)
per cent. per annum on the sum of Eleven Thousand, Two
Hundred and Fifty (11,250.) Dollars, from the tenth day
of November, 1910, to the first day of January, 1911, and

the remaining seventeen (17) installments shall be paid at intervals of three (3) months thereafter, during a period of fifty-one (51) months.

All unpaid installments shall bear interest at the rate of five (5) per cent. per annum. Interest on unpaid installments shall be paid at intervals of three (3) months and upon the days upon which installments shall be paid. Interest on unpaid installments shall be computed and paid as follows: On the day on which the fourth installment becomes due and payable, the party of the second part shall pay the fourth installment, and in addition, interest at the rate mentioned, on the sum of seventeen (17) installments for the three (3) months' time between the dates of payment of the third and fourth installments. The interest which the party of the second part shall pay, with each installment, at the end of the succeeding periods of three (3) months, shall be computed in like manner.

The following schedule shows the dates on which installments become due and payable, and the amount of interest which the party of the second part shall pay with each installment:

| Installment | Date | Amount of Installment | Interest | Installment and Interest |
|---|---|---|---|---|
| 1st and 2nd...Nov. | 10, 1910 | $1,250.00 | $112.84 | $1,362.84 |
| 3rd..........Jan. | 1, 1911 | 625.00 | 78.13 | 703.13 |
| 4th..........Apr. | 1, 1911 | 625.00 | 132.81 | 757.81 |
| 5th..........July | 1, 1911 | 625.00 | 125.00 | 750.00 |
| 6th..........Oct. | 1, 1911 | 625.00 | 117.19 | 742.19 |
| 7th..........Jan. | 1, 1912 | 652.00 | 109.38 | 734.38 |
| 8th..........Apr. | 1, 1912 | 625.00 | 101.56 | 726.56 |
| 9th..........July | 1, 1912 | 625.00 | 93.75 | 718.75 |
| 10th..........Oct. | 1, 1912 | 625.00 | 85.94 | 710.94 |
| 11th..........Jan. | 1, 1913 | 625.00 | 78.13 | 703.13 |
| 12th..........Apr. | 1, 1913 | 625.00 | 70.31 | 695.31 |
| 13th..........July | 1, 1913 | 625.00 | 62.50 | 687.50 |
| 14th..........Oct. | 1, 1913 | 625.00 | 54.69 | 679.69 |
| 15th..........Jan. | 1, 1914 | 625.00 | 46.88 | 671.88 |
| 16th..........Apr. | 1, 1914 | 625.00 | 39.06 | 664.06 |
| 17th..........July | 1, 1914 | 625.00 | 31.25 | 656.25 |
| 18th..........Oct. | 1, 1914 | 625.00 | 23.44 | 648.44 |
| 19th..........Jan. | 1, 1915 | 625.00 | 15.63 | 640.63 |
| 20th..........Apr. | 1, 1915 | 625.00 | 7.81 | 632.81 |
| Totals ............. | | $12,500.00 | $1,386.30 | $13,886.30 |

1     b. The party of the second part further agrees to pay
to the party of the first part, on or before the fifteenth day
of November, 1910, ninety (90) per cent. of the lease price
paid by the party of the first part to the manufacturers
and importers of licensed motion pictures, for leased motion pictures released by said manufacturers and importers
during the calendar week ending at midnight on the third
day of September, 1910, and in addition, interest at the
rate of five (5) per cent. per annum on the amount of
said ninety (90) per cent. of lease price, from the fifth
day of September, 1910, to the day on which payment is
2     made, subject to the condition that the party of the first
part shall not lease from said manufacturers and importers,
more than sixteen (16) reels of such motion pictures during
said week. Said ninety (90) per cent. of the lease price
is the actual cost of leased motion pictures to the party of
the first part after deducting the ten (10) per cent. rebates
which the manufacturers and importers of licensed motion
pictures allow and pay directly to the party of the first
part.
      c. The party of the second part further agrees to pay
3     to the party of the first part, on or before the fifteenth
day of November, 1910, or within five (5) days after the
party of the second part receives the aforesaid inventory
from the party of the first part, with interest at the rate of
five (5) per cent. per annum from the fifth day of September, 1910, the actual cost to the party of the first part of
all new merchandise, consisting of new motion picture projecting machines and stereopticons, new auxiliaries and attachments for projecting machines and stereopticons, new
standard parts of motion picture projecting machines and
stereopticons, new slides of songs, announcements, views
4     and advertisements, electric light carbons, new admission
tickets, new phonographic records and new supplies for
exhibitors of motion pictures, which the party of the
first part delivers to the party of the second part as part of
the property aforesaid at the place of business hereinbefore
mentioned of the party of the first part, but not including
any merchandise that has been rented to any exhibitor
or used in connection with the exhibition of motion pictures
at any time, or which is obsolete, and not including any
posters.

The "actual cost" of new merchandise which the party of the second part herein agrees to pay to the party of the first part, includes only the cost of transportation by freight or express, in addition to the manufacturer's or jobber's net prices after deducting all discounts, rebates and allowances.

d. In further consideration, the party of the second part agrees to issue or cause to be issued to and in the name of the party of the first part, SIX THOUSAND (6,-000.) DOLLARS par value, of seven (7) per cent. preferred capital stock of the party of the second part, consisting of SIXTY (60) SHARES, each of a par value of one hundred dollars; that the certificates of said stock shall be dated the tenth day of September, 1910, and that dividends on said stock begin to accrue on that day. Said preferred stock has a preference to the extent of seven (7) per cent. of its par value, in the net earnings of the party of the second part in each calendar year; if the net earnings in any calendar year should be less than the amount required to pay a dividend of seven (7) per cent. upon said preferred stock, the deficiency shall be paid from net earnings in the succeeding calendar year or years; and in the final distribution of the assets of the party of the second part, the holders of said preferred stock must be paid its par value and all accrued dividends before the holders of the common stock of the party of the second part receive any part of the assets. Said preferred stock does not entitle the holders thereof to vote at meetings of the holders of the capital stock of the party of the second part.

SEVENTEENTH: The party of the first part agrees to receive from the party of the second part, in full payment for the right, title and interest aforesaid in the property aforesaid, the sums of money and other considerations which the party of the second part hereinbefore agrees to pay and deliver to the party of the first part, under the terms and conditions specified in the sixteenth clause hereof.

IN WITNESS WHEREOF, the said parties hereto have caused this agreement to be executed by their respective

1   Presidents and attested under their corporate seals, in duplicate.

THEATRE FILM COMPANY,
By A. R. BOONE,
President.

Attest:

C. F. BAILEY,
Secretary.

Embossed seal: Theatre Film Supply Co. Birmingham, Ala. Corporate Seal.

2

GENERAL FILM COMPANY,
By J. J. KENNEDY,
President.

Attest:

WM. PELZER.
Secretary.

Embossed seal: General Film Company, Incorporated. Maine 1910.

State of Alabama, ⎱
County of Jefferson, ⎰ ss. :

3

On this 24th day of December, in the year of Nineteen Hundred and Ten, before me personally came A. R. Boone, to me known, who, being by me duly sworn, did depose and say, that he resided in Birmingham, County of Jefferson and State of Alabama; that he is the President of the THE-ATRE FILM SUPPLY COMPANY, one of the corporations described in, and which executed the above instrument; that he knew the seal of said corporation; that the seal affixed to said instrument was said corporate seal; that it was so affixed by order of the Board of Directors

4   of the said corporation, and that he signed his name thereto by like order.

W. B. Caldwell,
[SEAL.]            Notary Public,
Jefferson County, Ala.

State of New York, ⎱
County of New York, ⎰ ss. :

On this 2nd day of November, in the year of Nineteen Hundred and Ten, before me personally came JEREMIAH

J. KENNEDY, to me known, who, being by me duly sworn, did depose and say, that he resided in the Borough of Brooklyn, City of New York, State of New York; that he is the President of the GENERAL FILM COMPANY, one of the corporations described in, and which executed the above instrument; that he knew the seal of said corporation; that the seal affixed to said instrument was said corporate seal; that it was so affixed by order of the Board of Directors of the said corporation, and that he signed his name thereto by like order.

Clinton D. Ganse,

[SEAL.] Notary Public,

Kings County.

Certificate filed in New York County.

---

By Mr. KINGSLEY:

Q. Acton R. Boone, who was a witness in this proceeding, testified at pages 1213-1214, Vol. II of the record, after reciting the fact of the sale of the motion pictures, stock and equipment of the Theatre Film Supply Company of Birmingham, that none of the stock had been given him. Have you any explanation to make of that statement of Mr. Boone's? A. Yes. The stock was held as collateral—as part of collateral— also for $3,000 which was advanced him, subject to the condition that the stock should be held and all dividends accruing upon it, and all instalments becoming due under the contract, should be applied to the payment of the indebtedness of $3,000, and when that indebtedness was extinguished or paid, he was to receive his stock. At the same time, he was informed that when the stock was ready for delivery, he might pay whatever balance of his indebtedness remained unpaid and receive his stock at any time. He never offered, during my connection with the company, to make any payments on account of the money advanced. I have a copy of a letter, I think, in which that is set forth. I am not sure.

Q. Will you kindly produce it? Is this a correct copy of a letter which you sent to Acton R. Boone, March 21st, 1912? A. It is.

Q. Did you dictate the original of the letter of which this is a copy? A. I did, and signed it.

Q. Was this letter sent in response to a telegram which

1 Acton R. Boone sent to you, or to the General Film Company? A. It was sent in response to a joint telegram sent by Mr. Boone and Mr. Newsome, conveying the information that a serious flood had occurred in the section of the country in which they had theatres—

Mr. GROSVENOR: I object to the statement of the contents of the document, and I move to strike out the answer relating thereto.

2 By Mr. KINGSLEY:

Q. Proceed, Mr. Kennedy. A. That water was six feet in their theatres, and that the Theatre Film Supply Company needed $3,000 immediately to make repairs and to enable it to continue business, and that the Birmingham Film Supply also needed $2,000, and they requested that this money be advanced in addition to the moneys that I had personally advanced to the Theatre Film Supply Company. I telephoned the two other members of the Executive Committee, who refused to take any action, but told me that they would not object to my assuming
3 personally the responsibility for advancing the money.

Mr. KINGSLEY: I offer the copy of the letter in evidence.

The paper offered is received in evidence, marked "Defendants' Exhibit No. 166," and is as follows:

**Defendants' Exhibit No. 166.**

(Copy.)

4

March 21, 1912.

Theatre Film Supply Company,
    2104 First Avenue,
        Birmingham, Alabama.

Dear Sirs:

In reply to your telegram of to-day, we are enclosing our cheque No. 10273 to your order for $3,000. The cer-

tificates of preferred stock have not been issued and when
ready for issue, we will hold the preferred stock that you
own, as collateral on this loan, with interest at the rate of
five per cent., and we will apply on the loan and interest,
future dividends on the stock and unpaid and unassigned
installments.

When the certificates are ready to be issued, we will give
you an opportunity to borrow the amount of the loan on the
certificates, so that you can repay us, in which event your
unpaid and unassigned installments and dividends would
be released.

Owing to the urgency of the situation as set forth in
your telegram, we deemed it advisable to forward the money
that you require immediately, without losing the time that
would be necessary for obtaining formal notes and ar-
ranging details of the loan.

We are unable to take any action on your offer to sell
the stock at par for the reason that only the Board of
Directors can authorize the purchase of the stock and it
would be impossible to have your offer considered before
April 15th and possibly May 20th.

Respectfully,

GENERAL FILM COMPANY,
(Signed)   J. J. Kennedy,
President.

By Mr. KINGSLEY:

Q. Had there been a prior loan on Boone's stock? A.
Not by the company.

Q. Had there been one by you? A. Yes. I made two
prior loans, for which I had assignments. Mr. Boone,
shortly after he sold his exchange property to the company, claimed that he was in great financial distress and
requested me to lend him money, or to buy some of the
instalments which were about to become due under the
terms of the contract, at the same time offering me interest
at the rate of eight per cent. and a bonus of ten per cent.
I told Mr. Boone that I would lend him the money without
any bonus and at the rate of five per cent. for the actual
time the money was in his possession, that rate being the
same rate as he was receiving from the General Film Com-

1    pany.  I loaned him the money that he asked me to lend
him, and before that loan was paid off, he begged me to
assist him further.  I made him another loan under exactly
the same conditions, explaining that the company could
not establish the precedent of advancing money.  I therefore
derived no benefit from it, as he received the same interest
as he paid me.  There is considerable correspondence in connection with these transactions, most of which, I think, I
have here, if you care to look at it, and those are the
original assignments from the file of the General Film Com-
2    pany.
     Q. Are these letters which you have handed me, letters
which were received by you from the Theatre Film Supply
Company or from Acton R. Boone in connection with the
transactions which you have just described?  A. Yes.

        Mr. KINGSLEY:  I offer in evidence a letter dated
     Birmingham, August 24th, 1911, addressed to Mr. J.
     J. Kennedy, 52 Broadway, New York, signed "The-
     atre Film Supply Company, A. R. Boone, President."
        Mr. GROSVENOR:  Is this the letter that refers
3    to the second loan?

     The Witness:  I do not know without referring to the
letter and the dates of the loans.  I think this refers to the
second loan.

        The paper last offered by Mr. Kingsley is received
     in evidence and marked "Defendants' Exhibit No.
     167," and is as follows:

### Defendants' Exhibit No. 167.

4
                    Letterhead of
        SOUTHERN AMUSEMENT & SUPPLY CO.
                    Incorporated.

                    Birmingham, Ala., August 21 1911.
Mr. J. J. Kennedy,
    52 Broadway,
        New York, N. Y.

Dear Mr. Kennedy:—

    Without desiring to appear unduly hasty and presum-

ing that the matter has skipped your attention the writer 1
begs to remind you of your promise to assist us financially
by advancing us cash on four more of the deferred payments due from the General Film Co. and as we are now
very close to the time when funds will be needed by us most
urgently for use in constructing a new theatre at Pensacola,
Fla., we respectfully ask that you have the papers of assignment of these deferred payments drafted and sent to us for
execution at your earliest convenience.

We assure you of our great appreciation for the assistance you give us in these advances and it is only our pressing need for the funds with which to continue our work    2
which compels us to be urgent at this time in asking another
favor of you.

Thanking you for early reply and with our best regards
we are

Yours very truly

THEATRE FILM SUPPLY CO

A. R. Boone,
A. R. B. *K.                                        Prest.

Stamped: Received Aug. 23, 1911.   Ans. 8/26.   In- 3
dexed 9/2.

---

By Mr. KINGSLEY:

Q. I show you what purports to be a copy of a letter
dated August 26th, 1911, addressed to Mr. A. R. Boone, President of the Theatre Film Supply Company, Birmingham,
Alabama, signed J. J. Kennedy, and ask you if you recognize
it? A. I do. As a copy of a letter that I dictated and
signed.                                                   4

Q. Is this a true copy? A. It is.

Mr. KINGSLEY: I offer it in evidence.

The paper offered is received in evidence and
marked "Defendants' Exhibit No. 168," and is as follows:

1       **Defendants Exhibit No. 168.**

(Copy.)

August 26, 1911.

Mr. A. R. Boone, President,
    Theatre Film Supply Company,
        c/o Southern Amusement & Supply Company,
            Birmingham, Alabama.

Dear Sir:—

2       I am enclosing my cheque to your order for $2792.65 in payment for the installments with interest, that will become due and payable to you by the General Film Company on January 1, 1912, April 1, 1912, July 1, 1912, and October 1, 1912.

The amount of the enclosed cheque allows me five per cent. simple interest on the money invested after crediting the different payments as they become due. Interest is computed from and after September 1st, 1911.

I am also enclosing in triplicate, a form of assignment which is similar to the assignment under which I purchased

3   your last three payments from the General Film Company this year.

One copy of the assignment is intended for your files, and I will ask you to return two executed copies to me so that I can retain one and file one with the General Film Company.

I had not forgotten my promise to make you the advance represented by the enclosed cheque, as I was under the impression that you would not require it until September first, and I wanted to save you as much interest as possible.

4       You will, of course, affix your seal to each copy of the assignment that you send me.

Yours very truly,
    (Sd.) J. J. KENNEDY.

---

By Mr. KINGSLEY:

Q. I show you a letter addressed, "Mr. J. J. Kennedy, 52 Broadway, New York," dated Birmingham, August 31st,

1911, signed "Theatre Film Supply Company," and ask you ¹
if you recognize it? A. Yes. This is a letter that I received.

Mr. KINGSLEY: I offer it in evidence.

The paper offered is received in evidence and
marked "Defendants' Exhibit No. 169," and is as follows:

**Defendants Exhibit No. 169.**

Letterhead of ²

SOUTHERN AMUSEMENT & SUPPLY CO., Inc.

Birmingham, August 31st, 1911.

Mr. J. J. Kennedy,
No. 52 Broadway,
New York, N. Y.

Dear Sir:—

We are in receipt of your check for $2,792.65, also forms
of assignments, for which we thank you. ³

Our Mr. Boone is now at Augusta, Ga., and we have
this date mailed him assignments, to be signed, and returned to you.

Again thanking you, we remain,

Yours very truly,

THEATRE FILM SUPPLY CO.

WHS/S.

Stamped on face: Received Sep. 2, 1911. Indexed 9/8.

---

⁴

By Mr. KINGSLEY:

Q. I show you a letter addressed to Mr. J. J. Kennedy,
52 Broadway, New York, dated September 9th, 1911, signed
"Theatre Film Supply Company, A. R. Boone, President,"
and ask you if you recognize it. A. Yes, this is a letter that
I received.

Mr. KINGSLEY: I offer it in evidence.

The paper offered is received in evidence and

1    marked "Defendants' Exhibit No. 170," and is as follows:

**Defendants' Exhibit No. 170.**

Letterhead of

SOUTHERN AMUSEMENT & SUPPLY CO., Inc.

Birmingham, September 9th, 1911.

Mr. J. J. Kennedy,
2    No. 52 Broadway,
New York, N. Y.

Dear Sir:—

Yours of the 26th ulto. with check for $2,792.65 and instrument of assignment covering our transfer and sale to you of certain deferred payments due the Theatre Film Supply Co. by the General Film Co. was duly received and the papers were sent first to Mr. C. F. Bailey for execution as Secretary and then to the writer for execution as President, hence the delay in their return to you.

3    We now hand you one of the two copies and are retaining one for our files.

We wish to express to you our deepest appreciation for the very kind assistance you have rendered us by these cash advancements and trust that we will at all times merit your good will and consideration.

Yours very truly,

THEATRE FILM SUPPLY CO.,
A. R. Boone,
Prest.

4    A. R. B. *K.
Stamped: Received Sep. 12, 1911.   Indexed 10/1.

---

By Mr. KINGSLEY:

Q. Mr. Kennedy, you have told us about two loans made to Mr. Boone, the first loan of which you told us was the one made by the General Film Company and was in reality the third loan made him. Is that correct? A. It was the first and only loan made to him by the General Film Company, but it was made to him after I had made him two loans, <sup>1</sup> myself.

Q. You have identified the correspondence between yourself and Mr. Boone with regard to the second loan which you individually made him, have you not? A. Yes.

> Mr. GROSVENOR: You don't mean that you have identified all the correspondence, but only one or two letters?

The Witness: Such as were submitted to me for identification.

> Mr. GROSVENOR: By your counsel?

The Witness: Yes.

By Mr. KINGSLEY:

Q. I show you what purports to be a copy of a letter, dated December 29th, 1910, addressed, "Theatre Film Supply Company, Birmingham, Alabama," signed "J. J. Kennedy," and ask you if you recognize it. A. It is a copy of a letter that I dictated and signed and forwarded to that company.

Q. Is it a true copy? A. It is.

Q. Does it correctly state that transaction? A. It is a copy of a letter that was written and does correctly set forth the details of the transaction.

> Mr. KINGSLEY: I offer it in evidence.
> The paper is received in evidence and marked "Defendants' Exhibit No. 171," and is as follows:

## Defendants' Exhibit No. 171.

(Copy.)

December 29, 1910.

Theatre Film Supply Company,
    2104 First Avenue,
        Birmingham, Ala.

Dear Sirs:

In accordance with verbal agreement made with your

1   Mr. Boone, I am enclosing my cheque to your order for
$2,195.53, which amount is a loan to you, for which you
are to assign to me the installments which will become due
and payable to you by the General Film Company of No.
10 Fifth Avenue, this city, on April 1st, July 1st, and October 1st, 1911, as set forth on page 18 of your contract
dated 23rd day of August, 1910, with that Company.

The amount of this loan shall bear interest at the rate
of five per cent. annually.

A formal assignment of the aforesaid payments to me is
enclosed. The payment which the General Film Company
2   will owe you on April 1st, 1911, amounts to $757.81. This
amount will pay $748.46 of the loan and three months' in-
terest on $748.46 at five per cent. annually, amounting to
$9.35. The payment which the General Film Company will
owe you on July 1st, 1911, amounts to $750. This amount
will pay $731.71, of the loan and six months' interest on
$731.71 at five per cent. annually, amounting to $18.29. The
payment which the General Film Company will owe you on
October 1st, 1911, amounts to $742.19. This amount will
pay the balance of the loan, amounting to $715.36, and
3   nine months' interest on $715.36 at five per cent. annually,
amounting to $26.83.

Yours very truly,

(Sd.) J. J. KENNEDY.

Please affix your corporate seal and date the enclosed
assignment before you return it to me.

(Sd.) J. J. K.

---

By Mr. Kingsley:

4   Q. Does this letter relate to the first loan which you
made to Acton R. Boone? A. It relates to the first loan that
I made to him.

Q. At the time of the cancellation of the license of the
Western Film Exchange at St. Louis, did you know of the
reasons therefor? A. In a general way. At that particular
time I was not very active in the affairs of the Motion Picture
Patents Company, my activities being limited almost entirely to performing the duties of Treasurer. but I was familiar with the conditions

Q. Do you recall any of the reasons with sufficient clearness to be able to testify regarding them today? A. Yes. Mr. Crawford, who was at the head of that exchange, had been actively engaged, according to information which we considered reliable, in planning for some time to infringe the patents owned by the Motion Picture Patents Company. He had also been accused of using the motion pictures which were leased by his exchange and another exchange in which he was supposed to have an interest, unfairly, in favor of the theatres which he owned or controlled, or in which he had a large interest. He had been accused of forcing theatres to give him a percentage of their receipts in return for his not attacking them or competing with them unfairly. Later on, Mr. Kane, who was the manager of his exchange, called upon me to urge me to endeavor to have the license restored, and told me that he had warned Mr. Crawford that the things he was doing would not and could not be tolerated, and that the cancellation of his license was inevitable. Mr. Kane admitted that Mr. Crawford had been guilty of the various offenses with which he had been charged.

Mr. GROSVENOR: I object to this statement as hearsay, and to the conversation as incompetent, and I move to strike out all the testimony of the witness in the preceding answer, so far as the same is a repetition of hearsay and conversations.

The Witness: He stated that he was in the East as a special representative of Mr. Crawford and the exchange, and was empowered to make a settlement on any basis that he might consider advisable in connection with the restoration of his license. Later on, a Mr. Graham called, who pleaded for the restoration of the license as a personal matter, for the reason that he had a short while before, induced friends to invest over $50,000 in the exchange, and the conditions were such that he was afraid that the money would be lost, and that he would be ruined. At the same time he admited that Mr. Crawford had been guilty of the offenses with which he had been charged. I forget just what office he stated he filled in connection with the exchange.

1　By Mr. Kingsley:

Q. Did you say to Mr. Graham on that occasion, in terms or in substance, that in your opinion it was a grievous mistake that the license of this exchange had been cancelled? A. I did not, nor anything approximating any such statement.

Q. Did you say to Mr. Graham on that occasion, either in terms or in substance, that it was too bad, that they could not undo things that had been done? A. I did not.

Q. Were you a member of the General Film Company's
2　Executive Committee in 1910? A. I was.

Q. How many members of the Executive Committee were there? A. Three.

Q. Who were they? A. Mr. Berst, Mr. Smith and myself.

Q. Of those three members of the Executive Committee, who was most active in purchasing motion pictures, stock and equipment of rental exchanges? A. I was.

Q. Did the other members of the Executive Committee leave most of the details of such purchases with you? A. They left nearly all of the actual work of negotiating with
3　me, and I communicated with them by telephone from time to time, and kept them informed.

Q. What was the situation during 1910 with respect to negotiations with rental exchanges? Were they in the main begun by you or begun by the rental exchanges? A. We never began any negotiations. In every instance, except in the cases of exchanges which had negotiations directly with the Board of Directors, the negotiations were opened by the seller. We had many more requests to consider offers or to negotiate purchases than we complied with, at that time.
4
Q. Did you at any time use your influence as an officer of the General Film Company to induce the Motion Picture Patents Company to cancel the license of a rental exchange in order that it might be put out of business or in order that negotiations for the purchase of its motion pictures, stock and equipment by the General Film Company, might be facilitated? A. I did not, but on the other hand I suppressed evidence of violations on the part of exchanges.

Q. Did you at any time, as an officer of the Motion Picture Patents Company advise the cancellation of the license

of a rental exchange, that it might be put out of business 1
and that the General Film Company might be able to
purchase its motion pictures, stock and equipment more
readily?

Mr. GROSVENOR: Objected to as leading in form.

By Mr. KINGSLEY:

Q. You may answer. A. I did not. We always had
more exchange property offered to us than we were fitted
to handle. 2

Q. Did you at any time at a meeting of the producers
of motion pictures, vote to recommend the cancellation of a
rental exchange that it might be put out of business or
that the General Film Company might thereby purchase
its motion pictures, stock and equipment, more readily?
A. I never voted for the cancellation of an exchange after
the formation of the General Film Company.

Q. In purchasing the motion pictures, stock and equip-
ment of the rental exchange, while acting for the General
Film Company, did you pay anything for its license? A.
No. 3

Q. Was it necessary for a rental exchange, purchased
by the General Film Company, to have a license at the time
of the purchase? A. No. We purchased exchange property from an exchange that was unlicensed.

Q. Did you, at any time, while acting for the General
Film Company, pay a large price for the motion pictures,
stock and equipment of a rental exchange, which was not
making money, and which was doing an unprofitable business at the time? A. We never paid for any property that
we purchased from any exchange, a higher price than the
property was worth to us, in the conduct of our ordinary 4
business affairs.

Q. At the time of the organization of the General Film
Company, was it your intention or was it the intention of
your associates, so far as you know, to acquire all the rental
exchanges throughout the United States? A. It was not.
And the growth of the business was something that we were
entirely unprepared for.

1      Mr. GROSVENOR: You mean the growth of the business of the General Film Company?

The Witness: Yes. I mean the volume of property that we were requested to purchase was away in excess of anything that we had ever dreamed of.

By Mr. KINGSLEY:

Q. Was the organization of the Motion Picture Patents Company the result of a desire to monopolize the motion picture business throughout the United States, or of the desire to be able to do business free from litigation, and under authority of the various conflicting patents which dominated the art?

Mr. GROSVENOR: Objected to as leading in form.

The Witness: Will you read that question, please?

The Examiner repeats the question as follows:
"Q. Was the organization of the Motion Picture Patents Company the result of a desire to monopolize the motion picture business throughout the United States, or of the desire to be able to do business free from litigation and under authority of the various conflicting patents which dominated the art?"

The Witness: It was organized for the purpose of terminating the litigation and the very large expense that accompanied such litigation, and also for the purpose of establishing peaceful and safe conditions which would permit the normal growth and development of the business.

By Mr. KINGSLEY:

Q. Did any of the owners of rental exchanges whose motion pictures, stock and equipment you had purchased in behalf of the General Film Company, ever express dissatisfaction with their contracts to you?   A. I never heard of any dissatisfaction in that respect.

Q. Did any of them ever express satisfaction with their contracts? A. A great many.

Q. Did they speak to you personally on the subject? A. Yes. And commented on the fact that the prices were fair, and the General Film Company in many cases was referred to as their saviour.

Q. Do you know whether the General Film Company has carried out the terms of its contracts with the owners of exchanges from whom it purchased films, stock and equipment? A. It has, in every instance.

Q. Were you in touch with the business of the General Film Company after it began operations, June 6th, 1910? A. I was President of the company and directed its business until May 27th, 1912.

Q. Will you tell us something about the growth and development of the General Film Company, the methods it employed, and the economies that it introduced in handling motion pictures and serving exhibitors?

Mr. GROSVENOR: I object to all of that as immaterial and irrelevant, being purely of economic, if of any, value.

The Witness: Well, one of the things that it accomplished immediately, was the termination of what, in any other line of business would be considered an economic crime. The business had been conducted all over this country at just double the cost that should have been expended. In many cases a very large waste resulted from exchanges supplying picture service to exhibitors very remote from the location of the exchange, and in localities which could be more economically and better served by exchanges hundreds of miles nearer. For instance, an exchange in New York supplied Wilmington, North Carolina; Charlotte, Greensborough, North Carolina; Washington, Baltimore, Philadelphia, and other points in Pennsylvania, as well as points in New York and in New England, near the Canadian border. Exchanges in Philadelphia were supplying Baltimore, Washington and other points. Exchanges in Pittsburg were supplying exhibitors located almost adjacent to other exchanges. This resulted, in many instances, in motion pictures being more than fifty per cent. of their life in the possession of transportation companies, and as the

1   earning power of a film or motion picture was at that time
and is now, to a very large extent, based upon its age, every
day's time that a motion picture was in the possession of
a transportation company was just that much money lost.
If the business had been properly conducted, instead of
being in transit, it would be in service, thereby rendering
another motion picture unnecessary. This large expense
naturally had to be borne by either the exhibitor or by the
exchange losing money or making no profit. The General
Film Company at its start, impressed upon its representa-
2  tives in charge of its different depots or branch offices, the
fact that their service to exhibitors must be absolutely impartial and impersonal, and that a branch manager who
failed to satisfy the exhibitors in the territory immediately
tributary to his exchange, would be dismissed. The result
was that the quantity of film—motion pictures—required to
supply the same number of customers, or even a larger number, was reduced to between fifty and fifty-five per cent. of
the quantity formerly required, while at the same time the
General Film Company kept every contract and obligation
that it made with every exhibitor. Formerly, with approxi-
3  mately twice the quantity of motion pictures, exchanges
complained that they were unable to keep their agreements
with the exhibitors. I may specifically refer to the case of
the Biograph Company, of which I am President, and which
had a regular output varying from ninety-seven on one day
and ninety-nine, to one hundred and nineteen and one hundred and twenty copies. The output very quickly dropped
to fifty-seven copies, and yet the Biograph make was as
popular as any other make in motion pictures. Economies
were effected in other lines, and all the figures that show as
profits on the books of the General Film Company are not
4  profits as profits are ordinarily understood, but are economies, and if the business were conducted on the same old
lines, the profits would be very much greater, but the filling
of all contract obligations and promises, of course, increased
the cost relatively—to a relatively higher figure—than on
the old basis. Another point or object of the General Film
Company, and which it accomplished, was the placing of
more motion pictures in the territory which did not contain
enough very high-class theatres to justify a separate exchange making such large leases. Take, for instance, At-

lanta and that section of the country, the number of motion 1
pictures which the business justified an exchange in leasing
was very small. At the same time, there were a number of
very important houses which required a very much higher
class of service than could be supplied with the fewer number of motion pictures or the small number of motion pictures which the exchanges were able to supply, and exist.
The General Film Company was able to remedy those
conditions, and, if necessary, stand a loss while the business
in such sections was being developed.

By Mr. KINGSLEY: 2

Q. You have told us of the experience of the Biograph
Company in the curtailment of its production because of
the more efficient distribution of the General Film Company. Do you know whether other producers had a similar
experience or not? A. They all complained to me about
this reduction, and stated their reductions to be substantially the same as the reductions sustained by the Biograph
Company.

Q. Do you know, Mr. Kennedy, whether or not the
profits which the Biograph Company has received from the 3
General Film Company, have made good the curtailment of
production which was caused by the more efficient distribution of the General Film Company?

> Mr. GROSVENOR: I object to the use of the term
> "more efficient distribution," the same being a con-
> clusion of the counsel addressing the question to the
> witness.

The Witness: The profits paid to the Biograph Company, together with profits earned and not paid, amount 4
to less than two-thirds of the shrinkage sustained by the
Biograph Company.

> Mr. GROSVENOR: You mean by "the profits earned
> but not paid," the Biograph Company's pro rata
> share of the earnings of the General Film Company?

The Witness: I do.

1   By Mr. KINGSLEY:

Q. Do you know, Mr. Kennedy, whether or not other licensed producers of motion pictures who are stockholders in the General Film Company, have had a similar experience? A. I have had a great many complaints at different times from them during my connection with the company as President. In some instances they claim that they doubted their ability to continue producing motion pictures on the small volume of business. These statements were confirmed by the books of the company showing a decreasing number of
2   copies, motion pictures, required to serve the customers.

Q. At the time the General Film Company was acquiring the motion pictures, stock and equipment of various exchanges, were any purchases made in Canada? A. Yes. The property of the exchanges owned by Ernest Fenton and George Kleine were purchased.

Q. Have you prepared or supervised the preparation of a tabular statement showing the number of exchanges in the United States and Canada, the motion pictures, stock and equipment of which were purchased by the General Film Company up to December 30th, 1911? A. At my direction,
3   a statement was prepared, under my supervision, also; showing an analysis of the payments made under different classifications or headings, and contracts for each exchange in this country and in Canada.

Q. What were the divisions that you made? A. The divisions that are in the contract. That is to say, 90 per cent. of the last week's film bill of the exchange, the price paid for new merchandise which the exchange had on hand at the time it made delivery to the General Film Company, the amount of the company's preferred stock that was given in
4   part payment for the property, and the amount of the purchase price that was to be paid in cash. That was to be included or shown under the heading of instalments.

Q. Is this the statement to which you refer? A. Yes.

Q. Is it correct? A. It is.

Mr. KINGSLEY: I offer it in evidence.

The paper offered is received in evidence and is marked "Defendants' Exhibit No. 172," and is as follows:

# Defendants' Exhibit No. 172.

## COST OF BRANCHES AS PER BALANCE SHEET DECEMBER 30, 1911.

| | 90% of Films | Merchandise | Pref. Stock | Installments | Total |
|---|---|---|---|---|---|
| | $5,010.90 | $3,241.28 | $25,000.00 | $60,000.00 | $93,252.18 |
| Actograph Company, New York.............. | | | | | |
| Actograph Company, Albany................ | | | | | |
| Amalgamated Film Exchange, Portland....... | 5,044.35 | | | 75,000.00 | 115,044.35 |
| Amalgamated Film Exchange, Seattle........ | 1,932.94 | 750.35 | 35,000.00 | 36,000.00 | 52,179.59 |
| American Film Service, Chicago............ | 2,205.40 | | 13,500.00 | 37,000.00 | 52,205.40 |
| American Vitagraph Company, New York...... | 695.40 | 202.56 | 13,000.00 | 10,000.00 | 14,907.96 |
| Birmingham Film Supply Company........... | 1,615.15 | 2,536.51 | 4,000.00 | 16,000.00 | 25,151.66 |
| Buffalo Film Exchange................... | 2,794.20 | 7,688.09 | 6,000.00 | 40,000.00 | 70,482.29 |
| Charles A. Calehuff, Philadelphia.......... | 2,145.73 | 31.09 | 18,000.00 | 42,000.00 | 62,176.82 |
| Pennsylvania Columbia Film Exchange....... | 2,328.35 | 6,636.05 | 20,000.00 | 40,000.00 | 68,964.40 |
| William Henry Clune, Los Angeles.......... | 1,779.76 | 2,307.20 | 9,000.00 | 21,000.00 | 34,657.83 |
| Denver Film Exchange, Denver............. | 1,750.63 | 1,263.00 | 12,000.00 | 28,000.00 | 43,142.76 |
| Duquesne Amus Supply Co., Pittsburg........ | 2,650.98 | 2,034.10 | 16,000.00 | 35,000.00 | 55,685.08 |
| Electric Theatre Supply Co., Philadelphia... | 19,158.48 | 9,228.91 | 36,800.00 | 73,900.00 | 139,087.39 |
| Ernest Albert Fenton.................... | 1,154.93 | | 8,900.00 | 20,000.00 | 30,054.93 |
| Florence Film Company, Salt Lake.......... | 4,546.42 | 16,000.00 | 32,000.00 | 80,200.00 | 132,746.42 |
| Howard Moving Picture Co................. | 2,317.13 | 3,816.40 | | 43,900.00 | 50,033.53 |
| Imported Film & Supply Co., New Orleans.... | 1,371.05 | 609.76 | 8,000.00 | 22,000.00 | 31,980.81 |
| Kent Film Service Company, Toledo.......... | 3,592.50 | 3,418.15 | 20,800.00 | 52,100.00 | 79,910.65 |
| George Kleine, Boston................... | 12,007.04 | 10,141.68 | 36,800.00 | 73,900.00 | 132,848.72 |
| George Kleine, St. John, N. B............. | 2,029.43 | 1,165.51 | 16,400.00 | 38,700.00 | 56,129.43 |
| George Kleine, Chicago.................. | 678.74 | 1,689.80 | 6,400.00 | 16,000.00 | 24,244.25 |
| George Kleine, Denver................... | 2,192.02 | 341.65 | 14,200.00 | 35,500.00 | 53,581.82 |
| George Kleine, New York................. | 2,474.33 | 2,554.99 | 15,000.00 | 50,000.00 | 70,323.32 |
| H. Lieber Company, Indianapolis........... | 1,939.81 | 464.00 | 8,000.00 | 46,100.00 | 55,503.81 |
| S Lubn, Philadelphia.................... | 1,927.17 | 576.79 | 15,000.00 | 22,000.00 | 32,403.81 |
| Magnetic Film Service, Cincinnati......... | 1,940.71 | 1,975.18 | 15,000.00 | 35,000.00 | 53,915.89 |
| J. W. Melchior, Columbus................ | 1,551.72 | 3,106.79 | 20,000.00 | 25,000.00 | 39,658.52 |
| L. Mitchell, Little Rock & Memphis........ | 182.15 | 1,150.14 | 10,000.00 | 20,500.00 | 32,333.29 |
| Monarch Film Exchange, Oklahoma.......... | 1,594.60 | 1,943.39 | 9,500.00 | 28,500.00 | 36,237.99 |
| Montana Film Exchange, Butte............. | 1,155.95 | 778.36 | 4,200.00 | 13,000.00 | 19,932.31 |
| Tom Moore, Washington.................. | 2,146.89 | 2,604.01 | 5,000.00 | 15,000.00 | 21,000.00 |
| M P Supply Co., Rochester................ | 3,978.91 | 828.34 | 20,000.00 | 40,000.00 | 64,750.90 |
| M P Service Co., Syracuse................ | 1,160.98 | 846.45 | 23,000.00 | 60,000.00 | 87,807.25 |
| National Vaudette Film Co., Detroit........ | 2,500.35 | 730.46 | 5,000.00 | 15,000.00 | 22,007.43 |
| Novelty Film Exchange, San Francisco....... | 1,696.92 | 997.71 | 14,000.00 | 39,000.00 | 66,336.81 |
| Pearce & Scheck, Baltimore............... | | | 6,000.00 | 15,000.00 | 23,594.63 |
| People's Film Exchange, New York.......... | | | | | |
| Pittsburg Calcium Light, Rochester........ | | | | | |
| Pittsburg Calcium Light, Pittsburg, Cincinnati, | | | | | |

| | 90% of Films | Merchandise | Pref. Stock | Installments | Total |
|---|---|---|---|---|---|
| ..., .. .., Ms. Wil .rle.......... | 10,833.38 | 10,858.52 | 68,000.0 | 160, 0.0 | 250,295.16 |
| ..e M. P. Co., .in......... | 885.54 | 871.42 | 5,000.0 | 13, 0.0 | 19,756.96 |
| ..le Film Exchange.......... | 493.22 | 2,369.63 | 4,500.0 | 9,500.0 | 16,862.85 |
| George .... | 2,689.07 | 182.88 | 12,300.0 | 30,800.0 | 46,971.95 |
| ....m L. Tally, .os Angeles........ | 1,979.74 | 1,213.59 | 14,000.0 | 30, 0.0 | 47,193.33 |
| Theatre Film ..e., ...O.......... | .6.76 | 620.43 | 18,100.0 | 45,300.0 | 67,006.19 |
| Theatre Film ...r, ....Hm........ | 1,387.02 | .......... | 6, 0.0 | 12,500.0 | 19,887.02 |
| Turner & ....n, ..n ...o.......... | 4,393.19 | 8,318.89 | 25, 0.0 | 75, 0.0 | 112,707.08 |
| ...ed Film Exchange, ....d.......... | 961.09 | 761.38 | 6, 0.0 | 18,500.0 | 26,212.47 |
| C. E. .in ..e., .eolis.......... | 2,274.44 | 1,226.96 | 10, 0.0 | 38, 0.0 | 51,501.40 |
| P. L. Waters, New York.......... | 2,133.94 | 6,121.48 | 20,900.0 | 52,400.0 | 595.42 |
| Alfred ...es, New ..rk.......... | 1,706.12 | 575.01 | 10, 0.0 | 21, 0.00 | 33,281.13 |
| J D. ....n, Dallas.......... | 2,174.26 | 1,325.64 | 15,100.0 | 44,100.0 | 62,699.90 |
| ...le Film ...e. ...as City...... | 3,503.30 | 7,521.52 | 20, 0.0 | 75, 0.0 | 106,034.82 |
| S .Ne ..m, New ....e.......... | .......... | .......... | .......... | 8,935.21 | 8,935.21 |
| ...st Film Exchange, Chicago...... | .......... | .......... | 10,000.00 | 20, 0.0 | 30,000.0 |
| | $145,027.18 | $133,125.05 | $794,800.00 | $2,003,335.21 | $3,076,287.44 |

### UNITED STATES

| | |
|---|---|
| Cash ............ | $1,855,535.21 |
| Stock ............ | 721,200.00 |
| Merchandise ............ | 113,754.46 |
| 90% of last week's film bill ... | 113,860.66 |
| Total ............ | $2,804,350.33 |

### CANADA.

| | |
|---|---|
| Cash ............ | $147,800.00 |
| Stock ............ | 73,600.00 |
| Merchandise ............ | 19,370.59 |
| 90% of last week's film bill ... | 31,166.52 |
| Total ............ | $271,937.11 |

### SUMMARY.

| | |
|---|---|
| United States............ | $2,804,350.33 |
| Canada ............ | 271,937.11 |
| Total ............ | $3,076,287.44 |

FOLDOUT BLANK

Whereupon, at 5:15 P. M., on this Tuesday, the 17th
day of March, 1914, the hearings are adjourned until Friday
morning, March 20th, 1914, at 10:30.

---

IN THE

## DISTRICT COURT OF THE UNITED STATES

FOR THE EASTERN DISTRICT OF PENNSYLVANIA.

| | |
|---|---|
| UNITED STATES OF AMERICA, Petitioner, *v.* MOTION PICTURE PATENTS CO. and others, Defendants. | No. 889. Sept. Sess., 1912. |

NEW YORK CITY, March 20, 1914.

The hearings were resumed pursuant to adjournment, at
10:30 o'clock A. M., March 20, 1914, at Room 159, Manhattan Hotel, New York City.

> Present on behalf of the Petitioner, Hon. EDWIN
> P. GROSVENOR, Special Assistant to the Attorney General.
> JOSEPH R. DARLING, Esq., Special Agent.
> CHARLES F. KINGSLEY, Esq., GEORGE R. WILLIS,
> Esq., and FRED R. WILLIAMS, Esq., appearing
> for Motion Picture Patents Company, Biograph Company, Jeremiah J. Kennedy, Harry
> N. Marvin, Armat Moving Picture Company,
> Melies Manufacturing Co. and Gaston Melies.

1
    J. H. CALDWELL, Esq., and H. K. STOCKTON, Esq.,
        appearing for William Pelzer, General Film
        Company, Thomas A. Edison, Inc., Kalem'
        Company, Inc., Pathe Freres, Frank L. Dyer,
        Samuel Long and J. A. Berst.
    HENRY MELVILLE, Esq., attorney for George Kleine,
        Essanay Film Manufacturing Company, Selig
        Polyscope, George K. Spoor and W. N. Selig.
    JAMES J. ALLEN, Esq., appearing for Vitagraph
        Company of America, and Albert E. Smith.

2
    JEREMIAH J. KENNEDY, resumed the stand for fur-
ther direct examination.

    Q. Did you have any interview with the witness Mandel-
baum in connection with the exchange business, other than
the one which you described, when you were sworn in the
early part of the week? A. About the end of December,
1909, or early in January, 1910, Mr. Mandelbaum and Mr.
Gleichman called at my office and submitted to me a propo-
sitiou to undertake to combine all the film exchanges in this
3   country. His plan had been worked out, and was ready to be
put into effect. It provided for the giving of stock to exchanges who would accept stock in payment for their entire
exchange business, and it also provided for each exchange
that accepted stock, paying into the company in cash, half
as much in cash as the par value of the stock  that each
such exchange accepted for its own property. The money so
paid in was to be used to purchase exchanges who would not
take stock in whole or in part payment. His plan also provided for the trusteeing of the stock for a period of from
three to five years, under conditions which would enable me
4   to vote the stock and have absolute control of the proposed
company for whatever period might be agreed upon. He
urged the adoption of this plan, and stated that he felt sure
that 40 per cent. of the owners of the exchanges in this
country were prepared to enter into such an arrangement.
He also stated that he had conferred with a number of them
and knew what he was talking about. In urging me to undertake this consolidation, he called attention to the great

benefits that would be derived in the way of economies, and the ability of such an organization to charge very much higher prices than were then being received by exchanges for film service, and that such a corporation would dominate the entire film business. Furthermore, that any injury that I might suffer by the domination of such a company over the Motion Picture Patents Company, or any adverse effect that might come from it, would be offset by the very large compensation which such a company could give me, and such compensation would be assured, together with the absolute control in my hands for from three to five years.

Q. Did anything come of that interview? A. No, I declined to have anything to do with the proposal.

Q. Do you know whether or not different pictures made by a producer at different times differ in their cost of production? A. They vary within very wide limits. My statement in this respect is based upon my experience as an officer of the Biograph Company in producing motion pictures.

Q. Why is it that the producer in leasing motion pictures does not attempt to place different values on different pictures, but leases them all at a uniform price? A. The placing of a separate value on the pictures would be impracticable. It would involve separate negotiations and separate orders for each subject. It would prevent a regular supply being issued in such a manner as to meet the requirements of the exchanges and the exhibitors. The charging of higher or lower prices for pictures for greater or lesser merit has often been discussed. No plan, however, was ever devised which would be as effective as the plan— the present plan of averaging the price, under which plan orders can be placed in advance, the exchange assured of the receipt of the pictures which it requires on certain days, and the exhibitor likewise assured of his supply.

Q. Would you say that the standing order system tends to take away any incentive to improved quality of the producers' pictures? A. It does not, and it is the only practicable plan for marketing pictures of approximately 1,000 feet in length that has devised.

Q. Does your experience show that each improvement in the average quality of a producer's pictures is followed by an increased average number of copies sold of each pic-

1   ture?   A. That has been so in the case of the Biograph Company.

Q. Has that been your experience as a producer for some years?   A. It has been my experience as a producer since the Summer of 1907.

Q. Would you say that the cost of production is a direct measure of the value of a given picture to an exhibitor, or that that is a matter that is largely speculative and indeterminate?   A. That is entirely speculative. Some of the pictures which have cost the least, have been the most successful, and most in demand, while others that have been so costly as to involve a very serious loss, have been very unsuccessful and very unpopular.

2

Q. Has it been your experience as a producer of motion pictures, and as one conversant with the art and the business growing therefrom, that the demands of an exhibitor for a balanced program each day and for a non-conflicting and non-competing program, are sufficient to overbalance the desire for the more popular pictures, or even the more popular brands?   A. A balanced program is much more satisfactory to the exhibitor, even when the average quality is less, than is a program selected or composed of a few of the more popular brands or subjects.   The non-competing feature is also an important factor.

3

Q. Just what do you mean by that, Mr. Kennedy?   A. I mean that an exhibitor can conduct his business with greater success if he has a program that does not—that is not exactly the same as the program in an adjacent theatre. Even if the average merit of his program, or the subjects that he shows, is less than it might be, if competing houses or exhibitors show the same program, there nevertheless is a greater return, greater satisfaction on the part of the public, a greater patronage in motion picture places of exhibition, if the programs are different, that is, not competing.

4

Q. Then, if two theatres are in the immediate neighborhood of each other, there is a prime necessity for a difference in program?   A. Absolutely.

Q. If two theatres are in the immediate neighborhood of each other, and have different programs and do not conflict, do you say that one may stimulate the other's business, where, if they both have the same program or conflicting programs, they may stifle each other's business? A. Where the programs are different, the patronage of each is very much greater. More patrons are drawn to the locality in which both theatres are located, whereas if the programs are the same, each kills the other; in fact, the same amount of patronage may be said to be divided between two theatres to the injury of both.

Q. Is it a fact, nevertheless, that in spite of the various causes which enter into an exhibitor's selection of his program, that more copies of a popular make are leased than those of a less popular make? A. Yes. The exhibitors demand of their exchange a relatively larger percentage of the more popular subjects, or more popular make, and this in turn creates a demand for such production to the benefit of the producer.

Q. In your experience as a producer of motion pictures, have you ever made any picture or pictures, the first cost of which was so great that you knew you could not get a satisfactory direct return, but did so for the purpose of stimulating the business and increasing the popularity of your own productions generally? A. It has been a common practice amongst the licensed manufacturers, with whose work I am familiar, to produce at times pictures of such merit and cost, that the volume of business cannot possibly bring them back their direct expenses in producing such pictures. They do this for the purpose of maintaining the reputation of their make of pictures, and to keep their general average as high as possible in the estimation of the exchanges and the exhibitors.

Q. And they go still further than that, do they not, and also seek the approval of the public itself? A. Yes. They do that in various ways, such as by extensive advertising, and in every way possible.

Q. Do you recall having had negotiations on behalf of the General Film Company with one Warren R. Palmer, for the purchase of the motion pictures, stock and supply of the Motion Picture Supply Company? A. I had negotiations with him, and with his associate or partner, named Mock.

Q. Do you recall what arrangements were made for the payment of the moneys which the General Film Company agreed to pay for the property bought? A. The price was agreed upon, and the form of contract was sent to Mr.

1 Palmer at Rochester. It contained a statement to the
effect that the vendor vouched for the property which he
sold not being hypothecated, or that the seller was the real
owner of it, and the usual details relative to the giving
of a perfect title. Shortly afterwards, an attorney representing the Genesee Valley Trust Company called and tried
to arrange with me to accept on behalf of the General
Film Company, an assignment of the contract, together
with a modification of the statement that the property was
not hypothecated. He informed me that Mr. Palmer had
very little money when he started in the exchange business,
2 but that he had borrowed a considerable sum. He mentioned approximately $18,000. And that all or part of
this money was lent to him by the Trust Company, and
its payment guaranteed by a relative of Mr. Palmer, who,
I think he said, was Mr. Palmer's uncle. I refused to accept an assignment, as not being in the interest of the
General Film Company, and at a later date, a new form of
contract was prepared, which provided for the making of
payments—the forwarding of payments to Mr. Palmer's
company, in care of the Genesee Valley Trust Company, so
3 that the Trust Company could make arrangements with
Palmer and his associates for the Trust Company to get
the benefit of such remittances, the remittances, however,
being in the name of Mr. Palmer's company. I have the
original contract here if you want to see it. Mr. Palmer
stated to me at the time he sold, that his losses amounted
to between eighteen and twenty thousand dollars.

Cross examination by Mr. Grosvenor:

Q. Mr. Kennedy, what business were you engaged in
before the Summer of 1907, when you became interested in
4 the Biograph Company? A. The same business I am engaged in now, or profession.

Q. And what business is that? A. That is of civil engineering, broadly considered, including the departments of
mechanical and electrical engineering. I was also President of the Pneumatic Tube Companies in New York City,
in charge of the Mail Tube Companies, and was connected
with various other corporations. Do you want to go back
some time? I don't know the exact scope of your question.

Q. Have you kept up your interest in these other matters at the same time that you have been the President of the General Film Company? A. Yes.

Q. So that to-day your entire time is not devoted to the General Film Company? A. Not entirely.

Q. How much of your time is devoted to the General Film Company? A. Oh, I cannot say. That varies.

Q. Do you devote the bulk of your business hours to the affairs of the General Film Company? A. Well, I have no business hours, but I devote the bulk of my time to the General Film Company.

Q. And that has been true of the time in which you have been President of the General Film Company? A. Yes.

Q. Have you read with care the testimony which you gave two or three days ago, and which has been put in printed form? A. I have glanced over all of it. I do not know that I have read it with very great care.

Q. This morning, before the resumption of your direct examination, you made such corrections and amendments in your testimony as seemed to you advisable after reading it? A. No. To have the testimony appear as I intended it to appear.

Q. I say, you have made all such amendments and corrections as seemed to you desirable after reading it? A. All that I noticed.

Q. On page 3157 you testified: "Did any of the other producers of motion pictures, aside from the Edison Company and the Biograph Company, have any stock or any financial interest whatever in the Motion Picture Patents Company? A. None of them had any interest directly or indirectly, or any say in the management of the business or the affairs of the company. Their relations with the Motion Picture Patents Company were solely those of licensees to licensor." I show you, for the purpose of refreshing your recollection, exhibit to the petition numbered two, and also exhibit to the petition numbered three. Isn't it the fact that it was provided in the agreements which were contemporaneous with the beginning of business by the Patents Company, that 24 per cent. of certain royalties collected by the Patents Company were to be divided among the licensed producers? A. Yes, that is part of the relation of licensee and licensor.

1　　Q. Mr. Smith, Mr. Spoor and others of the defendants have testified that in 1909 and 1910, there were meetings from time to time of the licensed producers, at which meetings those present considered the question of recommending to the Patents Company the cancellation of the licenses of some of the rental exchanges. Is your recollection as to the transactions occurring in 1909 and 1910, opposed to theirs? A. Part of their relations as licensee and licensor gave them the assenting or dissenting voice in certain transactions.

2　　Q. Then your recollection is in accord with that of Mr. Smith and Mr. Spoor, in this matter? A. Substantially.

Q. It is true, is it not, that under the agreements entered into in 1908, the Patents Company was prohibited from issuing any license to any other producer except with the consent of the producers licensed in December, 1908, said consent being obtained by vote of the licensed producers, taken in the manner provided in the agreement? A. If the agreement provides for it, it is there, of course.

Q. I say, is it not the fact, that the agreements entered into in 1908, when the Patents Company started business, provided that the Patents Company should issue no additional licenses except when the licensed producers consented to the issuing of such an additional license? A. You are referring to the manufacturing licenses now?

Q. I am referring to the licenses under the camera and film patents, so-called. A. That is true with respect to licenses in the case of a given number, but it is my impression that the Patents Company had a perfect right to grant licenses under certain conditions, without referring to anyone.

Q. Is it not the fact that the given number to which you refer, was the number eight or nine, which embraced the total number of manufacturers who were licensed? A. I think it included ten.

Q. And ten was the number of original licensees? A. I think so.

Q. Now, isn't it the fact that the license agreements and papers and contracts executed in December, 1908, provided, that the Patents Company should issue no additional licenses, that is, no license beyond the number ten, except with the consent of the manufacturers who were licensed in

December, 1910? A. I think there was some such condition. I should say the license would set that forth quite clearly. If I have it, I can tell you. It is a very voluminous document, which has been obsolete for quite a while.

Q. I direct your attention to Paragraph 20 of Exhibit 3 to the petition, appearing at page 72 of the printed petition. Isn't it a fact that the license agreements and papers entered into in December, 1908, provided that the Patents Company should issue no additional license except with the consent of the manufacturers who entered into license agreements with it at that time? A. If that is a correct copy of the old license, I should say that that is true.

Q. Has the Patents Company issued any license since December, 1908, to any producer of motion pictures, except one issued in the Summer or latter part of 1913, to the Kinemacolor Company? A. I think it issued one to Gaston and George Melies.

Q. Gaston and George Melies are included within this number mentioned in the original agreement, namely, ten? A. I did not read that far.

Q. George Melies and Gaston Melies have always been one of the ten original licensees? A. I was under the impression there was very serious doubt about that, but that did not come within my province, and I am not qualified to give very direct information on it.

Q. Can you think of any producer other than the Melies and the Kinemacolor Company which has been issued a license by the Patents Company? A. No. Yes, I can. A manufacturing license was issued to George Kleine. That is my impression. But that did not even come under my observation.

Q. George Kleine is one of the original ten licensees, is he not? A. He was licensed to import motion pictures, but not to manufacture.

Q. When was the Melies license issued? A. I don't know.

Q. It was in the latter part of 1908 or the early part of 1909, was it not? A. I don't know. I think it was later.

Q. On page 3159 of your direct examination, referring to the relations of the Patents Company and the General Film Company, you stated, "The relations of the

1   two companies were solely those of licensor and licensee, in
fact, the management of the General Film Company was
always more or less hostile to the Patents Company. By
management in this case, I am referring to the Board of
Directors." The Board of Directors of the General Film
Company has been made up from the beginning, has it not,
of a representative of each of the licensed producers? A.
I cannot vouch for their being representatives. It is composed of Directors elected by the common stockholders.

Q. Has anyone at any time since the General Film Company was organized, been a Director of the General Film
2   Company, who was not an officer, a principal stockholder
or manager of one of the ten licensed producers? A. Two
men were elected Directors who had no connection with
any producer or importer.

Q. When was that? A. That is, Mr. Waters was elected,
I think, in May, 1912, and Mr. Pelzer was elected in January
of this year.

Q. Pelzer has many years been connected with the Edison
interests, has he not? A. Yes.

Q. And the Mr. Waters to whom you referred was the
man that was made general manager of the General Film
3   Company some time in 1910? A. Shortly after it was organized.

Q. And he is now the general manager? A. He is.

Q. Has there been any other person on the Board of
Directors of the General Film Company who was not a stockholder or principal officer or manager of one of the licensed
producers? A. There are two Directors now whose connection with licensed producers is entirely unknown to me, except the fact that they are elected by common stockholders,
and most of the common stock is held by the producers.

4   Q. Who are those two? A. Mr. McCarahan and Mr. Bonvillan.

Q. How long have these two men been Directors? A.
Mr. McCarahan has been a Director since late in January,
1914.

Q. Has he any connection with the motion picture business other than his directorship on the General Film Company? A. I understand he is in some way connected with
the special features that Mr. George Kleine is marketing.

Q. Mr. Kleine is one of the ten licensed producers? A.

Yes. But Mr. Kleine did not vote any stock for Mr. McCarahan.

Q. Who is this other man that you have named? A. Mr. Bonvillan.

Q. Has he had any previous experience with the motion picture business? A. I know nothing of his connection with the business prior to either December of last year or January of this year.

Q. What is his connection in the motion picture business today? A. He is connected in some capacity with Pathe Freres.

Q. Then the truth is, isn't it, Mr. Kennedy, that this man that you have just named, takes Berst's place as the representative of Pathe Freres on the Board of Directors of the General Film Company? A. I don't know.

Q. You suppose he does, don't you? A. I am not supposing anything of the kind.

Q. Does Pathe Freres have any other representative? A. Not that I know of.

Q. Isn't it a fact that each one of the licensed producers has had a representative on the Board of Directors ever since that company was organized? A. It is not.

Q. Which of the licensed producers has not had a representative on the Board of Directors at all times? A. The Biograph Company.

Q. Are you the President of the Biograph Company? A. Yes.

Q. And you are today the President of the General Film Company? A. I am.

Q. And you are a Director of the General Film Company? A. I am.

Q. And your company owns half the stock of the Patents Company? A. It does.

Q. And it has ever since the Patents Company was organized? A. It has.

Q. Can you name any other company that has not had a representative on the Board of Directors of the General Film Company at all times since the General Film Company was organized? A. I am not able to state positively yes or no. I do not know their relations. They may be in the same relative position that the Biograph Company was when it had no representation. The Board was full just the same.

1    Q. I say, do you know of any licensed company or producer that has not had a continuous representation on the Board of Directors of the General Film Company? A. None, except the Biograph Company.

Q. How long was the Biograph Company unrepresented on the Board of Directors of the General Film Company? A. I should say approximately a year.

Q. You organized the General Film Company? A. What do you mean by organized it?

Q. Are you unable to understand the word? A. I don't know just what you refer to. If you will specify the part that you think I took, or it is contemplated by your question, I will be able to give you direct information.

2

Q. Who did organize the General Film Company? A. I should say the first Board of Directors, with the exception of possibly Mr. Scull.

Q. And who were those? A. Mr. Rock, Mr. Kleine, Mr. Selig, Mr. Spoor, Mr. Berst, Mr. Gaston Melies, Mr. Siegmund Lubin and myself. I think there was one other, whose name I cannot recall at present.

Q. There was one representative on that first board from each of the licensed producers? A. There was one man connected with each of the producers or importers.

3

Q. You have always been Treasurer of the Patents Company? A. Yes.

Q. You have testified on direct examination, page 3159: "In fact, the management of the General Film Company was always more or less hostile to the Patents Company. By management in this case, I am referring to the Board of Directors." Did you consider yourself, as the Treasurer of the Patents Company, hostile to yourself as President of the General Film Company? A. No, I was figuring on a working quorum being hostile, and it always showed its hostility. That is, not less than seven Directors of the General Film Company. Their hostility was always very marked.

4

Q. Can you give any instance of the manifestation of such hostility? A. Various suggestions having to do with the reduction of the royalties, the changing of the license conditions to weaken the authority and domination of the Patents Company, and to obtain more freedom, if possible, than the Patents Company licenses and patent rights permitted.

Q. On page 3195 of the printed record, on your direct examination, you testified: "Q. At the time of the organization of the General Film Company, was it your intention, or was it the intention of your associates, so far as you know, to acquire all the rental exchanges throughout the United States? A. It was not, and the growth of the business was something that we were entirely unprepared for." Have you anything you wish to add to that answer? A. Nothing whatever.

Q. Let me ask you this question: At the time of the organization of the General Film Company, was it your intention, or was it the intention of your associates, so far as you know, to acquire all the licensed rental exchanges throughout the United States? A. It was not.

Q. What was the purpose of making up the estimate which was made up before the General Film Company started in business, of the value of the business of all the licensed rental exchanges? A. I had nothing to do with the making up of any estimate except an estimate that was made very quickly for the purpose of aiding Mr. John Collier some time previously, in preparing a chart to show the magnitude of the motion picture business in this country, and its importance as a factor in modern life, as he put it. More particularly, in connection with a meeting of the Playgrounds Association, which was to be held some months subsequently, and which it was expected would be attended by 1,800 delegates, who were very desirous of considering the motion picture as a new factor to be reckoned with and utilized.

Q. I direct your attention to Petitioner's Exhibit 78, printed at Volume 1 of the Record, page 251, being a letter addressed by you to Mr. William Pelzer, dated January 23rd, 1912, in which you say: "Some time before the General Film Company was organized, an estimate of the value of the business of exchanges leasing licensed motion pictures was made by men familiar with the manufacture of motion pictures, and also the business of exchanges. According to this estimate, the value of said business was $3,468,847." Did you make up that estimate? A. Mr. Collier and I made it up together at my office.

Q. When was this made up? A. To the best of my recollection, it was about August or September, 1909.

Q. Did you keep a copy of it? A. It was made on an ordinary scratch pad.

1    Q. I say, did you keep a copy of it? A. No, there was no occasion for keeping a copy of it.

Q. You did not keep a copy of any part of it? A. I probably had a scratch pad memorandum of it. Undoubtedly had at the time I wrote that, just the same as I had lots of other memoranda. I have looked—I brought all such memoranda as I have along with me today. I do not believe that is in it. I will look and see, if you want me to.

Q. Did you keep a copy of the estimate which you say you and this man Collier made up? A. The scratch pad memorandum was retained just as I retain all memoranda.

2    There was no formal estimate made. They were figures put down during a conversation and discussion lasting probably an hour or two.

Q. Well, did you give Mr. Collier any paper— A. I gave Mr. Collier no paper whatever. Mr. Collier departed with the information that had been developed or the opinions or conclusions that had been developed during our discussion, not only with relation to exchanges, but also with relation to theatres and manufacturing and importing.

Q. Then you gave Mr. Collier no paper of any kind? A.

3    I did not.

Q. And no report of the value— A. No.

Q. Of anything? A. No.

Q. The information that you gave him was purely oral, was it? A. I did not supply information. These figures were arrived at during a joint discussion.

Q. Then, if you gave Mr. Collier no written estimate, you did not keep any copy of any written estimate? A. I always keep copies of whatever memoranda I make for a certain length of time, until there is no probability of their being of any further use, and I have special facilities in my

4    office for keeping such memoranda and other data.

Q. Well, let me ask you this question: Was the estimate and value of all exchanges leasing licensed motion pictures which was made some time before the General Film Company was organized, was that estimate preserved by you? A. The memorandum or pad upon which the figures were jotted down as we talked the subject over, was kept until my departure from the General Film Company, possibly later. I brought an envelope along, which I find has some such information in. It may have this esti-

mate in. I do not know. I got it only this morning. It
was overlooked in the general house cleaning.

Q. Well, this is the fact, anyway: Before the General
Film Company was organized, an estimate was made of the
value of the business of all of the exchanges leasing licensed motion pictures? A. I will only answer that by
saying that an estimate was made during a discussion with
Mr. Collier, of the probable investment in manufacturing
and importing in motion pictures theatres, and in exchanges,
which covered the entire field, and which was information
which Mr. Collier was trying to collect data about.

Q. Well, where did you get this information which you
gave him? A. I did not collect any information at all.
The figures were jotted down offhand during our discussion,
just the same as we might jot down some figures here during this discussion.

Q. Then were they added up? A. There was no adding
up to be done unless probably one or two items. It was
not a formal undertaking.

Q. According to this letter, being Exhibit 78, you say,
"According to this estimate, the value of said business was
$3,468,847." Where did you get that figure? A. I did not
get it anywhere. I am perfectly willing to tell you my
recollection of how we arrived at it.

Q. Did you give that figure to Mr. Collier? A. We were
talking figures together. I did not have to give them
to him. He had the figures the same time I had. We were
discussing round figures. I remember very distinctly his
suggesting that the probable investment in motion picture
theatres was two hundred and forty millions. There was
no estimate made upon that at all. That was based on information he had.

Q. Try and bring your mind to bear on the subject we
have under discussion. I am not talking of the value of
motion picture theatres in the United States, in theatres
or anything else at that time, except this one question as
to the estimate made of the value of the business of licensed
exchanges at this time. A. I am trying to lay before you
the conditions under which these figures were arrived at.

Q. Well, an estimate was made, then, of the value of the
business of exchanges? A. A guess in figures was put down
on a scratch pad. Now, that is the extent of that estimate.

1  I think I can tell you how it was arrived at, and it can be checked now, probably.

Q. Exhibit 80, of the minutes of the Board of Directors, held October 11th, 1910, being at the record, Volume 1, page 266, at which, according to the minutes, the following were present: Messrs. Kennedy, Berst, Dyer, Kleine, Long, Lubin, Selig, Smith, Spoor and Pelzer, Secretary—state that you made a report, and so forth. Have you read these minutes recently? A. No.

Q. Did you discuss these minutes with your counsel, before testifying? A. Some of them, yes.

2  Q. And did you discuss with him this matter of an estimate having been made, or whether it was made before the General Film Company was organized? A. It was referred to quite a while ago.

Q. I say, you did discuss these subjects with your counsel before testifying? A. I did not discuss them. My counsel did not give me the notice he promised me. There was no time available.

Q. Did you go over this matter with your counsel? A. I did not—if you refer to what you have before you—

3  Q. Then please read these minutes. A. Where shall I begin?

Q. Read the entire minutes of that date, Exhibit 80. A. I have read them.

Q. These minutes refer to a report— A. Now, will you let me look at that just a moment, please? Yes, I remember the meeting very distinctly.

Q. These minutes refer to a report having been made by you on behalf of the Executive Committee, that the company had purchased thirty-nine exchanges. Was that report in writing? A. No. Verbal report.

4  Q. How long had the General Film Company been in business on October 11th, 1910? A. Since June 6th, 1910.

Q. It had been in business, then, four months and five days? A. Approximately, yes.

Q. When did the company form the intent to buy thirty-nine exchanges in four months?

Mr. KINGSLEY: I object to the question as incompetent, immaterial and irrelevant, and not properly deducible from any of the evidence given in this case,

not proper cross examination, and assuming a fact
which has not been testified to, and is not in evidence.

The Witness: Will you read that question?

The Examiner repeats the question as follows:
"Q. When did the company form the intent to buy
thirty-nine exchanges in four months?"

Mr. KINGSLEY: Same objection.

The Witness: It never formed such an intention.

By Mr. GROSVENOR:

Q. On direct examination you testified that the company
never intended to get all the licensed exchanges. What made
you start out to buy the exchanges so quickly? A. We were
practically forced to do so by the attitude of a number of
our Directors, and by the fact that we were urgently
solicited by would-be sellers to purchase.

Q. The Patents Company cancelled a number of licenses
in April, May, June and July, 1910, did it not? A. I know of
only two that were cancelled, and I have knowledge concerning the reasons. The two I refer to are the Imperial
Film Exchange and Miles Brothers.

Q. I direct your attention to Exhibit 61, Volume I, page
189, which states that the following licenses were cancelled:
Miles Brothers, Boston, Massachusetts, April 22nd, 1910;
Miles Brothers, New York, New York, April 22nd 1910;
Miles Brothers, San Francisco, California, June 22nd, 1910;
Kay Tee Film Exchange, Los Angeles, California, June 13th,
1910; O. T. Crawford Film Exchange Company, St. Louis,
Missouri, July 19th, 1910; Western Film Exchange, St. Louis,
Missouri, July 19th, 1910; Colorado Film Exchange, Denver,
Colorado, September 13th, 1910; H. & H. Film Service, Chicago, Illinois, October 11th, 1910. Does that refresh your
recollection as to the number of exchanges whose licenses
were cancelled in the period between April and October,
1910? A. Well, I was referring to the cancellations concerning which I had very definite knowledge or complete knowledge.

Q. Returning to these minutes, Exhibit 80, page 266, the

1   minutes read, folio 4: "Total payments authorized for all
exchanges in entire country; stock $988,800, cash, $2,480,-
000." What authorization does that paragraph in the minutes refer to? A. It does not refer to any authorization by
the Board. Those minutes are incomplete. I remember
when they were read for approval. It said only part of
what took place.

Q. Were these figures named in the minutes all read by
you to the Directors present? A. They were. But that is
not the same—

2   Q. The statement is also made, "Payments authorized
for exchanges owned October 10th, stock, $591,400, cash
$1,483,200." When were those payments authorized? A.
Such payments were never authorized by the Board
formally, or even informally, for that matter.

Q. Who did authorize them? A. A number of the Directors, in settling a method of computing the relative value of
the property—the value of the property of Mr. Kleine as
compared to other properties, agreed to a basis of computa-
tion which they would not object to, and would not criticize
if carried out in any transactions that might arise later, and
3   in that way, I used the conversation and statements referred
to as a basis for comparison as shown there. I have got to
tell you the whole story, and then it will be perfectly clear.

Q. In any event, Mr. Kennedy, you had, at the time this
meeting was held, paid $591,400 in stock and $1,483,200 in
cash for the exchanges thus far acquired? A. We had, if the
minutes contain those statements.

Q. What was this saving on—you state in the minutes
$55,500 in stock, and in cash $113,600? A. On the prices
paid on a reel basis as compared with the prices paid to Mr.
George Kleine, also computed on a reel basis, which is not
4   exact.

Q. And the basis which Mr. Kleine had computed you
called the authorized basis? A. I did not. When Mr. Kleine
agreed to sell the exchange property which he had, at a meeting of the Board of Directors, he stipulated after the price
had been agreed upon, that if a higher relative price should
be paid to anyone with whom we might have business relations later, for similar property, then such higher price
should apply to his property. During the balance of the
meeting, I gave considerable attention or consideration to the

difficulty that this imposed upon the Executive Committee, it
appearing to me to be almost impossible to make any exact
comparison of the values, for the reason that Mr. Kleine in
Chicago had only motion pictures without anything else. He
continued in the film business there after delivering his motion pictures. In New York he had motion pictures, merchandise, furniture and equipment. In Denver he had furniture and equipment, motion pictures, and, I understand, no
merchandise. After the meeting had adjourned, several
of the Directors, including myself, remained and I referred to this difficulty, and stated that it seemed to me that
the only way in which we could make any comparison between the value of Mr. Kleine's property and the value
of the other similar property, was on the basis of the
number of reels leased by the different vendors during
a period of, say, six months preceding the time of sale. Mr.
Kleine stated that he realized the difficulty in making an
exact or mathematical comparison, and said that basis would
be satisfactory to him. I asked the Directors who happened
to be seated there if in any future transactions that the
Executive Committee might have, it paid no more for similar property than the price that was paid to Mr. Kleine,
based entirely upon the reels, that is, the price divided by
the number of reels leased during the preceding six months,
—if they would approve such transactions when they came
before them at formal meetings of the Board for approval,
provided there were such transactions. They stated they
would. To get the matter squarely before the entire Board,
I used in all future computations the number of reels at the
price paid to Mr. George Kleine as the basis for arriving at
the amounts. And one of the reasons for bringing the matter
to the Board's attention in that form, was to get the whole
Board thoroughly familiar with Mr. Kleine's informal agreement or acceptance of that basis after the earlier meeting
had adjourned. Furthermore, the figures were used to show
the great danger to the company financially in carrying out
the wishes of a majority of the Board of Directors. And Mr.
Berst, Mr. Long, Mr. Selig and Mr. Kleine were particularly
insistent upon the General Film Company purchasing from
every exchange that offered its property, such property as it
offered at its fair value to the General Film Company, so as
to avoid any possibility of an impression of favoritism get-

1   ting abroad.   The volume of business that the Executive Committee transacted in the way of the purchase of the exchange property was so large as to menace it financially, particularly as it did not have the organization to properly handle and work the property.

Q. Mr. Kleine's exchanges were acquired by the General Film Company at the time it started in business, June 6, 1910?   A. They were acquired on May 27th or May 28th, 1910, at a meeting of the Board of Directors.

Q. They were the first exchanges, or among the first exchanges acquired?   A. They were.

2   Q. And in the purchase of those exchanges, you adopted a standard or a method for determining the value of the exchange?   A. We did not.

Q. Well, what was this basis which you have just testified to?   A. It was a basis used in making comparisons between property acquired and property not acquired in connection with Mr. Kleine's stipulation that if any property should be purchased later at a relatively higher price than was paid to him for similar property, such higher price should apply to the property that he sold.   That

3   forced the adoption, as I have stated before, of a basis of averaging prices according to the reels, regardless of the volume of business, the territory, or any other important factors in connection with such property.   But that did not have anything to do whatever with the prices paid for such property as was purchased.   In each case a separate estimate was made of the property offered for sale.   Its value to the General Film Company was determined.   All the factors relating—or affecting such value, were carefully considered, and in that way the purchase price was arrived at.

4   Q. When you bought Kleine's exchanges, you adopted some method of determining the value of his exchanges?   A. There was no method adopted then or at any other time, except to fix a value upon such property, the same as a real estate expert fixes a value upon a building by examining it and considering its location, its possible earning power, future development, and the various other factors which have to do with values.

Q. At the time you had this conversation with Kleine, you and he and other Directors, all knew that the General

Film Company was going to acquire other exchanges besides those acquired at the time the General Film Company started in business? A. We did not know anything of the kind.

Q. What was the purpose, then, of this conversation with Kleine, respecting this acquisition of other exchanges? A. It was a condition which should apply in the event of any additional similar property being purchased at a later time.

Q. Didn't you expect, at the time you had this conversation with Kleine, to acquire other exchanges? A. I don't know what I expected. There was no such purpose. I do not know that I had any expectations.

Q. You want the record to stand that you did or did not intend, at the time the General Film Company acquired the Kleine exchanges, to acquire other exchanges? A. I was about to add that that was not my intention, and I do not know of its being the intention of any other Director of the General Film Company.

Q. In other words, you had an open mind on the subject? A. Entirely open mind, and the idea was that if this method did not afford relief for the business and the evils in the business, that some other method would have to be found, some other form of relief for the exhibitor and the producer, particularly, and the honest exchange.

Q. Well, when did you make up this estimate of the value of all the other exchanges governed by the rate at which you had paid Kleine? A. Not before each of the Directors' meetings you have referred to. I think you have referred to figures submitted at two Directors' meetings.

Q. I have only referred to one meeting, the meeting of October 11th, 1910. A. I think there was another one also—

Q. There were several others? A. At which figures were submitted.

Q. How soon after this talk with Kleine did you make up your mind to buy other exchanges? A. Not until the next exchange asked us to purchase its property. I do not know when that was. We did not make up our mind then, and would not have purchased it if the price had not been attractive.

Q. Exhibit 62, printed in Volume I, page 190, and fol-

1 lowing, shows that on June 13th you acquired the Howard Moving Picture Company. A. That is wrong.

Q. When should it be? A. May 27th or May 28th.

Q. 1910? A. 1910. The date you refer to there is very probably the date on which the exchange property was delivered to the General Film Company, and not the date of the purchase at all.

Q. Then, in respect to each of the dates given in this exhibit, the fact is, the sale was consummated, or the negotiations reached an agreement some time prior to the date of delivery? A. If you will let me look at that I can
2 tell you in a moment about a few of them. Yes, it relates to the date on which the property purchased was delivered.

Q. Then, in respect to each of these purchases, the parties reached an agreement for the sale, some days prior to the date of delivery of the exchange? A. Oh, yes, sometimes weeks. Usually weeks. In Swaab's case, it was two months.

Whereupon, at 12:30 a recess was taken until 2:00 P. M.

3 The hearing was resumed at 2:00 o'clock.

---

JEREMIAH J. KENNEDY, resumed the stand.

Cross examination continued by Mr. GROSVENOR:

Q. Mr. Kennedy, please state the exchanges which were acquired by the General Film Company when it was organized, refreshing your recollection by examining either the exhibit which you introduced on your direct examination, being Defendants' Exhibit 172, or by using Government's Exhibit No. 62, or both of them? A. Will you read
4 the question, please?

The question is repeated by the Examiner as follows:

"Q. Mr. Kennedy, please state the exchanges which were acquired by the General Film Company when it was organized, refreshing your recollection by examining either the exhibit which you introduced on your direct examination, being Defend-

ants' Exhibit 172, or by using Government's Exhibit 1
No. 62, or both of them."

The Witness: I am somewhat in doubt as to just what
you mean by "organized." The company was organized
and held its first meeting in April. At a meeting of the
Board of Directors, held on May 27th, 28th, and, I think,
the 29th also, 1910, certain exchange property was offered
to the Board, and was purchased by the Board. Are those
the exchanges that you refer to?

By Mr. GROSVENOR: 2

Q. I want to know the names of the exchanges which
the General Film Company acquired before it commenced
doing business. A. The Howard Moving Picture Company, Boston. George Kleine, Boston.

Q. You may use Petitioner's Exhibit 62 if that will
help you to refresh your recollection. A. Well, there were
different days for delivery, and there were proposals accepted at later dates—I mean, there were prices discussed
at that meeting, which were rejected, and which were accepted at a later time. I can include all those and give you 3
the circumstances in connection with each one as I go along,
if you wish.

Q. No, I want to know the names of the exchanges which
you, that is, the General Film Company, had when you
started business on June 6th, 1910. A. Well, we started
on June 6th, 1910, but we had arranged to open other
exchanges on June 13th and later dates. Now, what I want
to know is, shall I include only the ones that we started
with, or the ones which we had arranged to acquire and
have delivery at a later date?

Q. In answering my question, you can divide the ex- 4
changes into two classes. Name those first which you
had acquired and whose properties you used in starting in
business on June 6th, and secondly, those which you had
already arranged to acquire, but whose property had not
yet been turned over to you. A. You have the Howard
Moving Picture Company, Boston? Just take that out and
put it in the second class. Perhaps I had better start all
over again.

Q. Yes. A. George Kleine, Chicago office. Siegmund

1   Lubin, Philadelphia. These two exchanges were opened on June 6th, 1910, that is to say, the exchange property connected with them was delivered to the General Film Company on that date. Howard Moving Picture Company, Boston, delivered its property on June 13th, 1910.

Q. Had that been contracted for prior to June 6th? A. Yes. The exchange property of George Kleine's Boston office was delivered on June 13th, 1910.

Q. Had that been contracted for before June 6th? A. Yes, all these had. George Kleine also made delivery of property in his New York office on June 6th, 1910. Those

2   were all, with the exception that the price for George Kleine's exchange property in Denver was agreed upon, but he refused to deliver until a later date, after the experiment of the General Film Company had been tried out, and the same applies to the exchange property of George K. Spoor in Chicago. Mr. P. L. Waters informed the Board that he was willing to accept the price which had been discussed and agreed upon, but the date for delivery would have to be made later, and at a time acceptable to him, but that if he delivered, he would accept the price that was

3   named.

Q. Referring again to the minutes for the meeting of October 11th, 1910, the balance of thirty-nine exchanges which the minutes state had been acquired on October 11th, 1910, were acquired by the company between June and October 11th, 1910? A. Yes.

Q. Why, in the minutes of October 11th, 1910, do you refer to the cost or estimate of acquiring all the exchanges in the entire country, if it was not your intention at that time to acquire them all? A. To show the rapidity with which we were called upon or requested to purchase exchange property, and to show the magnitude of our obliga-

4   tions in the event of the Board of Directors insisting upon the company's purchasing the properties of exchanges that were offered to us, so as to show no favoritism. I was opposed to the purchase of so much property so rapidly. To put the burden of responsibility entirely on the Board of Directors.

Q. Referring to the meetings of the Board of Directors of March 13th, 1911, being Petitioner's Exhibit 84, printed in the record, Volume 1, page 281 and following, that exhibit gives a list of the licensed exchanges not purchased at that time by the company. Please examine that list. A. I have examined it.

Q. The minutes state, page 282: "The following statement of licensed exchanges in the United States was submitted for the information of the Board." Was that statement submitted by you? A. Every statement submitted was submitted by me.

Q. Then that statement was submitted by you? A. Yes. If the statement was submitted. I have no recollection of it, of course.

Q. That statement shows: "Total number of licensed exchanges when General Film Company commenced business, June 6th, 1910, sixty-nine; number of exchange licenses cancelled since June 6th, 1910, eleven." Does the latter statement refresh your recollection as to the licenses of exchanges having been cancelled in the period of time that the General Film Company was acquiring these exchanges? A. I have no recollection to be refreshed. That information was common to everybody, and it was received in the ordinary course of business.

Q. It was known, then, generally, that the licenses of certain of the exchanges were being cancelled from time to time in the period, by the Patents Company? A. Yes. The Patents Company sent notices to that effect to all exchanges.

Q. You referred on direct examination to certain testimony given by Mr. Fox, a witness for the petitioner in this case. You recall having those interviews with Mr. Fox? A. I recall two interviews very clearly.

Q. Did you read the testimony given by Mr. Fox in this case? A. I just glanced over it. I am not familiar with it.

Q. The subject discussed at those meetings was the matter of the sale of the business of the Greater New York Film Rental Company to the General Film Company, is that right? A. That was the subject that was discussed at the request of Mr. Fox.

Q. I am not asking you at whose request it was discussed, but that was the subject which you and Mr. Fox met to discuss? A. It was.

Q. And you met— A. We did not meet to discuss it. I cannot agree to that.

ι  Q. What did you meet for? A. We did not meet at all, as your question implies. Mr. Fox, at the first meeting, came to the General Film Company's office. I was not there. I did not know of his coming. I learned of his presence after he had been there some time. The other interview to which I refer was at my office, and was at the request of Mr. Fox, who called.

Q. I am not asking you as to the request, and who called the meeting. The fact is that the subject you discussed when you did meet, was the sale of Mr. Fox's business, that is, the business— A. While we were together, that is the business that we discussed.

2

Q. That is, the sale of the business of the Greater New York Film Rental Company to the General Film Company? A. Yes.

Q. How many of the formerly licensed rental exchanges at the time that Mr. Fox called and saw you, were still doing business in licensed motion pictures? A. I remember, offhand, only two.

Q. And what two were those? A. One was called, I think, the Twin City Calcium Light & Film Company, and the other was the Greater New York Film Rental Company.

3

Q. One of the two companies you have named was Mr. Fox's company? A. Yes.

Q. Well, isn't it a fact that there were no other companies at that time handling licensed films, that is, the films of the licensed producers, except the General Film Company, the Greater New York Film Rental Company, and possibly this Twin City Calcium & Stereopticon Company of Minneapolis? A. I think I have already stated that offhand I could remember only two in addition to the General Film Company, and there is no "possibly" about the Twin City Company, because that company was not acquired, I am sure, until a later date.

4

Q. It was acquired by the General Film Company at a later date? A. At the earnest solicitation of its owner. The owner of the Twin City Company had solicited us to purchase his exchange property for, I should say, a year and a quarter, or more. I can give you the exact time, if you want me to refer to my records.

Q. A year and a quarter before Mr. Fox came to see you? A. It would be about the same.

Q. Before this date in November, 1911? A. He wrote

me in August, I think, 1910, and to the best of my recol- 1
lection, he came to New York and persuaded us to purchase the property that he had, in December, 1911.

Q. Then at the time Mr. Fox did see you about the sale
of the business of the Greater New York Film Rental
Company to the General Film Company, there were only
two exchanges other than the General Film Company handling the film of the licensed producers, which two exchanges were Mr. Fox's company, the Greater New York
Film Rental Company, and this Twin City Company? A.
Those are the only two that I remember.

Q. You would remember it if there were more than 2
those two, wouldn't you? A. I think I would, although out
of sixty, I might make a mistake.

Q. Then it is a fact, isn't it, frankly, that those are the
only two companies that were doing business in licensed
film other than the General Film Company at that time?
A. Those are the only two that I remember. That is my
answer to your question.

Q. Have you read over the testimony given by Mr.
Swaab, a witness for the petitioner, whose testimony you
referred to on your direct examination several days ago? 3
A. I don't remember referring to his testimony.

Q. Mr. Kingsley asked you certain questions about Mr.
Swaab's testimony, which questions you answered. Please
refer to the record at page 3165. A. I remember answering questions that Mr. Kingsley put to me relative to Mr.
Swaab's affairs.

Q. Have you read over the testimony given by Mr. Swaab
in this case? A. Only glanced over it. I have not had time
to read the testimony.

Q. You don't dispute the fact that you and Mr. Swaab
did have meetings at the times referred to? A. I do not dis- 4
pute the fact that Mr. Swaab came to the General Film Company's office and said he would remain there until he saw
me for the purpose of negotiating the sale of his exchange
property.

Q. And the matter discussed at your meeting or meetings with Mr. Swaab was the sale of the business of his company? A. And the management of it afterwards.

Q. Both those subjects were discussed? A. Yes, and
none other.

1  Q. The matter fell through, that is to say, the sale was not consummated? A. No, we refused to purchase.

Q. You do not dispute the fact that subsequently, Mr. Swaab's license was cancelled, do you? A. It is a matter of common knowledge.

Q. That it was cancelled? A. Yes.

Q. Have you read the testimony given by Mr. Mandelbaum, a witness for the petitioner, respecting whom you were asked several questions by Mr. Kingsley, your counsel, on direct examination? A. I have read some of it.

2  Q. Do you dispute the fact that Mr. Mandelbaum saw you at the times he testifies that he did see you in New York? A. I do not know about the dates, but I know we had interviews. I think I referred to them the other day.

Q. And they were about the times that he stated they were had? A. I do not know anything about the dates. I have no recollection of the dates.

Q. This interview, or interviews, were in New York? A. They were at New York.

Q. And the subject matter discussed was the sale of the business of his company, to the General Film Company? A. Not the business of his company.

3  Q. What was the subject under discussion? A. The sale of his stock and unexpired right in motion pictures, together with the purchase and sale of such new merchandise as he had.

Q. Was that matter consummated, that is to say, did you acquire Mr. Mandelbaum's company? A. We did not. I have already testified to that.

Q. Was Mr. Mandelbaum's license subsequently cancelled? A. I presume so. Notices were sent to that effect. Mr. Mandelbaum informed me that his license was cancelled.

4  Q. Have you read the testimony given by Mr. Ensor, a witness for the petitioner in this case, respecting whose testimony you were asked certain questions by Mr. Kingsley on your direct examination, several days ago? A. I have read it over very hurriedly.

Q. You do not dispute the fact that Mr. Ensor did come to New York and saw you at your office in connection with the sale of the business of his company, to your company? A. I do not dispute that fact at all.

Q. That was the matter that was discussed between you?

A. Yes. And in addition, his project to form a consolida- 1
tion which would control the film business in Colorado and
adjacent territory.

Q. What other company was doing a rental business in
the films of these producers in the territory in which Mr.
Ensor was doing business when the General Film Company
was organized? A. George Kleine had a branch in Denver,
and there was another exchange, the name of which I will
have to get from the list. It was managed or owned by a
man named Buckwalter, and was commonly referred to as
Buckwalter's exchange.

Q. Did you acquire that exchange? A. Yes, at a later 2
date.

Q. And you acquired the Kleine exchange? A. Yes.

Q. You may state whether or not the license of Mr. Ensor's company was subsequently cancelled? A. We received
notice to that effect.

Q. It was, then, so far as you know? A. So far as I
know.

Q. What was your objection, did you say, or explain it,
to Mr. Ensor's proposition to enter into an arrangement
with the General Film Company? A. For a long time it had 3
been common knowledge that the Colorado Film Exchange
was a stock jobbing proposition, and that stock was being
peddled at the rate of a dollar a share all over the section
of the country in which Mr. Ensor was located, that a great
deal of the stock had been taken by parties whom Mr. Ensor and others claimed had not paid for it, and there was
threatened litigation. Together with the fact that Mr. Ensor himself stated that he was not a practical film man. We
believed that we could not get a clear title to the property,
and for that reason, and for the reason that we did not want
to be involved in any litigation, we refused to have any deal- 4
ings with him.

Q. You testified on direct examination, page 3168, "He,"
that is, Ensor, "desired to enter into an arrangement with
the General Film Company for the control of that entire
territory between them, the General Film Company, and
the Colorado Company, to become secret partners." You
had objection to such an arrangement? A. Yes. It was not
the only time we refused to enter into such an arrangement.

Q. As a matter of fact, after Ensor's exchange had its

1  license cancelled, and you had acquired Kleine's exchange
and this other exchange out there which you referred to, you
did have the whole business?  A. The two exchanges that
we operated, they supplied all that territory, but not with
the object of charging extraordinary prices, but for the purpose of maintaining and building up the trade.

Q. You then got the whole business without entering into
any arrangement with Mr. Ensor?  A. Do you mean the
business in motion pictures in that territory?

Q. You got the entire business of handling the pictures
2  of these licensed producers in that territory?  A. Not in
that territory, but supplied from offices in that territory.
We had competition.

Q. What was the date of your interviews with Mr. Craw-
ford and Mr. Graham in regard to the affairs of the Western
Film Exchange?  A. I had no interview with Mr. Crawford.
I would not know him if I saw him.

Q. You did see parties who had interests in that exchange
on the subject of the purchase by the General Film Company of the business of the Western Film Exchange?  A.
With reference to the purchase of the business of the West-
3  ern Film Exchange?  I never discussed that with anyone.
I never had any such interview.

Q. The license of the Western Film Exchange was cancelled in July, 1910, was it not?  A. I don't know the date.
It was cancelled some time in the Summer, I should say.

Q. And was it cancelled in this period that you were
acquiring many of the other exchanges?  A. Oh, yes.

Q. Did you acquire Mr. Boone's company?  A. You mean
the Theatre Film Supply of Birmingham?

Q. Yes.  A. We did.  Not the company, but the property
which we could use.  He had other property which was ex-
4  cluded from the contract, the same as Pearce & Sheck, and
the Pittsburg Calcium Light & Film Company, and others.

Q. You are today President of the General Film Company?  A. I am.

Q. What per cent. of the total revenues of the General
Film Company is derived from the leasing of films to exhibitors?  A. I should say approximately between 90 and 95
per cent.

Q. And these films are the positive motion picture films
which are shipped out from your several branches to the

exhibitors?  A. Yes, but I am including with that, the large <sup>1</sup>
income from the sale and rental of posters.

Q. Those posters are shipped out in the same way from
your branch offices to the exhibitors?  A. No.  We are one
of the sources of supply.  There are several other sources;
they are supplied by the manufacturers, just the same, and
by the lithographers just the same as the General Film Company supplies them.

Q. I am talking now about your revenues.  The posters
that your company sends out are shipped out from your
branch offices to the exhibitors?  A. Yes.  But we do not
supply all, and have no control over them.

Q. That is to say, the licensed producers ship some posters
also?  A. Some of the licensed producers ship none.  For instance, the Biograph Company ships none.

Q. What per cent. of your total revenue is made up of
the leasing of films to the exhibitors?  A. No figures have
been made up to show that percentage, but I should say it is
approximately 90 or 91 per cent.

Q. Are these films shipped from the factories of the licensed producers to your branch offices?  A. They are delivered by the producers and importers to the transportation companies designated by us at the point of shipment.
Our responsibility commences when the producer and importer delivers to the transportation company that we designate, at the point of shipment.

Q. Then the transportation company carries them to your
branch offices?  A. Yes.

Q. And from your branch offices they are distributed to
these exhibitors?  A. Yes.

Q. And 90 per cent. of your revenues are derived from
this distribution to your exhibitors?  A. Yes.

Q. Then the exhibitors ship them back to you and you <sup>4</sup>
redistribute them to other exhibitors?  A. Yes.

Q. Are you acquainted with the affairs of the Biograph
Company prior to the Summer of 1907?  A. No, I did not
know of its existence.

Q. The by-laws of the Executive Committee of the General Film Company, which appear at Volume I of the Record, page 209, folio 4, provide that the Executive Committee
shall keep minutes.  Did this Executive Committee preserve
any minutes of the occurrences during the Summer of 1910

1 and during the year 1911? A. The Executive Committee had no by-laws, and if it had held any meetings, the minutes would have been kept in accordance with the requirements of the company's by-laws.

Q. The by-laws of the General Film Company, Petitioner's Exhibit 64, printed in the Record, page 201 *et seq.*, provide, Article VI, Section 9, "Executive Committee," the third paragraph in that section; "The Executive Committee shall exercise all the powers of the Board of Directors while the Board is not in session; shall keep minutes of the business transacted at all its meetings, and shall report to the Board

2 of Directors at each meeting of the Board, all the business that it transacted since the last meeting of the Board." You may state whether or not any minutes were kept of the meetings of the Executive Committee in 1910 and 1911. A. No minutes could have been kept, for the reason that there were no meetings.

Q. You constituted the Executive Committee? A. No, I was Chairman of the Executive Committee, and I drew those by-laws, and the Executive Committe was merely an emergeney body to act more quickly than the entire Board could

3 be brought into action.

Q. And you, in your own person, exercised all the powers of the Executive Committee, conferring over the telephone with Mr. Smith and Mr. Berst, the other members of the Executive Committee? A. At their request, I acted for them and reported to them informally.

Q. What was this dinner at which the subject of forming such a rental exchange, that is, a rental exchange owned by the producers, was broached? A. When was it?

Q. Yes. A. I think it was on December 20th, 1909.

Q. Was that a meeting held in celebration, that is, on the

4 anniversary of the birth of the Patents Company? A. For convenience, we arranged to get together once a year and discuss all our grievances with each other. It was a purely social affair.

Q. That was an idea which you sprung upon the others on the occasion of this anniversary of the formation of the Patents Company? A. It was a suggestion that appeared to me to go right to the point of the difficulties.

Q. How many reels does the Biograph Company produce today, a week? A. Well, that is indefinite. It produces three regular short subjects every week, and in addition, it produces one or more, sometimes only a fraction of one long subject of unusual expense and merit.

Q. Is there any competition as to price in the distribution of these regular releases of which you say you produce three a week, between yourself, that is, the Biograph Company, and the other licensed producers? A. Not that I know of. We all sell at the lowest price we can.

Q. And the lowest price at which you can sell them to the General Film Company is fixed by your license? A. Yes.

Q. So you don't mean to say, in saying that you sell at the lowest price you can, that there is competition between the ten different licensed producers in the fixing of that lowest price? A. I mean to say if we sold at the higher price, we would have no business. We have a perfect right to sell at any price we please. The present prices frequently involve very serious loss. But we have to stand that or go out of the business, so in that way there is competition.

Q. The price at which you distribute these reels to the General Film Company, that is, the regular releases, is the same as the price at which the other nine licensed producers distribute their regular releases to the General Film Company? A. Yes. It is the highest price the General Film Company will pay.

Q. When did you ever purchase exchange property from an exchange that was unlicensed? A. I don't know the exact time. I think I can get it from the record.

Q. Look at page 3195 of your testimony. A. I understood your question to refer to the date.

Q. "Q. Was it necessary for a rental exchange, purchased by the General Film Company, to have a license at the time of the purchase? A. No. We purchased exchange property from an exchange that was unlicensed." A. We did.

Q. In what cases? A. We purchased the exchange property formerly owned by the S. Nye Bass Film Exchange in New Orleans.

Q Do you know of any other case? A. No.

Q. Had that S. Nye Bass Company been a licensed exchange? A. Yes.

1      Q. At page 3195 you state, "We always had more exchange property offered to us than we were fitted to handle."
Have you anything to add to that answer? A. Nothing,
except to elaborate it.

Q. I wish you would. A. In reference to our fitness to
handle, I had in mind then the difficulty of obtaining
enough thoroughly skilled modern business men to handle
our business in the way we intended it should be handled,
in the way in which we wanted to handle it, and we were
then engaged in training men for those positions, having
in mind the fact that the branch managers are absolutely in-
2   dependent of the Board of Directors, and conduct the business of their branches the same as if it was their private
property.

Q. In other words, in the Summer of 1910, and the Fall
of that year, exchanges came to you to sell to you, faster
than you could buy them, and handle their properties? A.
Yes. And I protested to the Board against being obliged
to purchase such property in advance of our having the
organization to take care of it.

Q. Mr. Kingsley, on your direct examination, read to
3   you at page 3164, a statement given by Mr. Fox on his direct examination, who testified that you had said at this
interview, to him, "Well, this is the finish of my work. This
is the end of what I set out to do," and you denied having made that statement. Whether you made that statement or not, Mr. Kennedy, it is true that you had finished
the task of buying up exchanges at the time of the interview
with Mr. Fox? A. I had not finished any task. There never
was such a task, and I was involuntarily acting as an officer
of the General Film Company.

Q. In other words, you did not consider this buying up
4   of the·exchanges to be a task? A. No, I did not consider—
no task was set forth at any time. A task involves something to be done and accomplished, and there was nothing set forth to be done and accomplished in connection
with the General Film Company at any time.

Q. In other words, you were just doing this along without having any set purpose or plan to do it? A. The experiment of finding out whether the providing of a source
of supply of film, of motion pictures, conducted without
favoritism, would relieve the business from some of the

burdens and evils which were common to it, was only an experiment. It was tried with a view of finding out if it were a remedy. If not, some other remedy would be undertaken, and that was the only idea in starting the General Film Company.

Q. You started it, in your judgment, as an experiment? A. As an experiment, as the means most likely to afford the relief and accomplish the objects desired.

Q. When did the General Film Company cease to be an experiment?

Mr. KINGSLEY: I object to the question on the ground that it does not appear in the evidence that the General Film Company has ever ceased to be an experiment.

The Witness: It is still an experiment.

By Mr. GROSVENOR:

Q. And it was still an experiment at the time of your interview with Mr. Fox, at which time, as you have testified, none of the licensed exchanges were then in business except his, and this Twin City Calcium Company in the West? A. It was very much of an experiment, and a doubtful one.

Q. Did you consider the other exchanges doing business, also experiments? A. I never gave any thought to whether they were experiments or not, except when their owners referred to them as such.

Q. Then, in your judgment, the General Film Company was the only experiment in the exchange business? A. No, I say other exchange owners referred to their business as probably fleeting and evanescent, or an experiment, and that was the principal reason they gave for trying to induce the General Film Company or someone else to assume the risk.

Q. In what business were you engaged in the interim between your holding the office of President of the General Film Company? A. Engaged in conducting my regular engineering practice, as President of the Hall Switch & Signal Company, Vice-President and Treasurer of the Hall Signal Company, and various other business connections. I was also Treasurer of the Armat Company.

1    Q. What experience did you have in the motion picture business between the Spring of 1912, when you left the General Film Company, and January, 1914, when you returned to resume the presidency? A. A general experience as President of the Biograph Company, a producing concern, and also as a Director in the General Film Company part of the time.

Q. What other venture did you make or have in the motion picture business in that time? A. I do not know that I care to discuss my private ventures in the moving
2    picture business unless my counsel advises me to discuss them.

Q. Did you become the head or interested in a company known as the Kinetograph Company? A. I refuse to discuss the Kinetograph Company, on the ground it is my private business.

Q. The Kinetograph Company was a company which was licensed by the Patents Company, and which engaged for a time in the leasing and distribution of films in competition with the General Film Company? A. I am willing to accept your statement of that as a fact. I refuse to dis-
3    cuss it.

Q. I ask you, is that the fact? A. I refuse to discuss it, or anything relating to my private affairs.

Q. Is the Kinetograph Company still doing business? A. I repeat the same answer. I am perfectly willing to discuss anything with you on the advice of counsel.

Q. The Kinetograph Company endeavored to engage in business in competition with the General Film Company, and found it impossible to continue in business, isn't that right? A. No company that I have ever been connected with found it impossible to do anything it set out to do.

4    Q. Then the fact that the Kinetograph Company is no longer doing a rental business or a film business, is because you are no longer connected with that company? A. I have told you I refuse to discuss my private affairs.

Q. Is there any company that is today distributing licensed film, that is, the film of the ten licensed producers, other than the General Film Company and the Greater New York Film Rental Company? A. I do not know of any company that is handling the products of all of the licensed producers, but the product of some of the licensed

producers is being marketed independently of the General
Film Company, and in direct competition with it.

Q. You are unwilling to testify whether or not the business of the Kinetograph Company, in competition wth the
General Film Company, was profitable or unprofitable? A.
Perfectly willing to testify to anything that I am connected
with or have been conected with, if my counsel advises
me to do so. Not the slightest reluctance on my part.

Mr. GROSVENOR: Mr. Kingsley, will you advise
the witness?

Mr. KINGSLEY: You may say whether or not the
Kinetograph Company was profitable or unprofitable,
bearing in mind that you were developing the business at the time. That is, if you had sufficient experience to come to any conclusion on the subject.

The Witness: I did not consider it unprofitable.

By Mr. GROSVENOR:

Q. Did it pay any dividends? A. It did not.
Q. Is it doing any business today? A. I have answered
all your questions that I am going to answer, unless directed
by counsel.

Mr. GROSVENOR: I ask counsel for the witness to
request the witness to answer the question.

Mr. KINGSLEY: It is already in the record, time
after time, that the Kinetograph Company is not in
business. I concede that the Kinetograph Company is
not doing any business today, but as to any infer-
ences as to whether it might have been profitable or
not, or would have been profitable or not, or should
have paid a dividend or not, I make no concession.

By Mr. GROSVENOR:

Q. How long did the Kinetograph Company do business
in the distribution of the film of the licensed manufacturers? A. I refuse to discuss my private affairs unless
directed to do so by counsel.

Q. Of course, you understand, witness, when you say

1   that the affairs of the Kinetograph Company are your private affairs, you are making yourself and the Kinetograph
Company one and the same? A. I cannot help it.

> Mr. KINGSLEY: You may say how long it was in
> business, Mr. Kennedy, if you know.

The Witness: It commenced acquiring its stock of motion pictures late in November or early in December, 1912.
It stopped leasing film about the seventeenth of April, 1913.

2   Redirect examination by Mr. KINGSLEY:

Q. Did the Kinetograph Company have a license from
the Motion Picture Patents Company? A. It did.

Q. I understood you to say that the Biograph Company
is furnishing three releases a week. A. Three regular short
subjects a week.

Q. Are three releases a week sufficient to give an exhibitor a complete program? A. Not for a day.

Q. Does the exhibitor require a complete non-conflicting
program? A. It is absolutely necessary for his existence,
3   if he has a competitor.

Q. Does he necessarily use the pictures of more than
one producer in securing and showing such a program?
A. Yes. He is obliged to use the output of several producers.

Q. Can the exhibitor, under such conditions, obtain a
complete non-conflicting program without the co-operation
and aid of the rental exchange from which he secures service? A. That would be impossible.

Q. If he secures service from more than one exchange
at the same time, is it possible for him to avoid repeaters
4   and conflicts, if the rental exchanges are securing pictures
from the same producers? A. No.

Thereupon, AARON BRYLAWSKI, the next witness pro-   1
duced by the defendants, of lawful age, being first duly
sworn, deposed as follows:

Direct examination by Mr. KINGSLEY:

Q. Where do you live? A. Washington, D. C.

Q. In what business are you? A. Manager of motion
picture theatres.

Q. How many motion picture theatres do you manage?
A. Exclusively motion pictures?

Q. Yes. A. Five.                                       2

Q. Where are they located, and what are their seating
capacities? A. One is in South East Washington, with a
seating capacity of five hundred.

Q. Give us the streets, please? A. Eight hundred thirty-
five Eighth Street, South East.

Q. And the seating capacity? A. Five hundred. One is
1020 Seventh Street, North West, with a seating capacity
of two hundred and twenty. Another one is at No. 309
Ninth Street, with a seating capacity of two hundred and
ten. Another one is at No. 911 Pennsylvania Avenue, with
a seating capacity of one hundred and sixty, and another   3
one is at No. 477 Pennsylvania Avenue, with a seating
capacity of three hundred and fifty.

Q. How long have you been the manager of motion picture theatres in the City of Washington? A. Since 1909.

Q. In what month of 1909 did you go into the motion picture business? A. March, 1909.

Q. In March, 1909, when you went into the motion picture business, how many theatres did you have under your
immediate charge and supervision? A. Two theatres.

Q. Did you acquire any other theatres shortly after that?
A. On April 12th, 1909, I acquired the Pickwick.           4

Q. So that in April, 1909, you were in charge of three
motion picture theatres in the City of Washington? A. Yes,
sir.

Q. At that time did you have any difficulty in securing
programs for your three theatres which did not conflict?
A. Well, the following month I acquired another one.

Q. In May? A. Yes, in May, 1909, I acquired another
one, and in July, 1909, I acquired the Pastime. This was the
Colonial in 1909, and in September, 1909, the Cosmos and

1 the Crescent theatres, all in one neighborhood. That is, the Colonial was on Pennsylvania Avenue, No. 927, the Cosmos was on Pennsylvania Avenue, No. 921, and the Crescent was on Pennsylvania Avenue, No. 919, and the Pickwick was on Pennsylvania Avenue, No. 911, and the Palace was right around the corner from Pennsylvania Avenue, at No. 307 Ninth Street.

Q. So that, by September of 1909, you had five motion picture theatres in the immediate vicinity of each other? A. Yes, sir.

2 Q. Now, while you were managing these five motion picture theatres in the Autumn of 1909, from what rental exchange did you secure service? A. From the Actograph Company, for a part of them, and from Miles Bros. for another part, and from the Imperial, of Washington, and Baltimore, for the other part.

Q. While you were obtaining motion picture service for these five theatres from the four exchanges you have mentioned, did you have any difficulty with respect to conflicting programs and repeaters? A. All the time.

Q. Well, will you tell us something about your experience in that respect? A. The experience was such that I was compelled to dismiss them all, and confine myself exclusively to the Actograph Company.

Q. Did you find after you confined yourself exclusively to the Actograph Company that you could avoid much of the difficulty which resulted from the duplication of programs and repeaters? A. I could have avoided it if I had not had competition.

Q. Were these competitors being supplied by other exchanges? A. Yes, sir, immediately opposite us.

Q. What was the situation with respect to competition 4 between you and your competitors who were supplied by other exchanges after you began to take your exclusive service for all of your theatres from the Actograph Company? A. We were in continual competition. The same reels we would show on one day, they would insist upon showing on the same day.

Q. Did you afterwards advertise your program in advance? A. In 1910 I got out a little magazine to show what our different theatre programs were for the week.

Q. What time in 1910 was this? A. I started, I think, in May.

Q. Have you a copy of any of the programs that you got out in 1910? A. Yes, sir; I think this is in May. This is July, we started in June or the end of May. This is "Washington, D. C., July, 1910, No. 4, Vol. 1." So it must have been about the end of May.

Q. Were you issuing this program as a regular publication at that time? A. Yes, sir.

Q. Did you issue it under the name of the "National Motion Picture Magazine"? A. Yes, sir.

Q. Did this publication which you have handed me contain the programs of the Palace Theatre and the Pickwick Theatre? A. You will find that at the bottom of each little story, where the pictures were to be shown.

Q. Did this publication which you have handed me contain the complete programs of the Palace Theatre and the Pickwick Theatre, and the Colonial Theatre, and the Cosmos Theatre? A. Yes, sir.

Q. How long did you continue to issue the National Motion Picture Magazine? A. It did not contain the pictures of the Cosmos Theatre, because by virtue of the competition through the four theatres we eliminated the Cosmos and the Crescent in February of 1910, finding that we could not get enough pictures for all of them. We cut the Cosmos and the Crescent entirely out and put in a vaudeville theatre there.

Q. How many exclusively motion picture theatres did you have in the latter part of February, 1910? A. The Meader, South East, the Palace on Ninth Street, the Happyland, on Seventh Street, the Pastime, on Pennsylvania Avenue, and there was also one, the Metropolitan, on Pennsylvania Avenue, which is since extinct. The Pickwick, on Pennsylvania Avenue, and the Colonial, on Pennsylvania Avenue. The theatres that were together, the Palace, and the Pickwick, and the Colonial, those three theatres were in competition with one another. We lost the Colonial last July.

Q. How long did you continue the publishing of the National Motion Picture Magazine? A. I think, about six months.

Q. Did you find that that publication was an advantage

1 to you, or a disadvantage?  A. It was an advantage in the beginning, but it became a disadvantage.

Q. In what respect did it become a disadvantage, and why did you cease its publication?  A. Because our competitors knew what we were showing, and they anticipated us.

Q. Did they take advantage of the advertising contained in the National Motion Picture Magazine to anticipate your program, and show the pictures in advance of yours?  A. That I could not tell.  I could not tell how they done it, only what they done.

2 Q. What did they do?  A. They got the pictures and showed them the same day we did.

Q. After you ceased publishing the National Motion Picture Magazine, were they able to do that as they had done before?  A. Yes, they could have done it.

Q. Did they do it, as before?  A. They would have had more trouble to have gotten certain releases, but they could have found out what releases we were showing, and which they did find out.

Q. Did you have the same difficulty after you ceased
3 publishing the National Motion Picture Magazine, with respect to the duplication of your programs as you had encountered before?  A. Only for a while.

Q. When was it you resumed the practice of announcing your program in advance?  A. In 1913.

Q. At that time from what source did you obtain your motion picture service?  A. The General Film Company.

Q. How many theatres, at the present time, are you managing, in the immediate vicinity of one another on Pennsylvania Avenue, in Washington?  A. Just moving pictures?

Q. Yes?  A. Two.

4 Q. How long has it been since you operated three motion picture theatres in the immediate neighborhood of one another?  A. Last July.

Q. During the time you have been operating motion picture theatres on Pennsylvania Avenue, in the immedite neighborhood of one another, and only a few feet apart, have you been able to secure a satisfactory program for each of them?  A. Yes, within the last year.

Q. How have you been able to do that, Mr. Brylawski?  A. Through the General Film Company.

Q. In what respect has the service of the General Film

Company permitted you to give satisfactory programs to the patrons of each of these theatres? A. I secure their entire product, forty-two reels a week, which I divide between the two theatres, so that neither one would conflict with the other.

Q. Do you operate these two theatres so that each one has a separate and distinct and different program, which does not conflict with the program of either theatre? A. We operate in this way: We divide the product of the General Film Company so that certain reels are shown at each theatre each week.

Q. How far apart are these theatres, in feet? A. One hundred and fifty feet.

Q. What is the seating capacity of each? A. One hundred and sixty in one, and the other has two hundred and ten seats.

Q. And do each of them do a profitable business? A. I am sorry to say, no.

Q. Does either of them do a profitable business? A. They did, both of them did a profitable business at one time.

Q. In operating these two theatres, do you find that the immediate proximity of one to the other is an injury to the business? A. No, on the contrary, a theatre alone, isolated, does not do near as much business as when there are two or three of them together, provided, of course, that the programs offered in each of the theatres is different.

Q. Has that been your experience? A. Absolutely.

Q. If your two motion picture theatres were showing the same program, or conflicting programs, would it be possible to do the business you are now doing? A. No, sir. A party going to see one and seeing the same pictures, or, even one of the same three pictures, will simply go somewhere else, tures.

Q. Do you keep in touch with the patrons of your theatres, and by that I mean, do you hear what they have to say regarding your shows, and regarding the sort of programs you show? A. I couldn't make a success of it if I didn't know what our customers were doing.

Q. Do you find that customers sometimes leave one theatre and come into the other, still in pursuit of amusement? A. Yes, sir, often. They come down for the purpose

1   of spending a certain time, whether it is an hour and a
half, or two hours, and if the show is short they will go
to one place and then immediately leave that and go to
one as close as they can, providing they can see something
different. At times, being displeased with one show, they
go into the closest one, or next one, and see if they can
do any better, and if they are pleased with one, they surely
go into the next one, because they have enjoyed it.

Q. So that you have found that two theatres in the immediate neighborhood of each other with different programs
stimulate each other's business? A. Yes, sir, unques-
2   tionably.

Q. Then two theatres will have double patronage from the
same number of visitors? A. Frequently, often. I might
say time and again patrons have come out and said: "Now,
we will go around to the Palace. What have you got around
there?" They ask me: "Do you have a good show there?"
and I would say, "Yes, you will like it," or, "You will like it,
and if you don't, you will get your money back."

Mr. GROSVENOR: But you never have to give it
3   back?

The Witness: Yes, sir, I have had to give it back, sir.

By Mr. KINGSLEY:

Q. No large or considerable sums, Mr. Brylawski? A.
No. You asked me the question, I will tell you why. Sometimes they have come in there, and said, "I saw that picture
last night?" "Where at?" "I saw it around at the Pickwick last night." "Here is your money back." Such a thing
might occur by mistake, that is, the picture might have been
4   shown the previous night at the Pickwick.

Mr. GROSVENOR: That is in one of your theatres?

The Witness: Yes, sir.

By Mr. KINGSLEY:

Q. And only in cases of conflict you give them their money
back? A. Yes, sir.

Q. In cases where they have seen the picture? A. Yes, sir. Well, we ask them, or our door men have positive instructions if patrons come out and say they are not satisfied, simply to give them their ticket back, and mark it good for another day.

Q. Has it been your experience as an exhibitor of motion pictures that in cases of conflict they did speak about it? A. We have heard it. While we propose to use only first runs, not first runs either, but first runs in Washington, it has been by accident that a film which should have come to our place has been shown North East three miles away, and they have come to us and said: "I saw that picture yesterday," or "last night." They recall it.

Q. Have you had any instances in your recent experience of conflicts with licensed pictures, or with pictures furnished by the Greater New York Film Rental Company? A. Yes, sir, I am sorry to have to say it.

Q. And what was that experience? A. The Selig Company issued a serial story which was published in the Washington Star, of the "Adventures of Kathleen," and this picture, the Pickwick booked for the first two days, paying besides its regular service an additional price of six dollars and twenty-five cents a reel, or twelve dollars and fifty cents for the two pictures. The Pickwick was the first theatre to take it up, and showed the pictures on the first Monday of every issue with the understanding that it was to get it every two weeks—it come out every other Monday—for that purpose. The first Monday, the people they didn't know, didn't know what it was, and we lost money, but the subsequent weeks the serial stories were published in the Star, and the second Monday we did quite a business. When the third series came out we did a good business, and it was the first week for some time that we had made a little money. We continued that the fourth, and fifth weeks, and the sixth week our competitors, who were using the independent service proceeded and did show the same pictures exactly; and then we also showed the pictures South East on Saturday of the release date, and three weeks ago a little theatre in that neighborhood anticipated the Saturday's business by showing the "Kathleen" pictures on Thursday, and I called the manager of the theatre to account for it, and I said that we had never

1   done anything of that kind to them, and I wanted to know
why he tried to cut our throats, and I said, "You have got
only a small theatre, Mr. Anderson, of two hundred seats.
We have one of five hundred. You show four pictures and so
do we. We could show eight pictures, and it would hurt you,
but we never have done it. Now, why did you want to go to
work and anticipate a little patronage, and cut ours down,"
and he said he only took fourteen dollars from us, and I
said, "It don't matter how much you took, you took it away
from us, and it didn't do you any good." This picture was
not furnished to him by the General Film Company but by

2   the Greater New York Film Company.

Q. You mean the Greater New York Film Rental Company? A. Yes, sir. And they have done the same thing in
other sections of Washington, trying to anticipate where the
pictures were advertised. The Star Company makes a feature of it, a special advertising of it, that "Kathleen Pictures
will be shown here today" or, wherever they will be shown,
and they could well know where the picture was at, and so
they anticipated in other sections of the city with "Kathleen" to the detriment of ourselves, and of no good to them-

3   selves.

Q. Did you say that the "Kathleen" pictures were shown
at unlicensed houses? A. Yes, sir, shown at the Orpheum,
shown at the Garden, shown at the Eastern, shown at the
Plaza, and shown at the Garden, all unlicensed houses, and
that is the only licensed pictures they did show, just these
pictures, because they were advertised in advance by the Star
Company.

Cross examination by Mr. GROSVENOR:

4   Q. What was the release date of this Kathleen picture?
A. The first one, December 29th.

Q. I mean what is the day they were ready? A. Monday.

Q. Each Monday of every week? A. Every other Monday.

Q. What day did you contract to show them in Washington? A. Monday and Tuesday of release date.

Q. You showed them the day they were released? A. Yes,
sir.

Q. How could they have been shown before you showed

them by anybody else? A. They were shown the same day. 1

Q. Your objection is to somebody paying for and showing the same thing you are paying for on the same day? A. Yes, sir, especially, when I am doing the advertising, or after I have advertised the article, or the film—I can't object, but I dislike it. I dislike for someone to take advantage of my advertisement.

Q. The Star does a great deal of that advertising, does it not? A. Yes, sir. And the Star cut out a part of their advertisement—they saw the disadvantage of it.

Q. Were you paying for the advertisement in the Star? A. Yes, sir. 2

Q. For the story? A. Not for the story, but for the advertisement.

Q. For the advertisement of your theatre? A. Yes, sir, of where the picture would be shown.

Q. But the story, which serves as an advertisement to some extent, is published in the Star? A. Yes, sir.

Q. Without your having to pay for it? A. Yes, sir, without us having to pay for it, but at the same time, in return for that we put on our screens, our posters that the story itself can be read in the Star. We advertise them 3 as much as they do us. For instance, the next release, or the last release, was March 9th, that we showed the pictures. Now, we have on our screen on the outside that the story complete can be read in the Sunday Star, and they publish the story on the following Sunday.

Q. The Star has the same arrangement with other theatres besides yours, in Washington? A. With all those with the licensed people, yes.

Q. Your complaint, then, is that the others are getting some benefit of the advertisement of the Star? A. No, not those that are licensed. I have no objection be- 4 cause we can't get it for the entire time. We show it for the first and second days, and the third show is lost and the fourth show is lost, and we show it again on the fifth and on the twelfth again.

Q. All of your theatres are licensed theatres? A. Yes, sir.

Q. Has anybody else in Washington as many theatres as you have? A. Not that I know of.

1    Q. Have you always owned licensed theatres, during
these three years? A. No, sir, I have tried others.

Q. But you have found the licensed service is more satisfactory? A. Well, the licensed service, we can depend
on that better than the others.

Q. And, therefore, you think it necessary to have the
licensed service to enable you to run your theatres successfully? A. If we didn't have the licensed service, probably we could do it, but our customers are accustomed to
it, and we don't give them a different diet if they like the
2   diet, so we keep on furnishing it to them.

Re-examination by Mr. KINGSLEY:

Q. You find that the system of distribution of the General Film Company is better than the system of distribution
of the independents, do you not? A. That I could not tell
you. I don't know their distribution. The independents at
the present time, that is, the Mutual and the Universal,
I think, have got identically the same system that the licensed
have now.

Q. That is your information? A. Yes, sir. To the best
3   of my knowledge and belief. I am satisfied that they are
following the same principle, that they are eliminating
conflicting releases.

Whereupon, at 4:30 o'clock P. M., March 20th, 1914, the
hearings were adjourned until 10 o'clock A. M., March 24th,
1914, to be resumed at Room 159, Manhattan Hotel, New
York City.

4

IN THE

# DISTRICT COURT OF THE UNITED STATES

## FOR THE EASTERN DISTRICT OF PENNSYLVANIA.

|  |  |
|---|---|
| UNITED STATES OF AMERICA, Petitioner, *v.* MOTION PICTURE PATENTS CO. and others, Defendants. | No. 889. Sept. Sess., 1912. |

2

NEW YORK CITY, March 24th, 1913.

The hearing was resumed at the Hotel Manhattan, Room 159, pursuant to adjournment.

> Present on behalf of the Petitioner, Hon. EDWIN P. GROSVENOR, Special Assistant to the Attorney General.
>
> JOSEPH R. DARLING, Esq., Special Agent.  3
>
> CHARLES F. KINGSLEY, Esq., GEORGE R. WILLIS, Esq., FRED R. WILLIAMS, Esq. and MELVILLE CHURCH, Esq., appearing for Motion Picture Patents Company, Biograph Company, Jeremiah J. Kennedy, Harry N. Marvin, Armat Moving Picture Company, Melies Manufacturing Company and Gaston Melies.
>
> J. H. CALDWELL, Esq., and H. K. STOCKTON, Esq., appearing for William Pelzer, General Film Company, Thomas A. Edison, Inc., Kalem Company, Inc., Pathe Freres, Frank L. Dyer,  4 Samuel Long and J. A. Berst.
>
> HENRY MELVILLE, Esq., attorney for George Kleine, Essanay Film Manufacturing Company, Selig Polyscope, George K. Spoor and W. N. Selig.
>
> JAMES J. ALLEN, Esq., appearing for Vitagraph Company of America, and Albert E. Smith.

1    ARTHUR E. TALMADGE, a witness produced on behalf of the defendants, being first duly sworn, deposed:

Direct examination by Mr. KINGSLEY:

Q. Where do you live? A. 318 Hancock Street, Brooklyn.

Q. In what business are you engaged? A. Motion picture exhibitor.

Q. How long have you been a motion picture exhibitor? A. About three years.

Q. Are you the owner of any theatres in Brooklyn? A. I
2 am the owner of three at present.

Q. Are any of these theatres situated close together? A. Two of them are.

Q. How close are the two theatres? A. Within two blocks.

Q. Will you give us the names of these two theatres which are situated within two blocks of each other? A. The Photoplay Theatre at 98 Fifth Avenue, and Sterling Theatre at 127 Fifth Avenue.

Q. What is the seating capacity of the Photoplay Theatre? A. Two hundred and eighty seats.
3    Q. What is the seating capacity of the Sterling Theatre? A. Two hundred and ninety-eight.

Q. What service do you use in the Sterling Theatre? A. Association.

Q. By that you mean the licensed service? A. General Film.

Q. What service do you use at the Photoplay Theatre? A. Universal.

Q. Do you use the two kinds of service for the purpose of keeping the programs apart? A. I do.
4    Q. Do you find it necessary to secure your programs for these two theatres from different exchanges in order to have different programs? A. Absolutely necessary.

Q. How long have you been running the Photoplay Theatre and the Sterling Theatre in that neighborhood? A. I formerly owned the Sterling Theatre alone.

Q. Yes? A. That is wrong. I owned the Sterling Theatre with another partner. I bought out my other partner, and the proprietor of the Photoplay Theatre was formerly my opposition. We used to fight each other, using the same

service, and bills were running up to eighty and ninety dol- 1
lars a week some weeks to see who would get there first.

Q. At the time you were in competition with him, did
you have conflicting programs? A. No. We both ran Association.

Q. At that time were you able to keep apart? A. No.
We both ran General Film stuff. Both were fighting each
other.

Q. Then you were both showing the same program frequently? A. Yes, and it was hurting both of our businesses.
So I bought out my partner, and I took an interest in the
Photoplay, and the proprietor of the Photoplay came over 2
and took an interest in the Sterling, and we immediately
switched our program. Turned one house into a Mutual and
the other into an Association.

Q. After switching your programs, have you been able
to run both of those theatres at a profit? A. More profitably
than we did before.

Q. Is it possible to maintain two theatres profitably in
the same immediate neighborhood by supplying them with
different programs? A. It is possible.

Q. Has that been your experience? A. It has. 3

Q. Is it possible to maintain two theatres profitably in the
same immediate neighborhood by supplying them both with
the same program? A. That is not possible.

Q. What is the effect upon the business of two theatres
running in the same immediate neighborhood and depending
upon the same population for patronage if they show the
same programs? A. Well, you lose business. Because the
people will go to either one house or the other, but they won't
go to both.

Q. What is the effect upon the business of two theatres
running in the same immediate neighborhood, and depending 4
upon the same population for patronage, if they show different programs and avoid all conflicts? A. Well, where you
get five cents out of—five cents apiece out of a family where
they run the same, where you run different programs, you
have a good chance of getting ten cents, because in my place,
the Photoplay advertises what the Sterling is running, and
the Sterling advertises what the Photoplay is running, and a
great many people, after getting through the show at the
Sterling, they go over to the Photoplay, and those at the

1 Photoplay, when they get through there, go over to the Sterling, and it makes it very profitable.

Q. In the case which you have described, where two theatres give different shows, is there any considerable percentage of patrons who pay to see both shows? A. Yes, there is a large percentage.

Q. In a case such as you have described, where two theatres give the same show, is there any considerable percentage of patrons who pay to go to both houses? A. The percentage is very little, if any.

2 Q. Where two or more theatres side by side or in the immediate neighborhood, give the same shows, do they help or hurt one another's business? A. They hurt each other.

Q. Where two or more theatres side by side or in the immediate neighborhood, give different shows, absolutely free from all conflict, do they help or hurt one another's business? A. They help each other.

Q. Have you any idea as to the percentage of patrons who go from one house to the other when they are showing different programs? A. Well, I would say there is an average of at least twenty per cent. every day, and Saturday and

3 Sunday and holidays, when the people are out, why, I daresay it runs as high as fifty and sixty per cent. Probably higher.

Cross examination by Mr. GROSVENOR:

Q. How large are these theatres which you own in Brooklyn? A. How large are they?

Q. Yes. That is, how many people do they accommodate? A. Well, the Photoplay, about 280 seats, and the Sterling Theatre, about 295.

4 ————————

HARRY N. MARVIN, recalled for further direct examination, deposed:

Direct examination by Mr. KINGSLEY:

Q. Have the licensed manufacturers shown any favoritism in respect to leasing prices to rental exchanges? A. They have not.

Q. Are these the same throughout the United States? A. They are.

Q. Have any attempts been made, either by the Motion Picture Patents Company or the licensed producers, or both, to regulate the subleasing prices of the rental exchanges to exhibitors? A. None whatever.

Q. Did the Motion Picture Patents Company refuse to license any established manufacturer or any importer of desirable motion pictures at the time of its organization? A. It did not.

Q. It is charged in the petition in this action that defendants, through the Patents Company, were enabled to, and did determine whether new motion picture theatres should or should not be opened, and whether old ones should be closed, although defendants had no proprietary interest in such theatres. Is it a fact that defendants exercised any such power? A. No. The defendants never interfered nor attempted to interfere in any manner with the opening or closing of any theatre.

Q. Did the defendants set out to monopolize the business of all of the licensed rental exchanges in the United States? A. They did not.

Q. At what time was the Biograph Company doing business under a bond that compelled it to deposit the entire proceeds of its projecting machine business with a Trustee from week to week? A. During the period immediately following the decision of Judge Wheeler, sustaining the validity of the Edison patent, and holding that the Biograph Company's apparatus infringed the Edison patent, and continuing until the decision of Judge Wheeler was reversed by the Court of Appeals, the Biograph Company operated under a bond on condition that the entire profits resulting from this projecting machine business, which consisted in giving motion picture exhibitions in theatres and similar places, should be deposited with a Trustee.

Mr. GROSVENOR: That was back in 1901 and 1902, wasn't it?

The Witness: Well, I cannot remember the exact date, but it was during the period between the decision of Judge Wheeler and the decision of the Court of Appeals.

1    Mr. GROSVENOR: That was six or seven years before the Patents Company was organized, wasn't it?

The Witness: That was several years before.

Mr. GROSVENOR: I move to strike out the answer on the ground that it relates to a time too remote to have any bearing upon the issues in this case, the evidence in this case having shown that Judge Wheeler's opinion was given in 1901, and the reversal in 1902.

2    By Mr. KINGSLEY:

Q. Have you given all the reasons that actuated the Patents Company in imposing minimum price restrictions? A. Well, I don't recollect whether I stated as among those reasons the fact that the Edison Company and the Biograph Company, the owners of the Motion Picture Patents Company, were themselves producers of motion pictures, and they had considerable investment in the business at the time of the organization of the Motion Picture Patents Company, and they also owned patents covering various apparatus used in the art, and they felt that the permanence and growth of the business was of great importance to them, and they felt that in licensing others to join in the production and distribution business with them, that it was proper for their own protection, that some price regulation should be established, in order that the business which they conceived to be their business, since they believed that they owned the dominating patents and had created the business, should not be at the mercy of any shortsighted licensees who might, for the sake of a quick profit, demoralize the art in such a way as to jeopardize its future.

4    Mr. GROSVENOR: Whom do you mean by "they"?

The Witness: The Edison Company and the Biograph Company.

By Mr. KINGSLEY:

Q. Did anyone except you, know in advance of February 13th, 1913, that a cancellation notice was to be sent to the Greater New York Film Rental Company by the Motion

Picture Patents Company? A. Mr. Scull, I believe, was
acquainted with my intention of sending such a notice, and
our attorneys, Messrs. Leventritt, Cook & Nathan, under
whose direction the form of the notice was prepared. Those,
I believe, were the only ones who had any knowledge of the
notice prior to its being sent out.

Q. At page 250 of the printed record, in Petitioner's Exhibit 77, which purports to be an extract from testimony
given by you July 9th, 1910, in a suit brought by the Motion Picture Patents Company against the Chicago Film Exchange, occurs the following question and answer:

> "Q15. What proportion of the annual product of
> motion picture films manufactured and sold in this
> country is put out by the licensees of the Edison pat-
> ent in suit? A. About 90 per cent. of the films manu-
> factured and sold in this country are put out by licen-
> sees under the Edison patent above referred to. By
> licensees, I refer to the ten licensees above named."

Have you any explanation or amplification to make of
that answer? A. Well, that answer was limited, of course,
to motion pictures manufactured and sold or leased in this
country. It did not refer to motion pictures imported into
this country, and it did refer to the motion pictures sold
in this country for export.

By Mr. KINGSLEY:

Q. In Defendants' Exhibit 52, page 1357, Vol. III, which
is a letter written by C. C. Allen, of Newberg, Oregon, to the
Motion Picture Patents Company, he complains of the busi-
ness tactics and principles and practices of one H. C. Stevens,
Do you know what exchange was owned or managed by H.
C. Stevens?

> Mr. GROSVENOR: Is that a letter that you intro-
> duced?
> Mr. KINGSLEY: Yes.
> Mr. GROSVENOR: I make the same objection to that
> question which I made to the exhibit when it was
> introduced by counsel for the defendants.

1    The Witness: The Amalgamated Exchange, having an office at Portland, Oregon.

By Mr. KINGSLEY:

Q. In Defendants' Exhibit 60, page 1370, Vol. III, which is a letter written by A. J. Cavanaugh of Minneapolis, Minnesota, to the Motion Picture Patents Company, he refers to Mr. Van Duzee owning most of the motion picture houses in that city, and as favoring them in service. Do you know what exchange Van Duzee owned or managed? A. The
2    Twin City Calcium Company.

Q. Located where? A. At Minneapolis.

Q. Defendants' Exhibit 61, page 1371, Vol. III, which is a letter written by Otto N. Raths, of St. Paul, to the Motion Picture Patents Company, he alleges that "the agent of your exchange in Minneapolis has a personal interest in various theatres in this city." Do you know to whom he referred? A. He referred to Van Duzee, manager of that exchange, and owner of it.

Q. Will you name the exchange of which he was manager? A. Of the Twin City Calcium Company, that I men-
3    tioned in the previous answer.

Q. In Defendants' Exhibit 64, page 1376, Vol. III, which is a letter from Harry R. Rand to the Motion Picture Patents Company, he refers to one Florence, who had threatened to put him out of business. Do you know what exchange Florence owned or managed? A. Florence originally managed the Trent-Wilson Exchange in Salt Lake City, which exchange subsequently was known as the Florence Film Exchange, or Florence Exchange, largely owned and managed by Florence.

Q. Will you tell us where it was located? A. It was lo-
4    cated in Salt Lake City.

Q. And where was Harry R. Rand located? A. His principal location was Salt Lake City.

Q. Did the Motion Picture Patents Company at the time of the surrender of the license of the Imperial Film Exchange, receive any advice from Dwight Macdonald, relative to the matter? A. None whatever.

Q. At the time of the surrender of the license of the Imperial Film Exchange, did the Motion Picture Patents Company give Dwight Macdonald any instructions relative to

the matter, or have any relations with him relative thereto? 1
A. None whatever.

Q. When the film patent was reissued in 1904, was there any considerable quantity of foreign motion pictures in this country? A. There was not.

Q. Was it the purpose of the Motion Picture Patents Company, or of those who organized the Motion Picture Patents Company, to acquire all the patents relating to the motion picture art? A. No. They had no intention of acquiring all such patents, and they only did acquire a very small percentage of such patents.

Q. Did the Motion Picture Patents Company notify distributors and middle men, generally, of the proposed licensing arrangement in January, 1909? A. It did.

Q. What was the capitalization of the Biograph Company in 1908? A. Its capitalization then was and always has been two million dollars.

Q. At the time the witness Palmer sold the stock and equipment of the Motion Picture Service Company of Rochester to the General Film Company, were you present at the negotiations between him and Mr. Kennedy? A. I was not. I was never present during any negotiations concerning the purchase of any property by the General Film Company. I did see Mr. Palmer on some occasions long prior to the time at which these negotiations were had, but entirely with reference to matters pertaining to the conduct of his exchange as a licensee, and not in any respect with reference to the sale of any property.

Q. So if Mr. Palmer stated on his direct examination that you were present at the time he had certain negotiations with Mr. Kennedy, relative to the sale of the stock and equipment of his exchange, he is mistaken? A. He is.

Q. Do you know what was the principal feature of 4 the business carried on by Eberhard Schneider in 1907 and 1908? A. At that time the principal business of Eberhard Schneider was an optical business, and I believe during that period, he manufactured a few motion picture projecting machines.

Q. Was he at that time manufacturing motion pictures to any considerable extent? A. He was not.

Q. Is there at present any decree, order or injunction in force which prevents the licensed producers from ceas-

ing to serve the Greater New York Film Rental Company?
A. There is no such decree of any Court. I understand,
however, that pressure was brought to bear on the licensed
producers by representatives of the Department of Justice
that has induced them to continue to supply motion pictures to the Greater New York Film Rental Company.

Direct examination (continued) by Mr. CHURCH:

Q. Mr. Marvin, state whether you were and are familiar
with the practical motion picture art as it was practiced
say in January, 1908, prior to the time of the formation
of the Motion Picture Patents Company, and if yea, state
what your opportunities were for becoming familiar with it.
A. I was familiar with the art at that time. I was then
actively connected with the Biograph Company, one of the
prominent producers and distributors of motion pictures,
which company made use of cameras, films and projecting
machines in the conduct of its business. I was entirely
familiar with that apparatus, and I was also familiar
with similar apparatus employed by the competitors of that
company.

Q. What were the essential characteristics of the motion picture films, both positive and negative, in use and
on the market at the time inquired about? A. All of
those films consisted of an unbroken, transparent or translucent tape-like photographic film, having perforated edges,
and having uniform sharply defined equi-distant photographs of successive phases of moving objects arranged in
a continuous straight line sequence, observed from a single
point of view at rapidly recurring intervals of time, and
sufficient in number to cover an extended period.

Q. How, if at all, did the negative picture film and the
positive picture film of that date differ? A. The positive
motion picture film was a facsimile of the negative motion
picture film and differed from it only by having the lights
and shades of the photographs reversed.

Q. What were the essential characteristics of the motion picture cameras in use at the time mentioned, for producing by photography, negative motion picture films such
as described in your next to the last answer? A. All of
those motion picture cameras embodied a single stationary
lens, a single sensitized flexible tape-like photographic film

having perforated edges supported on opposite sides of the
lens, and movable longitudinally with reference thereto,
and having an intermediate section crossing the lens, a
main driving shaft adapted to be continuously rotated,
and a feeding mechanism positively engaging the intermediate section of the film, and adapted to move it across
the lens with an intermittent movement, and at a high
rate of speed, a shutter actuated by the main driving shaft,
and adapted to expose successive portions of the film during
the intervals of rest, and a take-up reel actuated with varying speed by the main driving shaft, and adapted to take up
the film after exposure. In addition to these characteristics, the cameras possessed continuously rotating sprocket
feed wheels, located between the intermittent feeding
device and the supports, and positively engaging the film,
one such feed wheel being located between the supply
reel and the intermittent feeding device, and its action
being to continuously and steadily and uniformly draw
film from the supply reel and deliver slack film to the
intermittent feeding device, the other continuously rotating sprocket feed wheel being located between the
intermittent feeding device and the take-up reel, and
its action being to continuously take up the slack film
supplied by the intermittent feeding device, and deliver it
to the take-up reel.

Q. Did the so-called Biograph camera, the invention of
Herman Casler, have the above characteristics of the
cameras just described by you, and if not, why not? A.
The Biograph camera, the invention of Casler, did not
possess all of the above characteristics, but differed from
the type of camera described, in several particulars. It
did not use a perforated photographic film, but used a
smooth, unperforated film. This film was not fed across the
lens uniformly by feeding devices that positively engaged
the film, but it was fed by friction, with a varying feed,
so that the successive portions of film exposed to the lens
were not uniformly spaced; the negative film resulting from
the operation of this camera differed from the negative film
resulting from the operation of the type of camera formerly
described, in that it did not possess a series of perforations
adapted to engage with feeding devices, and the series of
photographs on the film were not equi-distant, but were un-
evenly spaced, and the negative produced by this camera

1  could not be used for the purpose of printing fac-simile
positive copies for use on projecting machines.

Q. Will you please now describe the essential characteristics of the projecting machines that were in commercial use or on the market at the date before mentioned,
for projecting pictures of motion picture strips such as
you have described. A. All such projecting machines embodied the following common characteristics. They were
all adapted to use a single flexible transparent or translucent tape-like film such as I have already described.

2  They embodied upper and lower supports for the bulk of
the film. They embodied two feeding mechanisms, one
consisting of a pair of continuously rotating sprocket feed
wheels positively engaging the film, and having an intermediate section of slack film between them. The other
feeding device, consisting of a feeding device that positively
engaged the slack portion of the film and fed it with an
intermittent motion at a high rate of speed across a fixed
illuminated exposure window in such a manner that the
intervals of pause and illumination exceeded the intervals
of movement. These machines possessed a single stationary

3  lens, and a shutter adapted to intercept the light during the
period of movement of the film, and one or more times
during the period of rest. These machines also possessed a movable frame carrying the intermittent
feeding device and the slack portion of the film,
the frame, the feeding device and the film being capable of
adjustment with reference to the fixed exposure aperture.

Q. Was there upon those projecting machines, any framing device? A. Well, in describing a movable frame having
thereon the intermittent movement and the slack portion
of the film, which framing device was adjustable with ref-

4  erence to the fixed exposure aperture, I meant to describe
a framing device. Perhaps my language would have been
more descriptive if I had said that this frame possessed
means of varying the relative positions of the feeding device
and the slack portion of the film with reference to the
fixed exposure aperture, that arrangement constituting a
framing device, so-called.

Q. State whether or not there have been any projecting machines in commercial use in this country from the
beginning of 1908 down to the present time, that did not

embody all of the characteristics described by you in your 1
description of projecting machines. A. There have not.

Q. Can you, and will you, produce a camera typical of
the cameras on the market in January, 1908? A. I can,
and I here produce such a camera, which is of the type
known as the Warwick camera.

> Mr. CHURCH: The camera referred to by the wit-
> ness is offered in evidence, and the Examiner is re-
> quested to mark the same "Defendants' Exhibit 174."
> The exhibit is received in evidence, and is so
> marked. 2

By Mr. CHURCH:

Q. Can you, and will you, produce a projecting machine typical of the projecting machines on the market
in January, 1908, as you have testified? A. I can and
do produce such a projecting machine, which is known as
a Power Projecting Machine.

> Mr. GROSVENOR: What number of Power?
>
> 3
>
> The Witness: Number 5.

> Mr. CHURCH: I offer in evidence the projecting
> machine produced by the witness, and request that
> the same be marked "Defendants' Exhibit 175."
> The exhibit is received in evidence, and is so
> marked.

By Mr. CHURCH:

Q. Can you and will you produce a negative motion pic- 4
ture film typical of the negative motion picture films on the
market in January, 1908, as to which you have testified? A.
I can and do herewith produce such a negative.

> Mr. CHURCH: Counsel for the defendant offers in
> evidence the negative film produced by the witness,
> and requests that the same be marked in evidence as
> "Defendants' Exhibit 176."
> The exhibit is received in evidence, and is so
> marked.

1 By Mr. CHURCH:

Q. Can you and will you produce also a positive motion picture film typical of the positive motion picture films on the market in January, 1908, as to which you have testified? A. I can and do herewith produce such a positive motion picture film.

> Mr. GROSVENOR: Is this positive motion picture film which you now produce a positive copy of the negative which you also produced and which was marked "Defendants' Exhibit 176?"

2

The Witness: It is.

> Mr. CHURCH: Counsel for the defendant offers in evidence the positive motion picture film produced by the witness, and requests that the same be marked "Defendants' Exhibit 177."
> The exhibit is received in evidence, and is so marked.

3 By Mr. CHURCH:

Q. I have asked you to prepare an illustrative apparatus to serve as an aid to the Court in understanding the various features of cameras and of projecting machines known to you to be available and on the market in January, 1908, as testified to by you. If you have done so, will you please produce it and explain it as briefly as possible? A. I have prepared such an illustrative mechanism, and I am prepared to explain it. As the explanation, however, is somewhat tedious, I have written out a description in as brief language

4 as I could employ, which will perhaps save time if I am permitted to present or to read it. If it is not satisfactory, I will proceed to make the description without reference.

> Mr. CHURCH: Is there any objection to that, Mr. Grosvenor?
> Mr. GROSVENOR: I suggest that the witness first identify the illustrative mechanism, as he calls it, and then I will read the statement and determine.

A. I here produce the illustrative mechanism, and its 1
present condition illustrates some of the features embodied
in the cameras of the period concerning which I have testified, and it is arranged so as to be capable of modification
so as to show the different types of mechanism that I have
referred to, reference being made at the same time to photographs which I have had made, showing the mechanism as
arranged in several ways, illustrating features concerning
which I have testified.

Mr. CHURCH: Counsel for the defendant offers the
illustrative apparatus produced by the witness, in evi- 2
dence, and requests that the same be marked "Defendants' Exhibit 178."

The exhibit is received in evidence, and is so
marked.

By Mr. CHURCH:

Q. If you have prepared a description of this illustrative apparatus in its various adjustments, I wish you would
read it to the Examiner as a short mode of putting upon the
record a description of the apparatus. A. I have prepared 3
a brief description of this mechanism in its different aspects,
which I will read as I arrange the mechanism, to illustrate
the various features concerning which I have testified.

This mechanism as now arranged, and which arrangement is shown by Photograph No. 1, which I here produce,
illustrates the common features of cameras in use at the beginning of 1908, as described in the first part of my answer
to the question concerning such cameras.

In this mechanism and photograph will be noted, the
single stationary lens, marked "A" on the photograph; the
single flexible sensitized tape-like film, marked "B" on the 4
photograph; the supports on opposite sides of the lens,
marked "C" and "C1" on the photograph; the intermediate
section crossing the lens, marked "D" on the photograph; the
main driving shaft, marked "E" on the photograph; the intermittent feeding mechanism connected with the driving shaft,
which I here detach from the rest of the mechanism and exhibit, but which is obscured on the photograph by the fly-
wheel "F." (The witness here detaches the portion of the
mechanism referred to.)

1      It will be noted that this feeding mechanism engages the intermediate portion of the film, and is adapted to move the film across the lens at a high rate of speed and with an intermittent motion (the witness re-attaches the feeding device to the illustrative mechanism); the shutter adapted to expose successive portions of the film during the intervals of rest and marked "G" on the photograph; the take-up reel connected with the main shaft and marked "C1" on the photograph.

I have now arranged the illustrative mechanism so as to show the additional features described in the latter part of my former answer referred to, and the mechanism in this condition is now shown by the Photograph No. 2.

2

Referring to the mechanism in its present condition (Photograph No. 2), the continuously running sprocket feeding rollers will be noted, and are marked "M" and "M1" on the photograph, and the loop of slack film supplied to the intermittent feeding mechanism by the upper continuously operating feeding roller will be noted and is marked "I" on the photograph.

The slack film delivered by the intermittent feeding mechanism to the lower continually running sprocket wheel will also be noted, and is marked "J" on the photograph.

3

The illustrative mechanism also illustrates the mechanism of the projecting machines in commercial use in the beginning of 1908.

In the machine as now arranged and as it is shown by Photograph No. 3, will be noted the upper and lower supports for the bulk of the film, marked "K" and "K1" on the photograph; the transparent or translucent tape-like photographic film, marked "L" on the photograph, and one of the feeding mechanisms consisting of a pair of upper and lower continuously running sprocket wheels, marked "M" and "M1" on the photograph, engaging the film and having an intermediate section of slack film, marked "N" on the photograph, between them and the lens which is marked "A."

4

The stationary exposure window is obscured in the photograph.

I now supply the other feeding mechanism adapted to engage the intermediate portion of slack film and feed it across the illuminated exposure window at a high rate of speed, and with an intermittent motion, and the mechanism as now arranged with both feeding mechanisms is shown in Photograph No. 4, the intermittent feeding mechanism being obscured by the fly-wheel "F." The mechanism as now arranged and as shown in Photograph No. 4 shows all of the common characteristics of projecting machines about which I have already testified, marked on the photograph in the same manner as on Photograph No. 3, with the exception of the shutter, marked "O" on the photograph, and it will be noted that in the mechanism as now arranged, and as shown in Photograph No. 4, the shutter is of the same type as that formerly shown and used in cameras.

I now arrange the machine by substituting a shutter of a type in common use prior to 1908, as shown by Photograph No. 5, on which the shutter is marked "O1."

I now arrange the machine by substituting a different shutter so as to show one form of the type of shutter commonly used in the commercial projecting machines in the beginning of 1908, as shown by Photograph No. 6, in which the shutter is marked "O2."

I now again alter the machine by substituting another form of this type of shutter which is shown in Photograph No. 7, on which the shutter is marked "O3" and the mechanism as now finally arranged and shown in Photograph No. 7, embodies and illustrates all of the common features of construction described in my former answer as used in projecting machines in commercial use in the beginning of 1908.

It will be noted that the illustrative mechanism has a frame carrying the slack portion of the picture film and also carrying the feeding mechanism for feeding such slack portion of the film, and means for adjusting the position of the frame, the film, and the actuating mechanism, with respect to the fixed exposure window. This constitutes the so-called framing device.

Mr. CHURCH: Counsel for the defendants offers in evidence the several photographs referred to by the witness in his last answer, and requests that the same

1        be marked "Defendants' Exhibit 179, Photographs 1 to
         7 inclusive."
             The exhibit is received in evidence, and is so
         marked.

By Mr. CHURCH:

    Q. Will you please examine the drawing or chart I now
show you, and state what it represents and the purpose of
its production? A. That chart was prepared under my
direction to illustrate certain features of mechanism common
2 to cameras in use in the beginning of 1908. It illustrates, in
a diagrammatic manner, mechanism shown in Photograph
No. 1 of Exhibit 179 just introduced.
    Q. Will you refer briefly to the parts of the mechanism
shown on this chart? A. That chart indicates the stationary
lens, marked "Lens" on the chart, the sensitized photographic film marked "Edison film" on the chart, the upper
and lower supports for the film, the upper support being
marked "supply reel" and the lower support being marked
"take-up reel," the intermediate section of film being
marked "Edison film," main driving shaft, which is not
3 marked on the chart, but which is clearly discernible,
the intermittent feeding device engaging the intermediate
portion of film which is marked "Intermittent Feed" on
the chart, the shutter adapted to expose the portion of
the film during the period of rest marked "Edison shutter"
and the take-up reel that takes up the film after exposure,
being marked "Take-up reel" on the chart. The whole mechanism, it will be noted, is enclosed in a light-tight box.

         Mr. CHURCH: Counsel for the defendant offers in
4        evidence the chart referred to by the witness, and asks
         that the same be marked "Defendants' Exhibit 180."
             The chart offered is received in evidence and
         is so marked.

By Mr. CHURCH:

    Q. Please now examine the second chart that I now show
you, and state if you know what it represents and for what
purpose it was prepared. A. This chart was prepared for
the purpose of illustrating the common mechanical features
of cameras in use in the beginning of 1908.

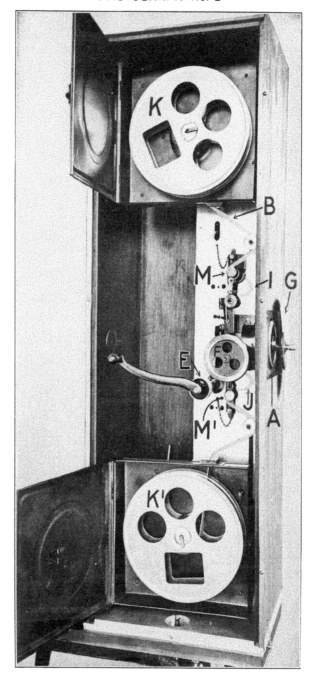

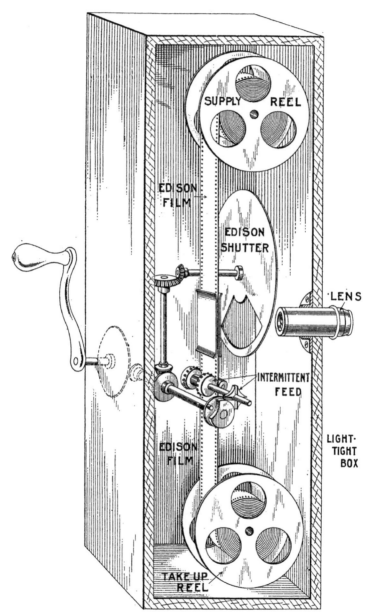

EARLY EDISON CAMERA

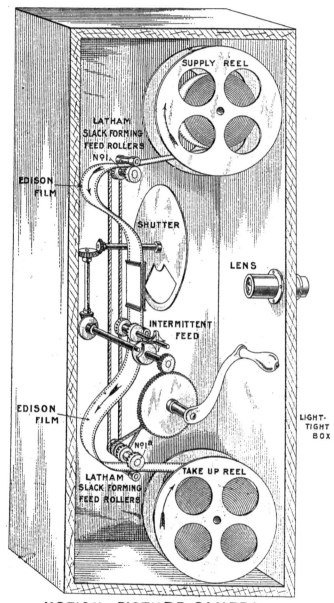

MOTION PICTURE CAMERA

Q. Please describe briefly the mechanism illustrated by this chart. A. In this chart will be noted the single stationary lens marked "Lens," the tape-like photographic film marked "Edison film," the upper and lower supports for the bulk of the film marked "supply reel," and "take-up reel," respectively, the continuously running sprocket feed rollers positively engaging the film and adapted to feed it regularly and uniformly and having an intermediate portion of the slack film between them, these feeding rollers being marked on the chart "Latham slack forming feed rollers No. 1" and "Latham slack forming feed rollers No. 1a" respectively, the intermittent feeding device positively engaging the intermediate section of the slack film and adapted to move it across the lens with an intermittent motion at a high rate of speed, marked "intermittent feed" on the chart, the shutter, marked "Shutter," adapted to expose the film during the period of rest, all of this mechanism being enclosed in a light-tight box. The main driving shaft is shown, but it is not marked on the chart.

Mr. CHURCH: Counsel for the defendant offers in evidence the chart last referred to by the witness, and requests that the same be marked "Defendant's Exhibit 181."

The exhibit is received in evidence and is so marked.

By Mr. CHURCH:

Q. Is the last chart referred to by you, Defendant's Exhibit 181, illustrative of the mechanism shown in any of the photographs that you have produced, and please state which? A. It is illustrative of the mechanism shown on photograph 2 of Defendant's Exhibit 179.

Q. I show you still another chart, the mechanism portrayed upon which I will ask you to briefly describe, and will also ask you to state for what purpose this chart is produced. A. This chart illustrates common features of projecting machines in general use at the beginning of 1908. It illustrates the mechanism shown in photograph No. 5 of Exhibit 179. In this chart will be noted the flexible transparent or translucent tape-like photographic film marked "Edison film," the upper and lower supports for the bulk of the film, marked respectively "supply reel" and "take-up

1   reel," the continuously running sprocket feed rollers positively engaging the film and feeding it uniformly, and marked
"Latham slack forming feed rollers" and "Latham slack
forming feed rollers," the intermittent feeding device positively engaging the slack portion of the film and adapted
to feed it positively with an intermittent motion at a high
rate of speed across the fixed illuminated exposure window
in such a manner that the intervals of pause and illumination shall exceed the intervals of movement.    This
mechanism is marked "intermittent feed" on the chart.
The fixed lens will be noted marked "lens," and the source

2   of light, which is marked "lamp." The shutter shown on this
diagram and marked "Armat shutter" is a type of shutter
in general use prior to the beginning of 1908.    It will be
noted that this shutter is adapted to intercept the light during the interval of movement of the film, but not during the
interval of pause and illumination.

> Mr. CHURCH: The chart last referred to and last
> described by the witness is here offered in evidence
> by counsel for the defendant, and it is requested
> that the same be marked "Defendant's Exhibit 182."

3   > The exhibit is received in evidence, and is so
> marked.

By Mr. CHURCH:

Q. I show you still another chart and ask you to state
what it represents.    A. This chart represents the several
features of construction common to the projecting machines in use at the beginning of 1908.    The central figure
upon this chart represents in a diagrammatic way such common features, and the smaller figures appearing in the

4   corners of the chart and connected to the central figure by
arrows, illustrate features of mechanism of an earlier
date, all of which are found embodied in the mechanism
illustrated in the central figure, as indicated by the arrows.
This central figure is similar in all respects but one to the
figures shown in the preceding Exhibit 182, but it will be
noted that on the present chart, the shutter is of a different
type than the shutter shown on Exhibit 182.    The shutter
illustrated on the central figure of the present chart, which
is an illustration of the mechanism shown in Photograph
No. 7 of Defendant's Exhibit 179, is adapted to intercept

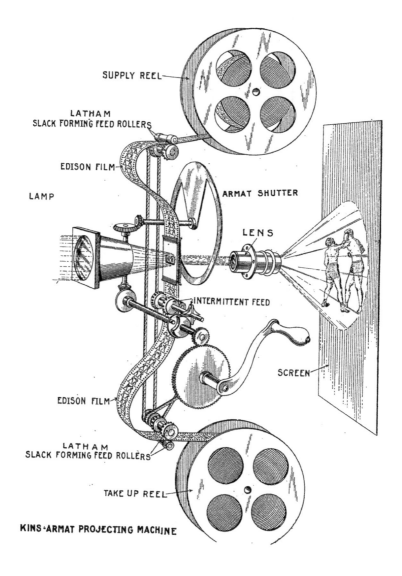

SUPPLY REEL

LATHAM
SLACK FORMING FEED ROLLERS

EDISON FILM

LAMP

ARMAT SHUTTER

LENS

INTERMITTENT FEED

SCREEN

EDISON FILM

LATHAM
SLACK FORMING FEED ROLLERS

TAKE UP REEL

KINS·ARMAT PROJECTING MACHINE

DEFENDANTS' EXHIBIT No. 183

LATHAM CAMERA

EDISON CAMERA

LATHAM SLACK FORMING FEED ROLLERS

EDISON FILM

MODERN PROJECTING MACHINE

MULTIPLE BLADE PROSS SHUTTER

ARMAT PROJECTING MACHINE

PROSS SHUTTER

—

the light during the interval of movement of the film and twice during the interval of pause and illumination.

Mr. CHURCH: The chart last referred to by the witness is offered in evidence, and it is requested that the same be marked "Defendant's Exhibit 183."

The exhibit is received in evidence, and is so marked.

By Mr. CHURCH:

Q. Please state whether or not the several patents re-cited as owned by the Motion Picture Patents Company in the license agreement between the Motion Picture Patents Company and the Biograph Company, dated December 18th, 1908 (being Exhibit No. 3 attached to the plaintiff's peti-tion), were, in fact, owned by the Motion Picture Patents Company at the date of the said license agreement, and have been continued to be owned by said company up to this time. A. All of those patents were owned by the Motion Picture Patents Company at the time stated, and the owner-ship of all of those patents has continued in the Motion Picture Patents Company up to the present time.

Q. Will you please give a list of the suits brought on the Edison camera re-issue Patent No. 12,037, after the assignment of that patent to the Motion Picture Patents Company, and the result of such suits? A. I have prepared such a list showing all such suits.

Mr. CHURCH: Counsel for the defendant offers the list produced by the witness in evidence, and re-quests that the same be marked "Defendants' Ex-bibit 184."

Mr. GROSVENOR: I make objection to the last column of this exhibit, the same being misleading, inasmuch as the same states or purports to give the dates on which several injunctions were issued in the cases named. It does not recite the fact that in each and every case where it is stated an injunction was granted in the case, the injunction has become valueless by reason of the re-issue of the patent, or by reason of other cause.

The list referred to is received in evidence and marked "Defendant's Exhibit 184," and is as follows:

## Defendants' Exhibit No. 184.

**SUITS BROUGHT ON THE CAMERA PATENT No. 12,037 AFTER THE ASSIGN-MENT OF THAT PATENT TO THE MOTION PICTURE PATENTS CO.**

| Defendants. | Bill Filed | District | Injunction Granted |
|---|---|---|---|
| Oklahoma Natural Mutoscene Co. | May 10, 1909 | Sup. Ct. Dist. Columbia | May 16, 1909 |
| New York Motion Picture Co. | Aug. 21, 1909 | East. Dist. N. Y. | Dec. 23, 1910 |
| Film Import & Trading Co. | Aug. 26, 1909 | South. Dist. N. Y. | Sept. 17, 1909 |
| Centaur Film Co. et al. | Nov. 6, 1909 | South. Dist. N. Y. | Aug. 30, 1910 |
| Pantograph Corporation | Nov. 29, 1909 | South. Dist. N. Y. | Mar. 21, 1910 |
| Carl Laemmle & Independent Moving Pictures Co. of America | Dec. 11, 1909 | South. Dist. N. Y. | Mar. 21, 1910 |
| Actophone Co. | Dec. 24, 1909 | South. Dist. N. Y. | Jan. 13, 1910 |
| David Horsley | Jan. 31, 1910 | Dist. of New Jersey | Apr. 7, 1910 |
| Great Western Film Co. | May 4, 1910 | North. Dist. Calif. | May 23, 1910 |
| Pacific Life Motion Picture Manufacturing Co. | June 27, 1910 | North. Dist. Calif. | Aug. 8, 1910 |
| The Champion Film Co. | Aug. 23, 1910 | South. Dist. N. Y. | Oct. 26, 1910 |
| Thanhouser Co. | Sept. 9, 1910 | South. Dist. N. Y. | .............. |
| Yankee Film Co. | Nov. 7, 1910 | South. Dist. N. Y. | Jan. 10, 1911 |
| William Steiner et al. | Nov. 12, 1910 | South. Dist. N. Y. | Jan. 10, 1911 |
| Carlton Motion Picture Laboratories | Nov. 14, 1910 | East. Dist. N. Y. | Dec. 27, 1910 |
| The Powers Co. | Nov. 19, 1910 | South. Dist. N. Y. | ............. |
| Adam Kessel, Jr., et al. | Nov. 28, 1910 | East. Dist. N. Y. | ............. |
| Fred Siegert & F. Berg | Mch. 18, 1911 | South. Dist. Calif. | Mch. 28, 1911 |
| C. Laemmle and Independent Moving Pictures Co. of America | Mch. 27, 1911 | South. Dist. N. Y. | ............. |
| J. Frank Whitfield | Apr. 4, 1911 | North. Dist. of Cal. | May 8, 1911 |
| Chas. F. Jenkins | May 8, 1911 | Supt. Ct. Dist. Columbia | ............. |

By Mr. CHURCH:    1

Q. State whether or not the several suits noted upon the list which is produced, have abated, and if so, for what reason, if you know. A. I understand that all of those suits have abated, owing to the surrender of the patent under which they were brought, and the re-issue of that patent.

Q. Why, if you know, was the re-issue No. 12,037 again surrendered and re-issued? A. For the purpose of eliminating the fourth claim of that patent.

Q. What, if any suits, have been brought by the Motion    2
Picture Patents Company on Edison camera re-issue No. 13,329, of December 5th, 1911, being the re-issue of re-issue No. 12,037, before referred to? A. A suit was brought against the Independent Moving Picture Company of America, and Carl Laemmle, on March 4th, 1912, in the Southern District of New York, and a suit was brought against the Imp Film Company, and Carl Laemmle, on the same day and in the same district. These two suits, I understand, have been progressed as one.

Q. Is there not another suit pending on that same re-issue in New Jersey, and if so, please state the name of it    3
and the title of it, if you know? A. There is also a suit pending against the Eclair Company in New Jersey. That suit was brought on the 9th of April, 1913.

Mr. GROSVENOR: Under the same patent?

The Witness: Under the same patent.

By Mr. CHURCH:

Q. The title of that suit is what? A. That suit was    4
brought against the Society Francaise des Films et Cine-matographe Eclair.

Q. Is there any suit now pending and being prose-cuted under Edison film re-issue No. 12,192 of January 12th, 1904, and if so, give the name of the defendant in that suit, and state where the suit is pending? A. A suit under Patent No. 12,192 was brought on the 9th of April, 1913, against the Society Francaise Eclair in New Jersey. That suit is now pending.

1      Q. You have heretofore testified (p. 1254, Vol. III of the record) that the Eastman Company was the source of supply of the unexposed photographic film stock used by the licensed manufacturers of motion pictures. Please now state whether or not that unexposed film stock referred to was useful for any other purpose. A. It was not useful for any other purpose, and I have never heard of its having been used for any other purpose.

Q. What were the standard dimensions, if any, of motion picture films in use, say in January, 1908, before the organization of the Motion Picture Patents Company? A. Those films are of indefinite length, and approximately 1⅜ inches in width. They possessed a row of perforations on each side of the film, having a clear space between the rows of perforations of approximately one inch available for picture purposes.

2

Q. When you speak of approximately, how much of a variation do you intend to convey by that language? A. A variation possibly of a few hundredths of an inch, such as might occur in variations in the slitting machine, by means of which this film is slit up into strips.

3      Q. State whether or not these films of standard dimensions had or had not the characteristics of the film described heretofore in your testimony this morning? A. Yes, all of the films to which I have referred this morning had the standard dimensions I have described.

Q. How long had those standard dimensions been established and who established them? A. Those standard dimensions were established by Edison along about 1891 or 1892, and they have not been varied from that time to the present.

4          Mr. GROSVENOR: That is 22 years ago?

The Witness: Yes.

By Mr. CHURCH:

Q. Do or do not the same standard dimensions prevail today? A. They do.

Q. Did any of the ten licensed manufacturers of motion picture films ever put out motion picture films of other than those standard dimensions, for commercial use on projecting machines? A. They do not.

Q. Did any of the cameras in use and on the market at the time of the organization of the Motion Picture Patents Company, produce motion picture films that were not of such standard dimensions? A. They did not.

Q. Did any of the exchanges licensed by the Motion Picture Patents Company handle or deal in any motion picture films that were not of such standard dimensions? A. They did not.

Q. Did any of the makes of projecting machines that were on the market or in use at the time of the formation of the Motion Picture Patents Company, handle motion picture films that were not of such standard dimensions? A. They did not.

Q. Did any of the exhibitors of motion picture films exhibit motion picture films that were not of such standard dimensions, or use a projecting machine adapted to handle any motion picture film that was not of such standard dimension? A. They did not.

Q. Did the General Film Company handle any motion picture films that were not of such standard dimensions or serve any exhibitors whose projecting machines were adapted to exhibit motion picture films that were not of such standard dimensions? A. They did not.

Q. Is it or is it not then true that any trade or business which the defendants herein or any one or more of them carried on prior to or since the bringing of this suit (so far as the same related to motion picture films or apparatus for producing or exhibiting motion picture films, or to systems of distribution of motion picture films, cameras, or projecting machines, through exchanges or otherwise) had relation solely to motion picture films of the aforesaid standard dimensions, and to apparatus for producing or exhibiting such standard film? A. All such business and apparatus have relation solely to motion picture films having such standard dimensions.

Q. You were, were you not, one of those who had to do with the devising of the plan involving:

1, the formation of the Motion Picture Patents Company to take over the various patents relating to the motion pic-

1    ture art, belonging to the different warring patent owners,
and, 2—

>    Mr. GROSVENOR: I object to that question as em-
>    bracing the term "warring patent owners" as being
>    the conclusion of the examiner.

By Mr. CHURCH:

Q. And, 2, the licensing of the various manufacturers,
exchanges and exhibitors by said company under those
2    patents? If yea, please tell us upon what theory and
with what intent you embarked in such enterprise? A.
I was one of those who had to do with the organization of
the Motion Picture Patents Company and with the devising
of the scheme of organization, and the intent in effecting that
organization was to terminate the legal strife over the various patents, and to procure revenue for the owners of the
patents under the patents, and by relieving those engaged
in the art from the continual menace of legal strife, to afford
them more means and opportunity for the exercise of the business concerned. And in devising the scheme for carrying
3    out those desired objects, the owner of the patents acted under the belief that they were justified on all grounds in en-
forcing in all reasonable ways, the exclusive rights and
monopolies conferred by the Government through the grant
of the several patents, and they believed that the owners of
the patents, as long as the patents existed, were authorized
to enforce in every reasonable manner possible, all of those
rights. And it was the intent to effect an organization lawful and equitable and desirable for the exercise of those several patent rights. They believed that they were justified
in imposing upon licensees under these patents, all the rea-
4    sonable customary restraints and conditions commonly or
frequently employed by owners of patents.

Q. State whether or not so far as your knowledge extends, you or any of your associates wittingly undertook to
cover by any licensing plan, any portion of the field which
the public in your estimation, had the right to occupy?

>    Mr. GROSVENOR: I object to that as calling for the
>    conclusion of the witness, and his own opinion as to
>    what the public were entitled to.

The Witness: My own intent, and so far as I know, the
intent of all others concerned in the organization of the Motion Picture Patents Company, was to in no way encroach
upon any right or liberty enjoyed by the public, but merely
to perfect some means by which litigation over rights not
enjoyed by the public could be terminated, and by means of
which, parties not then entitled to any liberty of action in
the practice of the art, might become possessed of lawful
rights, and thus practice the art without the menace of
suits under the patents.

Whereupon, at 12:45 P. M. of this Tuesday, the 24th day
of March, 1914, the hearings are adjourned to Saturday
morning, March 28th, 1914, at 10:30 o'clock A. M., at Room
159, Hotel Manhattan.

IN THE

## DISTRICT COURT OF THE UNITED STATES

FOR THE EASTERN DISTRICT OF PENNSYLVANIA.

UNITED STATES OF AMERICA,
                 Petitioner,

*v.*

MOTION PICTURE PATENTS Co. and others,
                 Defendants.

No. 889.

Sept. Sess., 1912.

NEW YORK CITY, March 28th, 1914.

The hearings were resumed, pursuant to adjournment, on Saturday, March 28th, 1914, at 10:30 o'clock A. M., at the Hotel Manhattan, New York City.

> Present on behalf of the Petitioner, Hon EDWIN P. GROSVENOR, Special Assistant to the Attorney General.
>
> JOSEPH R. DARLING, Esq., Special Agent.
>
> CHARLES F. KINGSLEY, Esq., GEORGE R. WILLIS, Esq., FRED R. WILLIAMS, Esq., and MELVILLE CHURCH, Esq., appearing for Motion Picture Patents Company, Biograph Company, Jeremiah J. Kennedy, Harry N. Marvin, Armat Moving Picture Company, Melies Manufacturing Company and Gaston Melies.
>
> J. H. CALDWELL, Esq., and H. K. STOCKTON, Esq., appearing for William Pelzer, General Film Company, Thomas A. Edison, Inc., Kalem Company, Inc., Pathe Freres, Frank L. Dyer, Samuel Long and J. A. Berst.
>
> HENRY MELVILLE, Esq., attorney for George Kleine, Essanay Film Manufacturing Company, Selig Polyscope, George K. Spoor and W. N. Selig.
>
> JAMES J. ALLEN, Esq., appearing for Vitagraph Company of America, and Albert E. Smith.

Thereupon, HARRY N. MARVIN resumed the stand for  1
further direct examination.

Direct examination continued by Mr. CHURCH:

Q. State whether or not the illustrative apparatus in Defendants' Exhibit No. 178 has ever been used for the practical
tical production and exhibition of motion pictures, and if
yea, state whether or not it is now capable of such use? A.
This illustrative mechanism has been used. It was used to
make the negative motion picture introduced in evidence and
marked Defendants' Exhibit No. 176, and it has been used  2
as a projecting machine in projecting the positive motion
picture Defendants' Exhibit No. 177, made from the above
mentioned negative motion picture. The apparatus is now
in condition suitable for practical use.

Q. Answering the question put you on page 3260 of the
record, you stated there were no projecting machines in commercial use in this country from the beginning of 1908 down
to the present time that did not embody all of the characteristics described by you in your description of projecting machines. I would now ask you whether or not the several projecting machines that have been referred to from time to time  3
by the witnesses in this case, namely, Power's Nos. 4, 5, 6, 6a;
Edison Exhibition, and Model B; Motiograph, 1, 1a and 2;
Kinodrome; Standard; and Simplex, were machines that fell
within the description given by you? A. All of those machines are machines that fell within the description given
by me.

Q. State, if you know, by whom the Power machines
were manufactured. A. They were manufactured by the
Power Manufacturing Company.

Q. The same question as to the Exhibition and Model B
machines. A. Edison Manufacturing Company or Thomas  4
A. Edison, Incorporated.

Q. By Power Manufacturing Company, do you mean
Nicholas Power Company? A. Yes, Nicholas Power being
the name of the man who invented the machine, according
to my understanding.

Q. Who put out the Kinodrome machines? A. George K.
Spoor, or the Essanay Company. I don't remember which.

Q. And what concerns put out the Standard machine so

1    called? A. That was put out, I believe, by the American
Company.

Q. Do you mean the American Moving Picture Company?
A. The American Moving Picture Company.

Q. How as to the Simplex machine? A. The Simplex
machines were put out by the Precision Manufacturing Company.

Q. Do you mean the Precision Machine Company? A.
The Precision Machine Company.

Q. And the Motiograph? A. The Enterprise Optical
Company.

2    Q. State whether or not the Simplex machines are machines put out under the license from the Patents Company.
A. They are.

Cross examination by Mr. GROSVENOR:

Q. Mr. Marvin, on your direct examination by Mr.
Church, you put in a room full of machines and diagrams.
Please state in your own language, the purpose of the intro-
duction of all those exhibits.

3            Mr. KINGSLEY: I object to the characterization
         that a room full of machines and diagrams were put
         in evidence. The fact that the counsel for the Gov-
         ernment was in the room at the same time the exhibits
         were introduced, shows that the room was not filled
         with machinery or exhibits.

The Witness: The purpose of introducing these machines
and diagrams was to enable the Court more readily to understand the various machines and apparatus that are concerned in this case.

4

By Mr. GROSVENOR:

Q. And was it in carrying out that purpose which you
have described, that on the various diagrams you have attempted to describe the various parts of the machines appearing on the diagrams? A. It was for the purpose of
giving a clear explanation of the various essential characteristics of this various apparatus that particular parts of
the apparatus have been designated on the charts in conformity with the description given of these several parts.

Q. Kindly look at Defendants' Exhibit No. 180, which
was introduced by you in the record, page 3266, and described by you.  I direct your attention to the label or
phrase appearing toward the center of that diagram, and
a little above the center, being the words "Edison film."
You may state whether the part of the film so designated on the diagram, which purports to be a copy of a
camera, has yet passed before the aperture so as to receive
the impressions of a picture.  A. From the diagram as it
appears—

Mr. GROSVENOR: I object to any answer except
yes or no.  I want to know plainly, yes or no, whether
that part of the film descending from what you call
the "supply reel" has at that point, passed before
the aperture.  I want the answer yes or no.

The Witness: That will depend upon the significance that
is given to the term "supply reel."  If we assume that that
is the reel from which the unexposed portion of the film is
taken, then the portion of the film to which you refer would
not be indicated as having passed before the lens, but if
we use the designation "supply reel" to indicate the supply
of exposed film, then the portion of the film to which you
refer would have already passed before the exposure window.

By Mr. GROSVENOR:

Q. Please state what you mean by the term "supply reel"
on your diagram.  A. In the diagram as here presented, it
was my intention in indicating the upper reel as the "supply reel" to indicate the reel from which the unexposed portion of film was taken.

Q. Has that part of the film to which I have directed
your attention, and which is labeled "Edison film" passed
before the aperture?  A. With that designation of the upper
supply reel, then that portion of the film referred to by you
is not represented as having passed before the aperture.

Q. Please state where that film which is so designated
has been obtained?  A. If I understand your question correctly, the portion of the film designated by me is supposed
to have been withdrawn from the reel marked "supply reel."

Q. And where was the film obtained from, which was

1    placed on the supply reel? A. I don't understand that question. This is a diagramatic representation of an imaginary film.

Q. Where would you get the film to place on an actual
camera if you had an actual camera to take the place of
that diagram? A. Well, such film, as to the raw stock and
sometimes as to the perforated film, is commonly obtained
in this country from the Eastman Company, Rochester, who
are the largest source of supply.

Q. Directing your attention to that place on the diagram
again, I ask you, would you describe the film at that posi-
2    tion as being raw stock? A. I would qualify that by the addition that the film has been perforated.

Q. Sometimes the perforated film comes from the Eastman Company, the manufacturer? A. The Eastman Company will supply perforated film on order, I believe.

Q. Other than making perforations on the film, has the
manufacturer, that is, the person intending to use the film
in his camera, done anything to the film at the time the film
appears at that point in the camera, that is, at the point
designated in your diagram? A. Well, that depends upon
3    conditions. Sometimes the film is treated to obviate the
difficulty of static electricity, treated by steaming. Sometimes it is exposed to certain chemical fumes for the purpose
of modifying the sensitiveness of the emulsion, and although
I have no direct knowledge, I have been informed that in
the use of certain film, it is specially treated by the manufacturer for the purpose of obtaining results for color
photography.

Q. The person using the camera has not had anything
to do with the manufacture of the film or with the placing
thereon of the sensitized emulsion, enabling it to receive the
4    impression when it passes through the camera? A. Other
than the modifications that I have referred to in my last
answer. The camera operator does not commonly manipulate the film in any way.

Q. Please state what had been done on the film by reason
of which you label it on your diagram at the point I have
indicated "Edison film." A. The film at that point is in a
condition which I understand was originated by Mr. Edison.

Q. You do not mean to imply that the film was made by
Edison? A. I understand that the film in the condition

in which it is supposed to be at the point indicated, was first
used in such a condition by Mr. Edison, and has been since
that time commonly characterized as Edison film.

Q. Did Edison make that film, witness? Answer the
question yes or no. A. Make what film, Mr. Grosvenor?

Q. Did he make the film which is represented on that diagram? A. As I have stated, that diagram represents an
imaginary film.

Q. Did Edison ever make any motion picture film? A.
I don't know.

Q. Is not your knowledge of the business sufficient to
enable you to answer the question yes or no, whether Edison
ever did make and sell and put on the market any motion
picture film? A. I don't know.

Q. Well, then, why do you call that "Edison film" if you
don't know whether or not Edison ever made any film? A.
I endeavored to explain that that diagram represents an
imaginary film of a type that I understand was created by
Mr. Edison.

Q. Do you mean to imply or testify that Edison created
—is that the word you used? A. Created is the word I used.
I did not say that he created the film. I said I understood
that he created a type of film.

Q. What type of film did Edison create? A. The type
indicated on the diagram.

Q. Did you ever see any type of film manufactured by
Edison on any camera? A. I don't know that I have ever
seen any film manufactured by Edison—

Q. I did not ask you whether you knew or not. I
asked you did you ever see any film, any type of film, on
any camera at any time in your experience in the motion
picture business, which was made by Edison? A. I do not
know that Edison ever made any film.

Q. Well, did you ever see any film made by Edison? A.
Well, that I cannot tell. I have seen lots of film, but I don't
know who made it.

Q. Don't you know, Mr. Marvin, that the question of who
did invent that film is a question which is in litigation between the Eastman Company and others, and that Edison
never claimed to invent that film? A. I think, Mr. Grosvenor, you are talking about one thing and I am testifying
about another.

1      Q. I want to ask you, what did Edison ever do to that
film before it came to that position in the camera, which
entitles you to term it at that point on your diagram "Edison film." A. I do not understand that anyone ever prepared or conceived any film of the type indicated by the diagram prior to the time that I understand that Mr. Edison
did it.

Q. Supposing you are going out with a camera which
has inside of it mechanism such as represented by that
diagram, to take a picture, and you have not any film to
put on the supply reel. Where will you get your film? A.
2    I might get it from the Eastman Company.

Q. And then when you get it from the Eastman Company, if it is not perforated, you perforate it, don't you?
A. Very likely.

Q. And then in ordinary practice, you put it on that
supply reel without doing anything else to the reel, don't
you? A. I might, if the weather was good.

Q. And then when you started your camera, the film
would pass down to that point, wouldn't it, without your doing anything to it? A. I would have to thread it.

3      Q. Other than threading it, that is, putting it on the reel
and threading it, you would not do anything to it after you
bought it from Eastman and perforated it, prior to the time
it reached that point on the diagram, would you? A. No,
I think not.

Q. Now, kindly direct your attention to the diagram below the aperture and above the take-up reel where these
words appear again toward the center of the diagram "Edison film." Please state what, if anything, has been done to
the film between the above point marked "Edison film" and
the lower point marked "Edison film" except to pass before
4    the aperture. A. Well, successive portions of the film have
been exposed to the action of light, and photographs made
thereon.

Q. And that has been done to it in passing from the upper to the lower points? A. Yes.

Q. Please look at Defendants' Exhibit No. 181, which
purports to be a diagram of a motion picture camera. I
direct your attention to a point a little above the center
where the words "Edison film" are printed with an arrow
pointing to the film. Is the type of film there used the same

type of film as that referred to in the prior diagram? A. Yes.

Q. Has anything been done by Edison to that film prior to its appearance at that point on the diagram? A. I do not understand your question. That is a diagramatic illustration of an imaginary film.

Q. Imagine to yourself that that is a camera and the diagram of a camera which it purports to represent, and that you are going out with such a camera, and that you have not any film to put on the supply reel? Where would you get your film to put on that supply reel? A. Well, I could get it from any one of a number of makers that supply Edison film.

Q. Would you get any of it from Edison? A. I might.

Q. Does Edison manufacture any film? A. I don't know that he does.

Q. You know that he does not, don't you, Mr. Marvin? A. No, I don't. I know that he has considered it sometimes. At least, I understand that he has.

Q. Has he manufactured any to sell? A. Not to my knowledge.

Q. Then why do you call that Edison film at that point on the diagram? A. Why, I understand that Mr. Edison created that type of film, and that that name is properly applied to any film of that type, no matter who makes it.

Q. I thought you said that Edison never made the film. A. I said he created the type.

Q. How do you mean, he created the type? What did he do in making the type? A. He just created it.

Q. How did he create it? A. I don't know; with his mind, I suppose.

Q. You don't mean to say that the raw film was made by Edison, do you? A. I don't know whether he made raw film or not. He has made a great many things.

Q. I am not asking you about other things. I am asking you, did he ever make raw film? A. I don't know.

Q. If you don't know that, how can you say that he created the type? A. He did not have to make raw film in order to create a type of film.

Q. Did Edison invent or create any sensitized emulsion to be placed on the raw base or on the base, enabling it to receive the impression, or a photograph? A. I don't know

Q. Please state what Edison did do by reason of which you say he created the type? A. Well, I understand—

1      Q. I am not asking you what you understand. I
say, please state what Edison did to the film, by reason
of which you say he created the type. A. I don't know
that he would have to do anything to a film to create a
type. He might create a type of film in his mind without
ever touching a piece of film. Inventions originate in the
mind, not in material.

       Q. I am not asking about what he might have done. I
am asking you for what he did do by reason of which you
say he created the type, and therefore label it on the diagram
"Edison film." That is what I am asking you. A. I started
2  to give you my understanding of it, but you seemed to object
to my language. If you want me to give it to you, I will
give it to you the best I can.

       Q. My question is clear. Please state what Edison did
to the film or in connection with any film by reason of which
you say that he created the type of film, and therefore label
it "Edison film" on your diagram. A. I understand that he
was the first to make use of such a long, unbroken, flexible,
transparent, translucent, tape-like, photographic film, having
perforated edges. I have never heard of anyone else who
3  made or used such a film which they had had made by
others, or made themslves, for such a purpose.

       Q. You say, "I understand that he was the first to
make use of such a long, unbroken, flexible, transparent,
translucent, tape-like, photographic film, having perforated
edges." Edison, then, was not the man that made the
article with those qualities which you have described, but
he was the first to make use of that article; is that what you
mean? A. No, I think he was the first to make it.

       Q. What did Edison do to make film flexible? A. I don't
know that he did anything to make film flexible.

4      Q. Did he ever do anything to make the film transparent?
A. I don't know that he did.

       Q. Did he ever do anything to make the film translucent?
A. I don't know that he did.

       Q. Did he ever do anything to make the film like a tape,
or tape-like? A. Well, I understand that he instructed the
manufacturers of the raw stock to supply it to him in that
form.

       Q. That is, he told the manufacturers who were making it
to make it in a long roll? A. I am not sure but what he

slit it up himself.  I don't know.  He may have done it
personally or had some assistants in his laboratory do it.
He may have asked his manufacturer to do it.  I am not
sure about it.

Q. Did Edison ever do anything to make the film photographic, that is, capable of receiving impressions from light?
A. Well, I don't know about that.  He may have coated it
with emulsion himself.

Q. You never profited in your business and the business
you did in motion pictures, by anything or any discovery
of Edison regarding coatings or photographic emulsions, did
you?  A. No, sir, we usually got the film from the Eastman
Company already coated.

Q. Isn't it a fact that Edison never did make and
sell any of that long, unbroken, flexible, transparent, translucent, tape-like, photographic film, having perforated edges?
A. I have already stated I did not know, and I do not know
whether he made and sold any of it or not.

Q. You never heard of his selling any such film, did you?
A. I do not know of his making it, but I understand that
he has sold thousands of feet of it.

Q. Do you mean thousands of feet of positive film with
pictures upon it, or do you mean thousands of feet of raw
stock without any pictures upon it for use by manufacturers?  A. Well, I know he has sold a great deal of positive film having pictures on it, and as to his having sold
negative film, about that, I have no personal knowledge.

Q. We are talking, Mr. Marvin, of film without any pictures, either negative or positive, which I believe you have
designated sometimes as raw stock.  Did you ever know of
Edison selling any such material, that is, raw stock without
pictures, negative or positive upon it, for use by manufacturers?  A. I presume he sold it.  I have no positive knowledge of it, though.

Q. Did you ever hear of him doing anything like that?
A. No, I cannot say that I have.

Q. Then when you used the term "thousands of feet" a
moment ago, you meant thousands of feet of positive film
with pictures upon it, or thousands of feet of negative film
with pictures upon it?  A. I think I so designated it in my
answer.

Q. That is what you meant, anyway, whether you so

1   designated it or not?  A. When I said thousands of feet, I
referred to exposed positive film.

Q. Please look at the diagram, Defendants' Exhibit No.
182. Should not those pictures be upside down on the film?
A. Is that a question?

Q. Yes.  A. Well, either the pictures should be upside
down on the film, or the indicated picture on the screen
should be upside down.

Q. That is to say, in order to make that an accurate diagram, the pictures should be reversed, that is, I mean com-
paring the picture on the screen with the picture on the film,
2   one should be upside down and the other right side up.  A.
Yes, to conform to ordinary commercial practice that would
be true, and the draftsman should have made one or the other
of the pictures reversed.

Q. Does this diagram, being Defendants' Exhibit No. 182,
give the same apparatus as that disclosed in diagram, Defendants' Exhibit No. 181, except that the lamp is added, and
the screen?  A. The apparatus indicated by Defendants' Exhibit No. 182 is the same in many respects as the apparatus
indicated by Defendants' Exhibit No. 181, but there are some
3   points of difference.

Q. Please point out the points of difference.  A. The
shutter indicated on Defendants' Exhibit No. 182 differs from
the shutter indicated on Defendants' Exhibit No. 181, and
the box or housing indicated on Defendants' Exhibit No. 181
is not present in Defendants' Exhibit No. 182; and in Defendants' Exhibit No. 182 a source of light or lamp and a condensing lens is indicated, which does not appear in Defendants' Exhibit No. 181.  The film indicated in Defendants'
Exhibit No. 181 is supposed to be undeveloped film.

Q. By "undeveloped" you mean it has not passed through
4   the camera?  A. No.  Part of it is indicated as having passed
through the camera in Defendants' Exhibit No. 181, and part
is represented as not having passed through the camera, but
none of it has been developed, whereas in Defendants' Exhibit
No. 182, a developed film is indicated, either positive or
negative.

Q. Do you observe any other differences?  A. Defendants'
Exhibit No. 182 has indicated an opening or window opposite the lens, whereas in Defendants' Exhibit No. 181, this
window is indicated as being closed or not existing.

Q. The only distinguishing feature between Defendants' Exhibit No. 182 and Defendants' Exhibit No. 181 relating to the principal mechanism that is in the center, is the difference in the shutter? A. That is the principal difference there.

Q. And is that the reason you call the exhibit, Defendants' Exhibit No. 182, a Jenkins-Armat projecting machine, namely, because it has a shutter that is different in size or in the size of its aperture, from the other projecting machines? A. Well, that is a characteristic which characterizes a type of projecting machine. This diagram is supposed to indicate a projecting machine and is distinguished from the former diagram, which indicated a camera.

Q. Why do you call it a Jenkins-Armat projecting machine? What is there about it that indicates Jenkins or Armat, except the shutter? A. That is the characteristic which leads to that designation.

Q. Then the reason you call that a Jenkins-Armat projecting machine is because it has the shutter known as the Jenkins-Armat shutter? A. Yes.

Q. Will you kindly look at Defendants' Exhibit No. 183, which has five diagrams upon it. The center is entitled "Modern projecting machine," the lower right-hand diagram is entitled "Armat projecting machine." Is there any difference between those two except that of the difference in shutters? A. No, the difference in the type of shutter indicated is the characterizing difference between the center diagram and the one appearing in the lower right-hand corner.

Q. And by reason of the difference in shutter, you call the one with the three apertures, the "Modern projecting machine" and you call the diagram in the lower right-hand corner the "Armat projecting machine," is that right? A. Yes, because the use of the Pross shutter which has supplanted the use of the so-called Armat shutter, characterizes the modern projecting machines.

Q. You testified on direct examination, page 3268, referring to Defendants' Exhibit 183, "This chart represents the several features of construction common to the projecting machines in use at the beginning of 1908. The central figure upon this chart represents in a diagramatic way, such common features, and the smaller figures appearing in the corners of the chart and connected with the central figure by

1  arrows, illustrate features of mechanism of an earlier date, all of which are found embodied in the mechanism illustrated in the central figure, as indicated by the arrows." That is an accurate statement of the diagram? A. I think so.

Q. Where did you get this projecting machine which you introduced as Defendants' Exhibit No. 175, page 3261? A. I got that from the Nicholas Power Company.

Q. When did you get it from them? A. A few days ago.

Q. And what did you ask them for? A. My instructions to the person who saw them was to get a machine, one of their types of machines such as they were putting out at the beginning of 1908.

2  Q. That is, to get a Model No. 5? A. No, I did not refer to the number of the model.

Q. What form of a shutter has that projecting machine? A. That has a Pross shutter, two-wing type.

Q. I will ask you to open the projecting machine and examine the shutter. A. (The witness complies with the request.)

Q. What do you find here (indicating Defendants' Exhibit No. 175)? How many do you find? A. It is a two-wing shutter.

3  Q. Then it is not a Pross shutter, is it? A. It is a Pross shutter, as I stated before.

Q. I thought your testimony was to the effect that the Pross shutter was a shutter with three apertures or wings. A. I don't remember having testified so.

Q. What is the distinguishing characteristic of a Pross shutter if it can be of two wings or three wings? A. A Pross shuter may be of any number of wings. It may even be of one wing. The characteristic of the Pross shutter is that it shall intercept the light during the time when the film is being moved, and one or more times during the interval of pause and illumination.

4  Q. Then if you take an Armat shutter and run it fast enough, it will serve the same purpose as the Pross shutter? A. That is not true, because the Armat shutter is arranged and geared in connection with the other mechanism so as to intercept the light only during the period of movement of the film. If, however, you wish to take a shutter constructed like the Armat shutter and change the gearing so as to change its mechanical function so that it may revolve twice for every

period of motion or of rest of the film, then a shutter which
when formerly arranged would be an Armat shutter, would
perform the function of the Pross shutter by intercepting the
light during the interval of movement, and also during the
interval of pause and illumination. Some machines have
been constructed in that way.

Q. The different manufacturers of projecting machines
have their shutters with apertures of varying size, that is to
say, each projecting machine manufacturer does not have a
shutter with the same size apertures as all the other manufacturers of projecting machines? A. Oh, the sizes of the
apertures differ on different machines.

Q. That is true today, isn't it? A. Yes.

Q. You did not mean then on your diagram that the mere
fact that the central figure had three wings in its shutter, whereas the Armat has only one wing, that the number of wings should be the distinguishing characteristic
of the machine in the center? A. Well, I intended to illustrate in as simple a manner as possible so as to give a fairly
intelligible description to a person of ordinary intelligence,
to indicate the difference in the characteristics of these two
types of shutters. I might have done it in other ways. This
way seemed to me a good way.

Q. Please look at the lower left-hand diagram entitled
"Latham camera" and state when, if ever, Latham made a
camera or sold a camera. A. I don't know as to what Latham's business in cameras was, but I do know that he used
such a camera in the Spring of the year 1896—hold on, 1895—
I cannot remember the exact month. I think it was in February or March.

Q. That diagram does not purport to represent the camera
Latham was using at that time, does it? A. It does not purport to be an accurate artistic copy, but it purports to indicate in a diagramatic way, the essential elements of the
camera that Latham used at that time.

Q. Is not the only difference between the figure at the
top named "Edison camera" and the one at the bottom,
labeled "Latham camera," at the left of the diagram, that
the lower picture has the so-called loop, and the diagram
labeled "Edison camera" does not have the loop? A. Yes,
the loop or slack forming feed mechanism which is present
in the Latham camera and absent in the so-called Edison

1    camera, is the characterizing difference between these two
cameras.

Q. I say, between those two diagrams that you have placed
there, the only difference as they stand is, that the lower
one has the loop and the upper one does not have the loop?
A. You mean the artistic difference, or do you mean the difference in the apparatus intended to be displayed by the diagram?

Q. I am referring to the apparatus displayed by the diagram. A. Well, the characterizing difference in those two
diagrams, I say, is the presence in one of the slack forming
2    continuously running feed rollers, and its absence in the
other.

Q. And where the rollers and the loop are present, you
have labeled it "Latham camera," and where they are not
present, you have labeled it "Edison camera"? A. Yes, that
is true.

Q. All the Edison cameras that have been sold, as far as
you know, have that loop in them, don't they? A. Well,
all the cameras of which I have any knowledge have the loop
in.

3    Q. And the Court of Appeals in this circuit held, did it
not, that the Latham invention, so far as it was an invention,
respecting a loop, did not apply to the cameras? A. I do
not understand they held any such thing as that. They could
not have, because the camera was the machine in which he
used the loop first.

Q. I am talking, Mr. Marvin, about the invention or the
patent of Latham concerning a loop, and which was in litigation. Wasn't it held by the Circuit Court of Appeals of this
circuit that Latham's patent was not valid so far as it applied to cameras? A. Now you are speaking of a patent.
4    Before you were speaking of an invention. My answer applied to an invention. I believe that the Court for some reason held that Latham was not entitled to patent protection
on his invention when his invention was used in a camera.
I do not understand the technical ground exactly.

Q. I show you Defendants' Exhibit No. 176 and Defendants' Exhibit No. 177. Defendants' Exhibit No. 176 is an ex-
bibit of a negative motion picture film? A. Yes.

Q. And Defendants' Exhibit No. 177 is the same series of
pictures on a positive motion picture film? A. Yes.

Q. Defendants' Exhibit No. 176, being the negative mo-

tion picture film, is the roll that went through the camera?
A. Yes.

Q. After it came out of the camera, what was done to it?
A. It was developed.

Q. And how was it developed? A. Well, it was developed by being passed through a series of chemical solutions and being dried.

Q. What was the purpose of passing it through the chemical solutions? I want you to give a brief description if you will be good enough to do so, of what happens to the film after it comes out of the camera. A. The film after it comes out of the camera is placed in a solution that fixes certain portions of the sensitized emulsion that have been exposed to the light, and the film is then put into another solution that dissolves out those portions that were not fixed by the previous process. The film is then washed in a neutralizing solution which checks further action of the chemicals, and is dried, the result of this fixing and washing out process being to make visible upon the film, the latent photographs made by the light.

Q. Then it comes out and is known as the negative? A. It is known as the negative.

Q. What is then done to the negative in order to produce the positive? A. The negative is passed through feeding devices engaging sprocket holes in the film, in contact with another similar strip of sensitized film, and light is allowed to pass through the negative on to the positive strip, making a facsimile series of latent photographs on the positive strip, which is then developed in a manner similar to that used in the development of the negative, the result being a facsimile motion picture strip known as a positive, on which the lights and shades of the negative are reversed.

Q. Can you use a film which you buy from Eastman indiscriminately for a negative film or positive film, or do you get two supplies from them, one for use as negative films, and one for use as positive films? A. Well, they can be used interchangeably, but in common practice it is not customary, because the film commonly used for making negatives must be of great quickness, and for making positives, a film having a less quick emulsion is somewhat preferable, so that it is common to use film of slightly different characteristics for negatives and positives.

1    Q. These slightly different characteristics between the films are given to the films by the manufacturer of the film? A. Yes. Those are chemical characteristics, not physical characteristics.

Q. On direct examination by Mr. Church, page 3269: "Q. Please state whether or not the several patents recited as owned by the Motion Picture Patents Company in the license agreements between the Motion Picture Patents Company and the Biograph Company, dated December 18th, 1908, being Exhibit No. 3 attached to the plaintiff's petition, were in fact owned by the Motion Picture Patents Company at the time of said license agreement, and have been continued to be owned by said company up to this time? A. All of those patents were owned by the Motion Picture Patents Company at the time stated, and the ownership of all of those patents has continued in the Motion Picture Patents Company up to the present time." The patents referred to were not acquired by the Patents Company from the various assignors until December 18th, 1908, being the day the Patents Company entered into licenses with the various manufacturing licensees? A. That is true. They were obtained on that day.

Q. It is also true, is it not, that the patents were acquired by the Patents Company from the various assignors of the patents subject to the condition that they should be re-assigned to each of the assignors in consideration of the sum of one dollar, in case the Patents Company become bankrupt, cease doing business, dissolve voluntarily or otherwise, or in case its charter were repealed? A. I believe that is true.

Q. On page 3272, you gave some testimony respecting standard dimensions. You did not mean to give rise to the inference that there was any patent on dimensions, or the dimensions of the several pictures? I am referring to positive motion pictures. A. I do not think I made any reference to patents.

Q. The standard dimension is one that has been adopted by all the manufacturers and followed during the last 22 years since it was first adopted by Edison about 22 years ago? A. Yes.

Q. Is a rheostat used with every projecting machine? A. A rheostat is commonly used with projecting machines when

they are used with direct current. When they are used with
alternating current, it is common to use what is known as a
choking coil.

Q. It is impossible to use a projecting machine without
one or the other of the two articles you have last named?
A. Oh, no. That merely is an accident of the ordinary source
of electrical supply available. In using a projecting machine
for projecting pictures in ordinary use, they are frequently
used in places where the current is direct current of about
110 volts. Somewhere about 50 volts is all that is required
for the operation of the lamp, and the resistance is used to
cut down the extra voltage, but where you encounter a source
of supply of lower voltage, the lamp might be used without
resistance, although it would be somewhat unstable.

Q. Have you attempted to display these pictures, Defendants' Exhibit No. 177, by means of this mechanism which you
have introduced, which pictures you state were taken, as I
understand, by the same mechanism? A. Oh, yes, we have
projected this identical film and others with that machine.

Q. In projecting them with that machine, have you used
a rheostat? A. Oh, yes, because the source of supply that
we had available was 110 volts or thereabouts.

Q. Is that rheostat made a part of the exhibit? A. Why,
I don't really know. It is not essential. That particular
rheostat there is a small rheostat adapted to cut down the
voltage very considerably so as to employ a small amount of
current in the arc light. We did that because we have prepared a small screen so as to save going into a large projecting room when we exhibited those pictures, and we did not
have any electrical connections in that room, which was at
the office of the Motion Picture Patents Company, suitable
to carry the heavy current commonly employed. Therefore
we put in small carbons, and used that small rheostat, which
cut the current down a great deal, but which gave a perfectly
good projection. There is no reason why the machine could
not be used with the full size arc lamp and rheostat and
project a picture as large as any commercial machine will do.

Mr. GROSVENOR: I introduce in evidence as throw-
ing light on these diagrams, and particularly on
what the film is, the opinion of Judge Coxe in the
United States Circuit Court of Appeals for the

1     Second Circuit, in the case of Goodwin Film & Camera Company against the Eastman Kodak Company.

Mr. KINGSLEY: Objected to as incompetent, immaterial and irrelevant, having no relation whatever to the issues in this case.

The opinion offered is received in evidence and marked "Petitioner's Exhibit No. 267," and the same is as follows:

**Petitioner's Exhibit No. 267.**

2

UNITED STATES CIRCUIT COURT OF APPEALS,

FOR THE SECOND CIRCUIT.

THE GOODWIN FILM AND CAMERA COMPANY,
         Complainant-Appellee,

*against*

3     EASTMAN KODAK COMPANY,
         Defendant-Appellant.

Before

LACOMBE, COXE and WARD,
    *Circuit Judges.*

On appeal from an interlocutory decree dated September 9, 1913, holding valid and infringed claims 1, 6, 8, 10 and 12 of Letters Patent No. 610,861 granted to Han-
4    nibal Goodwin of Newark, N. J., September 13, 1898, for improvements in photographic pellicles and processes of producing the same. The application was filed May 2, 1887, and the patent was granted eleven years and four months thereafter. The bill was filed December 15, 1902, four years after the patent issued and ten years and eight months before the decision of the District Court sustaining the five claims as stated. Over a quarter a century has thus elapsed between the filing of the application and the decree sustaining the patent.

The opinion of Judge Hazel is reported in 207 Fed. Rep. 351. The record contains 3,800 printed pages and the briefs aggregate 575 pages. 1

LIVINGSTON GIFFORD, J. J. KENNEDY and M. B. PHILIPP, for Appellant.

EDMUND WETMORE, EDWARD C. DAVIDSON and ROBERT D. EGGLESTON, for Appellee.

COXE, J.

Hannibal Goodwin was a clergyman residing at Newark, New Jersey, for thirty years prior to his death, which occurred December 31, 1900. His salary was small and for ten years prior to his death he had no regular charge. He was interested in chemistry and spent much of his spare time in chemical experimentation and research. The necessity for a transparent, sensitive pellicle for use in roller cameras had long been felt and Goodwin, though hampered by his inadequate surroundings, undertook the task of supplying it. The specification points out the manifest objections to supports of glass and of paper in combination with gelatin and other substances, and proceeds to state how they may be avoided. The patentee says: 3

> "I have provided a pellicle the principal ingredient of which is nitrocellulose, or any equivalent * * * which is transparent, and insoluble in the usual developing, fixing and intensifying solutions or liquids used in photography. * * * In carrying out the invention I provide a suitable surface, such as that of glass, and flow over the same a solution of nitrocellulose dissolved in nitrobenzole or other non-hydrous and non-hygroscopic solvents * * * and diluted in alcohol or other hydrous and hygroscopic diluent." 4

When dry this solution forms a flexible transparent sheet or pellicle which is insoluble in any of the fluids employed in dry plate photography. The foil when stripped from the glass constitutes a supporting pellicle for the sensitive film. The specification states further that previous efforts

1    to provide a transparent and flexible pellicle have been fail-
ures because they did not possess the properties of glass
and were incapable of resisting the usual developing, fixing and intensifying solutions used in photography.

The patentee asserts that he has produced a film which
is capable of resisting such fluids and of sufficient smoothness, hardness and toughness of surface for service in a
roller camera.   He says that in carrying out the invention
he provides a suitable surface such as glass and flows over
it the solution of nitrocellulose (as distinguished from
"commercial celluloid") dissolved in nitrobenzole or other
2    solvent not containing or capable of absorbing water.   The
equivalents for nitrobenzole are acetate of amyl and those
non-hydrous non-hygroscopic fluid solvents of nitrocellulose which do not mix with water, are not greasy and are
of slow volatility.   Nitrocellulose when so dissolved and
flowed over a smooth plate produces a smooth, transparent,
imporous, impermeable film capable of being subjected to
the photographic fluids without being affected thereby.   It
is further stated that the solution thus obtained by dissolving the nitrocellulose is diluted with alcohol or other
3    similar diluent which serves to dilute or expand the volume
of the dissolved nitrocellulose or increase its fluidity.   The
diluted solution is then applied to a smooth and hard surface, from which it may be stripped when dry.

Page two of the specification is largely devoted to a
discussion of matters which seem to us to have little bearing on the questions here involved and especially so as it is
stated that the entire page was inserted after the patentee
learned of the defendant's process.   The patentee on page
3 of the patent describes how he may reduce the cost by
enveloping or imposing on the nitrocellulose supporting
4    film a film of gelatin or coat a layer of gelatin with outer
films of the non-hygroscopic nitrocellulose film, so that
water or other solvents cannot gain access to the gelatin.
The remainder of the specification is devoted to a description of the various mays in which the pellicle may be constructed and to an explanation of the drawings of the
patent.

The claims in controversy are as follows:

    "1. An improvement in the art of making trans-

parent flexible, photographic-film pellicles, the same
consisting in dissolving nitrocellulose in a menstruum containing a hygroscopic element and an
element which is non-hygroscopic, the non-hygroscopic element being of itself a solvent of nitrocellulose, and of slower volatility than the hygroscopic
element, depositing and spreading such solution
upon a supporting surface, and allowing it to set
and dry and harden by evaporation, and spreading
a photographically-sensitive solution on the hardened film, and drying the film, substantally as set
forth."

"6. An improvement in the art of making transparent flexible, and elastic photographic pellicles,
the same consisting in dissolving nitrocellulose in
an eventual celluloidal menstruum which is anhy-
drous and non-hygroscopic, spreading such solution
upon a supporting-surface, allowing it to dry and
harden, spreading photographically-sensitive matter
thereon and again drying and stripping the pellicle
from said support, substantially as set forth."

"8. The process of making photographic pellicles,
which consists in subjecting nitrocellulose to the action of a menstruum combining fast and slow evaporating solvents, the slow evaporating solvent being
non-hygroscopic and non-greasy in nature and quality and acting as an eventual solvent as described,
spreading the solution upon a support and setting
the same by evaporation, then applying photographically-sensitive matter and stripping, all substantially as set forth."

"10. As a new article of manufacture, a transparent film-support for photographic purposes, the
same consisting of a thin, non-greasy, film, foil or
pellicle of a dried and hardened celluloidal solution
of nitrocellulose, combining in addition to the following essential properties of glass-plate supports,
viz., insolubility in developing fluids, insensibility to
heat and moisture, imporosity of structure, and hardness, smoothness, and brilliancy of surface, the further desirable properties of exceeding thinness, light-

1      ness in weight, toughness in texture and elasticity
in flexure; as and for the purposes specified."

"12. The process of manufacturing photographically-sensitive pellicles, consisting of flowing a non-
photographically-sensitive solution of nitrocellulose
dissolved in a non-hygroscopic liquid, or a liquid
which is eventually non-hygroscopic, and drying and
hardening such compound into a support for the
photographically-sensitive emulsion and imposing on
such support the said sensitive emulsion, substan-
2      tially as set forth."

Claim 10 covers the film support as a new article of
manufacture and the other claims cover the process by
which the pellicle is produced.

An examination of the first claim will demonstrate
sufficiently the various steps of the Goodwin process for
making a transparent, flexible photographic-film pellicle.
These are:

FIRST: Dissolving nitrocellulose in a menstruum con-
3      taining a hygroscopic and a non-hygroscopic element, the
latter being of itself a solvent of nitrocellulose and of
slower volatility than the former.

SECOND: Spreading such solution upon a supporting
surface.

THIRD: Allowing it to set, dry and harden by evaporation.

FOURTH: Spreading a photographically sensitive solution on the hardened film.

4      FIFTH: Drying the film.

At the time of Goodwin's invention the art was vehe-
mently demanding, as a substitute for the glass plates then
in use, a transparent photographic film capable of supporting the sensitive emulsion necessary in photography and
also capable of being rolled up. Goodwin entered the field
as an inventor for the sole purpose of overcoming the difficulties then existing and we think he did so when, speaking broadly, he discovered the process of dissolving nitrocellulose in a menstruum containing nitrobenzole and alco-

hol or their equivalents and then spreading the sensitive emulsion on the hardened film. He was subjected to almost unprecedented delays and disappointments in the Patent Office, which it is unnecessary to consider in detail, but he held tenaciously to his original conception of the invention.

Throughout the proceedings in the Patent Office and the courts Goodwin and his representatives have consistently asserted the proposition that he was the first to produce a pellicle by the above named process. Others may improve the process and may, perhaps, hold their improvements, if patented, against the owners of the Goodwin patent, but this does not give them the right to appropriate the basic invention. We are unable to find any proof in the record to support the contention that his process was known by others prior to the date of his application. On the contrary, the necessity for the patented pellicle became more and more apparent and the demand for it more and more insistent and many efforts were made to meet the demand, but with partial success only.

In 1887 an article appeared in the Photographic Times Almanac in which a well known authority on photographic subjects, Andrew Pringle, points out the pressing needs of the art in language which is prophetic of the Goodwin invention. He says:

> "When we get a support such as I have indicated, transparent, flexible, and in lengths, tourist photography will make a stride that will throw into obscurity all previous advances."

And yet at the time this article was published, there was in the Patent Office an application showing that this stride had actually been taken.

In an affidavit made by Mr. Eastman in 1890, after describing his efforts to produce a satisfactory film, he says:

> "From 1884 until the year 1888 I was constantly on the lookout for a fluid pyroxyline compound which would be suitable for the purpose of making such films."

It is unnecessary to advert to the other evidence in the record showing priority of invention in Goodwin. In ad-

1  dition to the presumption arising from the patent itself,
we have his clear description of the process which any in-
telligent chemist would understand and which, if followed,
must produce the desired film. Stripped of the unnecessary technical verbiage, which was largely produced by the
proceedings in the Patent Office, Goodwin's statement is so
plain that it would seem that a neophyte might follow the
instructions successfully.

We cannot resist the conclusion that Goodwin's application, as filed in 1887, disclosed for the first time the
fundamental and essential features of a successful, rollable
2  film and that, unless constrained by some controlling consideration to do otherwise, the effort of the court should
be to uphold the patent. The burden is on the defendants
to prove its invalidity. The presumptions are all in its
favor. Nothing in the prior art shows Goodwin's process
and the proposition that any skilled chemist, familiar with
the art as it existed prior to May 2, 1887, could construct
the Goodwin pellicle cannot be maintained. We do not
understand that the defendant now asserts that anyone
prior to Goodwin had produced a successful film roll sys-
3  tem. The defendant's brief says:

> "The Eastman Company, in 1888, devised and
> introduced its first 'Kodak' camera. * * * This
> 1888 Kodak * * * marked the beginning of
> amateur photography,"

but it is not pretended that a film other than one having
a paper support coated with sensitized gelatin, was used
prior to Goodwin's invention or, indeed, prior to May 2,
1887. The proposition that these paper films were used
4  because they were inexpensive and thus available for trying out the film roll system is not persuasive.

The Eastman Company did not commence its experiments looking to the substitution of pyroxyline for paper
as a film support until the latter part of 1888. These experiments were continued by Henry M. Reichenbach, the
company's chemist, until February, 1889, and on April 9,
1889, he filed his application for a patent as assignor to the
Eastman Dry Plate and Film Company and promptly received a patent dated December 10, 1889. During

all this period beginning with the experiments and
ending with the patent, Goodwin's application was
lying in the Patent Office. We are unable to see how
the Reichenbach patent anticipates or limits the claims of
the Goodwin patent. It may be that his process was an
improvement on Goodwin and that during the life of his
patent he was entitled to the exclusive use of such improvement, but it can have no retroactive effect, it cannot
destroy or limit an invention which was *in esse* before his
invention was conceived. The defendant's brief, after allud-
ing to the extensive manufacture of the Reichenbach film
since 1889, continues as follows: "This is the industry which
is enjoined by the decree of the court below—7 years after
the expiration of the Reichenbach patent 417202,—24 years
after the Eastman Company began the manufacture of
nitrocellulose film—and 26 years after the filing of the application on which the Goodwin patent issued. And this industry is enjoined on a patent the application for which
was uniformly rejected by the five different Examiners who
successively had it in charge during its eleven years' pendency in the Patent Office." Truly an extraordinary and
deplorable condition of affairs! But who was to blame for
it—Goodwin or the five examiners who improperly deprived
him of his rights during these eleven years? We are unable
to see what he could have done to enforce his rights during
this period or how any blame can attach to him for his
inaction.

We have examined the printed articles published, respectively, as follows: David in 1881, 1882 and 1883; Les
Mondes, 1883; Moniteur, 1885; British Journal of Photography, 1885; Year Book, 1869; Photographic News, 1881,
and the prior patents to Journond, 1885-6; Parkes, 1855-
6-65; Berard, 1857; Ollion, 1859-60, and do not find anticipation, even if these publications are considered in the
aggregate. No pellicle possessing the Goodwin characteristics, made prior to the patent, is produced and yet we are
asked to conclude that one could be produced by following
the directions contained in these articles. The defendant
must prove anticipation beyond a reasonable doubt and it
has not done so. The best references are undoubtedly the
Parkes patents and the disclosures of David to the French
Photographic Society. Parkes, in his 1855 patent, was not

1  concerned with photographic pellicles or the process of producing the same, but with making a substitute for india
rubber and gutta percha consisting of a waterproof coating
for fabrics which may also be used for book bindings, but-
ton making and similar purposes and may be pressed or
rolled into different forms or thin sheets. In 1856 he was
dealing with the substitution of collodion for glass as a
support for the prepared film in taking photographs. He
says, "or a thick layer of collodion may be first formed
on the glass, and on this layer the film of prepared collodion
may be produced, and the picture taken thereon and suit-
2  ably varnished or protected, afterwards the whole may be
stripped from the glass together."

The 1865 patent has to do with the manufacture of
"Parkesine," a product undoubtedly named in honor of the
inventor, and his claim is "the employment of nitrobenzole,
aniline and glacial acetic acid or either of them for dissolving pyroxyline in the manufacture of Parkesine and similar compounds of pyroxyline." He also claims the above
ingredients in the manufacture of collodion.

David's contribution to the art is found in photographic
3  journals which purport to give his remarks in explaining
experiments made by him. These were tentative efforts on
his part which he hoped might culminate in something
practical, but they never did. The various articles contain
expressions like the following: "He believes that this substance is sufficiently transparent and flexible to form good
material for photographic plates, provided it can be cut
sufficiently thin. His various attempts to cut it have not
been successful. I think they will have to render them
less inflammable, for if only a spark falls on one of these
leaves it is sufficient to produce rapid combustion. Mr.
4  David presents films produced with celluloid which probably might serve as a support for the sensitized prepara-
tions. He says *probably*, because he has not yet been able
to make the experiment. But we believe that the difficulty
of manipulation and the high price of liquid celluloid
would prevent this process from entering practical realms.
One of our members has tried this process, but has not
obtained good results in proceeding by successive coatings."

All this uncertainty and doubt is far from the clear and
explicit statement required to anticipate a patent. There
is no evidence that anyone ever did make the Goodwin pelli-

cle prior to his invention and we are convinced that no one could have made it by following the direction of Parkes or David.

It is unnecessary to consider the question of invention, in all the details pointed out in the defendant's briefs, for the reason that we are convinced that Goodwin was the first to dissolve nitrocellulose in nitrobenzole or its equivalents diluted in alcohol or its equivalents. This being so, his patent is entitled to a construction broad enough to enable its owner to reap the profits which naturally and fairly belong to the invention. The invention is one of more than ordinary merit and the claims should not be so construed that anyone may safely infringe who has wit enough to substitute equivalents for the elements named in the patent and to add or subtract therefrom, so long as the menstruum contains a hygroscopic and a non-hygroscopic element, the latter being a solvent of nitrocellulose and of slower volatility than the former. If the defendant uses a process having these elements, it matters not what else it uses or that its method is an improvement on the patented method.

Reverting to the first claim heretofore considered, there can be no doubt that the defendant's process employs all the elements there enumerated. The defendant contends that it does not employ the first element, as there stated, for the reason that in its process "the nitrocellulose is dissolved in a low boiling point, rapidly-evaporating, hygroscopic and miscible—with water-solvent, wood alcohol and acetone  *  *  *  and in the use of this solution with the other ingredients heretofore referred to (fusel oil and camphor) the defendant cannot operate 'under ordinary atmospheric conditions,' i. e., heat, during the spreading and drying of the nitrocellulose solution in order to secure the 'desired film.' "

Goodwin being the first to make the patented pellicle, is entitled to a fair range of equivalents, whether he claims them or not. His specification was addressed to chemists, not lawyers, and he was justified in assuming that a chemist would understand when he said in his original application that he used nitrobenzole or other solvent, that he meant other similar or equivalent solvent, one which would accomplish the same result in the same manner. A chemist knowing the ob-

1    ject to be attained, would hardly have selected a solvent which
could not accomplish that object. Knowing the properties of
nitrobenzole, he naturally would seek an equivalent having
similar properties and not one having properties which
would defeat the object in view. Later on, in response to a
demand from the Patent Office, Goodwin removed all doubt
by actually stating what we think the law implied, that
he used "Nitrobenzole or other non-hydrous and non-hygroscopic solvents such as may be employed in producing celluloid, as distinguished from collodion." This amendment was
within his rights;

2

Hobbs *v.* Beach, 180 U. S., 383;
Cleveland Foundry Co. *v.* Detroit Stove Works,
131 Fed. Rep., 853.

But without the amendment we can hardly imagine a
chemist stupid enough to select the "other solvent" from those
solvents which he must know would not do the work.

Goodwin says in the specification, "In carrying out the
invention I provide a suitable surface, such as that of glass,
3    and flow over the same a solution of nitrocellulose (by
which I do not mean a solution of the compound known as
'commercial celluloid' dissolved in alcohol or ether) dissolved in nitrobenzole", etc. The defendant now argues that
as commercial celluloid contains camphor this language
amounts to a disclaimer of camphor and that one who uses
camphor in any amount, however small, avoids infringement.
We think this contention is hypercritical and one which must
be rejected by any fair and reasonable construction of the
patent. Manifestly the patentee had in mind the amount of
camphor used in commercial celluloid, which is said to be
4    from 40 to 60 per cent. If he intended by the language to
disclaim anything, it was such excessive use which, the proof
shows, could not be successfully used to produce the result
he had in view. He was endeavoring to distinguish his solution of nitrocellulose from the solution used in celluloid. In
other words, he told the art that a solution containing from
40 to 60 per cent. of camphor would not do, but he never said
that 13 or 14 per cent. of camphor would not do. Surely
he did not intend to say that one who used his formula could

avoid infringement by using other ingredients which did not [1]
affect the ultimate result.

We do not deem it necessary to enter upon a discussion of
the Reichenbach interference further than to say that this, as
well as most of the complications in the case, would have been
avoided had the Goodwin patent gone to issue in due course,
as it should have done. The long delay and the contradictory
rulings of the Patent Office would have discouraged an inventor who had not supreme faith in the justice of his cause.
If we are right in thinking that Goodwin made a generic invention it follows that he is entitled to hold as infringers [2]
those who use the equivalents of nitrobenzole and alcohol.
In the process of the patent, and of the defendant, nitrocellulose is used. In both it is dissolved in a menstruum
containing a high boiling, non-hydrous, non-hydroscopic solvent like nitrobenzole or its equivalents and a diluent like
alcohol or its equivalents. In both the processes of the defendant nitrocellulose is dissolved in a menstruum consisting
of a high-boiling, non-hydrous, non-hygroscopic solvent and
a diluent of wood alcohol. In the process of 1898 the solvent
was amyl-acetate 5 parts, fusel oil about 16 parts and camphor 3 to 5 parts. The diluent was wood alcohol 104 parts. [3]
In the 1902 process the solvent was fusel oil 16 parts and
camphor 3 parts. The diluent was wood alcohol 40 parts
and acetone 40 parts. There can be no doubt that the defendant uses nitrocellulose and the diluent of the patent, viz.,
alcohol—wood alcohol being expressly referred to in the patent as an example of a diluent having a low boiling point and
a relatively quick evaporating quality. The only debatable
question relates to the equivalency of the defendant's solvent and we cannot doubt that the combination of fusel oil,
camphor and amyl-acetate of 1898 process and the fusel oil
and camphor of the 1902 process are equivalents of the high [4]
boiling, non-hydrous, non-hygroscopic solvent of the patent.
It matters not that the defendant's process produces better
results than that of the patent. Assuming this to be true, it
does not give the defendant the right to use Goodwin's discovery because it has introduced improvements. It would
be strange, indeed, if during the fifteen years which elapsed
from the date of the Goodwin application to the adoption of
the 1902 process there had been no progress in the art. Undoubtedly there was progress, but as we have had occasion to

1  point out before, one cannot use a patented invention because
he has improved it.

The other questions discussed are carefully considered
by Judge Hazel and we see no reason to add to his opinion in
this regard.

Our conclusion may be briefly stated—Believing, as we
do, that Goodwin was the first to produce a transparent sensitive pellicle for use in roller cameras, the conclusion naturally follows that his patent is entitled to a liberal construction. Doubts should be resolved in its favor and care taken
not to confuse the art at the date of issue with the art
2  as it existed at the date of the application, eleven years before. So considered and construed, we think the claims
in controversy valid and infringed.

We fully realize the incongruity of submitting a complicated question of chemistry to a tribunal composed of lawyers, even though assisted by such eminent chemists as Dr.
Chandler and Professor Main, who have made comprehens-
ible the salient features of an unusually complex and difficult
controversy.

It is said that a motion is pending in the District Court
3  for an order extending the time during which the complainant
may recover profits and damages to the date of the Goodwin
patent. This motion was postponed by stipulation until
after the decision of this court and we are asked to make this
affirmance "subject to the motion and stipulation referred
to." We do not see that any action by this court is necessary as the District Court will have full jurisdiction in the
premises.

The other assignments of error are sufficiently discussed
in Judge Hazel's opinion and we see no necessity for adding
to what is there so clearly stated.

4      The decree is affirmed.

———

Mr. GROSVENOR: I also introduce this as part
of the cross examination of this witness to go with
the diagrams introduced, and particularly with the
testimony given by him on cross examination relating
to those diagrams and the use of the term "Edison
film."

Mr. KINGSLEY: Objected to as incompetent, immaterial and irrelevant.

Mr. GROSVENOR: Do you make any objection for the reason that it is not certified?

Mr. KINGSLEY: No. I also object on the further ground that the cross examination has had no relevancy to the issues in this case, and has been founded upon an absolute misconception thereof on the part of the attorney representing the Petitioner.

Mr. GROSVENOR: I introduce that exhibit to show that the statements and the labels on the diagrams entitled "Edison film" are misleading, and this is introduced in part as an impeachment of the testimony and of the exhibits on that point.

Redirect examination by Mr. CHURCH:

Q. You have described the essential characteristics of a motion picture film, and you have also described the essential characteristics of a motion picture camera for producing such a film. The conception of which of these things, the film or the camera, in your judgment, preceded the other? A. If I am permitted to give an explanation of my opinion on that point, I should state that unquestionably the conception of the motion picture strip or film must have preceded the conception of the motion picture camera, and when I say must have preceded, I use the word with reference to any reasonable line of logical thought. For example, if I have before me as an inventor, the problem of obtaining a quick and convenient means of fire, I might conceive an elongated, tough, non-flexible structure having upon one end thereof an inflammable substance of such a nature as to be capable of cooperating with some other inflammable substance, so that when the two were brought together, a flame would result. That might take the form of a match. I should conceive, under those conditions, that I had invented a match, if no one had ever used a match before I did, although I did not invent the wood, nor did I give it any of those physical characteristics which it possesses, and although I did not invent the sulphur. If I was the first to put the sulphur on the end of the match and combine the two with other chemicals in such a way as to produce an effective, useful, operative thing which had not previously existed, I should think

1   that I had created that, but now would come the problem
of manufacture. How was I going to get matches enough
to be of any use? Obviously I could not whittle them out by
hand, and so I would have to go to work if I wished to make
my invention of any use, and invent a machine that would
make the match. Now, how could I think of inventing a
machine to make a match before I had the picture of the
match before me in my mind as something to be made? And
therefore I say that the conception of the film must have
preceded the conception of the machine to be used in making
the film.

2

Recross examination by Mr. GROSVENOR:

Q. What do you mean by "conception of the film"? A.
The invention of the film.

Q. By that you mean, then, that it was necessary for someone to invent the film before anyone could conceive the idea
of using the film? A. No, I did not say that a person must
invent the film before they conceived the idea of using a
film. I think the conception of use must come first. People
engaged in invention, particularly inventors of experience,

3   endeavor to supply by inventions, demands which they know
to exist.

Redirect examination by Mr. CHURCH:

Q. Then are we to understand that your idea is that the
conception of a motion picture film having the characteristics
of those already described by you, must have preceded the
conception of a machine for producing such a motion picture
film? A. Unquestionably the conception of the film in this
exact form that it was desired to have it, must have preceded

4   the invention of a machine to produce such a film.

Recross examination by Mr. GROSVENOR:

Q. But the conception of that film was not Edison's, was
it? A. I always supposed it was, Mr. Grosvenor. You state
that it was not, but I supposed that it was.

Q. In using the word "conception" you mean invention?
A. Yes.

Mr. GROSVENOR: I introduce as part of the cross ex-

amination, and for the purpose of discrediting the
witness' testimony on this point, and also these
diagrams and the use of the term "Edison film"
thereon, the question and answer of Mr. Edison in
the case of Thomas A. Edison *v.* American Mutoscope
Company, being the suit on the original Patent No.
589,168, a certain part of the record purporting to
be a part of the cross examination of Thomas A. Edison, a witness in that suit, appearing at pages 119
and 120, as follows:

"Q176. You did not regard the film, then, as a
thing of your invention?  A. No, I did not regard the
film as a part of my invention; no, sir.  I looked to
the people who made it for that."

Mr. KINGSLEY:  This record, Vol. I, at page 179,
contains a further colloquy in the opinion of the
Court of Appeals of the District of Columbia, dated
December 2nd, 1912, and I call attention to the fact
that the cross examination which petitioner's counsel wishes now to insert to the extent of two para-
graphs, is set out at greater length at page 179,
Volume I, of this record, in the opinion quoted, at
pages 175 to 183 inclusive.

Mr. GROSVENOR:  I ask to have copied at this
point, for convenience in examining the testimony of
the witness, Petitioner's Exhibit No. 54, Volume 1,
page 131.

Mr. KINGSLEY:  I object to encumbering the record
any further by repetition of exhibits already in, already printed.

Mr. GROSVENOR:  I also ask to have copied here
Petitioner's Exhibit No. 55, Volume 1, page 132.

Mr. KINGSLEY:  I object to it as surplusage, unnecessary labor and unnecessary repetition, the exhibits being already in evidence, and being set out
*in extenso* in Volume 1, and I ask that the Petitioner
refer to the exhibit by page number in the record already established.

At the request of counsel for the Petitioner, Petitioner's Exhibits Nos. 54 and 55 are reprinted at this
point, as follows:

1    **Petitioner's Exhibit No. 54.**

THE POSITION OF THE AMERICAN MUTOSCOPE
AND BIOGRAPH COMPANY.

"WE were urged to join the Edison-Pathe combination,
but we refused.

The Court of Appeals has twice repudiated the claims of
Edison that he is the creator of the moving picture art, and
has limited his patent to his own particular form of apparatus. The same court has also decided that our apparatus
2  does not infringe the Edison patent.

We stand absolutely independent and protected by our
own patents.

We have largely increased our capacity and are prepared
to regularly supply our own films and the films of the best
foreign manufacturers in any quantity.

We will, at our own expense, protect our customers from
any form of patent persecution in connection with film supplied by us.

Edison cannot obtain an injunction against any renter
or exhibitor for the reason that his film patent has not been
3  adjudicated and a decision cannot be obtained in less than
two years."

H. N. Marvin,
J. J. Kennedy."

—————

**Petitioner's Exhibit No. 55.**

BIOGRAPH COMPANY DEFINE THEIR POSITION.

4    In the year 1898 an action for infringement was brought
against the American Mutoscope and Biograph Company,
which had been for about three years in the business of manufacturing moving picture films, by Thomas A. Edison, under
a patent to the latter, No. 589168, dated August 21, 1907.
This patent contained four claims for a camera for taking
pictures of objects in motion and two claims for a moving
picture film.

The Court of Appeals for the Second Circuit decided
this suit in favor of the defendant, the American Mutoscope
and Biograph Company, on all points, finding Edison's

claims both for the camera and for the film to be void. Among other significant expressions in the opinion of the Court reported in Vol. 114 of the Federal Reporter, page 926, occur the following:

> "The photographic reproduction of moving objects, the production from the negatives of a series of pictures representing the successive stages of motion, and the presentation of them by an exhibiting apparatus to the eye of the spectator in such rapid sequence as to blend them together and give the effect of a single picture in which the objects are moving, had been accomplished long before Mr. Edison entered the field.
>
> It is obvious that Mr. Edison was not a pioneer, in the large sense of the term, or in the more limited sense in which he would have been if he had also invented the film. He was not the inventor of the film. He was not the first inventor of apparatus capable of producing suitable negatives, taken from practically a single point of view, in single line sequence, upon a film like this."

After the first failure Mr. Edison surrendered his patent and it was later reissued in two divisions. In reissue No. 12,037, dated September 30, 1902, he obtained four claims of limited scope based on the camera shown in the original patent. In reissue No. 12,038, of the same date, he secured two limited claims to a film. Both of these reissued patents were put in suit against the American Mutoscope and Biograph Company in the latter part of the year 1902.

In the suit under the reissued patent for the film, the defendant filed a demurrer which resulted in the withdrawal of the action by Mr. Edison. No further suit has been brought against the American Mutoscope and Biograph Company under any patent for a film and no such suit has been pressed, so far as we are aware, against any other person or corporation during the past five years.

The suit under the reissue for the camera, was carried through both the Circuit Court for the Southern District of New York, where the bill was ordered dismissed, and through the Court of Appeals for the Second Circuit,

1   which, on the main contention, sustained the finding of the Court below.

The American Mutoscope and Biograph Company at the time when the second action was brought against it, was using two forms of camera, one known as the Biograph camera, which it brought out in 1896 and for which it had obtained the controlling patents of unquestionable validity; and a foreign camera known as the Warwick camera, of which it had purchased a small number for special uses. The Court of Appeals held that the Biograph camera was not covered by the claims of the Edison patent and was not

2   an infrngement of that patent. The use of the Warwick camera was enjoined, but this caused no interruption whatever in the defendant's business operations, and for over a year the American Mutoscope and Biograph Company has manufactured many hundreds of thousands of feet of moving picture film with its Biograph camera.

The Court of Appeals in the second action found claim 4 of the Edison reissued patent for the camera, to be void, and in its opinion, which is reported in Volume 151 of the Federal Reporter, page 767, the Court says:

3

> "Upon the appeal in the first suit we discussed the prior art and the general character of the device sought to be patented at very great length. It is unnecessary to repeat that discussion. All that was said in the prior opinion, however, may be considered as embodied herein, since the conclusion hereinafter expressed is founded upon the findings then made, and which nothing in the present record or argument induces us to qualify in any manner. We held that Edison was not a pioneer in the large sense of the term, or in the limited sense in which

4

> he would have been if he had invented the film. He was not the inventor of the film. He was not the first inventor of apparatus capable of producing suitable negatives, taken from practically a single point of view, in single line sequence upon a film like his."

From the above it will be seen that none of the three suits brought by Edison against this company has been decided in Edison's favor, but on the contrary, that all three suits were decided adversely to Edison with the single exception that in the last action the Court found that three of the four claims of the Edison reissue were valid if limited to the special form of camera shown and described in his patent.

The camera of the Edison patent in question, is not, however, capable of producing long lengths of picture film, and has not been used by the Edison Manufacturing Company for a number of years, if ever, for the commercial manufacture of standard films. On the contrary, not only the Edison Company, but others engaged in the manufacture of such films have been compelled to adopt the camera of the Latham Patent No. 707,934, dated April 26, 1902.

The American Mutoscope and Biograph Company owns the Latham Patent and has a suit pending against the Edison Company for infringing it.

AMERICAN MUTOSCOPE & BIOGRAPH CO.

By Mr. Grosvenor:

Q. Before giving your testimony on direct examination by Mr. Church relating to these matters, did you refresh your memory by reading those exhibits which I have just introduced? A. I did not.

## Stipulation as to Custody of Defendants' Exhibits Nos. 174 to 183 Inclusive.

It is stipulated that Defendants' Exhibits Nos. 174 to 183 inclusive shall remain in the custody of counsel for the defendants, the same to be accessible to Government counsel if desired, and to be produced by the defendants at final hearing.

Whereupon, at 12.30 o'clock P. M. on this Saturday, the 28th day of March, 1914, the hearings are adjourned until Monday, March 30th, 1914, at 2 o'clock P. M., at Room 159, Hotel Manhattan, New York City.

1

IN THE

# DISTRICT COURT OF THE UNITED STATES

## FOR THE EASTERN DISTRICT OF PENNSYLVANIA.

UNITED STATES OF AMERICA,
Petitioner,

*v.*

2 MOTION PICTURE PATENTS Co. and others,
Defendants.

No. 889.

Sept. Sess., 1912.

NEW YORK CITY, March 30, 1914.

The hearings were resumed, pursuant to adjournment, at Room No. 159, Manhattan Hotel, New York City, on Monday, March 30th, 1914, at 2 o'clock P. M.

3

Present on behalf of the Petitioner, Hon. EDWIN P. GROSVENOR, Special Assistant to the Attorney General.

JOSEPH R. DARLING, Esq., Special Agent.

CHARLES F. KINGSLEY, Esq., GEORGE R. WILLIS, Esq., FRED R. WILLIAMS, Esq., and MELVILLE CHURCH, Esq., appearing for Motion Picture Patents Company, Biograph Company, Jeremiah J. Kennedy, Harry N. Marvin, Armat Moving Picture Company, Melies Manufacturing Co. and Gaston Melies.

4

J. H. CALDWELL, Esq., and H. K. STOCKTON, Esq., appearing for William Pelzer, General Film Company, Thomas A. Edison, Inc., Kalem Company, Inc., Pathe Freres, Frank L. Dyer, Samuel Long and J. A. Berst.

HENRY MELVILLE, Esq., attorney for George Kleine, Essanay Film Manufacturing Company, Selig Polyscope, George K. Spoor and W. N. Selig.

JAMES J. ALLEN, Esq., appearing for Vitagraph Company of America, and Albert E. Smith.

Thereupon HARRY N. MARVIN resumed the stand.  1

    Mr. GROSVENOR: No further cross examination of this witness.

Redirect examination by Mr. KINGSLEY:

    Q. Have you had occasion to notice within recent months whether or not any of the newspapers in the City of New York are giving special attention to motion picture dramas? A. I have noticed from time to time that the daily papers issued in New York have given an increasing  2 amount of space to accounts and references to motion picture dramas.

    Q. Has it come to your attention that the Evening Sun in connection with the Vitagraph Company of America, is offering prizes for moving picture scenarios? A. I have read articles concerning those prizes offered by the Evening Sun, from day to day.

    Q. I show you page 4 of to-day's Evening Sun, and ask you if that is typical of the publications which the Evening Sun has been making with respect to motion picture dramas and motion picture scenarios, within the past few months?  3 A. It is.

    Mr. KINGSLEY: I offer it in evidence.

    Mr. GROSVENOR: I enter an objection, on the ground that it is immaterial and irrelevant.

    The paper offered is received in evidence and is marked "Defendants' Exhibit No. 184," and is as follows:

4

1      **Defendants' Exhibit No. 184.**

(The Evening Sun.)

## "MOVIE" SCENARIO HELPS
## SEEKERS OF $1,000 PRIZE

---

### Publication of First Instalment Leads to Renewed Flood of Plays in the "Evening Sun" Contest.

2

---

Publication Saturday of the first section of the model Vitagraph scenario appears to have satisfied scores of intending competitors for THE EVENING SUN-Vitagraph $1,000 prize contest that their scenarios were in proper form, for to-day's mails brought in the greatest flood of manuscripts yet seen. Seemingly these ready ones were waiting only for a sight of the prepared scenario to make certain that the plays they had written out were in as good shape 3 as they could be put in.

The scenario that made such a hit is here continued to-day:

### THE BUTLER'S SECRET.

By Marguerite Bertsch.

SCENE 6.

*Entrance hall, Dixon home. Night.*

Wallace giving the impression that he has fallen while running through portieres, is picking himself up rather 4 frightened, just as his father dashes into scene from between portieres and seizes him, jerking him to his feet. Father and son face each other. Father horrified, "You!" Son uneasy. Father denounces son. Son, slightly intoxicated, begins to grasp the charge. Cut in:

. . . . . . . . . . . . . . . . . . . . . . . . . . . . . . . . . . . . . . . . . . . .

"WHY FATHER, I JUST THIS MINUTE CAME    :
:    HOME!"

Son denying charge, gives cut in.  Grows hot.  Argu- 1
ment between father and son.  Wallace sent from home,
never to return.  Enter the butler in violent emotion,
which he controls with effort, as Wallace walks from scene.
The butler seems torn between the desire to speak and
recall him and some other motive.  Dixon falls back against
portiere, clinging to it, heartbroken.

Dissolve back to:

### SCENE 7.

#### *Living room as in 3.*

Dixon still seated by fire dreaming, thinking.  He rises  2
with a sigh.  Butler enters.  Asks if there is anything he
can do for him.  Dixon sadly registers cut in:

"I CAN THINK OF NOTHING BUT THE NIGHT
THAT MY OWN SON TRIED TO ROB ME!"

Butler deeply moved.  Dixon registers he will need
nothing else, exits to retire for the night.  Butler looks  3
after him, then tenderly takes from his pocket a letter
which has brought him great joy, which he means to read
again.  Screen:

DEAR DAD:  I'VE BEEN ON THE LEVEL SINCE
THAT NIGHT, AM WORKING FOR A CARPENTER.
WHAT DO YOU THINK OF MY NEW PICTURE?

Barrow, deeply pleased by the letter, turns to look at  4
the photo.

Screen photo of Barrow's son, in overalls, with tools.
Other carpenters in background against shop, smiling at
him for having his picture taken.  Barrow gazing at picture.  Cut to:

1
### SCENE 8.

*Dixon's bedroom, same as 4.*

Dixon retiring for the night.  Cut to:

### SCENE 9.

. . . . . . . . . . . . . . . . . . . . . . . . . . . . . . . . . . . . . . . . . . . . . . . . . . .

DRIVEN HOME BY WANT.

. . . . . . . . . . . . . . . . . . . . . . . . . . . . . . . . . . . . . . . . . . . . . . . . . .

2  *Exterior Dixon home, showing light streaming from living room window out onto terrace.*

Wallace, shabby, haggard, half starved, returning home. Creeps along the wall as though trying to find some one without being seen.  Slips up to window, peeps in.  Sees the butler within, who is still gazing at the picture.  This is the man he is looking for.  Wants to signal to him by tapping on the window.  Hesitates, and then, desperate, does so cautiously.  Cut to:

### SCENE 10.

3
*Living room, same as 7.*

Barrow has heard tap on the window.  Slips picture and letter into pocket.  Listens again.  Goes to window, pulling aside the curtains.  Starts back, suprised at seeing Wallace.  Signals to him to go around to door, and he will let him in.  Exits quickly and softly to admit Wallace.

### SCENE 11.

*Entrance hall, Dixon home, showing view of front door.*

4      Barrow hurries into scene.  Looks about cautiously, then opens door, softly admitting Wallace.  Seems deeply concerned by the boy's forlorn appearance.  Wallace seizes Barrow's arm, looking at him earnestly.  Exacts a promise that he will keep his visit a secret from his father.  Barrow assures him he will not tell.  Wallace staggers back against wall, faint and hungry.  Butler realizes all at once the boy's desperate plight.  Registers he will get something to eat.  Tells him to follow.  Butler preceding to see that the coast is clear, they exit to kitchen.

To Be Continued To-morrow.

# DETAILS OF THE $1,000
## PHOTO PLAY CONTEST

1

THE EVENING SUN, in cooperation with the Vitagraph Company, offers:

$1,000 for the best Photo Play, whether Drama, Comedy or Melodrama, submitted under the conditions following:

$250 for the Second Best Photo Play so submitted.

$100 for the Third Best Photo Play so submitted.

In addition the Prize Plays will be produced by the Vitagraph Company in its best style and widely advertised as Prize Photo Plays. The names of the authors will appear on the films, and they will receive all due publicity. The prize winners, if suitable, will be produced at the Vitagraph Theatre, New York. The Vitagraph Company will also purchase, at its usual liberal rates, such others of the plays submitted as it can use, and reserves the right to so purchase any manuscript submitted provided the price offered is acceptable to the author.

2

THE EVENING SUN reserves the right to publish in fiction form the stories of the prize winning plays.

3

All plays must be capable of being made in America, must be from one to six reels in length and must be in THE EVENING SUN office at noon May 1. Contestants may send any number of plays, but only one prize will be awarded to any one person. Employees of THE EVENING SUN, THE SUN and the Vitagraph Company are barred. Only original work will be considered. Dramatizations of printed works are barred.

The prizes will be awarded by May 15, if possible, and awards will be made according to the best judgment of the five judges, who will be John Bunny and Maurice Costello of the Vitagraph Company, two experienced members of THE EVENING SUN staff and E. M. La Roche, associate editor of the *Motion Picture Story Magazine*. The judges may reject any and all plays. Should all be rejected, the offer will be renewed.

4

The controlling factor in the award will be the novelty, vitality and the acting value of the dramatic or comedy idea submitted.

1 Each scenario must be signed with a nom de plume or cipher and must be accompanied by a *scaled* envelope bearing the nom de plume or cipher and containing the competitor's name and address. Every care will be taken of manuscripts, but no responsibility for them will be accepted. Competitors should keep a carbon copy.

Scenarios *should be* typewritten in standard form with synopsis of 200 words. All that are not typewritten must have synopses.

Address Photo Play Contest, EVENING SUN, New York City.

2

---

## WHAT'S WORTH SEEING

## IN THE MOVIES TO-DAY

---

New releases briefly classified for those who seek good programmes. Plays unsuited to children are so described.

### PLAYS OF DISTINCTION.

3 NEVER AGAIN! (Vitagraph feature farce)—Distinctively Drewish. As some one has said, would make a bankrupt exhibitor laugh. The best farce in the French style in months. Sidney Drew, a staid pater-familias, sneaks off to a tango ball and the girl he takes an interest in is beloved of a fiery chef with a knife. Fine tango and one-step fun mixed in with the ballroom chase gives flavor to the action. S. Rankin Drew as the chef is almost as rich as Sidney Drew in a ballet costume pirouetting home. Sidney Drew's (stage) wife, daughters, sons-in-law, servants and friends get all tangled by the tangoer before the audience is released

4 from the spell of excessive laughter. Clara Young and Cortlandt Van Deusen help in giving color to the work. Anthony E. Wills, author.

IN THE DAYS OF HIS YOUTH (Rex)—Touching all of us. The father of two real boys has been out of touch with them and when a misthrown ball smashes glasses he uses the rod. This and other severities drive one lad to run away. The father, picking up the bats, is moved, first to remember his own boyish misdemeanors, then to forgiveness.

Return and reconciliation follow. Not much of a plot, one might say, yet the sincerity and care with which it is handled and the acting of Phillips Smalley and of the runaway, who is "just boy," make it a play among hundreds. Written by a woman, Lois Weber, it shows great knowledge of "boy."

BARNYARD FLIRTATIONS—Keystone out-Keystoned. To any one who knows this company's wonderful rough and tumble comedy that description will be sufficient. In this Fatty tries to catch two "chickens," one feathered, the other wearing skirts. The censors roared with laughter and audibly wondered how the actors could live through it. A smashing hit.

## PLAYS WELL WORTH SEEING.

THE HEAD WAITER (Frontier)—Restaurant hurly-burly. The restaurant owner's daughter loves Max Ascher, the head waiter, and the owner tries to get rid of him. How the rapid-fire mixup of waiters, food, cooks and patrons is kept going mystifies the layman. It brings roars of laughter.

PUTTING ONE OVER (Edison)—Demure daring by Dolly of the Dailies. Mary Fuller (Dolly) is a real reporter now and she lands a beat for her paper by posing as a reform agent and letting a crooked real estate operator bribe her with a $5,000 check. Here Dolly gets into the real swing of newspaper life and her flight by a fire escape is a foretaste presumably of exciting experiences to come. To a newspaper reviewer the following scenes in a newspaper office brought recollections of days of "big stories" in the office. Acton Davies wrote it.

THE BATTLE OF ELDERBUSH GULCH (Biograph feature)—Human as well as sensational. There really are good Indian war dramas and this is one. Dealing with the old fight about the pioneer's cabin, the massacre and the rescue, it handles them all so artistically as to make it a great film of its class. The incidents of the sacred children, the puppies and the baby they save relieve the tension of the Indian warfare scenes and still make a strong pull on the heartstrings. The child actress is far superior to the leading woman, who couldn't put any expression into her face. The verve with which the cavalry and Indian scenes were handled is beyond praise.

FORGETTING (Imp, to-day's release)—How one reel

can be better than two. Ethel Grandin as a neglected wife who finds herself strongly attracted to another man. She almost forgets her married condition. In time her husband is killed and happiness comes. Poignant in its sympathetic appeals. Finely acted and presented.

THE SURGEON'S EXPERIMENT (Majestic feature) —Educational and dramatic. The great surgeon cures a man of criminal tendencies by an operation. It teaches something while entertaining.

THE SMUGGLERS OF SLIGO (Reliance feature)— Staged with a fine eye to detail, it seems to have been made in Ireland. A well acted drama.

## THE RUN OF THE FILMS.

THE SLIPPERY SPY (Eclair)—Childish imaginings visualized. This starts with a better story than most of the children-as-grown-ups pieces and is fairly amusing.

THE BATTLE OF CHILI AND BEAN (Apollo, to-day's release)—Greaserish. Fred Mace in a burlesque battle that's not very good.

THE TOWN OF NAZARETH (American feature, to-day's release)—A country town story. It is told in slightly crude fashion, but the atmosphere is well preserved.

## "MAKESHIFT" PLAY A SUCCESS.

Failure of the expected Napoleonic film to arrive from Chicago at noon yesterday put the New York Theatre management in difficulties for two hours. In that time lively telegraphing and telephoning enabled it to put on at 2:30 o'clock "One Hundred Days," a splendid motion picture drama of Napoleon's last splurge. It shows in detail the great struggle following the return from Elba and culminating at Waterloo, which is realistically pictured. It follows Napoleon to St. Helena and shows his death in 1821. Enough of the scenes of his earlier life are shown as memories to give spectators a grasp of his full career.

The picture, made in France, is marked by a splendid characterization of Napoleon by an actor who not only resembles the Little Corporal but is able to play the part with power and restraint, and by a superb handling of thousands of troops in march and battle. The director keeps artistic effects prominent, yet the fighting, especially that about the farm house at Waterloo and the last battle of the Old Guard, is realistic. The number of excellent individual performances by soldiers in the ranks is great. The play made so great a hit with the management that an agreement for its retention for a run was made by telephone.

An artistic modern film that followed was "The Floor Above" (R. & M., four reels), from E. Phillips Oppenheim's "Mystery of Charlecot Mansions."

. James Kirkwood has staged with great care this story of the rich amateur detective who moves a slain man from the rooms of his sweetheart's actress sister to those of another tenant above. The completeness with which the difficult action is traced up and down stairs is to be admired as much as the fine acting in a restrained style.

---

By Mr. KINGSLEY:

Q. I show you Defendants' Exhibit No. 184, and call your attention to the fourth column, entitled "What Is Worth Seeing in the Movies To-day," which gives a list of motion picture dramas shown in the various theatres in the City of New York to-day, and which contains the names of the producers. Will you look at that list and tell us what dramas it contains which were produced by the licensed producers, and what dramas it contains which were produced by unlicensed producers? A. This account contains synopses of the following motion picture dramas produced by producers who are licensees of the defendant Motion Picture Patents Company, that is, "Never Again," Vitagraph; "Putting One Over," Edison; "The Battle of Elderbush Gulch," Biograph. It also contains synopses of the following motion picture dramas produced by producers who are not licensees of the defendant Motion Picture Patents Company, that is, "In the Days of His Youth," Rex; "Barnyard Flirtations," Keystone; "The Head Waiter," Frontier; "Forgetting," Imp; "The Surgeon's Experiment," Majestic; "The Smugglers of Sligo," Reliance; "The Slippery Spy," Eclair; "The Battle of Chili and Bean," Apollo; "The Town of Nazareth," American.

Q. Have you observed whether or not the daily news-

1   papers of the City of New York are giving considerable
space to descriptions of moving picture scenarios and
dramas at the present time? A. A number of New York
dailies are giving a very considerable amount of space to
such descriptions.

Recross examination by Mr. GROSVENOR:

Q. Mr. Marvin, this list does not purport to give a list
of all the pictures released today by the licensed producers,
does it? A. I do not know what it purports to give.

2   Q. Whether it purports to give it or not, it does not
give a complete list of the films released by the licensed
producers today, does it? A. It does not appear to give
a complete list of licensed or unlicensed pictures released
today, and the article does not seem to indicate any such
intention, it stating at the head of the article: "New releases briefly classified for those who seek good programs."

Q. Does this list give a list of all the pictures that are
released today by the licensed producers? A. I do not think
so, but I do not know what pictures are released today by
the licensed producers.

3   Q. Is it not the fact that the list includes some pictures
of unlicensed producers, which releases are not released to-
day, but on days following of this week? A. I do not know,
but from reading the accounts here given, I should suppose
that all of these pictures had been released either today or
previous to today.

Q. That list of unlicensed pictures is not a list of today's
releases, is it? A. I don't think so.

4   Mr. KINGSLEY: Counsel for the defendants offer
in evidence certified copies of the following letters patent of the United States, to wit, Edison
Re-Issue Patent No. 12,037, dated September 30th,
1902.

The same is received in evidence and is marked
Defendants' Exhibit 185.

Mr. KINGSLEY: We offer in evidence Edison Re-
Issue Patent No. 13,329, dated December 5th, 1911.

The same is received in evidence and is marked
Defendants' Exhibit 186.

Mr. KINGSLEY: We offer in evidence Edison Re-Issue Patent No. 12,192, dated January 12th, 1904.

The same is received in evidence and is marked Defendants' Exhibit 187.

Mr. KINGSLEY: We offer in evidence Smith Patent No. 673,329, dated April 30th, 1901.

The same is received in evidence and is marked Defendants' Exhibit 188.   ·

Mr. KINGSLEY: We offer in evidence Smith Patent No. 744,251, dated November 17th, 1903.

The same is received in evidence and is marked Defendants' Exhibit 189.

Mr. KINGSLEY: We offer in evidence Smith Patent No. 770,937, dated September 27th, 1904.

The same is received in evidence and is marked Defendants' Exhibit 190.

Mr. KINGSLEY: We offer in evidence Smith Patent No. 771,280, dated October 4th, 1904.

The same is received in evidence and is marked Defendants' Exhibit 191.

Mr. KINGSLEY: We offer in evidence Ellwood Patent No. 785,205, dated March 21st, 1905.

The same is received in evidence and is marked Defendants' Exhibit 192.

Mr. KINGSLEY: We offer in evidence Smith Patent No. 785,237, dated March 21st, 1905.

The same is received in evidence and is marked Defendants' Exhibit 193.

Mr. KINGSLEY: We offer in evidence Armat Patent No. 578,185, dated March 2nd, 1897.

The same is received in evidence and is marked Defendants' Exhibit 194.

Mr. KINGSLEY: We offer in evidence Armat Patent No. 580,749, dated April 13th, 1897.

The same is received in evidence and is marked Defendants' Exhibit 195.

Mr. KINGSLEY: We offer in evidence Jenkins & Armat Patent No. 586,953, dated July 20th, 1897.

The same is received in evidence and is marked Defendants' Exhibit 196.

Mr. KINGSLEY: We offer in evidence Steward & Frost Patent No. 588,916, dated August 24th, 1897.

1    The same is received in evidence and is marked Defendants' Exhibit 197.

Mr. KINGSLEY: We offer in evidence Casler Patent No. 629,063, dated July 18th, 1889.

The same is received in evidence and is marked Defendants' Exhibit 198.

Mr. KINGSLEY: We offer in evidence Armat Patent No. 673,992, dated May 14th, 1901.

The same is received in evidence and is marked Defendants' Exhibit 199.

2    Mr. KINGSLEY: We offer in evidence Latham Patent No. 707,934, dated August 26th, 1902.

The same is received in evidence and is marked Defendants' Exhibit 200.

Mr. KINGSLEY: We offer in evidence Pross Patent No. 722,382, dated March 10th, 1903.

The same is received in evidence and is marked Defendants' Exhibit 201.

## Stipulation as to Letters Patent Defendants' Exhibits 185 to 201 Inclusive.

3    It is stipulated by and between the respective counsel in this case that counsel for the defendants may reproduce uncertified Patent Office copies of the above mentioned letters patent, and bind them up into the record.

Mr. KINGSLEY: The defendants rest.

Whereupon, at 3 o'clock P. M., on this Monday, the thirtieth day of March, 1914, the hearings are adjourned until Monday, April 6th, 1914, for the taking of petitioner's
4    evidence in rebuttal, at a place to be later selected by petitioner's counsel.

No. 12.037.

Reissued Sept. 30, 1902.

T. A. EDISON.
KINETOSCOPE.
(Application filed June 10, 1902.

3 Sheets—Sheet 1.

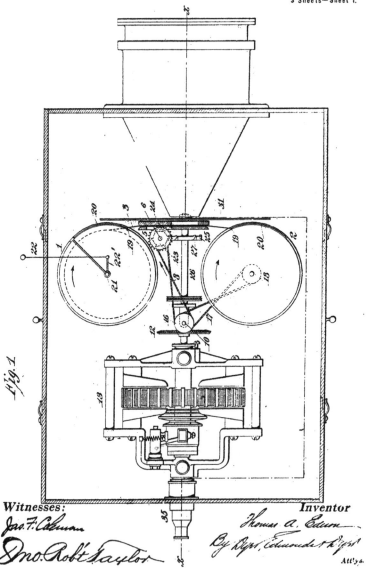

*Fig. 1*

Witnesses:

Jas. F. Coleman

Jno. Robt. Taylor

Inventor

Thomas A. Edison

By Dyer, Edmonds & Dyer
Att'ys.

No. 12,037.

**T. A. EDISON.**
**KINETOSCOPE.**
(Application filed June 10, 1902.)

Reissued Sept. 30, 1902.

3 Sheets—Sheet 2

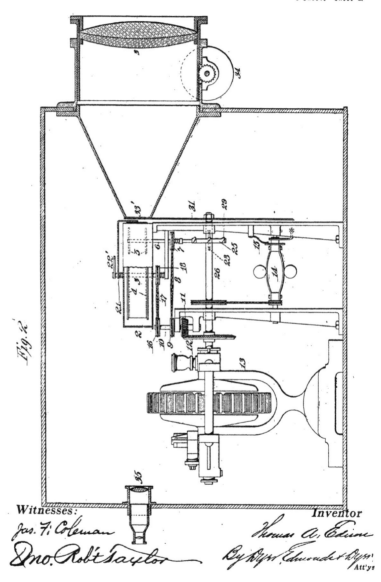

Fig. 2

Witnesses:

Jas. F. Coleman

Jno. Rob't Taylor

Inventor

Thomas A. Edison

By Dyer, Edmonds & Dyer

Att'ys

No. 12,037. Reissued Sept. 30, 1902.

# T. A. EDISON.
## KINETOSCOPE.
(Application filed June 10, 1902.)

3 Sheets—Sheet 3.

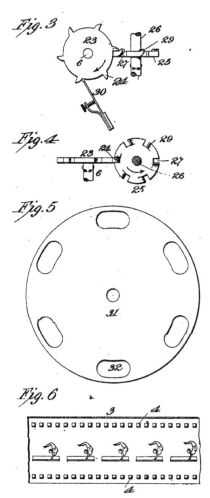

Fig. 3

Fig. 4

Fig. 5

Fig. 6

Witnesses:
Jas. F. Coleman
Jno. Robt Taylor

Inventor
Thomas A. Edison
By Dyer, Edmonds & Dyer Att'ys.

# UNITED STATES PATENT OFFICE.

THOMAS A. EDISON, OF LLEWELLYN PARK, NEW JERSEY.

## KINETOSCOPE.

**SPECIFICATION** forming part of Reissued Letters Patent No. 12,037, dated September 30, 1902.

Original No. 589,168, dated August 31, 1897. Application for reissue filed June 10, 1902. Serial No. 110,987.

### DIVISION A.

### REISSUED

*To all whom it may concern:*

Be it known that I, THOMAS A. EDISON, a citizen of the United States, residing at Llewellyn Park, in the county of Essex and State of New Jersey, have invented a certain new and useful Improvement in Kinetoscopes, (Case No. 928,) of which the following is a specification.

The purpose I have in view is to produce pictures representing objects in motion throughout an extended period of time which may be utilized to exhibit the scene including such moving objects in a perfect and natural manner by means of a suitable exhibiting apparatus, such as that described in an application filed simultaneously herewith, (Patent No. 493,426, dated March 14, 1893.) I have found that it is possible to accomplish this end by means of photography.

In carrying out my invention I employ an apparatus for effecting by photography a representation suitable for reproduction of a scene including a moving object or objects comprising a means, such as a single camera, for intermittently projecting at such rapid rate as to result in persistence of vision images of successive positions of the object or objects in motion as observed from a fixed and single point of view, a sensitized tape-like film, and a means for so moving the film as to cause the successive images to be received thereon separately and in single-line sequence. The movements of the tape-film are intermittent, and it is preferable that the periods of rest of the film should be longer than the periods of movement.

By taking the photographs at a rate sufficiently high as to result in persistence of vision the developed photographs will, when brought successively into view by an exhibiting apparatus, reproduce the movements faithfully and naturally.

I have been able to take with a single camera and a tape-film as many as forty-six photographs per second, each having a size measured lengthwise of the tape of one inch; and I have also been able to hold the tape at rest for nine-tenths of the time; but I do not wish to limit the scope of my invention to this high rate of speed nor to this great dispro-portion between the periods of rest and the periods of motion, since with some subjects a speed as low as thirty pictures per second or even lower is sufficient, and while it is desirable to make the periods of rest as much longer than the periods of motion as possible any excess of the periods of rest over the periods of motion is advantageous.

In the accompanying drawings, forming a part hereof, Figure 1 is a plan view, with the top of the casing removed, of a form of apparatus which I have found highly useful for the taking of the photographs. Fig. 2 is a vertical longitudinal section on line x x in Fig. 1. Figs. 3 and 4 are enlarged views of the stop mechanism of the photographing apparatus. Fig. 5 is a plan view of the shutter for the photographing apparatus, and Fig. 6 is a perspective view of a section of the tape-film with the positive photographs thereon.

Referring to the drawings, 3 indicates the transparent or translucent tape-film, which before the apparatus is put in operation is all coiled on a reel in the sheet-metal box or case 1, the free end being connected to an empty reel in the case 2. The film 3 is preferably of sufficient width to admit the taking of pictures one inch in diameter between the two edges of holes 4, Fig. 2, arranged at regular intervals along the two edges of the film, and into which holes the teeth of the wheels 5, Figs. 1 and 2, enter for the purpose of positively advancing the film. When the film is narrow, it is not essential to use two rows of perforations and two feed-wheels, one feed-wheel being sufficient. Said wheels are mounted on a shaft 6, which carries a loose pulley 7—that is, a pulley frictionally connected to its shaft and forming a yielding mechanical connection. This pulley is driven by a cord or belt 8 from a pulley 9 on the shaft 10, which shaft is driven by means of the beveled gears 11 12. The wheel 12 is preferably driven by an electric motor 13, which when the apparatus is in use is regulated to run at the desired uniform speed, being controlled by the centrifugal governor 14 and the circuit-controller 15 in a well-known manner. On the shaft 10 is another pulley 16, which is connected by a cross-belt

17 to a pulley 18, also frictionally connected to its shaft, and which carries the reel to which the tape is connected in casing 2. The film passes from the casing 1 through a slit formed by the edge 19 and the sliding door 20, which is normally thrown forward by the spring 21, Fig. 2, with sufficient force to clamp the film and hold it from movement. When the door 20 is retracted by pulling on the rod or string 22, which is connected to the arm 22', the film is liberated and allowed to advance. Film-case 2 is provided with a similar door, but the device for moving the door is not illustrated. This arrangement of the sliding door not only holds the film, but it tightly closes the casing, thus excluding light and protecting the sensitive film. The casings or boxes 1 2 are removable, so that they, with the inclosed film, may be taken bodily from the apparatus. The shaft 6, heretofore referred to, is provided with a detent or stop-wheel 23, the form of which is most clearly shown in Figs. 3 and 4. The wheel 23 is provided with a number of projecting teeth 24, six being shown, which teeth are adapted to strike successively against the face of the coöperating detent or stop-wheel 25 on the shaft 26, which is the armature-shaft of the motor or a shaft which is constantly driven by the motor. The wheel 25 has a corresponding number of notches 27 at regular intervals around its periphery. These notches are of such size and shape that the teeth 24 can pass through them, and when the wheels 23 and 25 are rotated in the direction indicated by the arrows each tooth in succession will strike the face of wheel 25, thereby bringing the film absolutely to rest at the same moment that an opening in the shutter exposes the film and will then pass through a notch, allowing the tape-film to be moved forward another step while it is covered by the shutter. To avoid the danger of the wheel 25 moving so quickly that a tooth cannot enter the proper notch, a laterally-projecting tooth 29 is provided adjacent to each notch. When a tooth 29 strikes a tooth 24, the latter tooth will be guided by the tooth 29 into the adjacent notch 27.

30 is a detent spring or pawl to prevent backward movement of the wheel 23.

I prefer to so proportion the parts above described that the wheel 23 is at rest for nine-tenths of the time in order to give to the sensitized film as long an exposure as practicable and is moving forward one-tenth of the time, and said forward movement is made to take place thirty or more times per second, preferably at least as high as forty-six times per second, although the rapidity of movement or number of times per second may be regulated as desired to give satisfactory results. The longer interval of rest of the film insures a good impression of the object projected thereon and results in a picture having clean and sharp lines, since the film has sufficient time to become steady and overcome the vibration caused by the sudden and rapid motions of the feed mechanism. On the shaft 26 or on any suitable shaft driven by the motor is a revolving disk 31, serving as a shutter for alternately exposing and covering the sensitive film. This disk, which is continuously revolving, is provided with six or any other suitable number of apertures 32 at regular intervals around it near the edge, they being so arranged that one of the apertures passes directly between the camera-lens 33 and the film each time the film is brought to rest, the light-rays passing through the opening 33' and falling on the film half-way between the reels on which the film is wound.

34 is a device for adjusting the camera-lens toward or from the film, and 35 is a device by means of which the operator can focus the camera on the object to be photographed.

Although the operation has been partially indicated in the description of the apparatus it will now be set forth more in detail.

The apparatus is first charged with a sensitive tape-film several hundred or even thousands of feet long and the motor is set in operation. Since the spring 21 causes the door 20 to clamp the film, as already described, the loose pulleys 7 18 slip without pulling said film along, but when a moving object—for example, a man gesticulating—is placed in the field of the camera and the handle 22 is pulled the film is released and the pulleys operate to pull the same along. At the same time the reel in case 2 is rotated to wind up the film, thus transferring it from the reel in case 1 to the reel in case 2. This movement is intermittent, the film advancing by very rapid steps, which are definitely and positively controlled by means of the peculiar detent or escapement described, and a photograph is taken after each step.

While I do not care to limit myself to any particular number of steps per second, there should be at least enough so that the eye of an observer cannot distinguish, or at least cannot clearly and positively distinguish, at a glance a difference in the position occupied by the object in the successive pictures, as illustrated in Fig. 7. A less speed in taking the pictures will cause a trembling or jerky appearance in the reproduced picture. When the movement of the object being photographed has ceased or the desired number of photographs has been obtained, the apparatus is stopped. The film is suitably treated for developing and fixing the pictures, when positive prints therefrom, Fig. 6, can be used in an exhibiting apparatus.

What I claim is—

1. An apparatus for taking photographs suitable for the exhibition of objects in motion, having in combination a camera having a single stationary lens; a single sensitized tape-film supported on opposite sides of, and longitudinally movable with respect to, the lens, and having an intermediate section crossing the lens; feeding devices engaging

such intermediate section of the film and moving the same across the lens of the camera at a high rate of speed and with an intermittent motion; and a shutter exposing successive portions of the film during the periods of rest, substantially as set forth.

2. An apparatus for taking photographs suitable for the exhibition of objects in motion, having in combination a camera having a single stationary lens; a single sensitized tape-film supported on opposite sides of, and longitudinally movable with respect to, the lens, and having an intermediate section crossing the lens; a continuously-rotating driving-shaft; feeding devices operated by said shaft engaging such intermediate section of the film and moving the same across the lens of the camera at a high rate of speed and with an intermittent motion; and a continuously-rotating shutter operated by said shaft for exposing successive portions of the film during the periods of rest, substantially as set forth.

3. An apparatus for taking photographs suitable for the exhibition of objects in motion, having in combination a camera having a single stationary lens; a single sensitized tape-film supported on opposite sides of, and longitudinally movable with respect to, the lens, and having an intermediate section crossing the lens; a continuously-rotating driving-shaft; feeding devices operated by said shaft engaging such intermediate section of the film and moving the same across the lens of the camera at a high rate of speed and with an intermittent motion; a shutter exposing successive portions of the film during the periods of rest; and a reel revolved by said shaft with variable speed for winding the film thereon after exposure, substantially as set forth.

4. An apparatus for taking photographs suitable for the exhibition of objects in motion, having in combination a single camera, and means for passing a sensitized tape-film across the lens at a high rate of speed and with an intermittent motion, and for exposing successive portions of the film during the periods of rest, the periods of rest being greater than the periods of motion, substantially as set forth.

This specification signed and witnessed this 17th day of April, 1902.

THOMAS A. EDISON.

Witnesses:
J. F. RANDOLPH,
J. A. BOEHME.

Defendants' Exhibit No. 186

Edison Reissue Patent No. 13,329
December 5, 1911

T. A. EDISON.
KINETOSCOPE.
APPLICATION FILED MAY 24, 1911.

Reissued Dec. 5, 1911.

13,329.
3 SHEETS—SHEET 1.

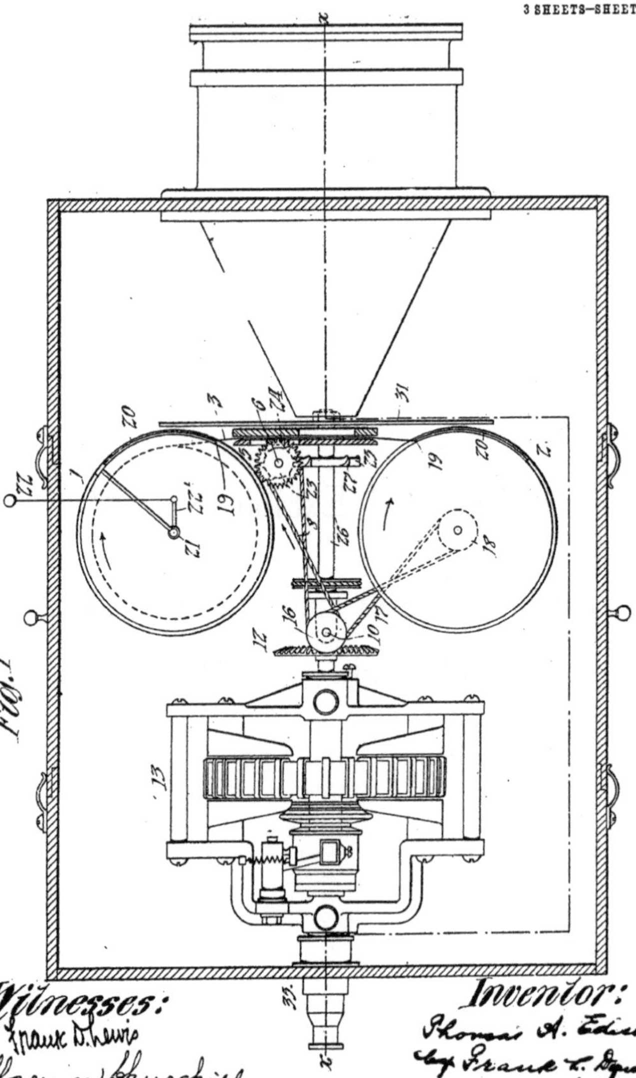

FIG. 1.

Witnesses:
Frank D. Lewis
Clarence Churchill.

Inventor:
Thomas A. Edison
by Frank L. Dyer
his Atty.

# T. A. EDISON.
## KINETOSCOPE.
### APPLICATION FILED MAY 24, 1911.

Reissued Dec. 5, 1911.

# 13,329.
### 3 SHEETS—SHEET 2

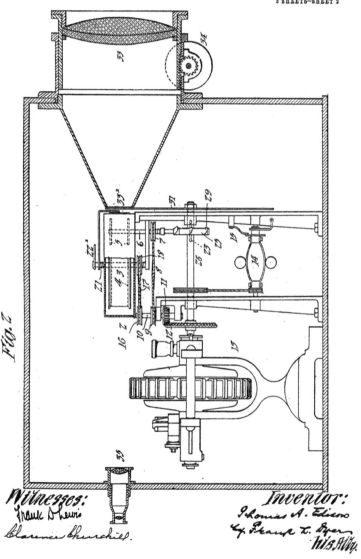

*FIG. 2.*

Witnesses:
Frank D. Lewis
Clarence Churchill.

Inventor:
Thomas A. Edison
by Frank L. Dyer
his Atty.

19

T. A. EDISON.
KINETOSCOPE.
APPLICATION FILED MAY 24, 1911.

Reissued Dec. 5, 1911.

13,329.
3 SHEETS—SHEET 3

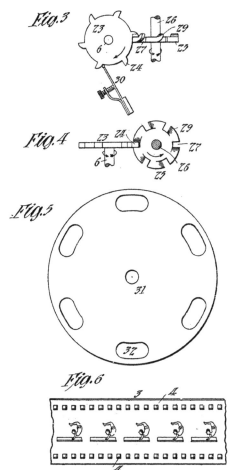

*Fig.3*

*Fig.4*

*Fig.5*

*Fig.6*

Witnesses:
Frank D. Lewis
Clarence Churchill.

Inventor:
Thomas A. Edison
by Frank L. Dyer
his Atty.

# UNITED STATES PATENT OFFICE.

THOMAS A. EDISON, OF LLEWELLYN PARK, NEW JERSEY, ASSIGNOR, BY MESNE AS-
SIGNMENTS, TO MOTION PICTURE PATENTS COMPANY, OF JERSEY CITY, NEW
JERSEY, A CORPORATION OF NEW JERSEY.

## KINETOSCOPE.

**13,329.**     Specification of Reissued Letters Patent.     **Reissued Dec. 5, 1911.**

Original No. 589,168, dated August 31, 1897. Original Reissue No. 12,037, dated September 30, 1902, Serial
No. 110,987. Application for this reissue filed May 24, 1911. Serial No. 629,240.

*To all whom it may concern:*

Be it known that I, THOMAS A. EDISON, a citizen of the United States, residing at Llewellyn Park, in the county of Essex and 5 State of New Jersey, have invented a certain new and useful Improvement in Kinetoscopes, (Case No. 928,) of which the following is a specification.

The purpose I have in view is to produce 10 pictures representing objects in motion throughout an extended period of time which may be utilized to exhibit the scene including such moving objects in a perfect and natural manner by means of a suitable exhibit- 15 ing apparatus, such as that described in an application filed simultaneously herewith, (Patent No. 493,426, dated March 14, 1893.) I have found that it is possible to accomplish this end by means of photography.

20 In carrying out my invention I employ an apparatus for effecting by photography a representation suitable for reproduction of a scene including a moving object or objects comprising a means, such as a single camera, 25 for intermittently projecting at such rapid rate as to result in persistence of vision images of successive positions of the object or objects in motion as observed from a fixed and single point of view, a sensitized tape- 3C like film, and a means for so moving the film as to cause the successive images to be received thereon separately and in single-line sequence. The movements of the tape-film are intermittent, and it is preferable that the 35 periods of rest of the film should be longer than the periods of movement.

By taking the photographs at a rate sufficiently high as to result in persistence of vision the developed photographs will, when 40 brought successively into view by an exhibiting apparatus, reproduce the movements faithfully and naturally.

I have been able to take with a single camera and a tape-film as many as forty-six pho- 45 tographs per second, each having a size measured lengthwise of the tape of one inch, and I have also been able to hold the tape at rest for nine-tenths of the time; but I do not wish to limit the scope of my invention to this 50 high rate of speed nor to this great disproportion between the periods of rest and the periods of motion, since with some subjects a speed as low as thirty pictures per second

or even lower is sufficient, and while it is desirable to make the periods of rest as much 55 longer than the periods of motion as possible any excess of the periods of rest over the periods of motion is advantageous.

In the accompanying drawings, forming a part hereof, Figure 1 is a plan view, with the 60 top of the casing removed, of a form of apparatus which I have found highly useful for the taking of the photographs. Fig. 2 is a vertical longitudinal section on line *x x* in Fig. 1. Figs. 3 and 4 are enlarged views of 65 the stop mechanism of the photographing apparatus. Fig. 5 is a plan view of the shutter for the photographing apparatus, and Fig. 6 is a perspective view of a section of the tape-film with the positive photographs 70 thereon.

Referring to the drawings, 3 indicates the transparent or translucent tape-film, which before the apparatus is put in operation is all coiled on a reel in the sheet-metal box 75 or case 1, the free end being connected to an empty reel in the case 2. The film 3 is preferably of sufficient width to admit the taking of pictures one inch in diameter between the rows of holes 4. Fig. 2, arranged at 80 regular intervals along the two edges of the film, and into which holes the teeth of the wheels 5, Figs. 1 and 2, enter for the purpose of positively advancing the film. When the film is narrow, it is not essential to use 85 two rows of perforations and two feed-wheels, one feed-wheel being sufficient. Said wheels are mounted on a shaft 6, which carries a loose pulley 7—that is, a pulley frictionally connected to its shaft and forming 90 a yielding mechanical connection. This pulley is driven by a cord or belt 8 from a pulley 9 on the shaft 10, which shaft is driven by means of the beveled gears 11 12. The wheel 12 is preferably driven by an electric 85 motor 13, which when the apparatus is in use is regulated to run at the desired uniform speed, being controlled by the centrifugal governor 14 and the circuit-controller 15 in a well-known manner. On the shaft 100 10 is another pulley 16, which is connected by a cross-belt 17 to a pulley 18, also frictionally connected to its shaft, and which carries the reel to which the tape is connected in casing 2. The film passes from 105 the casing 1 through a slit formed by the edge 19 and the sliding door 20, which is normally thrown forward by the spring 21, Fig. 2, with sufficient force to clamp the film and hold it from movement. When the door 20 is retracted by pulling on the rod or string 22, which is connected to the arm 22′, the film is liberated and allowed to advance. Film-case 2 is provided with a similar door, but the device for moving the door is not illustrated. This arrangement of the sliding door not only holds the film, but it tightly closes the casing, thus excluding light and protecting the sensitive film. The casings or boxes 1 2 are removable, so that they, with the inclosed film, may be taken bodily from the apparatus. The shaft 6, heretofore referred to, is provided with a detent or stop-wheel 23, the form of which is most clearly shown in Figs. 3 and 4. The wheel 23 is provided with a number of projecting teeth 24, six being shown, which teeth are adapted to strike successively against the face of the coöperating detent or stop-wheel 25 on the shaft 26, which is the armature-shaft of the motor or a shaft which is constantly driven by the motor. The wheel 25 has a corresponding number of notches 27 at regular intervals around its periphery. These notches are of such size and shape that the teeth 24 can pass through them, and when the wheels 23 and 25 are rotated in the direction indicated by the arrows each tooth in succession will strike the face of wheel 25, thereby bringing the film absolutely to rest at the same moment that an opening in the shutter exposes the film and will then pass through a notch, allowing the tape-film to be moved forward another step while it is covered by the shutter. To avoid the danger of the wheel 25 moving so quickly that a tooth cannot enter the proper notch, a laterally-projecting tooth 29 is provided adjacent to each notch. When a tooth 29 strikes a tooth 24, the latter tooth will be guided by the tooth 29 into the adjacent notch 27.

30 is a detent spring or pawl to prevent backward movement of the wheel 23.

I prefer to so proportion the parts above described that the wheel 23 is at rest for nine-tenths of the time in order to give to the sensitized film as long an exposure as practicable and is moving forward one-tenth of the time, and said forward movement is made to take place thirty or more times per second, preferably at least as high as forty-six times per second, although the rapidity of movement or number of times per second may be regulated as desired to give satisfactory results. The longer interval of rest of the film insures a good impression of the object projected thereon and results in a picture having clean and sharp lines, since the film has sufficient time to become steady and overcome the vibration caused by the sudden and rapid motions of the feed mechanism. On the shaft 26 or on any suitable shaft driven by the motor is a revolving disk 31, serving as a shutter for alternately exposing and covering the sensitive film. This disk, which is continuously revolving, is provided with six or any other suitable number of apertures 32 at regular intervals around it near the edge, they being so arranged that one of the apertures passes directly between the camera-lens 33 and the film each time the film is brought to rest, the light-rays passing through the opening 33′ and falling on the film half-way between the reels on which the film is wound.

34 is a device for adjusting the camera-lens toward or from the film, and 35 is a device by means of which the operator can focus the camera on the object to be photographed.

Although the operation has been partially indicated in the description of the apparatus it will now be set forth more in detail.

The apparatus is first charged with a sensitive tape-film several hundred or even thousands of feet long and the motor is set in operation. Since the spring 21 causes the door 20 to clamp the film, as already described, the loose pulleys 7. 18 slip without pulling said film along, but when a moving object—for example, a man gesticulating—is placed in the field of the camera and the handle 22 is pulled the film is released and the pulleys operate to pull the same along. At the same time the reel in case 2 is rotated to wind up the film, thus transferring it from the reel in case 1 to the reel in case 2. This movement is intermittent, the film advancing by very rapid steps, which are definitely and positively controlled by means of the peculiar detent or escapement described, and a photograph is taken after each step.

While I do not care to limit myself to any particular number of steps per second, there should be at least enough so that the eye of an observer cannot distinguish, or at least cannot clearly and positively distinguish, at a glance a difference in the position occupied by the object in the successive pictures, as illustrated in Fig. 7. A less speed in taking the pictures will cause a trembling or jerky appearance in the reproduced picture. When the movement of the object being photographed has ceased or the desired number of photographs has been obtained, the apparatus is stopped. The film is suitably treated for developing and fixing the pictures, when positive prints therefrom, Fig. 6, can be used in an exhibiting apparatus.

What I claim is—

1. An apparatus for taking photographs suitable for the exhibition of objects in motion, having in combination a camera having a single stationary lens; a single sensi-

tized tape-film supported on opposite sides of, and longitudinally movable with respect to, the lens, and having an intermediate section crossing the lens; feeding devices engaging such intermediate section of the film and moving the same across the lens of the camera at a high rate of speed and with an intermittent motion; and a shutter exposing successive portions of the film during the periods of rest, substantially as set forth.

2. An apparatus for taking photographs suitable for the exhibition of objects in motion, having in combination a camera having a single stationary lens; a single sensitized tape-film supported on opposite sides of, and longitudinally movable with respect to, the lens, and having an intermediate section crossing the lens; a continuously-rotating driving-shaft; feeding devices operated by said shaft engaging such intermediate section of the film and moving the same across the lens of the camera at a high rate of speed and with an intermittent motion; and a continuously-rotating shutter operated by said shaft for exposing successive portions of the film during the periods of rest, substantially as set forth.

3. An apparatus for taking photographs suitable for the exhibition of objects in motion, having in combination a camera having a single stationary lens; a single sensitized tape-film supported on opposite sides of, and longitudinally movable with respect to, the lens, and having an intermediate section crossing the lens; a continuously-rotating driving-shaft; feeding devices operated by said shaft engaging such intermediate section of the film and moving the same across the lens of the camera at a high rate of speed and with an intermittent motion; a shutter exposing successive portions of the film during the periods of rest; and a reel revolved by said shaft with variable speed for winding the film thereon after exposure, substantially as set forth.

4. An apparatus for taking photographs suitable for the exhibition of objects in motion, having in combination a camera having a single stationary lens; a single sensitized tape-film supported on opposite sides of, and longitudinally movable with respect to, the lens, and having an intermediate section crossing the lens; feeding devices engaging such intermediate section of the film and moving the same across the lens of the camera at a high rate of speed and with an intermittent motion, said feeding devices comprising means proportioned to cause the devices to so advance the film that its periods of rest shall exceed its periods of motion; and a shutter exposing successive portions of the film during the periods of rest, substantially as set forth.

5. An apparatus for taking photographs suitable for the exhibition of objects in motion, having in combination a camera having a single stationary lens; a single sensitized perforated tape-film supported on opposite sides of, and longitudinally movable with respect to, the lens, and having an intermediate section crossing the lens; feeding devices provided with teeth engaging the perforations of such intermediate section of the film and moving it across the lens of the camera at a high rate of speed and with an intermittent motion; and a shutter exposing successive portions of the film during the periods of rest, substantially as set forth.

In testimony whereof I have signed my name to this specification in the presence of two subscribing witnesses.

THOMAS A. EDISON.

Witnesses:
WARREN H. SMALL,
F. J. LEONARD.

---

No. 12,192.

REISSUED JAN. 12, 1904.

T. A. EDISON.
KINETOSCOPIC FILM.
APPLICATION FILED DEC. 17, 1903.

3 SHEETS—SHEET 1.

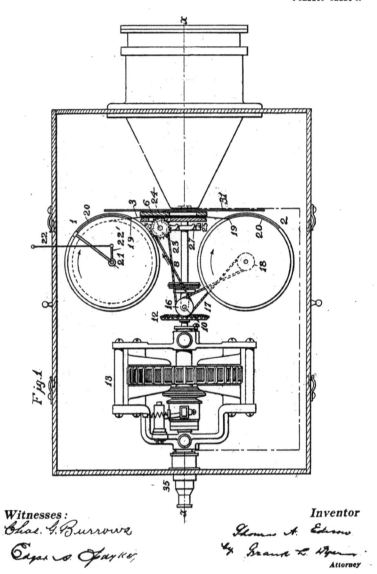

Fig.1

Witnesses:
Chas. G. Burrows
Edgar S. Fayke,

Inventor
Thomas A. Edison
by Frank L. Dyer
Attorney

No. 12,192.

REISSUED JAN. 12, 1904.

T. A. EDISON.
KINETOSCOPIC FILM.
APPLICATION FILED DEC. 17, 1903.

3 SHEETS—SHEET 2.

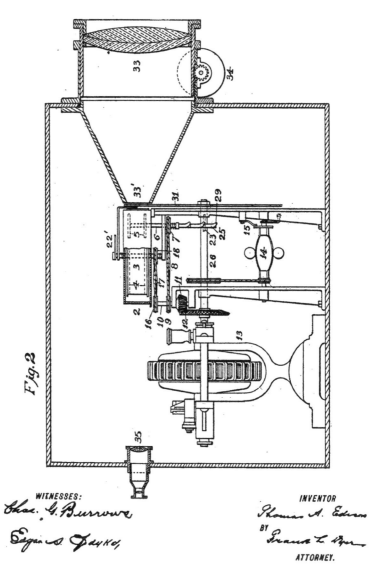

*Fig.2*

No. 12,192.

REISSUED JAN. 12, 1904.

T. A. EDISON.
KINETOSCOPIC FILM.
APPLICATION FILED DEC. 17, 1903.

3 SHEETS—SHEET 3.

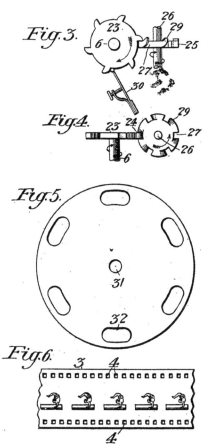

Fig.3.

Fig.4.

Fig.5.

Fig.6.

Witnesses:
C. K. Berryman
O. W. Edelin,

Inventor.
Thomas A. Edison
By Frank L. Dyer
Attorney

# UNITED STATES PATENT OFFICE.

## THOMAS A. EDISON, OF LLEWELLYN PARK, NEW JERSEY.

## KINETOSCOPIC FILM.

SPECIFICATION forming part of Reissued Letters Patent No. 12,192, dated January 12, 1904.

Original No. 589,168, dated August 31, 1897. Reissue No. 12,038, dated September 30, 1902. Application for present reissue filed December 17, 1903. Serial No. 185,597.

*To all whom it may concern:*

Be it known that I, THOMAS A. EDISON, a citizen of the United States, residing at Llewellyn Park, in the county of Essex and State 5 of New Jersey, have invented a certain new and useful Improvement in Kinetoscopic Films, (Case No. 928,) of which the following is a specification.

The purpose I have in view is to produce 10 pictures representing objects in motion throughout an extended period of time which may be utilized to exhibit the scene including such moving objects in a perfect and natural manner by means of a suitable exhibiting ap- 15 paratus, such as that described in an application filed simultaneously herewith, (Patent No. 493,426, dated March 14, 1893.) I have found that it is possible to accomplish this end by means of photography.

20 In carrying out my invention I employ an apparatus for effecting by photography a representation suitable for reproduction of a scene including a moving object or objects comprising a means, such as a single camera, 25 for intermittently projecting at such rapid rate as to result in persistence of vision images of successive positions of the object or objects in motion as observed from a fixed and single point of view, a sensitized tape-like 30 film, and a means for so moving the film as to cause the successive images to be received thereon separately and in single-line sequence. The movements of the tape-film are intermittent, and it is preferable that the periods of 35 rest of the film should be longer than the periods of movement.

By taking the photographs at a rate sufficiently high as to result in persistence of vision the developed photographs will, when brought 40 successively into view by an exhibiting apparatus, reproduce the movements faithfully and naturally.

I have been able to take with a single camera and a tape-film as many as forty-six pho- 45 tographs per second, each having a size measured lengthwise of the tape of one inch, and I have also been able to hold the tape at rest for nine-tenths of the time; but I do not wish to limit the scope of my invention to this high

rate of speed nor to this great disproportion 50 between the periods of rest and the periods of motion, since with some subjects a speed as low as thirty pictures per second or even lower is sufficient, and while it is desirable to make the periods of rest as much longer than the pe- 55 riods of motion as possible any excess of the periods of rest over the periods of motion is advantageous.

In the accompanying drawings, forming a part hereof, Figure 1 is a plan view, with the 60 top of the casing removed, of a form of apparatus which I have found highly useful for the taking of the photographs. Fig. 2 is a vertical longitudinal section on line *x x* in Fig. 1. Figs. 3 and 4 are enlarged views of the 65 stop mechanism of the photographing apparatus. Fig. 5 is a plan view of the shutter for the photographing apparatus, and Fig. 6 is a perspective view of a section of the tape-film with the photographs thereon. 70

Referring to the drawings, 3 indicates the transparent or translucent tape-film, which before the apparatus is put in operation is all coiled on a reel in the sheet-metal box or case 1, the free end being connected to an empty 75 reel in the case 2. The film 3 is preferably of sufficient width to admit the taking of pictures one inch in diameter between the rows of holes 4, Figs. 2 and 6, arranged at regular intervals along the two edges of the film, and 80 into which holes the teeth of the wheels 5, Figs. 1 and 2, enter for the purpose of positively advancing the film. When the film is narrow, it is not essential to use two rows of perforations and two feed-wheels, one feed- 85 wheel being sufficient. Said wheels are mounted on a shaft 6, which carries a loose pulley 7—that is, a pulley frictionally connected to its shaft and forming a yielding mechanical connection. This pulley is driven by a cord 90 or belt 8 from a pulley 9 on the shaft 10, which shaft is driven by means of the beveled gears 11 12. The wheel 12 is preferably driven by an electric motor 13, which when the apparatus is in use is regulated to run at the desired 95 uniform speed, being controlled by the centrifugal governor 14 and the circuit-controller 15 in a well-known manner. On the shaft

10 is another pulley 16, which is connected by a cross-belt 17 to a pulley 18, also frictionally connected to its shaft, and which carries the reel to which the tape is connected in casing 5 2. The film passes from the casing 1 through a slit formed by the edge 19 and the sliding door 20, which is normally thrown forward by the spring 21, Fig. 2, with sufficient force to clamp the film and hold it from movement. 10 When the door 20 is retracted by pulling on the rod or string 22, which is connected to the arm 22', the film is liberated and allowed to advance. Film-case 2 is provided with a similar door, but the device for moving the 15 door is not illustrated. This arrangement of the sliding door not only holds the film, but it tightly closes the casing, thus excluding light and protecting the sensitive film. The casings or boxes 1 2 are removable, so that 20 they, with the inclosed film, may be taken bodily from the apparatus. The shaft 6, heretofore referred to, is provided with a detent or stop-wheel 23, the form of which is most clearly shown in Figs. 3 and 4. The wheel 25 23 is provided with a number of projecting teeth 24, six being shown, which teeth are adapted to strike successively against the face of the coöperating detent or stop-wheel 25 on the shaft 26, which is the armature-shaft of the 30 motor or a shaft which is constantly driven by the motor. The wheel 25 has a corresponding number of notches 27 at regular intervals around its periphery. These notches are of such size and shape that the teeth 24 35 can pass through them, and when the wheels 23 and 25 are rotated in the direction indicated by the arrows each tooth in succession will strike the face of wheel 25, thereby bringing the film absolutely to rest at the same mo- 40 ment that an opening in the shutter exposes the film, and will then pass through a notch, allowing the tape-film to be moved forward another step while it is covered by the shutter. To avoid the danger of the wheel 25 45 moving so quickly that a tooth cannot enter the proper notch, a laterally-projecting tooth 29 is provided adjacent to each notch. When a tooth 29 strikes a tooth 24, the latter tooth will be guided by the tooth 29 into the adja- 50 cent notch 27.

30 is a detent spring or pawl to prevent backward movement of the wheel 23.

I prefer to so proportion the parts above described that the wheel 23 is at rest for nine- 55 tenths of the time in order to give to the sensitized film as long an exposure as practicable and is moving forward one-tenth of the time, and said forward movement is made to take place thirty or more times per second, pref- 60 erably at least as high as forty-six times per second, although the rapidity of movement or number of times per second may be regulated as desired to give satisfactory results. The longer interval of rest of the film insures a 65 good impression of the object projected there-

on and results in a picture having clean and sharp lines, since the film has sufficient time to become steady and overcome the vibration caused by the sudden and rapid motions of the feed mechanism. On the shaft 26 or on any 70 suitable shaft driven by the motor is a revolving disk 31, serving as a shutter for alternately exposing and covering the sensitive film. This disk, which is continuously revolving, is provided with six or any other suitable num- 75 ber of apertures 32 at regular intervals around it near the edge, they being so arranged that one of the apertures passes directly between the camera-lens 33 and the film each time the film is brought to rest, the light-rays passing 80 through the opening 33' and falling on the film half-way between the reels on which the film is wound.

34 is a device for adjusting the camera-lens toward or from the film, and 35 is a device by 85 means of which the operator can focus the camera on the object to be photographed.

Although the operation has been partially indicated in the description of the apparatus, it will now be set forth more in detail. 90

The apparatus is first charged with a sensitive tape-film several hundred or even thousands of feet long and the motor is set in operation. Since the spring 21 causes the door 20 to clamp the film, as already described, the 95 loose pulleys 7 18 slip without pulling said film along; but when a moving object—for example, a man gesticulating—is placed in the field of the camera and the handle 22 is pulled the film is released and the pulleys operate to 100 pull the same along. At the same time the reel in case 2 is rotated to wind up the film, thus transferring it from the reel in case 1 to the reel in case 2. This movement is intermittent, the film advancing by very rapid 105 steps, which are definitely and positively controlled by means of the peculiar detent or escapement described, and a photograph is taken after each step.

While I do not care to limit myself to any 110 particular number of steps per second, there should be at least enough so that the eye of an observer cannot distinguish, or at least cannot clearly and positively distinguish, at a glance a difference in the position occupied by 115 the object in the successive pictures, as illustrated in Fig. 7. A less speed in taking the pictures will cause a trembling or jerky appearance in the reproduced picture. When the movement of the object being photo- 120 graphed has ceased or the desired number of photographs has been obtained, the apparatus is stopped. The film is suitably treated for developing and fixing the pictures, when it is ready for use in an exhibiting apparatus. It 125 will be observed that all the photographs on the film are taken through the same camera-lens, which results in such a uniformity of photographs as would be unattainable were the photographs taken through different lenses. 130

What I claim is—

1. An unbroken transparent or translucent tape-like photographic film having thereon uniform sharply-defined equidistant photographs of successive positions of an object in motion as observed from a single point of view at rapidly-recurring intervals of time, such photographs being arranged in a continuous straight-line sequence, unlimited in number save by the length of the film, and sufficient in number to represent the movements of the object throughout an extended period of time, substantially as described.

2. An unbroken transparent or translucent tape-like photographic film provided with perforated edges and having thereon uniform sharply - defined equidistant photographs of successive positions of an object in motion as observed from a single point of view at rapidly-recurring intervals of time, such photographs being arranged in a continuous straight-line sequence, unlimited in number save by the length of the film, and sufficient in number to represent the movements of the object throughout an extended period of time, substantially as described.

This specification signed and witnessed this 15th day of December, 1903.

THOMAS A. EDISON.

Witnesses:
FRANK L. DYER,
HARRY G. WALTERS.

Defendants' Exhibit No. 188

Smith Patent No. 673,329
April 30, 1901

No. 673,329.

Patented Apr. 30, 1901.

A. E. SMITH.
KINETOSCOPE.

(Application filed Mar. 15, 1900.)

(No Model.)

4 Sheets—Sheet 1.

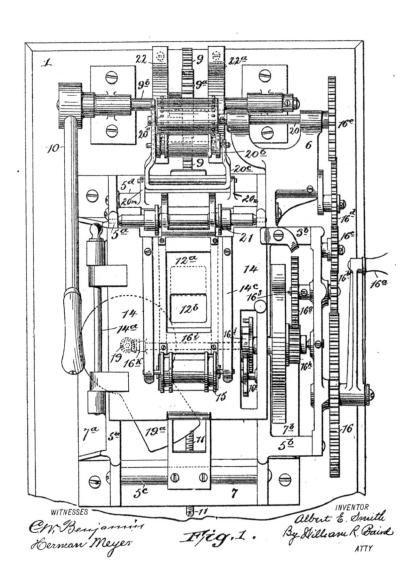

**Fig. 1.**

WITNESSES

C. W. Benjamin

Herman Meyer

INVENTOR

Albert E. Smith

By William R. Baird

ATTY

No. 673,329.

A. E. SMITH.
KINETOSCOPE.

Patented Apr. 30, 1901.

Application filed Mar 15, 1900.)

(No Model.)

4 Sheets—Sheet 2.

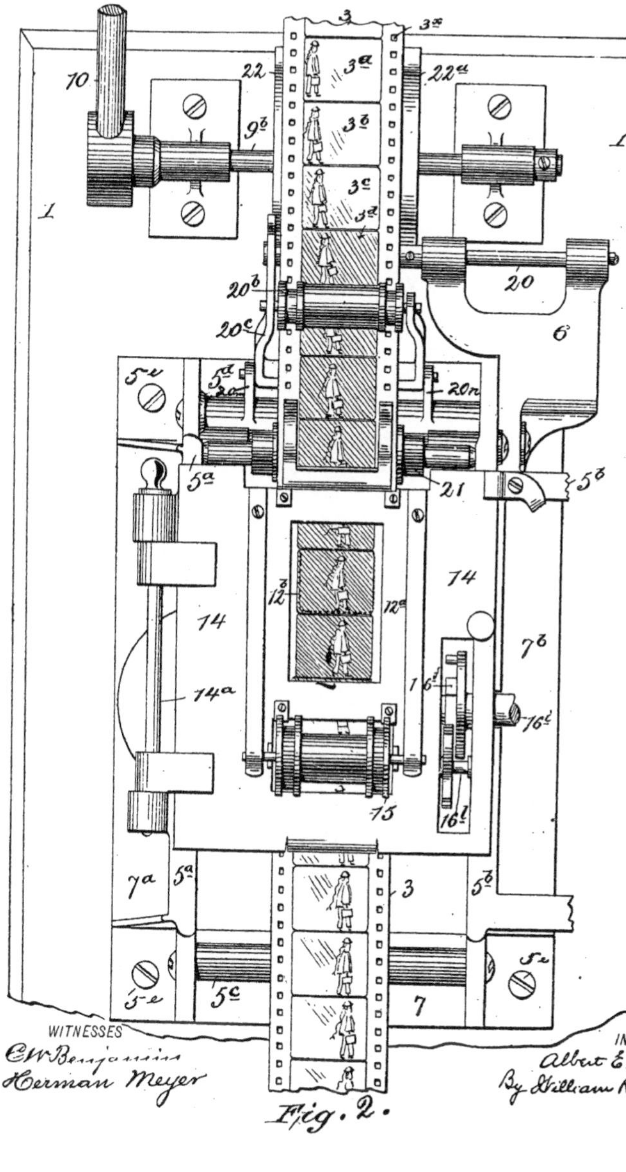

Fig. 2.

No. 673,329.

A. E. SMITH.
KINETOSCOPE.

(Application filed Mar. 15, 1900.)

Patented Apr. 30, 1901.

(No Model.)

4 Sheets—Sheet 3.

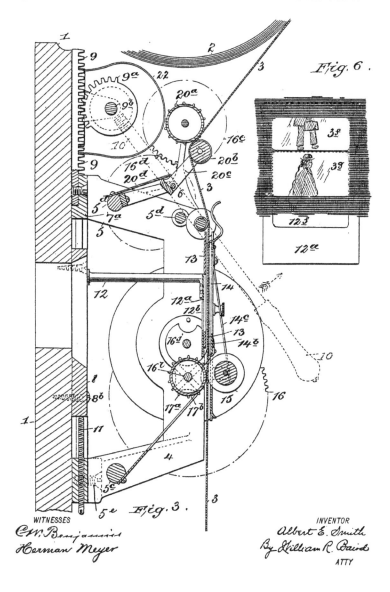

*Fig. 6.*

*Fig. 3.*

WITNESSES
C. W. Benjamin
Herman Meyer

INVENTOR
Albert E. Smith
By William R. Baird
ATTY

No. 673,329.

A. E. SMITH.
KINETOSCOPE.

(Application filed Mar. 15, 1900.)

Patented Apr. 30, 1901.

(No Model.)

4 Sheets—Sheet 4.

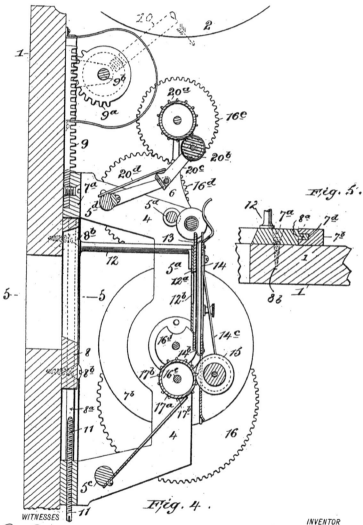

Fig. 5.

Fig. 4.

WITNESSES

C. W. Benjamin
Herman Meyer

INVENTOR

Albert E. Smith
By William R. Baird
ATTY

# UNITED STATES PATENT OFFICE.

ALBERT E. SMITH, OF BROOKLYN, NEW YORK, ASSIGNOR TO THE AMERICAN VITAGRAPH COMPANY, OF NEW JERSEY.

## KINETOSCOPE.

SPECIFICAT ON forming part of Letters Patent No. 673,329, dated April 30, 1901.

Application filed March 15, 1900. Serial No. 8,732. (No model.)

*To all whom it may concern:*

Be it known that I, ALBERT E. SMITH, a citizen of the United States, residing in the borough of Brooklyn, in the city of New York, in the county of Kings and State of New York, have invented a new and useful Improvement in Kinetoscopes, of which the following is a specification.

My invention relates to kinetoscopic apparatus, and especially to the type of apparatus designed for exhibiting in rapid succession a series of photographs of moving objects whereby the motion of the objects is apparently represented on a screen, and more particularly to the means employed for adjusting the film whereby it may be kept in proper position with reference to the aperture in the diaphragm opposite the source of light and for protecting the film from injury in its passage from the feed-roll to the carrier.

The main part of the apparatus, consisting of the feed-roll, the light and lenses, the guiding and propelling apparatus, the shutter-closing apparatus, and the means for producing the necessary intermittent motion of the film, are well known in the art and form no part of my present invention.

In the usual form of kinetoscopes known to me the film-carrier and the light-aperture are fixed with respect to each other, except in cases where the intermittent illumination of the film is produced by the reciprocation of one or the other. The film-strip is usually provided with small holes at its edges and is drawn forward by the engagement of such holes with sprockets or spurs on drums suitably placed for such purpose and intermittently rotated. When it is desired to use such an apparatus, the film is adjusted from the feed-roll so that one of its sections, containing a single view, is directly opposite the light-aperture in the diaphragm. It not infrequently happens in use, however, that the rapid motion of the film as it is propelled past the aperture causes the holes on its edges to spring out of engagement with the sprocket on the propelling-drum. This immediately causes the picture projected on the screen to be out of register with the field of light or mat projected on the screen by the passage of the light through the aperture in the diaphragm and produces the effect exhibited in Figure 6 of the drawings, where parts of two sections of the film are thrown upon the screen instead of the whole of one section. Endeavors have been made to obviate this difficulty by adjusting the diaphragm (and the aperture) with respect to the base of the apparatus; but this tended to throw the mat up or down on the screen, and possibly outside of the field of vision altogether, because a slight displacement of the aperture means a great displacement of the projected mat because of the refraction of the light through the lens. Moreover, such methods are impracticable by reason of the fact that an accidental displacement of the film usually takes place when it is being rapidly moved, and the exhibition is spoiled if the performance has to be stopped to make such a nice adjustment. There is also a form of apparatus in which the film is not provided with holes on its edges, but its propulsion is secured by means of its passage between pairs of rollers. In such construction an adjustment of the film with respect to the light-aperture is secured by varying the distance between the rollers of one pair, and thus permitting the film to slip into the desired position; but such means of adjustment are not applicable to the usual form of film. It was desirable, therefore, to secure the relative adjustment of the sections of the perforated film and the light-aperture in the diaphragm by some means which could be employed without disturbing the action of the apparatus or stopping the exhibition. It is the purpose of my invention to supply such means, and this I do by separating the frame supporting the film-carrier and its connected mechanism from the support for the diaphragm and its aperture and source of light-supply and providing a simple means of moving the first-mentioned frame with relation to such aperture, even while the motion of the film is continued, the film and the actuating mechanism therefor being mounted upon the adjusting-frame.

In the drawings, Fig. 1 is a front elevation of my improved kinetoscope without a film, but showing the means for carrying the film and propelling the same. Fig. 2 is a front elevation of the same, showing the film, but without showing the actuating mechanism of the film-rollers. Fig. 3 is a partial second side view of the same, showing the film-carrier in its uppermost position; and Fig. 4 is a similar view showing the film-carrier in its lowermost position. Fig. 5 is a vertical section on the plane of the line 5 5 in Fig. 4, and Fig. 6 is an illustration of the manner in which the film is at times out of register with the light-aperture in the diaphragm.

In the drawings, in which the same reference-numerals refer to the same parts in all of the figures, 1 is an upright frame or board on which my apparatus is mounted. Above it is mounted in any suitable manner a feed or supply roll 2 of the film 3, on which the pictures have been made in successive sections 3ª 3ᵇ 3ᶜ 3ᵈ, &c. From the feed-roll 2 the film 3 passes to the film-carrier 4. This carrier is made up of a frame 5, consisting of two standards 5ª and 5ᵇ, made of cast metal or other suitable material and provided at proper places with apertures which form journals for the axles of the several drums, rollers, and gear-wheels mounted thereon. The two standards 5ª and 5ᵇ are connected together by cross-pieces 5ᶜ and 5ᵈ, so as to make the frame 5 rigid.

A bracket 6, projecting from the upper part of the standard 5ᵇ, affords a suitable bearing for the axle 20 of a guide-sprocket drum 20ª and one of the cog-wheel pinions which actuates the said guide-sprocket drum.

The standards 5ª and 5ᵇ are rigidly bolted or otherwise secured by means of screws 5ᵉ to a rectangular frame 7, consisting of two vertical pieces 7ª and 7ᵇ, provided with longitudinal vertical slots 7ᶜ and 7ᵈ, adapted to reciprocate with tongues 8ª, projecting from the edges of a guide-plate 8, rigidly secured to the frame 1 of the apparatus by means of the screws 8ᵇ.

The frame 7 is provided at about the center of its upper edge with the vertical rack 9, adapted to engage with the teeth of a segmental pinion 9ª, mounted upon an axle 9ᵇ, adapted to oscillate in suitable bearings secured to the frame of the apparatus, the movement of the axle being secured by means of a handle 10 or similar suitable means.

The frame 7 is provided with a stop 11, consisting of a threaded rod placed within a threaded aperture in the lowermost member of the frame and adapted to abut against the fixed plate 8 when the film-carrier has reached its uppermost position.

The post or standard 12 projects outward from the plate 8 and supports at its outer extremity a vertical diaphragm 12ª, provided with an aperture 12ᵇ, through which the light intended to illuminate the picture formed by the representations upon the film is adapted to pass. In front of this diaphragm 12ª and mounted upon the standards 5ª and 5ᵇ is a flat friction-plate 13, and in the front of this is a friction-plate 14, swung upon a pintle 14ª, secured in bearings upon the standard 5ª. This

friction-plate 14 is supplied on its inner or under side with two friction-spring strips 14ᵇ, adapted to press against the film 3 when the latter is in position and against the surface of the plate 13 when it is not. In an aperture in this plate 14 is mounted a guide-roller 15, its axle resting in bearings formed by two slotted brackets secured to the outside of the plate and held in position within the slots of these brackets by two springs 14ᶜ, adapted to press against the axis of the roller.

Mounted upon the sides of the film-carrier is a train of gearing consisting of an actuating-wheel 16, (rotated by means of a suitable handle 16ª or other source of power,) two pinions 16ᵇ and 16ᶜ, a cog-wheel 16ᵈ, and the actuating cog-wheel 16ᵉ of the guide-sprocket 20ª. The pinion 16ᵇ is mounted upon an axle 16ᶠ, adapted to rotate in a bearing formed by an aperture in the standard 5ª and provided at its opposite extremity with a second cog-wheel 16ᵍ, adapted to mesh with another pinion 16ʰ, which in turn communicates motion to an axle 16ⁱ, adapted to rotate in bearings formed by suitable apertures in the standards 5ª and 5ᵇ, upon which axle are mounted a Geneva gear 16ʲ and a beveled pinion 16ᵏ. The Geneva gear 16ʲ intermittently rotates an axle 16ˡ, mounted in bearings formed in the standards 5ª and 5ᵇ below the axle 16ⁱ. Upon this axle 16ˡ is mounted the sprocket-drum 17ª, directly back of the guide-roller 15 and provided with the sprockets 17ᵇ, which engage with the holes in the film-strip and cause its intermittent downward motion. The beveled pinion 16ᵏ meshes with another beveled pinion 19, mounted upon the outer end of a shaft revolving in a bearing provided by a bracket secured to the standard 5ª, and which shaft actuates a revolving shutter 19ª, which, rotating in a vertical plane, intermittently cuts off the light from the source of illumination to the aperture 12ᵇ in the diaphragm 12ª. The Geneva gear and shutter and their connections are well-known constructions and form no part of my invention. A guide-sprocket drum 20ª is mounted above the friction-plate 14 at the inner end of the axle 20, and a guide-roller 20ᵇ, grooved to admit of the passage of the projecting sprockets on the drum 20ª, is mounted upon an axle supported by the bracket 20ᶜ, hinged in turn to two standards 20ᵐ and 20ⁿ, mounted upon the cross-piece 5ᵈ. The bracket 20ᶜ is held downward by means of the spring 20ᵈ, thus pressing the guide-roller 20ᵇ against the sprocket-drum 20ª.

In the actual operation of the machine the film 3 passes from the feed-roll 2 to the sprocket-guide 20ª, where the holes in the side of the film engage the sprockets on that guide, the film being held against the drum by the guide-roll 20ᵇ, under which it passes. It then passes over a loose roller 21, between the friction-plates 13 and 14, and under the roller 15 to the sprocket-drum 17ª, which by its intermittent forward motion, communicated to it by the Geneva gear 16$^j$, is adapted to pull the film downward and to bring each of its sections in succession opposite the aperture 12$^b$ in the stationary diaphragm 12$^a$. It sometimes happens that the film, being composed of stiff celluloid, springs backward in its passage from the feed-roll 2 to the guide-sprocket 20$^a$. It is then apt to strike against the adjusting-pinion 9$^a$. In order to avoid the injury which might result from such action, I have provided a shield over the pinion, consisting of two elastic pieces of metal 22 and 22$^a$, which, being placed between the film and the pinion, effectually prevents any contact between them.

The manner of operating this apparatus in making an exhibition is as follows: The film is first adjusted upon the sprockets of the guide 20$^a$ and drum 17$^a$ by means of the holes in the side of the film, so that one of the sections of the film coincides with the aperture 12$^b$ in the diaphragm 12$^a$. The actuating-gear being then set into operation, an intermittent rotary motion is communicated to the lower sprocket-drum 17$^a$ and the film is drawn downward, so that each successive section is brought in front of the aperture 12$^b$ in the diaphragm 12$^a$ and permitted to rest there for an instant, the revolving shutter 19$^a$ shutting off the light which otherwise would pass through the aperture 12$^b$. The rapid projection of the pictures upon the successive sections of the film causes the illusion of the representation of a moving scene upon the screen. Now if during the course of the exhibition it happens that the film should buckle and spring away from the sprocket-guide 20$^a$ when it is drawn forward again by the motion of the sprocket-drum 17$^a$ it misses one of the sprockets in the guide 20$^a$ and then the sections of the film will no longer coincide or register with the aperture 12$^b$ in the diaphragm 12$^a$. It will be remembered, however, that the diaphragm 12$^a$ is fixed. If, therefore, the handle 10, which actuates the pinion 9$^a$, be moved so as to bring the sections of the film as they are moved forward again in coincidence with the aperture 12$^b$ in the diaphragm 12$^a$, the mischief has been remedied and the picture no longer appears to be out of registry. It will be observed also that as the actuating mechanism of the film is all mounted upon the movable frame 4 no cessation of the forward motion of the film needs to take place while the adjustment referred to is being made, a result which prior to my invention had not been accomplished.

What I claim as new is—

1. In a kinetoscope, the combination with a fixed apertured diaphragm, of a frame adapted to carry the picture-film, actuating mechanism for the film, such mechanism being carried by said frame, and means for adjusting the position of the frame, the film and the actuating mechanism with respect to the diaphragm.

2. In a kinetoscope, the combination with a fixed apertured diaphragm, of a frame adapted to carry the picture-film and its actuating mechanism, and means for adjusting the position of the frame with respect to the diaphragm, consisting of a rack secured to the frame, a fixed pinion adapted to mesh with the rack and means for rotating the pinion.

3. The combination in a kinetoscope of a movable frame adapted to carry a picture-film and its propelling mechanism and provided with a rack, with a fixed diaphragm having a light-aperture and a support for said diaphragm, guides adapted to control the direction of motion of the frame and a pinion adapted to actuate the rack and frame.

4. In a kinetoscope, the combination with a fixed diaphragm provided with an aperture adapted to admit of the passage of the light, and film-actuating mechanism, of means for adjusting the position of a picture-carrying film with respect to the aperture, consisting of a movable frame upon which are mounted the film and its said actuating mechanism, said frame being designed to move the film with relation to the diaphragm, guides adapted to control the direction of the movement of said frame and means for producing said movement.

5. In a kinetoscope, a frame adapted to carry the film, propelling mechanism for the film also carried by said frame, a frame adapted to carry the diaphragm and its light-aperture and means for adjusting the relative positions of the two frames and holding them in position after adjustment, the film and the light-aperture being moved one in relation to the other in the frame adjustment.

6. In a kinetoscope, a frame adapted to carry the film and its propelling mechanism, a frame adapted to carry the diaphragm and its light-aperture and means for adjusting the relative positions of the two frames and holding them in position after adjustment, consisting of one frame and a pinion secured to the other and having an operating-handle.

Witness my hand this 13th day of March, 1900, in the presence of two subscribing witnesses.

ALBERT E. SMITH.

Witnesses:
J. STUART BLACKTON,
WM. T. ROCK.

Smith Patent No. 744,251

November 17, 1903.

A. E. SMITH.
KINETOSCOPE.
APPLICATION FILED MAR. 5, 1903.

NO MODEL.

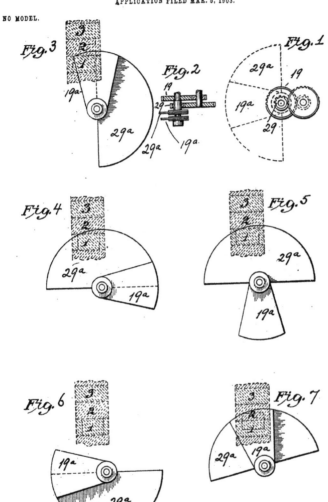

Albert E. Smith    Inventor
By His Attorney William R. Baird

# UNITED STATES PATENT OFFICE.

## ALBERT E. SMITH, OF BROOKLYN, NEW YORK.

## KINETOSCOPE.

SPECIFICATION forming part of Letters Patent No. 744,251, dated November 17, 1903.

Application filed March 5, 1903. Serial No. 146,274. (No model.)

*To all whom it may concern:*

Be it known that I, ALBERT E. SMITH, a citizen of the United States, and a resident of Brooklyn, in the county of Kings and State of
5 New York, have invented certain new and useful Improvements in Kinetoscopes, of which the following is a specification.

My invention relates to moving-picture machines; and its novelty consists in the means
10 employed to prevent or disperse the flicker of the picture projected upon the screen. In machines of this class comprising an intermittently-moving film actuated by means of sprocket-wheels or similar mechanism, where-
15 by a continuous film is forced intermittently forward in front of a film-aperture through which the light passes, a shutter is commonly employed to conceal from the observer the movement of the film from one of its posi-
20 tions of rest to the next position of rest. This shutter is usually made in the form of a sector constituting a revolving diaphragm actuated by gearing from the operating-crank of the machine, and it is so timed as to inter-
25 cept the light as the picture is moved. If this shutter is not employed, the motion of the film from one position of rest to another causes the picture projected upon the machine to look streaked and blurred, as though
30 the colors had run. When, however, the shutter is employed, although the difficulty referred to is obviated another arises—viz., there occurs a flicker on the picture, which produces a most unpleasant impression upon the ob-
35 server. Persons skilled in this art have long tried to overcome this flicker, but so far as I know have not measurably succeeded. The purpose of my invention is to lessen or dissipate it, and although I do not entirely remove
40 it I do remove so much of it that its disagreeable features are done away with.

I accomplish the purpose stated by interposing in the path of the light between the source of illumination and the screen upon
45 which the picture is projected means for very rapidly and intermittently intercepting the light. By "rapidly" I mean rapidly as compared with the rate of motion of the film, so that the light is cut off from four to twelve
50 times during each period of rest of the film. I do not confine myself to these precise limits of interception, but I give them as exam-

ples. Four is probably too slow, but, nevertheless, will produce an appreciable effect. Eight I have found to be a good number. I 55 do not wish to limit myself either to any particular size or shape of shutter. I have found that a disk of one hundred and eighty degrees for some subjects is advantageous, while a smaller disk is better for others. In 60 the case of pictures of any particular class the size and shape of the disk will have to be determined by previous experiment. The means which I employ for this purpose consists of a shutter mounted to revolve in a 65 plane at right angles to the path of the light, which path it crosses a number of times while the film is at rest. This shutter is actuated by intermediate multiplying-gearing driven from the crank of the apparatus. Of course 70 the effect of such numerous intersections of the light is to lessen somewhat the amount of illumination, but it also lessens the flicker referred to.

The principle upon which my invention is 75 based seems to be that the eye of the observer becomes so accustomed to the rapid intermission of the illumination by the revolution of the shutter referred to that when the main shutter is moved when the film is moved 80 from one position to another such movement of the main shutter is not particularly noticed, and the only perceptible effect to the observer is a slight but general toning down of the picture. 85

In the accompanying drawings, Figure 1 is a side elevation of the multiplying-gear by which the two shutters are rotated, the shutters themselves being shown in dotted outline. Fig. 2 is an elevation and partial sec- 90 tion of the same, only a portion of the shutters being shown. Figs. 3, 4, 5, and 6 represent different relative positions of the film and the two shutters as the latter are rotated.

The machines of the class to which my in- 95 vention relates are made of different forms by different makers. One approved form of the apparatus is shown and described in Letters Patent of the United States No. 673,329, issued to me April 30, 1901, and reference is 100 made to that patent for the details of the mechanism not directly connected with the subject-matter of this application. In the Letters Patent referred to there is shown the film-propelling mechanism, the surrounding parts, and the shutter to which I have above referred. This shutter is rotated at such a rate of speed and is so timed that it intercepts the light just as the film is moved from one position of rest to another. The means for rotating it consists of a pinion actuated by suitable gearing, which in turn is actuated from the handle of the machine. This mechanism is quite fully described in the patent above referred to, and such description need not be repeated here.

In the drawings, 19ª is the shutter adapted by its rotation to intermittently cut off the light from the film as it is moved from one position of rest to another, and 19 is the actuating-pinion. This shutter is preferably made in the form of a sector of a circle and of light flexible metal. Mounted upon the same shaft as the shutter 19ª is the second shutter 29ª, rotated by the pinion 29. This pinion 29 moves any desired number of times faster than the pinion 19. Consequently the shutter 29ª rotates that much faster and passes the larger number of times past the light-aperture of the machine and intercepts the light that much oftener.

Successive sections of the film are designated 1, 2, and 3. It will be understood that each of these sections displays a picture. In Figs. 3, 4, 5, and 6 the shutter 19ª is shown in the several successive positions which it would assume if it were revolving in the same direction as the hands of a watch. Now while it has been moving from the position shown in Fig. 3 to that shown in Fig. 6 and the film has been stationary the shutter 29 will have rotated several times, depending upon the relation of the actuating-gears 19 and 29, and will have been, for instance, during this time in the positions shown in the several figures with respect to that of the shutter 19ª.

In Fig. 7 is shown the position of the shutter 19ª just as the film is being moved downward to a new position, this shutter intercepting the light while the motion is taking place and the section 2 is moving from the position it occupied to the position which section 1 has occupied. In the meantime the shutter 29ª continues to rotate, whether it actually intercepts the light at that particular moment being immaterial.

The shutter 29ª may of course be placed at any other point in the path of the light from the source of illumination to the screen on which the picture is projected. I have found it convenient, however, to place it in close proximity to the shutter 19ª and to actuate it from the same mechanism. Of course the rotation of the shutter 29ª is actually continuous; but its interception of the light is intermittent, because it only passes the beam of light during a portion of its revolution.

Other means than a revolving shutter may be employed to carry out the principles of my invention; but I regard any such means as an equivalent if it has the functional effect of rapidly (as compared with the movement of the film) and intermittently intercepting the light passing through the film, and thus reducing the flicker upon the screen.

Having described my invention, what I claim as new is—

1. In a moving-picture machine an intermittently-moving shutter adapted to screen the film while it is being moved from one position to another, and means interposed between the source of light and the screen adapted to intermittently intercept the light consisting of a shutter moving much more rapidly than the first-named shutter.

2. In a moving-picture machine, a shutter adapted to screen the film while it is being moved from one position to another, a second shutter adapted to intermittently intercept the light while the film is at rest, a shaft common to both of said shutters and actuating mechanism for said shutters operating to drive the second shutter at a higher rate of speed than the first-mentioned shutter.

3. In a moving-picture machine, two relatively movable shutters and mechanism for operating said shutters at different speeds, for the purpose set forth.

4. In a moving-picture machine, a plurality of relatively movable light-intercepting means and means for operating the same at different speeds, for the purpose specified.

5. In a moving-picture machine, two relatively movable shutters, each the sector of a circle and one larger than the other, and mechanism for actuating the same, said mechanism operating to move one of the same much more rapidly than the other.

Witness my hand this 3d day of March, 1903, at the city of New York, in the county and State of New York.

ALBERT E. SMITH.

Witnesses:
HERMAN MEYER,
ERNEST H. BOISE.

Defendants' Exhibit No. 190

Smith Patent No. 770,937
September 27, 1904.

No. 770,937.

PATENTED SEPT. 27, 1904.

A. E. SMITH.
KINETOSCOPE.
APPLICATION FILED APR. 20, 1903

NO MODEL.

2 SHEETS—SHEET 1.

*Fig.1*

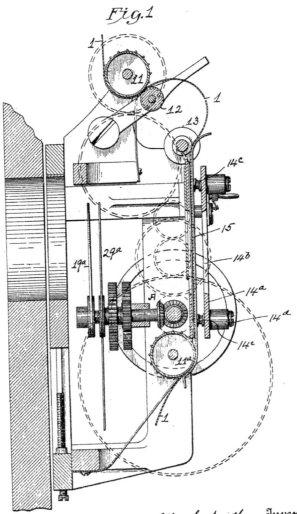

Witnesses
A. D. Wallace.
B. J. Smith

Albert E. Smith    Inventor
By His Attorney William R. Baird

No. 770,937.

PATENTED SEPT. 27, 1904

A. E. SMITH.
KINETOSCOPE.
APPLICATION FILED APR. 20, 1903.

NO MODEL.

2 SHEETS—SHEET 2.

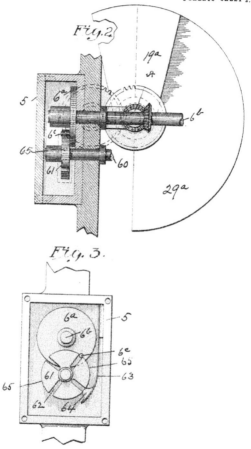

Fig. 2.

Fig. 3.

Albert E. Smith   Inventor
By His Attorney William R. Baird

# UNITED STATES PATENT OFFICE.

ALBERT E. SMITH, OF BROOKLYN, NEW YORK, ASSIGNOR TO THE VITA-
GRAPH COMPANY OF AMERICA, A CORPORATION OF NEW YORK.

## KINETOSCOPE.

SPECIFICATION forming part of Letters Patent No. 770,937, dated September 27, 1904.

Application filed April 20, 1903. Serial No. 153,354. (No model.)

*To all whom it may concern:*

Be it known that I, ALBERT E. SMITH, a citizen of the United States, and a resident of Brooklyn, in the county of Kings and State of New York, have invented certain new and useful Improvements in Kinetoscopes, of which the following is a specification.

My invention relates to kinetoscopes; and its novelty consists in the construction and mode of operation of sundry parts, as will be more fully hereinafter pointed out.

In the drawings, Figure 1 is a central vertical section and partial side elevation of a machine embodying my improvements. Fig. 2 is a section and partial plan view of the gearing and gear-box and a side elevation of the revolving shutters, and Fig. 3 is a front view of the intermittent gearing with the front cover of the gear-box removed.

In Letters Patent of the United States No. 673,329, granted to me April 30, 1901, there is shown and described a kinetoscope of the general type and style of my apparatus, and I refer to that patent for a full description of the details and common features of the apparatus.

In the drawings, 1 is the film fed from an upper supply-roll, (not shown,) passing under the upper sprocket-drum 11, above the guide-roll 12, and bending outward and then passing down in front of the guide-roll 13 and thence down to the lower sprocket-drum 11ᵃ. While taking this course the film 1 passes in front of the light-aperture 2 and is preferably held in proper relation thereto by suitable spring-pressed strips or devices 15, which bear upon the edges of the film where the sprocket-wheels are situated and do not bear upon any portion of its surface displaying the picture. A means which may desirably be employed to hold said plates yieldingly against the film comprises a plate 14ᵃ, having an aperture 14ᵇ registering with the light-aperture of the machine and provided with coiled springs 14ᶜ, suitably connected therewith and with said strips 15.

Mounted at one side of the frame of the apparatus is an air-tight case 5, consisting of bottom panels, side and edge panels, and a front cover secured in place by screws or any other suitable means. Within this case is arranged the intermittent gearing. It consists, first, of the actuating-wheel 6ᵃ, caused to rotate by the rotation of the shaft 6ᵇ, upon which it is mounted and provided with a fixed projecting pin or roller 6ᶜ.

Mounted on a shaft 60 parallel with the shaft 6ᵇ is a disk or wheel 61, provided with four radial slots 62, adapted to engage with the pin or roller 6ᶜ, and also having peripheral bearing-surfaces 65 between the slots. As the actuating-wheel 6ᵃ rotates the movement of the pin 6ᶜ turns the disk or wheel 61 one-fourth of a revolution while this pin is actually engaged in the radial slot 62. The disk or wheel 61 then remains at rest until the pin comes around again and engages with the next slot 62. A spring 63, provided with a lug or peg 64, is so arranged as normally to press against the peripheral bearing-surfaces 65 of the wheel or disk during the movement of said wheel or disk and upon the completion of said movement engages the contiguous slot 62. By this most simple and inexpensive means the movement of said wheel or disk is steadied and accidental rotation thereof prevented. As said disk or wheel is mounted on a shaft 60 the movement of which controls the movement of the film, it will be seen that the operation of the latter is similarly steadied. By this means a continuous rotary motion of the wheel 6ᵃ imparts an intermittent rotary motion to the wheel 61. The air-tight casing 5 is designed to protect this gearing from accidental injury, dust, and dirt.

The shutters 19ᵃ and 29ᵃ and their connections form the subject-matter of an application for Letters Patent of the United States, Serial No. 146,274, filed by me March 5, 1903; and consequently they will not be described in this connection further than to call attention to the fact that the shaft 6ᵇ is suitably geared, as shown generally at A in Figs. 1 and 6, within the main casing of the apparatus with the shutters and extends outward through the side of said main casing and is provided outside the same with the actuating-wheel 6ᵃ, above referred to.

What I claim as new is—

1. In a kinetoscope, a gearing comprising a shaft, a continuously-rotatable wheel mounted thereon and provided with a pin, a second shaft, a wheel mounted on said second shaft and provided with radial slots adapted to engage with the pin of the first wheel and a yieldably-supported holding-lug engaging the periphery of said wheel.

2. In a kinetoscope, the combination with a main casing or frame, shutter therein and film-carriers, of a pair of shafts, one of which is geared within the casing with said shutter and the other of which controls the movement of the film, each of said shafts extending from the interior of the main frame outward to the exterior thereof, means located outside said casing for transmitting movement from one shaft to the other and causing the film-controlling shaft to move intermittently, and a supplemental casing attached to the main casing and inclosing said means and the outer ends of said shafts.

3. Means for intermittently actuating the film of a kinetoscope, comprising a continuously-rotated wheel having a projection extending therefrom, a disk having radial slots arranged successively to be engaged by said projection and peripheral bearing-surfaces between said slots, and a spring having a lug to bear upon the periphery of said disk.

4. Means for intermittently actuating the film of a kinetoscope, comprising a continuously-rotated wheel having a projection extending therefrom, a disk having radial slots arranged successively to be engaged by said projection and peripheral bearing-surfaces between said slots, a flat spring secured at one end and having its other end provided with a lug to engage the periphery of said disk, and a casing for said parts.

5. The combination with the frame of a kinetoscope, of a casing secured to one side of said frame and means for feeding the film intermittently and comprising the following elements located in said casing, namely, a continuously-rotated wheel having a projection, a disk having radial slots arranged to be engaged by said projection and peripheral bearing-surfaces between said slots and a spring

having a lug to bear upon the periphery of said disk.

6. In a kinetoscope, means for intermittently actuating the film, comprising a continuously-rotating wheel having a projection, a disk having radial slots successively engaged by said projection and peripheral bearing-surfaces between said slots, and a spring having a lug to engage the periphery of said disk, in combination with means for holding the film in its passage across the light-aperture, comprising continuous bearing-surfaces yieldingly held in contact with the film.

7. In a kinetoscope, the combination with the film-carrier and shutter, of a continuously-rotating shaft connected with the shutter, a second shaft connected with the film-carrier, and means for transmitting intermittent movement to the latter shaft from the first-mentioned shaft, comprising an actuating-wheel on said first-mentioned shaft, having a projection, a disk on said second shaft, having radial slots and peripheral bearing-surfaces between said slots, and yieldably - supported steadying and holding means engaging the periphery of said disk.

8. In a kinetoscope the combination with the main casing or frame, shutter therein and film-carriers, of a pair of shafts, one of which is geared within the casing with said shutter and the other of which controls the movement of the film, each of said shafts extending from the interior of the main frame outward to the exterior thereof, means located outside said casing for transmitting intermittent movement to the film-controlling shaft from the other shaft, comprising an actuating-wheel having a projection and a disk having radial slots, mounted on the shafts respectively, said disk having peripheral bearing-surfaces between its slots, steadying and holding means engaging the periphery of said disk, and a supplemental casing attached to the main casing and inclosing the outer ends of said shafts and the parts mounted thereon.

Witness my hand this 16th day of April, 1903, at the city of New York, in the county and State of New York.

ALBERT E. SMITH.

Witnesses:
WILLIAM R. BAIRD,
B. J. SMITH.

Smith Patent No. 771,280
October 4, 1904.

No. 771,280.

PATENTED OCT. 4, 1904

A. E. SMITH.

WINDING REEL.

APPLICATION FILED FEB. 1. 1904.

NO MODEL.

3 SHEETS—SHEET 1.

Fig. 1

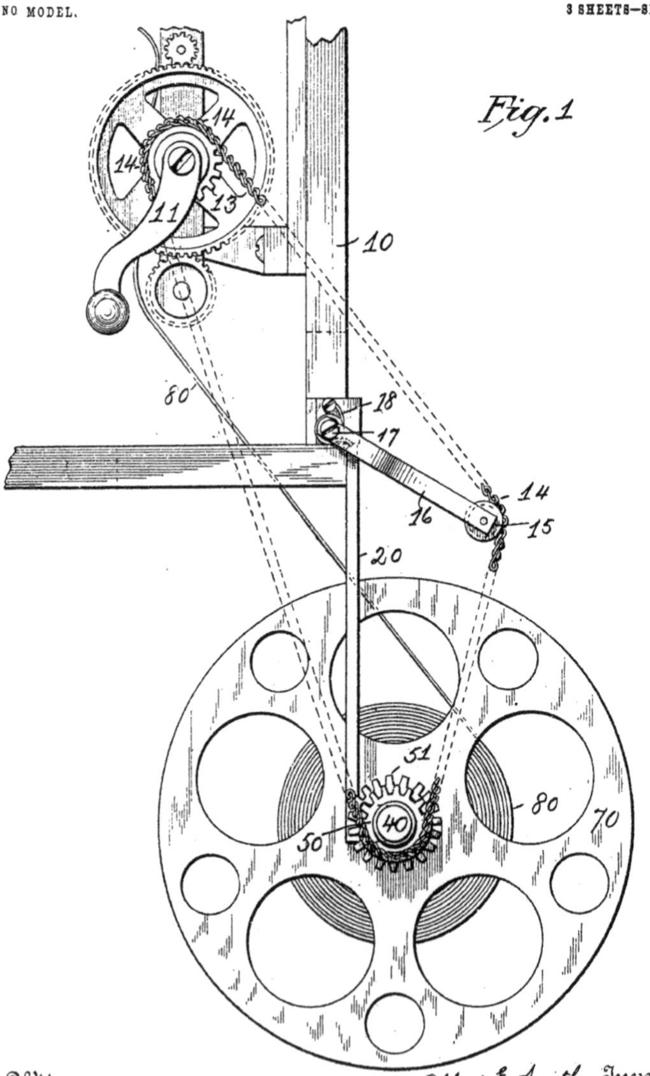


Witnesses
Estelle V. Titus.
Bartlett J. Smith

Albert E. Smith, Inventor
By His Attorney William R. Baird

No. 771,280.

PATENTED OCT. 4, 1904.

A. E. SMITH.
WINDING REEL.
APPLICATION FILED FEB. 1, 1904.

NO MODEL.

3 SHEETS—SHEET 2.

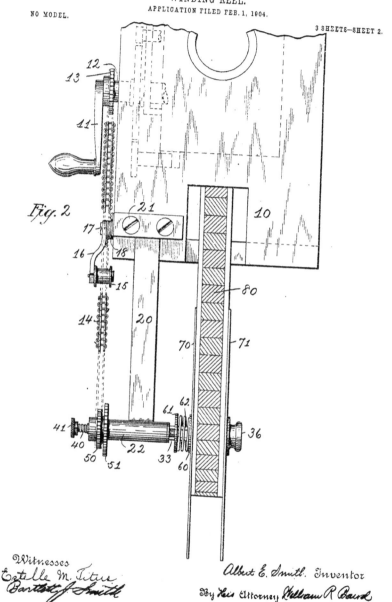

*Fig. 2*

No. 771,280. PATENTED OCT. 4, 1904.

A. E. SMITH.

WINDING REEL.

APPLICATION FILED FEB. 1, 1904.

NO MODEL. 3 SHEETS—SHEET 3.

Fig. 3

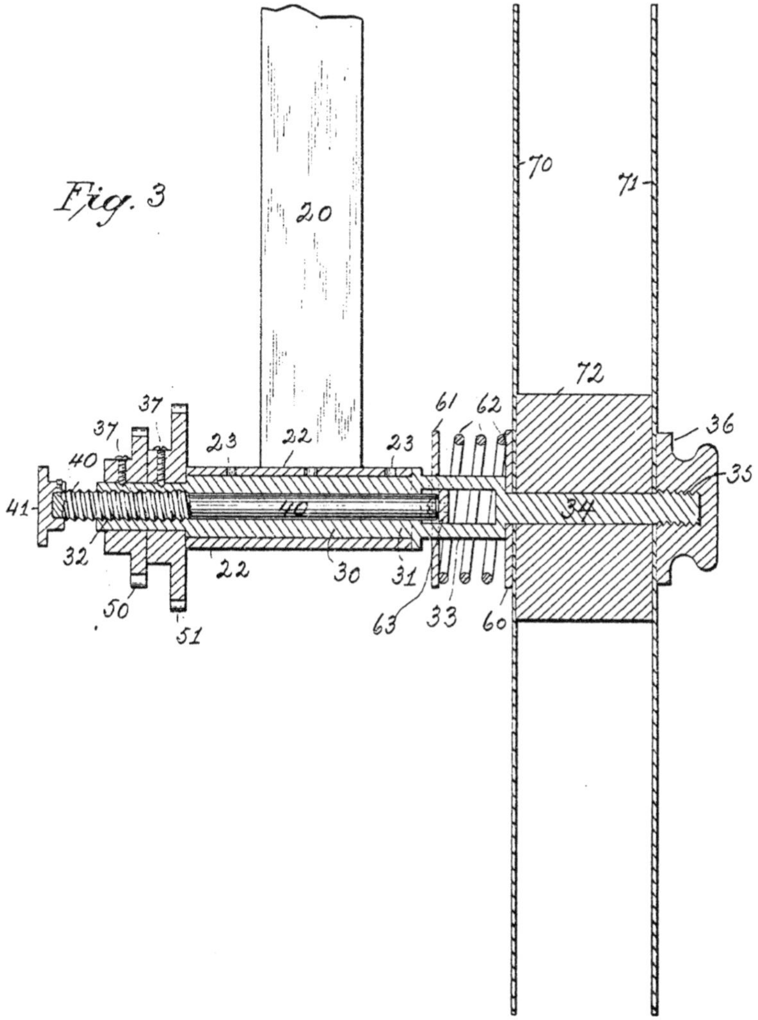


Witnesses
Estelle M. Titus.
Bartlett J. Smith

Albert E. Smith Inventor

By his Attorney William R. Baird

# UNITED STATES PATENT OFFICE.

## ALBERT E. SMITH, OF BROOKLYN, NEW YORK.

### WINDING-REEL.

SPECIFICATION forming part of Letters Patent No. 771,280, dated October 4, 1904.

Application filed February 1, 1904. Serial No. 191,445. (No model.)

*To all whom it may concern:*

Be it known that I, ALBERT E. SMITH, a citizen of the United States, and a resident of the borough of Brooklyn, in the county of Kings
5 and State of New York, have invented certain new and useful Improvements in Winding-Reels, of which the following is a specification.

This invention has reference to reels for
10 kinetoscopes, and more particularly to certain improvements in the means for taking care of the film after the same has passed the light-orifice of the machine.

The invention consists in certain peculiari-
15 ties in the construction of parts and in certain novel combinations of elements, substantially as hereinafter described, and particularly pointed out in the subjoined claims.

The purpose of my invention is to provide
20 means for winding the film upon a proper reel as it is discharged from the machine, so that it can be at once made ready for future use, and at the same time to provide means for varying the tension upon the reel-shaft and to
25 make the parts efficient, simple, and cheap.

In the drawings, Figure 1 is a side elevation of the lower portion of a kinetoscope provided with my improved device. Fig. 2 is a front elevation of the same, and Fig. 3 is an
30 enlarged vertical section of the reel and its connections.

In the drawings, 10 is the lower part of the frame of a kinetoscope.

11 is the main actuating-handle adapted to
35 turn the shaft 12, suitably connected to move the usual mechanism for propelling the film and moving the shutters, and which it is not necessary for our present purpose to describe.

13 is a sprocket-wheel rigidly secured to the
40 shaft 12 and adapted to propel the sprocket-chain 14 traveling over the same.

Depending from any part of the frame 10 is a bracket 20, suitably secured by any proper means, as the screws 21. Hanging from the
45 lower part of this bracket 20 is a horizontally-placed substantially cylindrical bearing 22, provided with apertures 23 23 for the introduction of lubricating-oil. Within this bearing is placed the reel-shaft proper, 30. It
50 comprises a hollow cylindrical portion 31,

threaded at 32 to receive a rod 40, a slotted cylindrical portion 33, and a solid round portion 34. This latter, passing through the core or hub of the reel and having a threaded extremity 35, is adapted to engage with a tension- 55 bearing knob 36.

Rigidly secured to the shaft 30 by any suitable means, as the screws 37 37, are a number of sprocket-wheels 50 51 having different radii. Loosely mounted on the end 34 of the 60 shaft is an annular disk 60, and mounted on the part 33 of the shaft is another annular disk 61. The latter is secured to the shaft and rotates with it. Between these two disks and secured to both is a coiled spring 62 encircling 65 the part 33 of the shaft 30. The rod 40, provided with a head 41, reciprocates within the shaft, its inner extremity impinging against a plate 63, secured to the disk 61, so that when the rod is rotated the disks are brought closer 70 together and the spring 62 between them is compressed.

The reel comprises two flat plates 70 and 71, apertured centrally to receive the part 34 of shaft 30 and provided with a hub or drum 72, 75 on which the film is to be wound.

15 is a tension-roller rotatably mounted on the end of an arm 16, hinged at 17 and provided with a coiled spring 18, which is secured both to the frame 10 and the arm 17 to cause the latter 80 always to swing outwardly and upwardly and toward the chain 14. Its function is to press yieldingly against the chain to keep it stretched and taut, although it may vary in length, as it does when the main shaft is, with the rest 85 of the mechanism, adjusted up and down in the operation of the machine.

The operation of the device is as follows: The parts being placed in the position shown in the figures, the chain 14 is coupled to the 90 wheel 50, the film being first led over the drum 72, and the machine is ready to be actuated. The rotation of the handle 11, which turns the whole mechanism, then turns the shaft 30 through the chain 14. This in turn ro- 95 tates the disk 61. The spring 62, being connected with this disk and with the disk 60, causes the latter to rotate. This presses against the plate 70, and thereby causes the rotation of the reel. At first the pressure upon 100

the disk 60 and against the plate 70 is slight, and is sufficient to cause the reel to rotate readily and to wind up the film. After a number of yards of film have been unwound on
5 the reel, however, the force necessary to turn it will be greater. If, then, the chain 14 is disconnected from the sprocket-wheel 50 and placed upon the larger wheel 51, the increased leverage adjusts the relative tensions of the
10 parts, and again the reel rotates readily. As more film continues to be wound upon the reel its effective diameter becomes greater, and again the pull on the film becomes too great. In fact, at times it would be sufficient
15 to break it, especially if it contains a weak spot, except for the device for relieving it which is provided. Then the rod 40 is brought into play. Being rotated, it moves inwardly the plate 63 and disk 61. This compresses
20 the spring 62 and presses the disk 60 more tightly against the plate 70 and of course increases the speed of rotation of the reel. If necessary, the rod 40 can be pushed in to compress the spring 62 until the friction between
25 the disk 60 and the plate 70 produces almost a rigid connection between them. It will be observed, however, that no matter what the speed of rotation of the reel or of the main shaft, yet the connection between the rotating
30 parts and the reel is a frictional one, and if the tension or downward pull on the film 80 becomes too great the reel slips and prevents its continuing to a breaking-point. In other words, a practically uniform tension is main-
35 tained upon the film and one at the same time which is safe.

If it is desired to rotate the reel without operating the handle 11 or turning the shaft 30 by means of the chain 14, the threaded rod is
40 turned to move the disk 61 toward the left when in the position shown in Fig. 3. This loosens the tension of the spring 62 and allows the reel to be turned without any difficulty. If it is desired to remove the reel altogether
45 from the shaft, the knob 36 is unscrewed from the threaded end 34 and the reel then readily slips off of the shaft.

I claim—

1. In a machine of the class described, a
50 winding-reel adapted to receive the film at its discharge, and means for rotating said reel comprising a shaft upon which the reel is mounted, said shaft having a projection contiguous to said reel, a plate loosely mounted
55 on said shaft between said projection and reel and engaged with the latter, a plate mounted on said shaft to rotate therewith, means for adjusting the latter plate toward the loose plate, and a spring interposed between said
60 plates.

2. In a machine of the class described, a winding-reel adapted to receive the film at its discharge, and means for rotating said reel, comprising a shaft upon which the reel is
65 mounted, a fixed and a loose plate on said shaft,

one of said plates being engaged with said reel, a spring interposed between said plates, and adjusted means for varying the distance between the plates, comprising an adjustable rod carried by the shaft and connected with one 70 of said plates.

3. In a machine of the class described, a winding-reel adapted to receive the film at its discharge, and means for rotating said reel comprising a shaft upon which the reel is 75 mounted, said shaft being hollow, a pair of plates one of which is loosely mounted on said shaft and is frictionally engaged with said reel, and the other of which plates is mounted to turn with said shaft, a plate mounted in the 80 hollow portion of said shaft and connected with the last-mentioned plate, an adjustable rod extending into said shaft and engaged with the plate therein, and a spring interposed between said pair of plates. 85

4. In a machine of the class described, a winding-reel adapted to receive the film at its discharge, and means for rotating said reel comprising a shaft upon which the reel is mounted, said shaft being hollow, a pair of 90 plates one of which is loosely mounted on said shaft and is frictionally engaged with said reel, and the other of which plates is mounted to turn with said shaft, a plate mounted in the hollow portion of said shaft and connected 95 with the last-mentioned plate, an adjustable rod extending into said shaft and engaged with the plate therein said rod having a threaded connection with said shaft and provided outside the same with a head, and a spring inter- 100 posed between said pair of plates.

5. In a machine of the class described, a winding-reel adapted to receive the film at its discharge, its shaft, and means for rotating said reel operated from the main shaft of the ma- 105 chine and comprising wheels of different radii mounted on the reel-shaft and means adapted to engage either of said wheels for connecting the same with said main shaft.

6. In a machine of the class described, the 110 combination with a main shaft, of a reel and its shaft, a plurality of wheels of different radii mounted on said reel-shaft, flexible means adapted to engage either of said wheels for operating the reel-shaft from the main shaft, 115 a tension-wheel engaged with said flexible connecting means, and a spring-pressed pivoted arm carrying said tension-wheel.

7. In a machine of the class described, the combination with a main shaft, a winding-reel 120 adapted to receive the film at its discharge and means for rotating said reel from said main shaft, comprising a shaft upon which said reel is mounted, a plurality of wheels of different radii mounted on said shaft, flexible means 125 connecting either of said wheels with said main shaft, and spring-pressed means for transmitting movement from said reel-shaft to said reel.

8. In a machine of the class described, the 130

combination with a main shaft, a winding-reel adapted to receive the film at its discharge and means for rotating said reel from said main shaft, comprising a shaft upon which said reel is mounted, a plurality of wheels of different radii mounted on said shaft, flexible means connecting either of said wheels with said main shaft, and means for transmitting movement from the reel-shaft to said reel, comprising a fixed and a loose plate on said shaft, one of said plates being engaged with said reel, a spring interposed between said plates, and adjusting means for varying the distance between said plates.

9. In a machine of the class described a winding-reel adapted to receive the film at its discharge, means for rotating the reel operated from the main shaft of the machine comprising a reel-shaft provided with a plurality of sprocket-wheels of different radii, whereby the speed of rotation of the shaft may be varied independently of the speed of rotation of the main shaft.

10. In a machine of the class described, a winding-reel adapted to receive the film at its discharge, means for rotating the reel operated from the main shaft of the machine comprising a reel - shaft provided with a plurality of sprocket-wheels of different radii, whereby the speed of rotation of the shaft may be varied independently of the speed of rotation of the main shaft and also comprising means for keeping the chain taut when its effective length is varied.

11. In a machine of the class described, a winding-reel adapted to receive the film at its discharge, means for rotating the reel operated from the main shaft of the machine comprising a reel - shaft provided with a plurality of sprocket-wheels of different radii, whereby the speed of rotation of the shaft may be varied independently of the speed of rotation of the main shaft and also comprising means for keeping the chain taut when its effective length is varied, consisting of a tension-roller yieldingly held against the chain.

12. In a machine of the class described, a winding-reel adapted to receive the film at its discharge, and means for rotating said reel, comprising a shaft upon which the reel is mounted, a plate loosely mounted on said shaft and engaged with said reel, a second plate carried by said shaft and partaking of the rotative movement thereof, said second plate being slidably mounted on said shaft, substantially as described, and for the purposes specified.

13. In a machine of the class described, a winding-reel adapted to receive the film at its discharge, and means for rotating said reel, comprising a shaft upon which the reel is mounted, a pair of plates each slidably mounted on said shaft and one of which engages said reel, means for causing the other of said plates to rotate with said shaft, means for adjusting the latter plate slidably on the shaft toward the other plate, and a spring interposed between said plates.

Witness my hand this 29th day of January, 1904, at the city of New York, in the county and State of New York.

ALBERT E. SMITH.

Witnesses:
HERMAN MEYER,
B. J. SMITH.

No. 785,205.

PATENTED MAR. 21, 1905.

W. ELLWOOD.
FLAME SHIELD FOR KINETOSCOPES.
APPLICATION FILED MAR. 30, 1904.

2 SHEETS—SHEET 1

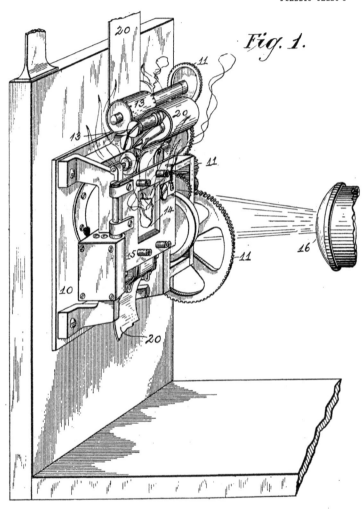

Fig. 1.

No. 785,205.                                    PATENTED MAR. 21, 1905.

W. ELLWOOD.
FLAME SHIELD FOR KINETOSCOPES.
APPLICATION FILED MAR. 30, 1904.

2 SHEETS—SHEET 2

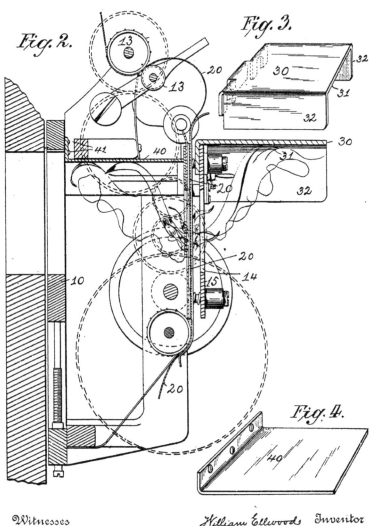

*Fig. 2.*

*Fig. 3.*

*Fig. 4.*

# UNITED STATES PATENT OFFICE.

WILLIAM ELLWOOD, OF BROOKLYN, NEW YORK. ASSIGNOR TO THE
VITAGRAPH COMPANY OF AMERICA, A CORPORATION OF NEW
YORK.

## FLAME-SHIELD FOR KINETOSCOPES.

SPECIFICATION forming part of Letters Patent No. 785,205, dated March 21, 1905.

Application filed March 30, 1904. Serial No. 200,704.

*To all whom it may concern:*

Be it known that I, WILLIAM ELLWOOD, a
citizen of the United States, and a resident of
Brooklyn, New York city, in the county of
5 Kings and State of New York, have invented
certain new and useful Improvements in
Flame-Shields for Kinetoscopes. of which the
following is a specification.

My invention relates to flame-shields for
10 kinetoscopes and similar forms of apparatus.

Moving-picture machines of the kind referred to comprise a long transparent film displaying a series of pictures, means for propelling the same rapidly intermittently in
15 front of a light-aperture, and a source of
proper illumination adapted to project rays of
light through the aperture in order that the
pictures may be thrown in succession enlarged
in size upon a suitable screen. A machine of
20 this class is shown and described in Letters
Patent of the United States No. 673,329, issued to Albert E. Smith, April 30, 1901, and
in one sense my invention is an improvement
upon that structure.

25 The transparent films employed are made of
pyroxylin or celluloid and are very inflammable. They are coiled above the machine on
a feeding-roll and below the machine are either
wound on a take-up reel or are allowed to fall
30 into a suitable receptacle. If in the course of
operating the machine the film-propelling
mechanism is stopped and the light is not shut
off at once, the rays impinge upon the section
of film in front of the light-aperture and in a
35 very short time set it on fire. Of course the
film may get afire from other causes; but this
is the chief one. As these machines are used
in theaters and are commonly placed in the
audience-room, a fire is apt to cause a panic
40 with disastrous results.

It has long been desired to provide some
means by which fires of the kind referred to
could be quickly extinguished. Endeavors
have been made to treat the film itself with
45 antiphlogistic material and to incase it in enveloping sleeves except at the point of use;
but all these methods, so far as they are known

to me, have tended to interfere with the transparency or efficiency of the film or with the
operation of the apparatus.                        50

I have discovered a simple and efficient
means for limiting the area of a fire of the
character referred to, so that it is almost immediately extinguished and does no harm, and
such means, in brief, consists of one or more    55
flame-shields placed above the exposed part
of the film and in relatively close proximity
thereto and adapted by reason of its size, arrangement, and material to prevent the spread
of the flame from the portion of the film in    60
proximity to the light-aperture to the portion
of said film above said light-aperture.

In the drawings, Figure 1 represents in perspective part of a moving-picture machine,
showing the source of the heat-rays and how   65
a film is ignited thereby. Fig. 2 is a vertical
central section through the apparatus, showing the flame-shields in place. Fig. 3 is a perspective of the front shield, and Fig. 4 of the
rear shield.                                      70

In the drawings, 10 is an upright frame or
support on which the apparatus is mounted.
Above it is a feed-roll secured in any suitable
manner, and proper propelling-gears 11 and
guiding devices 12 serve to conduct the film 20  75
from such feed-roll past a light-aperture 14 in
a shutter 15. 16 is the lantern provided with
a source of light-supply and adapted to project the light-rays to and through the light-
aperture. These parts are of usual construc-    80
tion and need no further or other description.

Mounted above the light-aperture and in
front of the apparatus (toward the lantern) is
a flame-shield 30. It is supported in any suitable manner and may be of any non-inflam-       85
mable material and any shape provided it presents a substantially horizontal impervious
obstacle 31 to the upward passage of the flames
on that side of the light-aperture. I prefer to
make this shield with depending flanges 32 32   90
in order to retard the spread of the flames
laterally; but in most cases they are not essential. Mounted also above the light-aperture and at the rear of the shutter is a second

flame-shield 40. It is supported in any suitable manner, as by the screws 41, from any portion of the apparatus. Like the similar shield 30, it may be of any desired shape and any non-inflammable material provided it presents a proper obstacle to the upward passage of the flames between the shutter 15 and the support 10. When these shields 30 and 40 have been put in position and the heat-rays from the lantern are permitted to impinge upon the film 20, the latter catches on fire and the flames spread upward to the front and rear; but their passage is checked by the shields and the fire dies out. It is impossible for it to follow the film upward between the shutter 15 and the diaphragm back of it for lack of air, and of course it cannot retreat downward. The result is that a hole is merely burned in the film, and the machine being again put into motion the exhibition can be continued uninterruptedly, the film itself can subsequently be pieced, and the burned spot cut out. If there existed a danger-spot similar to that at the light-aperture, it could be similarly protected by one or more flame-shields.

Having described my invention, what I claim as new is—

1. A moving-picture apparatus or the like, provided with a flame-shield comprising a substantially horizontal plate extending at an angle with the film and provided with one or more depending flanges, the whole placed above the danger-point and in close proximity thereto.

2. The combination with a kinetoscope comprising a film-propelling mechanism of a plurality of flame-shields placed in close proximity to the path of the film and extending outwardly therefrom.

3. The combination with a kinetoscope comprising a film-propelling mechanism of a plurality of flame-shields placed in close proximity to the path of the film and extending outwardly therefrom, one of said shields being provided with depending flanges.

4. A moving-picture apparatus provided with a plurality of flame-shields, arranged at opposite sides of the path traversed by the film in its passage across the light-aperture and in proximity to the latter and extending at an angle to the film and out of contact therewith throughout their length, said flame-shields comprising non-inflammable plates adapted to prevent the spread of the flame from the portion of the film in front of said aperture to that above the same.

Witness my hand this 29th day of March, 1904, at the city of New York, in the county and State of New York.

WILLIAM ELLWOOD

Witnesses:
ALAN CHARLES McDONNELL,
WILLIAM R. BAIRD.

Smith Patent No. 785,237
March 21, 1905.

A. E. SMITH.
FILM HOLDER FOR KINETOSCOPES.
APPLICATION FILED APR. 2, 1904.

2 SHEETS—SHEET 1.

*Fig. 1*

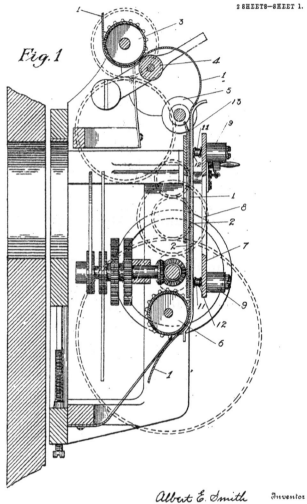

Albert E. Smith       Inventor

Witnesses
Estelle M. Titus
S. J. Cox

By William R. Baird

His Attorney

No. 785,237.

PATENTED MAR. 21, 1905.

A. E. SMITH.
FILM HOLDER FOR KINETOSCOPES.
APPLICATION FILED APR. 2, 1904.

2 SHEETS—SHEET 2.

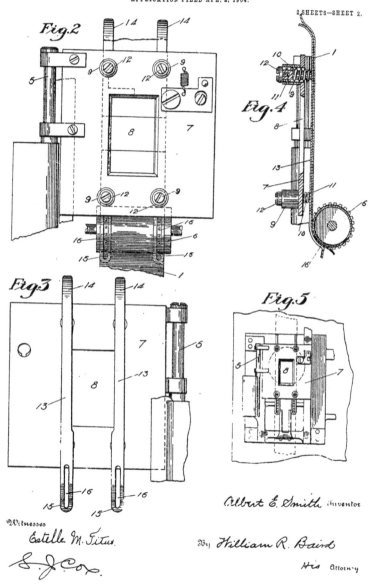

Witnesses
Estelle M. Titus.
S. J. Cox.

Albert E. Smith. Inventor

By William R. Baird

His Attorney

# UNITED STATES PATENT OFFICE.

## ALBERT E. SMITH, OF BROOKLYN, NEW YORK, ASSIGNOR TO THE VITAGRAPH COMPANY OF AMERICA, A CORPORATION OF NEW YORK.

### FILM-HOLDER FOR KINETOSCOPES.

SPECIFICATION forming part of Letters Patent No. 785,237, dated March 21, 1905.

Original application filed April 24, 1903, Serial No. 153,354. Divided and this application filed April 2, 1904. Serial No. 201,277.

*To all whom it may concern:*

Be it known that I, ALBERT E. SMITH, a citizen of the United States, and a resident of Brooklyn, in the county of Kings and State 5 of New York, have invented certain new and useful Improvements in Film-Holders for Kinetoscopes, of which the following is a specification.

This invention, which by requirement of the 10 Patent Office was divided from my application for Letters Patent filed April 24, 1903, Serial No. 153,354, consists in certain peculiarities in the construction of the means for holding the film in its passage across the light-15 apertures, substantially as hereinafter described. and particularly pointed out in the subjoined claims.

The particular object of the present invention is to provide a simple and practical means, 20 which will most efficiently hold the film in its passage across the light-aperture of the kinetoscope and will accommodate itself to irregularities in the film. This object is well accomplished by the construction shown in the 25 accompanying drawings. in which—

Figure 1 is a central vertical section and partial side elevation of a machine embodying my improvements. Fig. 2 is a front elevation of the friction-plate when in position to 30 hold the film. Fig. 3 is a similar view of the other side of the plate. Fig. 4 is a central vertical section and partial plan view of the cushion-spring and film. Fig. 5 is a miniature front elevation of the friction-plate and 35 its related parts.

The same reference characters designate the same parts in the several figures.

The general construction of the kinetoscope partially shown in the accompanying draw-40 ings resembles that disclosed in Letters Patent of the United States No. 673,329, granted to me April 30, 1901. For this reason and as the particular detail construction of kinetoscope is not essential to the present invention, 45 which relates to the film-holding plate or means for holding the film, a detail description of the parts is not deemed to be essential further than to state that 1 designates the film, which has perforated edges, and is fed from an upper supply-roll, (not shown,) passes un- 50 der the upper sprocket-drum 3, above the guide-roll 4 and bends outward, and thence passes downward in front of the guide-roll 5 and to the lower sprocket-drum 6. While taking this course the film 1 passes in front 55 of the light-aperture 2. It is in practice fed intermittently by the means shown in my application Serial No. 153,354, of which, as above stated, the present application is a division. 60

Hinged at 5 to swing upon bearings secured to the framework of the apparatus is a friction-plate 7, having an aperture 8, which registers with the general light-aperture 2 of the kinetoscope and provided on its outer side 65 with four projecting casings or pockets 9, which are arranged in two vertical pairs. Incased in said pockets are coiled springs 10, through which extend inwardly-projecting posts 11, which posts have threaded engage- 70 ment with screws or heads 12 at their outer ends. Each pair of posts is connected with a flat steel film-holding strip 13, of which strips there are two employed, arranged one at each side of the light-aperture. Each of said strips 75 13 is bent outward at its top 14 and inward at its bottom 15, and its lower portion is formed with an elongated slot 16, arranged opposite the teeth of the lower sprocket wheel or drum 6 in order to accommodate said teeth, and 80 thereby prevent the same from pressing the strips out of engagement with the film. Said strips thus constitute cushion-springs, and they are of sufficient width to afford a smooth firm bearing-surface against the two vertical 85 sides of the film as it moves downward. They bear upon the edges of the film where the sprocket-wheels are situated and do not bear upon any portion of its surface displaying the picture. They also follow the curve of 90 the film on its downward path and produce upon it a firm, uniform, and continuous pressure.

This device is much more efficient than a number of small springs arranged along the 95 path of the film. It not infrequently happens that the film is broken and has to be mended. At the place where so mended there is an extra thickness, and this is apt to catch upon the edges of individual springs arranged to hold it in place. With my improved cushion-spring, however, such portion of the film glides easily between the strip 15 and the guide-roller and passes on downward, gently pushing the strip back as it goes, and no interruption of the progress of the film can occur, although the film will be firmly held in place on both sides as desired.

It will be understood that the invention is not restricted in scope to the detailed construction described, which is merely selected because it is believed to exemplify the best embodiment of the invention. Changes in the details may be made without departing from the spirit of the invention.

Having thus described the invention, what I believe to be new, and desire to secure by Letters Patent, is—

1. In a kinetoscope, means adapted to hold the film in its passage across the light-aperture, comprising a friction-plate having an aperture to register with said light-aperture and provided at opposite sides of said aperture with a pair of relatively movable vertically-placed strips and with a plurality of springs arranged at different places in the length of each of said strips and pressing the same against said film, said strips engaging the edges of the film throughout their length and exerting a continuous pressure thereon.

2. In a kinetoscope, means adapted to hold the film in its passage across the light-aperture, consisting of a pair of continuous vertically-placed strips arranged at opposite sides of said aperture and engaging the edges of the film throughout their length, so as to exert a continuous pressure thereon, guiding means for said strips comprising posts arranged at right angles to said strips and connected therewith, and coiled springs mounted on said posts and engaged with said strips.

3. The combination with the frame of a kinetoscope, of the friction-plate provided with an aperture to register with the light-aperture of said frame, casings carried by said plate, spring-pressed posts in said casings and a pair of continuous strips each arranged at one side of said aperture and attached to a pair of said posts, said strips exerting a continuous pressure against the edges of the film at opposite sides of said aperture.

4. The combination with the frame of a kinetoscope, having a light-aperture, and means for feeding the film across the same comprising a sprocket to engage the film, of the friction-plate provided with an aperture to register with that of the frame, casings carried by said plate, spring-pressed posts in said casings, and a pair of continuous strips each arranged at one side of said aperture and extending above and below the same and attached to a pair of said posts, said strips exerting a continuous pressure against the edges of the film at opposite sides of said aperture and each having a bent and slotted end portion contiguous to said sprockets.

5. The combination with the frame of a kinetoscope, having a light-aperture, and means for feeding the film across the same, comprising a sprocket to engage the film, of a plate provided with an aperture to register with that of the frame, casings carried by said plate and having open outer ends, a post extending from each of said casings, a pair of continuous strips each arranged at one side of said aperture and attached to a pair of said posts, a coiled spring mounted on each post and engaging said strip, and an adjustable head for each post mounted in the open outer end of each casing and engaging the spring therein, substantially as described.

Witness my hand this 31st day of March, 1904, at the city of New York, in the county and State of New York.

ALBERT E. SMITH.

Witnesses:
ESTELLE M. TITUS,
WILLIAM R. BAIRD.

Defendants' Exhibit No. 194

Armat Patent No. 578,185
March 2, 1897.

# T. ARMAT.
## VITASCOPE.

No. 578,185.    Patented Mar. 2, 1897.

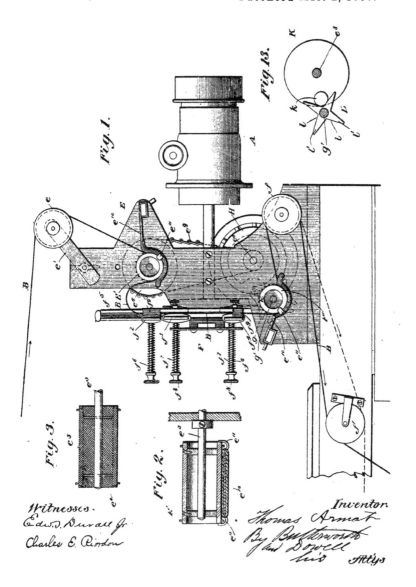

Fig.1.

Fig.13.

Fig.3.

Fig.2.

Witnesses.
Edw. D. Durall Jr
Charles E. Riordon

Inventor.
Thomas Armat
By Butterworth
and Dowell
his Att'ys

T. ARMAT.
VITASCOPE.

No. 578,185.

Patented Mar. 2, 1897.

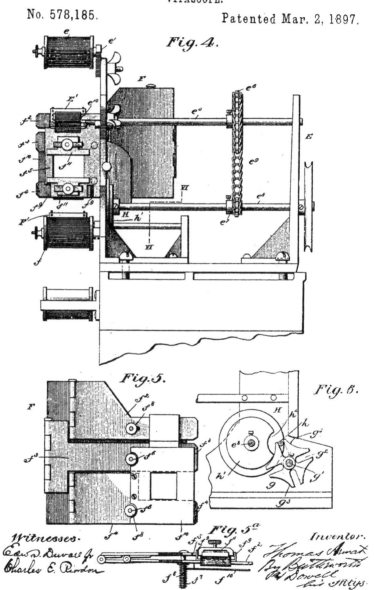

*Fig. 4.*

*Fig. 5.*

*Fig. 6.*

*Fig. 5ͣ*

Witnesses.
Edw. D. Duvall Jr
Charles E. Riordon

Inventor.
Thomas Armat
By Butterworth
& Dowell
his Attys.

T. ARMAT.
VITASCOPE.

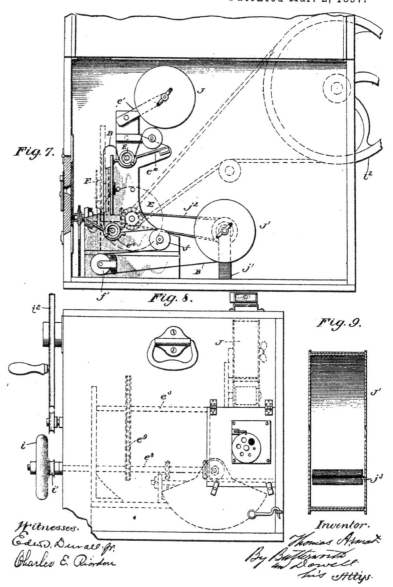

*Fig. 7.*

*Fig. 8.*

*Fig. 9.*

Witnesses.
Edw. Duvall Jr.
Charles E. Riordon

Inventor.
Thomas Armat
By Butterworth
his Attys.

**T. ARMAT.**
VITASCOPE.

No. 578,185.                          Patented Mar. 2, 1897.

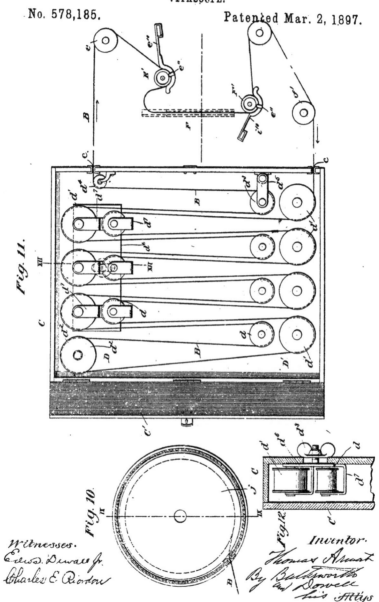

Fig. 11.

Fig. 10.

Witnesses.
Edw. Duvall Jr.
Charles E. Riordon

Inventor.
Thomas Armat
By Baldwin
and Dowell
his Attys

# UNITED STATES PATENT OFFICE.

## THOMAS ARMAT, OF WASHINGTON, DISTRICT OF COLUMBIA.

## VITASCOPE.

SPECIFICATION forming part of Letters Patent No. 578,185, dated March 2, 1897.

Application filed September 26, 1896. Serial No. 607,058. (No model.)

*To all whom it may concern:*

Be it known that I, THOMAS ARMAT, a citizen of the United States, residing at Washington, in the District of Columbia, have invented certain new and useful Improvements in Vitascopes; and I do hereby declare the following to be a full, clear, and exact description of the invention, such as will enable others skilled in the art to which it appertains to make and use the same.

This invention relates to apparatus for exhibiting pictures, but more particularly to that class of picture-exhibiting apparatus disclosed in my pending application, Serial No. 579,901, filed February 19, 1896, in which the impression is given to the eye of objects in motion.

The primary object of the invention is to provide improved and efficient means whereby a series of photographic or other pictures showing successively the different positions or attitudes assumed by a person or object in motion may be displayed in such a manner as to reproduce to the eye the appearance after a moving object through all the phases of such movement with a life-like and unblurred effect.

Another object is to provide simple and efficient mechanism for intermittently moving the film or band forming the picture-carrying surface, so as to successively place the objects thereon in position for reproduction, without liability of slipping and not moving the film the proper distance on account of the variations in its thickness or otherwise and without liability to injury from the knocking and jarring of the mechanism which is incident to the means usually employed or injury to the film by unnecessary strain and wear thereon.

Further objects are to provide simple and efficient mechanism capable of being also used in a photographic camera, to provide a tension and guiding device which will avoid the necessity of exerting a great pressure upon the film and which will instantaneously engage the film and hold it in its proper position without flexing or puckering at the point of exposure, and to provide simple and efficient means for holding the film while being operated.

With these and other objects in view the invention consists in the construction and combination of the several parts, substantially as hereinafter described, and then pointed out in the claims at the end of the description.

Referring to the accompanying drawings, forming a part of this specification, Figure 1 is a side elevation of a portion of an apparatus for reproducing pictures from a picture-carrying surface, illustrating my improved mechanism for operating and controlling the movements of the picture-carrying surface. Fig. 2 is a longitudinal section of one of the film-operating drums and the yielding pressure and guiding arm, and Fig. 3 is a detail longitudinal section of a modified form of drum. Fig. 4 is a rear elevation, on a smaller scale, of the film-operating mechanism and tensioning device with the projecting lens removed. Figs. 5 and 5ᵃ are a detail front elevation and plan, respectively, of the tension and guiding device. Fig. 6 is a fragmentary vertical sectional view, taken on the line VI VI of Fig. 4, illustrating in elevation the mechanism for operating one of the drums so as to intermittently move the film. Fig. 7 represents the interior of a camera casing or box with the mechanism in position for operating a photographic film. Fig. 8 is a front elevation of the camera-box, illustrating in elevation one means for imparting movement to the film-operating mechanism. Fig. 9 is a transverse vertical section of a casing or inclosure for containing the film-reel, the reel and film being removed. Fig. 10 is a longitudinal sectional view of the film-containing casing with the reel therein in position for use. Fig. 11 represents in side elevation, partly diagrammatic, a preferred arrangement of the film and support and casing or inclosure therefor. Fig. 12 is a vertical sectional view taken on the line XII XII of Fig. 11, and Fig. 13 is a vertical sectional view of a modified form of mechanism for intermittently operating the drum

In this apparatus, like that shown in my pending application above referred to, the picture is exposed for projection a much longer time than is required to displace it and substitute another in its stead, thus prolonging the period of illumination very greatly as compared with the period of interruption or change, and there is no necessity for obstruc-

tion of the light by the interposition of a
shutter or opaque substance across its path,
so that the impression of the picture on the
eye is so much longer and more permanent
than the distortion or shadow effect incident
to its movement, and the interval of change
or interruption is so infinitesimal that the
image of the picture is readily retained until
displacement and substitution takes effect,
and owing to the inability of the eye to receive an impression from every phase of motion the interruption or change is wholly imperceptible, and the result is a most vivid appearance of an object in motion, otherwise unchanging, clearly exhibiting all the phases of
such motion with life-like effect. This I accomplish by improved mechanism for moving
the film or other picture-carrying surface intermittently in such a manner that the interval of exposure and illumination of the picture shall so far exceed the interval of time
required to effect a change as to enable the
eye to receive a perfect impression or image
at each exposure and to retain it through the
interval of motion or change and until another picture has been superimposed, as it
were, upon the one displaced, thus taking advantage both of the inability of the eye to receive an impression of movement exceeding
a certain rapidity and upon that faculty of
the eye which enables it to retain an impression after each phase or view of the object
has vanished — the persistence of vision —
which enables me to change the pictures one
for another imperceptibly, so as to give to the
eye the impression of objects in motion.

In practice I employ, as usual, an illuminator and a condensing-lens (not shown) adapted to concentrate the rays of light upon a picture located in the focus of an objective lens
A, the latter, as well as the illuminator and
condensing-lens, being of the usual or of any
preferred construction and being arranged
in any suitable manner. The strip or film B
may be composed of any suitable transparent or translucent flexible substance adapted
to provide a surface for carrying pictures
produced thereon by photographic or other
means, the several pictures in the series representing, successively, different positions of
a moving object, so that the rapid exhibition
of the entire series of pictures in the order in
which they were made or taken may result in
the reproduction of the appearance of the
moving object in every phase of its motion.
This film may be either an endless or a continuous band and supported upon rollers or
in any other suitable manner, but I prefer to
make the film endless and arrange the same
as shown in Fig. 11. In this case a box or inclosure C is provided with a lid or cover C',
preferably partly or wholly of glass, so as to
permit the interior of the box or casing to be
readily seen, and slots or guiding portions c
through which the film may pass, said guiding portions being provided with a soft covering of suitable material to prevent injury

to the film during its rapid movement into
and out of the casing.

Within the casing are arranged an upper
and a lower bank of rollers or spools D D',
respectively, each comprising two series or
rows of rollers of any desired number and of
different diameters, the smaller rollers d being interposed between the outer or larger
rollers d'. The smaller rollers of each bank
are preferably arranged in the same vertical
plane as the larger rollers, so as to provide a
number of pairs according to the length of
the film it is desired to inclose within the casing, and the rollers of one bank are directly
opposed to the spaces between the rollers of
the other bank, so that the film may be made to
pass successively around or partially around
the larger rollers of one of the banks and the
smaller rollers of the other bank, as D' and D,
respectively, and then to the initial roller $d^2$
of the bank D to the initial smaller roller of
the bank D', and so on successively through
the series of rollers to the last roller $d^2$ of the
bank D' and then over a guide-roller $d^4$, arranged adjacent to the upper guiding portion
or slot c of the casing or box C, though it is
to be understood that the reverse of this winding may take place, as from the smaller rollers to the larger, or there may be provided
more than two banks of rollers if desired.

One of the rollers of the bank D', preferably roller $d^3$, may be journaled upon an arm,
as $d^5$, which has one end pivoted to the casing,
so as to permit free upward and downward
movement of the roller, said roller being of
sufficient weight, or independently weighted,
to provide sufficient tension on the film to take
up any slack therein, while either or both of
the banks or a number of the rollers thereof
may be made adjustable, as, for instance, the
three pairs of rollers of the bank D'. These
adjustable rollers or spools may be journaled
upon spindles extending outwardly from a
base-plate $d^6$, the outer ends of these spindles
being supported in preferably L-shaped
brackets $d^7$, extending outwardly from the
base-plate on the side opposite to where the
film passes around the rollers. The other rollers of each bank, except the tension-roller
$d^3$, are also preferably journaled in similar
brackets, which may be secured to the casing
or secured to or formed integrally with a plate
held or arranged in the casing in any suitable
manner.

The base-plate of the adjustable rollers is
provided with an outwardly-extending stem
or bolt which passes through a slot arranged
in the casing and has a nut $d^8$ arranged on its
outer end adapted to rigidly bind the base-
plate to the casing in various adjustments.
By this means a very long film may be protected and arranged in a very compact space,
so as to be readily fed into and out of the
inclosure or casing and provision made so as
to compensate for varying lengths of film.

The film B may pass from one casing C
to a roller or idler e, Fig. 1, journaled in

a bracket or arm $e'$, suitably held upon the frame E, and then around the lower surface of a feed-drum E'. This drum may be of any suitable construction, but preferably consists of a light hollow casing, as aluminium, provided with teeth or projections for engaging perforations or apertures in the film, and fitted over or upon and rigidly secured to one or more collars arranged upon a shaft $e^3$, as shown in Fig. 2, or said drum may consist of a hard-rubber spool or other body-portion $e^4$, secured to the shaft $e^3$, over which is forced a soft-rubber band or ring $e^3$, so as to be rigidly held between the outer flanges of the spool, as shown in Fig. 3, the band $e^5$ being provided with teeth or projections for engaging the apertures in the film. The shaft $c^3$ may be journaled in any suitable manner in the frame E, and may be provided with a sprocket-wheel $e^6$, which is connected to a sprocket-wheel $e^7$ on the driving-shaft $e^8$ by a chain $e^9$, or operated from said driving-shaft in any other preferred manner, so as to constantly rotate the feed-drum E' and feed the film. To one side of this feed-drum may also be placed an arm $e^{10}$, adjustably held to the frame, if desired, and provided with a curved spring or yielding portion adapted to bear underneath the film and press it gently against the periphery of the drum, so that the teeth will engage the perforations and prevent its slipping, the arm being preferably covered with plush or other soft material to prevent wearing or injuring the surface of the film, and with fingers or projections $e^{11}$, adapted to engage the edges of the film and aline the same, and to prevent enlarging or otherwise injuring the perforations or apertures in said film.

Owing to the rigidity or stiffness of the film it will be caused to move or be carried upwardly and outwardly a short distance away from the drum E' and its point of contact with the yielding portion of the arm $e^{10}$, so as to provide constant slack in the film at this point, and then with a return-bend it may pass in a substantially straight line through the tension and guiding device F, and thence around the drum F', (which may be similarly constructed to the feed-drum E' and provided with a similar pressure and guide arm,) from which the film may pass around an idler $f$, and thence around another idler or roller $f'$, as shown in full lines in Fig. 1, or in the manner indicated in dotted lines in said figure or in Fig. 11, when the casing therein shown is employed; both the rollers $f$ and $e$, as well as the others, if desired, being provided with a layer of plush or soft material to prevent injury to said film.

As a means for tensioning and frictionally holding the film so as to permit the series of pictures thereon to be brought successively into the illuminated field and retained therein for exposure for a predetermined time I preferably provide the tension device with three yielding members $f^2$, $f^3$, and $f^4$, though, of course, a greater number may be employed. These yielding members are each independently hinged or pivoted to a stationary member $f^5$, which is adapted to be rigidly secured to the frame E, and have their outer portions provided with a covering of soft material, as plush, overlying a yielding body, as rubber, if desired, so as to frictionally hold the film against the stationary member and prevent wear of the film, a layer of leather or other material being arranged upon the stationary member, so as to form an opposed bearing-surface for the film. A series of stems or bolts $f^6$ project outwardly from the stationary member $f^5$, each of which pass through an aperture in one of the yielding or hinged members and have a spiral spring $f^7$ interposed between the outer surface of each member and a nut $f^8$ arranged upon the outer end of said stem or bolt, so as to vary the pressure of each spring in order to exert the desired pressure upon the film. The members $f^2$ and $f^4$ have guides $f^9$, Figs. 1 and 5ª, passing through recessed portions of the stationary member, so as to engage the edges of the film and aline the same as it passes through the tension device, while upon the lower member $f^4$ a plate $f^{10}$ may be provided to protect the film from the heat of the illuminator and provide a space for the circulation of air between said plate and the film, so as to keep the latter cool. This plate is provided with an opening adapted to register with an opening in the stationary member or plate $f^5$, so as to permit exposure of the pictures carried by the film, the stationary member being preferably provided with one or more adjustable plates $f^{11}$, Fig. 4, for varying the size of the opening therein according to the position of the pictures or objects to be exposed relative to the perforations in the film, as the pictures on different films do not always occupy the same position with reference to the apertures or perforations.

The upper member $f^2$ preferably exerts less pressure than the other members and serves the double purpose of a brush to keep the film free from dust and to assist in holding the film so as to provide slack above the tension device and prevent flexing or puckering of said film at the point of exposure.

By providing three or more yielding members the tension of each member on the film may be greatly diminished, and at the same time the prompt action of one or more of the members is secured the instant the film has moved the desired distance.

For the purpose of intermittently moving or feeding the film or picture-carrying surface in such manner as to cause the series of pictures thereon to be brought into and permitted to remain in the illuminated field for an interval of time exceeding the time required to effect the displacement of any one picture and the substitution of another therefor, I prefer to employ a wheel or disk $g$, Figs. 1 and 6, which is secured to the shaft $g'$ of the drum F', preferably immediately inside of the upright or standard of the frame. This wheel or disk is provided with radial slots or recesses $g^2$, preferably four in number, extending to the periphery of said wheel, and may have depressed or concaved portions $g^3$ between the slots, so as to provide a wheel or disk substantially of the form of a Maltese cross.

Adjacent to the wheel $g$ and preferably secured to the driving-shaft $e^3$ is a rotating element H, provided with a lateral projection $h$, on which may be arranged a roller adapted to successively enter the slots or recesses $g^2$ and engage portions of the wheel, so as to intermittently move the latter when the element H is rotated. The element H may also be provided with a disk or circular plate $h'$, having a portion thereof recessed, as at $h^2$, to permit the wheel $g$ to rotate while engaged by the projection $h$, but which will engage the depressions in said wheel by its periphery as soon as the projection leaves any one of the slots, so as to cause the slots or recesses in the disk to always register with said projection and to hold the wheel and drum F' stationary for an interval of time in excess of the interval of time of each movement of said drum, the shafts $e^3$ and $e^8$ being so timed relatively to each other that the feed-drum E' and the drum F' will move the film the same distance in the same interval of time. It is to be understood, however, that a separate disk or wheel provided with concave depressions may be secured to the shaft $g'$ or arranged to rotate therewith and properly positioned with respect to a slotted disk and that a separate circular plate or disk may be provided for engaging these depressions, the latter being also rotated and positioned with respect to the projection $h$ of the rotating element. The rotating element is preferably of greater diameter than the wheel $g$ in order that said wheel may be rotated the required distance and be held stationary as long as possible relatively to the time occupied by each movement. This arrangement permits very small and light film - moving drums to be employed, and, as will be seen, the projection $h$ will gradually enter and leave the slots or recesses in the disk $g$, so as to gradually start and stop said drums, thus greatly removing the strain from the film incident to the necessarily instantaneous motion thereof, and furthermore provides an intermittently - operated drum which constantly engages the film, so as to prevent the possibility of the film slipping by reason of variations in its thickness.

The operation of the invention will be readily understood from the foregoing description when taken in connection with the accompanying drawings.

The parts being in the position shown in Figs. 1 and 11 and the driving-shaft $e^4$ operated by an electric motor or in any other suitable manner, so as to rotate the shaft $e^3$ and the feed-drum E' at the proper speed, the film B will be moved in the direction indicated by the arrows, but the pressure exerted by the tension device F' will hold the film stationary with the exposed picture in the field of illumination for a predetermined time, so as to provide sufficient slack in the film at the bend thereof above said tension device to permit a rapid movement of a given length sufficient to displace any one of the pictures in the series and permit another to be brought into position for exposure or reproduction. When the object has been held in the field of illumination the proper interval of time, the projection $h$ enters one of the slots in the disk $g$ and rotates said disk and the drum F' and moves the film so as to displace the exposed picture and bring another into the field of illumination, the yielding members of the tension device permitting the film to be forced or drawn downward, but the instant the drum F' ceases to rotate one or more of said members will engage the film and prevent further movement thereof until the drum is again rotated. The projection $h$ is so arranged that it carries the wheel or disk $g$ a part of a revolution equal to the distance between any two slots or recesses, in this case one-fourth of a revolution, and simultaneously with the exit of said projection from any one slot the periphery of the circular plate or disk $h'$ engages the depressions or concave portions $g^3$ of said disk, so that the drum F' will be held perfectly stationary in order to permit each phase or position of the object to be held in the field of illumination the proper interval of time and the next slot placed in position for the projection $h$ at the next rotation of the element H. During this interval of time the slack in the film between the drum F' and the idler $f$ will be gradually drawn into the box or inclosure C by the feed-drum E', but not at such a speed as to exert a tension or pulling strain upon the drum F', and in the same instant of time, while the picture is being exhibited, the slack in the film between the tension device and the drum E', which has been partially or wholly taken up by advancing the film, will be compensated by an additional amount of slack paid out by said latter drum, thus providing sufficient slack ahead of the tension device to permit the next succeeding picture to be brought quickly into the field of illumination. This operation will be repeated in regular sequence, the greater portion of the film being caused to move continuously, while that portion thereof which lies between the two drums is intermittently moved forward just far enough to expose a picture at each move, the interval of illumination of the picture being made to exceed the interval of movement or change preferably very greatly. In this manner the pictures on the picture-carrying surface or film may be successively displaced and substituted one for another with great rapidity, so that in exhibiting a series of similar pictures representing the same moving object in different phases of its motion the impression may be given to the eye of persons or objects in motion and with a vivid and life-like appearance. I thus provide simple and efficient means for positively engaging and operating the film, so that it may be moved the proper distance for exposing the successive pictures without liability to slipping due to the varying thickness of the film and without the knocking and jolting of the machinery incident to the necessarily rapid movement of the parts or unnecessary strain and wear upon the film. Also simple means are provided for tensioning and guiding the film and for placing and adjustably holding the film in a comparatively small space.

The film-operating mechanism may be used to advantage in a photographic camera, as shown in Figs. 7 and 8. The camera may be of the usual or of any preferred form, and the driving-shaft $e^2$ may be provided with a fly-wheel $i$ and a sprocket or pulley wheel $i'$, adapted to have motion imparted thereto by a belt or chain connecting said pulley or sprocket wheel to a much larger hand-wheel $i^2$, so as to permit very rapid movement of the film, though any other suitable means may be employed for rotating the driving-shaft. In this case, and in some instances with a re-producing apparatus, the film is wound upon a suitable reel and held in a casing or closure J, supported upon the arm $e'$, instead of the idler $e$, and after passing around the idler or roller $f'$ the film is passed backward and wound upon a reel $j$, Fig. 10, journaled within a casing J'. This latter casing is mounted and rigidly held upon a support, as at $f'$, and the reel on which the strip is to be wound is rotated by a slip-belt $j^3$ or by any other suitable frictional gearing. Each of these casings or closures, Figs. 9 and 10, preferably comprise two telescopic members adapted to be removably held together by friction or otherwise, and has a pin or shaft on which the reel $j$ is loosely journaled or to which the reel is secured, so as to rotate therewith. The members of each casing are provided with slits $j^3$, adapted to register with each other and permit the film to be wound upon or from the reel contained therein, the slits being provided with a suitable covering to prevent abrading the surface of the film. Such casings protect the film from light or exposure in a photographic apparatus and protect it from dust and the like when used in a reproducing apparatus.

Instead of the mechanism shown in Figs. 1 to 8, inclusive, for intermittently operating the drum and film I may provide a disk or wheel, as shown in Fig. 13. In this case the rotating element K has a lateral projection $k$, adapted to enter the slots or recesses $l$ and engage portions or arms $l'$ of the wheel L at each revolution thereof, so as to rotate said wheel and the drum F' the proper distance. The disk or circular plate $h'$ and the engaging portions therefor for positively hold-

ing the drum stationary and alining the slots or recesses for the projection $k$ both in this and in the preferred form may be dispensed with and the tension device utilized for stopping the film the instant the projection $k$ ceases to rotate the wheel and film-engaging drum.

In some instances I may provide an inclosure or casing for the mechanism and arrange a mirror at an angle and at a convenient distance from the projecting lens, so as to reflect the rays upward and backward upon a screen located above the mechanism in order to secure as large a picture as possible within a compact space when it is desired to place the apparatus in public places for exhibition by using coin-actuated mechanism or otherwise.

While, as described, the pictures are brought successively into an illuminated field and each picture illuminated without interruption from the instant it enters such field until displaced by the next picture in the series, I do not desire to be confined to the use of the invention without a shutter, inasmuch as such a device might be used under some circumstances, as, for instance, when constructed so as to interrupt the illumination only at that instant of time when the film is moving and without rendering the interruption perceptible to the eye.

It is obvious that the film may be fed to the tension device by other means than the use of a feed-drum and taken up by other means than that shown, that certain parts of the apparatus may be dispensed with or others substituted therefor, and that some parts of the operating mechanism and other parts of the apparatus may be employed with either a photographic or reproducing apparatus without departing from the spirit of my invention.

Having thus fully described my invention, what I claim as new, and desire to secure by Letters Patent of the United States, is—

1. The combination with a film or strip, of a tension device for yieldingly holding said film, a drum engaging the film, a wheel or disk provided with projections or portions forming a series of peripheral recesses, and a rotating element provided with a projection adapted to successively enter the recesses and engage a portion of the wheel at each revolution so as to intermittently rotate the drum and move the film with a gradual start-and-stop motion, whereby a very small and light drum may be employed and a positive intermittent motion imparted to the film so as to avoid racking and jolting of the mechanism and unnecessary wear and strain upon the film, substantially as described

2. The combination with a film or strip, of a tension device for yieldingly holding said film, a drum engaging the film, a wheel or disk provided with peripheral slots or recesses, and a rotating element provided with a lateral projection adapted to successively enter the slots or recesses and engage a portion of the wheel at each revolution so as to

intermittently rotate the drum and move the film through the tension device, whereby a very small and light drum may be employed and a positive intermittent motion imparted to the film so as to avoid racking and jolting of the mechanism and unnecessary wear and strain upon the film, substantially as described.

3. The combination with a film or strip, of a tension device for yieldingly holding said film, a drum engaging the film, a wheel rotating with said drum and provided with peripheral slots or recesses, a rotating element provided with a lateral projection adapted to successively enter the slots and engage portions of the wheel during a small portion of each revolution so as to intermittently rotate the drum and move the film through the tension device, and means for holding the drum and slotted wheel stationary during the greater portion of each revolution of the rotating element and for alining said wheel so as to permit the projection to readily enter the slots, whereby a very small and light drum may be employed and a gradual start-and-stop intermittent motion imparted to said drum so as to avoid racking and jolting of the machinery and unnecessary wear and strain upon the film, substantially as described.

4. The combination with a film or strip, of a tension device, a drum engaging the film so as to draw or force the same past said tension device, a peripherally-slotted wheel rotating with the drum and provided with concave depressions between said slots, a rotating element provided with a lateral projection adapted to enter the slots and engage portions of the wheel so as to intermittently rotate the same, and a disk or circular plate having a recessed portion adapted to engage the depression in the slotted wheel, whereby a very light and small drum may be employed and a gradual start-and-stop intermittent motion imparted to said drum so as to avoid racking and jolting of the mechanism and unnecessary wear and strain upon the film, substantially as described.

5. The combination with a film or strip, of a tension device, a drum engaging the film so as to draw or force the same through said tension device, a peripherally and radially slotted or recessed disk or wheel rotating with said drum and provided with concave depressions between said slots, a rotating element provided with a projection adapted to successively enter the slots and engage portions of the wheel so as to intermittently rotate the same, and a disk or circular plate having a peripheral recessed portion positioned with respect to the projection so as to permit rotary motion of the slotted wheel and having its periphery adapted to engage the depressions in said slotted wheel so as to hold the drum stationary for an interval of time in excess of the interval of rotation, whereby a very light and small drum may be employed

and a gradual start-and-stop intermittent motion imparted to said drum so as to avoid racking and jolting of the mechanism and unnecessary wear and strain upon the film, substantially as described.

6. The combination with a film or strip, of a feed-drum engaging the film so as to impart movement thereto when rotated, mechanism for rotating said drum, a tension device through which the film passes, a second drum engaging the film so as to move the film forward through said tension device, a peripherally-slotted wheel rotating with said latter drum and provided with concave depressions between said slots, a rotating element of greater diameter than the slotted wheel provided with a lateral projection adapted to enter the slots and engage portions of the wheel so as to intermittently rotate the same, and a recessed disk or circular plate having its periphery adapted to engage the depressions in the slotted wheel so as to intermittently hold said wheel stationary, whereby a very light and small drum may be employed and a gradual start-and-stop intermittent motion imparted to said drum so as to avoid racking and jolting of the mechanism and unnecessary wear and strain upon the film, substantially as described.

7. The combination with a film or strip, of a feed-drum engaging the film so as to impart movement thereto when rotated, a tension device through which the film passes, mechanism for constantly rotating the drum so as to provide slack on one side of the tension device, a second drum engaging the film so as to move said film forward through said tension device, a peripherally-slotted wheel rotating with said latter drum and provided with concave depressions between said slots, a rotating element comprising two disk-like portions, one of which has a lateral projection adapted to enter the slots and engage portions of the wheel so as to intermittently rotate the same, and the other with a peripherally-recessed portion located adjacent to the projection so as to permit rotary motion of the slotted wheel and having its periphery adapted to engage the depressions in said slotted wheel so as to intermittently hold said wheel stationary, whereby a very light and small drum may be employed and a gradual start-and-stop intermittent motion imparted to said drum so as to avoid racking and jolting of the mechanism and unnecessary wear and strain upon the film, substantially as described.

8. The combination with a film or strip, of a tension device, a drum engaging the film so as to draw or force the same past the tension device, a peripherally-slotted wheel rotating with said drum and provided with concave depressions between said slots forming a substantially Maltese-cross-shaped wheel, a rotating element provided with a lateral projection adapted to enter the slots and engage portions of the wheel so as to intermittently

rotate the same, and a recessed disk or circular plate adapted to engage the depressions in the slotted wheel so as to intermittently hold the drum stationary, whereby a very light and small drum may be employed and a gradual start-and-stop intermittent motion imparted to said drum so as to avoid racking and jolting of the mechanism and unnecessary wear and strain upon the film, substantially as described.

9. The combination with a film or strip, of a feed-drum engaging the film so as to impart movement thereto when rotated, a shaft to which said drum is secured, a tension device for holding the film, a second drum engaging the film so as to draw or force said film past the tension device, a peripherally-slotted wheel rotating with said drum, a rotating element provided with a lateral projection adapted to enter the slots and engage portions of the wheel so as to intermittently rotate the same, means for intermittently holding the slotted disk and drum stationary for intervals of time in excess of the intervals of rotation, a shaft to which the rotating element is secured, together with a sprocket-wheel and chain connection between this latter shaft and the feed-drum shaft so as to be simultaneously operated, whereby simple operating mechanism and a very light and small drum may be employed and a gradual start-and-stop intermittent motion imparted to said drum so as to avoid racking and jolting of the mechanism and unnecessary wear and strain upon the film, substantially as described.

10. The combination with a film or strip and means for intermittently moving the same so as to successively expose the pictures thereon, of a tension device provided with three or more yielding parts or members for holding the film so as to insure prompt action of one or more of said members the instant the film has moved the desired distance, substantially as described.

11. The combination with a film or strip and means for imparting movement to the same, of a tension device provided with three or more independent spring-pressed members or parts for yieldingly holding the film so as to insure prompt action of one or more of said members the instant the film has moved the desired distance; the upper member exerting less pressure than the others and serving to act as a brush to clear the film of dust as well as to exert tension on said film, substantially as described.

12. The combination with a film or strip, of a tension device comprising a stationary member, three spring-pressed members arranged one above the other and adapted to yieldingly press the film against said stationary member, and guides arranged upon the upper and lower members for alining the film; said upper member exerting less pressure upon the film than the other members and serving also as a brush to free the film from dust, substantially as described.

13. The combination with a film or strip, of a tension device, means for intermittently moving said film so as to impart a step-by-step movement thereto, and mechanism for feeding the film so as to provide slack therein between the same and said tension device; said tension device being provided with three yielding parts or members for holding the film so as to insure prompt action of one or more of said members the instant the film has moved the desired distance, substantially as described.

14. The combination with a film and means for operating the same so as to successively expose a portion thereof, of two or more banks of spools or rollers around which the film passes, each comprising two series or rows of rollers of varying diameters forming a series of pairs, the banks being opposed to each other, and the rollers of one bank opposed to the spaces between the rollers of the opposite bank, so that the film may pass around the larger rollers of one bank to the smaller rollers of the other bank successively, and then around the larger rollers of the latter bank to the smaller rollers of the first-mentioned bank in a similar manner, whereby a great length of film may be arranged in a very compact space, substantially as described.

15. The combination with an endless film and means for operating the same so as to successively expose a portion thereof, of a casing or closure provided with a cover or lid and guiding-slots through which the film may pass, and two banks of spools or rollers around which the film passes, each comprising two series or rows of rollers of varying diameters forming a series of pairs, the banks being opposed to each other and the rollers of one bank opposed to the spaces between the rollers of the opposite bank, so that the film may pass around the larger rollers of one bank to the smaller rollers of the other bank successively, and then around the larger rollers of the latter bank to the smaller rollers of the first-mentioned bank in a similar manner, whereby a great length of film may be arranged and protected in a very small space, substantially as described.

16. The combination with an endless film, and means for operating the same so as to successively expose a portion thereof, of a casing or closure provided with a cover or lid, guiding-slots through which the film passes, a guide-roller for the film arranged adjacent to one of the guiding-slots, and two banks of spools or rollers around which the film passes, each comprising two series or rows of rollers of varying diameters forming a series of pairs, the banks being opposed to each other and the rollers of one bank opposed to the spaces between the rollers of the opposite bank, so that the film may pass around the larger rollers of one bank to the smaller roll-

ers of the other bank successively, and then around the larger rollers of the latter bank to the smaller rollers of the first-mentioned bank in a similar manner; said banks having two or more of their rollers adjustable and one of the rollers journaled in an arm pivoted to the casing, whereby long and varying lengths of film may be arranged and protected in a very compact space, substantially as described.

17 . In a device of the character described, a drum comprising a body portion and a cov-ering of soft rubber provided with projections adapted to engage apertures or perforations in a film and serve as an abutting or engaging surface therefor, substantially as described.

In testimony whereof I affix my signature in presence of two witnesses.

THOMAS ARMAT.

Witnesses:
CHARLES E. RIORDON,
J. A. E. CRISWELL.

Armat Patent No. 580,749
April 13, 1897.

(No Model.)

# T. ARMAT.
## VITASCOPE.

No. 580,749. Patented Apr. 13, 1897.

Witnesses.
Edw. J. Duvall Jr.
Charles E. Riordon

Inventor.
Thomas Armat.
By Butterworth and Dowell
his Attys.

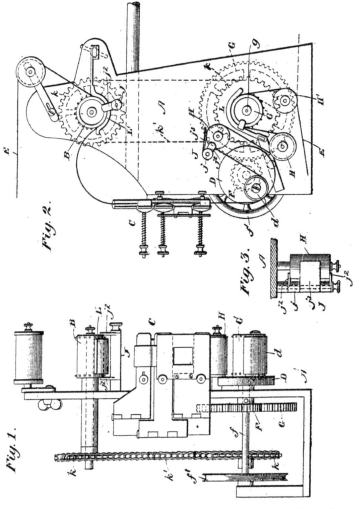

# UNITED STATES PATENT OFFICE.

## THOMAS ARMAT, OF WASHINGTON, DISTRICT OF COLUMBIA.

## VITASCOPE.

SPECIFICATION forming part of Letters Patent No. 580,749, dated April 13, 1897.

Application filed November 25, 1896. Serial No. 613,406. (No model.)

*To all whom it may concern:*

Be it known that I, THOMAS ARMAT, a citizen of the United States, residing at Washington, in the District of Columbia, have invented certain new and useful Improvements in Vitascopes; and I do hereby declare the following to be a full, clear, and exact description of the invention, such as will enable others skilled in the art to which it appertains to make and use the same.

This invention relates to apparatus for exhibiting pictures, but more particularly to that class of picture-exhibiting apparatus disclosed in my pending application, Serial No. 579,901, filed February 19, 1896, in which the impression is given to the eye of objects in motion.

The primary object of the invention is to provide simple and efficient means for imparting motion to the film-operating mechanism, whereby a series of photographic or other pictures showing successively the different positions or attitudes assumed by a person or object in motion may be displayed in such a manner as to reproduce to the eye the appearance of the moving object through all the phases of such movement with a life-like and unblurred effect.

Another object is to provide simple and efficient means for relieving the strain on the film between the tension device and the take-up drum while the film is being intermittently moved, and to prevent the teeth on the take-up drum from enlarging or otherwise injuring the apertures or perforations in the film or strip, whereby the life of the film, as well as its efficiency, is materially enhanced.

Further objects are to provide a simple and efficient guiding device for alining the film and to provide means adapted to be employed in a photographic apparatus.

The invention will be first hereinafter more particularly described and then pointed out in the claims at the end of the description.

Referring to the accompanying drawings, forming a part of this specification, Figure 1 is a front elevation of a portion of the apparatus embodying my invention with the film or strip removed. Fig. 2 is a side elevation of the mechanism shown in Fig. 1 with the film in position, and Fig. 3 is a detail plan view of one of the spools or drums and the guide-fingers for alining the film.

In the drawings, A may designate a suitable frame or support, B a feed-drum, C a tension device, and D a rotating element preferably provided with an eccentrically-arranged roller d, adapted to engage the film or strip E at each revolution, so as to intermittently move the film or a portion thereof through the tension device, all of which may be of any preferred form or construction or similarly constructed to that disclosed in my application before referred to or in my pending application, Serial No. 607,058, filed September 26, 1896.

The operation and movement of the film may be such that each successive picture is held a much longer time than is required to remove it and substitute another in its stead, thus prolonging the period of illumination very greatly as compared with the period of interruption or change; and there is no necessity for obstruction of the light by the interposition of a shutter or opaque substance across its path, so that the impression of the picture on the eye is so much longer and more permanent than the distortion or shadow effect incident to its movement, and the interval of change or interruption is so infinitesimal that the image of the picture is readily retained until displacement and substitution take effect; and owing to the inability of the eye to receive an impression from every phase of motion the interruption or change is wholly imperceptible, and the result is a most vivid appearance of an object in motion, otherwise unchanging, clearly exhibiting all the phases of such motion with life-like effect.

I have not illustrated an illuminator and a condensing-lens adapted to concentrate the rays of light upon a picture located in the focus of an objective lens, but this latter, as well as the illuminator and condensing-lens, may be of the usual or of any preferred construction and arranged in any suitable manner.

The film or strip may be composed of any suitable transparent or translucent flexible substance preferably provided with the usual apertures or perforations near its edges, and adapted to provide a surface for carrying pic-

tures produced thereon by photographic or other means, the several pictures in the series representing successively different positions of a moving object, so that the rapid exhibi-
5 tion of the entire series of pictures in the order in which they were made or taken may result in the reproduction of the appearance of the moving object in every phase of its motion. This film may be either an endless or
10 a continuous band or strip supported in any suitable manner and may be arranged and operated so that slack may be provided between the feed-drum B and the tension device in order that the entire film need not be
15 moved, as in my aforesaid applications.

Owing to the usual form and arrangement of the take-up drum and the mechanism for intermittently moving the film, and the high speed necessary for the proper action thereof,
20 it has been necessary to employ more or less complicated speed-reducing mechanism between said take-up drum and the film-operating mechanism, thereby materially increasing the cost of manufacture of the appara-
25 tus and causing considerable backlashing and jarring of the parts. To obviate these objectionable features, I secure a gear F to the shaft f of the rotating element D, adapted to mesh with a larger gear G, secured to the
30 shaft g, though in some instances a gear or gears adapted to mesh with each other and with the gears F and G may be employed, if desired.

The shaft f is preferably provided with a
35 driving-wheel f' or other means for rotating the same, while the shaft g has the take-up drum G' secured thereto, said drum being preferably provided with teeth or projections adapted to engage the perforations in the
40 film or strip. This take-up drum and its shaft are arranged to rotate relatively to the shaft of the rotating element according to the length of film and the number of pictures thereon moved at each revolution of said
45 shafts. In this instance the rotating element D moves the film or a portion thereof equal to the distance between any two successive pictures, so as to displace one picture and place another in its stead, and the gears F
50 and G and the take-up drum G' are so proportioned that the rotating element makes four revolutions to one revolution of said drum. By this means a small take-up drum may be employed and a simple and direct
55 gear connection made between the driving and the driven or take-up-drum shafts.

For the purpose of relieving the strain on the film and preventing the enlargement of the perforations therein as much as possible
60 I prefer to provide one or more idler drums or spools H, of any suitable material, preferably two, arranged on the support A between the take-up drum G' and the rotating element D. One of the spools H may be arranged
65 above the take-up drum G' and the other below said drum. The film after being arranged to be engaged by the roller of the rotating

element is passed around the upper surface of the upper spool, then around the lower surface of the lower spool and around the 70 take-up drum, and from there to either side of an idler roller or spool II'. The upper drum or spool II is preferably provided with a pressure and guiding device J to aline the film and prevent its jumping or buckling at 75 this point while being intermittently moved. This pressure and guiding device may comprise a sleeve j, rotatably arranged on a stem projecting outwardly from the support, having fingers j² thereon adapted to embrace the 80 edges of the drum, so as to aline the film, and with a pressure-plate j³ secured to the sleeve j' and adapted to exert sufficient pressure to retain the film against the drum, though the pressure-plate in some instances may be dis- 85 pensed with. The pressure-plate j³ is preferably covered with a yielding material, as leather, and is arranged to swing on the stem with the sleeve and guide-fingers j², so as to permit the film to be readily passed around 90 the drum or spool, both the pressure-plate and the guide-fingers being adapted to be held in an adjusted position by a thumb-nut arranged on the end of the stem or in any other suitable manner. 95

The feed-drum B and the take-up drum G' are preferably of the same diameter and are adapted to be rotated at the same rate of speed, so that one will take up exactly the same length of film as is fed by the other at 100 each revolution of said drums. The shafts of these drums may each have a sprocket-wheel k, around which passes a sprocket-chain k', though other means may be employed for connecting and rotating said shafts. 105

Each of the drums may be provided with a pressure and guiding device, as at J, or they may have an arm L, provided with guide-fingers adapted to aline the film. I may, however, employ a yielding arm, as L', without 110 the guide-fingers and instead of said guide-fingers use a guiding device, similar to the guiding device J, without the pressure-plate, as shown in connection with the feed-drum.

I thus provide simple and efficient means 115 for imparting motion to the film-operating mechanism and for alining and preventing injury to the film or to the apertures or perforations therein.

The mechanism, either in part or as a whole, 120 when desired, may be employed in connection with a photographic apparatus having the usual or any preferred mechanism for adapting the improvements herein described to such a device. 125

It is obvious that the shaft g may be employed as the driving-shaft, that a shutter may be employed, if desired, and that some of the parts may be dispensed with or others substituted therefor without departing from 130 the spirit of my invention.

Having thus fully described my invention, what I claim as new, and desire to secure by Letters Patent of the United States, is—

1. In an apparatus of the character described, the combination with a film or strip, of a tension device, a rotating element adapted to cause the film to intermittently move through said tension device, a drum for taking up the film as it is intermittently moved, together with a gear connection between said rotating element and the drum, said gear connection being so proportioned and timed that the interval of exposure of the film shall predominate the interval of motion, whereby simple and efficient mechanism may be provided for operating the film, substantially as described

2. In an apparatus of the character described, the combination with a film or strip, of a tension device, a shaft provided with a rotating element having an eccentrically-arranged roller thereon adapted to engage the film and intermittently move the same through said tension device, a shaft and a take-up drum secured to said shaft, a gear secured to the shaft of the rotating element, and a second gear of larger diameter secured to the take-up-drum shaft and meshing directly with the gear on the rotating-element shaft, said gear being so proportioned and timed that the interval of exposure of the film shall predominate the interval of motion, whereby simple and efficient mechanism may be provided for operating the film, substantially as described.

3. In a device of the character described, the combination with a film or strip, of a tension device, a feed-drum adapted to be continuously rotated and to provide slack in the film between said drum and the tension device, a take-up drum connected to the feed-drum so as to rotate in unison therewith, a rotating element interposed between the tension device and said take-up drum and adapted to intermittently move a portion of the film at each revolution, together with a direct gear connection between said rotating element and the take-up drum, said gear connection being so proportioned and timed that the interval of exposure of the film shall predominate the interval of motion, whereby simple and efficient mechanism may be provided for operating the film, substantially as described.

4. In an apparatus of the character described, the combination with a film or strip provided with apertures or perforations therein, a rotating element adapted to cause the film to intermittently move through said tension device, a drum provided with teeth engaging the perforations in the film and adapted to take up said film as it is intermittently moved, together with a pair of idler-spools interposed between the take-up drum and the rotating element and arranged above and below said drum on the same side thereof; said film being passed around the upper surface of the upper spool, and then around the lower surface of the lower spool to the take-up drum, whereby the strain on the film by the take-up drum may be relieved and the enlargement of the perforations thereof prevented, substantially as described.

5. In an apparatus of the character described, the combination with a suitable support, of a drum arranged thereon, a film or strip passing around said drum, and fingers arranged at the opposite ends of the drum adapted to aline said film, said fingers being adjustably held upon the support so as to swing away from the drum to permit the film to be passed around the latter, substantially as described.

In testimony whereof I affix my signature in presence of two witnesses.

THOMAS ARMAT.

Witnesses:
J. A. E. CRISWELL,
CHARLES E. RIORDON.

# C. F. JENKINS & T. ARMAT.
## PHANTOSCOPE.

No. 586,953.        Patented July 20, 1897.

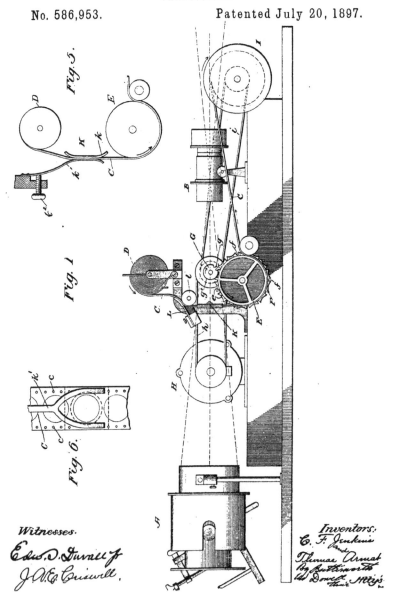

Fig. 5.

Fig. 1

Fig. 6.

Witnesses.

Edw. D. Duvall Jr

J. V. E. Criswell.

Inventors.
C. F. Jenkins
and
Thomas Armat
By Butterworth
& Dowell
their Att'ys

(No Model.) 2 Sheets—Sheet 2.

# C. F. JENKINS & T. ARMAT.

## PHANTOSCOPE.

No. 586,953. Patented July 20, 1897.

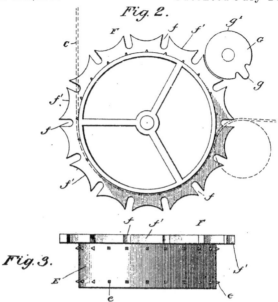

*Fig. 2.*

*Fig. 3.*

*Fig. 4.*

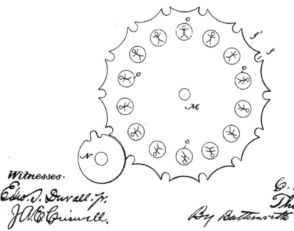

*Witnesses.*

Edw. J. Duvall, Jr.

J.A.E. Criswell.

*Inventors:*

C. F. Jenkins and Thomas Armat

By Butterworth & Dowell their Attys

# UNITED STATES PATENT OFFICE.

CHARLES FRANCIS JENKINS, OF RICHMOND, INDIANA, AND THOMAS ARMAT, OF WASHINGTON, DISTRICT OF COLUMBIA.

## PHANTOSCOPE.

SPECIFICATION forming part of Letters Patent No. 586,953, dated July 20, 1897.

Application filed August 28, 1895. Serial No. 560,793. (No model.)

*To all whom it may concern:*

Be it known that we, CHARLES FRANCIS JENKINS, residing at Richmond, in the county of Wayne and State of Indiana, and THOMAS
5 ARMAT, residing at Washington, District of Columbia, citizens of the United States, have invented certain new and useful Improvements in Phantoscopes; and we do hereby de-'clare the following to be a full, clear, and ex-
10 act description of the invention, such as will enable others skilled in the art to which it appertains to make and use the same.

This invention relates to apparatus for exhibiting pictures so as to produce the appear-
15 ance of objects in motion; and the primary object of the invention is to provide efficient means whereby a series of photographic or other pictures, showing successively the different positions or attitudes assumed by a per-
20 son or object in motion, may be displayed in such manner as to reproduce to the eye the appearance of the moving object through all the phases of such movement with a life-like and unblurred effect.

25 A further object is to provide means for effecting the displacement of a picture and the substitution of another in its stead in an interval of time less than the interval of illumination and exposure of the picture, so as to
30 cause the interval of illumination to predominate and render the act or effect of a change imperceptible to the eye.

Another object is to provide means for accomplishing the results stated without using
35 a shutter or equivalent device, such as has heretofore been necessary in apparatuses of a similar character, so as to utilize continuously and to the best advantage the light afforded by the illuminator and to avoid cast-
40 ing shadows or cloud effects produced by the passage of the shutter across the light.

The invention will first be hereinafter more particularly described with reference to the accompanying drawings, forming a part of
45 this specification, and then pointed out in the claims at the end of the description.

In the drawings, Figure 1 represents a side elevation of an apparatus or combination of devices which may be employed in practicing
50 the invention. Fig. 2 is a detail side view, on a slightly-enlarged scale, of the drum and mutilated gearing for intermittingly moving the tape-like film or other surface carrying the pictures to be exhibited. Fig. 3 is a plan view of the drum and larger mutilated gear 55 shown in Fig. 2. Fig. 4 represents in side elevation a modified form of a device embodying the invention; and Figs. 5 and 6 represent, respectively, a detail side view and a rear view of a tension device for yieldingly 60 holding the film or picture-carrying surface.

In devices or apparatuses such as have heretofore been devised for exhibiting life-like pictures or producing the appearance of motion it has been considered most feasible to 65 keep the series of similar pictures (whether on a disk, tape, or other surface) constantly moving at a regulated speed, corresponding with the speed at which the pictures were taken, and by means of a shutter or light ob- 70 structing surface to alternately cover and expose the pictures successively in a manner quite similar to the method of exposing the sensitive film or substance in taking the photographs, so as to bring the opening through 75 the shutter centrally over a picture at intervals practically equal to the intervals between exposure in taking the pictures, so that each picture may be seen only when it is in such a position that it will be exactly super- 80 posed upon the image not yet (owing to the persistence of vision) faded from the eye. The openings in such shutters, which are ordinarily in the form of revolving disks having openings near their circumferences, usu- 85 ally cover but a fractional part of the circumference of the disk, so that a view of the picture is afforded through an interval of time much less than the period of interruption, and as the illuminated pictures and the cloud ef- 90 fect or darkness of interruption caused by the passage of the shutter across the light are blended or mixed together in the eye of the observer the darkness continues to impress upon the retina so much longer than the light 95 that the value of the illumination is very greatly diminished and the picture appears to be poorly lighted or blurred.

In the case of our invention the conditions are quite different and the results produced 100

are therefore more satisfactory than and superior to anything of the kind heretofore obtained, for the reason that the picture is held a much longer time than is required to re-
5 move it and substitute another in its stead, thus prolonging the period of illumination very greatly as compared with the period of interruption or change, and there is no obstruction of the light by the interposition of
10 a shutter or opaque substance across its path, so that the impression of the picture on the eye is so much longer and permanent than the distortion or shadow effect incident to its movement, and the interval of change or in-
15 terruption is so infinitesimal that the image of the picture is readily retained until displacement and substitution takes effect, and owing to the inability of the eye to receive an impression from every phase of motion
20 the interruption or change is wholly imperceptible, and the result is a most vivid appearance of an object in motion, otherwise unchanging, clearly exhibiting all the phases of such motion with life-like effect.
25 In the arrangement illustrated in Fig. 1 of the drawings, A may denote an illuminator consisting, preferably, of an electric light and a condensing-lens, whereby the rays of light are concentrated upon a picture located in
30 the focus of an objective lens B.

C denotes a film or strip composed of any suitable transparent or translucent flexible substance adapted to provide a surface for carrying pictures produced thereon by photo-
35 graphic or other means, the several pictures in the series representing, successively, different positions of a moving object, so that the exhibition of the entire series of pictures in the order in which they were made or taken
40 may result in the reproduction of the appearance of the moving object in every phase of its motion. This film may be wound or coiled upon a reel or spool D, from which one of its ends may pass over the surface of a drum E,
45 said spool and drum being suitably journaled in standards or supports to permit the film to be wound upon one as it is unwound from the other and so arranged that as the film is moved the pictures thereon will be brought
50 successively into the focus of the object-lens.

Our invention depends for its successful operation both upon the inability of the eye to receive impression of movement exceeding a certain rapidity and upon that faculty of
55 the eye which enables it to retain an impression after the source of light has vanished— the persistence of vision—which enables us to change the pictures, one for another, imperceptibly. This we accomplish by moving
60 the film or other picture-carrying surface intermittingly in such manner that the interval of exposure and illumination of the picture shall exceed the interval of time required to effect a change sufficiently to enable the eye
65 to form a perfect impression or image at each exposure and to retain it through the interval of motion or change and until another pic-

ture has been superimposed, as it were, upon the one displaced, thus rendering the act or effect of displacement and substitution of pic- 70 tures wholly imperceptible and giving the impression to the eye of objects in motion.

Various contrivances and forms of mechanisms may be employed for effecting the intermittent movement, the requirement being 75 that the film or other surface shall be moved quickly between successive pauses far enough to expose the next succeeding picture in the series. In the apparatus shown in Figs. 1 and 2 we have affixed to one side of the drum 80 E a peripherally notched or toothed gearwheel F, which is driven by a smaller gearwheel or disk G, having a single tooth g, which is adapted to engage one of the notches f in the wheel F at every revolution and move the 85 latter a part of a revolution proportional to the relative diameters of the two gears, such part revolutions of the gear E being adapted to bring the several pictures successively into the focus of the object-lens. The pe- 90 riphery of the wheel F between each pair of notches f is formed with a concave or semicircular depression f', which is adapted to form a seat for the toothless peripheral portion g' of the gear G, whereby when the tooth 95 g has escaped from a notch the larger gear may be locked and held in a stationary position by said toothless portion of the gear G, engaging and moving in sliding contact with one of the depressions f' until the smaller 100 gear has made a complete revolution, whereupon the operation of moving the larger gear a part revolution and again locking it coincidently with the exposure of the picture on the picture-carrying surface will again be re- 105 peated, and so on indefinitely.

Any suitable motor may be employed for imparting motion to the driving-gear G. The letter H in Fig. 1 denotes a motor for this purpose connected by a belt h with the shaft 110 of the gear G. If desired, a reel, as at I, may receive the film or tape C as it is paid out by the drum E and may be rotated by the motor H by means of a belt i, connecting the shaft of the reel with the driving-shaft of the 115 gear G, or in any suitable manner. Every time the gear F is moved a part revolution the film C should be moved just far enough to displace the exposed picture and substitute another in its stead, and it is also desirable that 120 the film should be held quite taut in passing behind the lenses and maintained against flexure or bending at the point of exposure of the picture, and to this end it is preferably provided with a series of perforations along 125 its edges, as at c c, to engage teats or pins e e on the drum E to prevent slipping, and is yieldingly clasped by a tension device K, between the members of which it passes on its way from the spool D to the drum E, said ten- 130 sion device being suitably supported and in such position as to adapt it to prevent flexure of the film at the point of exposure of the picture and to aid in keeping the film taut.

This tension device may consist of a fixed member or plate $k$, Fig. 5, placed in front of the film, and a forked member $k'$, Figs. 5 and 6, of spring metal bearing on the opposite side of the film, so as to hold it with a yielding pressure against the plate, the latter having an opening therethrough arranged opposite the fork of the spring $k'$, which straddles the picture-surface, so that the view of the picture may be unobstructed. By means of a set-screw $k^2$, bearing upon the shank of the spring $k'$, the pressure of the latter upon the film may be varied at will. This tension device may be used either with or without a film-tightener L, Fig. 1, located nearer the reel D, though either or both of these devices may be dispensed with in some cases. The tightener L consists simply of a spring fixed at one end and having its free end padded and arranged to press the film yieldingly against a roller I, journaled below the spool D.

In the modification shown in Fig. 4 a series of similar pictures are arranged in a circle upon the upper surface of a circular plate or disk M, the periphery of which is formed with alternate notches and semicircular depressions the same as the gear-wheel F in the other figures, and adapted to be driven in the same manner by a smaller gear N, the pictures thereon being viewed through a magnifying-glass, which may be held in the hand. This picture-carrying surface or disk may be arranged to rotate in a horizontal plane or otherwise. In the horizontal position the pictures upon the plate are illuminated by light from above in case the plate is opaque, or from beneath if it be transparent. In the latter case the plate A may be made to revolve with its axis parallel with the axis of the object-lens of a microscopic or an ordinary projecting lantern with the pictures in the focus of the objective, so that the pictures may be projected upon a screen the same as ordinary transparencies are, except that the picture upon the screen will possess the same life-like effect which is observed through the magnifying-glass when the latter is used. This plate may take the place of an ordinary lantern-slide of a magic lantern, the lantern being otherwise the same as ordinarily used.

The series of pictures in the form shown in Fig. 4 are arranged in a circle, as at $o\ o$, near the periphery of the disk, but various modifications of this arrangement will readily suggest themselves to those skilled in the art, such as a spiral or serpentine arrangement, which will permit a larger number of pictures to be arranged spirally on the surface of the revolving disk.

It will be understood, of course, that the results hereinbefore described may be produced by other means than intermittent gearing, and we do not desire to be limited to the use of intermittent gearing, as other means may be employed for causing the light on the screen to exceed in duration the interval of change—that is, the time required to effect the removal of one picture and the substitution of another in its stead, which is essential to success.

We do not claim novelty in the pictures, but we are not aware that prior to our invention any instrument or apparatus has been devised by which life-like pictures may be given a very long illumination compared with the time necessary for effecting a change, and the fact that no feasible method has heretofore been devised to accomplish this result accounts for the very poor results so far attained in lantern-work.

From the foregoing description it will be seen that the pictures are brought successively into an illuminated field and that each picture is illuminated without interruption from the instant it enters such field until displaced by the next picture in the series, and that the several pictures in the series are successively substituted one for another with such rapidity that, although the exposed portion of the film or picture-carrying surface is continuously illuminated, the eye receives an impression of the picture which so greatly predominates any possible impression that might be made by the practically instantaneous motion of said film or surface, in substituting picture for picture, that the predominating impression which the eye receives, owing to its inability to receive two impressions at one and the same time, and to the persistence of vision, has the effect of rendering the movement of the film utterly imperceptible, while the successive impressions of different pictures are each retained until another picture in the series is superimposed, as it were, upon the previous impression or picture, thus rendering it possible to produce most vivid and life-like effects without any interruption whatever in the illumination, whether the film is moving or stationary, and without interposing a shutter and thereby causing a shadow or shade effect which reduces the vividness of the impression; but we do not desire to be confined to the use of the invention without a shutter, inasmuch as such a device might be used under some circumstances—as, for instance, when constructed so as to interrupt the illumination only at that instant of time when the film is moving and without rendering the interruption perceptible to the eye—but for all practical purposes a shutter of any kind is useless and objectionable and is preferably dispensed with.

Having thus fully described our invention, what we claim as new, and desire to secure by Letters Patent of the United States, is—

1. An apparatus for exhibiting pictures so as to give the impression to the eye of objects in motion, comprising a picture-carrying surface, means for supporting said surface and permitting it to be moved so as to cause the pictures or objects thereon to be successively exposed for the required interval of time in an illuminated field, and mechan-

ism adapted to intermittingly quickly move said surface at short intervals for exposing or exhibiting the pictures in the order of their succession, and for holding the surface stationary during the interval of illumination of each picture; the interval of illumination of the picture being made to exceed the interval of motion or change, substantially as described.

2. The combination, in an apparatus for exhibiting pictures so as to give the impression to the eye of objects in motion, of a movable picture-carrying surface and means for intermittingly moving said surface at short intervals exceeding the interval required in effecting the movement, so that the interval of pause and illumination shall exceed the interval of motion, substantially as described.

3. The combination, in picture-exhibiting apparatus for giving the impression to the eye of objects in motion, of a picture-carrying surface, means for supporting the same and means for feeding such surface intermittingly in such manner that the interval of illumination of the picture shall predominate the interval of motion, substantially as described.

4. The combination, in picture-exhibiting apparatus for giving the impression to the eye of objects in motion, of a picture-carrying surface, means for supporting and intermittingly quickly moving the same, and means for illuminating the pictures successively between the intervals of motion in such manner that the interval of pause and illumination of the picture shall predominate the interval of movement, substantially as described.

5. In a picture-exhibiting apparatus for giving the impression to the eye of objects in motion, the combination with a transparent picture-carrying surface, of means for intermittingly moving the same step by step so as to present to view the pictures thereon in the order of their succession; the interval of time between the exhibition of successive pictures being instantaneous while the period of illumination is comparatively greatly prolonged, substantially as described.

6. In picture-exhibiting apparatus for giving the impression to the eye of objects in motion, the combination with a picture-carrying surface, of mechanism for intermittingly moving said surface at short intervals so as to expose the pictures thereon successively in an illuminated field for an interval of time exceeding the interval of motion, comprising a peripherally-notched disk or wheel having semicircular or concave depressions between said notches, and a smaller gear having substantially a toothless periphery except at one point where a tooth is provided to engage the notches of the disk or wheel, so as to impart an intermittent step-by-step movement to the picture-carrying surface, and to hold the same immovable during the intervals of pause, substantially as described.

7. In picture-exhibiting apparatus for giving the impression to the eye of objects in

motion, the combination with the picture-carrying film and means for intermittingly moving said film so as to expose the pictures thereon successively in an illuminated field for an interval of time exceeding the interval of motion, of the tension device comprising two members between which the film is adapted to pass, one member being adapted to yieldingly press the film toward the other so that it is held taut and prevented from flexing or puckering at the point of exposure of the picture, substantially as described.

8. In a picture-exhibiting apparatus for giving the impression to the eye of objects in motion, the combination with an illuminator and a projecting lens, of a transparent picture-carrying surface arranged in the focus of the objective of the projecting lens, means for intermittingly moving the said surface in such manner that the interval of illumination shall exceed the interval of change, and a tension device adapted to keep the picture taut and prevent flexing or puckering at the point of exposure, substantially as described.

9. An apparatus for exhibiting pictures so as to give the impression to the eye of objects in motion, comprising a picture-carrying film or surface adapted to be given an intermittent step-by-step movement for bringing the pictures or objects thereon successively into position for exposure in an illuminated field, means for illuminating pictures or objects exposed in said field, and mechanism for quickly moving said surface at intervals so as to successively expose the pictures or objects thereon, the exposed picture or object being uninterruptedly illuminated during the period of exposure, the construction being such that the impression made by the illuminated picture while stationary so greatly predominates any impression liable to be caused by the motion of the film as to render the latter imperceptible to the eye, owing to the persistence of vision, substantially as described.

10. An apparatus for exhibiting pictures, comprising a movable picture-carrying surface or film adapted to be given an intermittent step-by-step movement, so as to bring a series of pictures or objects thereon successively into an illuminated field, means for illuminating the picture or object exposed in said field, and mechanism for intermittently moving said surface so as to quickly substitute one picture for another without interrupting the illumination; the construction being such that the motion of the film is rendered imperceptible to the eye by the predominating impression of the picture and the persistence of vision, substantially as described.

In testimony whereof we affix our signatures in presence of two witnesses.

CHAS. FRANCIS JENKINS.
THOS. ARMAT.

Witnesses:
J. A. E. CRISWELL,
WM. B. CROWELL.

Defendants' Exhibit No. 197

Steward & Frost Patent No. 588,916
August 24, 1897

# W. G. STEWARD & E. F. FROST.
## KINETOSCOPE.

No. 588,916.        Patented Aug. 24, 1897.

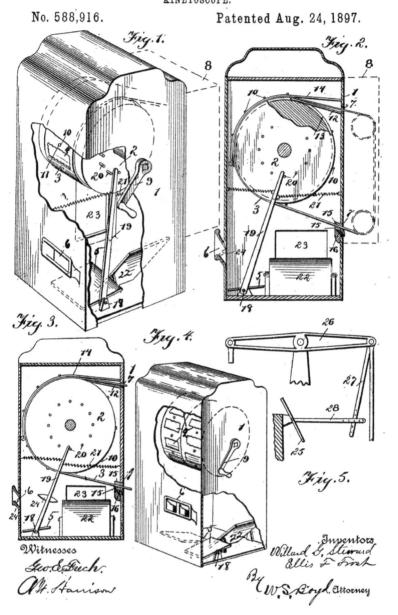

Fig. 1.    Fig. 2.    Fig. 3.    Fig. 4.    Fig. 5.

Witnesses
Geo. E. Buch.
A. H. Harison

Inventors
Willard G. Steward
Ellis F. Frost
By W. S. Boyd. Attorney

# UNITED STATES PATENT OFFICE.

WILLARD G. STEWARD AND ELLIS F. FROST, OF WASHINGTON, DISTRICT OF COLUMBIA, ASSIGNORS TO CHARLES M. CAMPBELL, OF SAME PLACE.

## KINETOSCOPE

SPECIFICATION forming part of Letters Patent No. 588,916, dated August 24, 1897.

Application filed June 1, 1896. Serial No. 593,912. (No model.)

*To all whom it may concern:*

Be it known that we, WILLARD G. STEWARD and ELLIS F. FROST, citizens of the United States, residing at Washington, in the District of Columbia, have invented certain new and useful Improvements in Kinetoscopes; and we do declare the following to be a full, clear, and exact description of the invention, such as will enable others skilled in the art to which it appertains to make and use the same, reference being had to the accompanying drawings, and to the figures of reference marked thereon, which form a part of this specification.

Our invention relates to optics; and it consists in the method of and apparatus for causing rays of light from a moving object, each to be held stationary through a given point. One means for accomplishing this object is fully described hereinafter and disclosed in the accompanying drawings, in which—

Figure 1 is a perspective view, partially broken away, of one form of an instrument embodying our invention. Fig. 2 is a vertical sectional view of the same, and Figs. 3, 4, and 5 are detail views.

Referring more particularly to the drawings, 1 indicates the box or casing, in which a wheel or roller 2 is mounted. Over this wheel is caused to pass a transparency 3 or other continuous strip of material provided with objects, pictures, or negatives 4.

5 indicates a reflector which is arranged in the box in such relative position to the wheel or roller as that the rays of light from the strip may be seen through the window or aperture 6 in the side of the box. These parts may be of such size and shape and arranged in such relation to each other as to secure the desired result. When it is desired to show a long series of pictures, the box may be made of a sufficient capacity to receive the entire length of the strip, or the box may be provided with slots or apertures 7 and 7', through which the strip may pass into and be stored in a separate compartment 8, (shown only in dotted lines,) or the strip may be permitted to run loosely upon the outside of the box.

The pictures or objects may be secured to or arranged upon the strip at intervals, so that as the wheel or roller is rotated by means of the crank 9 or any other suitable motor they will pass a given point at such times and with such speed as to produce the desired effect. The strip may be made to move uniformly with the periphery of the wheel in any desired manner, as by means of spurs or spikes 10, which may project through holes 11 in the strip.

To prevent the strip from becoming disconnected from the pins or spurs on the periphery of the wheel, a thin strip 12, of steel or other suitable material, may be secured at one side of the box with its free end extended over a portion of the periphery of the wheel. When the spurs 10 are used upon the wheel, it may be desirable to use strippers 13 to disengage the strip from the wheel by passing between it and the periphery of the wheel and forcing it from the pins should it adhere thereto and have a tendency to be carried around with the wheel. In the drawings we have shown the spurs arranged substantially centrally to the periphery of the wheel and the ends of the strippers lying within grooves 14, near the edges of the wheel. This will cause the strippers to lie substantially tangential to the periphery of the wheel and in a line with the movement of the strip and between the wheel and the slot 7 in the casing, where the strip passes out of the box.

In passing the strip to the wheel it may be found desirable to place it under tension, which can be done by passing it under a suitable brake. This brake can be located in the slot 7'—as, for instance, a cushion 15 on one or both sides of the strip—and an adjusting-wedge 16 inserted under one of the cushions to graduate the pressure of the brake.

To cause the pictures of the series to appear as at the same place, it is necessary that such movements be given to the reflector upon its axis or otherwise as will hold the direction of each of the rays of light stationary through a given point whatever may be the angle of the incident rays from the object to the reflector.

As the objects or pictures must succeed each other with sufficient rapidity to continuously impress the eye, it is evident that the reflector can only follow each picture a certain distance, when it must resume its initial

position and follow the succeeding picture. As the return movement of the reflector does not assist the correct representation of the pictures, it should be made as quickly as pos
5 sible, and, if desired, the rays of light from the pictures might be intercepted for that instant, so that there would be no reflection except during the forward movement of the reflector.

10 A plurality of reflectors may be arranged to successively reflect the succeeding pictures, one form of which is shown in Fig. 4.

In the drawings, which illustrate a machine having but one reflector 5, we have shown it
15 secured upon pivots 18 and provided with an arm 19, the free end of which engages with a series of pins 7, forming shoulders upon the wheel or roller 2. The parts are so arranged that one picture will pass a given point or be
20 exposed to view for each time that the reflector is oscillated or moved forward. The return movement of the reflector may be accomplished by any suitable mechanism—as, for instance, by a weight or spring 20—which
25 will draw the arm 19 back into its initial position to be engaged by the succeeding pin on the wheel.

Instead of the arms and pins above referred to the reflector and wheel or strip may be con-
30 nected and caused to move synchronously in any desired manner, the only requisite being that the return movement of the mirror be quick, so as to come as near making a continuous or unbroken reflection as possible.
35 The size of the reflector may be made to correspond with the size of the pictures, and the apertures or slots through the side of the casing, through which the pictures are observed, may be made accordingly.
40 When the parts are inclosed in a box, as shown, with the reflector below the strip, it is necessary to provide some means for illuminating the pictures, which can be done by an ordinary reflector 22, arranged in such man-
45 ner as to reflect the light passing through an aperture 23 in the side of the box upon the picture, or an ordinary lamp or incandescent or other light can be arranged within the box so as to illuminate the picture either by re-
50 flection or transparently—that is, the light transmitted through the transparency; but when the parts are arranged in an open framework or the reflector is located above the strip and the top of the box removed the means for
55 illumination may be dispensed with.

In using our machine one of the sides of the box is preferably made removable, so that the strip or objects to be used may be placed upon the wheel under the spring and the
60 brake properly adjusted. The removed portions are then replaced, the wheel rotated, and the objects are seen in the reflector.

If desired, the pictures may be placed directly upon the periphery of the wheel, in
65 which case the pins 10, strippers, and spring may be dispensed with. Lenses 24 may also be placed between the reflector and the pic-

tures or the eye, whereby the apparent size of the picture may be changed, and by using two
70 vis al openings and properly arranged pictures or objects the usual stereoscopic effects can be produced.

In addition to the foregoing adaptations and use our invention may be applied and used in the observation of any moving objects—
75 as, for instance, machinery. In this construction it is only necessary that the reflector be moved at such angular rate of speed with reference to that of the moving object to be observed as will cause the image of the object
80 to stand still when seen in the reflector. This may be accomplished in any suitable manner, as by connecting the reflector with the moving object, as shown in Fig. 5, in which 26 indicates the reflector, 26 a walking-beam of
85 an engine, (the object to be observed,) and 27 and 28 the means for connecting the two together. In this construction when the beam is moving in one direction the reflector is moved such a distance and at such a rate of
90 speed that the reflection of the virtual image of the portion of the beam being observed will appear at the same place during the entire length of the stroke, and as soon as the beam starts in the opposite direction the movement
95 of the reflector is changed accordingly and moved at such a rate of speed as will cause the image to still remain stationary

In view of the wide use and scope to which our invention may be applied we wish it to be
100 understood that we do not limit ourselves to the construction herein shown or described, but include all such changes and alterations as will come within the scope and spirit of our invention.
105 Having thus described our invention, we claim—

1. The herein-described method of directing light-rays, consisting in holding each of the rays of light from a series of moving ob-
110 jects stationary through a given point, substantially as set forth.

2. The herein-described method of forming an impression upon the eye, consisting in causing the rays of light from a series of mov-
115 ing objects, each to be held stationary through a given point, substantially as set forth.

3. In combination with a movable object, a movable reflector connected therewith, whereby the relative positions of the one to the other
120 are changed so that the rays of light from the object will each be held stationary by the reflector through a given point, substantially as set forth.

4. In a kinetoscope, the combination, with
125 a series of movable objects, of a movable reflector, and means for changing the relative positions of the objects and the reflector to each other, so that the rays of light from each succeeding object will each be held stationary
130 by the reflector through a given point, substantially as set forth.

5. In a kinetoscope, the combination, with a series of movable pictures, of a movable re-

flector, and means for changing the relative positions of the pictures and the reflector to each other, so that the rays of light from each succeeding picture will each be held station-
5 ary by the reflector through a given point, substantially as set forth.

6. In a kinetoscope, the combination, with a series of movable pictures, of an oscillating reflector, and means for changing the relative
10 positions of the reflector and the pictures to each other so that the rays of light from each picture will each be held stationary by the reflector through a given point, substantially as set forth.

15 7. In a kinetoscope, the combination, with a series of movable objects, of a movable reflector, and means for moving the reflector at such an angular rate of speed relatively to that of the objects that the rays of light there-
20 from each will be held stationary through a given point, substantially as set forth.

8. In a kinetoscope, the combination, with a series of movable pictures, of a movable reflector, and means for moving the reflector in
25 one direction at a greater rate of speed than in the other, so that the time of exposure will be greater than the time of change, substantially as set forth.

9. In a kinetoscope, the combination, with
30 a support, of a wheel journaled therein, an oscillating reflector, a series of pictures upon the wheel, and means for moving the wheel and the reflector in such relation to each other that the rays of light from the object
35 will each be held stationary through a given point, substantially as set forth.

10. In a kinetoscope, the combination, with a support, of a wheel journaled therein, an oscillating reflector, radially-projecting pins
40 upon the periphery of the wheel, a perforated strip upon the pins and provided with pictures, a retaining device upon the strip on the periphery of the wheel, and means for moving the pictures and the reflector in such
45 relation to each other that the rays of light will each be held stationary through a given point substantially as set forth.

11. In a kinetoscope, the combination, with a support, of a wheel journaled therein, an oscillating reflector, the periphery of the 50 wheel being grooved and provided with radially-projecting pins, strippers within the support, the free ends of which fit within the grooves of the wheel, a retaining device, and means for moving the wheel and the reflector 55 in such relation to each other that the rays of light from each succeeding picture will each be held stationary by the reflector through a given point, substantially as set forth.

12. In a kinetoscope, the combination, with 60 a support, of a wheel journaled therein, an oscillating reflector, a series of pins arranged in one side of the wheel, an arm from the axis of the reflector, the free end of which is adapted to be engaged by said pins, means 65 for returning said arm and reflector to their initial position, and a series of pictures upon the wheel, substantially as set forth.

13. In a kinetoscope, the combination, with a support, one wall of which is provided with 70 two slots, of a wheel and an oscillating reflector journaled within the support, a brake in one of the slots, and strippers extending from the other slot to the periphery of the wheel, a strip through said slots and extending around 75 the periphery of the wheel, and means for moving the pictures and the light in such relation to each other that the rays of light from each succeeding picture will each be held stationary by the reflector through a 80 given point, substantially as set forth.

14. In a kinetoscope, the combination, with a support, of a movable object therein, a source of illumination, and means for holding each of the rays of light therefrom sta- 85 tionary through a given point, and lenses for changing the apparent size of the object, substantially as set forth.

In testimony whereof we affix our signatures in presence of two witnesses.

WILLARD G. STEWARD.<br>ELLIS F. FROST.

Witnesses:
    Jos. H. Blackwood,
    W. S. Boyd.

No. 629,063.

H. CASLER.
KINETOGRAPHIC CAMERA.
(Application filed Feb. 26, 1896.)

Patented July 18, 1899.

(No Model.)

3 Sheets—Sheet 1.

*Fig.1,*

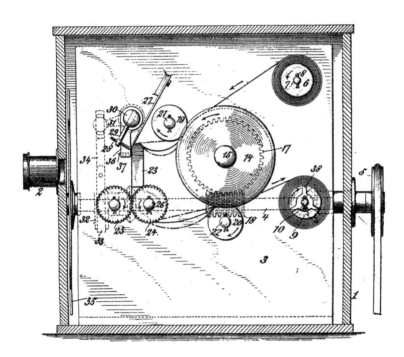

No. 629,063.

**H. CASLER.**
**KINETOGRAPHIC CAMERA.**
(Application filed Feb. 28. 1896.)

(No Model.)

Patented July 18, 1899.

3 Sheets—Sheet 2.

*Fig.2,*

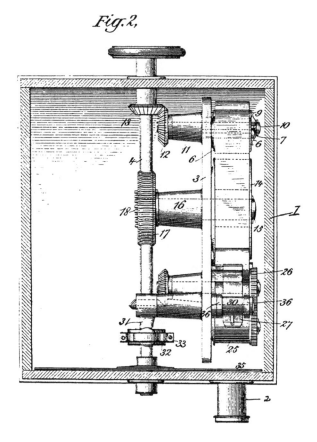

No. 629,063.

H. CASLER.
KINETOGRAPHIC CAMERA.
(Application filed Feb. 26, 1896.)

Patented July 18, 1899.

(No Model.)

3 Sheets—Sheet 3.

*Fig. 3,*

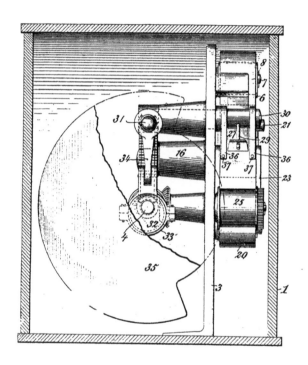

# UNITED STATES PATENT OFFICE.

HERMAN CASLER, OF CANASTOTA, NEW YORK, ASSIGNOR TO THE AMERICAN MUTOSCOPE COMPANY, OF NEW YORK, N. Y.

## KINETOGRAPHIC CAMERA.

SPECIFICATION forming part of Letters Patent No. 629,063, dated July 18, 1899.

Application filed February 26, 1896. Serial No. 580,811. (No model.)

*To all whom it may concern:*

Be it known that I, HERMAN CASLER, a citizen of the United States, residing at Canastota, in the county of Madison and State of New York, have invented a new and useful Improvement in Consecutive-View Apparatus; and I do hereby declare the following to be a full, clear, and exact description of the invention, such as will enable others skilled in the art to which it appertains to make and use the same.

My invention relates generally to consecutive-view apparatus and to strip or film feeding mechanism therefor, and particularly to photographic cameras employed for taking a rapid succession of views of objects in motion, from which the movements of said objects may be reproduced to the eye by means of a suitable apparatus; and my invention is particularly intended for the taking of pictures to be used in the instrument for reproducing the movements of objects from a succession of views thereof for which Letters Patent No. 549,309 were issued to me on November 5, 1895, or to be used in the other instrument for reproducing the movements of objects upon a screen for which I filed an application for Letters Patent of even date herewith, Serial No. 580,810.

Cameras heretofore devised for the taking of rapid successions of views of moving objects have been defective in that they have been incapable of taking pictures as large as is desirable or of giving sufficiently long exposure to each picture to enable photographs to be taken under ordinary conditions of illumination. In these cameras photographs are taken in a long flexible sensitive film, successive portions of which are moved into the field of a lens and held stationary while a shutter is opened to permit light passing through the lens to act upon the film. In order that the ordinary movements of objects may be satisfactorily reproduced, it is necessary that the series of views from which these movements are reproduced shall have been taken at about the rate of forty a second. While the shutter is open and the light is acting upon the film the portion of the film exposed to the light must be stationary, so that it is necessary to feed the film intermittently. If in order to produce the desired intermittent feeding of the film the movement of the entire film carrying and feeding mechanism be checked for each exposure, the vibration set up in the camera by the sudden stoppage of the rapidly-moving parts of the mechanism prevents a distinct picture from being obtained or makes it necessary that the shutter shall be opened each time for so brief a time that adequate exposure of the film is not obtained. If the spools from which the unexposed film is unwound and upon which the exposed film is wound are permitted to revolve continuously, while other mechanism, which feeds and guides the film across the field of the lens, is caused to move intermittently, stopping each time before the shutter is opened and commencing to move again after the shutter is closed, although by this means the weight of the intermittently moving parts is greatly reduced, it is still found that the sudden starting and stopping of these parts of the mechanism cause troublesome vibrations, which reduce greatly the time during which the shutter may be opened, and also that the intermittently-moving film-feeding mechanism is incapable of moving with sufficient rapidity and of feeding the film sufficiently rapidly to bring more than a very short length of fresh film into the field of the lens without setting up excessive vibration. These difficulties I have overcome in the camera herein described by causing all of the parts of the film-feeding mechanism to revolve continuously and uniformly, a catch being used to hold the film stationary while the shutter is open and the film-feeding rolls being permitted to slip over the film while the film is held by the catch. This catch is extremely light and easily moved, and its operation causes no vibration. All of the parts of the mechanism which carry or feed the film revolve continuously and uniformly, and therefore their operation causes no jar or vibration of the camera.

The above constitutes a most important feature and advantage of my camera and is its most characteristic feature. Other advantages I will hereinafter point out.

My invention consists in the novel means employed for intermittently feeding the film across the field of the lens, in the novel means employed for rendering the feeding of the film uniform, in the novel means employed for marking the film to permit exact registry of prints made therefrom, in the novel means employed for reeling up the film after exposure and preventing the accumulation of unreeled film in the camera, and in the novel combination, construction, and arrangement of the parts of the apparatus.

The objects of my invention are, first, to provide a camera for taking a rapid succession of views of moving objects which shall be capable of taking larger views and of giving longer exposures than the devices for similar purposes heretofore used; second, to provide a film or strip feeding mechanism capable of the intermittent feeding of longer lengths of film than has been practicable with the film-feeding mechanisms heretofore used and which shall be free from jar and vibration in its operation; third, to provide a film or strip feeding mechanism which shall not require previous perforation or other special preparation of the film and which shall not be liable to failure in operation owing to the slipping of the film; fourth, to provide a film or strip feeding mechanism which shall not wear, tear, or otherwise injure the film; fifth, to provide means for marking the film at the time and place of each exposure and to facilitate the bringing into registry of prints made from the film when the different views are to be mounted separately; sixth, to provide means for reeling up the film which shall prevent accumulation of loose film within the camera, and, seventh, to make the camera simple in construction, compact, portable, and easy of operation. These objects are attained in the camera herein described and illustrated in the drawings which accompany and form a part of this application, in which the same reference-numerals indicate the same or corresponding parts, and in which—

Figure 1 is a side view of the camera, the side of the inclosing case having been removed. Fig. 2 is a plan view of the camera, the top of the inclosing case having been removed; and Fig. 3 is a front view of the camera, the front of the inclosing case having been removed and a portion of the shutter-disk having been broken away.

In the drawings, 1 is the inclosing case of the camera.

2 is the lens, attached to the front of the case 1, and 3 is a vertical frame-plate secured at the bottom to the bottom of the case 1, which supports the film carrying and feeding mechanism.

4 is the driving-shaft of the camera. It is mounted in bearings in the case 1, and one end projects outside of the case and carries a pulley 5, by which it may be driven from a motor or other source of power.

6 is a spool carrying the strip of sensitive film upon which the photographs are to be taken. It is mounted to revolve upon a spindle 7, projecting from the frame-plate 3, and a spool from which the film has been unwound may be removed and a loaded spool placed on the spindle by removing the cotter-pin 8.

9 is a spool upon which the exposed film is wound. It is mounted upon a shaft 10, which is revolubly mounted in a bearing within a boss 11 of the frame-plate 3 and is driven from the driving-shaft 4 by bevel-gears 12 and 13. The spool 9 and shaft 10 are rotatably connected by a friction device hereinafter described.

14 is the main film-feeding drum. It is secured to a shaft 15, having a bearing in a boss 16 of the frame-plate 3, and is driven from the shaft 4 by a worm-wheel 17 and worm 18. Two small idle rolls 19 and 20 are mounted upon spindles 21 and 22 with their surfaces in contact with or in close proximity to the surface of the drum 14. These rollers are loose upon their spindles and are driven only by friction with the drum 14 or the film-strip interposed between the rollers and the drum. They serve to hold the film in contact with the surface of the drum. They are preferably composed of or have their surfaces covered with some yielding and elastic substance, so that possible injury to the film may be avoided.

23 is a plate secured to and projecting at right angles to the frame-plate 3 and located in the focal plane of the lens, which forms a support for the film during exposure and while the film is being punched, as hereinafter described.

24 and 25 are auxiliary film-feeding rolls, the function of which is to remove the exposed section of film and bring a fresh portion of the film into the field of the lens after each exposure. They are geared to revolve together at the same rate of speed, and roller 24 is mounted upon a shaft 26, having its bearing in the frame-plate 3 and driven by bevel-gears from the driving-shaft 4. These rolls feed the film forward intermittently, the film being held and prevented from feeding across the plate 23 during about one-half of the revolution of the shutter-disk by the catch hereinafter mentioned, during which time the rolls slip idly over the film. Since they act only intermittently and must during the time of their action feed forward as much film as has been fed forward by the drum 14 and roller 19 during a complete revolution of the shutter-disk, they are arranged to revolve at twice or more than twice the peripheral speed of the disk 14.

27 is a flat spring secured at one end to the frame-plate 3, the other end being arranged to press the film-strip against the top of the backing-plate 23. This spring forms the catch by which the film is held stationary in the field of the lens during exposure. Its free end is upturned and is provided with a slot 28, in which works a pin 29, secured to a revolubly-mounted rock-shaft 30, having bearings in the frame-plate 3. The rock-shaft

projects through the frame-plate and upon the rear side thereof carries an arm 31, which is directly over the shaft 4. Upon the shaft 4 is an eccentric 32, and the eccentric-strap 33 is connected to the arm 31 by an eccentric-rod 34, having a hinged connection with the eccentric-strap and a universal-joint connection with the arm 31. When the shaft 4 revolves, the rock-shaft 30 is caused to vibrate. The amplitude of this vibration is sufficient to cause the pin 29 to engage with the outer edge of the slot 28 each time and lift the spring 27 clear of the film and hold it so during the time the shutter of the camera is closed.

35 is the shutter-disk, by which the admission of light to the film is controlled. It is a thin disk mounted upon and secured to the driving-shaft 4 and situated just in rear of the lens. A portion of its periphery is cut away, so as to leave the lens uncovered during a portion of the revolution of the disk, and thus to permit the passage of light to the film. When the different views or prints made from the negative strip produced by this camera are to be mounted separately, as in the exhibition device shown and described in my above-mentioned patent, No. 549,309, it is necessary that some means shall be used for marking the position of each view on the strip or film accurately, so that the views of the prints made from the strip may be registered accurately when subsequently mounted separately. The marking of the film for this purpose I effect by punching two holes in the film each time a new length of film is fed forward. Upon the rock-shaft 30, upon either side of the pin 29, is mounted an arm 36, carrying a punch 37, which is arranged to punch a hole through the film each time the shaft 30 vibrates. The plate 23 is perforated to permit the punchings to escape. The holes thus punched are punched each time at the instant when the exposure is made and are always in precisely the same position with respect to the center of the view. In printing from the negative strip made in the camera after the pictures thereon have been developed a sensitized strip upon which the positives are to be printed is first run through the camera or through a similar punching mechanism, so as to have the holes punched at the same distance as are the holes in the negative strip. When the positive and negative strips are placed in the printing-frame for printing, the registration-holes are kept in registry while printing is going on by means of dowels or similar devices.

In preparing the camera for operation a strip of film is first placed in position by opening the side of the case 1, which exposes to view the mechanism, placing a spool of film on the spindle 7, and carrying the end of the film between the drum 14 and roller 19, over the plate 23 and under the catch 27, between the auxiliary feed-rolls 24 and 25, between the drum 14 and roller 20, and to the wind-

ing-spool 9, to which it is secured. The side of the case 1 is then closed, a loop being left between rollers 24 and 25 and rollers 14 and 20, and the camera is in readiness for operation.

In the drawings the parts of the mechanism are shown in the position occupied when the shutter is open and the exposure is completed. The spring or stop 27 is holding the film stationary against the top of the backing-plate 23. The drum 14 is rotating in the direction of the arrow shown in Fig. 1, drawing film from the spool 6, which collects in a loop between the drum and the plate 23, since the film is not being fed forward across the plate 23. A loop of exposed film, which has previously been formed, as will be seen hereinafter, between the auxiliary feed-rolls 24 and 25 and the drum 14, is being taken up through the feeding forward of the film by the drum 14 and roller 20, and the film thus fed forward is wound upon the rotating spool 9. As the shaft 4 rotates the edge of the shutter-disk 35 cuts off light from the lens. At the instant light is cut off the pin 29, moving upward, lifts the spring 27, thus releasing the film. The auxiliary feed-rolls 24 and 25 during the time that the shutter is open simply slip over the film, but are unable to feed it forward, because it is held by the spring 27; but when this spring has released the film the rolls 24 and 25 instantly feed it forward. These rolls move at twice the peripheral speed of the drum 14, as above stated. Therefore during the time the light is cut off they feed as much film across the plate 23 as has been fed into the loop between the drum 14 and plate 23 during a complete revolution of the shutter. The loop of film between the drum 14 and plate 23 is taken up, therefore, during the time that the shutter is closed, the extra film in this loop corresponding to the length of film required for a new exposure. At the same time another and corresponding loop is formed between the auxiliary feed-rolls 24 and 25 and the drum 14, since the film is fed onward much faster by the rolls 24 and 25 than it is taken up by the drum 14 and roll 20. Further rotation of the shaft 4 causes the shutter to open. Just before the shutter opens the spring 27, which has been descending with the pin 29, touches the film and holds it stationary against the plate 23. The auxiliary feed-rolls, being no longer able to move the film, slip over its surface. As soon as the shutter opens exposure begins and continues so long as the shutter is open—that is, during about half the revolution of the shutter-disk. The rock-shaft 30 still continues to move after the spring 27 has reached the film on the plate 23, and by its further movement causes the punches 37 to punch holes through the film, as above explained. These punches are withdrawn by the backward movement of the rock-shaft 30 before the pin 29 lifts the spring 27 and releases the film.

It will be noted that all of the parts of the

mechanism except the spring 27 and the rock-shaft 30 and parts connected therewith have a continuous uniform rotary motion, and therefore no jar or vibration results from their
5 motion. The spring 27 and the rock-shaft 30 and the parts connected therewith are so small and light, have such small amplitudes of movement, and are so firmly supported that no jar results from their movement.
10 The drum 14 and roller 19 are placed as close as possible to the plate 23, as are the auxiliary feed-rolls 24 and 25, so that the length of film set in motion by the rolls 24 and 25 may be as small as possible. This is
15 done so that the film may start to feed across the plate 23 promptly when released by the spring 27 and also to avoid the danger of tearing of the film, which results when a considerable length of film is started into motion
20 suddenly.

In practice in order to avoid any danger of the gradual accumulation of film in the loop between the drum 14 and the plate 23, due to possible slipping of the film between the aux-
25 iliary feed-rolls 24 and 25, I gear these rolls to revolve somewhat faster than would be theoretically required—that is, in the machine shown in the drawings to revolve with somewhat more than twice the peripheral speed of
30 the drum 14—so that each time that the film is fed forward by the rolls 24 and 25 the loop between the plate 23 and the drum 14 is entirely taken up. In order to provide for the gradual increase in diameter of the spool 9,
35 upon which the exposed film is wound, which tends to cause the spool to take up the film more and more rapidly, the spool is not directly connected to its shaft 10, but is mounted loosely upon it, while the legs of a tripod-
40 shaped spring-washer 38, itself so secured to the shaft 10 as to be caused to revolve therewith, press against the spool 9 and cause it to revolve by frictional contact. When the film between the spool 9 and the drum 14 is
45 tight, however, the spool will slip somewhat with respect to the shaft 10 and washer 38. All of the feeding-rolls revolve continuously and uniformly, and therefore when the film is to be fed across the field of the lens it is never
50 necessary to overcome the inertia of any of the parts of the apparatus, only the inertia of a very short section of the film requiring to be overcome. It is therefore possible to feed a considerable length of film across the
55 plate 23 in a brief time allotted for that purpose. As shown in the drawings, the shutter-disk is arranged to admit light during nearly one-half of its revolution. If desired, the shutter may be arranged to be open a much
60 greater portion of the revolution than one-half, all that is required being the cutting away of a greater portion of the periphery of the shutter, a proportionate increase in the peripheral speed of the auxiliary feed-rolls
65 24 and 25 with respect to the speed of the drum 14, and an adjustment of the amplitude of movement and of position of the pin 29,

so that the spring 27 may be released and lifted at the proper time; and because of the lightness of the parts and of the fact that all 70 of the parts which have directly to do with the feeding of the film move continuously, as does the great body of the film, a much higher speed of the rolls 24 and 25 is well within the limits of the machine. In this 75 manner the time allowed for each exposure may be considerably increased.

It will be noted that the greater portion of the work of feeding the film—viz., the drawing of the film from the roll 6—is done by the 80 drum 14 and that the rolls 24 and 25 are required to feed only a very short and loosely-held length of film, so that their hold on the film is very light and no injury results to the film because of the slipping of these rolls 85 upon it.

Having thus completely described my invention, what I claim, and desire to secure by Letters Patent, is—

1. In a consecutive-view apparatus, the 90 combination, with a supply-spool carrying a strip, a winding-spool upon which the strip may be wound, a main feeding-drum arranged to deliver the strip from said supply-spool and to carry it to the winding-spool, and means 95 for holding the strip in contact with the surface of said drum, of continuously-moving auxiliary feed-rolls having a higher peripheral velocity than said drum, acting upon the strip by frictional contact, and arranged to feed 100 the strip across the field of the apparatus, an intermittently-operating catch arranged to grasp the strip intermittently and thereby to prevent the feeding of the strip across the field of the apparatus, thereby causing the 105 auxiliary feed-rolls to slip thereon, a shutter arranged to cut off light from the strip while the same is moving in the field of the apparatus, and means for synchronously operating the shutter and catch, substantially as de- 110 scribed.

2. In a consecutive-view apparatus, the combination, with a lens, and film-feeding devices arranged to feed a strip of sensitive film across the field of said lens intermittently, of 115 a shutter arranged to cut off light from the film while the same is moving in the field of the lens, means for synchronously operating the shutter and film-feeding mechanism, and a marking device, arranged to mark the posi- 120 tion of each view upon the film, and operated each time the film-feeding mechanism operates, substantially as described.

3. In a consecutive-view apparatus, the combination, with a lens, and continuously- 125 moving film-feeding devices arranged to feed a strip of sensitive film across the field of the lens, of an intermittently-operating catch arranged to grasp the film intermittently, thereby momentarily preventing the feeding of the 130 film across the field of the lens, a shutter arranged to cut off light from the film while the same is moving in the field of the lens, means for synchronously operating the shutter and

catch, and a marking device, arranged to mark the position of each view upon the film, and operated each time the catch operates to hold the film, substantially as described.

4. In a consecutive-view apparatus, the combination, with a lens, and continuously-moving film-feeding devices arranged to feed a strip of sensitive film across the field of said lens, of an intermittently-operating catch arranged to grasp the film intermittently, thereby momentarily preventing the feeding of the film across the field of the lens, a shutter arranged to cut off light from the film while the same is moving in the field of the lens, means for synchronously operating the shutter and catch, and a punch operated synchronously with the shutter and catch, and arranged to mark the position of each view on the film, substantially as described.

5. In a consecutive-view apparatus, the combination, with a shutter arranged to interrupt the passage of light, and a continuously-moving driving-shaft arranged to operate said shutter, of a strip-feeding mechanism arranged to feed a flexible strip through the field of the apparatus, and comprising a main driving-drum, for delivering and carrying off the strip, driven from said shaft, means for holding the strip in contact with said drum on the delivery and take-off sides thereof, auxiliary feed-rolls driven from said driving-shaft and at a higher peripheral speed than said main driving-drum, and arranged to feed the strip across the field of the apparatus by frictional contact, and a catch arranged to grasp the strip and to prevent it from being fed across said field, and operated by said driving-shaft intermittently and synchronously with the shutter.

6. In a consecutive-view apparatus, the combination, with a shutter arranged to interrupt the passage of light, and a continuously-moving driving-shaft arranged to operate said shutter, of a strip-feeding mechanism arranged to feed a flexible strip through the field of the apparatus, and comprising a

main driving-drum, for delivering and carrying off the strip, driven from said driving-shaft, means for holding the strip in contact with said drum on the delivery and take-off sides thereof, a winding-spool frictionally driven from said driving-shaft and tending to revolve at a higher peripheral velocity than said main driving-drum, continuously-moving auxiliary feed-rolls likewise driven from said driving-shaft and at a higher peripheral speed than said main driving-drum, and arranged to feed the strip across the field of the apparatus by frictional contact, and a catch arranged to grasp the strip and to prevent it from being fed across said field, and operated by said driving-shaft intermittently and synchronously with the shutter.

7. In a consecutive-view apparatus, the combination, with a lens, a shutter arranged to interrupt the passage of light from said lens, and a continuously-moving driving-shaft arranged to operate said shutter, of continuously-moving feed-rolls driven from said driving-shaft for feeding a flexible strip of sensitive film across the field of the lens, and acting upon said strip by frictional contact, a plate for supporting said strip in the field of the lens, a spring arranged to press said strip against said plate and so to prevent the feeding thereof, a rock-shaft carrying an arm engaging said spring arranged to lift the same, means, operated by the driving-shaft for vibrating said rock-shaft synchronously with the operation of the shutter, thereby causing said spring to release the strip when the shutter is closed, and a punch, operated by said rock-shaft, and arranged to punch registration-holes in said strip each time the same is held by said spring, substantially as described.

In testimony whereof I affix my signature in presence of two witnesses.

HERMAN CASLER.

Witnesses:
A. A. SCHENCK,
K. F. CASSIDY.

Defendants' Exhibit No. 199

Armat Patent No. 673,992

May 14, 1901

No. 673,992.

**T. ARMAT.**
**VITASCOPE.**
Application filed Feb 19, 1896.

Patented May 14, 1901.

(No Model.)

3 Sheets—Sheet 1.

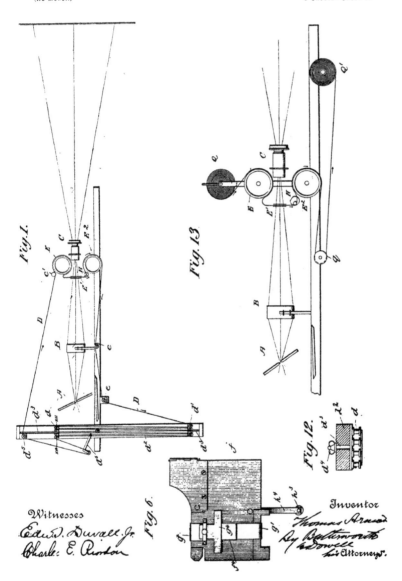

Inventor

Thomas Armat
By Butterworth
& Dowell
his Attorneys.

No. 673,992.

Patented May 14, 1901.

**T. ARMAT.**
**VITASCOPE.**
(Application filed Feb. 19, 1896.)

(No Model.)

3 Sheets—Sheet 2.

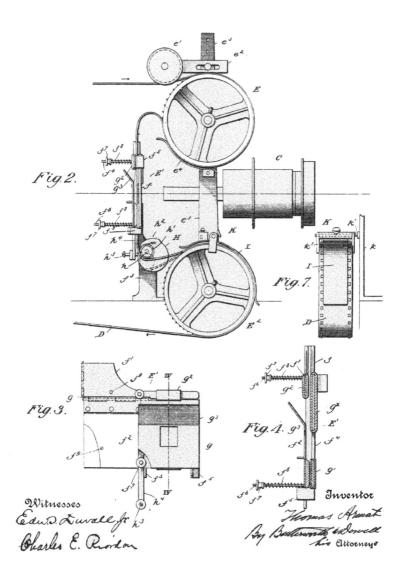

Fig.2.

Fig.7.

Fig.3.

Fig.4.

Witnesses
Edw. D. Duvall Jr.
Charles E. Riordan

Inventor
Thomas Armat
By Butterworth & Dowell
his Attorneys

No. 673,992.

T. ARMAT.

VITASCOPE.

(Application filed Feb. 19, 1896.)

Patented May 14, 1901.

(No Model.)

3 Sheets—Sheet 3.

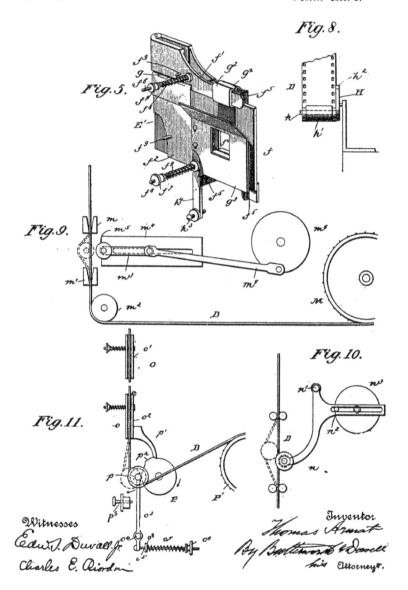

Fig. 8.

Fig. 5.

Fig. 9.

Fig. 10.

Fig. 11.

Witnesses

Edw. J. Duvall Jr.

Charles E. Riordan

Inventor

Thomas Armat

By Butterworth & Dowell

his Attorneys

# UNITED STATES PATENT OFFICE.

## THOMAS ARMAT, OF WASHINGTON, DISTRICT OF COLUMBIA.

## VITASCOPE.

SPECIFICATION forming part of Letters Patent No. 673,992, dated May 14, 1901.

Application filed February 19, 1896. Serial No. 579,901. (No model.)

*To all whom it may concern:*

Be it known that I, THOMAS ARMAT, a citizen of the United States, residing at Washington, in the District of Columbia, have in-
5 vented certain new and useful Improvements in Vitascopes; and I do hereby declare the following to be a full, clear, and exact description of the invention, such as will enable others skilled in the art to which it apper-
10 tains to make and use the same.

This invention relates to apparatus for exhibiting pictures, but more particularly to that class of picture-exhibiting apparatus in which the impression is given to the eye of
15 objects in motion.

The primary object of the invention is to provide improved and efficient means whereby a series of photographic or other pictures showing successively the different positions
20 or attitudes assumed by a person or object in motion may be displayed in such manner as to reproduce to the eye the appearance of the moving object through all the phases of such movement with a life-like and unblurred ef-
25 fect.

Another object is to provide means by which a continuous or endless strip or film forming the picture-carrying surface may be operated so as to successively place the ob-
30 jects thereon in position for reproduction without liability to injury from unnecessary strain and wear thereon and without the knocking and jarring of the mechanism which is incident to the means heretofore proposed.
35 Other objects are to provide means for preventing the film from flexing or puckering at the point of exposure (in order to assure a proper reproduction of the objects thereon) and for intermittently releasing the film, so
40 as to permit it to move a sufficient distance to expose a picture at each successive movement, and also to provide continuously-operated mechanism for moving the film, and means for intermittently moving it so as to
45 successively place the pictures in the field of illumination for reproduction.

These several objects may be accomplished by the use of the mechanism hereinafter described and without using a shutter or equiva-
50 lent device, such as is commonly used in apparatuses of a similar character, whereby the light for illuminating the picture to be projected or reproduced is utilized continuously and to the best advantage and the casting of shadows or cloud effects produced by the pas-
55 sage of the shutter across the light is avoided.

The invention will first be hereinafter more particularly described and then pointed out in the claims at the end of the description.

Referring to the accompanying drawings,
60 forming a part of this specification, Figure 1 is a diagrammatic view, in side elevation, of one form of picture-exhibiting apparatus embodying my invention. Fig. 2 is an enlarged
65 side elevation of a preferred form of mechanism for operating the picture-carrying surface or film, so as to place the objects thereon successively in position for reproduction. Fig. 3 is a front elevation of the tension and guiding device for the film. Fig. 4 is an en-
70 larged vertical sectional view taken on the line IV IV of Fig. 3. Fig. 5 is a perspective view of the tension and guiding device. Fig. 6 is an elevation of the tension and guiding de-
75 vice looking from the rear, illustrating an adjustable plate which may be employed for enlarging or decreasing the size of the opening therein according to the size of the object to be reproduced. Fig. 7 is a detail view
80 of one of the feed-drums, having a pressure and a guiding device for the film while passing around said drum. Fig. 8 is a detail view of a preferred form of device for intermittently operating the film. Figs. 9 and 10 are
85 side elevations of modified forms of mechanism for intermittently operating the film. Fig. 11 is a side view of another form of mechanism for intermittently operating the film, showing how pressure may be applied to and
90 released therefrom. Fig. 12 is a sectional plan on the line XII XII of Fig. 1, illustrating how the banks or series of rollers may be adjusted upon their support; and Fig. 13 is a diagrammatic view of a modified form of
95 apparatus in which a continuous instead of an endless strip or film is employed.

In devices or apparatuses such as have heretofore been devised for exhibiting life-like pictures or producing the appearance of
100 objects in motion it has been considered most feasible to keep the series of similar pictures (whether on a disk, tape, or other surface) constantly moving at a regulated speed corresponding with the speed at which the pic-

tures were taken and by means of a shutter or light-obstructing surface to alternately cover and expose the pictures successively in a manner quite similar to the method of exposing the sensitive film or substance in taking the photographs, so as to bring the opening through the shutter centrally over a picture at intervals practically equal to the intervals between exposure in taking the pictures, so that each picture may be seen only when it is in such a position that it will be exactly superposed upon the image not yet (owing to the persistence of vision) faded from the eye. The openings in such shutters, which are ordinarily in the form of revolving disks having openings near their circumferences, usually cover but a fractional part of the circumference of the disk, so that a view of the picture is afforded through an interval of time much less than the period of interruption, and as the illuminated pictures and the cloud effect or darkness of interruption caused by the passage of the shutter across the light are blended or mixed together in the eye of the observer the darkness continues to impress upon the retina so much longer than the light that the value of the illumination is very greatly diminished and the picture appears to be poorly lighted or blurred. In the case of my invention the conditions are quite different, and the results produced are therefore more satisfactory than and superior to anything of the kind heretofore obtained, for the reason that the picture is held a much longer time than is required to remove it and substitute another in its stead, thus prolonging the period of view or illumination very greatly as compared with the period of interruption or change, and there is no obstruction of the light by the interposition of a shutter or opaque substance across its path, so that the impression of the picture on the eye is so much longer and more permanent than the distortion or shadow effect incident to its movement and the interval of change or interruption is so infinitesimal that the image of the picture is readily retained until displacement and substitution takes effect, and owing to the inability of the eye to receive an impression from every phase of motion the interruption or change is wholly imperceptible, and the result is a most vivid appearance of an object in motion, otherwise unchanging, clearly exhibiting all the phases of such motion with life-like effect.

My invention depends for its successful operation both upon the inability of the eye to receive an impression of movement exceeding a certain rapidity and upon that faculty of the eye which enables it to retain an impression after the source of light has vanished—the persistence of vision—which enables me to change the pictures, one for another, imperceptibly. This I accomplish by moving the film or other picture-carrying surface intermittingly in such manner that the interval of exposure and illumination of the picture

shall exceed the interval of time required to effect a change sufficiently to enable the eye to form a perfect impression or image at each exposure and to retain it through the interval of motion or change and until another picture has been superimposed, as it were, upon the one displaced, thus rendering the act or effect of displacement and substitution of pictures wholly imperceptible and giving the impression to the eye of objects in motion. Various contrivances and forms of mechanisms may be employed for effecting the intermittent movement, the requirement being that the film or other surface shall be moved quickly between successive pauses far enough to expose the next succeeding picture in the series.

In the arrangement illustrated in Fig. 1 is shown an illuminator A and a condensing-lens B, the latter arranged adjacent to the illuminator and adapted to concentrate the rays of light upon a picture located in the focus of an objective lens C, all of which parts may be of the usual or of any preferred construction and arranged in any suitable manner. The strip or film D may be composed of any suitable transparent or translucent flexible substance adapted to provide a surface for carrying pictures produced or impressed thereon by photographic or other means, the several pictures in the series representing successively different positions of a moving object, so that the rapid exhibition of the entire series of pictures in the order in which they were made or taken may result in the reproduction of the appearance of the moving object in every phase of its motion. An upper and a lower bank or series of rollers $d$ $d'$, respectively, may be arranged upon a suitable support $d^2$, and the film may be made to pass around or partially around each roller in the series, passing alternately from an upper to a lower roller, or vice versa, so as to take up the surplus material and provide compact means by which a very long continuous or endless strip may be employed. These banks or series of rollers are preferably adjustably supported upon the standard $d^2$ in order to permit films of various lengths to be used, and for this purpose the frames of the rollers $d$ $d'$ may be provided with projecting screw-threaded bolts which may pass through slots $d^3$ in said support or standard and be secured thereto by a thumb-nut $d^4$ on the projecting threaded end of the bolt or otherwise, as shown in Fig. 12. From the last roller of the upper series or bank the film may pass around or over a roller or stud $d^5$, preferably first passing under a take-up roller arranged between said roller $d^5$ and the upper series or bank of rollers $d$, said take-up roller being arranged on an arm $d^6$, which has its inner end pivoted to the support, so that its outer end may move freely in order to provide a yielding surface over which the film may pass and to provide means for taking up the slack in said film, though as an additional means for taking up the slack the arm $d^6$ may be weighted or otherwise caused to exert a pressure upon the surface of the film. The film after leaving the roller $d^5$ is caused to pass around a drum or spool E, then through 5 a tension and guiding device E', and then around a drum or spool E², as hereinafter more fully explained, and then over one or more rollers $e$ to the lower series or bank of rollers $d'$ in the direction shown by the ar- 10 rows.

The drums or spools E and ·E² are preferably provided with peripheral teeth or, projections adapted to engage perforations in the film, so as to properly guide and hold it 15 against slipping. These spools may have their shafts journaled in any suitable support or standard and may be geared together by a sprocket-chain or otherwise, so as to rotate in unison, being so timed that each spool 20 will rotate the same number of times in the same space of time. The film is preferably gently pressed in its passage over the drum E by a roller $e'$ resting thereon, said roller being journaled in a bracket $e^2$, which is ad- 25 justably mounted upon a standard $e^3$, rising above the drum E. Below the drum E may also be placed a curved spring or yielding strip of metal $e^4$, which may be secured to the standard $e^3$, so as to bear underneath the film 30 and press it gently against the periphery of the drum. Owing to its rigidity or stiffness the film D will be caused to move of be carried upwardly or outwardly a short distance away from the drum E and its point of contact with 35 the spring $e^4$, so as to provide constant slack in the film at this point, and then with a return-bend it may pass in a substantially straight line through the tension and guiding device E' and thence to the drum E². 40 As a means for tensioning and frictionally holding the film so as to permit the series of pictures thereon to be brought successively into the illuminated field and retained for exposure therein for a predetermined time 45 I preferably employ a tension device E', having a stationary member $f$ and the pivoted or hinged members $f'$ and $f^2$, between which the film passes, as shown in Figs. 2 to 6, inclusive. The stationary member $f$ may be 50 supported in any suitable manner, as upon the standard $f^3$, and is provided with an opening $f^4$, through which the successive pictures may be exposed, and with the upper and lower guides $f^5$, against which the edges of 55 the film may abut, so as to be properly alined while passing between the yielding and stationary members. Pins or stems $f^6$ may project from the stationary member $f$ and pass through apertures in the yielding or movable 60 members $f'$ and $f^2$, each stem being provided with a nut $f^7$ at its outer end, between which and its corresponding yielding member is placed a coiled or other suitable spring $f^8$, so that said movable members may be held 65 with a yielding force in proper relation to the stationary member to clasp the film between the same, said yielding or movable

members being each also preferably provided with an aperture through which pins 70 $f^9$, projecting from the stationary member, may pass in order to serve as a guide therefor when moved on their pivots. The member $f^2$ may be pivoted or hinged, as at $g$, below the member $f'$ and is preferably angu- 75 lar in form and forced with greater pressure against the film than the member $f'$ in order to prevent flexing or puckering at the point of exposure and to yieldingly hold the film and to exert a pressure sufficient to prevent 80 the displacement thereof while the objects thereon are in position for reproduction. By employing two tension devices or a tension device having two members adapted to exert different pressures for yieldingly holding the 85 film or picture-carrying surface one of said members will act promptly in case the other should not, and thus insure the stoppage of the film the instant it has been advanced the desired distance and the holding of the same 90 stationary during the desired interval of exposure. In the form shown the pivot of the member $f'$ is arranged above and at right angles to the pivot of the member $f^2$. To cushion and provide a smooth brushing-sur- 95 face for the film between the members or any two or more of the same of the tension device, a strip of leather or other suitable material $g'$ and a strip of softer material $g^x$, as felt or plush, may be cemented or otherwise secured 100 on the stationary member $f$, between the guides $f^5$ and on opposite sides of the opening $f^4$, while on either or both of the movable or yielding members (preferably the member $f'$) may be secured felt, plush, or other suit- 105 able material, as at $g^2$, adapted to contact with the film and exert a yielding pressure thereon, so as to keep the film free from dust and to prevent it from slipping. Upon the movable member $f^2$ and secured thereto or 110 formed integrally therewith is a plate or shield $g^3$, having an aperture therethrough corresponding with the aperture $f^4$ of the stationary member, said shield being separated from the stationary member $f$ by a suitable space 115 in order to protect the film and tension and guiding device from the heat of the illuminator and to provide a space for the circulation of air, so as to keep the film cool, this result being facilitated by the fanning action of said 120 plate or shield under the action of the cam operating intermittently to release the tension on the film.

As the pictures on different films do not always occupy the same position with reference 125 to the perforations in the film, one or more adjustable plates, as $g^4$, Fig. 6, may be provided for varying the size of the opening $f^4$ of the stationary member according to the position of the pictures or objects to be ex- 130 posed relative to such perforations.

For the purpose of intermittently moving or feeding the film or picture-carrying surface in such manner as to cause the series of pictures thereon to be brought into and permitted to remain in the illuminated field for an interval of time exceeding the time required to effect the displacement of any one picture and the substitution of another therefor and to automatically release the pressure exerted upon the film by the yielding member of the tension device I may employ a rotating disk, cam, or other rotating element II, Figs. 1, 2, and 8, having thereon, preferably, an eccentric stud or pin $h$, which may have a friction-roller $h'$ journaled thereon and adapted to impinge against the film and advance the same a predetermined distance at each revolution of said disk or cam. The disk may be journaled in a suitable standard or frame-piece, as $f^3$, in such position that the stud or roller thereon may press downwardly upon the film at a point between the tension device E' and drum $E^2$, so as to cause the film to be moved or drawn downward the required distance at each revolution of said disk or cam. A cam-surface $h^2$ on the disk or cam H is adapted to engage the end of a screw $h^3$, arranged in a pendent arm $h^4$, which is secured to or formed integrally with the member $f^2$ of the tension device, in order to release the pressure on the film by said member prior to and while the film is being drawn downward by the roller $h'$. This roller is preferably provided with a suitable covering and may have reduced ends, as shown in Fig. 8, so that it may engage the surface of the film between the perforations in order to prevent enlarging or otherwise distorting the perforations. This arrangement permits the film to be constantly moved by the drums E E², while a portion thereof is intermittently fed forward and positively held during the interval of exposure, so as to present the successive pictures in the field of illumination, while maintaining sufficient tension thereon to prevent the film from slipping or moving more than the required distance.

In connection with one or both of the feed-drums E and E², I may employ a pressure device, such as shown at I in Figs. 2 and 7. This pressure device may consist of a spring having a portion thereof adapted to press the film yieldingly against the smooth face or periphery of the drum, between the rows of teeth thereon, so as to hold the film in place. A guide K may also be provided for either or both of the feed-drums, said guide being preferably supported upon a suitable standard $k$ and provided with depending arms or fingers $k'$, adapted to embrace the edges of the film, so as to aline the same and prevent the projections on the drum from enlarging or otherwise injuring the perforations in the film.

The feed-drums E and E² should be geared together, so as to run at a regulated speed and should revolve in unison with each other, each making a complete revolution in the same instant of time, and the disk or cam II should be so actuated and timed with respect to the rate of movement of the drums that

the film may be advanced the same distance for every revolution. Though no mechanism is shown for this purpose it is obvious that gearing, belts, chains, or any other suitable means may be employed and may be actuated by an electric or other suitable motor.

The operation of the invention will be readily understood from the foregoing description when taken in connection with the accompanying drawings, the parts being in the position shown in Figs. 1 and 2. If the feed-drums are rotated at a proper speed, the film D will be moved in the direction indicated by the arrows; but the pressure exerted by the tension device E will hold the film stationary with the exposed picture in the field of illumination for a predetermined time and until the disk II has rotated far enough to cause its roller $h'$ to contact with the film for advancing the latter, so as to displace the exposed picture and bring another picture into the field of illumination, there being sufficient slack in the film at the bend thereof above said tension device to permit a rapid movement of a given length sufficient to displace any one of the pictures in the series and permit another to be brought into position for exposure or reproduction. When the object has been held in the field of illumination the proper interval of time, the cam-surface $h^2$ of the cam or disk II will engage the set-screw $h^3$ and throw the member $f^2$ of the tension device outwardly on its pivot, so as to relieve the pressure exerted thereby upon the film, the member $f'$ being adapted to exert a constant but yielding pressure on the film to prevent the latter from slipping or being fed farther than is required to present the successive pictures in proper position. When the pressure exerted on the film by the member $f^2$ is relieved, the roller $h'$ on the disk H will simultaneously engage the film and move it downward a sufficient distance to displace one object or picture and place the next succeeding object in proper position for exposure. When the tension device and film are released by the cam $h^2$ and roller $h'$, respectively, on the disk H, the roller will revolve the remaining portion of a complete revolution before again moving the film, while the released tension device instantly regains its hold upon and holds that part of the film which is in the field of illumination stationary until the roller again contacts with the film. During this interval of time the slack in the film between the tension device and the drum E² will be gradually taken up by the last-mentioned drum, but not at such a speed as to exert a tension sufficient to move the film during the interval of exposure of the picture, and in the same instant of time, while the picture is being exhibited, the slack in the film between the tension device and the drum E, which has been taken up by advancing the film, will be compensated by an additional amount of slack paid out by the drum E, thus providing sufficient slack ahead

of the tension device to permit the next succeeding picture to be brought quickly into the field of illumination and allowing sufficient slack in that portion of the film which
5 has passed the tension device to be taken up by the succeeding drum during the inaction of the film-advancing device. This operation will be repeated in regular sequence, the film being caused to move over the sur-
10 face of the drums E and E² continuously, while that portion thereof which lies between the two drums is intermittently moved forward just far enough to expose a picture at each move, the film-advancing mechanism
15 being also continuously driven, but adapted to only intermittently advance the film, the interval of illumination of the picture being made to exceed the interval of movement or change preferably very greatly or
20 in the ratio of about one to ten. In this manner the pictures on the picture-carrying surface or film may be successively displaced and substituted one for another with great rapidity, so that in exhibiting a series of simi-
25 lar pictures representing the same moving object in different phases of its motion the impression may be given to the eye of persons or objects in motion and with a vivid or lifelike appearance. I thus provide means for
30 operating the film so that it may be moved the proper distance for exposing successive pictures without liability to injury thereto, and whereby the knocking and jolting of the machinery incident to the necessarily rapid
35 movement of the parts may be effectually prevented.

It is obvious that various devices may be employed for intermittently moving the film so as to successively place the pictures in the
40 field of illumination. In Fig. 9 the film passes between two suitable tension devices $m$ $m'$, then around a roller $m²$, and thence to the drum M, though other means for guiding said film may be used, if desired. Between the
45 guides $m$ $m'$ may be arranged an arm or crosshead $m³$, adapted to slide in a suitable support $m⁴$, one end of said cross-head being provided with a roller or other engaging portion $m⁵$, and the other end thereof connected to
50 suitable driving mechanism, as a crank and pitman $m⁶$ $m⁷$, respectively, so that when the cross-head is forced forward the roller will engage the film between the guides and force it outward, thereby causing the slack portion
55 of the film above the guide or tension device $m$ to move downward the desired distance to displace one picture and place another in its stead, the slack below the tension device $m'$ in the film being taken up by the drum M or
60 in any other preferred manner. The roller for actuating the film, instead of having a sliding reciprocating movement, as in Fig. 9, may be arranged on the end of an oscillating arm or lever $n$, Fig. 10, pivoted, as at $n'$, to
65 a suitable support, so as to swing in the arc of a circle. In this case the lever $n$ may have a slotted portion in which a pin or stud $n²$,

projecting from a rotary disk or crank $n³$, may work, so as to tilt said lever on its pivot and force the film outward, as shown in dot-
70 ted lines.

Fig. 11 illustrates a modified form of tension guiding device and means for intermittently operating the film. The stationary member $o$ of the tension device O in this in-
75 stance may be in two parts, as shown, (or in one piece, if preferred,) and has an upper yielding member $o'$, which exerts a constant yielding pressure upon the film, and a lower pivoted or hinged and yielding member $o²$,
80 adapted to exert a greater pressure upon the film than the member $o'$ in substantially the same manner as in the tension device E'. A lever $o³$ may be pivoted, as at $o⁴$, to a suitable support and has on one end thereof a rod or
85 stem $o⁵$, provided with an adjusting-nut $o⁶$, and a spring $o⁷$, interposed between said nut and a suitable stop or fixture $o³$, through which the rod $o⁵$ slides, so that the rod will be normally forced inward, and on the opposite end
90 of said lever may be journaled a roller $p$ adapted to engage the film and tending to normally force the same outward, as shown in dotted lines. The yielding member $o²$ of the tension device is provided with a depend-
95 ing arm or finger $p'$, adapted to be engaged by the cam-surface $p²$ of the disk or cam P at a predetermined time, so that when said member is thrown outward sufficiently to relieve the pressure on the film the spring $o⁷$ will force
100 the end of the lever $o³$, with the roller $p$ thereon, in the direction indicated by the arrow, until the lever reaches the adjustable stop $p³$, at which time the picture in the field of illumination will be displaced and another
105 substituted therefor. At P' is a drum for taking up the slack in the film and holding the lever $o³$ against the tension of the spring $o⁷$ until the pressure on the film by this member $o²$ of the tension device is relieved by the
110 cam P.

In Fig. 13 the film is shown as a continuous strip or band instead of an endless strip, as shown in Fig. 1. In this case the film may be unwound from a reel or spool Q' and af-
115 ter passing around the feed-drums E and E², as heretofore explained, may be caused to pass around a roller $q$ and then to the reel or spool Q', the latter being operated in any suitable manner, as by frictional engagement
120 devices, to take up the slack in the film as it is unwound from the drum E without causing unnecessary tension upon said film. The reel Q' may, however, be placed in such position that the film may be wound directly
125 thereon from the drum E².

It will be understood, of course, that the film may be fed to the tension device and taken up after leaving the same by other means than by the use of the feed-drums,
130 that certain parts of the apparatus may be dispensed with or others substituted therefor, and that some parts of the operating mechanism and other parts of the apparatus may

be employed in other connections or for other purposes than exhibiting pictures without departing from the spirit of my invention.

From the foregoing description it will be seen that the pictures are brought successively into an illuminated field and that each picture is illuminated without interruption from the instant it enters such field until displaced by the next picture in the series and that the several pictures in the series are successively substituted one for another with such rapidity that although the exposed portion of the film or picture-carrying surface is continuously illuminated the eye receives an impression of the picture which so greatly predominates any possible impression that might be made by the practically instantaneous motion of said film or surface in substituting picture for picture that the predominating impression which the eye receives, owing to its inability to receive two impressions at one and the same time and to the persistence of vision, has the effect of rendering the movement of the film utterly imperceptible, while the successive impressions of different pictures are each retained until another picture in the series is superimposed, as it were, upon the previous impression or picture, thus rendering it possible to produce most vivid and life-like effects without any interruption whatever in the illumination, whether the film is moving or stationary and without interposing a shutter, and thereby causing a shadow or shade effect which reduces the vividness of the impression, but I do not desire to be confined to the use of the invention without a shutter, inasmuch as such a device might be used under some circumstances—as, for instance, when constructed so as to interrupt the illumination only at that instant of time when the film is moving and without rendering the interruption perceptible to the eye; but for all practical purposes a shutter of any kind is useless and objectionable and is preferably dispensed with.

Having thus fully described my invention, what I claim as new, and desire to secure by Letters Patent of the United States, is—

1. In a picture-exhibiting apparatus for giving the impression to the eye of objects in motion, the combination with a picture-carrying strip or film, a tension device adapted to keep the film taut and prevent flexing or puckering at the point of exposure, means for intermittently moving the film through the tension device at short intervals exceeding the interval required in effecting the movement, so that the period during which each picture is stationary and visible shall exceed the period occupied in substituting one picture for another, and mechanism for feeding the film so as to provide slack therein between the same and said tension device, whereby the film may be moved with great rapidity without unnecessary strain and wear upon the film, substantially as described.

2. In a picture-exhibiting apparatus for giving the impression to the eye of objects in motion, the combination with a picture-carrying strip or film, a tension device adapted to keep the film taut and prevent flexing or puckering at the point of exposure, means for intermittently moving the film through the tension device at short intervals exceeding the interval required in effecting the movement, so that the interval of pause and illumination shall exceed the interval of motion, and mechanism for feeding the film so as to provide slack between the same and said tension device, whereby the film may be intermittently moved with great rapidity without unnecessary strain and wear upon the film, substantially as described.

3. In a picture-exhibiting apparatus for giving the impression to the eye of objects in motion, the combination with an illuminator and a projecting lens, of a picture-carrying strip or film having a portion thereof arranged in the focus of the objective of the projecting lens, a tension device adapted to keep the exposed portion of the film taut and prevent flexing or puckering at the point of exposure, means for intermittently moving the film at short intervals exceeding the interval required in effecting the movement, so that the interval of pause and illumination shall exceed the interval of motion; mechanism for taking up the film as it is intermittently moved, and mechanism for feeding the film so as to provide slack therein between the same and said tension device, whereby that portion of the film between the feeding and take-up mechanisms may be intermittently moved with great rapidity without unnecessary strain and wear upon the film, substantially as described.

4. The combination, in an apparatus for exhibiting pictures so as to give the impression to the eye of objects in motion, of a picture-carrying film or strip, a pair of feed-drums adapted to be continuously rotated so as to give a continuous movement to the film, a tension device interposed between the feed-drums adapted to hold and keep the film taut so as to provide slack on one side thereof, together with means for intermittently moving the film between the drums at short intervals exceeding the interval required in effecting the movement, so that the interval of pause and illumination shall exceed the interval of motion, substantially as described.

5. In a picture-exhibiting apparatus, the combination with a picture-carrying film and means for giving movement to the same, of a tension device provided with a yielding member adapted to hold and prevent movement of the film for a predetermined interval of time, together with mechanism for intermittently moving the film and simultaneously engaging a portion of the yielding member so as to release the pressure exerted thereby upon the film, whereby the pictures may be successively placed in position for ex-

posure with great rapidity without unnecessary strain and wear upon the film, substantially as described.

6. In a picture - exhibiting apparatus, the
5 combination with a picture-carrying surface or film and means for intermittingly moving the same so as to successively expose the pictures thereon, a tension device for yieldingly holding the film, having two parts or mem-
10 bers adapted to exert different pressures, so as to insure prompt action of one or the other of said parts the instant the film has moved the desired distance, substantially as described.

15 7. In a picture - exhibiting apparatus, the combination with an illuminator and a projecting lens, of a picture - carrying strip or film having a portion thereof arranged in the focus of the objective of the projecting lens,
20 a tension device having two members adapted to exert different pressures so as to keep said portion of the film taut and prevent flexing or puckering at the point of exposure, means for intermittently moving said portion
25 so as to impart a step-by-step movement thereto and successively place the pictures in position for exposure, mechanism for taking up the film as it is intermittently moved, and mechanism for feeding the film so as to pro-
30 vide slack therein between the same and said tension device, whereby that portion of the film between the feeding and take-up mechanisms may be intermittently moved with great rapidity without unnecessary strain and
35 wear upon the film, substantially as described.

8. In a picture - exhibiting apparatus, the combination with a picture-carrying film, of a tension device therefor having two members adapted to exert different pressures so
40 as to keep the film taut and prevent flexing or puckering at the point of exposure, mechanism for taking up the film after leaving the tension device, means located intermediate said tension device and the take - up
45 mechanism for intermittently moving the film, together with means for feeding the film so as to provide slack between the same and said tension device, whereby the pictures may be successively placed in position for exposure
50 with great rapidity without unnecessary strain and wear upon the film, substantially as described.

9. The combination with a film or strip and means for imparting movement thereto, of a
55 tension device provided with a yielding member adapted to hold and keep the film taut and prevent flexing or puckering at the point of exposure, a rotatable element adapted to contact with a portion of the yielding mem-
60 ber so as to relieve the pressure exerted thereby upon the film, together with means for intermittently moving the film through the tension device, substantially as described.

10. The combination with a film or strip, of
65 a pair of feed-drums adapted to be continuously rotated so as to give a continuous movement to the film, a tension device interposed

between the feed-drums and provided with a yielding member adapted to hold and keep
70 the film taut, so as to provide slack on one side thereof, a rotary disk or cam adapted to contact with a portion of the yielding member so as to release the pressure thereof on said film, and having thereon a projecting
75 portion adapted to engage the film and intermittently move the same when the pressure of said yielding member is released, substantially as described.

11. In combination with the film and means
80 for imparting movement thereto, the tension device comprising three members between which the film is adapted to pass, one member being stationary and the others adapted to press the film against said stationary mem-
85 ber with different pressures so that when the pressure of one of the yielding members is released the other may exert a pressure sufficient to prevent slipping of the film without preventing its proper movement, whereby
90 the film may be successively moved a uniform distance, substantially as described.

12. The combination with a film or strip, of a tension device comprising a stationary member, two spring - pressed yielding members
95 adapted to press the film against said stationary member with different pressures, guides for alining the film, and means whereby one of the yielding members may be actuated so as to release the pressure exerted
100 thereby upon the film, substantially as described.

13. The combination with a film or strip, of a tension device comprising a stationary member, two yielding members hinged thereto
105 adapted to press the film against said stationary member with different pressures, guides for alining the film, means whereby one of the yielding members may be actuated so as to release the pressure thereof upon the
110 film, and a plate or shield carried by one of the yielding members and separated therefrom sufficiently to provide space for the circulation of air, whereby the film may be protected from the heat of the illuminator and
115 the parts kept cool by the fanning action of said plate, substantially as described.

14. The combination with a film or strip and means for imparting movement thereto, of a support, banks or series of rollers separated
120 from each other and adjustably held upon said support so that the film may pass alternately from a roller of one series to the next succeeding roller of the other series, together with an arm pivotally held to the support
125 and provided with a roller adapted to engage the film and exert a tension thereon, substantially as described.

In testimony whereof I affix my signature in presence of two witnesses.

THOMAS ARMAT.

Witnesses:
J. A. E. CRISWELL,
CHARLES E. RIORDON.

**W. LATHAM.**

**PROJECTING KINETOSCOPE.**

Application filed June 1, 1896.

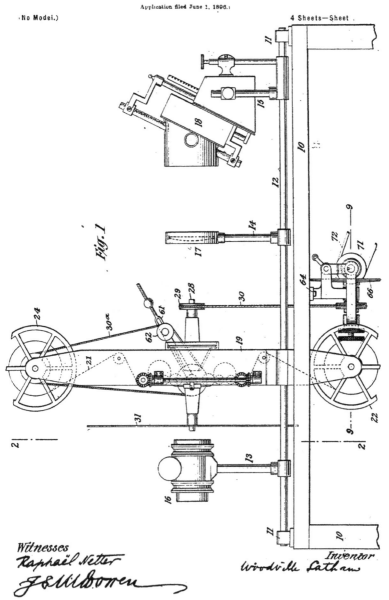

*Fig. 1*

No. 707,934

Patented Aug. 26, 1902.

W. LATHAM.

PROJECTING KINETOSCOPE.

(Application filed June 1, 1896.)

(No Model.)

4 Sheets—Sheet 2.

Fig. 2

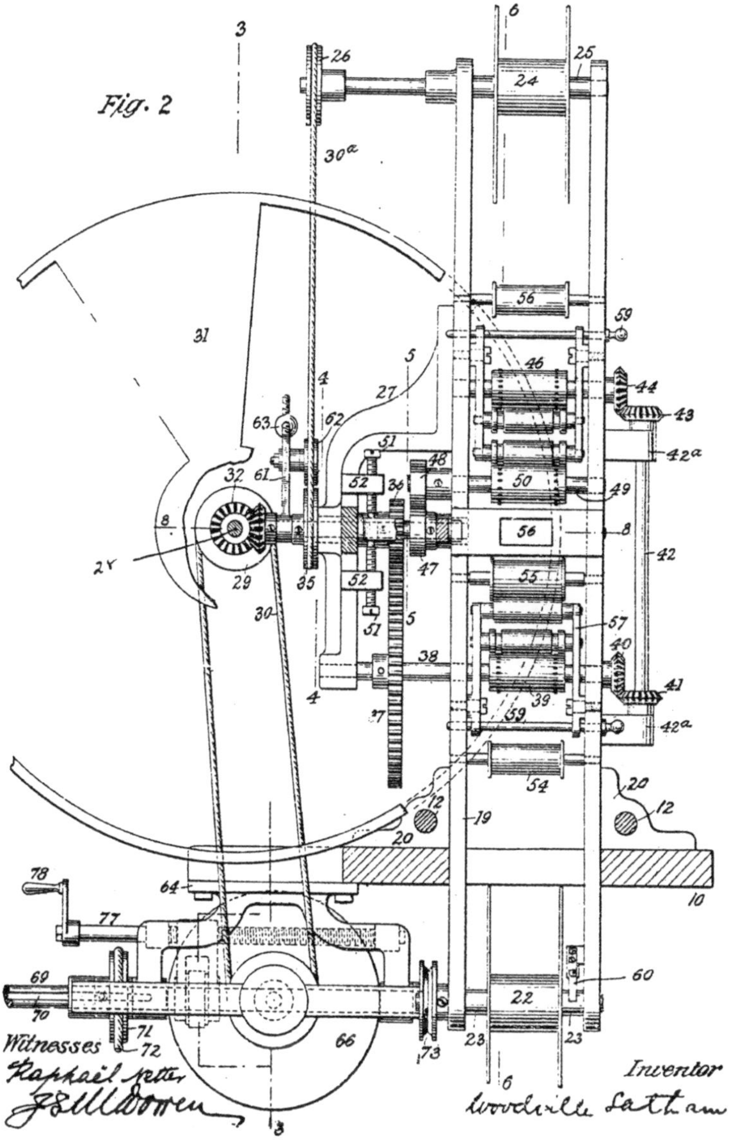

Witnesses

Raphaël Netter

J. S. McDowen

Inventor

Woodville Latham

**W. LATHAM.**
**PROJECTING KINETOSCOPE.**
Application filed June 1, 1896.

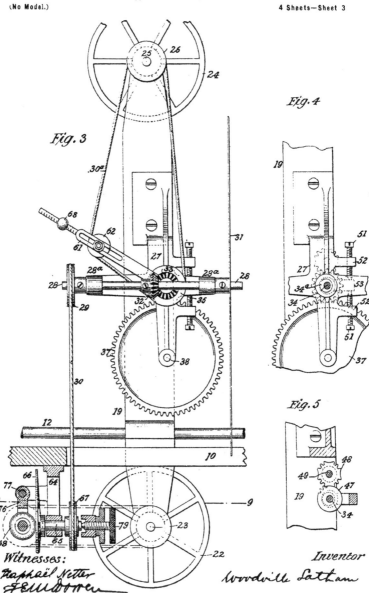

*Fig. 3*

*Fig. 4*

*Fig. 5*

Witnesses:
Raphaël Netter
J. Ellis Bower

Inventor
Woodville Latham

No. 707,934.

W. LATHAM.
PROJECTING KINETOSCOPE.
(Application filed June 1, 1896.)

Patented Aug. 26, 1902.

(No Model.)

4 Sheets—Sheet 4.

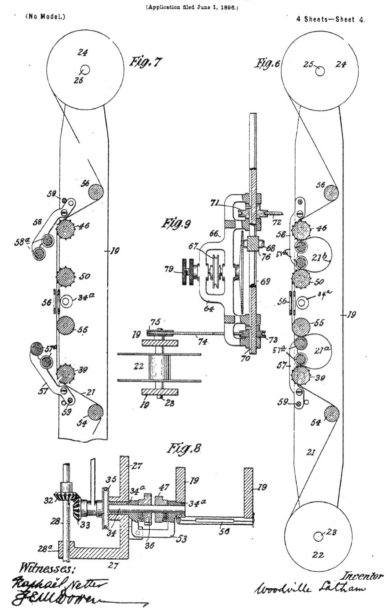

Fig. 7

Fig. 6

Fig. 9

Fig. 8

Witnesses:
Raphaël Netter
F. Ell. Bower

Inventor
Woodville Latham

# UNITED STATES PATENT OFFICE.

WOODVILLE LATHAM, OF NEW YORK, N. Y., ASSIGNOR, BY MESNE ASSIGN-
MENTS, TO E. & H. T. ANTHONY & CO.. OF NEW YORK, N. Y., A COR-
PORATION OF NEW YORK.

## PROJECTING-KINETOSCOPE.

SPECIFICATION forming part of Letters Patent No. 707,934, dated August 23, 1902.

Application filed June 1, 1896. Serial No. 593,747. (No model.)

*To all whom it may concern:*

Be it known that I, WOODVILLE LATHAM, a citizen of the United States, and a resident of New York, in the county and State of New York, have invented certain new and useful Improvements in Projecting-Kinetoscopes, of which the following is a specification.

The present invention has reference to apparatus for projecting successively and at frequent intervals on a screen or other plane surface an extended series of photographs of moving objects, whereby the movement of the objects may be accurately exhibited.

The purpose of the invention is to provide an apparatus capable of continuously projecting or exhibiting upon a suitable surface a great number of pictures taken from moving objects and arranged upon a strip or film of great length, whereby each picture in the strip is brought to rest at the moment of projection, so that there is given to the eye an impression of objects in motion in a manner now well understood.

In an apparatus organized so that the picture-bearing strip is caused to move continuously and uninterruptedly across the optical axis a light of very high intensity is necessary to give satisfactory results; but a light of such power is not required for satisfactory projection by means of an apparatus embodying the principle of the present invention. The stoppage of each picture during its exposure permits the requisite quantity of light to pass through the condenser, the picture, and the objective to the screen or plane surface upon which the image is projected when the light employed is only of a moderately-high power.

The invention therefore consists in an apparatus for projecting successively a large number of pictures of moving objects, embodying, among other things, means for bringing each picture to rest at the moment of projection, means for reducing the strain the picture-film would otherwise suffer from its rapid interruption and renewal of its movement, and means for maintaining uniformity of movement of the film as it unwinds from the delivering-reel and as it winds upon the receiving-reel, all as set forth in the claims at the end of this specification.

In the accompanying drawings, which form part of this description, one form of apparatus embodying the invention is illustrated.

In the drawings like features are designated in the several figures by like numerals of reference.

Figure 1 is a side elevation of the apparatus. Fig. 2 is a cross-section on the line 2 2 of Fig. 1, partly broken away. Fig. 3 is a section on broken line 3 3 of Fig. 2 looking toward the machine. Fig. 4 is a fragmentary section on line 4 4 of Fig. 2. Fig. 5 is a similar section on the line 5 5 of Fig. 2. Fig. 6 is a vertical section through the machine, showing the slack in the film, taken on the line 6 6 of Fig. 2. Fig. 7 is a similar section showing the devices for pressing the film into contact with the guide-rollers and drums thrown out of action. Fig. 8 is a sectional view on the line 8 8 of Fig. 2; and Fig. 9 is a section on the line 9 9 of Figs. 1 and 3 through the power-transmitting appliances, showing the relation of the parts when winding back the film to the delivering-reel.

The several parts of the apparatus may be mounted upon an optical bench (indicated in the drawings at 10) of any convenient design. At the ends of the bench 10 are the brackets 11, furnishing supports for the pair of longitudinal rods 12, upon which are mounted the standards 13 14 15, said standards being bifurcated to connect with the rods 12. The standard 13 supports a projecting-objective 16, which may be readily adjusted to bring it in proper relation to the picture being projected, and standard 14 supports the condensing lens or lenses 17, while the standard 15 supports the lamp 18, which in this instance is shown as a focusing arc-lamp. The lamp 18 is preferably adjustable on its support both vertically and laterally, and the standards for the condensing-lens and the lamp are so constructed that they may be adjusted longitudinally on the rods 12 so as to obtain the proper relative relation between the lamp and the condenser and the condenser and the picture-strip. The mechanism for supporting and propelling the shutter and the picture-bearing strip is arranged above and below the optical bench 10 on standards 19, which extend vertically above the bench and for a short distance beneath and are braced by the brackets 20, which also furnish bearings for the longitudinal rods 12, as seen in Fig. 2. The picture-bearing strip or film, which may be of any desired length without in any way affecting the operation of the machine, is indicated at 21 in the several views. It is wound upon the delivering-reel 22, the shaft of which, 23, is journaled in the lower ends of the standards 19. The receiving-reel 24 is similarly mounted at the top of standards 19, its shaft 25 having bearings in said standards and being extended at one side beyond the standard to receive a pulley 26 for the belt 30ᵃ, transmitting the motion of the driving-shaft to the receiving-reel. The function of these two reels is merely to support the bulk of the film while successive sections of it are subjected to the feeding and exposing mechanism. One of the reels supplies the film for exposure, and the other coils up and takes care of the film after exposure. The picture-bearing strip 21 is conducted through and over its guiding and controlling mechanism, mounted in standards 19, and secured to the hub of reel 24. The said strip when in the position it is caused to assume when the apparatus is projecting has two slack sections contiguous to the sprocketed feed-drums for the purposes presently explained.

To one side of the standards 19 there is fixed a bracket 27, in which the main shaft 28 is mounted in bearings 28ᵃ. At one end of this shaft 28 there is keyed a pulley 29 to receive the driving-belt 30, and at its opposite end is fixed the hub of the shutter 31. On the main shaft 28 is keyed the bevel-gear 32, which meshes with a bevel-gear 33, fixed to the end of shaft 34, which revolves in bearings 34ᵃ in bracket 27 and adjacent standard 19, the revolution of the shaft 28 being thereby transmitted to shaft 34. The shaft 34 has keyed to it a pulley 35, which receives the belt 30ᵃ, transmitting motion to the receiving-reel, and it has also keyed to it the small gear-wheel 36, which engages with the large gear-wheel 37, keyed to shaft 38, having bearings in bracket 27 as well as in standards 19, said shaft carrying the toothed drum 39 and having keyed to its outer end a bevel-gear 40, which meshes with another bevel-gear 41, fixed to the upright shaft 42, supported in brackets 42ᵃ on standard 19, and having at its upper end a bevel-gear 43, which meshes with a like gear 44 on the end of shaft 45, which carries a toothed drum 46 and has bearings in standards 19. By this mechanism the toothed drums 39 and 46 are caused to revolve continuously at a uniform rate when power is communicated to the main shaft 28. It is obvious that other forms of gearing may be employed

to drive said toothed drums 39 and 46 in unison. Shaft 34 has also keyed to it broken gear 47, Fig. 5, which is adapted to engage with a broken gear 48, fixed to shaft 49, having bearings and standards 19 and carrying a toothed drum 50. The gear 48 on the shaft of drum 50 is provided with a series of four toothed sections and a series of four plain sections, the surfaces of the latter being made to conform to the toothless portion of the circumference of the broken gear 47, so that while the gear 47 revolves continuously it intermeshes with gear 48 only momentarily as it completes each revolution, moving the gear 48 intermittently, and thus producing momentary stoppage of the drum 50 once with each complete revolution of shaft 34. At the moment of stoppage of the drum 50 the smooth surfaces of the gears are in sliding contact and remain so until the shaft 34 completing another revolution the teeth of the two gears again intermesh, revolving the drum 50 one-fourth of a revolution, and so on continuously, said drum momentarily stopping as the picture-bearing strip is moved through the apparatus the length of one picture, thus bringing each picture to rest at the moment of projection, and hence in a device of the construction described the period of rest of the film is four times greater than its period of movement. To prevent any vibration of the picture at the moment of projection, the smooth surfaces of the broken gears 47 and 48 should preferably be held in close sliding contact, and with this end in view the bearings 34ᵃ 34ᵃ (see Figs. 4, 5, and 8) of the shaft 34 are made eccentric, so that by means of the adjusting-screws 51 51, passing through lugs 52 on bracket 27 and bearing at their points on opposite sides of the yoke 53, connected to or formed with said bearings, the shaft 34 may be slightly raised or lowered, as required. This mode of adjustment has been found in practice to be efficient and to satisfactorily answer the purposes intended.

Because of the rapid interruption and resumption of the movement of the picture-film it is necessary to provide means for reducing the strain on the same to prevent its being ruptured by the teeth of the sprocket-drum 50, which actuates or feeds the film intermittently by engaging in holes at its edges, and it is also necessary or desirable to provide means for maintaining uniformity of tension of the film as it unwinds from the delivering-reel and winds upon the receiving-reel. The manner whereby these objects are effected will now be described.

The numerals 54, 55, and 56 indicate rollers for supporting and guiding the picture-bearing strip 21 and are arranged to freely revolve on fixed shafts supported in the standards 19. The picture-bearing strip or film 21, which has photographically produced upon it a series of pictures representing the successive stages or positions of the moving object or ob-

jects to be reproduced, is conducted from the delivering-reel 22 over the guide-roller 54, toothed or sprocketed drum 39, guide-roller 55, past exposure-window 56ª, which is at-
5 tached to the standards 19 in the line of the optical axis of the apparatus, toothed drums 50 and 46, and guide-roller 56 to the receiving-reel 24, to the hub of which its end is secured. The strip or film is perforated at regular in-
10 tervals along its lateral edges to correspond exactly with the sprocket-like teeth arranged on the circumference of the drums 39, 46, and 50, near their ends, respectively.

In Fig. 6 the parts of the mechanism for
15 controlling and guiding the picture-bearing strip or film, as well as the strip itself, are in position for projecting, and in Fig. 7 the parts are shown in the position they are made to assume when the picture-bearing strip is be-
20 ing wound back from the receiving to the delivering reel.

To secure the necessary engagement between the picture-bearing strip 21 and the feeding-drums 39, 46, and 50, so that the strip
25 may be fed or moved with greater accuracy and certainty, the frames 57 and 58, pivoted, as shown, to the standards 19, are provided, and they are supplied with the freely-revolving rollers 57ª and 58ª. (See Fig. 7.) The
30 rollers 58ª, carried by frame 58, are adapted to coöperate with the toothed drums 46 and 50, and they have circumferentially near their ends grooves, as shown in Fig. 2, to receive the teeth or sprockets of said feed-drums
35 when the frame is fixed in the position it occupies when the apparatus is projecting, and the rollers 57ª of frame 57, one of which coöperates with toothed drum 39, are similarly constructed for the same reason, the upper
40 roller 57ª, which coacts with the toothless guide-roller 55, being grooveless on its circumference. The frames 57 58 are held in the two positions which they are adapted to occupy, as in Fig. 6 when projecting or as in
45 Fig. 7 when the picture-bearing strip is released so as to be wound back from the upper to the lower reel by the removable rods which pass through suitable holes in the standards 19 and engage with the ends of the frames,
50 as shown in Figs. 6 and 7. When in the position shown in Fig. 6, the rollers carried by frame 57 are between the sprocket-drum 39 and the guide-roller 55, while the rollers carried by frame 58 are between the sprocket-
55 drums 46 and 50. Within the planes occupied by the two sets of rollers 57ª and 58ª when the apparatus is adjusted for projecting—i. e., when in operation—the film or picture-bearing strip 21 is thrown out in the form
60 of a loop, as shown at 21ª 21ᵇ, one of these slack portions being at one time above window 56ª and the other at another time above the same. The extent of each of said slack portions is preferably that of the height of a
65 picture or slightly more. It will be understood from the description that follows that the loops of slack below and above the ex-

posure-window are alternately thrown out and then taken up by the operation of the sprocket-drums, respectively, and that they
70 produce and take up the slack by their own positive action entirely independent of the film-supporting reels at the extremes of the apparatus. In the operation of the machine the rollers 57ª 58ª hold the strip in proper
75 contact with the respective feed-drums and guide-roller 55, as will be understood from Fig. 6, and insure proper contact between the strip and the respective drums. The picture-bearing strip is carried through the ap-
80 paratus with great rapidity, and because of the rapid interruption and resumption of its movement it would not be possible for the strip to withstand the strain brought upon it for any considerable time if there were not
85 provision made for the slacks in the film, as just explained. The instant each picture of the strip is brought in the line of the optical axis the toothless surfaces of the broken gears 47 48 are in sliding contact, their re-
90 spective cogs being out of engagement, with the effect of causing stoppage of revolution of the toothed drum 50 and consequent momentary stoppage of the film between said toothed drum 50 and the toothless roller 55
95 beneath the optical axis; but the revolution of shaft 38 being continuous the toothed drums 39 and 46, which latter is positively geared from said shaft, as explained, also revolve continuously, taking up the slack 21ᵇ
100 between toothed drums 46 and 50 and also replacing the slack 21ª between toothed drum 39 and roller 55, thus restoring the slack 21ª, to be again taken up when the broken gears 47 48 again momentarily intermesh. It will
105 thus be seen that as the slack 21ᵇ is taken up at the moment of stoppage of the toothed drum 50 the slack 21ª is simultaneously being restored, and this action is continuous and positive and independent of the other
110 parts of the machine while the operation of projection is going on. There is therefore but little, if any, additional strain on the film incident to the rapid interruption and resumption of its movement through the appa-
115 ratus.

The construction and operation of the devices which produce and take up the loops of slack film and also those which intermittingly feed or, so to speak, "jerk" the film from
120 picture to picture across the exposure-window or axis of the lens form an exceedingly important part of this invention. It will be noted that they are entirely separate and distinct from the reels which support the
125 weight of the bulk of the film and which are consequently relatively heavy, so that the length and consequent weight of the film may be indefinitely extended without affecting the operation of the machine. The in-
130 termittingly-feeding devices, on the other hand, which comprise only the broken gear 48 and the feed-drum 50 with its shaft, are very light, and consequently have very little

inertia, and since also the small portion of the film which this part of the apparatus actuated has scarcely any weight these parts will instantly stop and start with great rapidity and with a minimum of strain or jar upon the mechanism and with the least possible wear on the holes for the sprocket-teeth in the film, and in order that the slack may be formed and the intermittent movements across the optical axis effected with accuracy and certainty it is desirable, although not essential, that the rollers which effect these movements be provided with the sprocket-teeth shown or their equivalent, so that they may positively engage with the film and positively move it without the possibility of any slipping, which is apt to occur when frictional contact alone is relied on, because such slipping will preclude proper registration between the picture and the optical axis. In order that these parts may operate as described, it is essential that the loop of slack film be maintained at all times ready for the intermittingly-acting device and also that the slack-manipulating and the intermittingly-moving devices be positively driven by mechanism which will absolutely insure the presence of the slack and the accurate movement of the film. The reason these parts and their arrangement and method of operation are such important and valuable features of the invention is because their action is necessarily exceedingly rapid, and if the intermittingly-feeding mechanism were heavy, so as to have much inertia, or if any considerable portion of the film or either of the reels which support it were stopped and started at each transition from picture to picture there would be such strain brought to bear on the sprocket-holes in the film as would speedily tear it adjacent to such holes, thus ruining it, and since these films are expensive, a good one being capable of making large profits for its owner, any means which will prolong their life is of great value in this art.

Another feature peculiar to my invention and one which distinguishes it from certain other apparatus is the important fact that the intermitting feed devices and the slack-former being entirely separate and distinct from the other parts are alone relied upon for securing accurate registration of the successive pictures with the axis of the projecting-lens. The supply and coiling reels at the extremes of the machine may operate with only substantial accuracy and still the results will be satisfactory, because they have nothing to do except to properly support and take care of the film, supplying it at one side and taking it away at the other. The intermitting feed devices and the slack-producing devices, on the other hand, which lie between the two reels and immediately adjacent to the exposure-window, control and manipulate that special and limited part of the film which is at that instant relied upon for the desired results, and it is a comparatively easy matter to accomplish exactness in operation when this part of the mechanism is separate and distinct from the other.

Uniformity of tension of the film as it unwinds from the delivering-reel, to prevent the film from buckling and insure its proper entrance to the apparatus, is secured by any suitable friction device applied to the shaft 23 of said reel. In the drawings is shown a metallic strap with an adjusting-screw for this purpose. This friction device is indicated by 60.

The rate of winding of the picture-bearing strip upon the receiving-reel is regulated by automatically controlling the revolution of the reel by means of the idler 61, which is shown loosely journaled on shaft 34. The idler is provided with a slot, as shown, in which is adjustably fixed roller 62, and around this roller is passed the belt 30ª. By adjusting roller 62 in the slot the pressure on the belt is varied. As the reel 24 becomes larger by the winding of the film thereon the idler may be manipulated to loosen the belt 30ª and to cause it to slip on pulley 26 of the reel-shaft. This slipping is or may be a continuous one from beginning to end of the operation of the machine, but it is such a gentle slipping that no appreciable heat is produced and no appreciable wearing of the belt. The outer end of the idler is screw-threaded and provided with a weight 63, by means of which a nicer adjustment of the pressure exerted by the idler is obtained. By this means the rate of revolution of the receiving-reel is automatically maintained in proper correspondence with that of the feed-drum 46.

The shutter 31, carried by the shaft 28, has but a small solid section. Its use is to cover the film during the interval of movement of each picture.

The power may be imparted to the main shaft 28 through a friction regulating and controlling appliance attached to the bottom of the optical bench by means of the bracket 64. In this bracket is journaled the shaft 65, carrying at one end a friction-plate 66 and having keyed to its opposite end a pulley 67, adapted to receive the belt 30, which passes over pulley 29 on the main shaft 28. The friction-plate 66 coöperates with a friction-roller 68, keyed to shaft 69, the said shaft having a longitudinal groove 70 and being provided with pulley 71, receiving the belt 72 to the motor, and also with pulley 73, adapted to receive belt 74, (see Fig. 9,) which is made use of to transmit the power of the motor to the delivering-reel when winding back the film from the receiving-reel, the shaft of said reel being provided with pulley 75 to receive said belt. The pulleys 71 and 73 are connected to shaft 69 by feathers entering the groove of said shaft, as shown in Fig. 9, so that while these pulleys cannot turn on the shaft the shaft can be moved through the hubs of the pulleys, which is done when adjusting the friction-roller 68 with relation to the friction-plate 66. The hub of the friction-roller is connected by an arm 76, having a screw-threaded sleeve through which passes screw-threaded shaft 77, supported in bracket 64 and adapted to be turned by crank 78 to permit the adjustment of the friction-roller toward or from the center of the friction-plate to increase or diminish the rate of speed of the friction-plate shaft 65 in a manner well understood, the rate of speed of the main shaft 28, connected to the friction-plate shaft 65 through belt 30, being thus determined and regulated as desired. The pressure of the friction-plate 66 against the friction-roller 68 is regulated by means of the milled-head screw 79, the point of which enters a depression in the end of the friction-plate shaft, as shown in Fig. 3. In Fig. 9 the friction-speed-regulating appliances are shown adjusted for winding back the film from the receiving and delivering reel, the friction-roller 68 having been shifted across the center of the friction-plate so as to reverse the revolution of the shaft 65. When winding back the film, the pulleys 73 and 75 are connected by belt 74 and the frames 57 58 are swung back, as shown in Fig. 7, so as to relieve the film of all binding tension.

The reels may be of size suitable to carry any length of picture-bearing strip that may be desired.

In operating the apparatus power is transmitted from the motor (not shown) by belt 72 and through friction-plate shaft by belt 30 to main shaft 28 of the apparatus. The operation of the gearing and the manner in which the teeth of the feed-drums engage the perforations in the edges of the picture-bearing strip and move it from the delivering to the receiving reel and across the opening 56 in the line of the optical axis of the apparatus, with a momentary stoppage of the film crossing the optical axis as the central portion of each picture is brought in the line of the optical axis, will all be understood from the preceding description. Whenever the central portion of a picture is in the line of the optical axis and the picture comes to rest, the light will pass simultaneously through the condensing-lens, through the picture, and through the objective outward to the screen or other plane surface. The light of course must be so adjusted as to cover the whole of the picture. The pictures are projected successively, with such great rapidity, each succeeding picture showing a slightly-advanced stage of motion, that the effect on the eye of the observer is exactly the same as if a moving object or objects were being looked at directly.

It is to be understood that many of the mere details of the apparatus herein described may be varied without departing from the principle of my invention—as, for example, while the mechanism shown and described for forming the slack in the film and causing the picture-bearing strip to travel in such manner that there is a real stoppage of the film as each picture is presented in the line of the optical axis is the form and character preferred by me, it is obvious that the principle of the invention may be retained with differently-organized gearing and the employment of other appliances than those shown and described.

Having described my invention, I claim as new—

1. The combination with devices for supporting the bulk of a flexible film before and after exposure, of feeding mechanisms located between the devices for supporting the film and separate and distinct therefrom, one of said feeding mechanisms being constructed to uniformly feed the film and produce a predetermined supply of slack, and the other adapted to intermittently feed the slack across the exposure-window.

2. The combination with devices for supporting the bulk of the film before and after exposure, of feeding mechanisms located between the devices for supporting the film and separate and distinct therefrom, one of said feeding mechanisms being constructed to uniformly feed the film and produce a predetermined supply of slack, and the other adapted to intermittently feed the slack film across the exposure-window, and constructed also to cause the intervals of rest of the film to exceed its intervals of movement.

3. The combination with devices which support the bulk of the film and supply it for exposure and receive it after exposure, of positively-driven devices separate and distinct from the film-supporting devices, located between them and at opposite sides of the exposure-window, and which respectively engage with and accurately and uniformly feed the film, and which respectively produce and take up slack in it, and an intermittently-acting device located between said last-named devices which intermittently moves the slackened part of the film across the exposure-window.

4. The combination with devices which support the bulk of a flexible strip or film and supply it for exposure and receive it after exposure, of positively-driven devices separate and distinct from the film-supporting devices and which engage the film and accurately compel its movement, and which feed the film by uniform and continuous rotary action, and an intermittently-acting device located between said last-named devices and which moves the slackened part of the film picture by picture across the exposure-window and causes its period of rest to exceed its period of movement.

5. The combination with devices which support the bulk of a flexible film and supply it for exposure and receive it after exposure, of positively-driven devices separate and distinct from the film-supporting devices and located between them at opposite sides of the exposure-window, and which engage the film

and accurately insure its feeding, which last-named devices respectively produce and take up slack in the film, and an intermittently-acting device provided with teeth which engage in holes in the film whereby it feeds the film across the exposure-opening.

6. The combination with devices which support the bulk of a flexible film and supply it for exposure and receive it after exposure, of a positively-driven device entirely disconnected from the said film-supporting devices located between the film-supplying device and the exposure-window and which produces a loop of slack film, and an intermittently-acting device which engages with the film and feeds the slackened part of it across the exposure-window, and causes its period of rest to exceed its period of movement.

7. The combination with devices adapted to support the bulk of a flexible film and supply it for exposure and receive it after exposure, of positively-driven toothed rotary devices located between and entirely disconnected from said supporting devices and at opposite sides of the exposure-window, said toothed devices being adapted to carry and feed the flexible film by the engagement of their teeth with equally-spaced holes made in the edges of the film and to respectively produce and take up slack in the film, and an intermittently-acting rotary feeding device also provided with teeth which engage with the holes in the film, whereby the film is intermittently fed across the exposure-opening.

8. The combination with two reels which support the bulk of a flexible film, one of which supplies it for exposure and the other receives it after exposure, of a positively-driven device separate and distinct from the said reels and located between the supply-reel and the exposure-window and which produces a loop of slack film, and an intermittently-acting device likewise positively driven which moves the film picture by picture into the optical axis at the exposure-window and causes each picture to remain momentarily at rest in the optical axis.

9. The combination with two rotary reels which support the bulk of a flexible film, one of which supplies the film for exposure and the other coils it up after exposure, of two rotary feeding mechanisms located between said reels and separate and distinct from them, one constructed to feed the film intermittently and cause it to move picture by picture across the axis of the lens and to come to rest in said axis, the other constructed to feed the film continuously and uniformly and thus provide a constant supply of slack film and gearing positively connecting the said two feeding mechanisms for maintaining a fixed relation between them.

10. The combination with two rotary reels adapted to support the bulk of a flexible film, one of which supplies the film for exposure and the other receives it after exposure, of two toothed rotary feeding-rollers located between said film-supporting reels and separate and distinct therefrom and adapted to carry and feed the film by the engagement of their teeth with equally-spaced holes in the edges of the film, actuating mechanism and connecting-gearing between said feeding-rollers which positively actuates one of the feeding-rollers so as to feed the film intermittently and cause its interval of rest to exceed its interval of motion and which positively actuates also the other feeding-roller continuously and thus provides a constant supply of slack film.

11. The combination with the main shaft provided with a broken gear mounted in eccentric bearings and a feed-drum whose shaft is provided with a broken gear which meshes with the first-named broken gear, of means for adjusting said bearings to regulate the contact between said gears.

Signed at New York, in the county and State of New York, this 25th day of May, 1896.

WOODVILLE LATHAM.

Witnesses:
  J. E. M. BOWEN,
  ALEXIS C. SMITH.

Defendants' Exhibit No. 201

Pross Patent No. 722,382

March 10, 1903

No. 722,382.

PATENTED MAR. 10, 1903.

J. A. PROSS.

ANIMATED PICTURE APPARATUS.

APPLICATION FILED JAN. 19, 1903.

NO MODEL.

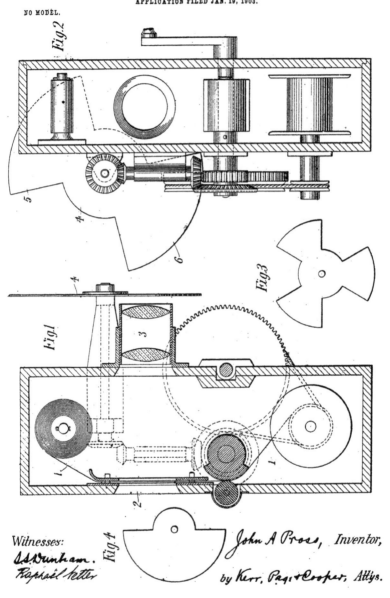

*Fig.2*

*Fig.3*

*Fig.1*

*Fig.4*

Witnesses:

S. S. Dunham.

Raphaël Netter

John A Pross, Inventor,

by Kerr, Page & Cooper, Attys.

# United States Patent Office.

JOHN A. PROSS, OF CANASTOTA, NEW YORK, ASSIGNOR TO AMERICAN
MUTOSCOPE & BIOGRAPH COMPANY, OF NEW YORK, N. Y., A COR-
PORATION OF NEW JERSEY.

## ANIMATED-PICTURE APPARATUS.

SPECIFICATION forming part of Letters Patent No. 722,382, dated March 10, 1903

Application filed January 19, 1903. Serial No. 139,531. (No model.)

*To all whom it may concern:*

Be it known that I, JOHN A. PROSS, a citizen of the United States, residing at Canastota, county of Madison, State of New York, have invented certain new and useful Improvements in Animated-Picture Apparatus, of which the following is a specification, reference being had to the drawings accompanying and forming a part of the same.

My invention relates to machines for exhibiting animated pictures, and has for its object to improve the effects produced by such machines.

Heretofore it has been found impossible to avoid the wavering or flickering caused by the rapid succession of the different views of the moving object, although numerous attempts have been made to accomplish the same—as, for example, by the use of a specially-constructed shutter which obscures the field during the substitution of one picture for the preceding or by the use of a rotating optical system which keeps each successive view momentarily at rest on the screen, although the picture-bearing band itself be continuously moving. Such expedients have been found satisfactory to a certain extent; but they have all possessed in practice certain disadvantages, and I have therefore been led to devise my present invention, which not only is simple in construction and operation and adapted for use with any form of apparatus, but also greatly reduces the undesirable "flicker" which has always been present in the projection of pictures showing objects in motion. The invention involves a departure from hitherto accepted theories, under which it has always been thought desirable in order to reduce the flicker to the minimum to make the period of exposure of each picture as long as possible in comparison with the period of obscuration during substitution or change consistent with producing the illusion of motion. I have found, however, that by interposing an opaque shutter to obscure the field during the period of substitution or change and also one or more times during the period of rest or exposure the objectionable flickering is very greatly reduced.

The invention therefore, broadly stated, consists in means for obscuring the picture during the period of change and also one or more times between changes. I have shown it in the accompanying drawings employed with a projecting apparatus in which the picture-bearing strip or film is moved intermittently, so as to hold each picture stationary in the field for a certain proportion of the time, which may be substantially equal to the period of motion by which one picture succeeds another, but is preferably considerably longer.

It should be understood, of course, that the use of my invention is not limited to the apparatus just mentioned, but may be employed with advantage in connection with any mechanism in which the picture or the image remains stationary for a period of time.

Referring now to the drawings for a better understanding of the invention, Figure 1 shows a simple apparatus arranged to operate in accordance with my invention. Fig. 2 is a rear view of the same with the end of the case and other parts removed. Figs. 3 and 4 show modified forms of shutters.

By means of feed devices of a suitable kind the picture-bearing band or film 1 is intermittently moved past the aperture 2, behind which is located a source of light. In front of the film or band is the objective 3. At any convenient position—as, for example, immediately in front of the objective—is a shutter 4 of suitable form. The shutter is preferably of the form shown in Fig. 2, having two blades 5 6, each substantially equal in extent to the open or cut-away spaces between them. The obscuring device or shutter is rotatably mounted in any convenient way and has means to revolve the same once for each picture. It will thus be seen that each picture or phase of motion will be thrown on a screen twice, once immediately after it moves into the field, followed by a short period when the shutter intercepts the light, then again when the shutter moves away before the picture is carried out of the field; or, stated otherwise, the period during which the picture is in the field is broken by a period of obscuration. This operation has the effect of very materially reducing the flicker. It is not necessary, of course, that the openings in the shutter be exactly ninety degrees, as they may be increased or decreased at will; but it is essential to the best results that they be symmetrically arranged; nor is it necessary that the shutter have only two openings, since the same effect may be obtained with one of three blades, as shown in Fig. 3, by rotating it at lower speed, or by a half-and-half shutter, Fig. 4, at higher speed.

Under some circumstances it may be desirable to intercept the light two or more times during the period of exposure instead of once, and this may be accomplished, as will readily be understood, by increasing the speed of rotation of the shutter or without changing the speed by a shutter having a larger number of blades and openings. Such devices, however, are clearly within the scope of my invention.

One very important result accomplished by my invention is that it makes it possible to exhibit moving pictures at a very much lower rate of speed than has heretofore been necessary for good results. Where the ordinary form of mechanism is employed, in which the picture-bearing strip is obscured only during the substitution of the pictures, the flickering is less objectionable if the frequency of the transposition of the pictures is very great— say forty or fifty pictures per second; but this involves the use of a large amount of film. If the attempt is made to economize in film by exhibiting only twelve or fifteen pictures per second, the flickering becomes very noticeable and objectionable; but by obscuring the picture one or more times during each period, according to the speed of change, the number of flickers per second is increased two or three fold, and the effect upon the eye is much less disagreeable. This operation is analogous to the case of an incandescent electric lamp, which when operated by current of low frequency has an objectionable pulsation, whereas if operated upon a current of the proper high frequency appears to give a steady uniform light. I have also discovered that while the result aimed at—namely, increased steadiness and freedom from flicker—is accomplished to a degree by the employment of a multiplicity of shutter-blades and an interruption of the light several times during each exposure and transposition regardless of the proportion and arrangement of the opaque and transparent portions of the shutter, yet under certain conditions better results are obtained when the openings in a shutter are equal to each other in extent and symmetrically arranged with reference to the axis of rotation in the case of a rotating shutter and with reference to the extent and movement when a reciprocating shutter is employed. All of these forms, however, are within the scope of my invention.

I have found that the loss of illumination caused by the interposition of the opaque portions of the shutter during the periods of exposure of the picture is more than counterbalanced by the elimination or reduction of the flickering normally present when the alternations of light and shade follow each other more slowly.

The mechanism herein shown and described represents merely one embodiment of my invention, which obviously may be embodied in apparatus of widely-varying forms, so long as they are arranged to intercept the light one or more times during each period of exposure as well as during the period of substitution or change.

What I claim is—

1. In an apparatus for projecting a series of pictures of successive phases of moving objects, the combination with means for exposing the pictures in rapid succession, of means for intercepting the light during each period of substitution of the pictures, and also one or more times in each period of exposure, as and for the purposes set forth.

2. In an apparatus for projecting a series of pictures of successive phases of moving objects, the combination with means for exposing the pictures in rapid succession, of a shutter arranged to intercept the light during the periods of substitution of the pictures, and also one or more times between successive substitutions, as and for the purposes set forth.

3. In an apparatus for projecting a series of pictures of successive phases of moving objects, the combination with means for exposing the pictures in rapid succession, of a rotary shutter arranged to intercept the light during the periods of substitution of the pictures, and also one or more times between successive substitutions, as set forth.

4. In an apparatus for projecting a series of pictures of successive phases of moving objects, the combination with means for exposing the pictures in rapid succession of a rotary shutter having a plurality of blades and openings symmetrically arranged, adapted to intercept the light during the periods of substitution, and also one or more times between successive substitutions, as set forth.

5. In an apparatus for projecting a series of pictures of successive phases of moving objects, the combination with means for exposing the pictures in rapid succession, of a rotary shutter having a plurality of symmetrically-arranged blades of substantially equal extent, adapted to intercept the light during the periods of substitution of the pictures, and also one or more times between successive substitutions, as set forth.

6. In an apparatus for projecting a series of pictures of successive phases of moving objects, the combination with means for exposing the pictures in rapid succession, of a rotary shutter having a plurality of symmetrically-arranged blades and openings of substantially equal extent, adapted to intercept the light during the periods of substitution of the pictures, and also one or more times between successive substitutions, as set forth.

JOHN A. PROSS.

Witnesses:
HERMAN CASLER,
J. S. PICKEL.

1

# DISTRICT COURT OF THE UNITED STATES

FOR THE EASTERN DISTRICT OF PENNSYLVANIA.

| | |
|---|---|
| UNITED STATES OF AMERICA,<br>Petitioner,<br><br>v.<br><br>MOTION PICTURE PATENTS CO. and others,<br>Defendants. | No. 889.<br><br>Sept. Sess., 1912. |

2

NEW YORK CITY, April 6, 1914.

Hearings in this case were resumed at the Hotel Mc-Alpin, on April 6th, 1914, at 2.30 P. M., for the purpose of taking evidence in rebuttal on behalf of the petitioner herein.

Present on behalf of the Petitioner, Hon. EDWIN P. GROSVENOR, Special Assistant to the Attorney General.

3

JOSEPH R. DARLING, Esq., Special Agent.

CHARLES F. KINGSLEY, Esq., GEORGE R. WILLIS, Esq., FRED R. WILLIAMS, Esq., and MELVILLE CHURCH, Esq., appearing for Motion Picture Patents Company, Biograph Company, Jeremiah J. Kennedy, Harry N. Marvin, Armat Moving Picture Company, Melies Manufacturing Co. and Gaston Melies.

J. H. CALDWELL, Esq., and H. K. STOCKTON, Esq., appearing for William Pelzer, General Film Company, Thomas A. Edison, Inc., Kalem Company, Inc., Pathe Freres, Frank L. Dyer, Samuel Long and J. A. Berst.

4

HENRY MELVILLE, Esq., attorney for George Kleine, Essanay Film Manufacturing Company, Selig Polyscope, George K. Spoor and W. N. Selig.

JAMES J. ALLEN, Esq., appearing for Vitagraph Company of America, and Albert E. Smith.

1 **Petitioner's Evidence in Rebuttal.**

The petitioner then offered the following evidence in rebuttal.

Thereupon FREDERICK C. BEACH, being first duly sworn by the Examiner, deposed:

Direct examination by Mr. GROSVENOR:

Q. Mr. Beach, what is your business? A. Publisher and patent solicitor.

2

Q. Are you connected with the publication called the Scientific American? A. Yes, sir.

Q. Are you one of the owners of that magazine? A. I am, yes, sir.

Q. Do you know Mr. Frederick A. Talbot? A. Yes, sir.

Q. Does Mr. Talbot have any relation to the Scientific American? A. Yes, he has. He is English correspondent.

Q. How long has Mr. Talbot been the English correspondent of the Scientific American? A. About 15 years.

Q. Has Mr. Talbot written from time to time, articles on photography for the Scientific American? A. Well, he

3 has written some articles on that, and some on cameras.

Q. Has he written any articles for the Scientific American relating to the motion picture art? A. Yes.

Q. Do you know of Mr. Talbot writing any articles of a similar character for any English journal? A. Yes. I know that he has written articles for a journal called the British Journal of Photography.

Q. Please state what that journal is.

Mr. KINGSLEY: I object to that as incompetent,
4 immaterial and irrelevant, calling for a conclusion of the witness, and not binding upon any of these defendants.

The Witness: The British Journal of Photography is a technical journal on photographic subjects, generally; one of the oldest journals published.

By Mr. GROSVENOR:

Q. Please state from your knowledge of the work done

by Mr. Talbot whether or not he is generally recognized as
an authority on photography.

> Mr. KINGSLEY: I object, on the ground it is in-
> competent, immaterial and irrelevant, calls for a
> conclusion of the witness; on the further ground the
> witness has not been shown to be competent to give
> expert testimony, and the question is in effect calling
> for expert testimony.
> Mr. KINGSLEY: Is this from your knowledge of
> his work?

The Witness: This is from my knowledge, yes. He is
recognized on general things relating to photography.

By Mr. GROSVENOR:

Q. I show you a book entitled "Moving Pictures," by Frederick A. Talbot. Please state whether that is a book written
by Mr. Talbot, regarding whom you have been testifying.

> Mr. KINGSLEY: I object to that on the ground
> it calls for a conclusion of the witness. The mere
> fact that the book purports to have been written by
> Frederick A. Talbot is no proof that the book was
> written by him. The chances are that it was not.

The Witness: I should say that it was put together by
him. I do not know that all of the book was originated by
him. I think it was compiled by him. That is the way
I would put it.

By Mr. GROSVENOR:

Q. Is that a book which is distributed and sold by the
Scientific American? A. Yes, sir.

Q. You may state whether or not that book is considered by you to be a standard book on the motion picture
art.

> Mr. KINGSLEY: Objected to as calling for a con-
> clusion of the witness. I also object to the question
> on the further ground that the witness is not shown
> to be qualified to testify with respect to what is or

1       is not a standard book upon the motion picture art, or any other art.

The Witness: I consider it to be a standard compilation on the art. I do not know that it is the original ideas of the author.

Mr. KINGSLEY: I move to strike out the answer as being incompetent, immaterial and irrelevant, having no probative force, and not binding upon any of these defendants.

2

By Mr. GROSVENOR:

Q. Where is Mr. Talbot to-day, Mr. Beach? A. He is a resident of England, South Sea, England.

Mr. KINGSLEY: Do you know where he is to-day?

The Witness: I do not know, no, sir.

Mr. GROSVENOR: I offer this book in evidence, to wit, the book referred to by the witness, "Motion Pictures, How They are Made and Worked," by Frederick A. Talbot, published in 1912. This exhibit is offered for the purpose of having readily available for use as a reference by the Court and counsel, a standard history and description of the motion picture art. I herewith present two copies, one copy for counsel for the defendants, and one for the Examiner. I shall present at the final hearing, three additional copies of this book, one for each of the judges who may hear the case.

The Examiner: The book is marked Petitioner's Exhibit No. 268.

Mr. KINGSLEY: I object to the introduction of the book entitled "Moving Pictures" by Frederick A. Talbot, in evidence in this case, on the ground that it is incompetent, immaterial and irrelevant, that according to the testimony of the witness now on the stand, it is nothing but a compilation, that there is nothing in his evidence and nothing in the proof in this case to indicate that it is a standard work, that there is nothing in evidence to indicate

that Talbot, in compiling this book, was actuated by 1
a desire to compile a standard work, that he probably threw together a mass of disconnected material for the purpose of making up a book for sale.
I also object to the introduction of this book in evidence, on the ground that there is nothing here
shown to the effect that Talbot is himself an expert
with respect to the motion picture art, or photography. I also object to the introduction of this work
in evidence, on the further ground that although it
purports to have been printed in 1912, there is nothing to show that it was not written long anterior to 2
that date, and according to the evidence of the witness now on the stand, it is but a compilation of the
works of various individuals.

By Mr. GROSVENOR:

Q. Mr. Beach, in using the word "compilation" as applied to that book, did you mean a bringing together into
one book of various articles written by Mr. Talbot, or the
bringing together into one book of various articles written
by different individuals? A. I should say that it was writ- 3
ten by Mr. Talbot, containing the various different features
of the moving picture machine, in order to make it a read-
able, understandable book.

Q. That is to say, the book is written by him, and he
has embodied in it information which he has gained in
regard to the art from various sources?

Mr. KINGSLEY: I object to the question on the
ground that it calls for a conclusion of the witness,
the witness manifestly being unable to say whether
Talbot has successfully embodied the information 4
which he has received from various sources, in the
articles which appear in this work. He may have, in
fact, embodied a large amount of misinformation,
and probably has.

The Witness: Yes.

Mr. KINGSLEY: That is your opinion of what he
has done?

The Witness: That is my opinion.

1          Mr. KINGSLEY: You don't know whether it is information or misinformation, as a matter of fact? I am asking you what you know, not what you think.

The Witness: I should say it is reliable information.

          Mr. KINGSLEY: Have you read the book?

The Witness: No, I have not.

2          Mr. KINGSLEY: Then how do you know it is reliable information?

The Witness: Because he has written so many articles for the Scientific American that I am pretty well sure.

          Mr. KINGSLEY: Is that the source of your authority?

The Witness: Yes.

3          Mr. KINGSLEY: Is that the reason for your opinion that it is responsible and reliable, because he has written numerous articles for the Scientific American?

The Witness: That would be the reason, yes.

          Mr. KINGSLEY: I move to strike out the witness' evidence with respect to Talbot's work, on the ground that he manifestly does not know whether it is correct or incorrect, whether it is expert or inexpert.

4          Mr. GROSVENOR: I am afraid counsel for the defendants is not acquainted with the reliability of the Scientific American. It is a scientific magazine.

          Mr. KINGSLEY: I am talking about this witness' testimony, not about the Scientific American.

Cross examination by Mr. KINGSLEY:

Q. As I understand it, you have never read this book at all. A. I have read parts of it.

Q. This book or some articles that you think appear in
this book? A. Part of this book.

Q. What part of this book have you read? A. I think
I read the first part of it.

Q. On what subject was the first part of the book written? A. The part that tells about the beginning of the art
of moving pictures.

Q. How far did you read? A. About ten or fifteen
pages.

Q. Now, as a matter of fact, you did not read those
ten or fifteen pages until the last few days? A. I did not
read them until recently, no.

Q. When you say "recently," you mean within the last
48 hours, don't you? A. Yes, sir.

Q. You read these first few pages here because you knew
you were going to testify with regard to this book, didn't
you? A. Yes, I suppose so. Well, we have the book on
file at the Scientific American office, and that is where I
read it.

Mr. KINGSLEY: Will you please read my question and read Mr. Beach's answer to him, and give
him another chance to answer it, because he will see
he has not answered it?

The question and answer are repeated to the witness as follows:

"Q. You read these first few pages here because
you knew you were going to testify with regard to
this book, didn't you? A. Yes, I suppose so. Well,
we have the book on file at the Scientific American
office, and that is where I read it."

The Witness: That is correct.

By Mr. KINGSLEY:

Q. Are you a photographer? A. Yes, sir. I have been
a photographer for the past 50 years.

Q. Have you ever made any moving pictures? A. No,
sir.

Q. What was the subject of the first twelve or fifteen
pages of this book entitled "Moving Pictures" that you read
within the past 48 hours? A. It related to the history—a
brief history of the art.

1     Q. Did it discuss, "What is Animated Photography"? A. I think so, yes, sir.

Q. Was this the first knowledge that you had of what is animated photography, when you read it? A. No.

Q. After reading twelve or fifteen pages, you desisted, did you not? You did not go ahead with the reading? A. I glanced through the book.

Q. Do you know Mr. Talbot? A. I have never seen him, but I know him, from the fact that he is a correspondent of the Scientific American and has been for several years.

Q. How many years? A. About fifteen.

2     Q. On what various subjects has he written? A. He has written recent articles on the use of the moving picture machine, and on a new moving picture machine, also.

Q. What other subjects has he written on? A. I could not go over a whole list of them unless I went through the files—

Q. Give us a list of some of them besides photography. A. I could not enumerate offhand all the articles, because it covers such a long period of time, but I have brought papers here to show articles he has written for the Scientific American relating to moving pictures and to

3     moving picture machines.

Q. Outside of moving pictures, hasn't he written a great many articles for you? A. Yes.

Q. Doesn't he write on a variety of subjects outside of photography and moving pictures? A. Yes.

Q. He is one of your regular contributors, isn't he, on a number of subjects of more or less scientific aspects? A. Yes, scientific subjects.

Q. He is in a sense, a scientific reporter, is he not? A. Yes.

4     Q. And writes from a variety of standpoints, and with respect to a variety of subjects? A. Yes.

Q. And in so writing, phrases his articles in a popular way? A. Well, he writes them so that they will be understood. I do not know what you mean by "in a popular way."

Q. When you say that they will be readily understood —by whom do you mean that they will be readily understood—by scientists or by the general public? A. I think by the general public. There is an article here of a new kind of a hand camera, moving picture camera (indicating loose copies of Scientific American). Here is an article by Mr. Talbot on the subject of Kinematographing the Matterhorn (indicating).

Mr. GROSVENOR: What is the date of the issue?

The Witness: The date of the issue is March 21st, 1914.

By Mr. KINGSLEY:

Q. Did you know by what publisher "Moving Pictures," by Frederick A. Talbot had been published? A. In this country by Lippincott & Company.

Q. Is Frederick A. Talbot also the author of the work known as "Conquests of Science" published by J. B. Lippincott Company? A. I could not tell. I have not looked that up.

Q. Is Mr. Talbot the author of the work known as the "Railway Conquest of the World," published by the same company? A. I don't know.

Q. Is Mr. Talbot author of the work known as "Steamship Conquest of the World" published by the same company? A. I have not looked it up.

Q. Then you are not prepared to say to-day that Mr. Talbot is an authority with respect to the Railway Conquest of the World? A. I am not.

Q. You are not prepared to say to-day that he is an authority with respect to the Steamship Conquest of the World? A. No, sir.

Q. You have not evinced any interest in his work entitled "Railway Conquest of the World" or the other work, entitled "Steamship Conquest of the World"? A. No, sir.

Q. You were not asked to read either of those within the past 48 hours, or to glance them over? A. No, sir.

Redirect examination by Mr. GROSVENOR:

Q. The name of the company which publishes the Scientific American is Munn & Company, Incorporated? A. Yes, sir.

Q. Does Munn & Company and the Scientific American have a catalogue of the scientific and technical books which it sells to the general public? A. It has, yes, sir.

1      Q. Is this catalogue generally limited to books of that character, that is, scientific or technical, or having a popular interest, or to books that relate to scientific and technical subjects having popular interest, that is, that describe scientific and technical subjects in a popular way, so as to be interesting to people generally? A. It is.

Q. Is this book which I show you your catalogue for 1914? A. Yes, sir.

Mr. GROSVENOR: Please mark that Petitioner's Exhibit for identification.

2      The book identified by the witness is marked "Petitioner's Exhibit for Identification No. 269."

By Mr. GROSVENOR:

Q. I direct your attention to page 93 of that catalogue, to the list of books under the title "Photography" and to an advertisement in the column with the heading "Photography" of a book, "Romance of Modern Photography, Its Discovery and Its Achievements," by Charles R. Gibson. Is that book a book which you advertise for sale 3      as a book dealing with photography?

Mr. KINGSLEY: Objected to as incompetent, immaterial and irrelevant.

The Witness: It is.

By Mr. GROSVENOR:

Q. I show you a book entitled "Romance of Modern Photography," by Charles R. Gibson. Please state whether 4      or not this is the book which you advertise in your catalogue? A. It is, yes, sir.

Mr. GROSVENOR: I offer in evidence, but not to be copied in the record,—the book entitled "Romance of Modern Photography," by Charles R. Gibson, F.R.S.E. The purpose of the introduction of this book is to have readily available and accessible for the use of the Court and counsel, history of photography, and a description of the modern art of photography.

Mr. KINGSLEY: Objected to on the ground that it is incompetent, immaterial and irrelevant, that it is not shown that the author Gibson is an authority on the subject of photography, that the work itself purports to be a romance, and is necessarily largely imaginative; on the further ground, that the only proof respecting the value of this work is the testimony of the witness now on the stand, to the effect that its name appears in a catalogue issued by a firm of which he is a member.

Mr. GROSVENOR: I produce two copies, one for the Examiner, and one for counsel for the defendants, and I will produce three more copies at the final hearing, one copy for each of the three judges who may hear the case.

Mr. KINGSLEY: I also object to the introduction of this work in evidence, on the ground that the author in his preface himself says "It is not the author's purpose in the present volume to give any instruction in the practice of photography. There are many useful works dealing with the practical side of the subject. His object is to tell the romantic story of the discovery of this wonderful art and the steps by which its range has been extended until it can achieve results which only a few years ago would have been thought impossible."

The book offered is received in evidence and marked "Petitioner's Exhibit No. 270."

Recross examination by Mr. KINGSLEY:

Q. Do you know anything about Gibson? A. I know that he is in our catalogue. That is all.

Q. He has not even joined the list of your contributors, has he? A. No. Not that I know of. I see that he writes a great many books of romance. The romance of this, of that, and the other thing.

Q. He is a steady workman in that field? A. It looks so, yes.

Q. Is he the author of that work known as "The Romance of Modern Electricity"? A. The same book, yes, sir.

Q. Is he the author of the work known as "The Romance of Modern Manufacture"? A. Yes, sir, I think so.

1      Q. Do you happen to think of any other romantic works
of which he is the author?  A. I have seen a list of them
somewhere.

Q. There is, then, a longer list than the one in this book
here?  A. I don't know, but I think there is.

Q. About how many romances would you say he has
written?  A. I don't know.

Q. Have you read any of his romances?  A. No, I have
not.  Because I am more of a technical man than a romance man.

Q. Not even to the extent of ten or fifteen pages?  A.
2      No.

Mr. KINGSLEY:  I offer in evidence the last full
page of the cover of the work entitled "Moving Pictures," by Frederick A. Talbot, which is an an-
nouncement of the alleged fascinating and instructive accounts of the Railway Conquest of the World,
and of the Steamship Conquest of the World.

The same is received in evidence and is marked
"Defendants' Exhibit No. 202."

3      **Defendants' Exhibit No. 202.**

*Conquests of Science Series*

THE RAILWAY CONQUEST OF THE WORLD

By Frederick A. Talbot

A fascinating and instructive account of Railway
Building all over the world since the earliest days of Rail-
roading.  The author describes for us the difficulties and
obstacles which were overcome by the men of genius whose
names are immortalized in Railway annals.  The technical
4      terms are expressed in a popular manner and the narrative
is interspersed with many stories of adventures and hu-
morons incidents.  It is not merely a chronicle of Railway
history, but is a real romance of great achievements heroic-
ally performed.

As the English correspondent of the Scientific American,
Mr. Talbot came in touch with many great engineers and
knows his subject thoroughly.

About 100 illustrations from photographs.
Numerous maps and diagrams.
8vo.  Cloth, $1.50 net.

STEAMSHIP CONQUEST OF THE WORLD  1

By Frederick A. Talbot

In this work Mr. Talbot traces the remarkable conquest of the sea from the earliest days of wooden-hulled steamships until the present time of gigantic steel liners. He describes the various dangers which have been overcome by man's ingenuity, and intersperses his narrative with stories of the disasters and accidents which have been the means of bringing about the invention of new life-saving devices and more comfortable quarters for those who travel the ocean highways. There are also chapters devoted to the planning and building of ocean liners, and the latest methods which have been used to make them unsinkable. Some of the other subjects dealt with in an interesting and instructive manner are derelicts, floating docks, salvage, how a liner is run, wireless telegraphy, charting new seas, famous vessels, etc.

142 illustrations from photographs.

8vo. Cloth, $1.50 net.

J. B. LIPPINCOTT COMPANY  3

Publishers                    Philadelphia

---

By Mr. KINGSLEY:

Q. Do you know that in your catalogue, and by that I mean the catalogue of Munn & Company, Incorporated, there appears this entry: "Railway Conquest of the World, by Frederick A. Talbot, price 1.50"? A. If it is there, I suppose it is.

Q. Do you know that it is there? A. I don't know.  4

Q. You don't know the work at all, do you? A. No.

Q. You have paid no attention to it? A. No, sir.

Whereupon, at 3:45 o'clock P. M., on this Monday, the 6th day of April, 1914, the hearings are adjourned until 2:30 o'clock P. M. on Tuesday, April 7th, 1914, at the Hotel McAlpin, New York City.

1

IN THE

## DISTRICT COURT OF THE UNITED STATES

FOR THE EASTERN DISTRICT OF PENNSYLVANIA.

UNITED STATES OF AMERICA,
                    Petitioner,

*v.*

No. 889.
Sept. Sess., 1912.

2    MOTION PICTURE PATENTS CO. and others,
                    Defendants.

NEW YORK CITY, April 7, 1914.

The hearings were resumed, pursuant to adjournment, at the Hotel McAlpin, New York City, on Tuesday, April 7th, 1914, at 2:30 o'clock P. M.

Present on behalf of the Petitioner, Hon. EDWIN P. GROSVENOR, Special Assistant to the Attor-

3            ney General.

JOSEPH R. DARLING, Esq., Special Agent.

CHARLES F. KINGSLEY, Esq., GEORGE R. WILLIS, Esq., FRED R. WILLIAMS, Esq., and MELVILLE CHURCH, Esq., appearing for Motion Picture Patents Company, Biograph Company, Jeremiah J. Kennedy, Harry N. Marvin, Armat Moving Picture Company, Melies Manufacturing Co. and Gaston Melies.

J. H. CALDWELL, Esq., and H. K. STOCKTON, Esq., appearing for William Pelzer, General Film

4            Company, Thomas A. Edison, Inc., Kalem Company, Inc., Pathe Freres, Frank L. Dyer, Samuel Long and J. A. Berst.

HENRY MELVILLE, Esq., attorney for George Kleine, Essanay Film Manufacturing Company, Selig Polyscope, George K. Spoor and W. N. Selig.

JAMES J. ALLEN, Esq., appearing for Vitagraph Company of America, and Albert E. Smith.

Mr. GROSVENOR: Petitioner's Exhibit No. 220 for identification, which was produced by Mr. Pelzer, as appears in the record at Volume 1, page 389, and subsequently introduced by me at Volume II, page 1217, has not been copied in the record. I ask to have that copied at this point.

### Petitioner's Exhibit No. 220.

#### REPLEVIN SUITS INSTITUTED BY MANUFACTURERS LICENSED BY MOTION PICTURE PATENTS COMPANY.

| ACTION. | COURT. | DATE. |
|---|---|---|
| Edison Mfg. Co. vs. Seabury | Supreme Ct., Westchester Co., New York | Sept. 4, 1909 |
| Lubin Mfg. Co. vs. Seabury | Supreme Ct., Westchester Co., New York | Sept. 4, 1909 |
| Kalem Co. vs. Seabury | Supreme Ct., Westchester Co., New York | Sept. 4, 1909 |
| Selig Polyscope Co. vs. Seabury | Supreme Ct., Westchester Co., New York | Sept. 4, 1909 |
| Biograph Co. vs. C. M. Kessel and F. H. Graf, doing business under the name of Empire Film Co. | Municipal Court, City of New York, 9th District | Sept. 7, 1909 |
| Biograph Co. vs. John Cachapus et al. | Municipal Court, City of New York, 5th District | Oct. 13, 1909 |
| Vitagraph Co. of America vs. John Cachapus et al. | "    " | .. |
| Edison Mfg. Co. vs. Edward Dunn | Municipal Court, City of New York, 2nd District | Nov. 30, 1909 |
| Pathe Freres vs. Edward Dunn | "    " | "    " |
| Selig Polyscope Co. vs. C. M. Kessel and F. H. Graf | Municipal Court, City of New York, 1st District | Jan. 12, 1910 |
| Pathe Freres vs. C. M. Kessel and F. H. Graf | "    " | "    " |
| Edison Mfg. Co. vs. C. M. Kessel and F. H. Graf | | |
| Biograph Co. vs. Samuel Warwick | Municipal Court, City of New York, 2nd District | Jan. 12, 1910 |
| Selig Polyscope Co. vs. Knieriem & Meehan | Municipal Court, City of New York, 2nd District. | Jan. 14, 1910 |
| Biograph Co. vs. Benjamin Marks | Municipal Court, City of New York, 1st District | Feb. 10, 1910 |
| Biograph Co. vs. Jerome Rosenberg | "    " | Feb. 23, 1910 |
| Edison Mfg. Co. vs. Jerome Rosenberg | "    " | "    " |
| Selig Polyscope Co. vs. Jerome Rosenberg, | | "    " |
| Essanay Film Mfg. Co. vs. Jerome Rosenberg, | | |
| Lubin Mfg. Co. vs. Jerome Rosenberg, | | |

1

| ACTION. | COURT. | DATE. |
|---|---|---|
| Biograph Co. vs. Benjamin Marks, | Municipal Court, City of New York, 1st District | Feb. 24, 1910 |
| Biograph Co. vs. Walter Rosenberg, | Municipal Court, City of New York, 1st District | Mar. 8, 1910 |
| Edison Mfg. Co. vs. Walter Rosenberg, | Municipal Court, City of New York, 1st District | Mar. 8, 1910 |
| Selig Polyscope Co. vs. Walter Rosenberg, | "       " | .. |
| Essanay Film Mfg. Co. vs. Walter Rosenberg, | ..       .. | ..       .. |
| Vitagraph Co. of America vs. Walter Rosenberg, | | |
| Kalem Co. vs. Walter Rosenberg, | | |
| Lubin Mfg. Co. vs. Walter Rosenberg, | | "       " |
| Edison Mfg. Co. vs. Walter Rosenberg, | "       " | Mar. 9, 1910 |
| Kalem Co. vs. Walter Rosenberg, | | "       " |
| Biograph Co. vs. Anthony Jenelli, | "       " | Mar. 8, 1910 |
| Selig Polyscope Co. vs. Carrick & Burnstein, doing business as Federal Film Co., | Municipal Court, City of New York, 1st District | Mar. 12, 1910 |
| Biograph Co. vs. Pechette, | "       " | Mar. 17, 1910 |
| Kalem Co. vs. Pechette, | | "       " |
| Pathe Freres vs. Wm. Morris, Inc., | | Apr. 15, 1910 |
| Pathe Freres vs. Wm. Hammerstein, | | "       " |
| Pathe Freres vs. Fulton Amusement Co., | | "       " |
| Pathe Freres vs. Wm. Morris, Inc., | | Apr. 20, 1910 |
| Pathe Freres vs. Wm. Hammerstein, | | "       " |
| Pathe Freres vs. Fulton Amusement Co., | | "       " |
| Pathe Freres vs. Miner & Marion's Jardin de Paris Girls Co., | | Apr. 25, 1910 |
| Selig Polyscope Co. vs. Advance Amusement Co., | | Apr. 28, 1910 |
| Selig Polyscope vs. Burkett & George, | Common Pleas, Dauphin Co., Pennsylvania | Mar. 26, 1909 |
| Kalem Co. vs. Sellers et al., | "       " | .. |
| American Mutoscope & Biograph Co. vs. Burkett & George, | "       " | |
| Pathe Freres vs. Burkett & George, | "       " | Mar. 25, 1909 |
| Pathe Freres vs. Horowitz, | Common Pleas, Philadelphia Co., Pennsylvania | Mar. 12, 1909 |
| Lubin Mfg. Co. vs. J. Stamford, | "       " | Mar. 13, 1909 |
| Pathe Freres vs. Kohler, | Common Pleas, Philadelphia Co., Pennsylvania | Mar. 13, 1909 |
| American Mutoscope & Bio. Co. vs. L. P. Saul, | Common Pleas, Allegheny Co., Pennsylvania | Mar. 12, 1909 |
| Edison Mfg. Co. vs. Samuel McKim, | "       " | Mar. 11, 1909 |
| Edison Mfg. Co. vs. Wm. Erwin, | Common Pleas, Allegheny Co., Pennsylvania | Mar. 11, 1909 |

2

3

4

1

| ACTION. | COURT. | DATE. |
|---|---|---|
| Geo. Kleine vs. Allison et al., | Common Pleas, Allegheny Co., Pennsylvania | Mar. 11, 1909 |
| Pathe Freres vs. Baldauff, | "        " | .. |
| Selig Polyscope Co. vs. Jackson, | "        " | "    " |
| Lubin Mfg. Co. vs. Scott, | Athens Co., Ohio | Sept. 9, 1909 |
| Edison Mfg. Co. vs. Kohler, | Common Pleas, Philadelphia Co., Pennsylvania | Sept. 20, 1909 |
| Biograph Co. vs. Kline, | First District Court, Newark, N. J. | Nov. 3, 1909 |
| Selig Polyscope Co. vs. Sohlank, | First District Court, Newark, N. J. | Dec. 2, 1909 |
| Selig Polyscope Co. vs. MacMahon, | District Court, New Britain, Conn. | Nov. 5, 1909 |
| Biograph Co. vs. Much, | District Court, Elizabeth, N. J. | Jan. 3, 1910 |
| Kalem Co. vs. Doran, | District Court, Amesbury, Mass. | ..   .. |
| Pathe Freres vs. American Express Co., | | Apr. 30, 1910 |
| Biograph Co. vs. Charles Rehn, | Municipal Court, City of New York,    District | May 7, 1910 |
| Essanay Film Mfg. Co. vs. Charles Rehn, | "        " | ..   .. |
| Pathe Freres vs. Edward Hesse, | York, Pennsylvania | May 13, 1910 |
| Pathe Freres vs. John C. Weideman, | Baltimore, Md. | Aug. 4, 1910 |
| Essanay Film Mfg. Co. vs. John C. Weideman, | "        " | "    " |
| Selig Polyscope Co. vs. John C. Weideman, | "        " | |
| Biograph Co. vs. John C. Weideman, | | |
| Vitagraph Co. of America vs. John C. Weideman, | | |
| Kalem Co. vs. John C. Weideman, | "        " | |
| George Kleine vs. John C. Weideman, | "        " | "    " |
| Biograph Co. vs. George Wright, trading as Georgia Film Exchange, | Atlanta, Ga. | Sept. 14, 1910 |
| Essanay Film Mfg. Co. vs. George Wright, trading as Georgia Film Exchange, | .. | "    " |
| Edison Mfg. Co. vs. George Wright, trading as Georgia Film Exchange, | | |
| George Kleine vs. George Wright, trading as Georgia Film Exchange, | | |
| G. Melies vs. George Wright, trading as Georgia Film Exchange, | | |
| Selig Polyscope Co. vs. George Wright, trading as Georgia Film Exchange, | | |

2

3

4

1

## ACTION.

| | | |
|---|---|---|
| Kalem Co. vs. George Wright, trading as Georgia Film Exchange, | Atlanta, Ga. | Sept. 1 |
| Lubin Mfg. Co. vs. George Wright, trading as Georgia Film Exchange, | `` `` | `` |
| Pathe Freres vs. George Wright, trading as Georgia Film Exchange, | Atlanta, Ga. | Sept. 1 |
| Vitagraph Co. of America vs. George Wright, trading as Georgia Film Exchange, | `` | `` |
| Biograph Co. vs. Imperial Film Exchange, | Sup. Ct., New York County, New York | Sept. 14 |
| Biograph Co. vs. Wm. Kelly, | Common Pleas, York County, Pennsylvania | Nov. 30 |
| Selig Polyscope Co. vs. Wm. Kelly, | `` `` | `` |
| Pathe Freres vs. Wm. Kelly, | `` `` | `` |
| Pathe Freres vs. Wm. Kelly, | `` `` | Apr. 12 |
| Edison Mfg. Co. vs. Wm. Kelly, | | `` |
| Biograph Co. vs. Wm. Kelly, | `` `` | `` |
| Vitagraph Co. of America vs. Wm. Kelly, | `` | |
| Biograph Co. vs. Lewis Swaab, | Common Pleas, Philadelphia Co., Penna. | Jan. 24 |
| Edison Mfg. Co. vs. Lewis Swaab, | `` `` | |
| Essanay Film Mfg. Co. vs. Lewis Swaab, | `` `` | |
| Kalem Co. vs. Lewis Swaab, | `` `` | `` |
| George Kleine vs. Lewis Swaab, | `` | `` |
| Lubin Mfg. Co. vs. Lewis Swaab, | `` `` | `` |
| G. Melies vs. Lewis Swaab, | | |
| Pathe Freres vs. Lewis Swaab, | `` `` | |
| Selig Polyscope Co. vs. Lewis Swaab, | `` `` | |
| Vitagraph Co. of America vs. Lewis Swaab, | | |
| Biograph Co. vs. W. Scott Wilkie, | County Court, Carroll Co., Arkansas | Aug. 31 |
| Edison Mfg. Co. vs. W. Scott Wilkie, | `` `` | `` |
| Essanay Film Mfg. Co. vs. W. Scott Wilkie, | `` | |
| Kalem Co. vs. W. Scott Wilkie, | | |
| Lubin Mfg. Co. vs. W. Scott Wilkie, | | |
| Pathe Freres vs. W. Scott Wilkie, | | |
| Selig Polyscope Co. vs. W. Scott Wilkie, | | |
| Vitagraph Co. of America vs. W. Scott Wilkie, | | |

2

3

4

1

| ACTION. | COURT. | DATE. | |
|---|---|---|---|
| Biograph Co. vs. The International Film Traders, Inc., | Municipal Court, City of New York,      District | May 19, 1911 | |
| Essanay Film Mfg. Co. vs. The International Film Traders, Inc., | "          " | ..      .. | |
| Kalem Co. vs. The International Film Traders, Inc., | "          " | | |
| George Kleine vs. The International Film Traders, Inc., | "          " | | |
| Lubin Mfg. Co. vs. The International Film Traders, Inc., | | | |
| Pathe Freres vs. The International Film Traders, Inc., | ..          .. | "      " | 2 |
| Selig Polyscope Co. vs. The International Film Traders, Inc., | ..      .. | | |
| Vitagraph Co. of America vs. The International Film Traders, Inc., | ..      .. | | |
| Biograph Co. vs. Jackson Hoyt, | Jacksonville, Fla. | Mar.      1911 | |
| Edison Mfg. Co. vs. Jackson Hoyt, | "          " | "      " | |
| Essanay Film Mfg. Co. vs. Jackson Hoyt, | "          " | "      " | |
| Kalem Co. vs. Jackson Hoyt, | .. | | |
| George Kleine vs. Jackson Hoyt, | " | | |
| Lubin Mfg. Co. vs. Jackson Hoyt, | " | | |
| Pathe Freres vs. Jackson Hoyt, | .. | "      " | 3 |
| Selig Polyscope Co. vs. Jackson Hoyt, | "          " | "      " | |
| Biograph Co. vs. George Bradenburgh, | Common Pleas, Philadelphia Co., Pennsylvania | 1911 | |
| Edison Mfg. Co. vs. George Bradenburgh, | "          " | | |
| Essanay Film Mfg. Co. vs. George Bradenburgh, | ..          .. | | |
| Kalem Co. vs. George Bradenburgh, | .. | | |
| George Kleine vs. George Bradenburgh, | | | |
| Lubin Mfg. Co. vs. George Bradenburgh, | | | |
| Pathe Freres vs. George Bradenburgh, | "          " | "      " | 4 |
| Selig Polyscope Co. vs. George Bradenburgh, | | | |
| Vitagraph Co. of America vs. George Bradenburgh, | | | |
| Vitagraph Co. of America vs. John Wright, | Municipal Ct., City of N. Y.,      District | Jan.   6, 1913 | |
| Biograph Co. vs. George Geaneas & Bro., | Municipal Ct., New York City, 1st District | Nov.   6, 1912 | |
| Edison Mfg. Co. vs. George Geaneas & Bro., | "          " | ..      .. | |

| ACTION. | COURT. | DATE. |
|---|---|---|
| Essanay Film Mfg. Co. vs. George Geaneas & Bro., | Municipal Ct., New York City, 1st District | Nov. 6, 1912 |
| Kalem Co. vs. George Geaneas & Bro., | "        " | |
| George Kleine vs. George Geaneas & Bro., | "        " | |
| Lubin Mfg. Co. vs. George Geaneas & Bro., | | |
| G. Melies vs. George Geaneas & Bro., | ::        :: | ..        .. |
| Pathe Freres vs. George Geaneas & Bro., | "        " | |
| Selig Polyscope Co. vs. George Geaneas & Bro., | | |
| Vitagraph Co. of America vs. George Geaneas & Bro., | | |
| Biograph Co. vs. McIntyre & Richter, | | Aug. 1, 1912 |
| Edison Mfg. Co. vs. McIntyre & Richter, | "        " | ..        .. |
| Essanay Film Mfg. Co. vs. McIntyre & Richter, | "        " | |
| Kalem Co. vs. McIntyre & Richter, | "        " | ..        .. |
| George Kleine vs. McIntyre & Richter, | "        " | |
| Lubin Mfg. Co. vs. McIntyre & Richter, | | |
| G. Melies vs. McIntyre & Richter, | | |
| Pathe Freres vs. McIntyre & Richter, | | |
| Selig Polyscope Co. of America vs. McIntyre & Richter, | | |
| Vitagraph Co. of America vs. McIntyre & Richter, | | |
| Vitagraph Co. of America vs. Rohlendsen, | Circuit Ct., Cook County, Illinois | Mar. 11, 1909 |
| Selig Polyscope Co. vs. Robinson & Normal, | " | |
| Vitagraph Co. of America vs. Jacobson & Carlson, | "        " | "        " |
| Vitagraph Co. of America vs. Schmuck, | Justice's Court, Auburn, Indiana | Oct. 7, 1910 |
| ................... vs. Sodini, | Justice's Court, Clinton, Iowa | Nov. 10, 1909 |

HECTOR J. STREYCKMANS, subpœnaed on behalf of the Petitioner, already sworn, deposed:

Direct examination by Mr. GROSVENOR:

Q. I show you a copy of the Show World of March 7, 1908, and direct your attention to an article entitled "Kleine Talks. Biograph Company Denies Validity of Patents." Were you connected with the Show World at the time of the date of that issue, March 7, 1908? A. Yes.

Q. Please state whether or not you saw Mr. George Kleine in regard to this interview on the subject covered by this interview before it was printed in the Show World. A. The interview was given to me by Mr. Kleine, was submitted to him for approval, was set up in type, and the proof sheets were also submitted to him for his final O. K. before the papers were run off.

Q. And then it was after the proof had been returned by him that it was printed? A. It was printed.

Q. And is this a copy of the proof as it was when it was returned to you by him? A. Absolute copy of the proof as returned by him with his approval.

Mr. GROSVENOR: I offer it in evidence.

Mr. KINGSLEY: Objected to as incompetent, immaterial and irrelevant, as being hearsay and as not being binding upon any of the defendants, and as not relating to the issues in this action.

Mr. GROSVENOR: That exhibit is offered in part on the theory of admissions, the person giving the interview, George Kleine, being a defendant in this suit.

The paper offered is received in evidence and marked "Petitioner's Exhibit No. 271," and the same is as follows:

### Petitioner's Exhibit No. 271.

## KLEINE TALKS—BIOGRAPH COMPANY DENIES VALIDITY OF PATENTS.

George Kleine, president of the Kleine Optical Company, was interviewed last week by a reporter for THE SHOW WORLD, and he authorized the publication of his views re-

1   garding the moving picture industry, which are as follows:

"The moving picture business of the United States is now divided into two distinct sources of supply, and neither the rental exchange nor the exhibitor can secure films from both.

"The Edison Manufacturing company, acting under its own patents, has licensed certain manufacturers to make and sell moving picture films.

"The Biograph company, under its patents, has licensed the Kleine Optical company, representing nine European manufacturers; Italian Cines; Williamson & Co., London, 2   and Williams, Brown & Earl, who import certain other lines of English films.

"As the bearing of these patent claims is of the utmost importance, and appears to be so slightly understood, not only by the rental exchanges but by the exhibitors as well, I will attempt to explain the situation as briefly as possible, as I understand it.

## EDISON PATENTS LITIGATION.

"Mr. Edison received letters patent No. 589,168 on Aug. 3   31, 1897, covering moving picture cameras and films. Litigation ensued between himself and the Biograph company, the latter being made defendants as infringers of this patent. The question was fought through the courts during an extended period, and the final decision upon this patent was rendered by the U. S. Circuit Court of Appeals on March 10, 1902, by Judges Wallace, Lacombe and Townsend, disallowing the Edison claims in toto.

"The court stated in effect that application should have been made to cover the specific apparatus used by Edison, and that the attempt to cover the entire moving picture art, 4   broadly, could not stand.

"Edison then applied at the patent office for a re-issue, dividing his original claim into two applications for patents, one of them covering his specific type of moving picture camera and the other covering motion picture films. Letters patent No. 13,037 were granted thereon, Sept. 30, 1902.

"Suits were then brought against the Biograph company and others for infringement of the camera claim, and these were strenuously defended for the Biograph company by

Messrs. Kerr, Page & Cooper, whom I consider the most  1
thoroughly informed firm of patent attorneys on moving picture matters in the United States.

## DECISION APPLIED TO CAMERA ONLY.

"This litigation passed through the lower and the higher
courts, and a decision was rendered early in 1907. In order
to understand the question properly it must be emphasized
that this decision applied to the camera only, and not to
motion picture films, which the court dismissed in the
following terms:                                              2

" 'In the prior suit the circuit court sustained claims
Numbers 1, 3 and 5, and those only came to this court upon
the appeal. It was held that the patentee was not entitled
to such broad claims, the decree of the circuit court was reversed, and the bill dismissed.

" 'Thereupon the patentee applied for, and obtained, a
re-issue in two patents, one for the film as a new article of
manufacture (the subject of original claim Number 6),
which is not involved in this case, and the other (camera
patent), which is now sued upon.'

3

## VALIDITY OF PATENTS ESTABLISHED.

"This decision was advantageous to both litigants, as it
established the validity of the Edison and the Biograph
patents on cameras, i. e., the court declared that the Biograph company owned an original, valid patent covering its
own apparatus, entirely distinct from the Edison camera,
and the patents covering the latter were also upheld.

"According to the present situation, therefore, no moving
picture negative can be made in the United States without
infringing either the Edison or the Biograph camera patent. The rights of these two patentees are independent of   4
each other, and each can license a manufacturer to make
moving picture negatives in the United States upon his own
apparatus.

"We now come to the Edison patent covering films.
Clauses 5 and 6 of the original application by Edison,
covering films as 'an unbroken transparent or translucent
tape-like photographic film, having therein equi-distant
photographs of successive positions of an object in motion,
all taken from the same point of view, such photographs

1  being arranged in a continuous, straight-line sequence, unlimited in number, save by the length of the film.'

### QUESTION OF PERFORATED EDGES.

"Paragraph 6 of the original application covers films
in the same terms, adding the phrase 'with perforated edges.'

"If these claims were declared valid, Edison would control the making of motion picture films, with or without
perforated edges. However, these claims have never been
fought through the courts, although I have been informed
2  that suits having been brought from time to time against
Pathe Freres, the Vitagraph Company of America, and
possibly others unknown to me. They were never adjudicated nor brought to a conclusion.

"The question that arises, therefore, which is of greatest
interest to film buyers and users, is, what is the possibility
of the courts declaring the validity of the Edison film patents?

"I consider the decision of the Circuit Court of Appeals,
referred to above, of March 10, 1902, as a precedent of the
greatest value in enabling us to reach a conclusion as to
3  the probable action of the court when this matter comes
before it.

### EXTRACTS FROM DECISION.

"That decision commented upon the film claims as follows:

" 'It is obvious that Mr. Edison was not a pioneer, in
the large sense of the term, or in the more limited sense
in which he would have been if he had also invented the
film. He was not the inventor of the film. He was not the
4  first inventor of apparatus capable of producing suitable
negatives, taken from practically a single point of view, in
single-line sequence, upon a film like his, and embodying
the same general means of rotating drums and shutters for
bringing the sensitized surface across the lens, and exposing
successive portions of it in rapid succession.'

"The Court then says regarding original claim No. 5:

" 'The fifth claim of the patent is obviously an attempt by
the patentee to obtain a monopoly of the product of the apparatus described in the patent, so that in the event it

should turn out that his apparatus was not patentable, or the product could be made by apparatus not infringing his, he could nevertheless enjoy the exclusive right of making it. A claim for an article of manufacture is not invalid merely because the article is the product of a machine, whether the machine is patented or unpatented: but it is invalid unless the article is new in a patentable sense—that is, unless its original conception or production involved invention, as distinguished from ordinary mechanical skill. If it is new only in the sense that it embodies and represents superior workmanship, or is an improvement upon an old article in degree and excellence, within all authorities the claim is invalid.  *  *  *

## LENGTH OF FILM NOT DEFINED.

" 'By the terms of the claim the length of the film is not defined, nor is the number of photographs which it is to represent defined. It is to be an unbroken, transparent or translucent, tape-like photographic film; it is to have thereon equi-distant photographs of successive positions of an object in motion; these photographs are to be arranged in a continuous straight-line sequence, and the number of them is not limited, save by the length of the film. The film was not new, and if the other characteristics of the product are not new, or are new only in the sense that they add to the article merely a superiority of finish, or a greater accuracy of detail, the claim is destitute of patentable novelty.

" 'In view of these proceedings, and the acquiescence of the patentee in the limitations imposed upon the claim by the patent office, its novelty depends mainly upon the length of the film. This feature of the claim is satisfied by any film which is long enough to carry a sufficient number of successive pictures to reproduce, when properly used, some definite cycle of movements to convey the impression of reality to the observer. A film having this characteristic was not new, in the sense that its production involved invention. The Du Cos (patented in 1864) apparatus was capable of taking the requisite number of pictures in series suitable for using in an exhibiting apparatus. Prof. Morton, the expert for the complainant (Edison) in his testimony, conceded that a series of photographs of an object

1    in motion could have been taken upon a paper strip by the
camera of the certificate of addition of the Du Cos patent,
and these negatives might have been transferred to a translucent paper strip, as a series of positives and that it would
require no invention, in view of the insructions which
Du Cos gives as to doing this, to prepare such a strip of
paper with a series of pictures upon it. He differentiates the
film of the claim from the film which could have been thus
produced in the fact that the pictures, not having been
taken from a single lens, would not all be taken from the
same point of view. This conclusion, however, overlooks

2    the fact that practically the images were produced from
the same point of view, in the Du Cos apparatus,—the
single aperture through which the lenses operate, and that
it is quite immaterial whether the same point of view is obtained by the use of a single lens, or by the use of a number of lenses, for the purpose of meeting this characteristic
of the claim.

    " 'We conclude that the court below erred in sustaining
the validity of the claims in controversy, and that the decree should be reversed, with costs, and with instructions

3    to the court below to dismiss the bill.'

### MERITS OF LATHAM PATENTS.

    "On the other hand, the Biograph company own the
Latham patent, which has been very little known except
by those who have made a special study of motion picture
inventions. Disregarding the other claims of this patent, I
consider the first paragraph of the utmost importance, so
far as the legal aspect of the question is concerned. The
merits of the patent have not yet been passed on by the
courts.

4    "The main point involved covers the use of the loop between the upper sprocket of a projecting machine, or
camera, and the film gate. I know of no camera or projecting machine using a film longer than 75 feet which can
possibly evade the use of the loop. The claim is simple, but
radical. If it is declared valid by the courts, no camera
nor projecting machine crank will turn in the United
States unless authorized by the Biograph Company, engaging films longer than 75 feet.

    "Suits were brought against the Edison Manufactur-

ing company by the Biograph company several days ago, 1
for infringement of this patent.

## CONTRACT WITH BIOGRAPH COMPANY.

"In order to guarantee protection to buyers and users of
the films marketed by the Kleine Optical company, we have
made a contract with the Biograph company covering all
of these films, and in accordance with its terms any suit
that may be brought against purchasers or exhibitors for
alleged infringement of the Edison film patent because of
the use of our films will be defended by the Biograph com- 2
pany, free of charge; and, furthermore, immunity is given
against prosecution for infringement of the loop patent of
the Biograph company, to those using films licensed by the
Biograph company.

"As to the general policy of my company, it will place
upon the market all desirable novelties made by the nine
European manufacturers whose product we control in this
country, and also films made by the Biograph company. In
addition, we shall handle films imported by Italian Cines,
Williamson & Co., and Messrs. Williams, Brown & Earl.

"It shall be our purpose to exploit these films through- 3
out the United States, making them easily available to all
exhibitors, either through our various rental bureaus, or
renting companies with which I am personally affiliated, as
well as through any independent rental exchange that
wishes to purchase these films.

## ESTABLISHING NEW CONNECTIONS.

"New connections are being established as rapidly as
possible. Missouri points will be supplied with independent films from a new office in St. Louis established by the
Kleine Optical company of Missouri. 4

"A new rental bureau will be in operation at Birmingham, Ala., Monday, March 2. Our other rental bureaus at
Seattle, Denver, Des Moines, Indianapolis, Montreal and
New York are fully equipped to give the most efficient
service.

"We have been in constant communication by cable,
since the convention at Buffalo, with the European manufacturers whom we represent, and they have entered into
the spirit of the situation in a most enthusiastic manner,

promising a series of film novelties that will excel from every standpoint.

"All films that we control, and those of affiliated concerns, acting under the Biograph license, will be sold outright, without restrictions as to their use.

"The question that has become of vital importance to rental exchanges is the purchase of films. After mature consideration the Kleine Optical company will hereafter abolish the system of standing orders for new subjects. I have long recognized that to insist upon the purchase of all new subjects, long before they are seen, or even manufactured, is an injustice to the rental exchanges, and an imposition upon the exhibitors who are compelled to use undesirable films, forming a material percentage of the total output, frequently against their will. In the early days of the exhibiting business as it now exists this could not be considered unreasonable, as the supply of subjects was limited, and every film was usable that was not obscene, extremely vulgar, or highly sensational.

### CENSORSHIP POLICY FOLLOWED.

"We have always followed the policy of censorship at the root, and have never imported films that could be considered objectionable from any view-point. This is due to our system of inspecting samples of every subject before our stock was shipped from Europe.

"The standing order system is oppressive also because it compels the rental exchange to accept an indefinite quantity of films, subject to great variations from week to week. No exchange, under this rule, can state in advance the total sum of its film bills,—a condition which would not be tolerated in any other line of trade.

"In harmony with this position, we have decided upon a uniform price for films to all rental exchanges in good standing, irrespective of size or quantity purchased. A large exchange will have no advantage, because of heavier purchases, over the small concern.

"In view of the fact that we charge a selling price for films, we think it but just that the buyer own the goods that he has paid for, without restriction, and do not attach any conditions calling for the return of our films at the expiration of a stated period.

## PURCHASERS MAY RENT FILMS.

"Purchasers of our films are at liberty to rent them to others, without restrictions as to rental prices, or manner of use.

"A movement has originated in Chicago among owners of nickelodions which bids fair to spread to all large cities of the United States. These exhibitors have formed an association called the Moving Picture Theatre Protective Association of Chicago, with varied objects, among them being resistance to oppressive city ordinances and in general to further the interests of the members.

"A forward step has been taken by this association in the matter of film rentals. A new renting exchange has been formed, called the Independent Film Exchange, incorporated under the laws of Illinois, of which I have the honor to be president.

"Reciprocal arrangements have been made by which this exchange will rent films in Chicago only to members of the Moving Picture Theatre Protective Association, which will confine its rentals to the Independent Film Exchange. This system will strengthen both the exchange and the association. I am prepared to assist in the furthering of this movement throughout the United States in any city capable of supporting such an exchange.

"The activities of these exchanges are not to be confined to their home cities, the exclusive feature being applied only in the city of origin. I will be pleased to hear from owners of picture theatres in other cities, and will give information as to details of organization. The efforts of these local associations need not be confined to the rental of films, but can include united action upon any question of interest.

"Attention need hardly be drawn to the strength of such an association against all opposing interests that may be inimical.

## FUTURE OF INDUSTRY PROMISING.

"I would say to those pessimists who are doubtful as to the future of the moving picture industry, that, in spite of the present unsettled—not to say critical—condition of affairs, the future appears to me to be more promising than ever. Case after case can be cited demonstrating the increasing interest in motography upon the part of the gen-

1 eral public. If there were any evidence of a lessening of
this public interest, I would consider the situation of serious
concern.

"It should be gratifying, however, to every one interested
that public interest is growing, and the general average tone
of moving picture shows is improving. So far as my observation extends, it is demonstrated that for every small
store show that closes, a large moving picture theatre is
opened.

"I need only mention the use of Keith's theatres, in New
2 York city, exclusively for moving picture shows, replacing
vaudeville; also, the Garrick at St. Louis, the Lyric at
Cleveland, the Orpheum at Chicago, and the Hopkins at
Louisville,—all of them pretentious houses, many involving
the payment of enormous rentals.

## WILL IMPROVE EXHIBITIONS.

"The introduction of moving pictures into theatres of
this character must undoubtedly tend to improve the character of the exhibition, as well as enlist the patronage of a
class of people who have heretofore known nothing of that
3 branch of entertainment, having been inclined to consider
this class of amusement beneath them.

"In Paris, France, the Hippodrome is to be devoted exclusively to moving pictures. This seats some 7,000 people,
and will have an orchestra of 60 pieces. The films for this
resort will be supplied in the main by the European manufacturers whose product will be marketed in this country
under the Biograph license, and the same subjects will be
available for the most humble neckelodion in the smallest
country town.

"It appears to be inevitable, much as I regret it, that
4 there will be two factions in the motion picture field for
some time to come; and that circumstances force me and
the Kleine Optical company, with which I have been identified since its inception, into a position of business opposition to many personal friends engaged in this business,
for whom I have the highest regard. I can only say in conclusion that if competition becomes bitter, the conflict will
be conducted, as far as we are concerned, along clean and
wholesome lines, without personalities, and while our campaign may be aggressive it is unavoidable, and has been
forced upon us by conditions."

By Mr. GROSVENOR:        1

Q. I show you another issue of the Show World of April 4th, 1908, and an article at page 11 purporting to be an article by George Kleine, President of the Kleine Optical Company, Chicago, Illinois. Please state whether that is a statement received by you in the same manner from Mr. Kleine. A. It was handled in the same manner. It was given to me by Mr. Kleine, was written out, submitted to him, and the proof sheets submitted to him again for his final O. K., before the paper was run off.

Q. Then the article was run off from proof sheets re-        2
turned by him? A. It was printed from the same type that the proof sheets were made from. Identical.

Mr. GROSVENOR: I offer that entire article in evidence.

Mr. KINGSLEY: Same objection on behalf of the defendants.

The paper offered is received in evidence and marked "Petitioner's Exhibit No. 272," and the same is as follows:

3

---

## Petitioner's Exhibit No. 272.

# KLEINE DISPUTES VALIDITY
# OF THE EDISON PATENTS

---

*Deprecates Attempt Made to Question Quality and Volume
of Product of Independent Film Manufacturers—        4
Quotes Attorney John R. Nolan, Who Holds
Edison Patents are Invalid.*

### By George Kleine.

*President of the Kleine Optical Co., Chicago and New York.*

In a recent issue of a theatrical paper an unidentified film manufacturer, said to operate under the Edison standard, when asked why the Edison campaign was commenced in Chicago instead of New York, is quoted as follows:

1     "Since the decision in the United States Court establishing the Edison camera patent as against all the manufacturers except the Biograph Company was handed down, there has been only one case brought against an infringing maker and carried through.

    "This was against the Selig Polyscope company in Chicago. The decision in this case was rendered in the United States Circuit Court only two months ago, and was in favor of the Edison company. The case was pretty thoroughly threshed out at that time.

2     "The Edison attorneys believe that this court, having upheld the Edison camera patent in a former action, will be more likely to support the film patent of the same concern, which is so closely related to the camera patent. It was for this reason that the case was brought in the Chicago court which heard the Selig-Edison case."

### OUTLINE OF LITIGATION.

    The following is a brief outline of the litigation referred to.

3     On November 7, 1902, suit was filed by the Edison Manufacturing company against the Selig Polyscope company on the Edison reissue patent No. 12037 covering the camera. Under agreement between the parties this suit was allowed to rest without prosecution until Feb. 25, 1907, because of the pendency of the suit against the Biograph company at New York on the same patent. After the decision of the Court of Appeals in New York in that case the prosecution of the suit against Selig was taken up at Chicago, and a motion for a preliminary injunction was made and argued, the contention being made that the defendant's camera was substantially the same as the Warwick camera which had been held to infringe on the Edison patent.

4     On October 30, 1907, Judge Kohlsaat granted a preliminary injunction in favor of the Edison Manufacturing company against the Selig Polyscope company.

    In spite of this temporary injunction the Selig Polyscope company continued without interruption to make and sell motion picture films.

    Why was there no action taken against the defendant company for what appeared to be violation of an injunction?

    On Nov. 13, two weeks after the injunction, the Selig

Polyscope company issued What the Pipe Did, 465 feet; on
Dec. 12, Eviction, 585 feet; on Dec. 23, Two Orphans, 1,035    1
feet; Jan. 3, The Four-Footed Hero, 600 feet; Jan. 9, Newly-
wed's Breakfast, 290 feet; on the same date, Financial Scare,
435 feet; on Jan. 16, Irish Blacksmith, 640 feet; Jan. 23,
Miser's Fate, 400 feet; Jan. 30, Monte Cristo, 1,000 feet.

## RAISES INTERESTING QUESTION.

If the acceptance of a license from the Edison Manufacturing company is based upon Edison's legal strength, why
was Mr. Selig allowed to make such excellent films as the    2
Two Orphans and Monte Cristo, which must have been sold
in quantities, without interference, before the Edison license was offered and accepted?

There is no pretense that the Selig Polyscope company
was operating under the Edison license during the interval
between October 30, 1907, the date of the decree, and about
Feb. 1, 1908.

Why were Mr. Selig and the Selig Polyscope company
not molested by the Edison Manufacturing company for what
appeared to be violation of an injunction?

The temporary injunction necessarily applied to a par-    3
ticular type of camera upon which suit was brought in 1902.
During the years intervening between the date of the original
suit and Oct. 30, 1907, did the Selig Polyscope company continue to use this type of camera?

## ONLY ONE ANSWER TO QUESTION.

I can find but one answer to the question and that is that
the Selig Polyscope company must be in possession of another
moving picture camera which does not infringe the Edison
patent.    4

If Mr. Selig is in possession of such a camera, wherein
lies the necessity of his accepting a license to operate under
the Edison Camera Patent; or under the Edison Film Patent, if the strength of the latter lies, as is stated in the paragraph quoted above, in its close relation to the Edison camera
patent?

If the film patent rests upon the camera patent, wherein
do films infringe which are made from negatives produced
by a non-infringing camera?

If Mr. Selig owns a non-infringing camera, possibly other

1    Edison licensees own non-infringing cameras; and why accept Edison licenses if that be the fact?

Does the answer rest in the necessity of finding some means to justify and validate the attempt to restrict the number of film subjects placed upon the market and to legalize certain other operations which would otherwise be considered as in restraint of trade?

Some Edison licensees are attempting to deprecate the quality and volume of the Independent supply of films. The answer will be found in our four-page advertisement in this issue of THE SHOW WORLD. Sample prints of every sub-
2    ject can be seen at our Chicago office. We have a full stock of some in Chicago, while the balance is in transit, or about to be shipped from Europe. They will be released from day to day in such quantities as will not disturb market conditions for Independent exchanges, giving a continuous supply, rather than an enormous output within a limited period, thereby obviating a congestion and avoiding an oversupply at any one time.

## HOLDS PATENTS INVALID.

3    Certain interests not generally known in the motion picture trade, wishing to obtain an opinion covering the validity of the Edison patents on films, empowered their patent attorney, John R. Nolan, No. 111 Broadway, New York, to make a thorough and impartial investigation of the merits of the claim. In a written opinion which is comprehensive and unbiased, he decides clearly and unqualifiedly against the validity of the Edison patents.

Several points are brought out by Mr. Nolan which have not been previously emphasized, and which will prove interesting to everyone concerned with motion picture films. I
4    quote from his opinion:

"In compliance with your request for my opinion as to the scope and validity of reissue patent No. 12,192, dated Jan. 12, 1904, to Thomas A. Edison, for Kinetoscopic Film, I have to advise you as follows:

"I have examined the said re-issue; the original patent No. 589,168, dated August 31, 1897; the first re-issue No. 12,038, dated Sept. 30, 1902, and the decision of the U. S. Circuit Court of Appeals for the Second Circuit, involving the original patent.

"As a result of my investigation, I am of opinion that claim 1 of this re-issue is void for the reason, amongst others, that the subject thereof is substantially the same as that of claim 5 of the original patent, which was declared invalid by the Court of Appeals for the Second Circuit. I am also of the opinion that claim 2 of this re-issue is invalid for the reason that the perforating of the edges of the film did not involve patentable invention in view of the prior state of the art.

### OPERATES AS AN ESTOPPEL.

"Whether the decision of the Court of Appeals referred to be right or wrong, the express acquiescence of Edison therein by his surrender and re-issue of the original patent, operates as an estoppel to his now claiming the film forming the subject of the adjudicated claim.

"It is to be noted that in these claims (Re-issue No. 12,038) Edison substituted for the word 'equidistant' the words 'uniform sharply-defined'; that he substituted for the words, 'all taken from the same point of view' the words 'as observed from a single point of view at rapidly recurring intervals of time,' and that he inserted at the end of the claim (relative to the photographs), the words 'sufficient in number to represent the movements of the object throughout an extended period of time.'

"It was evidently an attempt to expand the claims by eliminating the word 'equidistant.' The other changes were doubtless designed to include supposedly novel features which would overcome the criticisms of the Court to the original claims."

### EDISON SURRENDERS RE-ISSUE.

After reviewing the ensuing litigation between the Biograph company and Edison, Mr. Nolan continues:

"Pending this suit, and before the decision on the demurrer, Edison surrendered re-issue No. 12,038, and secured the present re-issue No. 12,192, in the claims of which latter he inserted the word 'equidistant.'

"The simple question is: Do the claims of re-issue define patentable subject matter over the claims of the original patent? In my opinion they do not, for the following reasons:

1    The terms 'uniform sharply-defined' were necessarily included by implication in the adjudicated claim of the original patent and that the Court so regarded them, may be fairly deduced from its language as follows:

" 'The film was not new, and if the other characteristics of the product are not new, or are new only in the sense that they add to the article merely a superiority of finish or a greater accuracy of detail, the claim is destitute of patentable novelty.'

"In Union Paper Collar Co. v. Van Deusen, 23 Wall., 530,566, the Supreme Court of the United States reiterated the rule:

2

" 'Articles of manufacture may be new in the commercial sense when they are not new in the sense of the patent law. New articles of commerce are not patentable as new manufactures unless it appears in the given case that the production of the new article involved the exercise of invention or discovery beyond what was necessary to construct the apparatus for its manufacture or production.'

## EQUIVALENT LANGUAGE USED.

3    "Respecting the words 'as observed from a single point of view at rapidly recurring intervals of time,' I am unable to see wherein they differentiate in substance from the language for which they were substituted, namely—'all taken from the same point of view.' It is quite clear, I think, that if 'equidistant photographs of successive positions of an object in motion' are 'all taken from the same point of view,' such positions are 'observed from a single point of view at rapidly recurring intervals of time.' Even though the language may be somewhat more elastic than that for which it was substituted, it must, I think, be regarded substantially as equivalent thereto.

4

"As to the words 'and sufficient in number to represent the movements of the object through an extended period of time,' it seems clear that this language must fairly be implied in the original claim. It is manifest that if the photographs represent successive positions of an object in motion, such photographs being arranged in a continuous straight-line sequence unlimited in number save by the length of the film, they are 'sufficient in number to represent the movements of the object through an extended period of time.' Such period is necessarily a variable quantity determined by the nature of the subject."

## OPTICAL THEATER PATENT.

Mr. Nolan then refers to a French patent granted for an "Optical Theater," and continues:

"This French patent I regard as a complete anticipation of the two claims of the Edison re-issue patent, particularly so in the light of the Du Cos and other prior art patents.

"As above indicated, claim 2 differs from claim 1 by the inclusion of perforations in the edges of the film, but, as will be noted, the film of the French patent is provided with perforations. That these perforations are in the middle and not at the edges of the film, is, in my opinion, immaterial in the sense of the patent law, as it is a common mechanical expedient to provide flexible carriers of various kinds with perforated edges or marginal teeth for engagement by feed wheels.

## INSISTS RE-ISSUE PATENTS ARE VOID.

"In conclusion, my opinion, therefore, is that the re-issue patent No. 12,192 is invalid:

"(1) Because the subject of the claim is not patentably different from that of the claims of the original patent;

"(2) Because the subject of the claims did not involve the exercise of invention beyond what was necessary to devise the apparatus of the production of the film, and

"(3) Because the subject of the claims is anticipated by the prior art patents."

In conclusion, I am quite content to set the opinion of Messrs. Kerr, Page & Cooper, and that of Mr. John R. Nolan, against that of the learned counsel for the opposition.— GEO. KLEINE.

---

LEWIS M. SWAAB, subpœnæd on behalf of the petitioner, already sworn, deposed:

Direct examination by Mr. GROSVENOR:

Q. Mr. Swaab, you appeared as a witness for the Government some months ago? A. Yes, sir.

1    Q. At that time you testified in relation to certain suits pending. Please state whether there has been a trial of any of those suits since the day you testified, and if so, please name the suits. A. We had a trial of the Vitagraph, on a writ issued by the Vitagraph Company, about the middle of March, last month.

Q. That is, you had the trial in March, 1914? A. Yes, sir, 1914.

Q. That was the replevin suit of the Vitagraph Company? A. One of the replevin suits.

2    Q. Which was one of the suits referred to and testified to by you on your previous examination? A. Yes, sir.

Q. Please state what was the result in that action.

> Mr. KINGSLEY: Objected to as incompetent, immaterial and irrelevant, as not binding upon any of the defendants in this action, and not relating to the issues in this action.
>
> Mr. CALDWELL: And on the further ground it is not the proper way of proving a verdict rendered by a jury, or a judgment entered upon a verdict of a jury.

3

The Witness: After a trial of five days, the jury rendered a verdict in my favor for $20,424.00 against the Vitagraph Company.

By Mr. GROSVENOR:

Q. Have any of the other suits respecting which you testified on your previous examination, been as yet brought to trial?

4    > Mr. KINGSLEY: Same objection.

The Witness: No, sir.

————

ALFRED WEISS, a witness subpœnaed on behalf of the petitioner, being first duly sworn by the Examiner, deposes:

Direct examination by Mr. GROSVENOR:

Q. Mr. Weiss, in the first six months of 1910, in what

business were you engaged?   A. Moving picture film business.
Exchange business.

Q. What was the name of your rental exchange?   A.
Alfred Weiss Film Exchange.

Q. Was that one of the licensed exchanges, that is, one
of the companies which had taken a license from the Patents
Company?   A. Yes, sir.

Q. You were doing business with all the licensed
manufacturers?   A. Yes, sir.

Q. Was the Kalem Company one of the companies with
which you were doing business?   A. Yes, sir.

Q. Do you know a man named Mr. Wright?   A. Yes, sir.

Q. Was he connected with the Kalem Company?   A. Yes,
sir.

Q. In what capacity?   A. At that time General Sales
Manager.   I really cannot tell you in what capacity.

Q. You had business dealings with Mr. Wright, did you?
A. Yes, sir.

Q. Did you have any conversation with Mr. Wright in
regard to the formation of the General Film Company, on
or about May or June, 1910?   A. Yes, sir.

Q. About what was the time?   A. A week or two before
the General Film Company acquired my office, Mr. Wright
came up—

Q. When did the General Film Company acquire your
office?   A. July 4th, 1910.

Q. Please state to the best of your recollection what Mr.
Wright said and what you said, and where the interview
was.

> Mr. KINGSLEY: Objected to as incompetent, imma-
> terial and irrelevant, as not binding upon any of these
> defendants, it not appearing that Mr. Wright is a de-
> fendant, or that Mr. Wright was an officer of any of
> the defendant corporations.

The Witness: Mr. Wright came up one afternoon and
after we were talking some business transactions in general—

By Mr. GROSVENOR:

Q. That is, business transactions with the Kalem Company?   A. Yes, sir.

1    Q. Where was this? At your office? A. That was
at my office, No. 219 Sixth Avenue, a few weeks before
I sold out. We were discussing the General Film Company,
and Mr. Wright said to me, he said, "Weiss, you had better
wake up and see that you close up some kind of a deal with
the General Film Company; it will be to your advantage;
they will pay you a good price for your exchange; they will
make a stockholder out of you and give you a very good
position, and you will have a steady income on the order
like life insurance, or so." That was his advice he gave me.

2
By Mr. GROSVENOR:

Q. Was anything said about the general plan of the General Film Company? A. Well, I asked him—rumors went
around in those months that if an exchange will refuse—

> Mr. KINGSLEY: I object to the witness retailing
> any rumors that he may have heard in June, 1910,
> or at any other time.

By Mr. GROSVENOR:
3
Q. Tell it in your best way. A. I was told by other exchange people that it is advisable to sell to the General Film
Company—

> Mr. KINGSLEY: I object to the witness testifying
> to any rumors, about what third persons or unau-
> thorized persons may have said to him, as not bind-
> ing upon any of these defendants.

The Witness: I asked Mr. Wright in case I would refuse
to sell my office to the General Film Company, what would
4    happen. Mr. Wright told me first that he advised me in a
friendly way it is much better to sell, and he told me, he
said, "Mr. Weiss, you know how it is, today the licensed
manufacturers control the market, they have got you right
in their hands, they can cancel your license in no time, now
you had better sell and be one of us."

By Mr. GROSVENOR:

Q. What, if anything, did you say in reply? A. Nothing
at that time, but—

Q. You may state whether or not you saw or had any ¹
communication with Mr. Waters subsequent to this talk
with Mr. Wright.

Mr. KINGSLEY: Objected to as leading in form.

The Witness: About a week after that Mr. Waters called
me up on the telephone.

By Mr. GROSVENOR:

Q. Which Mr. Waters was that? A. Mr. P. L. Waters, ²
General Manager of the General Film Company. And he
asked me, "Weiss, do you want to do business with us?"
And I told him, "Well, I don't know, I may." He said,
"You had better come down to the office at No. 10 Fifth
Avenue and see me." And I went down there, and Mr.
Waters took me into another room, and I met Mr. Kennedy
and Mr. Berst there, and Mr. Kennedy asked me that day,
he said, "Well, Mr. Weiss, how much do you want for your
exchange?" And I was not in a position to name him any
figures, I did not care to name any figures, and Mr. Kennedy
went over to some shelf or closet or safe, or whatever it was, ³
I don't remember now, and he had some papers, and he took
the papers, and showed them to Mr. Berst, and a couple
of minutes after, Mr. Kennedy told me, "Mr. Weiss, we offer
you for your office, $31,000." We will pay you one week's
film rental, we will pay you for all the new supplies you
have on hand, and we will give you out of the $31,000, $10,-
000 preferred stock for which we will pay you seven per
cent. interest." That was the proposition Mr. Kennedy
made me.

Q. Did you eventually sell your exchange to the General
Film Company? A. I did.                                    ⁴

Q. And what was the figure at which you sold? A. At
the same figures what Mr. Kennedy offered me that day.

Q. Did you subsequently enter the employ of the General
Film Company, and if so, in what capacity? A. As manager
for the Alfred Weiss branch.

Q. How many branches of the General Film Company
were there in New York City at that time? A. To my knowledge that was the third or the fourth one. I don't remember exactly.

1      Q. Did the General Film Company subsequently open other branches in New York City? A. They acquired all the branches in New York City, with the exception of the Greater New York Rental Company.

Q. Were you a branch manager of the General Film Company during the period that the Greater New York Film Rental Company was the only exchange dealing in licensed pictures in competition with the General Film Company? A. I was.

Q. Please describe the methods employed by the branch
2    exchange of the General Film Company of which you had charge, in order to get business, and particularly the methods of the competition adopted towards the Greater New York Film Rental Company, if any such methods were adopted. A. We had instructions from the home office in case the Greater New York had a customer in a certain neighborhood and we served the opposition customers with General Film service, to give to our customers a brand new service, not charging any extra money for it, and furnish that service so long until we had the Greater New York customer in our offices.

3      Q. State whether or not that was giving the customer a better service than your regular service for the same price, or not. A. We gave them a better service, a much better service.

Q. Was that policy adopted in any places where there was not competition with the Greater New York Film Rental Company? A. No, sir.

Q. As I understand it, then, you gave a better program for the same price to such a customer than you did to your other customers? A. Yes.

4          Mr. GROSVENOR: I offer in evidence the opinion of the Circuit Court of Appeals of the Second Circuit, dated March 18th, 1911, appearing at 187 Federal Reporter, 1017, in Motion Picture Patents Company vs. Yankee Film Company and versus William Steiner, et al.

The same is received in evidence and is marked "Petitioner's Exhibit No. 273," and is as follows:

## Petitioner's Exhibit No. 273.        1

MOTION PICTURE PATENTS CO. v. YANKEE FILM
CO. SAME v. WILLIAM STEINER, et al. (Circuit Court
of Appeals, Second Circuit. May 18, 1911; 187 Fed. 1007).
Appeals from the Circuit Court of the United States for the
Southern District of New York. The patent in suit (Edison
reissue patent No. 12,037) has four claims. In March, 1907,
it was declared valid by this Court as to claims 1, 2, and 3,
and invalid as to claim 4. The bills of complaint in these
suits were filed in November, 1910, and the complainant has
never filed a disclaimer of claim 4. For opinion below, see    2
183 Fed., 989. See also, 188 Fed., 338. Kenyon & Kenyon
(William Houston Kenyon, William J. Wallace and Seward
Davis, of counsel), for appellants. J. Edgar Bull, for appellee. Before COXE, WARD and NOYES, Circuit Judges.

> PER CURIAM. The principal question presented
> upon these appeals is whether the complainant by its
> failure to enter a disclaimer of the claim declared in-
> valid by this court has "unnecessarily neglected or
> delayed" and so lost its right to maintain suits for
> the infringement of the other claims. Were we certain    3
> that all the facts were before us we should con-
> sider it our duty to examine the question upon its
> merits for the purpose of determining whether the
> Circuit Court should be directed to dismiss the bills.
> But the complainant insists that it has not had full
> opportunity to present the facts, and, in view of this
> contention, we shall go no further than to say that,
> in our opinion, the case presented is too doubtful to
> warrant the issuance of preliminary injunctions. The
> orders of the Circuit Court are reversed, with costs.
> (187 Fed., p. 1007.)                                     4

Mr. GROSVENOR: I offer in evidence part of the
testimony given by Mr. Harry N. Marvin in the case
of the Greater New York Film Rental Company
against the Biograph Company and the General Film
Company, in an action pending in the United States
District Court, Southern District of New York, the
testimony having been given September 9th, 1913, and

1      the part offered being pages 2907 through 2915 to the
point marked.

Mr. KINGSLEY: Objected to as incompetent, immaterial and irrelevant, as not relating to the issues
in this action, and as not binding upon any of the defendants herein.

Mr. CALDWELL: And on the further ground that
the witness Marvin was a witness for the Government
and has also been a witness for the defendant, and
his attention was not called to this examination when
he was on the stand, and on the further ground that
2      the witness Marvin is in court now and can be called
by counsel for the petitioner if he so desires.

Mr. GROSVENOR: You make no objection on the
ground that I have not produced the stenographer who
made the record?

Mr. CALDWELL: No.

Mr. KINGSLEY: No.

The exhibit offered is received in evidence and is
marked "Petitioner's Exhibit No. 274," and the same
is as follows:

3      ## Petitioner's Exhibit No. 274.

Q. Do you recall that after the notice of cancellation
in this case to the complainant was sent, that you personally
sent a letter to the Greater New York Film Rental Company, withdrawing the notice of cancellation that was
served? A. Yes.

Q. Did you consult or confer with anybody before you
sent that letter of withdrawal? A. Yes.

Q. With whom did you confer? A. I consulted with Mr.
4      Kennedy, and I consulted with either Mr. Pelzer or Mr.
Scull, whichever one was Director; I think it was Mr.
Pelzer. I am not sure whether I consulted with Mr. Dyer
or not, but my impression is that I did consult with him.

Q. In what form did the request come to you, to send a
notice to the complainant withdrawing the cancellation? A.
Well, Mr. Kennedy called me on the telephone.

Q. It was a telephone conversation? A. It was a telephone conversation; Mr. Kennedy called me on the telephone.

Q. I asked the means by which it was done? A. This

conversation I am about to speak of, was a telephone conversation.

> The Master: Tell what he said over the telephone.
> Mr. Rogers: I have not asked him that.
> The Master: I want him to tell.

The Witness: Mr. Kennedy said that Mr. Fox was then in his office, and was negotiating for the sale of his exchange, or the property of his exchange, to the General Film Company, and it seemed to be likely that they would reach an agreement, and in view of that fact he thought that it would be wise to withdraw the notice of cancellation so as to avoid inconvenience and embarrassment to the customers of the Greater New York Film Rental Exchange, and to save Mr. Fox personally the embarrassment of having his license cancelled.

> The Master: And also for the benefit of the General Film Company, if it should acquire the property?

The Witness: No, it would not affect the General Film Company in any way, shape, form or manner.

> The Master: Would it not be better to buy a going concern with a lot of satisfied customers than a concern with its customers all dissatisfied?

The Witness: I will explain why that would not be true.

> The Master: You may do so.

The Witness: Because if the licensed customers should for any reason leave the Greater New York Film Exchange, they would go to the General Film Company, so that the General Film Company had nothing to gain by the fact that the license was in existence or not at the time that it purchased the property, and it was privileged to purchase the property even after the license was cancelled. That had nothing to do with the purchase of the property.

> The Master: I understand.

1     Q. You are quite certain that Mr. Kennedy said to you
that Mr. Fox was in his office at that time? A. Yes.

      Q. Did you consult with anybody else besides the per-
sons whose names you mentioned before you sent that notice of cancellation? A. I think I telephoned to one or two
of the manufacturers.

      The Master: You mean the notice of withdrawal?

      The Witness: Yes.

2     Q. Wasn't that because Mr. Kennedy told you to call up
one or more of the manufacturers? A. When Mr. Kennedy
made the suggestion, I told him that it would be necessary
to consult with the other members of the board before sending such a notice, and I thought it was desirable to consult
with some of the manufacturers. And I think Mr. Kennedy
suggested that I try to reach them by telephone, so as to save
delay.

      Q. Didn't he also in that conversation say to you that you
should call some [one] up on the long distance telephone,
mentioning the names? A. He may have mentioned calling
3   up some Chicago people.

      Q. You did, didn't you? A. I don't remember whether I
telephoned to Chicago, I may and I may not.

      Q. Had you ever gone through a procedure of that kind
before, when the General Film Company had purchased a
business of a rental company? A. Why, nothing of the sort
came up except in connection with the Peoples Exchange, and
I don't think that there was considered to be the urgency
about that, that there was in this case, and I think that the
consultations were done in other ways, although it may have
4   been by telephone. I don't remember.

      Q. Did you consult with the majority of the manufac-
turers before you sent to the People's Film Exchange a notice
of withdrawal or suspension of cancellation? A. I don't remember; I presume that I did, but I am not sure.

      Q. Didn't Mr. Kennedy in his conversation with you on
the telephone, say to you that he thought it was best to get
the consent of the majority of the manufacturers before you
sent the notice of withdrawal to the complainant? A. I don't
recollect his saying that; he may have said so, but I don't
remember.

Q. I don't want you to be exact? A. I am doing the best 1
I can, Mr. Rogers.

Q. I want to know whether he did say something about
consulting with the majority of the manufacturers; was the
term "majority" used? A. I do not recall that he used that
term.

Q. You would not say that he did not use it? A. No, he
may have used it; but I do not recall.

Q. With which of the manufacturers did you confer or
consult before you sent the notice of withdrawal? A. I think
I consulted with either Mr. Marion or Mr. Long, of the Kalem
Company; and with Mr. Berst, and I think likely I consulted 2
with Mr. Spoor, or Mr. Kleine, or Mr. Selig, in Chicago; I
don't remember which one of them.

Q. Didn't you confer with Mr. Smith about it? A. I don't
remember; I think possibly I may have, but I really don't
remember just who I did consult with.

Q. Wasn't the reason you consulted with these manufacturers, because the manufacturers had, at a meeting on November 13, 1911, either acquiesced in the recommendation of
the Motion Picture Patents Company, or come to a decision
that the Motion Picture Patents Company should cancel the 3
license of the complainant? A. It was our custom not to
grant licenses nor to cancel them without consulting with
the manufacturers, and we usually gave heed to their recommendations, and as a matter of courtesy, after we had taken
this act, it seemed proper, in revoking it, that we should consult with them and advise them of our reasons for revoking
it, and allow them to express their views, if they had any.

Q. Was there an incident that you can recall, where the
Motion Picture Patents Company made a recommendation,
or where you made a recommendation that the manufacturers
did not acquiesce in, and where you took contrary action to 4
that which was recommended? A. There were a number of
cases in which we took action contrary to the opinions of
some of the manufacturers; whether we acted contrary to the
opinions of the majority or not, I would not say; I doubt if
we did.

Q. At this meeting of the manufacturers on November 13,
1911, did Mr. Albert Smith make a statement of any kind?
A. I think very likely he did; most everybody spoke.

Q. Were there any in that room on that day who, before

1 the decision was arrived at, made some protest against the license of the Greater New York Film Company being cancelled? A. I don't recall any.

Q. Then immediately after you made your statement, at that meeting, was there acquiescence by all those who were present, that the license of the complainant be cancelled? A. No; I should say there was quite a fairly lengthy discussion about it.

Q. Was there a single individual in that room who expressed the opinion that the license of the complainant should not be cancelled? A. Well, there were some who expressed the regret that it should be necessary to do it, because they would lose business by losing a customer, but I don't know that their final conclusion was that it should not be cancelled; I don't recollect any one who took a definite position of that sort.

2

Q. Immediately after that meeting was held, you sent the first notice of cancellation to the complainant, did you not? A. It was either, I think, on that day or the day following. I would not be sure about that.

Q. Who did you speak to about the license of the complainant, after you sent the notice of withdrawal, and before you sent the second notice of cancellation? A. I don't know that I consulted with anyone other than the directors of the Patents Company about that action.

3

Q. I didn't ask you who you consulted with; I ask who you spoke with about it? A. I mean that I spoke to them.

Q. Who first asked you, if anybody, to again take up the question of the license of the Greater New York Film Rental Company? A. To take up the cancellation of the license, you mean?

Q. Yes, I mean speaking now after the withdrawal?

4

      The Master: The second cancellation, we are talking about.

The Witness: My impression is, that I was advised that the negotiations for the purchase of the property of the Greater New York had been broken off, and that then I myself raised with the other directors the question of the propriety of sending another notice of cancellation; and they all agreed that it should be sent.

Q. Was that immediately after you were notified that the
negotiations between the General Film Company and the
complainant had been broken off?  A. I don't remember the
exact circumstances, but my impression is that it was very
soon afterwards.

Q. Who told you that the negotiations had broken off?  A.
I think Mr. Kennedy did.

Q. Between December 2nd and December 7th, 1911, about
how frequently had you seen Mr. Kennedy?  A. Well, I
should say possibly about once a week.

Q. Did you tell the other men, or your co-directors in the
Motion Picture Patents Company, what Mr. Kennedy had
told you about the result of the negotiations between the General Film Company and the complainant?  A. I may have
told them that he had informed me that the negotiations had
been broken off, or I may have asked them if they had heard
of it; at any rate, I became acquainted with the fact that they
knew it; whether they knew it before I did or not, I don't
know; they may have done so.

Q. So that before the second notice of cancellation was
sent, the fact was known to all of the directors of the Motion
Picture Patents Company, that the negotiations had terminated?  A. Why, yes; that is why the notice was sent, or sus-
pended, because they did not deem necessary to carry it out;
and when it could not be done, it became necessary to send
a new notice of cancellation.

----

Mr. CALDWELL: If counsel for the petitioner will
include all of the witness Marvin's testimony in that
case, we will withdraw our objection.

Mr. GROSVENOR: The trouble is the examination
is three or four hundred pages long, or at least several
hundred pages long. It would unduly protract the
record. The exhibit above is offered in part under
the theory of admissions made by the defendants in
regard to the matters now in controversy.

Mr. GROSVENOR: I offer also part of the testimony
given by Mr. Frank L. Dyer in the same suit, that is,
in the suit of the Greater New York Film Rental Company vs. The Biograph Company and the General Film
Company, in the District Court of the United States,
Southern District of New York, the testimony having

1    been given October 23rd, 1913, the questions being the
last question at the bottom of page 3908 and the answer at the top of page 3909.

Mr. CALDWELL: Same objection.

Mr. GROSVENOR: And also, at page 3968, being the
four lines at the bottom of that page, and the six lines
at the top of page 3969.

Mr. CALDWELL: That is objected to, on the ground
that Mr. Dyer was a witness in this case subsequent
to the time when he was examined in the case from
which these extracts are taken, and his attention was
2    not directed to these questions and answers at that
time, counsel for the petitioner having then full opportunity to cross examine him thereon, and Mr. Dyer is
now available as a witness in this case if petitioner
chooses to call him, and I offer to produce him.

Mr. KINGSLEY: I also object to it on the ground
it is incompetent, immaterial and irrelevant, that the
testimony of the witness Dyer relates to issues not
embraced in this action, and that his testimony taken
now in this fragamentary way cannot bind any of the
defendants in this case.

3    Mr. GROSVENOR: You make no objection, though,
to the want of production of the stenographer who
took the record?

Mr. KINGSLEY: No such objection has been made.

The exhibit offered is received in evidence and is
marked "Petitioner's Exhibit No. 275," and the same
is as follows:

### Petitioner's Exhibit No. 275.

4    "Q. In other words, Mr. Dyer, it had been decided, had
it not, that the General Film Company was to be a company
which was to be run exclusively by licensed manufacturers
or the representative of licensed manufacturers?

"THE MASTER:

"Q. That was the understanding, was it not? A. My recollection is that it was considered, of course, that the General
Film Company would be a licensee of the Patents Company,
and would have a very close connection with the Patents
Company as a licensee; that it would be very undesirable

for us in case the license of a manufacturer was cancelled and ¹
he became an outlaw and an infringer, to have him connected
with the General Film Company."

＊　　＊　　＊　　＊

"Q. When was it decided that the Motion Picture Patents
Company would grant licenses to rental exchanges?

"THE MASTER:

"Q. Was it at that meeting?  A. To the best of my knowledge, it was understood when the Patents Company plan
was hit upon, that that would be done.                             ²

"Q. The Patents Company's plan was hit upon in September of that year, was it not?  A. I think, about that time;
some months before December.

"Q. So that in your last answer you referred to September of 1908?  A. Yes."

_____

Whereupon, at 3:45 P. M., on this Tuesday, the 7th day
of April, 1914, the hearings are adjourned until Friday,
April 10th, 1914, at 10 o'clock A. M., at the Hotel McAlpin, ³
New York City.

4

IN THE

## DISTRICT COURT OF THE UNITED STATES

FOR THE EASTERN DISTRICT OF PENNSYLVANIA.

| | |
|---|---|
| UNITED STATES OF AMERICA, <br> Petitioner, <br><br> *v.* <br><br> MOTION PICTURE PATENTS Co. and others, <br> Defendants. | No. 889. <br> Sept. Sess., 1912. |

2

NEW YORK CITY, April 10, 1914.

The hearings were resumed at the Hotel McAlpin, on April 10th, 1914, at 10:30 o'clock A. M., pursuant to adjournment, for the taking of further evidence in rebuttal on behalf of the petitioner.

3

Present on behalf of the Petitioner, Hon. EDWIN P. GROSVENOR, Special Assistant to the Attorney General.

JOSEPH R. DARLING, Esq., Special Agent.

CHARLES F. KINGSLEY, Esq., GEORGE R. WILLIS, Esq., FRED R. WILLIAMS, Esq., and MELVILLE CHURCH, Esq., appearing for Motion Picture Patents Company, Biograph Company, Jeremiah J. Kennedy, Harry N. Marvin, Armat Moving Picture Company, Melies Manufacturing Co. and Gaston Melies.

4

J. H. CALDWELL, Esq., and H. K. STOCKTON, Esq, appearing for William Pelzer, General Film Company, Thomas A. Edison, Inc., Kalem Company, Inc., Pathe Freres, Frank L. Dyer, Samuel Long and J. A. Berst.

HENRY MELVILLE, Esq., attorney for George Kleine, Essanay Film Manufacturing Company, Selig Polyscope, George K. Spoor and W. N. Selig

JAMES J. ALLEN, Esq., appearing for Vitagraph Company of America, and Albert E. Smith.

ALFRED WEISS resumed the stand for cross examina-  1
tion.

Cross examination by Mr. KINGSLEY:

Q. Who do you say gave you instructions from the home
office in case the Greater New York had a customer in a certain neighborhood, "And we served the opposition customers
with General Film service, to give to our customers a brand
new service, not charging any extra money for it, and furnish
that service so long until we had the Greater New York customer in our offices"? A. Mr. Naulty.                        2

Q. What was the date of the instructions given you by
Mr. Naulty? A. That I don't remember.

Q. Who was in charge of the office when you began working for the General Film Company? A. Mr. Waters.

Q. How long did Mr. Waters remain in charge of the
office? A. He resigned, I believe, in July or in August, 1912.

Q. Were you allowed to conduct the exchange after you
sold to the General Film Company, according to the policies
and plans you had been pursuing before you sold? A. Yes.

Q. Did you have any competition with the Greater New
York Film Rental Company before you sold to the General  3
Film Company? A. Yes, sir.

Q. Did you try to take customers away from them during
the progress of that competition? A. Yes.

Q. Did they try to take customers away from you? A.
Yes.

Q. Did they sometimes get one of your customers from
you? A. Yes.

Q. Did you sometimes get one of their customers from
them? A. Yes.

Q. After you had entered into a contract with the General
Film Company and went to work for that corporation, was  4
the film exchange which you conducted, profitable? A. Yes,
sir.

Q. Were you making money in July and August and
September of 1910? A. Yes, sir.

Q. When was it that you sold to the General Film Company? A. The Fourth of July, 1910.

Q. Was the exchange just as profitable under your management after the Fourth of July, 1910, as it had been before July 4th, 1910? A. No, sir.

1    Q. Did you own any theatres at that time? A. Yes, sir.

Q. How many? A. Three.

Q. Do you own any theatres now? A. Yes, sir.

Q. How many? A. One.

Q. Did you own any theatres at the time you left the employ of the General Film Company? A. Yes, sir.

Q. How many? A. One.

Q. During the period that you were managing the Weiss
Branch of the General Film Company, did you supply service
to your own theatres from that branch? A. Yes.

2    Q. Did you give your own theatres a good service? A.
Yes, sir.

Q. Did you give your theatres a service such as you say
you were instructed from the home office to give competitors
of the customers of the Greater New York Film Rental Company? A. I never had any instructions how to serve my own
theatre.

Q. What is that? A. I never had any instructions how
to serve my own theatre.

Q. And did you serve your own theatres just as you saw
fit? A. Yes, sir.

3    Q. Did you ever receive any instructions from Mr.
Waters not to interfere with the customers of the Greater
New York Film Rental Company? A. Yes, sir.

Q. Are you in the film business at present? A. Yes, sir.

Q. When did you leave the General Film Company? A.
I think it was the last week in January, 1912.

Q. With what company or corporation did you affiliate
yourself then? A. With Mr. Waters and the Kinetograph
Company.

Q. How long were you with the Kinetograph Company?
A. Eight weeks.

4    Q. During the eight weeks that you were with the Kinetograph Company, did it conduct a competition with the General Film Company? A. Yes, sir.

Q. Was it a spirited competition? A. Yes, sir.

Q. Was the Kinetograph Company subsequently sold to
the General Film Company? A. Yes, sir.

Q. And after its sale, did you resign? A. No, I was discharged.

Q. You were discharged at the time of the sale of the
Kinetograph Company to the General Film Company. What

did you then do? A. I made immediately connection with the Mutual Film Corporation.

Q. The Mutual Film Corporation is a concern which is dealing in unlicensed motion pictures, is it not? A. Yes, sir.

Q. Have you been with the Mutual Film Corporation since that time? A. Yes, sir.

Q. Are you still with it? A. Yes, sir.

Q. In what capacity are you now employed by the Mutual Film Corporation? A. As District Manager.

Q. As District Manager of the Mutual Film Corporation, are you conducting a competition with the General Film Company? A. Yes, sir.

Q. Is it a spirited competition? A. No.

Q. You try to get customers away from them? A. If they come to us, we take them on.

Q. Do they try to take customers away from you? A. Yes, sir.

Q. I think you said that after you went to work for the General Film Company that the business of the Weiss Exchange was not so profitable as it had been before? A. Yes.

Q. Did it fall off immediately? A. No, gradually.

Q. Did it fall off the first two or three weeks to amount to anything? A. That I don't remember.

Q. But it did fall off, you think, gradually? A. Gradually.

Q. For how long a time was that? A. The Summer season came. In the Summer time the film business is very poor.

Q. Is that a natural consequence of the season? A. Yes.

Q. And after the Summer, did it pick up again? A. If Mr. Waters would give me all the films that were necessary for my branch, it would pick up.

Q. I am not asking you that. Did it pick up again afterwards? A. No, it went up one week and went down the next week.

Q. Did it keep going right down? A. Oh, no, we increased our business.

Q. You finally increased it, did you? A. Yes.

Q. How long was it before you increased it? A. It is necessary to repeat that again. The moment Mr. Waters gave me more film, I increased the business. The moment they cut down on the film, it decreased.

1    Q. When was that? A. It was about a year after I managed the branch for the General Film Company.

Q. Were you cut down on films immediately after you
went to work for the General Film Company? A. No. But
the other branches, they received eight—

Q. I am just asking you this. Were you cut down on
films immediately after you went to work for the General
Film Company? A. No.

Q. Wasn't the amount of your films, as a matter of fact,
increased after you went to work for the General Film Company? A. No.

2    Q. Didn't you have larger orders after that? A. We
had larger orders, but I was in direct competition with the
other branches, and the other branches always had six or
eight films a week more than I had.

Q. But you were in competition with the other branches
of the General Film Company? A. Yes, sir. And for this
reason our business improved very, very slow.

Q. But it did improve, did it not, under your careful
and systematic management? A. A little.

Q. Is there any case where you were serving a customer
3    who was in competition with one of your own theatres? A.
Yes, sir.

Q. Did you have a case where you were serving a customer who was competing with one of your own theatres,
who left you and went to the Greater New York Film Rental
Company, in order to get a better service? A. No, sir.

Q. No such case? A. No.

Q. Did you have a case of a customer who was competing with one of your theatres who left you and went with
another branch of the General Film Company because he
could get a better service than you could furnish him in com-
4    petition with your own theatre? A. No, sir.

Q. Did you make out weekly statements of the business
done by the Alfred Weiss Branch of the General Film Company at No. 10 Fifth Avenue in 1910? A. Yes, sir.

Q. I show you a weekly statement of business done by the
Alfred Weiss Branch of the General Film Company, 10 Fifth
Avenue, New York, dated week ended July 11, 1910. Was
that the address of your branch? A. Two hundred and nineteen Sixth Avenue.

Q. So that this is really the address of the main office
that is on there? A. That I don't know.

Q. What was the address of the main office at that time?     1
A. No. 10 Fifth Avenue.

Q. Is this a blank which was made out and signed by you at your branch?  A. Yes, sir.

Q. Is that your signature at the end?  A. Yes, sir.

Q. Was it correct at the time you made it out?  A. Yes, sir.

Mr. KINGSLEY: I ask to have that marked for identification.

The paper identified by the witness is marked "Defendants' Exhibit for Identification No. 203."     2

By Mr. KINGSLEY:

Q. I show you a weekly statement of business done, Alfred Weiss Branch of the General Film Company, dated week ended July 16th, 1910, signed Alfred Weiss, Manager. Is that a statement made out by you for the use of the Home Office?  A. Yes, sir.

Q. Is it correct?  A. Yes, sir.

Mr. KINGSLEY: I ask to have it marked for identification.     3

The paper identified by the witness is marked "Defendants' Exhibit for Identification No. 204."

By Mr. KINGSLEY:

Q. I show you a weekly statement of business done, Alfred Weiss Branch of the General Film Company, week ended July 23rd, 1910, signed Alfred Weiss, Manager. Is that a statement made out and signed by you?  A. Yes, sir.

4

Q. Is it correct?  A. Yes, sir.

Mr. KINGSLEY: I ask to have it marked for identification.

The paper identified by the witness is marked "Defendants' Exhibit for Identification No. 205."

By Mr. KINGSLEY:

Q. I show you a statement marked weekly statement of

1   business done, Alfred Weiss Branch of the General Film
Company, week ended July 30th, 1910, signed Alfred Weiss,
Manager. Was that statement made out by you? A. Yes,
sir.

Q. Is it correct? A. Yes, sir.

Mr. KINGSLEY: I ask to have that marked for identification.

The paper identified by the witness is marked "Defendants' Exhibit for Identification No. 206."

2           Mr. KINGSLEY: That is all.

Redirect examination by Mr. GROSVENOR:

Q. Mr. Weiss, you stated on cross examination in response
to the question regarding receiving instructions from Mr.
Waters not to interfere with the customers of the Greater
New York, that you did receive such instructions. When
was it that you received such instructions from Mr. Waters?
A. We received from Mr. Waters—from the General Film
Company—a circular letter stating that under no consideration we should take any Greater New York customer on in
3   our office or solicit any Greater New York customer.

Q. When was this? A. That was—let me think for a mo-
ment. The time an injunction was served. The time the
Greater New York had an injunction out against the General
Film Company.

Q. Had you received any such instructions, that is, that
you were not to interfere with the customers of the Greater
New York Film Company prior to the issuing of the injunction to which you have referred? A. No, sir.

Q. Then in giving the answer that you did on cross examination, you had reference solely to these instructions re-
4   ceived by you from Mr. Waters after the issuing of that
injunction? A. Yes, sir.

Q. Did you receive any subsequent instructions from Mr.
Waters after the injunction was dissolved? A. Yes, sir.

Q. What was the character of those instructions? A. To
solicit Greater New York business, and in case they come to
our office, to take them on again.

Q. You may state whether or not, after the receipt of this
second letter of instructions from Mr. Waters, your branch
of the General Film Company returned to, and resumed the

tactics previously employed regarding the customers of the    1
Greater New York Film Rental Company?

Mr. KINGSLEY: I object to the question as containing a characterization of the examiner.

A. The second instruction we received over the telephone. Mr. Waters called us up and told us over the telephone that we can go ahead now and take the Greater New York customers on. We did not receive any instructions in writing.

Q. Then after this telephone communication with Mr.    2
Waters, did your branch, or not, resume the methods which you have previously described for obtaining the customers of the Greater New York Film Rental Company? A. No. We went right out and took their business.

Q. Whose business? A. The Greater New York's business. The Greater New York's customers.

Q. Did you or not employ the methods that you described on your direct examination respecting giving a better service for the same price? A. That was only done in certain instances where the Greater New York were directly in competition with our customers.    3

Q. Did you resume those methods after this telephone communication with Mr. Waters? A. Yes, sir.

Recross examination by Mr. KINGSLEY:

Q. Did you have any solicitors out for your branch at all? A. We had solicitors out. They were paid by the Home Office. They were soliciting for all the branches.

Q. Did you have any solicitors out under your charge? A. No.

Q. Were there any solicitors who reported to you? A.    4
Yes, sir.

Q. Who were they? A. Mr. Harstn.

Q. When did he work for you? A. He never worked for me. He worked for Mr. Waters.

Q. When did he work under your direction or report to you? A. He never worked under my direction, but he reported once a week in case he had a customer for me.

Q. If he did not have a customer he did not report to you? A. No.

1    Q. How many times did he report to you in 1911?   A.
Very seldom.

Q. Were you a witness in the case of the Greater New
York Film Rental Company against the General Film Company and the Biograph Company?   A. Yes, sir.

Q. Do you remember that you gave testimony there one
day, and that I examined you?   A. Yes, sir.

Q. Did I ask you this question, and did you make this
answer: "Q. You did not have solicitors, did you?   A. No."?
A. Yes, sir.

2    Q. Do you recall that on that occasion I also asked you
this question: "Q. How many weeks did this competition in
which you were giving away so much free film, last?   A. A
couple of months."?   A. Yes, sir.

Q. I asked you that question and did you make that answer?   A. Yes, sir.

Q. Over what period did this time which you have described as a couple of months, extend?   A. It was about a
month after Mr. Waters resigned.

Q. Do you recall that on that occasion I asked you this
question: "Q. In the early days of your connection with the
3    General Film Company, were you permitted to conduct the
branch, using your own discretion as to the manner of conducting it?   A. Yes, sir."?   A. Yes, sir.

Q. And made that answer to the question I have read
you, did you?   A. Yes, sir.

Q. What was your position in the Kinetograph Company?   A. Manager.

Q. General manager?   A. No, sir.

Redirect examination by Mr. GROSVENOR:

4    Q. You have just been asked by Mr. Kingsley regarding
question and answer given by you in the Greater New York
Film Rental Company case at page 4034 as follows: "Q.
You did not have solicitors, did you?   A. No." At the time
you gave that answer, were you immediately thereafter
asked the following question: "Q. You used to deal with
these men yourself?   A. They came to our office"?   A. Yes,
sir.

Q. Is there anything you wish to add to any of the answers which you have given, either on direct examination or
cross examination?   A. In regard to this answer, when I

stated that I had no solicitors, I state that over again, that
I never had any solicitors, but this particular man, Mr.
Harstn, was engaged by Mr. Waters to solicit for the five
branches, and as I stated before, once in a while Mr. Harstn
came in and gave me the customer to supply. I just
state the fact that I was correct in my statement when I
stated that I had no solicitors.

Q. While you were with the branch of the General Film
Company, was some of the business with the new customers
done as a result of those customers coming to your offices,
or the proposed customers coming to your offices and talking
over prices and programs with you there? A. Yes, sir.

Q. That is the common method of doing business in the
rental exchange busines? A. The exhibitor comes first in
and gets a quotation on different grades of service, and then
he generally cancels the order with his present branch or
present office, and makes the change beginning next week
or next Monday. Allow me to state one more thing. When
those statements were submitted to me before—

Q. Which statements do you have reference to? A.
Those statements are sent to the home office.

Q. The statements that were marked Defendants' Exhibits for identification numbers 203, 204, 205 and 206? A.
Those statements were shown to me before, and you will
find that in July, 1910, the time I sold my office to the General Film Company, you will find the business there from
two thousand to twenty-one hundred dollars. Coming back
to the cross examination Mr. Kingsley gave me before, you
compare those statements to the year after, and you will
find $4,000 business there, with all that, that Mr. Waters
kept me down with the buying of additional films. That is
all I have to say.

Q. How much were you making individually a year out
of your rental exchange business before you sold it to the
General Film Company in June or July, 1910? A. The way
I conducted my business, I made from fifteen to twenty
thousand dollars, net profits.

Recross examination by Mr. KINGSLEY:

Q. Had you been making it at the rate of fifteen or twenty
thousand dollars a year up to the time that you sold to the
General Film Company? A. Before I sold—

1     Q. Now answer me. Had you been making fifteen or
twenty thousand dollars a year up to the time you sold
to the General Film Company? A. Yes, sir.

Q. Were you making it on the day that you delivered
your property to the General Film Company? A. No, sir.
Before the Patents Company was formed, I had an outlay
of a thousand dollars a month selling my old films to
South America, to Germany, to Europe, to Russia, Austria
and Hungary, and the moment the Patents Company was
formed, they took away ten thousand dollars profit from
me by making me sign one agreement. In addition to that,
2     I conducted three theatres, and you will find the Patents
Company agreement where they say that no exchange man
has any right to conduct theatres, but rent films only, and I
was foolish enough at that time that I went to work and disposed of two good theatres that made me all kinds of money.

Q. Didn't you have those three theatres when you sold to
the General Film Company? A. Yes, sir.

Q. Now I want to ask you, you signed the exchange license
agreement, didn't you? A. Yes, sir.

Q. You knew what was in it, didn't you? A. Yes, sir.

3     Q. You did not need Mr. Wright to come and tell you what
was in it, or anyone else? A. At the time I signed the exchange agreement with the Motion Picture Patents Company, I did not know that there was such a party as Mr.
Wright in existence.

Q. But even afterwards, you did not need Mr. Wright to
tell you what was in it? A. Mr. Waters gave me the advice
to sign it, and I done business with Mr. Waters.

Q. Did you know what was in it when you signed it? A.
Yes, sir.

Q. Do you remember that you were asked a number of
4     questions and made a number of answers in the case of the
Greater New York Film Rental Company against the Biograph Company and the General Film Company when you
were giving your direct testimony? A. Yes, sir.

Q. Do you recall that Mr. Rogers asked you this question: "Q. After you agreed to take the offer they made, how
much did they pay you cash down, I mean on the $31,000?
A. I had to wait two months, maybe longer than two months.
In the meantime I transferred this business on Mr. Kennedy's word over to the General Film Company, deposited all
my money, and delivered it to the General Film Company, and

I think it was ten weeks after that that they made a payment 1
of two thousand and, I think, a few hundred odd dollars."?
A. That is correct.

Q. You were asked that question and you made the answer
which I have read you? A. Yes, sir.

Q. Were you then asked this question by the Master, and
did you make the answer which I shall read you? "The Master: Were you receiving a salary as manager for the General
Film Company during those ten weeks? A. Yes, sir."?
A. Yes, sir.

Q. Did he then ask you this question and did you make
this answer: "Q. During those ten weeks, as far as you now 2
recall, what were the approximate profits of the exchange?
A. From $300 to $500 a week"? A. Yes, sir.

Q. Did you so answer him? A. Yes, sir.

Q. And did you, during those ten weeks from July 4th,
1910, make a profit of from three thousand to five thousand
dollars for the General Film Company for the aggregate
period? A. I never stated three thousand to five thousand
dollars.

Q. All right. Did you during the ten weeks succeeding
July 4th, 1910, make a profit of three hundred to five hundred 3
dollars a week? A. Yes, sir.

Q. For the Alfred Weiss Branch of the General Film
Company? A. Yes, sir.

Q. Were the deferred cash payments made to you as they
became due? A. Yes, sir.

Q. Was the preferred stock delivered to you? A. Yes, sir.

Q. Has the preferred stock carried a dividend of seven per
cent. per annum? A. Yes, sir.

Q. Have the dividends on this preferred stock been paid
to you promptly as they became due? A. Yes, sir.

Q. I show you a weekly statement of business done, Alfred 4
Weiss Branch of the General Film Company, week ending
August 10th, 1910, and signed Alfred Weiss, Manager. Was
that statement made by you? A. Yes, sir.

Q. Is it correct? A. Yes, sir.

Mr. Kingsley: I ask to have it marked for identification.

The paper identified by the witness is marked "Defendants' Exhibit for Identification No. 207."

1   By Mr KINGSLEY:

Q. I show you a weekly statement of business done, Alfred Weiss Branch of the General Film Company, week ended August 13th, 1910, Alfred Weiss, Manager. Was that statement made by you? A. Yes, sir.

Q. Is it correct? A. Yes, sir.

Mr. KINGSLEY: I ask to have it marked for identification.

The paper identified by the witness is marked "Defendants' Exhibit for Identification No. 208."

2   By Mr KINGSLEY:

Q. I show you a weekly statement of business done, Alfred Weiss Branch of the General Film Company, week ended August 20th, 1910, signed Alfred Weiss, Manager. Was that statement made by you? A. Yes, sir.

Q. Is it correct? A. Yes, sir.

Mr. KINGSLEY: I ask to have it marked for identification.

The paper identified by the witness is marked 3   "Defendants' Exhibit for Identification No. 209."

By Mr KINGSLEY:

Q. I show you a weekly statement of business done, Alfred Weiss Branch of the General Film Company, week ended August 27th, 1910, signed Alfred Weiss, Manager. Was that statement made by you? A. Yes, sir.

Q. Is it correct? A. Yes, sir.

Mr. KINGSLEY: I ask to have it marked for identification.

4   The paper identified by the witness is marked "Defendants' Exhibit for Identification No. 210."

By Mr KINGSLEY:

Q. I show you a weekly statement of business done, Alfred Weiss Branch of the General Film Company, week ended September 3rd, 1910, signed Alfred Weiss, Manager. Was that statement made by you? A. Yes, sir.

Q. Is that statement correct? A. Yes, sir.

Mr. KINGSLEY: I ask to have it marked for identification.

The paper identified by the witness is marked "Defendants' Exhibit for Identification No. 211."

By Mr KINGSLEY:

Q. I show you a weekly statement of business done, Alfred Weiss Branch of the General Film Company, week ended September 10th, 1910, signed Alfred Weiss, Manager. Was that statement made by you? A. Yes, sir.

Q. Is is correct? A. Yes, sir.

Mr. KINGSLEY: I ask to have it marked for identification.

The paper identified by the witness is marked "Defendants' Exhibit for Identification No. 212."

Mr. GROSVENOR: I offer in evidence a list of the suits brought under the Latham Patent No. 707,934, by the Motion Picture Patents Company, between June 14th, 1909, and July 15th, 1911.

The same is received in evidence and marked "Petitioner's Exhibit No. 275a," and is as follows:

## Petitioner's Exhibit No. 275a.

SUITS BROUGHT UNDER THE LATHAM PATENT, NO. 707,934, BY THE MOTION PICTURE PATENTS CO., BETWEEN JUNE 14, 1909, AND JULY, 15, 1911.

| ACTION. | COURT. | DATE. |
| --- | --- | --- |
| Motion Picture Patents Co. vs. Viascope Mfg. Co. | U. S. Cir. Ct., No. Dist., Ills. | June 14, 1909 |
| Motion Picture Patents Co. vs. Indep. Moving Pictures Co. | U. S. Cir. Ct., So. Dist., N. Y. | Feb. 10, 1910 |
| Motion Picture Patents Co. vs. Anera Theatre Co. | do | July 15, 1911 |
| Motion Picture Patents Co. vs. Automatic Vaudeville Co. | do | July 15, 1911 |
| Motion Picture Patents Co. vs. J. Wesley Rosenquest Amusement Co. | do | July 15, 1911 |
| Motion Picture Patents Co. vs. William N. Swanson trading as Wm. N. Swanson & Co. | U. S. Cir. Ct., No. Dist., Ills. | July 15, 1911 |
| Motion Picture Patents Co. vs. The Madison Amusement Co. | U. S. Cir. Ct., So. Dist., N. Y. | July 15, 1911 |
| Motion Picture Patents Co. vs. Leon O. Mumford | U. S. Cir. Ct., Dist. of N. J. | July 15, 1911 |
| Motion Picture Patents Co. vs. David Newman | U. S. Cir. Ct., Dist. of Maryland | July 15, 1911 |
| Motion Picture Patents Co. vs. Carl G. Harig and Sylvester G. Staylor, trading as Cupid Amusement Co. | do | July 15, 1911 |

Mr. GROSVENOR: I also introduce in evidence a list of the suits brought under the Pross Patent No. 722,-382, by the Motion Picture Patents Company, between June 14th, 1909, and July 15th, 1911.

The same is received in evidence and marked "Petitioner's Exhibit No. 276," and is as follows:

## Petitioner's Exhibit No. 276.

### SUITS BROUGHT UNDER THE PROSS PATENT, NO. 722,382, BY THE MOTION PICTURE PATENTS CO., BETWEEN JUNE 14, 1909, AND JULY 15, 1911.

| ACTION. | COURT. | DATE. |
| --- | --- | --- |
| Motion Picture Patents Co. vs. Viascope Mfg. Co. | U. S. Cir. Ct., No. Dist. of Ills. | July 14, 1911 |
| Motion Picture Patents Co. vs. Anera Theatre Co. | U. S. Cir. Ct., So. Dist. of New York | July 15, 1911 |
| Motion Picture Patents Co. vs. Automatic Vaudeville Co. | do | July 15, 1911 |
| Motion Picture Patents Co. vs. J. Wesley Rosenquest Amusement Co. | do | July 15, 1911 |
| Motion Picture Patents Co. vs. William N. Swanson trading as Wm. N. Swanson & Co. | U. S. Cir. Ct., No. Dist. of Ills. | July 15, 1911 |
| Motion Picture Patents Co. vs. The Madison Amusement Co. | U. S. Cir. Ct., So. Dist. of New York | July 15, 1911 |
| Motion Picture Patents Co. vs. Leon O. Mumford | U. S. Cir. Ct., Dist. of N. J. | July 15, 1911 |
| Motion Picture Patents Co. vs. David Newman | U. S. Cir. Ct., Dist. of Maryland | July 15, 1911 |
| Motion Picture Patents Co. vs. Carl G. Harig and Sylvester G. Staylor, trading as Cupid Amusement Co. | do | July 15, 1911 |

Mr. KINGSLEY: I object to both of these, on the ground that they are incompetent, immaterial and irrelevant.

Mr. GROSVENOR: There is no objection that the list is not properly proved?

Mr. KINGSLEY: No.

Mr. GROSVENOR: I also offer in evidence the Opinion of the Circuit Court of Appeals, Second Circuit, August 10th, 1912, in the case of Motion Picture Patents Company against The Independent Moving Picture Company of America, 200 Federal Reporter, 411, this Opinion being on the Latham patent, and having been referred to in the testimony of sev-

eral of the witnesses. I ask the Examiner to copy
into the record pages 411 to 424, and the heading, the
statement of facts, and the Opinion of the Court, also
the dissenting opinion of Judge Coxe.

The same is received in evidence and marked "Petitioner's Exhibit No. 277," and is as follows:

## Petitioner's Exhibit No. 277.

### MOTION PICTURE PATENTS CO. v. INDEPENDENT MOVING PICTURES CO. OF AMERICA.

(Circuit Court of Appeals, Second Circuit. August 10, 1912.)
No. 228.

PATENTS (§ 328*)—INFRINGEMENT—PROJECTING KINETO-
SCOPE.

The Latham patent No. 707,934 for a projecting kinetoscope cannot be construed as to any of its claims as including a camera, but must be limited to a projecting apparatus, especially in view of the proceedings in the Patent Office preceding the introduction of such claims by way of amendment. As so construed, *held* not infringed.

Coxe, Circuit Judge, dissenting.

Appeal from the District Court of the United States for the Southern District of New York; Learned Hand, Judge.

Suit in equity by the Motion Picture Patents Company against the Independent Moving Pictures Company of America. Decree for defendant, and complainant appeals. Affirmed.

The patent in question, No. 707,934, was granted to Woodville Latham August 26, 1902, for new and useful improvements in projecting kinetoscopes.

The specification says:

"The present invention has reference to apparatus for projecting successively and at frequent intervals on a screen, or other plane surface, an extended series of photographs of moving objects, whereby the movement of the objects may be accurately exhibited.

"The purpose of the invention is to provide an ap-

---

*For other cases see same topic and section number in Dec. & Am. Digs. 1907 to date, and Reporter Indexes.

1

paratus capable of continuously projecting or exhibiting upon a suitable surface a great number of pictures taken from moving objects and arranged upon a strip of film of great length, whereby each picture in the strip is brought to rest at the moment of projection, so that there is given to the eye an impression of objects in motion, in a manner now well understood.

2

"In an apparatus organized so that the picture-bearing strip is caused to move continuously and uninterruptedly across the optical axis a light of very high intensity is necessary to give satisfactory results; but a light of such power is not required for satisfactory projection by means of an apparatus embodying the principle of the present invention. The stoppage of each picture during its exposure permits the requisite quantity of light to pass through the condenser, the picture, and the objective to the screen or plane surface upon which the image is projected when the light employed is only of a moderately high power.

3

"The invention therefore consists in an apparatus for projecting successively a large number of pictures of moving objects, embodying, among other things, means for bringing each picture to rest at the moment of projection, means for reducing the strain the picture-film would otherwise suffer from the rapid interruption and renewal of its movement, and means for maintaining uniformity of movement of the film as it unwinds from the delivering reel, and as it winds upon the receiving reel, all as set forth in the claims at the end of this specification."

4

The claims involved are the first, third, fifth, and eighth. They relate to the film-feeding mechanism, and are as follows:

"(1) The combination with devices for supporting the bulk of a flexible film before and after exposure, of feeding mechanisms located between the devices for supporting the film and separate and distinct therefrom, one of said feeding mechanisms being constructed to uniformly feed the film and produce a predetermined supply of slack, and the other adapted to intermittently feed the slack across the exposure window."

"(3) The combination with devices which support the bulk of the film and supply it for exposure and receive it after exposure, of positively driven devices separate and distinct from the film-supporting devices, located between them and at opposite sides of the exposure window, and which respectively engage with and accurately and uniformly feed the film, and which respectively produce and take up slack in it, and an intermittently acting device located between said last-named devices which intermittently moves the slackened part of the film across the exposure-window."

"(5) The combination with devices which support the bulk of a flexible film and supply it for exposure and receive it after exposure, of positively driven devices separate and distinct from the film-supporting devices and located between them at opposite sides of the exposure-window, and which engage the film and accurately insure its feeding, which last-named devices respectively produce and take up slack in the film, and an intermittently acting device provided with teeth which engage in holes in the film whereby it feeds the film across the exposure-opening."

"(8) The combination with two reels which support the bulk of a flexible film, one of which supplies it for exposure and the other receives it after exposure, of a positively driven device separate and distinct from the said reels and located between the supply-reel and the exposure-window and which produces a loop of slack film, and an intermittently acting device likewise positively driven which moves the film picture by picture into the optical axis at the exposure-window and causes each picture to remain momentarily at rest in the optical axis."

The District Court was of the opinion that the claims were limited to the use of the apparatus in projecting machines; and, as the defendant uses its machine as a camera

1  for taking pictures, and not for projecting them on a
screen, it does not infringe.

The following is the opinion of the District Court, by
Hand, District Judge:

"In spite of the many questions which this case
raises, there is only one that I shall consider, because
it seems to me quite fatal to this suit, although it
does not, directly at any rate, affect the validity of
the patent itself. I mean the point that the patent
does not cover a camera, which is the only infringing device in evidence. I confess that when this point
2  was raised upon the hearing I was at first blush
strongly disposed against it, because it seemed then
to be an effort to take advantage of what was at
best a doubtful vagueness in the claims, coupled with
the mere title of the invention, which, perhaps, had
been thrust upon the patentee by the classification
of the Patent Office. However, even with this pre-
disposition against the defense, a more thorough examination of the way the patent came to be granted
has satisfied me that to construe it as covering
3  cameras will be to make successful, or at any rate
to take one step towards making successful, the
evasion of the whole effect of the long and carefullly
considered litigation in the Patent Office. It is quite
true that the point turns only upon the fact that at
the outset the patentee claimed one invention only,
when he might, perhaps, have claimed two, and there
is a color of injustice in holding him only to what
he claimed; but that injustice is certainly answered
by the fact that the bargain between himself and
the sovereign he dedicates to the latter all that he
4  does not claim; and it is a hardship to those who
may have acted upon the strength of his disclaimer
to lose in turn the fruits of their own industry and
invention, because he, who thought it first without
value, now finds that he was mistaken. This case
presents an especially clear instance of this very
thing. However, it is of no consequence what the
reason may be, or, indeed, whether they are in the
least reasonable; the courts have always forbidden
such a fundamental change in the claims as amounts
to a new invention.

"Coming from these general considerations down [1]
to the especial facts of this case, I shall consider
the application and claims as originally filed by
the patentee on June 1, 1896, more than a year
after he or Lauste had concededly perfected a camera,
but (except for the experiments prior to May,
1895, which were held insufficient in the Patent
Office) less than five months before he had perfected
his projector.

"The petition is for 'improvements in apparatus
for projecting on a screen pictures of moving ob- [2]
jects.'   The specification recites the same phrase,
and in the preamble states: 'The present invention
has reference to apparatus projecting continuously
on a screen, or other plane surface, many thousands
of photographs of moving objects, whereby the movement of objects is accurately exhibited.'   The patentee then proceeds to state that the purpose of the
invention was to avoid the necessity of the light of
the highest intensity on account of the stoppage
of each picture during its exposure.   This being the
purpose of the invention, the inventor speaks as fol- [3]
lows of the invention itself: 'My present invention
accordingly consists of an apparatus for projecting
continuously a great number of pictures of moving
objects, embodying means for bringing each picture
to rest at the moment of projection, means for
reducing the strain the picture-film would otherwise
suffer from the rapid interruption of its movement,
and means for maintaining the uniformity of tension of the film as it unwinds from the delivery
wheel, and as it winds upon the receiving wheel,
all set forth in the claims.'   Then follows a descrip- [4]
tion of the figures and mode of operation, which
throughout show in many instances that the invention is a projector only.   Throughout the strip is
spoken of as a 'picture-film' or 'picture-bearing
strip.'   It will serve no useful purpose to select all
the instances of the use of these terms; for I do not
understand that the complainant contends that the
disclosure was not strictly limited to a projecting
machine; his position being, correctly enough, that,

whatever the disclosure, the patentee is entitled to its uses.

"Coming then to the claims as originally filed, one finds that claims 1, 2, 3, and 4 are limited to an 'apparatus for projecting on a screen, or other plane surface, pictures of moving objects.' So far the inventor was strictly consistent with the description of what his invention consisted of. Claims 5, 6, and 8 begin as follows: 'Combination with a perforated picture-bearing strip and feeding appliances therefor,' which likewise clearly limits the claim to the definition in the specification; that is, to a 'machine for projecting pictures.' There remain 7, 9, and 10. Claim 10 likewise gives as a part of the combination a 'picture-bearing strip.' Claim 7 in general terms describes the mechanism by which one shaft shall transmit a continuous movement to two drums and an intermittent movement to a third. Claim 9 describes on a diagram the details of the mechanism by which the intermittent motion is acquired. Claims 7 and 9 are equally applicable to a camera as to a projecting machine.

"Nothing further was done of any consequence in the office until, on January 23, 1897, an interference was declared upon a common claim for a projecting machine. While it is true that this interference concerned chiefly the relation between the period of illumination to that of motion, it is to be noted that the issue as framed included not only that, but also 'the mechanism for feeding the film so as to provide slack therein between the same and said tension device whereby the film may be intermittently moved with great rapidity without unnecessary strain and wear on film.' Nothing was done for more than three years, during which the interference was pending, The dates of the decisions are, however, quite significant. The examiner for the interference filed his decision on June 14, 1899, which granted priority to Latham. That decision was based upon the theory that Latham's experiments in the spring of 1895, whether with or without the shutter, constituted an adequate reduction to operation of the machine as a projector. The examiners in chief reversed this de-

cision on November 16, 1899, proceeding specifically
upon the theory that the invention of the camera
was not an invention of a projecting machine; that
a projecting machine was not a use for a camera;
that therefore there must be some proof that Latham
had used with substantial success his machine as a
projector prior to November, 1895, the date of Armat's invention; and that there was no such proof in
the case. The second appeal, which was to the Com-
missioner, was decided by him on February 5, 1900,
and proceeded upon substantially the same grounds
as the decision of the examiner in chief. The final
appeal was taken to the Court of Appeals of the
District of Columbia, which filed its decision on January 8, 1901, affirming the decisions below, upon the
especial ground that Latham had not perfected his
machine as a projecting machine in the spring of
1895. After that decision it was therefore conclus-
ively settled that Latham could never get a patent
for a projecting machine, which covered the substance of the issue which had been framed. While
it was open to him, therefore, upon his prior application to get a patent for anything not covered by the
interference, nothing else was open to him. On March
23, 1901, he filed 7 new claims, which, so far as the
matter in question is concerned, are essentially the
same as those eventually allowed. Each one of those
claims reads quite as well upon the camera as upon
the projector, except claim 12. Thus of the 14 claims
then present before the Patent Office the first 11,
when read alone, had become ambiguous.

"Two questions arise: First. As a mere matter of
interpretation, should the claims be held to include a
camera? Second. If that be a fair interpretation,
has the patentee, by amendment, put in a new 'invention?' Railway Co. v. Sayles, 97 U. S. 554, 24 L.
Ed. 1053; Hobbs v. Beach, 180 U. S. 397, 21 Sup. Ct.
409, 45 L. Ed. 586; Gilmer v. Geisel (C. C.) 187
Fed. 606; Id., 187 Fed. 941, 109 C. C. A. 620; Hes-
tonville, etc., Ry Co. v. McDuffee, 185 Fed. 798, 109
C. C. A. 606. This is certainly not permissible where,
as here, the amendments which create the 'new inven-

tion' have never been sworn to by the inventor. Eagleton Mfg. Co. v. West Mfg. Co., 111 U. S. 490, 4 Sup. Ct. 593, 28 L. Ed. 493; American Lava Co. v. Steward, 155 Fed. 731, 84 C. C. A. 157.

"First as to the question of interpretation. In principle certainly there can be no doubt that the so-called doctrine of 'equivalents' has no application, when the claims are not ambiguous. The words in the claims must, of course, be read intelligently, and without illiterate literalism. Where there is any ground for ambiguity, the usual canons of interpretation fit a patent as well as any other document. The doctrine of equivalent is especially applicable in answer to the argument that the claim reads only on the disclosures. Indeed, a leading case, Winans v. Denmead, 15 How. 330, 14 L. Ed. 717, arose when the claim did read on the disclosure literally. It was quite clear there that the inventor did not mean by his claim only the exact disclosure, even if he used words which literally meant so. But then, as is now so universal, the elements of the claims are described in terms of general applicability, while the inventor should be allowed whatever latitude arises from the use of words, at best but ambiguous instruments, still if it be clear that whatever latitude be given, the words he has chosen do not cover the infringement without an obvious abuse of them, then he must fail. I am aware that there have been decisions (e. g., McSherry Mfg. Co. v. Dowagiac Mfg. Co., 101 Fed. 716, 41 C. C. A. 627; Kings County Raisin & Fruit Co. v. U. S. Consolidated Raisin Co., 182 Fed. 59, 104 C. C. A. 499), which proceed upon the theory that it may be apparent that the invention does not reside in the claim, and that there may be infringement, where concededly one element of the claim is lacking. With the greatest deference, since these decisions are not authoritative upon me, I must regard them as not in accord with the very great weight of authority, which finds the invention in the claim alone. If this be true, I must confess that, as a mere matter dialectic, I cannot understand how the court may substitute a new element of the claim for one

chosen by the inventor, even where the former operates in the same way to effect the same result.
Hard cases should not make bad law; and a patentee
who has had the whole field to choose from cannot
justly complain if he be held to his choice. Out of
all of the discussion which this subject has called
forth, I can see nothing that finally remains, except
that a court should, on the one hand, try sympatheti-
cally and intelligently to understand what the inventor meant by the words he used, and, on the other,
should hold him to that meaning, or candidly avow
that his patent is not the measure of his rights.

"Now, when the patentee says that his invention
consists of an apparatus for projecting pictures, he is
speaking not of a single disclosure, used for purposes
of illustration, but of what the 'invention' is, and the
'invention' is to be found in his claims. It is precisely equivalent to saying, 'What is to be found in
my claims is an apparatus,' etc. Any ordinarily in-
telligent man reading that preamble and then reading the claims would surely think that the claims
were only for a projector. This is especially evident
when one looks at Latham's patent for a camera and
a projector, filed six months later, which shows that
he distinguished between projector and camera, and
that when he thought a machine capable of both he
said so clearly. In view of this application filed
after the application for the patent in suit, but before these amendments were made, and with it, as it
were, staring the patentee in the face, can there
really be any ground for insisting that the patent
should now be allowed to cover cameras? Consider,
further, that in the amendments on January 17,
1902, after all the litigation, and while he had all
the facts before him, Latham's attorney repeats the
substance of the old specifications, so that they took
the eventual form of the preamble and appear as on
page 1, lines 8 to 51. It was then by a deliberate
reaffirmation of the invention as consisting of a
projector that the claims were inserted. It must be
apparent that if the intention had been really to include cameras the applicant would not have left in
the application those original statements which di-

rectly contradicted what he is supposed to have intended by the change. Why did he do this? Obviously either because he meant nothing of the sort, or because he was afraid to avow his intention and to take his chance of passing it upon the examiner. Either admission is fatal to his now contending that his language effected the change he now claims.

"Again, the whole theory of the changes also precludes the view that it meant to extend the claims to cameras. Latham had been beaten in the interference proceedings because he failed to antedate his feature of 'pause *and illumination*'; pause being the kernel of his invention up to that time. His first amended claims really repeated the substance of the old ones; for they all had as a feature that the period of rest should exceed that of motion. His attorney, in his argument, said quite frankly that the whole interference issue had been a mistake, and that in any case the decision depended strictly upon the distinction between 'illumination' and 'rest.' He neglected to say that the original claims made no such distinction, but contented themselves with speaking of the momentary 'rest' of the film. The first amendments did not succeed; but the attorney tried again, and submitted, on January 17, 1902, substantially the claims which were eventually allowed. Now it is true that some of these claims (i. e., 1, 3, 7, 11, and 12) do not refer to the period of rest; but the last two are limited claims, and the other three were put in out of abundant caution. My point is that the chief theory of the patent still remained the securing of the period of rest, as it always had been; and this was the important thing for a projector and the reason why Latham had originally limited it to a projector, thinking for other purposes the positive feed devices inferior to his friction feed, which he did apply to cameras as well.

"Therefore I insist that the whole proceedings show from the outset a continual purpose to cover only projectors, starting expressly with that purpose, and changing only with another purpose in mind, at least avowedly. It is not, therefore, a narrow or technical construction of the patent. It is a con-

struction which tries to understand the proceedings 1
as a whole, and really to interpret them. It is rather
the complainant which, seizing upon words of general applicability and neglecting to read them in
their history, is really twisting them beyond their
proper scope through the invocation of liberal canons which have here no application.

"But even if all this be not so; and if I were
obliged to hold, as matter of fair interpretation, that
the claims cover a camera, so to interpret them
would allow the introduction of a 'new invention,' 2
within the rule I have mentioned above, because,
whatever may be the fair meaning of the clai:·
as allowed, no one can for a moment doubt that, as
first presented, they were by their terms confined to
projectors, with the exception of claims 7 and 9. This
is so clear that I shall not elaborate it. Of the two
other claims, one was for a detail of the mechanism
disclosed, and the other reads upon the figures, and
cannot be the basis of expanding the patent.

"What, then, is meant by a 'new invention?' I
do not think that it means that the change between 3
the original specifications and the amendments must
be itself patentable. Certainly that has not been the
test suggested in the cases. Rather it means that
there need only be a new element added to the claim,
or one taken away, or one substituted for another,
without any original suggestion of it in the patent.
The rule is the same in this respect as to amendments that obtains as to reissues (Railway Co. v.
Sayles, supra), and the distinction is shown in Morse
Chain Co. v. Link Belt Co. (C. C.) 182 Fed. 825,
and 189 Fed. 584, 110 C. C. A. 564. Now, in the 4
case at bar, there was, as I have said, absolutely no
indication anywhere that the invention included cameras. The patented combination in the first six
claims contained as one of its elements a projector.
What the amendment did was to substitute for that
element another, making the element read as it was,
'in a projector or camera.' That certainly created
another invention, regardless of whether it was a
patentable advance to put the disclosure into a camera, the negative of which I may assume for argu-

1

ment. To say that this is only to put the invention
to a new use is to fail to recognize that the projector was an element in the original claim itself.
To disclose a combination as fitted for one use, no
element of which is included within the elements
which the applicant selects to put into his claim,
does not limit the invention by the use disclosed. One
may put the same 'invention' to a different use, because it will still have the same constituent parts;
but if, as here, the 'use' includes certain of the elements which go into the claim, you cannot change

2

the 'use' without changing the substance of the 'invention.' That is this case, at least except as to
claims 7 and 9, which, as I have said, referred to the
precise disclosure, and cannot be the basis of expanding the patent.

"So much for the argument drawn from the formal change in the claims; but the vice goes to the
essence. In his second patent, which, as I have
said, he made expressly applicable to cameras and
projectors, which operated by friction devices only,
and the claims of which do not mention the pause

3

feature, Latham had spoken of that device as 'the
only one of which I have any knowledge that is capable of giving anything like accurate results' 'for
scientific purposes.' That means that the 'positive
feed' of the patent in suit gave nothing like accurate
results, as well as being apt to tear the films. Page
1, lines 19 to 22. Turning next to the patent in
suit, we see the 'invention,' as defined in the specifications, originally consisted, and still consist, of the
positive feed only as a means to the full rest for pur-

4

poses of illumination. The purpose of his invention
was 'the stoppage of each picture during its exposure
[to] permit the requisite quantity of light to pass
through the condenser,' etc. It consists of three elements—means of bringing the film to rest, means of
reducing the strain on the film arising from the rapid
interruption and renewal, which the period of rest
requires, and means for uniform winding and un-
winding. Here is no suggestion that the accuracy
of measurement is a factor, or that the positive

feed is important, except as the pause requires rapid
interruption and renewal. It is perfectly consistent
with the second application, which was for accuracy
of registration. Coming next to the original claims,
the consistency continues. The first four are clearly
directed at securing the necessary pause. Claims 6 and
7 are of the same character and refer to the same period of rest. Claim 5 does not mention the period of
rest, but refers to the mechanism by which the intermittent rotation of the drum is secured. It is somewhat ambiguous as to the pause feature, if taken
alone, but not when taken in connection with the
accepted construction of claim 10; for it contains the
pause feature as much as the latter. Claims 8 and 9
are for mere details of the mechanism. Claim 10 was
that upon which the interference issue was raised,
and includes the pause; at least, the applicant could
hardly dispute it, after going through all the courts
and accepting the issue as a true statement of that
claim. The claims after January 17, 1902, do contain the 'positive feed,' some of them alone, and
some still as a means of securing the required rest;
and it was then the change first occurred.

"Now, all this shows that at first Latham conceived his 'invention,' considering that term collo-
quially, to reside not at all in the positive feed
(which he repudiated altogether when used in a camera), except as a means to secure the rest. That was
essential in a projector, indifferent in a camera, and
he left it out, because he then thought it worthless
for any camera use.

"I am now assuming, for argument, that the
changed claims now cover cameras, which before they
did not. If so, then the complainant's dilemma is
this: In so far as the 'invention' resides now in the
'positive feed' feature, it is a complete abandonment
of his position for nearly six years after the application was filed. In so far as it resides in the 'rest'
feature, it completely ignores the interference litigation as though it had never occurred. As to the
former, I think I have already shown it in enough
detail. There was no suggestion anywhere of it till
the date I mention. There was repudiation of its

1   accuracy in the second patent. The means to secure
the rest were of consequence only in so far as they
actually did assure the period of rest. If the patent
abandons that and substitutes the 'positive feed' as
the patent, it has become a 'new invention' in every
sense.

"Moreover, there are more important considerations than the mere lapse of time. Armat and Casler
had machines which, in respect of 'positive feed' as
the complainant now understands it, infringe his
present claims. Furthermore, in respect of that fea-
2   ture, probably his camera use is sufficient to antedate them. By his change of front he has included
those whom before he did not, except by the original
feature of his claims, upon which he was beaten, and
this by the selection of a feature he had originally
abandoned. Now, the policy of the statute was to
prevent that very thing. It was to prevent a man's
gambling upon his ingenuity, avoiding the expense of
a patent till his invention proved successful, and,
then after others had acted upon his inaction, getting
a monopoly for the full period of 17 years. If Latham
3   had waited so long without filing any application, he
could not have succeeded; and the rule against allowing him to amend is designed to prevent his doing by
indirection what he could not do directly.

"Coming now to the 'rest' feature, the complainant's case is even worse; for his attorney quite naively
got those claims upon the theory that the interference issue was a mere nullity and effected nothing.
Now, it is not necessary to determine how far the
issue was correct, and how far 'pause and illumina-
4   tion,' have anything to do with 'rest.' It may be that
Latham suffered by the reduction of his claims,
though I think it quite clear that he did not, but he
fought it out upon that issue for nearly five years;
and it is really rather too hard a position to take in
a court, however it may be before an examiner, that
such an assent does not estop him. While Latham's
attorney conceded that Armat got the benefit of the
interference, yet, since he denied that Latham's claims
were embodied at all in the issue, it is hard to see
what Armat did get. The matter is, indeed, quite

confused; for the only relevant claim Latham then
had was original claim 10, and that was a very special one.   However, it said nothing of 'illumination' as distinct from 'rest'; and the patent was
throughout based on the supposition that the 'illumination' and the 'rest' occupied the same period.   The
court did not deny that the patent so intended; but
they did deny that the use in the spring of 1895 reduced that feature to practice, though Latham's attorney seems to have supposed that the courts had
confused the two.   To reinstate the 'rest' claims, of
which claim 8 in suit is one, was really a most extraordinary vagary of the lay mind, as it seems to me,
and deprived Armat of not only the substance of
his success, as did the substitution of the 'positive
feed' claims, but of even of the semblance of any
fruits of victory whatever.   It cannot be necessary
to show that the Patent Office is not the place in
which to play fast and loose like that.

"Much of the last argument goes beyond the question of whether the claims over a camera; but I mean
to decide nothing else.   My point is that if they do
include a camera they were brought in by an amendment, which was in part a radical departure from
the invention, after six years, and when others had
secured rights, with much expense, upon the faith
of the application as it was—in remainder, a mere
disregard of all the proceedings theretofore had in
the Patent Office.   What the effect of this may be
upon the claims for any other purpose, I leave to be
decided when it may arise.

"The bill will be dismissed for noninfringement,
with costs."

Kerr, Page, Cooper & Hayward, of New York City
(Thomas B. Kerr and Parker W. Page, both of New York
City, of counsel), for appellant.

Kenyon & Kenyon, of New York City (William Hons-
ton Kenyon and Richard Eyre, both of New York City, of
counsel), for appellee.

Before COXE, WARD, and NOYES, Circuit Judges.

PER CURIAM. The majority of the court are of the
opinion that the decree appealed from should be affirmed,

1   with costs, upon the opinion of Judge Hand; and it is so
ordered.

COXE, Circuit Judge (dissenting). The dismissal of
the bill by the District Court upon the sole ground of non-
infringement, for the reason that the claims in question
relate to a projector, whereas defendant uses a camera,
presents a question which may be broadly stated as follows:
Should these claims, the language of which covers a feeding
mechanism which is capable of being used in the defendant's camera, as well as in the projector described in the
patent, be so limited that they cover the use of the feeding
2   mechanism in the projecting apparatus only?

In approaching the consideration of this question it
must be remembered that the claims in controversy are not,
so far as their language is concerned, limited to any particular machine and that the combinations described are as
capable of use in a camera as in a projector. So far as the
combinations which we are now considering are concerned,
they might as well have been illustrated in a camera as in
a projector and the description and drawings might as
well have been confined to a camera as to a projector. The
machine can be used as well to take pictures as to project
3   them upon a screen. I do not understand that this proposition is seriously disputed. The camera and the projector
belong to analogous arts and can be used interchangeably
in each. Take from the projector the well-known parts, the
objective, the condenser and the light, which are intended
to throw the pictures in rapid succession upon the screen,
and a successfully operating camera remains. Add these
parts to the camera and the result is a machine capable of
exposing the pictures to an audience.

The combination for a projector requires more elements
4   than for a camera, but if the camera be new and useful,
there is no reason why the inventor may not cover by his
claims the combination which comprises the camera. Of
course, in considering the single defense of non-infringement, novelty and invention must be conceded.

The defense here, as I understand it, is predicated of the
proposition that Latham's achievement must be rigidly limited to a projecting device and though he may have made
a meritorious invention of a camera, he is nevertheless limited to his title of "Projecting-Kinetoscope." If this con-

tention be sustained, any one can use the exact structure shown, provided he does not use it in a projecting machine. I am unable to assent to this proposition. It is a fundamental canon of construction of patent law that where the court is convinced that the the patentee has made a valuable invention, the patent shall be interpreted, if possible, to give him the full results of his labors. He may have so entangled himself in a maze of contradictory verbiage that it is impossible to do this, but if two constructions can be given his claims, it is the duty of the court to adopt the one which vitalizes rather than the one which destroys them.

The inventor is entitled to all the uses to which his invention may be put and the court should, if possible, see that he secures its full benefits. He should not be impaled on the point of a too literal construction. In the present instance I see no reason why Latham, if it be shown that he was the first to invent the improved camera, should not reap the rewards of this division of his invention. His claims cover it and there is nothing in the description which definitely limits its use to the exposing rather than the taking of pictures. If these claims do not cover a camera what do they cover?

Take the first claim, for instance. Construct a machine in exact accordance with the directions of the specification and having all the elements of the claim, what will be the result?

Such a machine will contain: 1. Devices for supporting the bulk of a flexible film before and after exposure. 2. Feeding mechanism located between the devices for supporting the film and separate and distinct therefrom. 3. One of said feeding mechanisms being constructed to feed the film uniformly and produce a predetermined supply of slack. 4. The other adapted to feed the slack intermittently across the exposure-window. Would such a machine project pictures upon a screen? None of the necessary accessories of such a machine is included in the combination. The condenser, the objective and the light are not elements and the use of the combination as a projector is not mentioned. What is to be done with such a machine? It cannot be used as a projector, for it has not the necessary parts, and, if the defendant be correct, it cannot be used as a camera because the patent must be limited to a projector. I cannot

1 think that the patentee should be left in this dilemma with a claim practically valueless—a derelict of the patent law. On the contrary, I think that Latham invented a machine capable of use as a camera, that he has described this machine in his specification, illustrated it by his drawings and covered it by his claims.

The construction of the machine and the uses of which it is capable are manifest, and, this being so, the patentee should not be deprived of the fruits of his invention, even assuming that he has given it a wrong name. Nomenclature must yield to facts.

2 In short, my conclusion, upon this branch of the case, is that if Latham has invented a new and useful camera, he cannot be defeated upon the theory of non-infringement because he described and illustrated his invention in a projector.

The patent should be construed with reference to what the description shows and the claims cover and not according to the title forced upon the applicant by the examiner.

As was said by the court in Bell v. Daniels, 1 Fish Pat. Cas. 372, Fed. Cas. No. 1,247:

3

"The plaintiff is not controlled by his title, but the patent, specification and drawings are all to be examined, and are all to have a fair and liberal construction in determining the nature and extent of the invention."

See, also, Inman v. Beach, 71 Fed. 420, 18 C. C. A. 165; Hobbs v. Beach, 180 U. S. 385, 21 Sup. Ct. 409, 45 L. Ed. 586; Cleveland Foundry Co. v. Detroit Co., 131 Fed. 583, 68 C. C. A. 283.

4 The contention that the words, "In a projecting-kinetoscope" should be read into claims which do not contain them is wholly untenable both as an original proposition and also because the courts have repeatedly held that such limitations of the claims are unwarranted. An inventor cannot anticipate every use to which his invention may be put and is not called upon in limine to deprive himself of such uses by putting his invention in a strait-jacket.

The employment of Latham's combination as a camera did not require invention; any mechanic skilled in the art would know enough to do this. It was simply applying it to a different, though analogous use.

It has been assumed through all stages of this litigation that a camera could be used as a projector and vice versa. Thus the Court of Appeals of the District of Columbia says:

> "A picture-taking camera, like many of those heretofore referred to as patented, could undoubtedly be utilized as an apparatus for exhibiting pictures also, by substituting a picture film in the carrying device and then applying the apparatus of the magic lantern."

The District Judge also says that claims 7 and 9, as originally filed, "are equally applicable to a camera as to a projecting machine."

I have thus far proceeded upon the hypothesis that Latham was the first to make the invention which is the subject of the claims in controversy.

The invention consists of a film-feeding mechanism operated by continuously rotating sprockets, a loop being produced and maintained in the slack film. Also a sprocket, rotating intermittently, which feeds the slack loop across the optical axis section by section. It is described in the specification as consisting in employing "means for bringing each picture to rest at the moment of projection, means for reducing the strain the picture-film would otherwise suffer from the rapid interruption and renewal of its movement, and means for maintaining uniformity of movement of the film as it unwinds from the delivering reel, and as it winds upon the receiving reel."

The invention introduced a decided improvement to the art and one which can be used with equal advantage in a projector and a camera. If it were a new and useful improvement as to one, it was equally so as to the other.

Bearing in mind that the invention with which we are concerned consists of the apparatus which produces this intermittent movement of the film across the exposure opening, I am unable to find any proof in the record which anticipates.

Latham's application was filed June 1, 1896. His invention was made on or prior to February 26, 1895, and

1   was put into practical operation on that date, as a camera, its use as a projector having been also demonstrated.

The complaint admits that the invention of Latham was shortly after February 26, 1895,

> "invented independently in France by M. J. H. Joly, who used it both in cameras and projectors, and still later in the year 1895, in this country, by Thomas Armat, who used it exclusively in projecting machines."

2   This admission undoubtedly anticipates the filing date of June 1, 1896, and throws upon the complainant the burden of establishing the date of the invention at a period anterior to the dates of the Joly and Armat structures. This has been done. I do not deem it necessary to discuss the testimony in detail because it fully establishes the fact of the completion and reduction to practice by Latham, on the evening of February 26 or the morning of February 27, 1895.

The defendant took no evidence on this issue. It is as-
3  serted that the evidence is insufficient because the device relied on was not a projector, but a camera. I have already shown that the two devices were used interchangeably and, where it appears that the inventor was the first to make the precise structure which he now claims, it is not material what he called it or how he first used it in the moving picture art. He was entitled to any use to which it might be legitimately put in that art.

The testimony does not bear out the defendant's other contentions that the adaptation and use of the device as a projector is not satisfactorily established, that it was an
4  abandoned experiment and was not the work of Latham, but of his mechanic, Eugene Lauste.

The conception was Latham's, worked out and made operative by skilled mechanics employed by him.

Latham says:

> "When the idea came into my head * * * it was necessary for me to get the help of skilled mechanics."

It would be necessary to ignore arbitrarily the testimony

in order to reach a conclusion that some one other than Latham conceived the invention. If Latham conceived it, the fact that he employed others to embody his idea in a working machine does not deprive him, and his assigns, of the fruits of the invention.

Of course the process of taking and projecting pictures varies in several details, many of which are pointed out in the defendant's brief, but I do not deem it necessary to consider them at length, in view of the controlling circumstance that the machine, the physical thing, is capable of taking and projecting pictures. The picture-bearing strip might as well have been described as "a strip designed for bearing pictures"; it is the same strip in either case. When used as a camera the pictures are impressed upon the strip during the passage through, when used as a projector the same pictures, on the same strip, are passed through in the same manner.

It would seem to be an exceedingly harsh doctrine to hold that when one has invented a complicated and delicately organized machine, consisting of a combination of reels, drums, pulleys and sprockets, designed to manipulate the film; invention and infringement must depend upon the color or length of the film. The combination is the same whether the film is impressed with the pictures while passing through, or whether the same film with the pictures completed is passed through.

If the camera of February 26th did not embody the invention in issue, nothing could do so, it *was* the invention in issue.

The Edison patent No. 493,426 shows a continuously moving film with no intermittent motion. The Edison patent No. 589,168 is for a "Kinetographic Camera." He says:

> "The purpose I have in view is to produce pictures representing objects in motion throughout an extended period of time which may be utilized to exhibit the scene including such moving objects in a perfect and natural manner by means of a suitable exhibiting apparatus, such as that described in an application filed simultaneously herewith (Patent No. 493,426, dated March 14, 1893). I have found

1        that it is possible to accomplish this end by means
         of photography."

The complainant's expert, Mr. Waterman, asserts, and
I see no reason to differ from him, that the apparatus here
described can be used equally well for taking pictures and
projecting them. It comprises a supply and a take-up reel
with an escapement between them having a sprocket wheel
engaging the holes perforated at regular intervals on the
two edges of the film to feed it along intermittently across
an exposure opening.

2        There is not, however, the distinguishing characteristic
of the Latham patent, the second feeding mechanism which
continuously maintains a loop and relieves the pressure on
the intermittently feeding sprocket.

Thomas Armat testifies that the Edison Company began
to put out projecting machines in the fall of 1896 or the
spring of 1897. He says:

        "These last mentioned machines, however, at this
        date did not at first embody the feature of providing
3       slack between the supporting reel and the intermit-
        tently moving device, and they had a very short life
        as thus put on the market."

The problem I am now considering was solved, not by
Edison, but by Latham.

The patents to Marcy, though prior in time, do not disclose the Latham invention. The film is pinched between
two rollers and is advanced by the revolving of the larger
roller, at a uniform rate. There are no sprocket wheels and
no holes in the edges of the film to engage such sprockets,
4   the film is moved by friction and therefore lacks the uniform and definite action of the Latham device.

The Chinnock camera, assuming it to have been completed and operative prior to the Latham invention, which
proposition is disputed and in doubt, does not anticipate for
reasons similar to those just above stated regarding the
Marcy camera. The film is advanced by continuously
driven friction rolls, and is arrested and released by a
clamp intermittently operated. There is also a pair of
friction rolls below the exposure opening; they are of a

greater diameter than the upper rolls and revolve at a
higher speed but are arranged to slip over the film when it
is clamped. The function of these rollers is to pull down
a certain amount of film and they are, therefore, made
larger in diameter and are driven at a higher speed. With
the addition of these rolls, the Chinnock device is substantially similar to the Marcy device. It does not have the
essential features of the Latham invention, as before pointed
out, viz., the loop of slack film produced by the film-feeding
mechanism operated by continuously rotating sprockets together with an intermittently operating sprocket which
feeds the slack across the exposure window.

I do not deem it necessary to refer to the friction roll
printing press patents further than to say that I consider
them as belonging to a different art and much more remote
than the patents already considered.

The complainant is criticized for "reading into the
claims" the sprocket type of feed, but as the claims must
be construed in the light of the specification and as the description describes the sprocketed feed drums, the teeth of
which engage the holes in the films, and as the drawings
clearly show these features, I see no just basis for the criti-
cism.

It is also charged that the complainant has been guilty
of laches in permitting infringements to proceed during
five and a half years which elapsed after the patent was issued. Undoubtedly there was this delay, but in view of the
protracted litigation which had impoverished the then owners of the patent, I cannot find that this delay amounted to
laches. Under its present owners infringers have been vig-
orously prosecuted and it is alleged that all of the infringers have taken out licenses under the patent.

The patent encountered unusual vicissitudes from the
moment the application was filed and its progress through
the Patent Office met with opposition and discouragement
at almost every stage. I cannot find, however, that anything occurred there to deprive Latham of his invention.
The issue in the interference between him and Armat was a
narrow one, and though it was decided in favor of Armat,
it is plain that this occurred because of the restricted scope
of the issue between them. No one can read the decision of
the Court of Appeals without being convinced that it was

reached because of the narrow issue presented in the interference. For instance, the court says:

> "We are free to confess in this case, that, the inspection of the original machine, and the proof of its efficient performance in intermittently moving the film for the taking of pictures, in connection with the evidence of the first private trials in exhibiting pictures, has strongly inclined us to decide in favor of its reduction to practice."

But they were unable to do this because of "all of the limitations and requirements of the issue." If the questions had been those with which we are now concerned, I am persuaded that the court would have reached a different conclusion. I am not convinced that Latham's conduct in the Patent Office was unfair or disingenuous, unless persistent and untiring effort to secure what he believed to be his rights can be so characterized. He fought on until he secured claims which covered not a different invention, but the invention which he had reduced to practice in February, 1895. I am convinced that Latham made a valuable invention, not an epoch-making invention, it is true, but one which introduced a much-needed improvement into the motion picture art. It remedied the difficulties which had baffled inventors of unquestioned genius and placed the art upon a successful commercial basis. In such circumstances, it is, in my opinion, the duty of the court to save rather than to destroy the patent.

For these reasons I am unable to concur in the disposition of this appeal by the majority of the court. I think that the decree should be reversed and the cause remanded to the District Court with instructions to enter a decree in favor of the complainant with costs.

---

Whereupon, at 11:30 A. M., the hearings were adjourned on this Friday, April 10th, 1914, to Wednesday, April 15th, 1914, at 10:30 A. M., at the Hotel Manhattan, New York City.

IN THE 1

# DISTRICT COURT OF THE UNITED STATES

## FOR THE EASTERN DISTRICT OF PENNSYLVANIA.

UNITED STATES OF AMERICA,
Petitioner,

*v.*

No. 889.
Sept. Sess., 1912.

MOTION PICTURE PATENTS CO. and others,
Defendants.

2

NEW YORK CITY, April 15, 1914.

The hearings were resumed, pursuant to adjournment, at 10:30 o'clock A. M. on this April 15th, 1914, at Room 159, Hotel Manhattan, New York City.

Present on behalf of the Petitioner, Hon. EDWIN P. GROSVENOR, Special Assistant to the Attorney General. 3

JOSEPH R. DARLING, Esq., Special Agent.

CHARLES F. KINGSLEY, Esq., GEORGE R. WILLIS, Esq., FRED R. WILLIAMS, Esq., appearing for Motion Picture Patents Company, Biograph Company, Jeremiah J. Kennedy, Harry N. Marvin, Armat Moving Picture Company, Melies Manufacturing Co. and Gaston Melies.

J. H. CALDWELL, Esq., and H. K. STOCKTON, Esq , appearing for William Pelzer, General Film Company, Thomas A. Edison, Inc., Kalem Company, Inc., Pathe Freres, Frank L. Dyer, Samuel Long and J. A. Berst. 4

HENRY MELVILLE, Esq., attorney for George Kleine, Essanay Film Manufacturing Company, Selig Polyscope, George K. Spoor and W. N. Selig.

JAMES J. ALLEN, Esq., appearing for Vitagraph Company of America, and Albert E. Smith.

Thereupon ALFRED D. BRICK, the next witness called by Petitioner in rebuttal, of lawful age, being first duly sworn by the Examiner, deposed as follows:

Direct examination by Mr. GROSVENOR:

Q. Mr. Brick, what is your occupation? A. I am a perforator.

Q. Are you engaged in the motion picture business? A. Yes, sir.

Q. With what company are you connected? A. The Universal Film Manufacturing Company.

Q. Are you familiar with the type of film that is used in cameras and for developing pictures by the Universal Film Manufacturing Company? A. Yes, sir.

Q. I show you a strip of film, being marked "Petitioner's Exhibit No. 278 for Identification." Please state if that is a type of the negative or positive film used by you, and if so, which is it? A. This is a type of film, negative film, which goes into the camera.

Q. From what source is that sample that I have shown you (Petitioner's Exhibit No. 278) obtained? A. From the regular stock.

Q. And from whom do you get your regular stock? A. From the Eastman Kodak Company.

Q. Is this in the condition it is in when received by you from them? A. Yes, sir, that is its condition.

Q. What is done by your company to this film before it is put in the camera? A. Just perforated, sir.

Q. Do you do anything else to it? A. No, sir.

Q. I show you "Petitioner's Exhibit No. 279 for Identification." Please state whether or not that is a sample of the positive film which you use. A. This is a sample of the positive film which we use.

Q. And where do you get the positive film from? A. From the Eastman Kodak Company.

Q. Do you do anything to this film before it is used as positive film? A. No, only it is printed on.

Mr. GROSVENOR: I offer both of these exhibits in evidence.

"Petitioner's Exhibits Nos. 278 and 279" were left by the Examiner in the custody of Petitioner's counsel, by consent of counsel.

Cross examination by Mr. KINGSLEY:  1

Q. Are these samples of negative and positive films, which you have identified, samples which you yourself furnished the attorney for the Government? A. Yes, sir.

Q. In perforating film so that it may be used in the camera for a negative, or so that it may be used for printing positives, is it necessary to do the work accurately? A. Yes, sir.

Q. How many perforations is it necessary to have in each running inch of film? A. That I could not answer; I never measured them.  2

Q. How many perforations do you make in each running inch of film in ordinary use? A. About four holes.

Q. And by that you mean there are four holes to the picture? A. Yes, sir.

Q. Are these perforations made equidistant from one another? A. Yes, sir.

Q. Do you have a machine to make these perforations? A. Yes, sir.

Q. Is it a specially devised machine, which makes them with absolute accuracy? A. Yes, sir.

Q. I show you Defendants' Exhibit No. 176. Is that a  3
fairly representative perforated negative motion picture? A. Yes, sir.

Q. So far as the perforations are concerned? A. Yes, sir.

Q. Do you know what is the standard width of motion picture film? A. No, sir, I could not say for sure.

Q. Does it always come of the same width? A. Yes, it always comes the same width.

Q. Did you ever see any motion picture film that was of a different width from that with which you are familiar? A. No, sir.

Q. I show you Defendants' Exhibit No. 177, being a motion picture positive. Is that a representative motion picture positive, so far as the perforations on the edges are concerned? A. Yes, sir.  4

Q. In referring to the raw stock which you obtained from the Eastman Kodak Company, do you usually speak of it as "film"? A. Yes, sir.

Q. And are negative motion pictures frequently referred to as "film"? A. Yes, sir.

1      Q. Are positive motion pictures generally referred to as
"film"? A. Yes, sir.

Q. As a matter of fact, after a film has been received from
the Eastman Kodak Company and perforated and passed
through the camera, it is no longer film in the original sense,
is it? A. They call it a reel then.

Q. Has it become a motion picture after it has been passed
through the camera? A. It is a motion picture then.

Q. It is no longer a film, but has become a motion picture? A. A motion picture.

2      Q. And the positives which are printed from the negative
motion pictures which have been taken from the camera, are
also motion pictures, are they not? A. Yes, sir.

Redirect examination by Mr. GROSVENOR:

Q. How do you perforate these films? A. By machine.

Q. And where do you get your machine? A. From Bell &
Howell.

———————

Thereupon JULES E. BRULATOUR, the next witness
3  produced by the petitioner in rebuttal, of lawful age, being
first duly sworn by the Examiner, deposed as follows:

Direct examination by Mr. GROSVENOR:

Q. Mr. Brulatour, what is your occupation? A. Motion
picture business, the distributing of motion picture films.

Q. Have you been connected with the Eastman Kodak
Company for several years? A. Yes, for three years. I have
been with that company over three years.

Q. Does the Eastman Kodak Company sell a standard
4  type of film for use in motion picture cameras? A. Yes, sir.

Q. Called "negative film"? A. We have negative and
positive.

Q. You have one type or standard for use in motion picture cameras, and another type or standard for use in printing positives from the negative? A. Yes, sir.

Q. The most of the film which you sell, both the negative
and the positive, is unperforated, is it not? A. Oh, yes, the
great majority of it.

Cross examination by Mr KINGSLEY: 1

Q. How long have you been connected with the Eastman Company? A. Why, I have this contract—the contract has been renewed since the original one, but over three years, three years in February.

Q. Were you with them before February three years ago? A. I was selling Lumiere film, a foreign film, made in Lyons, France.

Q. You mean by that Lumiere raw stock? A. Yes, sir, for moving pictures.

Q. What is the standard width of moving picture film? 2 A. Well, it is approximately one and three-eighths of an inch.

Q. Is that the standard all over the world? A. Yes, sir.

Q. And there is no other standard for motion picture film? A. No, sir.

Q. And did that originate in this country, that standard width, or don't you know about that? A. I am not positive about that. That would be calling for my opinion; I could not tell you positively.

Q. In perforating a negative motion picture film, is it necessary that the perforations be made with absolute accuracy? A. Oh, yes, it is very desirable. 3

Q. It is therefore necessary that producers of motion pictures, when they perforate negative film, perforate it with absolute accuracy? A. Oh, yes.

Q. And does the success of the motion picture depend to some extent upon the accuracy with which the perforations are made? A. Yes, the success of the fixity on the screen depends on it in a great measure.

Q. And why is it perforated? A. It is perforated so that it can be projected, and so that it can be used in the cameras, because the mechanisms of the cameras and of all projecting machines are provided with sprockets that move the film. 4

Q. Then the perforations are necessary, if I understand you correctly, to the successful use of the film in the commercial types of cameras and projecting machines now in successful use in this country? A. Yes, absolutely. I have not seen any machine yet in which you could do away with it.

Q. Is it necessary to have the perforations which you have described for negative motion picture film made also in the positive motion picture film? A. Yes, sir.

1      Q. And is it necessary to have them made in it for the same reason? A. Yes, sir.

Q. Mr. Brulatour, is it customary in your line to speak of the raw stock which you distribute as "film"? A. Yes, sir.

Q. And is it customary to speak of the negative after it comes from the camera as "film?" A. Yes, sir, it is always film.

Q. Is it customary to speak of the positives, after they have been made and are sent out, as "film?" A. After it is printed, you mean?

2      Q. Yes. A. Yes, they generally denote it as being a "reel of film," and that indicates to the mind that it is printed up and finished. "Film" generally means unexposed or undeveloped, but when a man says a "reel of film" to an experienced mind it means film that is printed up and ready for the projecting machine.

Q. The raw stock, which you distribute, is "film," is it not? A. Yes, sir, it is film, absolutely nothing else.

Q. After a reel of negative motion picture film has been passed through the camera, it is no longer "film" in the sense in which you used the term when you took it from

3      the factory? A. No, sir.

Q. After it has passed through the camera, is it then film, or is it a motion picture negative? A. It is a motion picture negative after the exposure has been made on it. It is negative film when you put it in and after the exposure has been made it becomes doubly negative, and the process has been gone through, but until the developing, it is really not fully negative film, because the process has not been completed.

Q. After it has been passed through the camera, it is no longer "film" in the commercial sense? A. No, sir.

4      Q. As you used the term when you referred to raw stock? A. Yes, sir.

Q. It is thereafter something different from what you sold? A. Yes, sir.

Q. And after it is developed it is a motion picture negative? A. Yes, sir, absolutely.

Redirect examination by Mr. GROSVENOR:

Q. But it is not a motion picture negative until it is developed? A. No, sir, but it is no longer film as I sold it, because it cannot be used for anything else. It is neither a picture nor raw stock. It has lost its identity as raw stock, and it has not acquired its identity as a negative film.

Recross examination by Mr. KINGSLEY:

Q. After raw stock, called positive film, is made into positive motion pictures, it is no longer "film" in the sense in which you use the term when you refer to the product you distribute? A. No, sir, not at all. It is different, so far as I am concerned.

Q. And it is no longer available for use as film? A. No, sir.

Q. It is now a perforated, completed motion picture? A. A finished commercial article.

Redirect examination by Mr. GROSVENOR:

Q. The finished positive, then, is an entirely different product from the negative? A. Oh, yes, the finished positive is a different product from the finished negative.

Recross examination by Mr. KINGSLEY:

Q. In what sense? A. In this sense: Where the light portion, or the white portion in the positive is light, in the negative it will be black, and vice versa.

Q. You are referring to the reversal of the light and shade? A. Yes, sir.

Q. And otherwise they are exactly the same? A. Yes, sir.

Q. Did you ever see negatives projected? A. Yes, sir.

Q. Frequently? A. Not commercially or in theatres, or anything of that sort, but in studios and different factories. In factories, they always do that before printing, that is, the most of them do. That takes an experienced eye to follow it, it is very hard.

Q. Are the perforations used throughout the world standard or uniform as to the number and the spacing and the arrangement of the perforations, so that all film will run on any commercial camera or projecting machine? A. Yes, sir.

Q. In the common parlance of the trade, are motion

1 pictures sometimes referred to as "film," and is such use of the term sometimes confusing as to motion pictures and raw stock? A. Well, that question I could answer this way—it depends on the sense in which the word is used. If I am talking to an exchange man, for instance, and he speaks of his "film" I know he means his finished product, and if I am talking to somebody at the factory, for instance, of the Kodak Company, and he and I refer to "film," I know that means the unexposed film.

Q. How long have you been in the motion picture film business altogether? A. Probably six years, I guess. About
2 six or seven years, probably, since the Patents Company was formed.

Q. Before you went into the motion picture business at all, did you have any knowledge of it, or did you then have any idea of the distinctions of the word "film" as used in the business? A. Yes, I was in the material and photographic business before, that is how I drifted into it. I had the agency for the Lumiere Company of France, for their different photographic material.

Q. You mean the word "film" is particularly confusing
3 to persons who have no knowledge of the motion picture business? A. Yes, sir.

Q. Do you know of such instances? A. Yes, sir, it would be to this extent: If you refer to the roll film for kodaks, or film for the moving picture business, or a flat film used in place of plates, of the same type of film. The Seed Company of St. Louis, used to sell a flat film. That was a film used in place of the plate in the camera.

Q. Did you state that before the Patents Company was formed you were distributing Lumiere film? A. No, not film then. I had the agency, but I didn't sell any.

4 Q. Did the Lumiere Company make film? A. Oh, yes, at Lyons, France.

Q. And you had the agency for that? A. I had the agency, yes, sir.

Q. Did the Lumiere Company manufacture moving picture film? A. Yes, sir.

Q. And when did they begin to put it out in a form available for use on cameras and projecting machines in this country? A. Well, the first film that I imported in this country was imported probably—oh, not very long after

the formation of the Patents Company. I don't know exactly 1
the date, but it was not very long after that, but not in very
large quantities.

Q. Do you know when motion picture film, and by that I
mean the raw stock, was first available in its present form
in this country? A. Not of my own knowledge, no.

Redirect examination by Mr. GROSVENOR:

Q. Mr. Brulatour, you have used the term "raw stock"
several times in the course of your cross examination. As I
understand the use of the term, you apply the words "raw 2
stock" to the film which you sell? A. Yes.

Q. And it is all ready when you sell it to put in the
camera, except for perforations? A. Yes, sir.

Q. In that condition you call it "raw stock"? A. Yes,
sir, it is a name that we have given to it—it is really a
misnomer, but it is a name that has been given to the film,
and that has stuck to it.

Q. It is a finished product? A. Yes, sir, and exposure
has not been made on it, and it has not been developed.

Q. And you term it "raw stock"? A. Yes, sir.

Q. Until it has been exposed? A. Yes, sir. 3

Q. And then it becomes a hybrid article, neither raw
stock, nor a picture, nor a negative? A. As a matter of fact
neither, but to the eye it keeps its original identity.

Q. Until it is developed, or until the image is fixed or developed? A. Yes.

Thereupon the Petitioner rested its case in rebuttal.

4

1

UNITED STATES OF AMERICA,
     Petitioner,

    *v.*

2 MOTION PICTURE PATENTS CO. and others,
        Defendants.

No. 889.
Sept. Sess., 1912.

NEW YORK CITY, April 15, 1914.

The hearings were continued on this April 15th, 1914, at Room 159, Hotel Manhattan, New York City, for the purpose of taking evidence on behalf of the defendants in surrebuttal.

> Present on behalf of the Petitioner, Hon. EDWIN
> 3 P. GROSVENOR, Special Assistant to the Attorney General.
> JOSEPH R. DARLING, Esq., Special Agent.
> CHARLES F. KINGSLEY, Esq., GEORGE R. WILLIS, Esq., FRED R. WILLIAMS, Esq., appearing for Motion Picture Patents Company, Biograph Company, Jeremiah J. Kennedy, Harry N. Marvin, Armat Moving Picture Company, Melies Manufacturing Co. and Gaston Melies.
> J. H. CALDWELL, Esq., and H. K. STOCKTON, Esq.,
> 4 appearing for William Pelzer, General Film Company, Thomas A. Edison, Inc., Kalem Company, Inc., Pathe Freres, Frank L. Dyer, Samuel Long and J. A. Berst.
> HENRY MELVILLE, Esq., attorney for George Kleine, Essanay Film Manufacturing Company, Selig Polyscope, George K. Spoor and W. N. Selig.
> JAMES J. ALLEN, Esq., appearing for Vitagraph Company of America, and Albert E. Smith.

## Defendants' Evidence in Surrebuttal.    1

Thereupon WILLIAM WRIGHT, the first witness produced by the defendants in sur-rebuttal, of lawful age, being
duly sworn by the Examiner, deposed as follows:

Direct examination by Mr. KINGSLEY:

Q. What is your business?  A. I am Sales Manager for
the Kalem Company.

Q. How long have you been Sales Manager for the Kalem
Company?  A. Between three and four years.

Q. Were you with the Kalem Company prior to becom-  2
ing its Sales Manager?  A. Yes, sir.

Q. In what capacity?  A. I represented the Kalem Company in Chicago, soliciting orders for the sale and leasing
of film.

Q. Were you with the Kalem Company in 1910?  A. Yes,
sir.

Q. In 1910 were you acquainted with Alfred Weiss, one
of the witnesses in this action?  A. Yes, sir.

Q. Did you have any conversation with Mr. Weiss in
1910, some time prior to July 4th, in which you advised him  3
to sell his rental exchange to the General Film Company?
A. No, sir.

Q. Did you ever have any conversation in 1910, or at
any other time, with Alfred Weiss, in which you advised
him to sell his rental exchange or any of the property of
his rental exchange to the General Film Company or anybody else?  A. No, sir.

Q. Did you have any conversation with Alfred Weiss in
1910, or at any time, in which you discussed the desirability
of his selling his rental exchange, or some of the property
of his rental exchange, to the General Film Company, or  4
to any other firm, corporation, or individual?  A. No, sir.

Q. Did you, in the early Summer of 1910 call upon
Weiss at his office, No. 219 Sixth Avenue, and there say to
him in words or in effect: "Weiss, you had better wake up
and see that you close up some kind of a deal with the
General Film Company; it will be to your advantage; they
will pay you a good price for your exchange; they will
make a stockholder out of you and give you a very good
position, and you will have a steady income on the order
like life insurance, or so"?  A. No.

Q. Did you have a conversation with Weiss at his office

1 at No. 219 Sixth Avenue, prior to July 4th, 1910, in which you said to him, either in words or in substance: "Mr. Weiss, you know how it is, today the licensed manufacturers control the market, they have got you right in their hands, they can cancel your license in no time, now you had better sell and be one of us"? A. No.

Q. Now, did you have a conversation with Mr. Weiss and make either of the two statements outlined in the two foregoing questions, at any other place or at any other time than at his office, No. 219 Sixth Avenue? A. No.

2 Q. Were you at all interested in the purchase of the stock and equipment of rental exchanges by the General Film Company? A. No.

Q. Did you know anything about the affairs of the General Film Company so far as the purchase of stock and equipment of rental exchanges was concerned? A. No, sir.

Q. Did you have any authority to speak for the General Film Company? A. No.

Q. Did you speak to Weiss, or to any other rental exchange man, at any time, with reference to the sale of his stock and equipment to the General Film Company? A. Yes.

3 Q. What other men did you speak to? A. William H. Clune, of Los Angeles, California, and Joseph Hopp, of Chicago.

Q. Are you positive that you never spoke to Weiss on that subject? A. Yes, sir.

Cross examination by Mr. GROSVENOR:

Q. Mr. Wright, what was your position with the Kalem Company in June, 1910? A. Sales Manager.

Q. What were your duties as Sales Manager? A. Soliciting the leasing of film.

4 Q. You addressed your solicitations to the owners of the rental exchanges? A. Yes, sir.

Q. And it was in that line of business that you had occasion to meet Mr. Weiss? A. I met Mr. Weiss once only, in his office.

Q. And in what relation did you meet him or in what capacity did you see him? A. I saw him early in 1910, and asked him to lease film from us.

Q. Mr. Weiss did take film from the Kalem Company,

did he not, in 1910?  A. My recollection is that at that
time he was not leasing film from us.

Q. That is, at the time you went to see him?  A. Yes,
sir.

Q. Now, my question is:  Mr. Weiss did take film from
the Kalem Company in 1910?  A. I think that his last
order was in January of 1910, and if my recollection serves
me right, there is an interim there—as a matter of fact, I
don't think his exchange took any film from us until after
it was acquired by the General Film Company, and then
Mr. Weiss called me on the 'phone and said he had a sur-
prise for me.

Q. Have you, before testifying, refreshed your recollection by looking up any records to determine whether or not
the Weiss Exchange did take film from you in the first
months of 1910?  A. No.

Q. Are you still Sales Manager for the Kalem Company?  A. Yes, sir.

Q. You say you did meet Mr. Weiss?  A. He called at
our office some time during 1910.

Q. Have you ever been to his office?  A. I have been to
his office several times, but saw him only once, and that
was early in 1910, several months before any purchases
were made, or any General Film Company business.

Q. Did you go to his office several times in the year
1910 before the General Film Company acquired the Weiss
Exchange?  A. I probably called at his office three or four
times, but I didn't see him; he was out.

Q. Did you go to his office on these occasions with the
object of having his exchange take film from the Kalem
Company?  A. Yes, sir.

Q. You went there making solicitations?  A. I went
there for that purpose, but not seeing him there, I turned
around and walked out.

Q. Are you one of the officers of the Kalem Company?
A. I am the Vice-President of it, now.

Q. Are you one of the owners of the company?  A. I
am, in the amount of one share of stock.

Q. Were you an officer of that company in 1910?  A.
No, sir.

Q. In making solicitations, or endeavoring to sell the
film of the Kalem Company, it was necessary for you to

1  keep up with the changes and business conditions? A. Yes, naturally.

Q. And you naturally read the trade papers? A. Yes, sir.

Q. Then you were advised to that extent of the formation of the General Film Company and of the fact that it was entering upon the rental exchange business? A. Yes, sir.

Q. You had that information in April and May and June of 1910? A. I don't remember the dates, but during 1910 naturally I was familiar with what was going on, because it was public property.

2

Redirect examination by Mr. KINGSLEY:

Q. Were you soliciting orders when you went to Mr. Weiss' office and didn't find him? A. Yes, sir.

Q. Did you find it necessary in 1910 to go out and solicit orders in order to meet the competition of the other producers of motion pictures? A. Yes, sir, and ever since I have been connected with the business I have found it very necessary.

3  Q. Do you still find it necessary as Sales Manager of the Kalem Company? A. Yes, sir, more so than ever.

Q. Do you find it necessary to advertise? A. Very extensively.

Q. Do you advertise extensively? A. Yes, sir.

Q. Do you send out circulars to the exhibitors and to the managers of rental exchanges? A. Yes, sir.

Q. Do you have a large bill for advertising? A. Very large.

Recross examination by Mr. GROSVENOR:

4  Q. What was the extent of your information regarding the plans of the General Film Company from reading papers and from keeping up with trade conditions and trade news in June, 1910, Mr. Wright? A. Well, during that Summer I knew that the General Film Company was acquiring various exchanges.

Q. You knew that it was entering very largely upon the business of a rental exchange? A. I do not remember how many exchanges they acquired during that time, but I know they did acquire some.

Q. You knew they had acquired more in a short time than

any other corporation had acquired within the same period of time? A. I couldn't say anything about that.

Q. Did you then know of any other corporation which, in the same period of time, had acquired as many exchanges? A. I am not in a position to answer that; I have no knowledge as to other corporations.

Q. Do you know to-day of any corporation that has acquired within the same period of time as many exchanges as the General Film Company acquired at that time? A. Why, the Universal at one fell swoop, or at one time, formed a combination that took in practically all of the independent exchanges that there were. The thing was consummated, as I remember it, at one or two meetings.

Q. Now, if you can recall that, Mr. Wright, can't you recall that when the General Film Company was organized, or shortly thereafter, it acquired all the licensed exchanges in New York except one? A. Well, I don't know that, but I rmember that it acquired several of them within a month or two here.

Q. Can you recall that it acquired a great many others besides those that it acquired in New York about the same time? A. Well, within a number of months it acquired a great many of the exchanges.

Q. That is, in the Summer of 1910, and in the early Fall of 1910? A. Yes, sir.

Redirect examination by Mr. KINGSLEY:

Q. By that do you mean that the exchanges acquired were licensed exchanges? A. Yes, sir.

---

Thereupon THOMAS YARROW HENRY, the next witness produced by the defendants in sur-rebuttal, of lawful age, being first duly sworn by the Examiner, deposed as follows:

Direct examination by Mr. KINGSLEY:

Q. What is your business? A. Accounting.

Q. Are you connected now with any firm or corporation? A. The General Film Company.

Q. How long have you been with the General Film Company? A. From the end of July, 1910.

1　　Q. Are you familiar with the books and accounts of the Alfred Weiss Branch of the General Film Company during the ten weeks succeeding July 4th, 1910? A. I am, thoroughly.

　　Mr. Grosvenor: I object to all of the testimony of the witness thus far on this subject, and move to strike it out, the profits of the Weiss Exchange after July, 1910, being immaterial, the same being but a branch of the General Film Company.

2　　Mr. Kingsley: The attorney for the petitioner has questioned Mr. Weiss as to the profits of the Alfred Weiss Branch—what the General Film Company made —and he answered from fifteen thousand to twenty thousand dollars.

　　Mr. Grosvenor: My questions to Mr. Weiss were directed to the profits of his company before he sold out.

　　Mr. Kingsley: Mr. Weiss on cross examination testified that for ten weeks after he transferred his property to the General Film Company he was in charge, and that he had received no contract, but that

3　nevertheless he went on for the ten weeks until he did receive a contract, during which period he made from three hundred to five hundred dollars a week for the General Film Company, accumulating the same in bank.

　　Mr. Grosvenor: That is, after he was turned out. It is objected to on the same ground, and if the testimony is intended to discredit or contradict or impeach the testimony of the witness Weiss, it is also incompetent under the rules, as counsel has undertaken to

4　contradict collateral testimony brought out by him on cross examination and relating to matters not brought out on direct examination, and therefore it is improper under the rules referring to impeachment of witnesses.

By Mr. Kingsley:

　　Q. Mr. Henry, did you make up a statement showing the receipts and expenses of the Alfred Weiss Branch of the General Film Company for the week ending July 9th, 1910, and for the nine succeeding weeks? A. I did.

**Defendants' Exhibit No. 213.**

WEISS 1910 BRANCH.

| | | FILM RENTALS ACCOUNT | | | | | | | | COLLECTIONS AND OUTSTANDINGS | | | | | |
| | | | | Film Rentals Less Returns | | | | | Net Profit | Customers Balances | | | | Customers | Increase, |
| Week Ending | No. of Reels | Gross Film Rentals | *Returns *and Allowances | and Al- lowances | *Net *Releases / *Cost of Film Rentals | Gross Profit on Film Rentals | *Royalties *Paid | *Oper- or *ating *Expenses | or *Loss on Film Rentals | from Previous Week | Net Business for Week | Total Due | *Collections of Week | *Balances at End of Week | *Decrease, of Customers Balances |
|---|---|---|---|---|---|---|---|---|---|---|---|---|---|---|---|
| **1910** | | | | | | | | | | | | | | | |
| July 9.... | 18 | 2207.79 | | 2207.79 | *1745.77 | 462.02 | *100. | *301.30 | 60.72 | | 2268.62 | 2268.62 | *1539.15 | 729.47 | 729.47 |
| 16.... | 22 | 1913.75 | | 1913.75 | *2138.47 | *224.72 | *88. | *226.72 | *539.44 | 729.47 | 1986.55 | 2716.02 | *1519.74 | 1196.28 | 466.81 |
| 23.... | 14 | 1923.55 | | 1923.55 | *1350.36 | 573.19 | *86. | *232.45 | 254.74 | 1196.28 | 2008.75 | 3205.03 | *2263.38 | 941.65 | 264.63 |
| 30.... | 18 | 1949.65 | | 1949.65 | *1731.00 | 218.65 | *88. | *211.05 | *80.40 | 941.65 | 2018.55 | 2960.20 | *1807.85 | 1152.35 | 210.70 |
| Aug. 6.... | 18 | 1863.16 | | 1863.15 | *1749.94 | 113.21 | *86. | *334.40 | *307.19 | 1152.35 | 1943.25 | 3095.60 | *2046.40 | 1049.20 | *103.15 |
| 13.... | 18 | 1981.41 | | 1981.41 | *1741.59 | 239.82 | *92. | *222.17 | *74.35 | 1049.20 | 2060.06 | 3109.26 | *2031.81 | 1077.45 | 28.25 |
| 20.... | 18 | 2075.70 | | 2075.70 | *1747.66 | 328.04 | 1*00. | *234.20 | *6.26 | 1077.45 | 2158.15 | 3235.60 | *2273.60 | 962.— | *115.45 |
| 27.... | 18 | 2067.30 | *31.52 | 2035.78 | *1748.75 | 287.03 | *96. | *221.15 | *20.12 | 962.— | 2066.48 | 3028.48 | *2175.45 | 853.03 | *108.97 |
| Sept. 3.... | 18 | 2159.00 | | 2159.00 | *1744.08 | 414.92 | *104. | *344.90 | *33.98 | 853.03 | 2297.95 | 3150.98 | *2333.45 | 817.53 | *35.50 |
| 10.... | 18 | 2437.92 | | 2437.92 | *1757.92 | 680.— | *126. | *264.05 | 299.95 | 817.53 | 2848.62 | 3666.15 | *2389.35 | 1276.80 | 459.27 |
| | 180 | 20579.22 | *31.52 | 20547.70 | *17485.54 | 3092.16 | *966. | *2582.49 | *456.33 | ....... | 21656.98 | 21656.98 | *20380.18 | 1276.80 | 1276.80 |
| | | | | | | | | | | | | | | | 729.47 |
| | | | | | | | | | | | | | | | 547.33 |
| | | | | | | | | | | | | | | | 1276.80 |

*Indicates red ink.

Q. Did you check that statement up with the reports made by Alfred Weiss, the Manager of the Alfred Weiss Branch of the General Film Company? A. I did, personally.

Q. Is this statement a correct statement? A. It is.

Q. Is it made in your own handwriting? A. Yes, sir.

Mr. KINGSLEY: I offer this statement in evidence.

Mr. GROSVENOR: I renew my objection to it, without restating the same as above given.

The statement produced by the witness and offered in evidence by the defendants' counsel is marked by the Examiner "Defendants' Exhibit No. 213," and is as follows:

1

Mr. KINGSLEY: I offer in evidence the article appearing in Harper's Weekly, of June 13th, 1891, at page 446, entitled "Edison Kinetograph, by George Parsons Lathrop." This number of Harper's Weekly belongs to the Library, and we have agreed not to mark or deface it, and we will produce the article and furnish it to the Examiner to be incorporated as a part of the record.

Mr. GROSVENOR: I have no objection to a reproduction instead of the production of this article, but I do object to the introduction of the article as evidence on the ground, among others, that it is too remote, appearing on its face to be dated some seventeen years prior to the formation of the combination alleged to be unlawful and the commencement of the acts complained of, and, also, on the ground that it is immaterial, incompetent and irrelevant.

The article, when received by the Examiner, will be marked "Defendants' Exhibit No. 214."

## Defendants' Exhibit No. 214.

3

Mr. GROSVENOR: I further object to the introduction of the article, as it appears on its face that it relates to the "Peep-hole" invention of Edison, and relates to matters not involved in this suit, and to patents also not involved in this suit.

Mr. KINGSLEY: The defendants rest.

Thereupon the defendants rested their case.

## Stipulation as to the Return of Exhibits.

4

It is stipulated by counsel that the Examiner may return to counsel all exhibits which have not heretofore been returned to counsel, that is to say, counsel for the petitioner will retain in his possession the exhibits of the petitioner, and counsel for the defendants will retain in their possession the exhibits of the defendants, the same to be available to either side at any time for examination before the hearing, and the

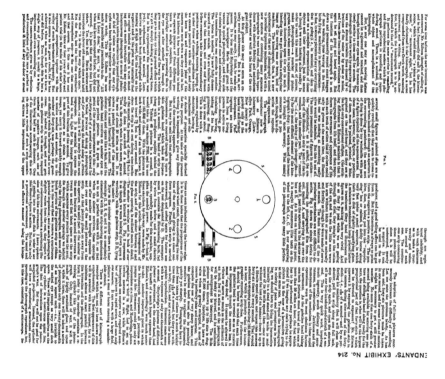

Fig. 1.

Fig. 2.

seen from space. The original and unique

A. Pencil.  B. Phonograph.  C. Kinetograph.  D. Pulley.

sixth of one brain, they are linked so closely as in the Japanese Ning and Ching, and by a bond of their own in their works. The so-called link-and-button form is found in that arrangement of the brain, which a little study of the kinetograph, combined in a box on the same frame, will readily confirm. In its heart of the kinetograph is an electric battery, and a single electric motor connected with color-picture printing. The phonograph is fitted with the lenses for sending forth its magnifying beams for interval sound, and the kinetograph is supplied forth large moving shapes upon a screen beyond.

To say that the kinetograph can be anything more than a marvellous toy would be hasty. It surpasses great possibilities, and immeasurably in a degree as many that the common retina is open in the very simple of amusement are very large. Mr. Edison's unique task and half-lost kinetographs reproduce by spectacles every fitful movement of the face, the above people laughing, smiling, crying, and no way to make—will exhibit the gestures and thoughtful facial expressions of orators, humorists, and actors. By means of them one will be able to report the lifelike shadow-play off scenes of all sorts; the enjoyment of whole operatic, athletic scenes, ballet dances, circus rings, street scenes (with their accompanying noises, and in some cases sung and still), harvest and practice, entire companies of soldiers at work (which the kinetograph alone, by preserving scenes of choice living in the same form, and for the kinetograph itself a great fund of entertainment). As the sound-wave of the phonograph are so greatly increased, so that figures of desirable will move their lips to high examples of the word had the kineto-graph even, that it will come day reproduce the complete turmoil of Niagara. It can picture a locomotive with all its mighty force in full swing of motion, or other machinery and operatives at work. What objections some people see nothing so much from a lifelike faithful moving sights or incidents, and the animating presence of scene! Children could have kinetographs monographs, full of authentic appearances taken from life, and moving up in its instead of by cruel imitation. We seem to be at a time when every man may realize the told philosophical of a theatrical scene in his world of man's own—by mounting in his room a tape which will fill it with all the fierce and world of true to-day, the actual globe. By supplying illustrations of this kind for schoolrooms and travels, and by preserving for future ages obtained pictures of such person as at the bidding of such scenes, the kinetograph may yet play a part of incalculable importance in human life.

FOLDOUT BLANK

that the figures, if desired, will move three times as fast as the actual persons could, a variety of comic and grotesque exaggerations might be produced by this means. It seems to me just as evident that the kinetograph may become very useful for instruction in sundry directions. Why not apply it to acting, for the preservation and study of high examples of that art? Mr Edison expects even that it will some day reproduce the majestic tumult of Niagara. It can picture a locomotive with rods and wheels in full swing of motion, or other machinery and operatives at work. What object-lessons might it not bring to us from foreign lands of literally moving sights or accidents, and the animated presence of far-off peoples! Children could have kinetographic menageries, full of authentic specimens taken from life, and moving as in life instead of by crude imitation. We seem to be nearing a time when every man may realize the old philosophical idea of a microcosm—a little world of one's own—by unrolling in his room a tape which will fill it with all the forms and motions of the habitable globe. By supplying illustrations of this kind for school-books and travels, and by preserving for future ages vitalized pictures of each passing generation or of historic events, the kinetograph may yet play a part of incalculable importance in human life.

same to be produced at the final hearing in Philadelphia, if 1 required.

The Examiner: All of the exhibits produced by the petitioner have been delivered to Edwin P. Grosvenor, Esq.

All of the exhibits produced by the defendants have been delivered to Charles F. Kingsley, Esq.

## Stipulation Waiving Signatures of Witnesses.

It is stipulated by counsel that the signatures of the wit- 2 nesses to their several depositions are hereby waived by both sides.

## Stipulation as to Certification of Record.

It is stipulated that the Examiner shall certify as the record in this case a copy of the revised printed record agreed upon by counsel for both sides, together with all the exhibits in the case, and that until the completion of said revision of the record, the Examiner is requested by counsel to withhold his certificate, and the filing of the record in this case; Pro- 3 vided that if the revised record is not agreed upon by May 15th, 1914, either side may apply to the Examiner for a hearing on the question as to whether or not he will certify the original record.

## Petitioner Closed.

## Defendants Closed.

Thereupon, at 11:45 A. M., April 15th, 1914, the hearings in this case were closed.

4

# UNITED STATES OF AMERICA

v.

## MOTION PICTURE PATENTS CO. ET AL.

### GENERAL INDEX TO RECORD—ALPHABETICALLY ARRANGED.

ADAMS, PETER:

|  | VOL. | PAGE |
|---|---|---|
| Direct Examination | II | 858– 859 |
| Cross Examination | | 859– 860 |
| Redirect Examination | | 860 |

AIKEN, FRED C.:

| | | |
|---|---|---|
| Direct Examination | IV | 2329–2342 |
| Cross Examination | V | 2475–2566 |
| Redirect Examination | | 2566–2567 |
| Redirect Examination | | 2567–2570 |
| Recross Examination | | 2567 |
| Recross Examination | | 2570–2571 |

ANDERSON, WILLIAM J.:

| | | |
|---|---|---|
| Direct Examination | II | 860– 862 |
| Cross Examination | | 862– 863 |
| Redirect Examination | | 864– 866 |
| Redirect Examination | | 866– 867 |
| Recross Examination | | 866 |

ANTHONY, FREDERICK A.:

| | | |
|---|---|---|
| Direct Examination | IV | 2064–2074 |
| Cross Examination | | 2074–2075 |

**Armat Moving Picture Company:**

| | | |
|---|---|---|
| Agreement, Preliminary, for Assignment of Patents between Patents Co. and Armat Co., dated Dec. 18, 1908; printed as Exhibit 1 to Answer of Armat Co.; Petitioner's Exhibit 4 | I | 15 |

ARMAT MOVING PICTURE CO., Continued:    VOL.     PAGE

License Agreement under the Projecting Machine Patents between Patents Co. and Armat Moving Picture
Co., dated Jan. 7, 1909; printed as
Exhibit 5 on page 87 of the Petition     I       244

License Agreement dated Dec. 12,
1900, between Armat Co. and E.
Burton Holmes, Defendants' Ex-
hibit 121 ......................    IV      2119

License Agreement, dated March 14,
1902, between Armat Co. and B. H.
H. Lawrence, Defendants' Exhibit
122 ...........................    IV      2122

Agreement, dated Feb. 19, 1904, between
Armat Co. and Biograph Co., re
Letters Patent 586,953, Defend-
ants' Exhibit 127...............    IV      2160

Letter, Armat Co. to H. N. Marvin,
Trustee, attached to Defendants'
Exhibit 127, Feb. 19, 1904, Defend-
ants' Exhibit 128...............    IV      2163

Agreement dated March 21, 1908, between Armat Co. and Biograph Co.,
Defendants' Exhibit 130.........    IV      2166

Writ of Injunction, dated Jan. 8, 1903,
out of Circuit Court for the Southern District of New York on the
part of Armat Co. directed to Edison Mfg. Co., on Letters Patent
586,953, Defendants' Exhibit 126.    IV      2136

ARMAT, THOMAS:

Direct Examination ..............    IV      2118–2138
Direct Examination ..............            2158–2174
Cross Examination ...............            2174–2185

ATWATER, L. W.:

| | VOL. | PAGE |
|---|---|---|
| Direct Examination ................ | IV | 2004–2009 |

AUGER, EDWARD:

| | | |
|---|---|---|
| Direct Examination ................ | IV | 2275–2280 |
| Cross Examination ................ | | 2429–2433 |
| Redirect Examination .............. | | 2433–2434 |
| Recross Examination .............. | | 2434–2435 |

BALSLEY, CHARLES H.:

| | | |
|---|---|---|
| Direct Examination ................ | II | 867– 869 |
| Cross Examination ................ | | 870– 873 |
| Redirect Examination .............. | | 873– 877 |
| Recross Examination .............. | | 877 |

BATES, THOMAS H.:

| | | |
|---|---|---|
| Direct Examination ................ | II | 969– 983 |
| Cross Examination ................ | | 1006–1018 |
| Redirect Examination .............. | | 1018–1019 |

BAUERFREUND, ADOLPH:

| | | |
|---|---|---|
| Direct Examination ................ | IV | 1944–1946 |
| Cross Examination ................ | | 1946–1947 |

BAUMANN, CHARLES O.:

| | | |
|---|---|---|
| Direct Examination ................ | V | 2864–2883 |
| Cross Examination ................ | | 2885–2891 |
| Redirect Examination .............. | | 2891–2892 |

BEACH, FREDERICK O.:

| | | |
|---|---|---|
| Direct Examination ................ | VI | 3328–3332 |
| Cross Examination ................ | | 3332–3335 |
| Redirect Examination .............. | | 3335–3337 |
| Recross Examination .............. | | 3337–3339 |

BENNETHUM, GEORGE W.:

| | | |
|---|---|---|
| Direct Examination ................ | II | 900– 904 |
| Cross Examination ................ | | 904– 905 |

BERST, J. A.:                                  VOL.    PAGE

   Direct Examination ................ III   1761–1790
   Direct Examination ................ IV    1947–1955
   Cross Examination .................        1955–1970

**Biograph Company:**

   Agreement, Preliminary, for Assign-
     ment of Patents between Biograph
     Co. and Patents Co., dated Dec. 18,
     1908; printed as Exhibit 1 to An-
     swer of Biograph Co.; Petitioner's
     Exhibit 3 ..................... I       15

   License Agreement under Camera and
     Film Patents between Patents Co.
     and Biograph Co., dated Dec. 18,
     1908; printed as Exhibit 3 to Peti-
     tion; Petitioner's Exhibit 6 ...... I    23

   Memorandum of Agreement between
     Biograph Co., Williams, Brown &
     Earle, Kleine Optical Co. and C. E.
     Dressler & Co., dated Feb. 18, 1908;
     Petitioner's Exhibit 57.......... I      140

   License Agreement under the Project-
     ing Machine Patents between Pat-
     ents Co. and Biograph Co., dated
     April 20, 1909; similar to Ex-
     hibit 5 to Petition ............. I      244

   Agreement between Armat Moving Pic-
     ture Co. and Biograph Co., re Let-
     ters Patent No. 586,953, dated Feb.
     19, 1904; Defendants' Exhibit 127 IV   2160

   Agreement between Armat Moving Pic-
     ture Co. and Biograph Co., dated
     March 21, 1908; Defendants' Ex-
     hibit 130 ..................... IV      2166

Biograph Co., Continued:    VOL.    PAGE

Agreement between Patents Co., Edison
Co. and Biograph Co., dated Feb.
14, 1911; Petitioner's Exhibit 136    I    643

Agreement between Biograph Co. and
General Film Co., dated April 21,
1910, similar to Exhibit 8 at page
116 of Petition................    I    552

License Agreement, June 6, 1912, between Patents Co. and Biograph
Co.; printed as Exhibit 3 to Answer of Patents Co.; Defendants'
Exhibit 47 ....................    III    1309

License Agreement, dated June 20, 1913,
between Patents Co. and Biograph
Co.; similar to Defendants' Ex-
hibit 48 ......................    III    1310

Supplemental License Agreement, Patents Co. and Biograph Co., dated
Jan. 26, 1909; printed as Exhibit
2 to Answer of Patents Co.; Defendants' Exhibit 49............    III    1329

Contract dated April 21, 1910, between
Biograph Co. and General Film Co.,
relating to common stock of General Film Co. owned by Biograph
Co.; Petitioner's Exhibit 242 ....    III    1682

Letter to Editor of Moving Picture
World from Biograph Co., pub-
lished in issue of March 23, 1907;
Petitioner's Exhibit 56..........    I    136

BIOGRAPH CO., Continued:                    VOL.     PAGE

  Statement entitled "The Facts" or "Bio-
    graph Company Define Their Posi-
    tion," issued to the Trade by Bio-
    graph Co., published in Moving Pic-
    ture World March 14, 1908; Peti-
    tioner's Exhibit 55.............    I      132
  See also ........................    VI     3310

  Statement entitled "The Position of the
    American Mutoscope & Biograph
    Co.," published in Moving Picture
    World Feb. 15, 1908, signed by H.
    N. Marvin and J. J. Kennedy; Pe-
    titioner's Exhibit 54...........    I      131
  See also ........................    VI     3310

BLACKTON, J. S.:

  Direct Examination ...............    IV     1873–1887
  Direct Examination ...............           1984–1996
  Cross Examination ................           2080–2091

BOEHRINGER, E.:

  Direct Examination ...............    V      2838–2841
  Cross Examination ................           2841
  Redirect Examination .............           2842

BOONE, ACTON R.:

  Direct Examination ...............    II     1205–1209
  Cross Examination ................           1210–1211
  Redirect Examination .............           1211–1212
  Redirect Examination .............           1213–1214
  Recross Examination ..............           1212–1213
  Recross Examination ..............           1214–1216

BOYER, CHARLES W.:

  Direct Examination ...............    II     1019–1022
  Cross Examination ................           1023–1027

BRADEN, JOHN:

  Direct Examination ...............    II     992– 993
  Cross Examination ................           993– 994

BRALEY, ORA L.:                           VOL.     PAGE

Direct Examination ............... V    2636–2641
Cross Examination ................        2641–2642

BRANDON, WILLIAM C.:

Direct Examination ............... IV   2385–2390
Cross Examination ................        2571–2574

BRANDT, WILLIAM:

Direct Examination ............... IV   1887–1890
Cross Examination ................        1890–1892
Redirect Examination .............        1892–1893

BRICK, ALFRED D.:

Direct Examination ............... VI   3418
Cross Examination ................        3419–3420
Redirect Examination .............        3420

BROWN, FLOYD:

Direct Examination ............... V    2750–2760
Cross Examination ................        2760–2763
Redirect Examination .............        2763
Redirect Examination .............        2764–2765
Redirect Examination .............        2767
Recross Examination ..............        2764
Recross Examination ..............        2765–2766

BROWN, THOMAS A.:

Direct Examination ............... V    2722–2724
Cross Examination ................        2725–2731

BRULATOUR, JULES E.:

Direct Examination ............... VI   3420
Cross Examination ................        3421–3422
Redirect Examination .............        3422–3423
Redirect Examination .............        3425
Recross Examination ..............        3423
Recross Examination ..............        3423–3425

BRYLAWSKI, AARON:                          VOL.     PAGE

Direct Examination ............... VI     3239–3246
Cross Examination ................         3246–3248
Redirect Examination .............         3248

CARLTON, JAMES L.:

Direct Examination ............... II     770– 781
Cross Examination ................         799– 800

CHOYNSKI, MORRIS A.:

Direct Examination ............... V      2732–2737

CLAPHAM, A. J.:

Direct Examination ............... II     1028–1033
Cross Examination ................         1033–1057
Redirect Examination .............        1057
Recross Examination .............         1057

CLARK, JAMES B.:

Direct Examination ............... V      2576–2599
Cross Examination ................         2599–2605
Redirect Examination .............        2605–2606

COHEN, GEORGE:

Direct Examination ............... IV     1929–1937
Cross Examination ................         1937–1939
Redirect Examination .............        1939
Recross Examination .............         1939
Redirect Examination .............        1940

COLLIER, JOHN:

Direct Examination ............... V      2894–2910
Direct Examination ...............        2940–2941

COOK, FRANK:

Direct Examination ............... V      2703–2708
Cross Examination ................         2708–2709

CROSS, GLENN A.:                              VOL.     PAGE

    Direct Examination ................    V     2685–2689
    Cross Examination .................          2689

CUMMINGS, JOSEPH M.:

    Direct Examination ................    V     2809–2818
    Cross Examination .................          2819–2820
    Redirect Examination ..............          2820

DECREE APPOINTING EXAMINER............    I        1

DEFENDANTS' EVIDENCE ...............III–VI   1246–3326

DEFENDANTS' SURREBUTTAL ..............   VI     3427–3434

DENNISTON, JOSEPH R.:
    Direct Examination ................    V     2662–2666
    Cross Examination .................          2667

DEVERY, WILLIAM:

    Direct Examination ................   II      832– 857
    Cross Examination .................          984– 991
    Cross Examination .................          994–1001
    Redirect Examination ..............          1001–1004
    Redirect Examination ..............          1006
    Redirect Examination ..............          1089–1090
    Redirect Examination ..............          1092
    Recross Examination ...............          1004–1006
    Recross Examination ...............          1090–1092

DYER, F. L.:

    Direct Examination ................   III    1469–1650
    Cross Examination .................          1666–1684
    Redirect Examination ..............          1684–1686
    Redirect Examination ..............          1690
    Recross Examination ...............          1686–1690

    Article printed in Show World March
       21, 1908, entitled "Film Magnates
       in Chicago Conference; Edison
       Company Issues Important State-
       ment;" Petitioner's Exhibit 255..    V     2520

DYER, F. L., Continued:             VOL.     PAGE

Bulletin No. 27 of Film Service Association, being Letter dated Oct. 3, 1908, from F. L. Dyer to Dwight MacDonald regarding the return of old film to Manufacturers; Petitioner's Exhibit 97..............    I     430

Interview with Frank L. Dyer in Show World April 4, 1908, *re* the Latham Patent; Petitioner's Exhibit 173..   II    922

Testimony of F. L. Dyer in case of Greater New York Film Rental Co. v. Biograph Co. and General Film Co., in the District Court of the United States, Southern District of New York, Oct. 23, 1913; Petitioner's Exhibit 275.............   VI   3376

Testimony of F. L. Dyer in case of Motion Picture Patents Co. v. Independent Moving Picture Co., Feb. 27, 1911; Petitioner's Exhibit 172   II    919

**Eastman Kodak Company:**

Agreement, Patents Co., Edison Mfg. Co. and Eastman Kodak Co., Jan. 1, 1909; Petitioner's Exhibit 133..    I     558

Agreement, Patents Co. and Eastman Kodak Co., dated Jan. 15, 1909; Petitioner's Exhibit 134........    I     582

Agreement, Patents Co., Edison Mfg. Co. and Eastman Kodak Co., Feb. 14, 1911; Petitioner's Exhibit 135.    I     632

Opinion of Judge Coxe in the case of The Goodwin Film & Camera Co. v. Eastman Kodak Co., United States Circuit Court of Appeals, Second Circuit; Petitioner's Exhibit 267 .....................   VI   3294

**Edison Manufacturing Company:**     VOL.     PAGE

Agreement, Preliminary, for Assignment of Patents between Patents
Co. and Edison Mfg. Co., dated
Dec. 18, 1908, printed as Exhibit 2
to Petition; Petitioner's Exhibit 2     I     15

License Agreement under Camera and
Film Patents, Patents Co. and Edison Mfg. Co., Dec. 18, 1908; similar to Exhibit 3 to Petition; Peti-
tioner's Exhibit 6 . . . . . . . . . . . . . .     I     23

Agreement between Edison Mfg. Co. and
Kalem Co., dated Jan. 31, 1908,
printed as Exhibit 1 to Answer of
T. A. Edison, Inc.; similar agree-
ments were executed by the other
Edison licensees, Pathe, Lubin,
Selig, Essanay, Vitagraph and
Melies; Petitioner's Exhibit 92. . .     I     356

License Agreement under the Projecting Machine Patents between Patents Co. and Edison Mfg. Co.,
dated Jan. 7, 1909; similar to Ex-
hibit 5 to Petition . . . . . . . . . . . . . .     I     244

Agreement between Patents Co., Edison
Mfg. Co. and Eastman Kodak Co.,
dated Jan. 1, 1909; Petitioner's
Exhibit 133 . . . . . . . . . . . . . . . . . . .     I     558

Agreement between Patents Co., Edison
Mfg. Co. and Eastman Kodak Co.,
dated Feb. 14, 1911; Petitioner's
Exhibit 135 . . . . . . . . . . . . . . . . . . .     I     632

Agreement between Edison Mfg. Co. and
General Film Co., dated April 21,
1910, printed as Exhibit 8 on page
116 of Petition. . . . . . . . . . . . . . . .     I     552

EDISON MFG. CO., Continued:        VOL.     PAGE

Agreement between Patents Co., Edison
    Mfg. Co. and Biograph Co., dated
    Feb. 14, 1911; Petitioner's Ex-
    hibit 136 .....................    I      643

Agreement, dated Dec. 7, 1904, between
    Paley and Steiner, Melies, Pathe
    and Schneider, about defense of
    suits on Edison patents; Defend-
    ants' Exhibit 112 ..............  III    1765

Supplemental License Agreement, Pat-
    ents Co. and Edison Mfg. Co., dated
    on or about Jan. 26, 1909; similar
    to Exhibit 2 to Answer of Pat-
    ents Co.; Defendants' Exhibit 49..  III   1329

License Agreement between Patents
    Co. and Edison Mfg. Co., dated
    June 6, 1912; similar to Exhibit 3
    to Answer of Patents Co.; Defend-
    ants' Exhibit 47................  III    1309

License Agreement, dated June 20, 1913,
    between Patents Co. and Edison
    Mfg. Co.; similar to Defendants'
    Exhibit 48 ....................   III    1310

Article entitled "The Mechanism," from
    pages 8 and 9 of Edison Catalogue,
    Form 300, regarding Projecting
    Kinetoscopes, March 15, 1906; Pe-
    titioner's Exhibit 236a (p. 1652).  III   1663

Article printed in The Show World
    March 7, 1908, entitled "Opposing
    Moving Picture Interests Fire
    First Guns in Great War for Su-
    premacy"; Petitioner's Exhibit
    263 ..........................     V     2503

EDISON MFG. CO., Continued:  VOL.  PAGE

Article in Show World May 16, 1908,
  entitled "Film Battle Waged in
  Court; Arguments Heard and War
  is Stayed by Agreement. Attorneys Consent to Truce," etc., *re*
  case of Kleine Optical Co. v. Edison Mfg. Co., by H. J. Streyckmans; Petitioner's Exhibit 259...  V  2545

Article in Show World March 28, 1908,
  entitled "Edison Fires Second Gun
  in Film Battle"; Petitioner's Exhibit 256 ......................  V  2528

Article printed in Show World May 2,
  1908, entitled "Film Association
  Announces Victory in Edison Litigation;" Petitioner's Exhibit 258  V  2541

Catalogues of Edison Co., Forms 300,
  320, 335, 410, 470 and 500; Petitioner's Exhibits for identification
  236a to 241, inclusive ..........  III  1152

Form of Contract used by the Edison
  Licensees in 1908 in Dealing with
  Film Exchanges; Petitioner's Ex-
  hibit 91 ......................  I  350

Kleine's Answer in case Edison Mfg.
  Co. v. Kleine Optical Co., in Circuit Court for the Northern District of Illinois, in suit on Reissue
  Patent 12,192, April 2, 1908; Petitioner's Exhibit 171.............  II  906

Label used by Edison on Film Prior to
  the Reissue of the Film Patent;
  Defendants' Exhibit 105.........  III  1492

Label used by Edison on Film after the
  Reissue of the Film Patent; Defendants' Exhibit 106...........  III  1493

EDISON MFG. CO., Continued: VOL. PAGE

Opinion of the Circuit Court of Appeals, 2nd Circuit, in the first case on the Camera and Film Patent No. 589,168, between the Edison and Biograph Cos., and reported in 114 Fed., 926; Opinion by Circuit Judge Wallace; Petitioner's Exhibit 58 ...................... I 151

Opinion of the Circuit Court of Appeals, 2nd Circuit, in the second case on the Camera Patent, Reissue No. 12,037, reported in 151 Fed., 767; Opinion by Circuit Judge Lacombe; Petitioner's Exhibit 59... I 166

Opinion of Judge Kohlsaat in Thomas A. Edison v. Selig Polyscope Co., on Reissue 12037, filed Jan. 29, 1910, as of Oct. 24, 1907, in the U. S. Circuit Court for the Northern District of Illinois, Eastern Division; Defendants' Exhibit 111 III 1617

Reissued Letters Patent No. 12,192, dated Jan. 12, 1904, printed as Exhibit 9 on page 123 of Petition. See, also, Defendants' Exhibit 187 VI 3326

Writ of Injunction, dated Nov. 1, 1907, out of Circuit Court for Northern District of Illinois, Eastern Division, on the part of T. A. Edison directed to Selig Polyscope Co., on Reissue Letters Patent No. 12,037; Defendants' Exhibit 113 ........ IV 1979

Writ of Injunction, dated Sept. 18, 1900, out of Circuit Court for the Southern District of New York, on the part of T. A. Edison directed to Vitagraph Co. and another, on Letters Patent No. 589,168; Defendants' Exhibit 114............ IV 1985

EDISON MFG. Co., Continued.    VOL.    PAGE

Writ of Injunction, dated Jan. 8, 1903,
out of Circuit Court for the Southern District of New York on the
part of Armat Moving Picture Co.,
directed to Edison Mfg. Co., on
Letters Patent No. 586,953; Defendants' Exhibit 126............ IV   2136

EDWARDS, CALVIN S.:

Direct Examination ................ IV   2365–2374
Cross Examination ................    2374–2382
Redirect Examination ..............    2382–2383
Recross Examination ..............    2383–2385
Recross Examination ..............    2463

ENSOR, J. M.:

Direct Examination ................ II   1126–1135
Cross Examination ................    1135–1137
Redirect Examination ..............    1137–1138

**Essanay Film Manufacturing Company:**

License Agreement under Camera and
Film Patents, Patents Co. and
Essanay Mfg. Co., Dec. 18, 1908,
similar to Exhibit 3 to Petition;
Petitioner's Exhibit 6 .......... I    23

Agreement between Essanay Film Mfg.
Co. and General Film Co., dated
April 21, 1910, similar to Exhibit
8 on page 116 of the Petition...... I    552

Agreement between Edison Mfg. Co.
and Essanay Film Mfg. Co., dated
Jan. 31, 1908, similar to Exhibit
1 to Answer of T. A. Edison, Inc.;
Petitioner's Exhibit 92 .......... I    356

ESSANAY FILM MFG. CO., Continued.  VOL.  PAGE

License Agreement between Patents
Co. and Essanay Mfg. Co., dated
June 6, 1912, similar to Exhibit
3 to Answer of Patents Co.; Defendants' Exhibit 47 ............ III  1309

Supplemental License Agreement, Patents Co. and Essanay Mfg. Co.,
dated on or about Jan. 26, 1909,
similar to Exhibit 2 to Answer of
Patents Co.; Defendants' Exhibit
49 .......................... III  1329

License Agreement, dated June 20, 1913,
Patents Co. and Essanay Mfg. Co.;
similar to Defendants' Exhibit 48 III  1310

ETRIS, ROBERT:
Direct Examination ................ IV  2058–2064
Direct Examination ................  2112–2116
Cross Examination ................  2186–2196
Redirect Examination .............  2196–2197
Recross Examination .............  2197

EVANS, JOHN G.:
Direct Examination ................ V  2857–2858
Cross Examination ................  2859
Redirect Examination .............  2859

**Exhibits, Petitioner's:**

VOL.   PAGE

1   Charter of Motion Picture Patents Co., dated Sept. 9, 1908, printed as Exhibit 1 to the Petition.................   I     14

2   Preliminary Agreement for Assignment of Patents—Patents Co. and Edison Mfg. Co., Dec. 18, 1908, Exhibit 2 to the Petition ........................   I     15

3   Preliminary Agreement for Assignment of Patents—Patents Co. and Biograph Co., Dec. 18, 1908, Exhibit 1 to Answer of Biograph Co. ..................   I     15

4   Preliminary Agreement for Assignment of Patents—Patents Co. and Armat Co., Dec. 18, 1908, Exhibit 1 to Answer of Armat Co. .....................   I     15

5   Preliminary Agreement for Assignment of Patents—Patents Co. and Vitagraph Co., Dec. 18, 1908.................   I     16

6   License Agreement under Camera and Film Patents, Patents Co. and Biograph Co., Dec. 18, 1908, Exhibit 3 to Petition ........................   I     23

CIRCULAR LETTERS TO FILM RENTAL EXCHANGES, ISSUED BY THE PATENTS CO., EXHIBITS 7 TO 33.

7   Circular to Film Rental Exchanges, Jan. 9, 1909 ........................   I     29

8   Circular to Film Rental Exchanges, Jan. 12, 1909, and Copy of Exchange License Agreement .................   I     36

9   Circular by Patents Co. to Licensed Exchanges, re List of Licensed Exhibitors, Feb. 5, 1909.................   II    930

PETITIONER'S EXHIBITS, Continued:                VOL.   PAGE

10  Circular to Licensed Film Rental Ex-
     changes, Jan. 30, 1909..............    I      45

11  Circular to Licensed Film Rental Ex-
     changes, Feb. 8, 1909...............    I      47

12  Circular to Licensed Film Rental Ex-
     changes, Feb. 10, 1909..............    I      50

13  Circular to Licensed Exchanges, Feb. 24,
     1909, being a list of Licensed Manu-
     facturers, Importers, and Exchanges.    I      52

14  Circular to Licensed Exchanges, Feb. 27,
     1909, being a list of Licensed Manufac-
     turers of Moving Picture Machines...    I      59

15  Exchange Bulletin No. 1, Feb. 26, 1909..   I      60

16  Exchange Bulletin No. 2, March 3, 1909..   I      61

17  Exchange Bulletin No. 3, March 20, 1909.   I      64

18  Exchange Bulletin No. 5, April 7, 1909..   I      66

19  Exchange Bulletin No. 8, May 15, 1909..    I      69

20  Exchange Bulletin No. 10, July 27, 1909.   I      71

21  Exchange Bulletin No. 11, Aug. 21, 1909.   I      72

22  Exchange Bulletin No. 14, Aug. 23, 1909.   I      73

23  Exchange Bulletin No. 16, Sept. 7, 1909.   I      74

24  Exchange Bulletin No. 18, Dec. 4, 1909..   I      75

25  Exchange Bulletin No. 22, April 19, 1910.  I      76

26  Exchange Bulletin No. 23, April 23, 1910.  I      77

PETITIONER's EXHIBITS, Continued:    VOL.   PAGE

27  Exchange Bulletin No. 25, July 19, 1910.    I    78

28  Exchange Bulletin No. 26, Sept. 14, 1910.    I    78

29  Exchange Bulletin No. 28, Nov. 21, 1910.    I    79

30  Exchange Bulletin No. 29, Nov. 22, 1910.    I    80

31  Exchange Bulletin No. 30, Jan. 3, 1911..    I    80

32  Exchange Bulletin No. 32, June 30, 1911.    I    81

33  Exchange Bulletin No. 33, Sept. 13, 1911.    I    82

CIRCULAR LETTERS AND BULLETINS
TO LICENSED EXHIBITORS ISSUED
BY THE PATENTS CO. EXHIBITS 34–53.

34  Circular Letter to exhibitors of moving
    pictures, Jan. 22, 1909, giving a list of
    licensed manufacturers, importers and
    exchanges ......................    I    87

35  Exhibitors' Application, January, 1909..    I    94

36  Notice to Exhibitors, Jan. 27, 1909......    I    95

37  Circular to Exhibitors from Licensed Ex-
    changes, Jan. 27, 1909..............    I    97

38  Circular Letter, Feb. 1, 1909...........    I    97

39  Circular Letter, Feb. 2, 1909...........    I    99

40  Form used in writing to an exhibitor rel-
    ative to the opening of a new theatre
    in his vicinity ...................    I    102

41  Printed form of Letter used by Patents
    Co., early in 1909, in Refusing to Re-
    fund License Fee .................    I    102

PETITIONER'S EXHIBITS, Continued:  VOL.  PAGE

42  Licensed Exhibitor's Certificate.........  I  103

43  Exhibitors' Bulletin No. 1, Feb. 15, 1909..  I  104

44  Exhibitors' Bulletin No. 2, Feb. 27, 1909  I  105

45  Exhibitors' Bulletin No. 3, Mar. 20, 1909  I  108

46  Exhibitors' Bulletin No. 4, April 7, 1909  I  111

47  Exhibitors' Bulletin No. 5, Sept. 15, 1909  I  112

48  Exhibitors' Bulletin No. 6, Dec. 6, 1909..  I  114

49  Exhibitors' Bulletin No. 7, Mar. 16, 1910  I  115

50  Exhibitors' Bulletin No. 8, May 10, 1910  I  115

51  Exhibitors' Bulletin No. 9, June 1, 1910.  I  116

52  Exhibitors' Bulletin No. 10, July 2, 1910.  I  116

53  Exhibitors' Bulletin No. 12, May 29, 1911  I  117

54  A statement by H. N. Marvin and J. J.
    Kennedy, entitled "The Position of the
    American Mutoscope and Biograph
    Co.," published in the Moving Picture
    World, Vol. 2, p. 112, in the issue of
    Feb. 15, 1908.....................  I  131
    See also .........................  VI  3310

55  A statement entitled "The Facts," issued
    to the trade by the Biograph Co. and
    published in the Moving Picture
    World, Vol 2, p. 205, issue of March
    14, 1908 ........................  I  132
    See also .........................  VI  3310

56  Letter to Editor Moving Picture World
    from American Mutoscope and Bio-
    graph Co., published in issue of March
    23, 1907, Vol. 1, p. 43..............  I  136

PETITIONER'S EXHIBITS, Continued: VOL. PAGE

57 Memorandum of Agreement between American Mutoscope and Biograph Co. and Williams, Brown & Earle, Kleine Optical Co. and Charles E. Dressler & Co., dated Feb. 18, 1908............... I 140

58 Opinion of the Circuit Court of Appeals, 2nd Circuit, in the first case on the camera and film patent No. 589,168, between the Edison and Biograph Cos., and reported in 114 Fed., 926, opinion by Circuit Judge Wallace........... I 151

59 Opinion of the Circuit Court of Appeals, 2nd Circuit, in the second case on the camera patent, Reissue No. 12,037, reported in 151 Fed., 767, opinion by Circuit Judge Lacombe............... I 166

60 Opinion of the Circuit Court of Appeals, District of Columbia, on Reissue No. 12,192, the film patent, opinion by Chief Justice Shepard ............. 1 175

61 List of film exchanges whose licenses have been cancelled or terminated by the Motion Picture Patents Co.......... I 188

62 Statement showing price and dates of delivery of exchange equipment and stock of motion pictures and merchandise bought by General Film Co. (See also, Defendants' Exhibit 172, Vol. VI, p. 3200.) ................. I 190

63 List of branches of General Film Co. on Jan. 12, 1912..................... I 199
    See also, Defendants' Exhibit 108...... III 1608

64 Extracts from By-Laws of General Film Co. .............................. I 201

PETITIONER'S EXHIBITS, Continued:          VOL.   PAGE

65  Letter, Thomas Armat to H. N. Marvin,
       July 30, 1908......................   I    234

66  Letter, H. N. Marvin to Thomas Armat,
       Oct. 5, 1908......................    I    235

67  Letter, H. N. Marvin to Frank L. Dyer,
       Oct. 28, 1908.....................    I    236

68  Letter, Kleine Optical Co. to H. N. Mar-
       vin, Oct. 30, 1908.................    I    237

69  Letter, H. N. Marvin to George Kleine,
       Nov. 2, 1908......................    I    238

70  Letter, H. N. Marvin to George Kleine,
       Nov. 6, 1908 .....................    I    241

71  Letter, H. N. Marvin to George Kleine,
       Nov. 23, 1908.....................    I    242

72  Letter, H. N. Marvin to Frank L. Dyer,
       Nov. 23, 1908.....................    I    243

73  Letter, H. N. Marvin to Thomas Armat,
       Nov. 24, 1908.....................    I    244

74  Letter, Thomas Armat to H. N. Marvin,
       Nov. 23, 1908.....................    I    245

75  Letter, George F. Scull to H. N. Marvin,
       Dec. 24, 1908.....................    I    246

76  Letter, George F. Scull to H. N. Marvin,
       Dec. 30, 1908.....................    I    248

77  Extract from testimony given by defend-
       ant H. N. Marvin July 9, 1910, in case
       of Motion Picture Patents Co. v. Chi-
       cago Film Exchange...............    I    249

PETITIONER'S EXHIBITS, Continued:    VOL.  PAGE

78  Letter, J. J. Kennedy to Wm. Pelzer, Jan.
    23, 1912 .........................    I    251

79  Extracts from Minutes of a meeting of di-
    rectors of General Film Co. on June
    23, 1910 .........................    I    262

80  Minutes of a regular meeting of the Board
    of Directors of the General Film Co.,
    held Oct. 11, 1910.................    I    265

81  Minutes of a regular meeting of the Board
    of Directors of the General Film Co.,
    held Nov. 10, 1910.................    I    271

82  Minutes of a regular meeting of the Board
    of Directors of the General Film Co.,
    held Dec. 19, 1910, at 80 Fifth Avenue    I    273

83  Minutes of a regular meeting of the Board
    of Directors of the General Film Co.,
    held at 80 Fifth Avenue, Jan. 16, 1911    I    278

84  Minutes of a regular meeting of the Board
    of Directors of the General Film Co.,
    held at 80 Fifth Avenue, March 13,
    1911 .............................    I    281

85  Minutes of a meeting of the Board of Di-
    rectors of the General Film Co., held
    at 80 Fifth Avenue, March 15, 1911...    I    286

86  Minutes of an adjourned meeting of the
    Board of Directors of the General Film
    Co., held at 80 Fifth Avenue, April
    18, 1911 .........................    I    287

87  Minutes of an adjourned meeting of the
    Board of Directors of the General Film
    Co., Aug. 14, 1911.................    I    289

PETITIONER'S EXHIBITS, Continued:  VOL.  PAGE

88  Form of notice to suspend service of theatres sent by Motion Picture Patents
Co. to exchanges ...................  I  336

89  Another form of notice to suspend service of theatres by Motion Picture Patents Co. to exchanges...............  I  337

90  List of members of Film Service Association .............................  I  343

91  Copy of form of contract used by the Edison licensees in 1908 in dealing with
film exchanges ...................  I  350

92  Copy of agreement between the Edison
Mfg. Co. and Kalem Co., Jan. 31,
1908. Similar agreements were executed by each of the Edison licensees.
This exhibit is printed as Exhibit No.
1, to answer of Thomas A. Edison,
Inc. ............................  I  356

93  Advertisement of a special feature production (by Kalem Co., for July 1,
1912) .........................  I  375

94  Names of manufacturers of films and
prices in 1907 to Greater New York
Film Rental Co. ..................  I  382

95  Names of manufacturers of projecting machines and prices of same to Greater
New York Film Rental Co., 1907-1912  I  384

96  Letter, George Kleine to Greater New
York Film Rental Co., Jan. 23, 1909  I  384

97  Bulletin No. 27 of Film Service Association, being letter dated Oct. 3, 1908,
Frank L. Dyer to Dwight MacDonald
regarding the return of old film to
manufacturers ...................  I  430

PETITIONER'S EXHIBITS, Continued: VOL. PAGE

98 Form of contract between rental exchange and exhibitors used by the Greater New York Film Rental Co. during the period of the Film Service Association I 431

99 Bulletin No. 1, Film Service Association, Feb. 14, 1908 ...................... I 437

100 Bulletin No. 2, Film Service Association, Feb. 24, 1908..................... I 439

101 Bulletin No. 10, Film Service Association, March 24, 1908................... I 441

102 Bulletin No. 14, Film Service Association, April 20, 1908 ................... I 442

103 Letter, Motion Picture Patents Co. to Greater New York Film Rental Co., July 13, 1910..................... I 448

104 Letter, Motion Picture Patents Co. to Greater New York Film Rental Co., July 21, 1911..................... I 449

105 Letter, Motion Picture Patents Co. to Greater New York Film Rental Co., Sept. 13, 1909.................... I 451

106 Letter, Motion Picture Patents Co. to Greater New York Film Rental Co., Sept. 23, 1909.................... I 452

107 Letter, Motion Picture Patents Co. to Greater New York Film Rental Co., Sept. 23, 1909.................... I 452

108 Letter, Motion Picture Patents Co. to Greater New York Film Rental Co., Sept. 30, 1909..................... I 453

PETITIONER'S EXHIBITS, Continued:          VOL.   PAGE

109  Letter, Motion Picture Patents Co. to
     Greater New York Film Rental Co.,
     Sept. 30, 1909.....................   I     454

110  Letter, Motion Picture Patents Co. to
     People's Amusement Palace, Sept. 22,
     1909 ..............................   I     455

111  Letter, Motion Picture Patents Co. to
     Greater New York Film Rental Co.,
     Sept. 30, 1909.....................   I     456

112  Letter, Motion Picture Patents Co. to
     Greater New York Film Rental Co.,
     Sept. 30, 1909.....................   I     457

113  Letter, Motion Picture Patents Co. to
     Greater New York Film Rental Co.,
     Nov. 16, 1909......................   I     458

114  Letter, Motion Picture Patents Co. to
     Greater New York Film Rental Co.,
     Nov. 26, 1909......................   I     459

115  Letter, Motion Picture Patents Co. to
     Greater New York Film Rental Co.,
     Nov. 18, 1909......................   I     460

116  Letter, Motion Picture Patents Co. to
     Greater New York Film Rental Co.,
     Nov. 26, 1909......................   I     461

117  Letter, Motion Picture Patents Co. to
     Greater New York Film Rental Co.,
     Dec. 29, 1909......................   I     462

118  Letter, Motion Picture Patents Co. to
     Greater New York Film Rental Co.,
     Jan. 27, 1910......................   I     463

PETITIONER'S EXHIBITS, Continued:                VOL.  PAGE

119  Letter, Motion Picture Patents Co. to
     Greater New York Film Rental Co.,
     Feb. 14, 1910......................    I    464

120  Letter, Motion Picture Patents Co. to
     Greater New York Film Rental Co.,
     March 15, 1910.....................    I    465

121  Letter, General Film Co. to Norten &
     Gentile, Nov. 13, 1912 (see also IV,
     2191) .............................    I    467

122  Letter, Kalem Co. to Greater New York
     Film Rental Co., June 24, 1910......    I    469

123  Telegram, Selig Polyscope Co. to Greater
     New York Film Rental Co., April 29,
     1912 .............................    I    470

124  Pink card, issued by Patents Co., being a
     notice to suspend service of a theatre,
     June 9, 1911 ....................    I    472

125  Pink card, issued by Patents Co., being a
     notice to suspend service of a theatre.    I    473

126  Pink card, issued by Patents Co., being a
     notice to suspend service of a theatre,
     Sept. 14, 1911....................    I    473

127  License agreement between Motion Pic-
     ture Patents Co. and Gaumont Co.,
     March 2, 1909 ....................    I    398

128  List of preferred stockholders of General
     Film Co. for 1912.................    I    541

129  List of officers and directors of General
     Film Co. as of Jan. 1st, 1912.........    I    546

PETITIONER'S EXHIBITS, Continued:                VOL.    PAGE

130  Agreement between Patents Co. and Gen-
     eral Film Co., dated April 21, 1910,
     printed as Exhibit No. 7 to the petition    I    547

131  Statement of the undivided net profits of
     the General Film Co. credited to man-
     ufacturers, after payment of dividends,
     Dec. 30, 1911.....................    I    548

132  Distribution of undivided net profits of
     General Film Co. for years 1910 and
     1911 credited after payment of divi-
     dends on preferred and common stock
     on basis of feet of film leased from li-
     censed manufacturers .............    I    549

133  Agreement between Motion Picture Pat-
     ents Co., Edison Mfg. Co. and East-
     man Kodak Co., Jan. 1, 1909........    I    558

134  Agreement between Motion Picture Pat-
     ents Co. and Eastman Kodak Co., June
     15, 1909 ........................    I    582

135  Agreement, Patents Co., Edison Co., and
     Eastman Kodak Co., Feb. 14, 1911...    I    632

136  Agreement, Patents Co., Edison Co., and
     Biograph Co., Feb. 14, 1911........    I    643

137  Letter, Motion Picture Patents Co. to
     Greater New York Film Rental Co.,
     Nov. 14, 1911 ....................    II    672

138  Letter, Motion Picture Patents Co., to
     Greater New York Film Rental Co.,
     Dec. 1, 1911.....................    II    688

139  Letter, Pathe Freres to Greater New
     York Film Rental Film Co., Nov. 20,
     1911 ...........................    II    689

PETITIONER'S EXHIBITS, Continued: VOL. PAGE

140 Letter, Motion Picture Patents Co. to
Greater New York Film Rental Co.,
Dec. 7, 1911...................... II 692

141 Letter, Motion Picture Patents Co. to
Greater New York Film Rental Co.,
May 16, 1912..................... II 694

142 Letter, Motion Picture Patents Co. to
Greater New York Film Rental Co.,
Feb. 13, 1913.................... II 696

143 For identification. Extract from Pam-
phlet entitled "Edison Projecting
Kinetoscopes" ................... II 801

144 Check of Lewis M. Swaab, dated Philadelphia May 30, 1910, payable to the
order of Motion Picture Patents Co... II 804

145 Letter, Motion Picture Patents Co. to
Lewis M. Swaab, May 12, 1910...... II 805

146 Letter, Lewis M. Swaab to Motion Picture
Patents Co., May 13, 1910.......... II 805

147 Letter, Motion Picture Patents Co. to
Lewis M. Swaab, May 26, 1910...... II 806

148 Letter, Lewis M. Swaab to H. N. Marvin,
Pres. Motion Picture Patents Co., May
27, 1910 ......................... II 806

149 Letter, Motion Picture Patents Co. to
Lewis M. Swaab, May 28, 1910...... II 807

150 Letter, Lewis M. Swaab to Motion Picture
Patents Co., May 30, 1910.......... II 808

151 (Skipped)

PETITIONER'S EXHIBITS, Continued:                VOL.   PAGE

152  Correspondence between Lewis M. Swaab
     and General Film Co. from Aug. 6th
     to Aug. 29, 1910.................... II    816

152a Letter, Motion Picture Patents Co. to
     Lewis M. Swaab, Dec. 21, 1910...... II    819

152b Letter, Lewis M. Swaab to Motion Picture
     Patents Co., Dec. 22, 1910.......... II    820

152c Letter, Lewis M. Swaab to J. A. Berst,
     Dec. 23, 1910..................... II    821

153  Telegram, J. A. Berst to L. M. Swaab,
     Dec. 15, 1910 .................... II    818

154  Telegram, L. M. Swaab to J. A. Berst,
     Dec. 16, 1910..................... II    819

155  Letter, Motion Picture Patents Co. to
     Louis M. Swaab, Jan. 3, 1911........ II    823

156  Statement entitled "Special Payments
     Made by Licensed Exchange Ex-
     hibitors" (not introduced) ........ II    830

157  Report of Special Master in the Matter
     of Imperial Film Exchange, an alleged
     bankrupt, June 20, 1910............ II    841

158  Order of District Judge Hough in the
     Matter of Imperial Film Exchange,
     an alleged bankrupt, dated June 28,
     1910 ............................. II    853

159  Letter, Motion Picture Patents Co. to
     Wm. J. Anderson, Dec. 8, 1910....... II    864

PETITIONER'S EXHIBITS, Continued:  VOL.  PAGE

160 Letter, Motion Picture Patents Co. to
Wm. J. Anderson, Dec. 30, 1910..... II 865

161 Letter, Motion Picture Patents Co. to
Imp. Theatre, Uniontown, Pa., Sept.
14, 1912.......................... II 868

162 Letter, Pathe Freres to Chas. H. Balsley,
Sept. 7, 1912..................... II 874

163 Letter, Chas. H. Balsley to Pathe Freres,
Jan. 1, 1913...................... II 875

164 Letter, Pathe Freres to Chas. H. Balsley,
Jan. 3, 1913...................... II 875

165 Letter, Chas. H. Balsley to Motion Picture Patents Co., Jan. 6, 1913....... II 876

166 Letter, Motion Picture Patents Co. to
Chas. H. Balsley, Jan. 9, 1913....... II 876

167 Letter, General Film Co. to Wm. J. Anderson, Jan. 16, 1911................. II 867

168 Letter, Motion Picture Patents Co. to
G. W. Bennethum, Nov. 15, 1911..... II 901

169 Letter, Geo. W. Bennethum to Motion
Picture Patents Co., Nov. 20, 1911.... II 902

170 Letter, Motion Picture Patents Co. to
Geo. W. Bennethum, Nov. 27, 1911.... II 903

171 Kleine's Answer in case of Edison Mfg.
Co. v. Kleine Optical Co........... II 906

172 Testimony of Frank L. Dyer in case of
Motion Picture Patents Co. v. Independent Moving Picture Co., on Feb.
27, 1911 ......................... II 919

PETITIONER'S EXHIBITS, Continued:  VOL.  PAGE

173  Interview of Frank L. Dyer in The Show
     World of April 4, 1908, relating to
     the Latham Patent.................  II   922

174  Charter, General Film Company of New
     Jersey, Feb. 10, 1910...............  II   925

175  Letter, Kleine Optical Co. to Edison Mfg.
     Co., Feb. 19, 1908 .................  II   968

176  Letter, Lubin Mfg. Co. to Thos. H. Bates,
     April 10, 1911....................  II   971

177  Letter, Motion Picture Patents Co. to
     Thomas H. Bates, Oct. 20, 1911......  II   975

178  Letter, Thomas H. Bates to Motion Pic-
     ture Patents Co., Nov. 3, 1911.......  II   976

179  Letter, Motion Picture Patents Co. to
     Thos. H. Bates, Jan. 2, 1912.........  II   978

180  Letter, Motion Picture Patents Co. to
     Thomas H. Bates, Jan. 10, 1912......  II   978

181  Certificate given to Thomas H. Bates by
     Arthur F. Symonds, Mgr., Savoy
     Theatre, Boston, Oct. 13, 1911.......  II   982

182  Letter, Motion Picture Patents Co. to
     C. W. Boyer, Dec. 23, 1912..........  II  1020

183  Letter, Motion Picture Patents Co. to
     Rosedale Theatre, Chambersburg, Pa.,
     Jan. 11, 1913.....................  II  1021

184  Letter, Motion Picture Patents Co. to
     Rosedale Theatre, Jan. 14, 1913.......  II  1021

185  Letter Motion Picture Patents Co. to
     Chas. W. Boyer, Jan. 22, 1913.......  II  1022

PETITIONER's EXHIBITS, Continued:    VOL.    PAGE

186  Circular Letter of Motion Picture Patents Co. to exhibitors, *re* Standard Film Exchange, Sept. 22, 1910 ....... II    1061

187  Letter, Motion Picture Patents Co. to Standard Film Exchange, Sept. 15, 1909 ........................... II    1064

188  Letter, Motion Picture Patents Co. to Standard Film Exchange, Sept. 22, 1909 ........................... II    1065

189  Letter, Motion Picture Patents Co. to Standard Film Exchange, April 28, 1909 ........................... II    1070

190  Letter, Motion Picture Patents Co. to Standard Film Exchange, Sept. 30, 1909 ........................... II    1070

191  Letter, Motion Picture Patents Co. to Standard Film Exchange, Jan. 25, 1910 ........................... II    1071

192  Letter, Motion Picture Patents Co. to Standard Film Exchange, March 14, 1910 ........................... II    1072

193  Letter, Motion Picture Patents Co. to E. Soling, Chicago, Ill., May 2, 1910.. II    1073

194  Letter, Motion Picture Patents Co. to Standard Film Exchange, June 9, 1910 ........................... II    1074

195  Letter, Motion Picture Patents Co. to Standard Film Exchange, July 12, 1910 ........................... II    1075

196  Letter, Standard Film Exchange to Motion Picture Patents Co., July 15, 1910 ........................... II    1075

Petitioner's Exhibits, Continued:        VOL.    PAGE

197  Letter Motion Picture Patents Co. to
       Standard Film Exchange, July 19,
       1910 ............................    II    1076

198  Letter, General Film Company to Edgar
       Thorp, Aug. 9, 1911...............    II    1083

199  Letter, Edgar Thorp to General Film Co.,
       Aug. 10, 1911.....................    II    1084

200  Letter, General Film Co. to Edgar Thorp,
       Aug. 11, 1911.....................    II    1085

201  Letter, Motion Picture Patents Co. to
       Orpheum Theatre (Thorp), Aug. 16,
       1911 ............................    II    1086

202  Letter, MacDonald & Bostwick to Imperi-
       al Film Exchange, April 18, 1910....    II    1089

203  Letter, General Film Co. to J. H. Henry,
       Feb. 8, 1912.................    II    1102

204  Letter, General Film Co. to J. H. Henry,
       March 28, 1913...................    II    1103

205  Telegram, Motion Picture Patents Co. to
       Colorado Film Exchange Co., Sept.
       14, 1910..........................    II    1130

206  Circular letter to exhibitors on letter-
       head of General Film Company, dated
       Denver, Col., Sept. 15, 1910.........    II    1131

207  Letter, Motion Picture Patents Co. to J.
       M. Ensor & Co., June 20, 1913........    II    1138

208  Letter, Motion Picture Patents Co. to
       The Lake Shore Film & Supply Co.,
       Feb. 17, 1911.....................    II    1142

PETITIONER's EXHIBITS, Continued:  VOL. PAGE

209 Letter, Edison Mfg. Co. (Signed, Frank L. Dyer, V. P.), to The Lake Shore Film & Supply Co., Jan. 7, 1910......  II  1144

210 Copy of Letter signed J. J. Kennedy to The National-Vaudette Film Co., Detroit, Mich., Oct. 27, 1910...........  II  1146

211 Letter, John Pelzer to E. Mandelbaum, Jan. 18, 1911.....................  II  1148

212 Copy of Letter, Julius H. Michael to Motion Picture Patents Co., April 14, 1912 .............................  II  1158

213 Letter, Motion Picture Patents Co. to Grand Theatre, Cleveland, O., July 10, 1910 .............................  II  1159

214 Letter, Motion Picture Patents Co. to Philadelphia Film Exchange, Feb. 26, 1909 .............................  II  1164

215 Letter, American Mutoscope & Biograph Co. to Philadelphia Film Exchange, Feb. 27, 1909 ....................  II  1165

216 Telegram, Motion Picture Patents Co. to Frank A. Fisher, Philadelphia, Pa., Feb. 26, 1909.....................  II  1166

217 Affidavit of James J. Lodge in the case of Greater New York Film Rental Co. v. Motion Picture Patents Co., verified Dec. 15, 1911......................  II  1183

218 Statement made Jan. 11, 1912, by Durant Church to William Pelzer as to Replevin Suits instituted by Mr. Church (See Pet'r's Ex. 220, Vol. VI, p. 3341.)  II  1217

PETITIONER'S EXHIBITS, Continued:  VOL.  PAGE

219  Statement made by MacDonald & Bost-
     wick as to Replevin Suits instituted by
     Motion Picture Patents Co., and re-
     ferred to in Exhibit 218............  II  1217
     (See Pet'r's Ex. 220, Vol. VI, p.
     3341.)

220  Replevin Suits instituted by Manufactur-
     ers Licensed by Motion Picture Pat-
     ents Co., from March 11, 1909, to Jan.
     6, 1913 (being Statement Produced by
     Mr. Pelzer on Direct Examination—
     Vol. I, p. 389, introduced for identifi-
     cation Vol. II, p. 1217, and printed in
     Vol. VI) ........................  VI  3341

221  Letter, Motion Picture Patents Co. to
     Miles Brothers, April 21, 1910.......  II  1219

222  Exchange Bulletin, Motion Picture Pat-
     ents Co. to Miles Bros., Inc., March
     10, 1909 ........................  II  1220

223  Exchange Bulletin, Motion Picture Pat-
     ents Co., April 23, 1910, regarding
     cancellation of license of Miles Bros...  II  1221

224  Exchange Bulletin, Motion Picture Pat-
     ents Co., April 19, 1910, regarding
     cancellation of licenses of Miles Bros.
     and Imperial Film Exchange........  II  1222

225  Letter, Eastman Kodak Co. to Miles
     Bros., May 22, 1908...............  II  1223

226  Letter, Eastman Kodak Co. to Miles Bros.,
     June 12, 1908 ...................  II  1224

227  Letter, Motion Picture Patents Co. to
     Miles Bros., Dec. 21, 1909..........  II  1225

228  Telegram, Motion Picture Patents Co. to
     Western Film Exchange, July 19, 1910  II  1227

PETITIONER'S EXHIBITS, Continued:    VOL.   PAGE

229   Telegram, Motion Picture Patents Co. to
O. T. Crawford Film Exchange Co.,
July 19, 1910.....................   II   1228

230   Circular of Yale Film Exchange Co., to
Managers of Moving Picture Shows,
Kansas City, Mo., July 20, 1910......   II   1229

231   Bulletins Nos. 2 and 3, by Yale Film Exchange Co. to Moving Picture Exhib-
itors in St. Louis, Aug. 1, 1910......   II   1232

232   Telegram, Pathe Freres to Western Film
Exchange, St. Louis, Mo., July 20, 1910   II   1236

233   Letter, Motion Picture Patents Co. to
National Theatre, Cleveland, Ohio,
July 10, 1912.....................   II   1242

234   Letter, Motion Picture Patents Co. to
Novelty Theatre, Wichita, Kansas,
Dec. 5, 1912.....................   II   1242

235   List of Licenses Cancelled by Patents
Company on Account of Exhibition of
Unlicensed Motion Pictures, dated
March 21, 1913...................   II   1243

235   For identification. Memorandum used
by Marvin to Refresh his Recollection
with Reference to Cancellations, etc.,
of Exchanges.....................   III   1427

236   List of Theatres to which Patents Company Refused to Grant Licenses, dated
March 25, 1913...................   II   1243

237   List of Theatres whose Names were sent
to the Exchanges by Patents Company
with Statement that they should not
be Supplied with Service, dated March
25, 1913.........................   II   1243

PETITIONER'S EXHIBITS, Continued:          VOL.   PAGE

238  List of Theatres whose Licenses were
     Cancelled on Account of Loaning or
     Subrenting Licensed Motion Pictures,
     dated March 25, 1913..............   II    1243

239  List Showing new Licenses Granted to
     Theatres by Patents Company where
     the License had been Previously Can-
     celled, dated March 25, 1913........   II    1244

236a For identification.  Catalogue of Edison
     Mfg. Co., endorsed "Form 300, March
     15, 1906" ........................   III   1652

237a For identification.  Catalogue of Edison
     Mfg. Co., endorsed "Form 320, Feb-
     ruary 1, 1907" ...................   III   1654

238a For identification.  Catalogue of Edison
     Mfg. Co., endorsed "Form 335, Feb-
     ruary 15, 1908" ..................   III   1654

239a For identification.  Catalogue of Edison
     Mfg. Co., entitled "Edison Kineto-
     scopes" and endorsed "Form 410, De-
     cember 1, 1908" ..................   III   1656

240  For identification.  Catalogue of T. A.
     Edison, Incorporated, entitled "Edison
     Kinetoscopes" and endorsed "Form
     470, January 1, 1910"..............   III   1657

241  For identification.  Catalogue of T. A.
     Edison, Incorporated, entitled "Edison
     Kinetoscopes" and endorsed "Form
     500, August 1, 1911"..............   III   1657

242  Contract dated April 21, 1910, between
     Biograph Co. and General Film Co.  III   1682

PETITIONER'S EXHIBITS, Continued:                    VOL.   PAGE

243   Letter, General Film Co. to J. S. Bassett,
        Independence, Ia., May 9, 1911......   IV   2417

244   Letter, General Film Co. to J. S. Bassett,
        Independence, Ia., May 12, 1911......   IV   2418

245   Letter, General Film Co. to J. S. Bassett,
        Independence, Ia., May 16, 1911......   IV   2419

246   Letter, General Film Co. to J. S. Bassett,
        Independence, Ia., June 28, 1911.....   IV   2420

247   Letter, General Film Co. to J. S. Bassett,
        Independence, Ia., July 1, 1911......   IV.   2421

248   Letter, General Film Co. to J. S. Bassett,
        Independence, Ia., July 4, 1911......   IV   2422

249   Letter, General Film Co. to J. S. Bassett,
        Independence, Ia., July 8, 1911.......   IV   2422

250 Memorandum of Independent and Li-
        censed Theatres in Iowa and Nebras-
        ka, November, 1913...............   IV   2428

251   For Identification.   Memorandum book
        of witness Kinson showing towns in
        his territory and theatres in each
        town  ..........................   IV   2459

252   Advertisement printed in Moving Picture
        World Nov. 16, 1907, entitled "Con-
        vention of Manufacturers and Film
        Renters," re Meeting at Fort Pitt
        Hotel, Pittsburgh .................   V   2477

253   Article printed in Moving Picture World
        Nov. 23, 1907, entitled "The Pittsburgh
        Conference" ......................   V   2480

PETITIONER'S EXHIBITS, Continued:            VOL.   PAGE

254  Two Articles printed in Moving Picture
     World Feb. 15, 1908, *re* the Buffalo
     Meeting, entitled "The United Film
     Service Association and the Film Man-
     ufacturers" and "The Platform of the
     Association" ......................   V    2494

255  Article printed in Show World March 21,
     1908, entitled "Film Magnates in Chi-
     cago Conference; Edison Company Is-
     sues Important Statement" .........   V    2520

256  Article printed in Show World March 28,
     1908, entitled "Edison Fires Second
     Gun in Film Battle"...............   V    2528

257  Article printed in Show World April 25,
     1908, entitled "Important Bulletin of
     Film Association" ................   V    2536

258  Article printed in Show World May 2,
     1908, entitled "Film Association An-
     nounces Victory in Edison Litigation"   V    2541

259  Article printed in Show World May 16,
     1908, entitled "Film Battle Waged in
     Court; Arguments Heard and War is
     Stayed by Agreement. Attorneys Con-
     sent to Truce," etc., by H. J. Streyck-
     mans ...........................   V    2545

260  For identification. List of Theatres Us-
     ing Service from the Atlanta, Ga.,
     Branch of General Film Co., compris-
     ing eight sheets and a heading sheet,
     December, 1913 ..................   V    2574

261  For identification. List of Theatres Us-
     ing Service from the Memphis, Tenn.,
     Branch of General Film Co., also List
     of Independent Customers in Arkan-
     sas, Tennessee, Kentucky, Mississippi
     and Missouri, comprising eight sheets,
     December, 1913 .................   V    2574

PETITIONER'S EXHIBITS, Continued:    VOL.  PAGE

262  For identification. List of Motion Picture Theatres now Operating in Florida, Dec. 4, 1913, comprising two sheets  V  2574

263  Article printed in Show World March 7, 1908, entitled "Opposing Moving Picture Interests Fire First Guns in Great War for Supremacy".........  V  2503

263a  For identification. List of Towns Served by the Indianapolis Branch of General Film Co., giving number of Picture Theatres in each, Character of Service, and Whether Licensed or Unlicensed, December, 1913 ............  V  2763

264  Skipped.

265  Skipped.

266  Skipped.

267  Opinion of Judge Coxe in the case of The Goodwin Film & Camera Co. v. Eastman Kodak Co., United States Circuit Court of Appeals, Second Circuit.....  VI  3294

268  Book entitled "Motion Pictures, How They Are Made and Worked," by Frederick A. Talbot, published in 1912....  VI  3330

269  For identification. Munn & Company's Catalogue of Scientific and Technical Books for 1914....................  VI  3336

270  Book entitled "Romance of Modern Photography," by Charles R. Gibson, F. R. S. E. .........................  VI  3337

271  Article by George Kleine in Show World March 7, 1908, entitled "Kleine Talks —Biograph Company Denies Validity of Patents" ......................  VI  3347
    (See also Pet'r's Ex. 263, Vol. V, p. 2509.)

PETITIONER'S EXHIBITS, Continued:    VOL.    PAGE

272   Article by George Kleine in Show World
      April 4, 1909, entitled "Kleine Dis-
      putes Validity of Edison Patents"....  VI    3357

273   Opinion of Circuit Court of Appeals, Sec-
      ond Circuit, March 18, 1911, in case of
      Motion Picture Patents Co. v. Yankee
      Film Co., and M. P. P. Co. v. William
      Steiner (187 Fed., 1017)............  VI    3368

274   Testimony given by Harry N. Marvin in
      case of Greater New York Film Rental
      Co. v. Biograph Co. and General Film
      Co., in the District Court of the United
      States, Southern District of New York,
      Sept. 9, 1913 ....................  VI    3370

275   Testimony given by Frank L. Dyer in
      case of Greater New York Film Rental
      Co. v. Biograph Co. and General Film
      Co., in the District Court of the United
      States, Southern District of New York,
      Oct. 23, 1913.....................  VI    3376

275a  Suits brought under the Latham Patent
      No. 707,934, by Motion Picture Pat-
      ents Co., between June 14, 1909, and
      July 15, 1911.....................  VI    3391

276   Suits brought under the Pross Patent
      No. 722,382, by Motion Picture Pat-
      ents Co., between June 14, 1909, and
      July 15, 1911.....................  VI    3392

277   Opinion of the Circuit Court of Appeals,
      Second Circuit, in case of Motion Pic-
      ture Patents Co. v. The Independent
      Moving Picture Company of America
      (200 Fed., 411), Aug. 10, 1912, on the
      Latham Patent No. 707,934..........  VI    3393

278   Strip of Negative Motion Picture Film   VI    3418

279   Strip of Positive Motion Picture Film   VI    3418

**Defendants' Exhibits:**                                   VOL.   PAGE

1   Final Bulletin of Film Service Association, Jan. 9, 1909..................    I    499

2   By-Laws, Film Service Association......    I    506

3   Skipped.

4   Skipped.

5   For identification. Sheet entitled "Swanson St. Louis Film Co." ............    I    516

6   For identification. Sheet entitled "Swanson Omaha Film Co."..............    I    516

7   For identification. Two sheets entitled "William A. Swanson Dixie Film Co., New Orleans" ....................    I    516

8   For identification. Three sheets entitled "William A. Swanson & Co., Chicago"    I    517

9   Opinion, Supreme Court of Pennsylvania, Eastern District, in Lubin Mfg. Co. v. Lewis M. Swaab, March 31, 1913.....    II    888

10   Letter, Wm. Steiner, Pres. Imperial Film Exchange, to Patents Co., April 15, 1910 .............................    II    994

10a   Decision, Circuit Court of Appeals, Second Circuit, May 16, 1912, *in re* Imperial Film Exchange, an alleged bankrupt .............................    II    997

11   Letter, T. A. Edison, Inc., to Thomas H. Bates, April 28, 1912..............    II    1009

12   Letter, Thomas H. Bates to Patents Co., July 31, 1911.....................    II    1010

DEFENDANTS' EXHIBITS, Continued:          VOL.   PAGE

13  Letter, Patents Co. to Thomas H. Bates,
        Aug. 5, 1911...................... II   1011

14  Letter, Thomas H. Bates to Motion Pic-
        ture Patents Co., Oct. 14, 1911....... II   1012

15  Letter, Thomas H. Bates to Motion Pic-
        ture Patents Co., Aug. 16, 1912....... II   1013

16  Letter, Motion Picture Patents Co. to
        Thomas H. Bates, Aug. 26, 1912...... II   1015

17  Letter, Chas. W. Boyer to Motion Picture
        Patents Co., Jan. 24, 1913........... II   1023

18  Letter, Chas. W. Boyer to Motion Picture
        Patents Co., Jan. 14, 1913........... II   1024

19  Letter, Chas. W. Boyer to Motion Picture
        Patents Co., Jan. 20, 1913........... II   1025

20a Bill of Western Amusement Co., Inc.,
        dated Oct. 15, 1909................. II   1037

20b Bill of Western Amusement Co., Inc.,
        dated Oct. 15, 1909................. II   1038

20c Bill of Western Amusement Co., Inc.,
        dated blank ..................... II   1039

21  Letter, Moving Picture Patents Co. to
        A. J. Clapham, Jan. 5, 1910......... II   1040

22  Letter, A. J. Clapham to Motion Picture
        Patents Co., Jan. 11, 1910........... II   1041

23  Letter, Motion Picture Patents Co. to
        A. J. Clapham, Feb. 4, 1910......... II   1044

24  Letter, A. J. Clapham to Motion Picture
        Patents Co., Jan. 12, 1910........... II   1045

DEFENDANTS' EXHIBITS, Continued: VOL. PAGE

25 Letter, A. J. Clapham to Motion Picture
Patents Co., Jan. 24, 1910........... II 1046

26 Letter, Motion Picture Patents Co. to
Theatre Film Service Co., Feb. 8, 1910 II 1047

27 Letter, Theatre Film Service Co. to Motion Picture Patents Co., Feb. 11, 1910 II 1048

28 Letter, Theatre Film Service Co. to Motion Picture Patents Co., Jan. 8, 1910 II 1055

29 Advertisement of Empire Theatre, Win-
chester, Va., Feb. 12, 1912........... II 1107

30 Letter, J. H. Henry to Mr. Cohen, General
Film Exchange, Washington, Feb. 8,
1912 .............................. II 1110

31 Letter, Motion Picture Patents Co. to
Mr. R. Solz, Nov. 6, 1912............ II 1115

32 Letter, Motion Picture Patents Co. to
Mr. R. Solz, Nov. 21, 1912........... II 1116

33 Agreement between R. Solz and Motion
Picture Patents Co., Dec. 31, 1912.... II 1117

34 Letter, Lake Shore Film & Supply Co. to
M. H. Mark, Buffalo, N. Y., Nov. 30,
1909 .............................. II 1152

35 Letter, J. H. Michael to Motion Picture
Patents Co., April 11, 1912......... II 1160

36 Advertisement of Philadelphia Film Exchange in Motion Picture World,
March 20, 1909.................... II 1168

37 Advertisement of Philadelphia Film Exchange in Motion Picture World,
March 27, 1909.................... II 1169

DEFENDANTS' EXHIBITS, Continued:          VOL.   PAGE

38   Advertisement of Philadelphia Film Ex-
     change in Motion Picture World,
     April 3, 1909...................,....   II    1170

39   Opinion in the case of Geo. Melies Co. v.
     Motion Picture Patents Co. *et al.* in
     the United States Court of Appeals for
     the Third Circuit, October Term, 1912  II    1191

40   Letter, Motion Picture Patents Co. to
     People's Film Exchange (Notice of
     Cancellation), March 28, 1911.......   III   1280

41   Exchange Bulletin No. 12, Aug. 21, 1909.  III   1299

42   Exchange Bulletin No. 20, Dec. 7, 1909..  III   1300

43   Exchange Bulletin No. 36, Aug. 27, 1912.  III   1302

44   Form of Exhibitor's Royalty Receipt....  III   1304

45   Statement of Film Royalties Paid to Pat-
     ents Company by Licensed Manufac-
     turers and Importers, 1909 to 1913...  III   1305

46   Statement of Cancellations and Reinstate-
     ments by M. P. P. Co. of Licenses of
     Exhibitors Taking Service from Great-
     er New York Film Rental Co. ......   III   1308

47   License Agreement, June 6, 1912, between
     Patents Company and Biograph Com-
     pany, being Exhibit 3 printed at page
     150 of Answer of M. P. P. Co. Simi-
     lar agreements were executed with
     each of the other licensed manufac-
     turers .........................   III   1309

48   License Agreement, June 20, 1913, be-
     tween Patents Company and George
     Kleine. Similar agreements were ex-
     ecuted with each of the other licensed
     manufacturers ..................   III   1310

DEFENDANTS' EXHIBITS, Continued:   VOL.   PAGE

49   Supplemental License Agreement, Patents
     Company and American Mutoscope &
     Biograph Company, Jan. 26, 1909, be-
     ing Exhibit 2 printed at page 144 of
     Answer of M. P. P. Co.   Similar
     agreements were executed with each of
     the other licensed manufacturers ....   III   1329

50   Exchange License Agreement, Motion Pic-
     ture Patents Co. and (blank), June,
     1913 .............................   III   1330

51   License Agreement, Patents Company and
     Kinemacolor Co. of America, Aug. 4,
     1913 .............................   III   1335

52   Letter, C. C. Allen to Motion Picture Pat-
     ents Co., dated Newberg, Ore., March
     17, 1910 .........................   III   1357

53   Letter, William Hunt to Motion Picture
     Patents Co., letterhead Elite Theatre,
     Woodland, Cal., March 8, 1910.......   III   1359

54   Letter, William Hunt to Motion Picture
     Patents Co., letterhead Elite Theatre,
     Woodland, Cal., April 6, 1910.......   III   1360

55   Letter, F. H. Mitchell to Motion Picture
     Patents Co., dated Berkeley, Cal., Nov.
     30, 1910 .........................   III   1362

56   Letter, C. A. Riffle to Motion Picture Pat-
     ents Co., dated San Rafael, Cal., June
     2, 1910 ..........................   III   1362

57   Letter, Keller Bros. to Motion Picture
     Patents Co., dated Frederick, Md.,
     May 18, 1909.....................   III   1364

58   Letter, Hood & Schultz to Motion Picture
     Patents Co., dated Baltimore, Md.,
     July 23, 1910.....................   III   1366

DEFENDANTS' EXHIBITS, Continued: VOL. PAGE

59. Letter, W. J. Swarts to Motion Picture Patents Co., Butte, Mont., April 17, 1911 .............................. III 1369

60 Letter, A. J. Kavanagh to Motion Picture Patents Co., Minneapolis, June 23, 1909 ............................. III 1370

61 Letter, Gaiety Theatre to Motion Picture Patents Co., dated St. Paul, Minn., June 23, 1909.................... III 1371

62 Letter, Motion Picture Patents Co. to Kestner & Young, Feb. 21, 1910...... III 1373

63 Letter, The Princess Theatre to Motion Picture Patents Co., dated Bellefontaine, O., May 3, 1910.............. III 1374

64 Letter, Harry R. Rand to Motion Picture Patents Co., June 24, 1910.......... III 1376

65 Letter, Harry R. Rand to Motion Picture Patents Co., Oct. 28, 1910........... III 1378

66 Letter, Harry R. Rand to Mr. Buckwalter, Oct. 14, 1910..................... III 1379

67 Letter, Charles A. Persons to Motion Picture Patents Co., dated Canandaigua, N. Y., March 2, 1909.......... III 1380

68 Letter, Charles A. Persons to Motion Picture Patents Co., March 5, 1909.. III 1381

69 Letter, Lew F. Cullins to Motion Picture Patents Co., dated The Dalles, Ore., Feb. 18, 1910..................... III 1383

70 Letter, Lew F. Cullins to Motion Picture Patents Co., Oct. 14, 1910........... III 1384

DEFENDANTS' EXHIBITS, Continued:     VOL.   PAGE

71   Letter, J. T. Fleischman to Motion Picture Patents Co., dated Portland, Ore., Nov. 12, 1909..................... III   1385

72   Letter, J. T. Fleischman to Motion Picture Patents Co., dated Portland, Ore., Dec. 15, 1909..................... III   1386

73   Letter, Henry Newman to Motion Picture Patents Co., dated Astoria, Ore., May 3, 1910.......................... III   1387

74.   Letter, Henry Newman to Motion Picture Patents Co., May 3, 1910............ III   1388

75   Letter, B. E. Gellerman to Motion Picture Patents Co., dated Portland Ore., Feb. 8, 1910.......................... III   1389

76   Letter, Ed. J. Wagner to Motion Picture Patents Co., dated Hartford, Wis., Oct. 6, 1909....................... III   1390

77   Letter, C. J. Jelier to Motion Picture Patents Co., dated Racine, Wis., July 23, 1909 ............................ III   1391

78   Letter, W. Clark to Motion Picture Patents Co., dated Rockford, Ill., June 10, 1909......................... III   1393

79   Letter, The Kent Film Service Co. to Motion Picture Patents Co., dated Toledo, O., Aug. 15, 1910.................. III   1395

80   Letter, H. Wolff to Motion Picture Patents Co., dated Sacramento, Cal., Dec. 19, 1910......................... III   1396

81   Letter, John Carter to Motion Picture Patents Co., dated Baltimore, Md., Sept. 7, 1910....................... III   1397

DEFENDANTS' EXHIBITS, Continued:  VOL.  PAGE

82  Letter, Yale Amusement Co. of Oklahoma
to The Monarch Film Exchange, Nov.
27, 1909, enclosing letter Mitchells'
Film Exchange, Little Rock, Ark., to
John Buchanan and Affidavit of R. B.
Smith and Arthur Cooley.......... III  1399

83  Letter, Wilcox & Wilcox to Motion Picture Patents Co., dated Santa Maria,
Cal., Dec. 21, 1909................ III  1402

84  Letter, The Kent Film Service Co. to
Motion Picture Patents Co., dated
Aug. 15, 1910.................... III  1403

85  Letter, A. W. Rhorer to Motion Picture
Patents Co., dated Athens, Ga., Sept.
4, 1909.......................... III  1404

86  Letter, Motion Picture Patents Co. to A.
W. Rhorer, Sept. 9, 1909........... III  1406

87  Letter, A. W. Rhorer to Motion Picture
Patents Co., Sept. 14, 1909......... III  1407

88  Letter, J. Warner to A. D. Flinton c/o
Yale Film Exchange, Kansas City, and
Affidavit of Mr. Warner, Dec. 15,
1909 ............................ III  1409

89  Letter, C. Baumbach to Motion Picture
Patents Co., dated Baltimore, Md.,
June 17, 1910.................... III  1413

90  Letter, Charles W. Demme to Motion Picture Patents Co., dated Baltimore,
Aug. 3, 1910..................... III  1414

91  Letter, Red Mill Moving Picture Parlor
to Motion Picture Patents Co., dated
Baltimore, March 28, 1911.......... III  1415

DEFENDANTS' EXHIBITS, Continued:     VOL.  PAGE

92   Letter, E. W. Sprosty to Mr. Mandelbaum
of the Lake Shore Film Exchange of
Cleveland, dated Jan. 17, 1910...... III  1417

93   Letter, Ferdinand Shoemaker to Motion
Picture Patents Co., dated Crow
Agency, Mont., July 2, 1910......... III  1419

94.  Letter, C. F. Hanke to Motion Picture
Patents Co., dated Washington, July
15, 1910.......................... III  1420

95   Letter, Motion Picture Patents Co. to
Ferdinand Shoemaker, July 23, 1910.. III  1421

96   Letter, George F. Scull to Lieut. Com. G.
H. Holden, April 30, 1909........... III  1423

96a  Copy of Circular Letter on Letterhead of
H. & H. Film Service Co., dated Chicago, Oct. 3, 1910................. III  1433

97   Letter, The Laemmle Film Service Co. to
Mr. Geo. Hines, Chicago, April 12, 1909 III  1439

98   Letter, Vaudette Film Exchange to Motion Picture Patents Co., Nov. 3, 1909 III  1452

99   Letter, Western Film Exchange, Milwau-
kee, to Mr. J. Elliott, Minneapolis
(no date) ....................... III  1455

100  Statement of Exchange Licenses Granted
or Offered Subsequent to Feb. 1, 1909. III  1458

101  Letter, Birmingham Film Supply Co. to
Motion Picture Patents Co., May 17,
1910 ............................. III  1460

102  Letter, Birmingham Film Supply Co. to
Motion Picture Patents Co., July 21,
1909 ............................. III  1461

DEFENDANTS' EXHIBITS, Continued:        VOL.    PAGE

103  Letter, The H. Lieber Co. to Motion Pic-
       ture Patents Co., April 10, 1909..... III    1463

104  Letter, Clune Film Exchange to Motion
       Picture Patents Co., Nov. 22, 1909.... III   1465

105  Label used by Edison on film prior to
       the reissue of the film patent ....... III    1492

106  Label used by Edison on film after the
       reissue of the film patent ........... III    1493

107  Exhibitors' Bulletin No. 11 by Motion
       Picture Patents Co., Nov. 21, 1910... III    1571

108  List of Branches of General Film Co.,
       dated Nov. 10, 1913................ III    1608
     See also, Petitioner's Exhibit 63....... I      199

109  List of Exchanges Maintained byMutual
       Co., produced by Frank L. Dyer .... III    1610

110  List of Distributing Offices Handling Uni-
       versal Service in United States and
       Canada, produced by Frank L. Dyer III    1613

111  Opinion of Judge Kohlsaat in Thomas A.
       Edison v. Selig Polyscope Co., filed
       Jan. 29, 1910, as of Oct. 24, 1907, in
       the U. S. Circuit Court for the North-
       ern District of Illinois, Eastern Divi-
       sion ........................... III    1617

112  Agreement, Dec. 7, 1904, between Paley
       & Steiner, George Melies, Pathe Cine-
       matograph Co., and Eberhard Schnei-
       der about defense of suits on Edison
       patents ......................... III    1765

113  Writ of Injunction, dated Nov. 1, 1907,
       out of Circuit Court for Northern Dis-
       trict of Illinois, Eastern Division, on
       the part of T. A. Edison directed to
       Selig Polyscope Co. on Reissue Letters
       Patent 12,037 ................... IV     1979

DEFENDANTS' EXHIBITS, Continued:     VOL.   PAGE

114  Writ of Injunction, dated Sept. 18, 1900,
     out of Circuit Court for the Southern
     District of New York on the part of
     T. A. Edison directed to American
     Vitagraph Co. and Walter Arthur, in-
     dividually, on Letters Patent No.
     589,168 .......................... IV   1985

114a For identification. Copy of Scenario of
     "From the Manger to the Cross," copy-
     righted 1912 by Kalem Co........... IV   1915

115  Credit Memorandum of Edison Mfg. Co. to
     Blackton & Smith, dated Orange, N.
     J., Oct. 31, 1900.................... IV   1988

116  Letter, The American Vitagraph Co. to
     W. E. Gilmore c/o Edison Mfg. Co.,
     Orange, N. J., Jan. 12, 1901......... IV   1989

117  Receipt, dated March 24, 1905, for $400
     paid by Vitagraph Co. to Kerr, Page
     & Cooper as retainer in suit against
     Vitagraph Co. by T. A. Edison on re-
     issued Patents 12,037 and 12,192..... IV   1992

118  Letter, S. O. Edmonds to Vitagraph Co.
     of America, dated March 15, 1907.... IV   1993

119  Letter, Armat Moving Picture Co. to
     Vitagraph Co., Washington, D. C.,
     Nov. 27, 1902..................... IV   1994

120  Letter, P. B. Chase to Vitagraph Co.,
     dated Nov. 29, 1902............... IV   1995

121  License Agreement dated Dec. 12, 1900,
     between Armat Moving Picture Co.
     and E. Burton Holmes............. IV   2119

DEFENDANTS' EXHIBITS, Continued: VOL. PAGE

122 License Agreement dated March 14, 1902,
between Armat Moving Picture Co.
and B. H. H. Lawrence.............. IV 2122

123 Circular, dated Washington D. C., about
1901, entitled "Final Notice to Infringers of the Armat Patents," on
the letterhead of the Armat Moving
Picture Co........................ IV 2127

124 Circular, entitled "A Warning," aecom-
panying Defendants' Exhibit 123.... IV 2128

125 Circular, on letterhead of Armat Moving
Picture Co., dated Washington March
25, 1902, sent out with copy of Defendants' Exhibit 124.................. IV 2132

126 Writ of Injunction, dated Jan. 8, 1903,
out of Circuit Court for the Southern
District of New York on the part of
Armat Moving Picture Co., directed to
Edison Mfg. Co., on Letters Patent
586,953 .......................... IV 2136

127 Agreement, dated Feb. 19, 1904, between
Armat Moving Picture Co. and American Mutoscope & Biograph Co., on Letters Patent 586,953................ IV 2160

128 Letter, Armat Moving Picture Co. to H.
N. Marvin, Trustee, attached to Defendants' Exhibit 127.............. IV 2163

129 Agreement, dated Oct. 17, 1904, between
Armat Moving Picture Co. and American Mutoscope & Biograph Co., attached to Defendants' Exhibit 127.... IV 2164

130 Agreement, dated March 21, 1908, between
Armat Moving Picture Co. and American Mutoscope & Biograph Co........ IV 2166

DEFENDANTS' EXHIBITS, Continued: VOL. PAGE

131 Advertisement of Motion Picture Distributing & Sales Co., in Motion Picture World July 23, 1910, with List of Independent Buying Exchanges July 13, 1910...................... V 2874

132 Advertisement of Motion Picture Distributing & Sales Co., in Motion Picture World Oct. 29, 1910, with List of Buying Exchanges Oct. 22, 1910...... V 2877

133 Bulletin of National Board of Censorship Representing Work Done Week Ending Feb. 21, 1914 (See Exhibit 146).. V 2903

134 Reply Postal Card used by Motion Picture Patents Co. in requesting information on theatres, Form 298.............. V 2916

135 Reply Postal Card used by Motion Picture Patents Co., in requesting information on theatres, Form 311.............. V 2918

136 Reply Postal Card used by Motion Picture Patents Co., in requesting information on theatres, Form 314.............. V 2920

137 Reply Postal Card used by Motion Picture Patents Co., in requesting information on theatres, Form 452.............. V 2921

138 Reply Postal Card used by Motion Picture Patents Co., in requesting information on theatres, Form 467.............. V 2922

139 Reply Postal Card used by Motion Picture Patents Co. in requesting information on theatres, Form 299....... V 2924

140 Reply Postal Card used by Motion Picture Patents Co. in requesting information on theatres, Form 313....... V 2925

DEFENDANTS' EXHIBITS, Continued: VOL. PAGE

141 Reply Postal Card used by Motion Picture Patents Co. in requesting information on theatres, Form 483........ V 2928

142 Circular Letter (Sheet 1) with Form of Reply attached (Sheet 2) used by Patents Company in requesting information on theatres, Form 315....... V 2930

143 Circular Letter to Exhibitors used by Patents Co. in requesting information on theatres, Form 10................. V 2932

144 Statement by Patents Co. as of July 21, 1913, showing Licensed and Nonlicensed Motion Picture Theatres in United States .................... V 2934

145 Statement by Patents Co. as of July 21, 1913, showing Licensed and Nonlicensed Motion Picture Theatres in Cities of 100,000 and over in United States ......................... V 2936

146 Report of Work of Censoring Committee of National Board of Censorship on Motion Pictures (see Exhibit 133)... V 2940

147 Map of Georgia..................... V 2976

148 Towns in Georgia within dotted lines on Map having Moving Picture Shows (Sheet 1); Towns in Georgia within dotted lines on Map not having Moving Picture Shows (Sheet 2)......... V 2978

149 Map of Ohio...................... V 2980

150 Towns in Ohio within Black Line on Map not having Moving Picture Shows (Sheet 1); Towns in Ohio within Black Line on Map having Moving Picture Shows (Sheet 2)............ V 2981

DEFENDANTS' EXHIBITS, Continued: VOL. PAGE

151 Analysis of Difference between July and
December (1913) Checking of Towns
in Georgia Investigated by W. W. R.
Greene ........................ V 3022

152 Analysis of Difference between July, 1913,
and January, 1914, Checking of Towns
in Ohio Investigated by W. W. R.
Greene ........................ V 3023

153 Analysis of Difference between Number of
Theatres Testified by W. C. Brandon
as Existing in Territory of States of
Georgia and Alabama, December, 1913,
and Results of Checkings of Miss
Matthews and W. W. R. Greene for
same period ..................... V 3024

154 Statement, Oct. 31, 1910, showing Number of Places in United States in
which Motion Pictures were Exhibited, Separated as to Licensees and
Non-licensees of Patents Co........ V 3026

155 Statement, Jan. 30, 1911, showing Number of Places in United States in
which Motion Pictures were Exhibited, Separated as to Licensees and
Non-licensees of Patents Co......... V 3028

156 Statement, July 3, 1911, showing Number of Places in United States in
which Motion Pictures were Exhibited, Separated as to Licensees and
Non-licensees of Patents Co......... V 3030

157 Statement, Dec. 18, 1911, showing Number of Places in United States in
which Motion Pictures were Exhibited, Separated as to Licensees and
Non-licensees of Patents Co......... V 3032

DEFENDANTS' EXHIBITS, Continued: VOL. PAGE

158 Statement, July 7, 1912, showing Number of Places in United States in which Motion Pictures were Exhibited, Separated as to Licensees and Non-licensees of Patents Co.......... V 3034

159 Statement, Oct. 31, 1910, showing Cities in United States of 100,000 and over in which Motion Pictures were Exhibited, Separated as to Licensees and Non-licensees of Patents Co.......... V 3036

160 Statement, Jan. 30, 1911, showing Cities in United States of 100,000 and over in which Motion Pictures were Exhibited, Separated as to Licensees and Non-licensees of Patents Co.......... V 3038

161 Statement, July 3, 1911, showing Cities in United States of 100,000 and over in which Motion Pictures were Exhibited, Separated as to Licensees and Non-licensees of Patents Co.......... V 3040

162 Statement, Dec. 18, 1911, showing Cities in United States of 100,000 and over in which Motion Pictures were Exhibited, Separated as to Licensees and Non-licensees of Patents Co.......... V 3042

163 Statement, July 7, 1912, showing Cities in United States of 100,000 and over in which Motion Pictures were Exhibited, Separated as to Licensees and Non-licensees of Patents Co.......... V 3044

164 Docket Entries of Dyer & Dyer, Gifford & Bull and Kerr, Page & Cooper re various suits by Edison on Letters Patent No. 589,168, and Reissue Patents Nos. 12,037, 12,038 and 12,192, brought between 1897 and 1909.............. VI 3093

DEFENDANTS' EXHIBITS, Continued:      VOL.    PAGE

165   Contract between Theatre Film Supply Co., Birmingham, Ala., and General Film Co., dated Aug. 23, 1910....... VI   3170

166   Letter, General Film Co. to Theatre Film Supply Co., March 21, 1912......... VI   3184

167   Letter, Theatre Film Supply Co. to J. J. Kennedy on letterhead of Southern Amusement & Supply Co., Aug. 21, 1911 ............................. VI   3186

168   Letter, J. J. Kennedy to A. R. Boone, President, Theatre Film Supply Co., Aug. 26, 1911..................... VI   3188

169   Letter, Theatre Film Supply Co. to J. J. Kennedy, Aug. 31, 1911............. VI   3189

170   Letter, Theatre Film Supply Co. to J. J. Kennedy, Sept. 9, 1911............. VI   3190

171   Letter, J. J. Kennedy to Theatre Film Supply Co., Dec. 29, 1910............ VI   3191

172   Statement of cost of branches of General Film Co. as per balance sheet of December 30, 1911.................... VI   3200

173   Skipped.

174   Motion Picture Camera, known as the Warwick Camera ................. VI   3261

175   Projecting Machine, known as the Power Projecting Machine ............... VI   3261

176   Negative Motion Picture Film ......... VI   3261

DEFENDANTS' EXHIBITS, Continued:            VOL.   PAGE

177  Positive Motion Picture Film .........   VI   3262

178  Defendants' Illustrative Apparatus.....  VI   3263

179  Photographs, marked 1 to 7, showing De-
     fendants'    Illustrative   Apparatus,
     Defts' Ex. 178 ....................   VI   3266

180  Chart explanatory of Photograph No. 1
     Defts' Ex. 179...................   VI   3266

181  Chart explanatory of Photograph No. 2,
     Defts' Ex. 179...................   VI   3267

182  Chart explanatory of Photograph No. 5,
     Defts' Ex. 179...................   VI   3268

183  Chart explanatory of Photograph No. 7,
     Defts' Ex. 179...................   VI   3269

184  List of Suits brought on Camera Patent
     No. 12,037 after the Assignment of
     that Patent to Motion Picture Patents
     Co.  ...........................   VI   3270

184a Motion Picture Scenario, etc., from Even-
     ing Sun March 30, 1914............   VI   3316

185  Edison Reissue Patent No. 12,037, dated
     Sept. 30, 1902...................   VI   3326

186  Edison Reissue Patent No. 13,329, dated
     Dec. 5, 1911....................   VI   3326

187  Edison Reissue Patent No. 12,192, dated
     Jan. 12, 1904...................   VI   3326

188  Smith Patent No. 673,329, dated April 30,
     1901  ..........................   VI   3326

DEFENDANTS' EXHIBITS, Continued:  VOL.  PAGE

189  Smith Patent No. 744, 251, dated Nov. 17,
1903 ........................... VI  3326

190  Smith Patent No. 770,937, dated Sept. 27,
1904 ........................... VI  3326

191  Smith Patent No. 771,280, dated Oct. 4,
1904 ........................... VI  3326

192  Ellwood Patent No. 785,205, dated March
21, 1905......................... VI  3326

193  Smith Patent No. 785,237, dated March
21, 1905......................... VI  3326

194  Armat Patent No. 578,185, dated March 2,
1897 ........................... VI  3326

195  Armat Patent No. 580,749, dated April 13,
1897 ........................... VI  3326

196  Jenkins and Armat Patent No. 586,953,
dated July 20, 1897................ VI  3326

197  Steward and Frost Patent No. 588,916,
dated Aug. 24, 1897............... VI  3326

198  Casler Patent No. 629,063, dated July 18,
1889 ........................... VI  3326

199  Armat Patent No. 673,992, dated May 14,
1901 ........................... VI  3326

200  Latham Patent No. 707,934, dated Aug.
26, 1902 ........................ VI  3326

201  Pross Patent No. 722,382, dated March
10, 1903 ........................ VI  3326

DEFENDANTS' EXHIBITS, Continued:          VOL.   PAGE

202   Last page of paper wrapper of Book enti-
      tled "Moving Pictures," by Frederick
      A. Talbot, advertising the Books enti-
      tled "Railway Conquest of the World"
      and "Steamship Conquest of the
      World," by the same author......... VI    3338

203   For identification. Statement of Busi-
      ness done by the Alfred Weiss Branch
      of the General Film Co. for the week
      ended July 11, 1910................ VI    3382

204   For identification. Statement of Busi-
      ness done by the Alfred Weiss Branch
      of the General Film Co. for week
      ended July 16, 1910................ VI    3383

205   For identification. Statement of Busi-
      ness done by the Alfred Weiss Branch
      of the General Film Co. for week
      ended July 23, 1910................ VI    3383

206   For identification. Statement of Busi-
      ness done by the Alfred Weiss Branch
      of the General Film Co. for week
      ended July 30, 1910................ VI    3384

207   For identification. Statement of Busi-
      ness done by the Alfred Weiss Branch
      of the General Film Co. for week
      ended Aug. 10, 1910................ VI    3389

208   For identification. Statement of Busi-
      ness done by the Alfred Weiss Branch
      of the General Film Co. for week
      ended Aug. 13, 1910................ VI    3390

209   For identification. Statement of Busi-
      ness done by the Alfred Weiss Branch
      of the General Film Co. for week
      ended Aug. 20, 1910................ VI    3390

DEFENDANTS' EXHIBITS, Continued: VOL. PAGE

210 For identification. Statement of Business done by the Alfred Weiss Branch of the General Film Co. for week ended Aug. 27, 1910............... VI 3390

211 For identification. Statement of Business done by the Alfred Weiss Branch of the General Film Co. for week ended Sept. 3, 1910................ VI 3391

212 For identification. Statement of Business done by the Alfred Weiss Branch of the General Film Co. for week ended Sept. 10, 1910............... VI 3391

213 Statement showing Receipts and Expenses of the Alfred Weiss Branch of the General Film Co., for week ended July 9, 1910, and for the nine succeeding weeks ........................... VI 3433

214 Article Published in Harper's Weekly June 13, 1891, page 446, entitled "Edison Kinetograph, by George Parsons Lathrop" ........................ VI 3434

FEINLER, CHARLES A. :                    VOL.    PAGE

    Direct Examination ................. V    2613–2618
    Cross Examination ................. 2618–2619
    Redirect Examination .............. 2619

**Film Service Association:**

    Advertisement printed in Moving Pic-
        ture World Nov. 16, 1907, entitled
        "Convention of Manufacturers and
        Film Renters," *re* meeting to be
        held at Fort Pitt Hotel, Pittsbugh,
        Nov. 16 and 17, 1907, Petitioner's
        Exhibit 252 ................... V    2477

    Article entitled "The Pittsburgh Con-
        ference" printed in Moving Picture
        World Nov. 23, 1907; Petitioner's
        Exhibit 253 ................... V    2480

    Two Articles printed in Moving Picture
        World Feb. 15, 1908, entitled "The
        United Film Service Association
        and the Film Manufacturers" and
        "The position of the American
        Mutoscope & Biograph Co.;" Peti-
        tioner's Exhibit 254............. V    2494

    Article Printed in Show World April
        25, 1908, entitled "Important Bul-
        letin of Film Service Association;"
        Petitioner's Exhibit 257 ........ V    2536

    Article Printed in Show World May 2,
        1908, entitled "Film Association
        Announces Victory in Edison Liti-
        gation;" Petitioner's Exhibit 258.  V    2541

    Bulletin No. 1 of Film Service Associa-
        tion, Feb. 14, 1908; Petitioner's
        Exhibit 99.....................  I     437

FILM SERVICE ASSOCIATION, Continued:  VOL.  PAGE

Bulletin No. 2 of Film Service Association, Feb. 24, 1908; Petitioner's Exhibit 100 .................... I    439

Bulletin No. 10 of Film Service Association, March 24, 1908; Petitioner's Exhibit 101 .................... I    441

Bulletin No. 14 of Film Service Association, April 20, 1908; Petitioner's Exhibit 102..................... I    442

Bulletin No. 27, being letter dated Oct. 5, 1908, from F. L. Dyer to Dwight MacDonald regarding return of old film to Manufacturers; Petitioner's Exhibit 97.............. I    430

Final Bulletin No. 39, dated Jan. 9, 1909, being Report of Annual Meeting held at Hotel Imperial, New York; Defendants' Exhibit 1..... I    499

By-Laws; Defendants' Exhibit 2...... I    506

Form of Contract between Rental Exchange and Exhibitors used by Greater New York Film Co. during period of Film Service Association; Petitioner's Exhibit 98.......... I    431

List of Members of Film Service Association, February, 1908; Petitioner's Exhibit 90.................. I    343

FORSTER, JOSEPH:

Direct Examination ................ III  1864–1869
Cross Examination ................      1870–1871
Redirect Examination ..............      1871–1872
Recross Examination ..............      1872

Fox, William:                               VOL.      PAGE

Direct Examination ................ II     658– 700
Cross Examination ................          781– 795
Redirect Examination ..............         795– 796
Recross Examination ..............          796– 797

**General Film Company of Maine:**

Advertisement of a Special Feature Pro-
    duction by Kalem Co. for July 1,
    1912; Petitioner's Exhibit 93.....   I      375

Agreement, General Film Co. and Pat-
    ents Co., April 21, 1910, printed as
    Exhibit 7 to Petition; Petitioner's
    Exhibit 130 ...................       I      547

Agreement between General Film Co.
    and Edison Mfg. Co., dated April
    21, 1910, printed as Exhibit 8
    on page 116 of Petition. Simi-
    lar agreements were executed by
    each of the other licensed manu-
    facturers .....................       I      552

By-Laws of General Film Co., Extracts
    from; Petitioner's Exhibit 64....    I      201

Branches of General Film Co., as of
    Jan. 12, 1912; Petitioner's Ex-
    hibit 63 ......................       I      199

Branches of General Film Co., as of
    Nov. 10, 1913; Defendants' Exhibit
    108 ..........................       III    1608

Charter, General Film Company of
    Maine, April 21, 1910; printed as
    Exhibit 6 to Petition............    II      924

Circular Letter to Exhibitors from Den-
    ver, Colo., dated Sept. 15, 1910, on
    letterhead of G. F. Co.; Petition-
    er's Exhibit 206...............      II     1131

GENERAL FILM COMPANY, Continued:  VOL.  PAGE

Contract between Theatre Film Supply
    Co., Birmingham, Ala., and Gen-
    eral Film Co., Aug. 23, 1910; De-
    fendants' Exhibit 165............ VI  3170

Contract dated April 21, 1910, between
    Biograph Co. and General Film
    Co., relating to common stock of
    General Film Co. owned by Bio-
    graph Co.; Petitioner's Exhibit 242 III  1682

Correspondence, General Film Co. and
    L. M. Swaab between Aug. 6th and
    Aug. 29th, 1910, introduced as one
    Exhibit; Petitioner's Exhibit 152. II  816

Dividends Paid on Preferred and Com-
    mon Stocks of General Film Co.,
    Dec. 31st, 1910, to Dec. 31st, 1912. I  327

Undivided Net Profits of General Film
    Co. remaining after Payment of
    Dividends on Preferred and Com-
    mon Stocks—June 6th, 1910, to
    Dec. 31st, 1910, and Year 1911.... I  328

List of exchanges from whom purchas-
    es were made up to June 23rd,
    1910 ......................... I  325

List of Preferred Stockholders of Gen-
    eral Film Co. for 1912; Petition-
    er's Exhibit 128 ................ I  541

List of Officers and Directors of Gen-
    eral Film Co. as of Jan. 1, 1912;
    Petitioner's Exhibit 129......... I  546

GENERAL FILM COMPANY, Continued:          VOL.          PAGE

Minutes of Meetings of Board of Directors of General Film Co.; Petitioner's Exhibits 79, 80, 81, 82, 83,
84, 86, 87 ......................          I          262– 289

Net Profits of General Film Co., June
6th to Dec. 31st, 1910, and Year
1911 .........................          I          326

Statement of Cost of Branches of General Film Co. as per balance sheet
of Dec. 30, 1911; Defendants' Ex-
hibit 172 .....................          VI          3200
(See also Petitioner's Exhibit 62,
I, p. 190.)

Statement showing Price and Dates of
Delivery of Exchange Equipment
and Stock of Motion Pictures and
Merchandise Bought by General
Film Co.; Petitioner's Exhibit 62          I          190
(See also Defendants' Exhibit 172,
VI, p. 3200.)

Statement of Undivided Net Profits of
General Film Co., Credited to Manufacturers, after Payment of Dividends, Dec. 30, 1911; Petitioner's
Exhibit 131 ...................          I          548

Statement of Distribution of Undivided
Net Profits of General Film Co.,
for Years 1910 and 1911, Credited
after Payment of Dividends on
Preferred and Common Stock on
Basis of Feet of Film Leased from
Licensed Manufacturers; Petition-
er's Exhibit 132 ...............          I          548

**General Film Company of New Jersey:**

Charter, General Film Company of
New Jersey, Feb. 10, 1910; Peti-
tioner's Exhibit 174.............          II          925

GIBBONS, N. H.:                                    VOL.    PAGE

    Direct Examination ................. V    2783–2785
    Cross Examination ................         2785

GILLIGHAM, ALBERT J.:

    Direct Examination ................. IV   2199–2220
    Cross Examination ................         2220–2226
    Redirect Examination ..............        2226–2227
    Recross Examination ..............         2227

GOFF, ALBERT W.:

    Direct Examination ................. IV   2342–2348
    Cross Examination ................         2463–2466
    Redirect Examination ..............        2466–2468
    Recross Examination ...............        2466–2468

GRAHAM, J. C.:

    Direct Examination ................. II   1226–1238
    Cross Examination ................         1238–1244

GRAHAM, HOWELL:

    Direct Examination ............... V     2845–2849
    Cross Examination ................         2849–2850
    Redirect Examination ..............        2850–2851
    Redirect Examination ..............        2851–2852
    Recross Examination ..............         2851
    Recross Examination ..............         2852

GREENE, WALTER W. R.:

    Direct Examination ............... V     2974–2983
    Cross Examination ................         2983

GREENBURG, ABRAHAM:
    Direct Examination ............... IV    2100–2104
    Cross Examination ................         2104–2106
    Redirect Examination ..............        2106
    Recross Examination ..............         2106

HAAS, OTTO:                            VOL.    PAGE

Direct Examination ................ V   2842–2845
Cross Examination ................     2845

HALL, OTTO P.:

Direct Examination ................ V   2852–2856
Cross Examination ................     2856
Redirect Examination ...............    2856
Recross Examination ...............    2856

HANSEN, MATTHEW:

Direct Examination ................ IV   2052–2056
Cross Examination ................     2056–2057
Redirect Examination ...............    2057

HARDIN, JOHN:

Direct Examination ................ III   1650–1662
Cross Examination ................     1662–1663
Redirect Examination ...............    1663
Recross Examination ...............    1663–1664

HARING, CHARLES F.:

Direct Examination ................ IV   2038–2045
Cross Examination ................     2045–2050
Redirect Examination ...............    2050–2051
Recross Examination ...............    2051

HATCH, STANLEY W.:

Direct Examination ................ IV   2348–2352
Cross Examination ................     2352–2355
Cross Examination ................     2450
Redirect Examination ...............    2450–2452

HENNEGAN, JOHN F.:

Direct Examination ................ V   2694–2700
Cross Examination ................     2700–2701

HENRY, J. HENKEL:

Direct Examination ................ II   1101–1104
Cross Examination ................     1104–1111
Redirect Examination ...............    1112

HENRY, THOMAS YARROW:                          VOL.    PAGE

   Direct Examination ................ VI   3431–3433

HERBST, WILLIAM P.:

   Direct Examination ................ IV   2300–2304
   Cross Examination .................       2304–2307

HOPP, JOSEPH:

   Direct Examination ................ II   1058–1078
   Cross Examination .................       1078–1082

HOWARD, FRANK J.:

   Direct Examination ................ III  1838–1856
   Cross Examination .................       1856–1861
   Redirect Examination ..............       1861
   Recross Examination ...............       1862

HUNTER, JAMES W.:

   Direct Examination ................ V    2620–2623
   Cross Examination .................       2624

JEFFERYS, FRED.:

   Direct Examination ................ III  1827–1835
   Cross Examination .................       1835–1837
   Redirect Examination ..............       1837

JONES, C. R.:

   Direct Examination ................ V    2625–2629
   Cross Examination .................       2629–2630

**Kalem Company, Inc.:**

   Advertisement of a Special Feature for
      July 1, 1912 .................. I    375

   License Agreement under Camera and
      Film Patents, Patents Co. and
      Kalem Co., Dec. 18, 1908, similar
      to Exhibit 3 to Petition; Petition-
      er's Exhibit 6 ................. I    23

KALEM CO. (INC.), Continued:          VOL.     PAGE

    Agreement between Edison Mfg. Co.
       and Kalem Co., dated Jan. 31,
       1908; similar to Exhibit 1 to An-
       swer of T. A. Edison, Inc.; Peti-
       tioner's Exhibit 92.............          I       356

    Agreement between Kalem Co. (Inc.)
       and General Film Company, dated
       April 21, 1910; printed as Exhibit
       8 on page 116 of Petition........          I       552

    License Agreement between Patents
       Co. and Kalem (Inc.), dated June
       6, 1912, similar to Exhibit 3 to An-
       swer of Patents Co.; Defendants'
       Exhibit 47 ...................          III      1309

    Supplemental License Agreement, Pat-
       ents Co. and Kalem Co., dated on
       or about Jan. 26, 1909, similar to
       Exhibit 2 to Answer of Patents
       Co.; Defendants' Exhibit 49......          III      1329

    License Agreement, dated June 20,
       1913, between Patents Co. and
       Kalem Co., similar to Defendants'
       Exhibit 48 ...................          III      1310

    Letter, Kalem Co. to Greater New York
       Film Rental Co., dated June 24,
       1910; Petitioner's Exhibit 122....          I       469

KARSON, LOUIS:
    Direct Examination ...............          II       1093–1099
    Cross Examination ................                   1099–1101

KATZ, SAMUEL:                                    VOL.      PAGE

    Direct Examination ................ V    2737–2740
    Cross Examination ................         2740

KENNEDY, J. J.:

    Direct Examination ................ VI   3156–3206
    Cross Examination ................        3206–3238
    Redirect Examination ..............       3238

    Letter, J. J. Kennedy to William Pel-
      zer, Jan. 23, 1912; Petitioner's
      Exhibit 78 .................... I        251

    Letter, J. J. Kennedy to National-
      Vaudette Film Co., Detroit, Mich.,
      Oct. 27, 1910; Petitioner's Ex-
      bibit 210 ..................... II       1146

    Statement entitled "The Position of the
      American Mutoscope & Biograph
      Co." published in Moving Picture
      World Feb. 15, 1908, signed by
      Kennedy and Marvin; Petitioner's
      Exhibit 54 .................... I        131
    See also ........................ VI     3310

KENNEY, FRANK M.:

    Direct Examination ................ V    2667–2673
    Cross Examination ................        2673–2674
    Redirect Examination ..............       2674–2675

KENNEY, W. ALLEN:

    Direct Examination ................ V    2716–2719
    Cross Examination ................        2719–2721
    Redirect Examination ..............       2721–2722

KENT, LELAND B.:

    Direct Examination ................ V    2655–2659
    Cross Examination ................        2659–2660
    Redirect Examination ..............       2661
    Recross Examination ..............        2661

KERTSCHER, WILLIAM F.:                  VOL.    PAGE

Direct Examination ................ IV    1940–1943
Cross Examination ................        1943
Redirect Examination .............        1943–1944

KESSLER, JOHN DANIEL:

Direct Examination ................ V     2675–2678
Cross Examination ................        2678–2679

KINSON, W. F.:

Direct Examination ................ IV    2315–2321
Cross Examination ................        2452–2453
Cross Examination ................        2459
Redirect Examination .............        2453–2454

**Kleine, George:**

License Agreement under Camera and
    Film Patents, Patents Co. and
    George Kleine, Dec. 18, 1908 simi-
    lar to Exhibit 3 to Petition; Peti-
    tioner's Exhibit 6 ............. I       23

Agreement between George Kleine and
    General Film Co., dated April 21,
    1910, similar to Exhibit 8 to Pe-
    tition ....................... I        552

License Agreement between Patents
    Co. and George Kleine, dated June
    6, 1912, similar to Exhibit 3 to
    Answer of Patents Co.; Defend-
    ants' Exhibit 47................ III    1309

License Agreement, Patents Co. and
    George Kleine, June 20, 1913; De-
    fendants' Exhibit 48 ........... III    1310

Supplemental License Agreement,
    Patents Co. and George Kleine,
    dated on or about Jan. 26, 1909,
    similar to Exhibit 2 to Answer of
    Patents Co.; Defendants' Exhibit
    49 .......................... III      1329

GEORGE KLEINE, Continued:  VOL.  PAGE

Answer of Kleine Optical Co. in case
of Edison Mfg. Co. v. Kleine Optical Co., April 2, 1908; Petitioner's Exhibit 171.................  II  906

Article in Show World May 16, 1908,
by Streyckmans, *re* Petition of
Kleine Optical Co. v. Edison Mfg.
Co.; Petitioner's Exhibit 259.....  V  2545

Article by George Kleine in Show
World March 7, 1908, entitled
"Kleine Talks—Biograph Com-
pany Denies Validity of Patents";
Petitioner's Exhibit 271.........  VI  3347
(See also Petitioner's Exhibit 263,
Vol. V, p. 2509.)

Article by George Kleine in Show
World April 4, 1909, entitled
"Kleine Disputes Validity of Edison Patents"; Petitioner's Exhibit 272 ......................  VI  3357

Letter, George Kleine to Greater New
York Film Rental Co., Jan. 23,
1909; Petitioner's Exhibit 96.....  I  384

Letter, Kleine Optical Co. to Edison
Mfg. Co., Feb. 19, 1908; Petitioner's Exhibit 175................  II  968

KOERPEL, JONAS A.:

Direct Examination ................  III  1792–1807
Cross Examination ................     1807–1814
Redirect Examination .............     1814–1815
Recross Examination .............     1815

LANDAU, WILLIAM A.:    VOL.    PAGE

Direct Examination ................ IV    1893–1897
Cross Examination ................. 1898

LEBEAU, RALPH:

Direct Examination ............... IV    2356–2360
Cross Examination ................. 2360–2363
Cross Examination ................. 2459–2460
Redirect Examination .............. 2460–2463

LESSY, MICHAEL:

Direct Examination ............... II    1163–1167
Cross Examination ................. 1167–1170
Redirect Examination .............. 1170

LODGE, JAMES J.:

Direct Examination ............... II    1171–1174
Cross Examination ................. 1174–1189
Redirect Examination .............. 1189–1190
Recross Examination ............... 1190–1205

LONG, SAMUEL:

Direct Examination ............... IV    1898–1917
Cross Examination ................. 1917–1927
Redirect Examination .............. 1927
Cross Examination ................. 1971–1982

**Lubin Manufacturing Company:**

License Agreement under the Camera
    and Film Patents, Patents Co. and
    Lubin Mfg. Co., Dec. 18, 1908,
    similar to Exhibit 3 to Petition;
    Petitioner's Exhibit 6 ......... 1    23

Agreement between Edison Mfg. Co.
    and Lubin Mfg. Co., dated Jan. 31,
    1908, similar to Exhibit 1 to An-
    swer of T. A. Edison, Inc.; Peti-
    tioner's Exhibit 92 ............ 1    356

LUBIN MANUFACTURING CO., Continued:   VOL.   PAGE

License Agreement under the Projecting Machine Patents between Patents Co. and Lubin Mfg. Co., dated
Jan. 7, 1909, similar to Exhibit
5 to Petition ................. I   244

Agreement between Lubin Mfg. Co. and
General Film Co., dated April 21,
1910, similar to Exhibit 8 on page
116 of Petition ............... I   552

Supplemental License Agreement, Patents Co. and Lubin Mfg. Co., dated
on or about Jan. 26, 1909, similar to Exhibit 2 to Answer of
Patents Co.; Defendants' Exhibit
49 .......................... III   1329

License Agreement between Patents
Co. and Lubin Mfg. Co., dated
June 6, 1912, similar to Exhibit 3
to Answer of Patents Co.; Defendants' Exhibit 47 ............... III   1309

License Agreement, dated June 20,
1913, between Patents Co. and
Lubin Mfg. Co., similar to Defendants' Exhibit 48 ........... III   1310

Opinion of the Supreme Court of Pennsylvania, Eastern District, in case
of Lubin Mfg. Co. v. Swaab, dated
March 31, 1913; Defendants' Exhibit 9 ....................... II   888

LUBIN, SIEGMUND:

Direct Examination ............... V   3045–3050
Cross Examination ............... VI   3081–3089
Redirect Examination ............. 3089
Recross Examination ............. 3089–3090

MACHAT, NATHAN:              VOL.    PAGE

Direct Examination ................ III   1815–1823
Cross Examination ................      1823–1826
Redirect Examination ..............      1826–1827

MANDELBAUM, EMANUEL:

Direct Examination ................ II   1139–1149
Cross Examination ................      1149–1155

MARSEY, HARRY:

Direct Examination ................ IV   1997–2001
Cross Examination ................      2001–2003
Redirect Examination ..............      2003–2004

MARVIN, HARRY N.:

Direct Examination (for Petitioner).. I     7– 257
Cross Examination, Waived by Counsel
    for Defendants ................      257
Direct Examination (for Defendants). III   1246–1467
Direct Examination ................ VI   3253–3278
Cross Examination ................      3278–3307
Redirect Examination ..............      3307–3308
Redirect Examination ..............      3315–3324
Recross Examination ..............      3308–3313
Recross Examination ..............      3324

Extract from Testimony given by H. N.
    Marvin, July 9, 1910, in case of
    Patents Co. v. Chicago Film Ex-
    change; Petitioner's Exhibit 77.. I    249

Letter, Thomas Armat to H. N. Mar-
    vin, July 30, 1908; Petitioner's
    Exhibit 65 ..................... I    234

Letter, H. N. Marvin to Thomas Armat,
    Oct. 5, 1908; Petitioner's Exhibit
    66 ............................ I    235

Letter, H. N. Marvin to F. L. Dyer,
    Oct. 28, 1908; Petitioner's Ex-
    hibit 67 ....................... I    236

HARRY N. MARVIN, Continued:                VOL.      PAGE

Letter, Kleine Optical Co. to H. N. Marvin, Oct. 30, 1908; Petitioner's
Exhibit 68 .....................     I      237

Letter, H. N. Marvin to George Kleine,
Nov. 2, 1908; Petitioner's Exhibit
69 ...........................     I      238

Letter, H. N. Marvin to George Kleine,
Nov. 6, 1908; Petitioner's Exhibit
70 ...........................     I      241

Letter, H. N. Marvin to George Kleine,
Nov. 23, 1908; Petitioner's Ex-
hibit 71 ......................     I      242

Letter, H. N. Marvin to F. L. Dyer,
Nov. 23, 1908; Petitioner's Ex-
hibit 72 ......................     I      243

Letter, H. N. Marvin to Thomas Armat,
Nov. 24, 1908; Petitioner's Ex-
hibit 73 ......................     I      244

Letter, Thomas Armat to H. N. Marvin,
Nov. 23, 1908; Petitioner's Ex-
hibit 74 ......................     I      245

Letter, G. F. Scull to H. N. Marvin,
Dec. 24, 1908; Petitioner's Ex-
hibit 75 ......................     I      246

Letter, G. F. Scull to H. N. Marvin,
Dec. 30, 1908; Petitioner's Ex-
hibit 76 ......................     I      248

Statement entitled "The Position of the
American Mutoscope & Biograph
Co.," published in Moving Picture
World, Feb. 15, 1908, signed by
Marvin and Kennedy; Petition-
er's Exhibit 54..................     I      131
See also ......................     VI     3310

HARRY N. MARVIN, Continued:    VOL.    PAGE

Testimony given by H. N. Marvin in
case of Greater New York Film
Rental Co. v. Biograph Co. and
General Film Co., in the District
Court for the Southern District of
New York, Sept. 9, 1913; Petition-
er's Exhibit 274............... VI   3369

MATTHEWS, MISS ANNA S.:
Direct Examination .............. V   2913–2938
Direct Examination ..............     3019–3045
Cross Examination ............... VI  3147–3154
Redirect Examination ............     3154

**Melies, George and Gaston:**

License Agreement under the Camera
and Film Patents between Patents Co. and George and Gaston
Melies, dated about Feb., 1909,
similar to Exhibit 3 to Petition;
Petitioner's Exhibit 6 .......... I   23

Agreement between George and Gaston Melies and General Film Co.,
dated April 21, 1910, similar to
Exhibit 8 on page 116 of Petition ........................ I   552

Agreement between Edison Mfg. Co.
and George and Gaston Melies,
dated Jan. 31, 1908; similar to Exhibit 1 to Answer of T. A. Edison,
Inc.; Petitioner's Exhibit 92..... I   356

Agreement, dated Dec. 7, 1904, between
George Melies and others, *in re*
suits on Edison Patent 589,168 and
Reissues; Defendants' Exhibit 112 III  1765

Supplemental License Agreement, Patents Co. and George and Gaston
Melies, dated on or about Jan. 26,
1909, similar to Exhibit 2 to Answer of Patents Co.; Defendants'
Exhibit 49 .................... III  1329

MELIES, GEORGE AND GASTON, Continued: VOL.   PAGE

License Agreement between Patents
Co. and George and Gaston Melies,
dated June 6, 1912; similar to
Exhibit 3 to Answer of Patents
Co.; Defendants' Exhibit 47 ..... III  1309

License Agreement, dated June 20, 1913,
between Patents Co. and George
and Gaston Melies, similar to Defendants' Exhibit 48 ............ III  1310

Opinion in case of George Melies Co. v.
Patents Co. and Others, October,
1912; Defendants' Exhibit 39..... II  1191

MICHAEL, JULIUS H.:

Direct Examination ................ II  1155–1159
Cross Examination ................ 1160–1162

MILDER, MAX:

Direct Examination ................ V  2821–2831
Cross Examination ................ 2832–2838
Redirect Examination .............. 2838

MILES, HERBERT:

Direct Examination ................ II  1218–1225

MOGLER, JOSEPH:

Direct Examination ................ V  2795–2799

MORGAN, HOUSTON N.:

Direct Examination ................ V  2768–2776
Cross Examination ................ 2777

MORGAN, JOSEPH P.:

Direct Examination ................ IV  2307–2312
Cross Examination ................ 2312–2314
Redirect Examination .............. 2314
Redirect Examination .............. 2315
Recross Examination .............. 2315

MORRIS, SAMUEL E.:

Direct Examination ................ V  2650–2655

**Motion Picture Patents Company:** VOL. PAGE

Charter of Motion Picture Patents Company, dated Sept. 9, 1908, printed as Exhibit 1 to Petition; Petitioner's Exhibit 1 .......... I 14

Agreement, Preliminary, for Assignment of Patents, Patents Co. and Biograph Co., dated Dec. 18, 1908, printed as Exhibit 1 to Answer of Biograph Co.; Petitioner's Exhibit 3, ............................. I 15

Agreement, Preliminary, for Assignment of Patents, Patents Co. and Edison Mfg. Co., dated Dec. 18, 1908, printed as Exhibit 2 to Petition; Petitioner's Exhibit 2 ...... I 15

Agreement, Preliminary, for Assignment of Patents, Patents Co. and Armat Co., dated Dec. 18, 1908, printed as Exhibit 1 to Answer of Armat Co.; Petitioner's Exhibit 4 I 15

Agreement, Preliminary, for Assignment of Patents, Patents Co. and Vitagraph Co. of America, dated Dec. 18, 1908; Petitioner's Exhibit 5 ..................... I 16

License Agreement under Camera and Film Patents, between Patents Co. and Biograph Co., dated Dec. 18, 1908; similar agreements executed by each of the other Licensed Manufacturers; printed as Exhibit 3 to Petition; Petitioner's Exhibit 6 I 23

Supplemental License Agreement, Patents Co. and Biograph Co., Jan. 26, 1909, printed as Exhibit 2 to Answer of Patents Co.; similar agreements executed by each of the other Licensed Manufacturers; Defendants' Exhibit 49 ........... III 1329

MOTION PICTURE PATENTS CO., Continued:   VOL.   PAGE

License Agreement, June 6, 1912, between Patents Co. and Biograph
Co., under Camera and Film Patents, printed as Exhibit 3 to
Answer of Patents Co.; similar
agreements executed by each of
the other Licensed Manufactur-
ers; Defendants' Exhibit 47..... III   1309

License Agreement, Patents Co. and
George Kleine, dated June 20,
1913, under Camera and Film
Patents; similar agreements executed by each of the other Licensed Manufacturers; Defend-
ants' Exhibit 48 ............... III   1310

License Agreement between Patents
Co. and Gaumont Co., March 2,
1909, under Camera and Film Patents; Petitioner's Exhibit 127 ... I   398

License Agreement, Patents Co. and
Kinemacolor Co. of America, Aug.
4, 1913, under Camera and Film
Patents; Defendants' Exhibit 51 III   1335

License Agreement under the Projecting Machine Patents between Patents Co. and Armat Moving Picture Co., dated Jan. 7, 1909, printed as Exhibit 5 to Petition; similar agreements also executed between Patents Co. and Edengraph
Mfg. Co., Edison Mfg. Co., Enterprise Optical Mfg. Co., Lubin Mfg.
Co., Nicholas Power Co., Eberhard
Schneider, Selig Polyscope Co.,
Spoor & Co., Vitagraph Co. of
America, dated Jan. 7, 1909; American Moving Picture Machine Co.,
dated Feb. 13, 1909, Biograph Co.,
dated April 20, 1909, and Gaumont
Co., dated early in 1909.......... I   244

MOTION PICTURE PATENTS CO., Continued: VOL. PAGE

Exchange License Agreement attached
to Circular of Patents Co., to
Film Rental Exchanges, dated Jan.
12, 1909; identical with Exhibit
4 to Petition; Petitioner's Exhibit 8 ...................... I 36

Exchange License Agreement between
Patents Co. and Kinetograph Co.,
dated Dec. 28, 1912, being Form
of License Agreement between Patents Co. and the Rental Exchanges; printed as Exhibit 4 to
Petition; Petitioner's Exhibit 130a I 548

Exchange License Agreement, Patents
Co. and blank; Form adopted in
June, 1913; Defendants' Exhibit
50 .......................... III 1330

Licensed Exhibitor's Certificate, valid
to June 30, 1909; Petitioner's Exhibit 42 ...................... I 103

Agreement, Patents Co., Edison Mfg.
Co., and Eastman Kodak Co., Jan.
1, 1909; Petitioner's Exhibit 133.. I 558

Agreement, Patents Co. and Eastman
Kodak Co., dated Jan. 15, 1909;
Petitioner's Exhibit 134 ........ I 582

Agreement, Patents Co., Edison Mfg.
Co. and Eastman Kodak Co., Feb.
14, 1911; Petitioner's Exhibit 135 I 632

Agreement, Patents Co., Edison Mfg.
Co. and Biograph Co., Feb. 14,
1911; Petitioner's Exhibit 136... I 643

MOTION PICTURE PATENTS CO., Continued: VOL. PAGE

Agreement, Patents Co. and General
Film Co., dated April 21, 1910,
printed as Exhibit 7 to Petition;
Petitioner's Exhibit 130 ........ I 547

Affidavit of James J. Lodge in case
of Greater New York Film
Rental Co. v. Motion Picture Patents Co., verified Dec. 15, 1911;
Petitioner's Exhibit 217 ........ II 1183

Pink Cards Issued by Patents Co., being
notice to suspend service of a Theatre, June 9, 1911; Petitioner's
Exhibits 124, 125 and 126........ I 472

Circulars to Film Rental Exchanges;
Petitioner's Exhibits 7 to 33..... I 29- 82

Circular to Licensed Exchanges, Feb.
24, 1909, being List of Licensed
Manufacturers, Importers and Exchanges; Petitioner's Exhibit 13.. I 52

Circular to Licensed Exchanges, Feb.
27, 1909, being List of Licensed
Manufacturers of Moving Picture
Machines; Petitioner's Exhibit 14. I 59

Circulars and Bulletins to Licensed Exhibitors; Petitioner's Exhibits 34
to 53 ......................... I 87- 117

Circular Letter, Patents Co. to Exhibitors, re Standard Film Exchange,
dated Sept. 22, 1910; Petitioner's
Exhibit 186 ................... II 1061

Circular by Patents Co. to Licensed
Exchanges, re List of Licensed Exhibitors, Feb. 5, 1909; Petitioner's Exhibit 9................. II 930

MOTION PICTURE PATENTS CO., Continued:   VOL.      PAGE

Correspondence, Patents Co. and L. M.
    Swaab; Petitioner's Exhibits 144,
    145, 146, 147, 148, 149, 150, 152a,
    152b, and 155 .................   II     805

Exhibitors' Application for License,
    January, 1909; Petitioner's Ex-
    hibit 35 ......................   I      94

Form of Notice to Suspend Service of
    Theatres sent by Patents Co. to
    Exchanges, dated Nov. 16, 1911;
    Petitioner's Exhibit 88..........   I     336

Another Form of Notice to Suspend
    Service of Theatres by Patents Co.
    to Exchanges, dated Nov. 1, 1912;
    Petitioner's Exhibit 89..........   I     337

Form Used in Writing to an Exhibitor
    Relative to the Opening of a New
    Theatre in His Vicinity; Petition-
    er's Exhibit 40.................   I     102

Printed Form of Letter Used by Pat-
    ents Co. early in 1909, when Re-
    fusing to Refund License Fee;
    Petitioner's Exhibit 41..........   I     102

Letter, Standard Film Exchange to Pat-
    ents Co., July 15, 1910; Petition-
    er's Exhibit 196................   II    1175

Letter, Imperial Film Exchange to Pat-
    ents Co., dated April 15, 1910; De-
    fendants' Exhibit 10............   II     994

MOTION PICTURE PATENTS CO., Continued: VOL. PAGE

Letter, MacDonald & Bostwick to Imperial Film Exchange, April 18, 1910; Petitioner's Exhibit 202.... II 1089

Letters, Patents Co. to Greater New York Film Rental Co.; Petitioner's Exhibits 103 to 120, inclusive ......................... I 448– 465

Letters, Patents Co. to Greater New York Film Rental Co.; Petitioner's Exhibits 137, 138, 140, 141, and 142 ...................... II 672

List of Licensed Manufacturers, Importers and Exchanges, contained in Circular to Licensed Exchanges, dated Feb. 24, 1909; Petitioner's Exhibit 13 .................... I 52

List of Licensed Manufacturers, Importers and Exchanges, contained in Circular Letter to Exhibitors, dated Jan. 22, 1909; Petitioner's Exhibit 34 .................... I 87

Additional List of Licensed Film Exchanges, contained in Notice to Exhibitors, Jan. 27, 1909; Petitioner's Exhibit 36............. I 95

List of Licensed Manufacturers of Moving Picture Machines, Feb. 27, 1909; Petitioner's Exhibit 14..... I 59

List of Film Exchanges whose Licenses were Cancelled or Terminated by the Patents Co. down to January, 1912; Petitioner's Exhibit 61.... I 188

MOTION PICTURE PATENTS CO., Continued: VOL. PAGE

List of Licenses Cancelled by Patents
Co., on Account of Exhibit of Unlicensed Motion Pictures, dated
March 25, 1913; Petitioner's Exhibit 235 ...................... II 1243

List of Theatres to which Patents Co.
refused to grant Licenses, dated
March 25, 1913; Petitioner's Exhibit 236 ...................... II 1243

List of Theatres whose names were sent
to the Exchanges by Patents Co.,
with Statement that they should
not be supplied with Service,
dated March 25, 1913; Petitioner's Exhibit 237................ II 1243

List of Theatres whose Licenses were
Cancelled on Account of Loaning
or Subrenting Licensed Motion Pictures, March 25, 1913; Petitioner's Exhibit 238................ II 1243

List showing new Licenses granted to
Theatres by Patents Co. where the
License had been previously Cancelled, dated March 25, 1913; Petitioner's Exhibit 239............ II 1244

Opinion in case of Geo. Melies Co. v.
Patents Co. et al., in the United
States Court of Appeals for the
Third Circuit, October Term, 1912;
Defendants' Exhibit 39.......... II 1191

MOTION PICTURE PATENTS CO., Continued: VOL. PAGE

Opinion of the Circuit Court of Appeals,
District of Columbia, in case of
Chicago Film Exchange v. Patents
Co., on Film Patent Reissue No.
12,192, by Chief Justice Shepard,
dated Dec. 2, 1912; Petitioner's
Exhibit 59 ..................... I 175

Statement entitled "Special Payments
made by Licensed Exchange Exhibitors"—not introduced; Petitioner's Exhibit 156 ........... II 830

Statement of Film Royalties paid to
Patents Co. by Licensed Manufacturers and Importers, 1909 to
1913; Defendants' Exhibit 45.... III 1305

Statement of Cancellations and Rein-
statements by Patents Co., of Licenses of Exhibitors taking service from Greater New York Film
Rental Co.; Defendants' Exhibit
46 .......................... III 1308

Statement of Exchange Licenses Granted or Offered Subsequent to Feb. 1,
1909; Defendants' Exhibit 100.... III 1458

Statements by Patents Company showing number of places in United
States in which motion pictures
were exhibited, separated as to Licensees and Non-Licensees of Patents Co., Defendants' Exhibits 144,
154, 155, 156, 157 and 158.
As of Oct. 31, 1910 .............. V 3026
As of January 30, 1911 .......... V 3028

MOTION PICTURE PATENTS CO., Continued: VOL.    PAGE

    As of July 3, 1911 .............. V    3030
    As of December 18, 1911 ......... V    3032
    As of July 7, 1912 ............. V    3034
    As of July 21, 1913 ............ V    2934

    Statements by Patents Company show-
      ing Cities in United States of 100,-
      000 and over in which Motion Pic-
      tures were Exhibited, separated as
      to Licensees and Non-Licensees of
      Patents Company, Defendant's Ex-
      hibits 145, 159, 160, 161, 162 and
      163.
    As of October 31, 1910 ........... V    3036
    As of January 30, 1911 .......... V    3038
    As of July 3, 1911 ............. V    3040
    As of December 18, 1911 ......... V    3042
    As of July 7, 1912 ............ V    3044
    As of July 21, 1913 ............ V    2936

    Replevin Suits instituted by the Manu-
      facturers Licensed by Motion Pic-
      ture Patents Company, from March
      11, 1909, to Jan. 6, 1913; Petition-
      er's Exhibit 220 ............... VI    3341
  See also.......................... I     389
  See also.......................... II   1217

    Suits brought under the Latham Pat-
      ent No. 707,934, by Motion Picture
      Patents Co., between June 14,
      1909, and July 15, 1911; Petition-
      er's Exhibit 275a .............. VI    3391

    Suits brought under the Pross Patent
      No. 722,382, by Motion Picture Pat-
      ents Co., between June 14, 1909,
      and July .15, 1911; Petitioner's
      Exhibit 276..................... VI    3392

Motion Picture Patents Co., Continued: VOL. PAGE

Suits brought on Camera Patent No.
12,037, after the Assignment of
that Patent to Motion Picture Patents Co., Defendants' Exhibit 184. VI 3270

Testimony of F. L. Dyer in case of Patents Co. v. Independent Moving
Picture Co., Feb. 27, 1911; Petitioner's Exhibit 172............. II 919

**Moving Picture World:**

Statement entitled "The Position of the
American Mutoscope & Biograph
Co.," published in Moving Picture
World Feb. 15, 1908, signed by H.
N. Marvin and J. J. Kennedy; Pe-
titioner's Exhibit 54............ I 131
See also ....................... VI 3310

Statement entitled "The Facts," or
"Biograph Company Define their
Position," issued to the trade by
Biograph Co., published in Moving
Picture World March 14, 1908;
Petitioner's Exhibit 55.......... I 132
See also ....................... VI 3310

Advertisement printed in Moving Pic-
ture World Nov. 16, 1907, entitled
"Convention of Manufacturers and
Film Renters," re Meeting at Fort
Pitt Hotel, Pittsburgh; Petition-
er's Exhibit 252............... V 2477

Article printed in Moving Picture
World Nov. 23, 1907, entitled "The
Pittsburgh Conference;" Petition-
er's Exhibit 253............... V 2480

MOVING PICTURE WORLD, Continued:          VOL.     PAGE

Two Articles printed in Moving Picture World Feb. 15, 1908, *re* the
Buffalo Meeting, entitled "The
United Film Service Association
and the Film Manufacturers" and
"The Platform of the Associa-
tion"; Petitioner's Exhibit 254...   V    2494

Advertisement of Philadelphia Film
Exchange in Motion Picture World
March 20, 1909; Defendants' Ex-
hibit 36 ......................   II    1168

Advertisement of Philadelphia Film
Exchange in Motion Picture World
March 27, 1909; Defendants' Ex-
hibit 37 ......................   II    1169

Advertisement of Philadelphia Film
Exchange in Motion Picture World
April 3, 1909; Defendants' Ex-
hibit 38 ......................   II    1170

Advertisement of Motion Picture Dis-
tributing & Sales Co., in Motion
Picture World July 23, 1910, with
List of Independent Buying Ex-
changes July 13, 1910; Defendants'
Exhibit 131 ..................   V    2874

Advertisement of Motion Picture Distributing & Sales Co., in Motion
Picture World Oct. 29, 1910, with
List of Buying Exchanges Oct. 22,
1910; Defendants' Exhibit 132....   V    2877

MURRAY, WILLIAM T.:

Direct Examination ...............   V    2859–2861
Cross Examination ................        2861
Redirect Examination .............        2861–2862
Recross Examination ..............        2862

NEWSOME, H. M.:  VOL.  PAGE

    Direct Examination ................ V 3009–3017
    Cross Examination ................ 3017–3019

NICHOLS, HARRY E.:

    Direct Examination ................ IV 2321–2328
    Cross Examination ................ 2454–2456
    Redirect Examination ............. 2456–2457
    Redirect Examination ............. 2457–2458
    Recross Examination .............. 2457

NOTICE OF FIRST HEARING ............ I 4

**Opinions:**

OPINION of the Circuit Court of Appeals,
2nd Circuit, in the first case on the
Camera and Film Patent No. 589,168,
between the Edison and Biograph Cos.,
and reported in 114 Fed., 926, by Circuit Judge Wallace; Petitioner's Exhibit 58 ......................... I 151

OPINION of the Circuit Court of Appeals
2nd Circuit, in the second case on the
Camera Patent, Reissue No. 12,037, reported in 151 Fed., 767, by Circuit
Judge Lacombe; Petitioner's Exhibit
59 .............................. I 166

OPINION of Judge Kohlsaat in Thomas A.
Edison v. Selig Polyscope Co., on
Camera Patent Reissue 12,037, filed
Jan. 29, 1910, as of Oct. 24, 1907, in
the U. S. Circuit Court of Appeals for
the Northern District of Illinois, Eastern Division; Defendants' Exhibit 110 III 1617

OPINION of Circuit Court of Appeals, Second
Circuit, March 18, 1911, in cases of Motion Picture Patents Co. v. Yankee Film
Co., and M. P. P. Co. v. William Steiner (187 Fed., 1017); Petitioner's Ex-
bibit 273 ......................... VI 3368

OPINIONS, Continued:                              VOL.    PAGE

OPINION of the Circuit Court of Appeals
District of Columbia, on Film Patent
Reissue No. 12,192, by Chief Justice
Shepard, dated Dec. 2, 1912; Peti-
tioner's Exhibit 60 ................    I      175

OPINION of the Supreme Court of Pennsyl-
vania, Eastern District, in Lubin Mfg.
Co. v. Lewis M. Swaab; Defendants'
Exhibit 9 ........................    II      888

OPINION in the case of Geo. Melies Co. v.
Motion Picture Patents Co. *et al.*, in the
United States Court of Appeals, Third
Circuit, October Term, 1912; Defend-
ants' Exhibit 39 ...................    II     1191

OPINION of Judge Coxe in the case of The
Goodwin Film & Camera Co. v. Eastman Kodak Co., United States Circuit
Court of Appeals, Second Circuit; Petitioner's Exhibit 267................    VI     3294

OPINION of Circuit Court of Appeals, Second
Circuit, in the case of Motion Picture
Patents Co. v. Independent Moving Picture Company of America (200 Fed.,
411), Aug. 10, 1912, on the Latham Patent No. 707,934; Petitioner's Exhibit
277 ..............................    VI     3393

ORDER of District Judge Hough in the Matter of Imperial Film Exchange, alleged
bankrupt, confirming the Report of the
Special Master and Dismissing the Petition of the Vitagraph Co. and others
to have said Exchange adjudged an involuntary bankrupt, June 28, 1910; Defendants' Exhibit 158...............    II      853

OPINION of the Circuit Court of Appeals
2nd Circuit, dated May 16, 1912, in the
Matter of Imperial Film Exchange,
alleged bankrupt, affirming Order of
District Court, dismissing Petition
and reversing confirmation of Master's
Report; Defendants' Exhibit 10a.....    II      997

PALMER, WARREN R.:        VOL.    PAGE

Direct Examination ................ V   2941–2946
Cross Examination ................      2946–2948
Redirect Examination ..............      2949
Redirect Examination ..............      2950
Recross Examination ..............      2949–2950

**Patents:**

Armat Patent No. 578,185, dated March
    2, 1897; Defendants' Exhibit 194.   VI   3326

Armat Patent No. 580,749, dated April
    13, 1897; Defendants' Exhibit 195.   VI   3326

Armat Patent No. 673,992, dated May
    14, 1901; Defendants' Exhibit 199.   VI   3326

Casler Patent No. 629,063, dated July
    18' 1899; Defendants' Exhibit 198.   VI   3326

Edison Reissue Patent No. 12,037, dated
    Sept. 30, 1902; Defendants' Ex-
    hibit 185 ..................... VI   3326

Edison Reissue Patent No. 12,192, dated
    Jan. 12, 1904; printed as Exhibit
    9 to Petition and Defendants' Ex-
    hibit 187 ..................... VI   3326

Edison Reissue Patent No. 13,329, dated
    Dec. 5, 1911; Defendants' Exhibit
    186 .......................... VI   3326

Ellwood Patent No. 785,205, dated
    March 21, 1905; Defendants' Ex-
    hibit 192 ..................... VI   3326

Jenkins & Armat Patent No. 586,953,
    dated July 20, 1897; Defendants'
    Exhibit 196 ................... VI   3326

PATENTS, Continued:                    VOL.    PAGE

Latham Patent No. 707,934, dated August 26, 1902; Defendants' Ex-
hibit 200 ......................  VI   3326

Pross Patent No. 722,382, dated March
10, 1903; Defendants' Exhibit 201  VI   3326

Smith Patent No. 673,329, dated April
30, 1901; Defendants' Exhibit 188  VI   3326

Smith Patent No. 744,251, dated Nov.
17, 1903; Defendants' Exhibit 189  VI   3326

Smith Patent No. 770,937, dated Sept.
27, 1904; Defendants' Exhibit 190  VI   3326

Smith Patent No. 771,280, dated Oct.
4, 1904; Defendants' Exhibit 191.  VI   3326

Smith Patent No. 785,237, dated March
21, 1905; Defendants' Exhibit 193.  VI   3326

Steward & Frost Patent No. 588,916,
dated Aug. 24, 1897; Defendants'
Exhibit 197 ...................  VI   3326

**Pathe Freres:**

Agreement between Pathe Freres and
General Film Co., dated April 21,
1910; similar to Exhibit 8 on page
116 of Petition................   I     552

Agreement between Edison Mfg. Co.
and Pathe Freres, dated May 20,
1908, similar to Exhibit 1 to Answer of T. A. Edison, Inc.; Petitioner's Exhibit 92 .............   I     356

PATHE FRERES, Continued:                VOL.      PAGE

License Agreement under the Camera
and Film Patents, Patents Co. and
Pathe Freres, dated on or about
Dec. 18, 1908, similar to Exhibit
3 to Petition; Petitioner's Ex-
bibit 6 ........................    I      23

Supplemental License Agreement, Patents Co. and Pathe Freres, dated
on or about Jan. 26, 1909, similar
to Exhibit 2 to Answer of Patents
Co.; Defendants' Exhibit 49 .....  III    1329

License Agreement between Patents
Co. and Pathe Freres, dated on or
about June 6, 1912; similar to Exhibit 3 to Answer of Patents Co.;
Defendants' Exhibit 47 .........   III    1309

License Agreement, dated on or about
June 20, 1913, between Patents
Co. and Pathe Freres; similar to
Defendants' Exhibit 48 .........   III    1310

Letter, Pathe Freres to Greater New
York Film Rental Co., Nov. 20,
1911; Petitioner's Exhibit 139....  II    689

PEARSON, ELMER R.:

Direct Examination ................  IV   2262–2268
Cross Examination .................       2268–2269
Cross Examination .................       2407–2411
Cross Examination .................       2424–2428
Redirect Examination ..............       2411–2412
Recross Examination ...............       2412–2413
Redirect Examination ..............       2413

PELTIER, ROBERT G.:                          VOL.     PAGE

    Direct Examination ................     V     2643–2646
    Cross Examination ................           2646–2648
    Redirect Examination ..............          2648–2649
    Redirect Examination ..............          2649
    Recross Examination ..............           2649

PELZER, WILLIAM:

    Direct Examination ................     I     258– 291
    Direct Examination ................           325– 342
    Direct Examination ................           388– 397
    Direct Examination ................           538– 557
    Direct Examination ................    II     830– 832

PENMAN, JOHN, JR.:

    Direct Examination ................     V     2630–2634

PETITIONER'S EVIDENCE ................      I       7– 646
                                           II     647–1244

PETITIONER'S REBUTTAL ................     VI     3328-3425

POWELL, ADOLPH:

    Direct Examination ................     V     2740–2744
    Cross Examination ................           2744–2745
    Redirect Examination ..............          2745
    Recross Examination ..............           2745

PRELLER, WILLIAM C.:

    Direct Examination ................    IV     2269–2275
    Cross Examination ................           2413–2423
    Redirect Examination ..............          2423–2424
    Recross Examination ..............           2424

REBUTTAL, Petitioner's ................    VI     3328–3425

**Replevin Suits:**                          VOL.    PAGE

Replevin Suits Instituted by Manufacturers Licensed by Motion Picture
Patents Co., from March 11, 1909,
to Jan. 6, 1913, being Statement
produced by Mr. Pelzer on Direct
Examination—Vol. I, p. 389, introduced for identification Vol. II,
p. 1217, and printed in Volume
VI; Petitioner's Exhibit 220..... VI    3341

Statement made Jan. 11, 1912, by Durant Church to William Pelzer as
to Replevin Suits Instituted by
Mr. Church; Petitioner's Exhibit
218 ...........................  II    1217
(See Petitioner's Exhibit 220, Vol.
VI, p. 3341.)

Statement made by MacDonald & Bostwick as to Replevin Suits Instituted by Motion Picture Patents
Co., and Referred to in Petitioner's Exhibit 218; Petitioner's Exhibit 219 .....................  II    1217
(See Petitioner's Exhibit 220, Vol.
VI, p. 3341.)

ROSENBLUH, LOUIS:
Direct Examination ................  I    357– 387
Direct Examination ................       420– 475
Cross Examination .................  II   700– 730
Redirect Examination ..............       730– 733
Recross Examination ...............       733– 734

ROSENQUEST, J. WESLEY:
Direct Examination ................  V    2910–2913
Cross Examination .................       2913

RUBEN, ISAAC H.:                          VOL.    PAGE

Direct Examination ................    V    2709–2714
Cross Examination .................         2714–2715
Redirect Examination ..............         2715

RULING OF JUDGE RAY on Question Asked L.
M. Swaab by Counsel for Defendants
(Vol. II, pp. 897, 932)..............    II    954,  983

SAWIN, CHESTER W.:

Direct Examination ................    IV    2292–2298
Cross Examination .................         2469–2472
Redirect Examination ..............         2472–2474

SAWYER, ARTHUR H.:

Direct Examination ................    II    736– 741
Cross Examination .................         827– 830

SCHECK, PHILIP J.:

Direct Examination ................    IV    2391–2398
Cross Examination .................         2398–2401
Redirect Examination ..............         2401

SCHERER, HARRY W.:

Direct Examination ................    V    2606–2611
Cross Examination .................         2611–2613
Redirect Examination ..............         2613
Recross Examination ..............         2613

SCHUCHERT, J. A.:

Direct Examination ................    IV    2009–2034
Direct Examination ................         2036–2037
Cross Examination .................         2091–2097
Redirect Examination ..............         2097–2098

SCHWALBE, HARRY:

Direct Examination ................    IV    2138–2148
Cross Examination .................         2150–2158

**Selig Polyscope Company:**

VOL.    PAGE

Agreement between Edison Mfg. Co.
and Selig Polyscope Co., dated Jan.
31, 1908; similar to Exhibit 1 to
Answer of T. A. Edison, Inc.; Petitioner's Exhibit 92............ I    356

License Agreement under Camera and
Film Patents, Patents Co. and
Selig Polyscope Co., Dec. 18, 1908,
similar to Exhibit 3 to Petition;
Petitioner's Exhibit 6 ......... I    23

License Agreement under the Projecting Machine Patents between Patents Co. and Selig Polyscope Co.,
dated Jan. 7, 1909; similar to Ex-
bibit 5 to Petition ............ I    244

Agreement between Selig Polyscope Co.
and General Film Co., dated April
21, 1910; similar to Exhibit 8 on
page 116 of Petition............ I    552

License Agreement between Patents
Co. and Selig Polyscope Co., dated
June 6, 1912; similar to Exhibit
3 to Answer of Patents Co.; Defendants' Exhibit 47 ........... III    1309

License Agreement, dated June 20, 1913,
between Patents Co. and Selig
Polyscope Co.; similar to Defendants' Exhibit 48 ............. III    1310

Supplemental License Agreement, Patents Co. and Selig Polyscope Co.,
dated on or about Jan. 26, 1909,
similar to Exhibit 2 to Answer of
Patents Co.; Defendants' Exhibit
49 .......................... III    1329

SELIG POLYSCOPE CO., Continued:          VOL.     PAGE

Opinion of Judge Kohlsaat in case of
    T. A. Edison v. Selig Polyscope Co.,
    on Camera Patent Reissue 12,037,
    filed Jan. 29, 1910, as of Oct. 24,
    1907, in the U. S. Circuit Court for
    Northern District of Illinois, East-
    ern Division; Defendants' Exhibit
    111 .............................  III   1617

Writ of Injunction, dated Nov. 1, 1907,
    out of Circuit Court for Northern
    District of Illinois, Eastern Divi-
    sion, on the part of T. A. Edison
    directed to Selig Polyscope Co., on
    Reissue Letters Patent No. 12,037;
    Defendants' Exhibit 113.........  IV   1979

Telegram, Selig Polyscope Co. to Great-
    er New York Film Rental Co.,
    April 29, 1912; Petitioner's Ex-
    hibit 123 ......................   I    470

SHIRLEY, SAMUEL H.:

Direct Examination ...............  IV   2280–2286
Cross Examination ................        2437–2440
Redirect Examination .............        2440–2442
Redirect Examination .............        2442
Recross Examination ..............        2442
Recross Examination ..............        2443

Show World:

Article printed in The Show World
    March 7, 1908, entitled "Opposing
    Moving Picture Interests Fire
    First Guns in Great War for Su-
    premacy"; Petitioner's Exhibit 263   V    2503

Article by George Kleine in Show World
    March 7, 1908, entitled "Kleine
    Talks—Biograph Company Denies
    Validity of Patents"; Petitioner's
    Exhibit 271 ...................  VI   3347
    (See also Petitioner's Exhibit 263,
    Vol. V, p. 2509.)

SHOW WORLD, Continued:        VOL.    PAGE

Article printed in Show World March
21, 1908, entitled "Film Magnates
in Chicago Conference; Edison
Company Issues Important State-
ment"; Petitioner's Exhibit 255...    V    2520

Article in Show World March 28, 1908,
entitled "Edison Fires Second Gun
in Film Battle"; Petitioner's Exhibit 256 .....................    V    2528

Article printed in Show World April
25, 1908, entitled "Important Bulletin of Film Association"; Petitioner's Exhibit 257.............    V    2536

Article printed in Show World May 2,
1908, entitled "Film Association
Announces Victory in Edison Liti-
gation"; Petitioner's Exhibit 258..    V    2541

Article printed in Show World May 16,
1908, entitled "Film Battle Waged
in Court; Arguments Heard and
War is Stayed by Agreement. Attorneys Consent to Truce," etc., re
case of Kleine Optical Company v.
Edison Mfg. Co., by H. J. Streyckmans; Petitioner's Exhibit 259...    V    2545

Article by George Kleine in Show
World April 4, 1909, entitled
"Kleine Disputes Validity of Edison Patents"; Petitioner's Exhibit
272 ..........................    VI    3357

SIMONS, EDWIN M.:

Direct Examination ...............    V    2690–2693
Cross Examination ................      2693

SLOCUM, HENRY R.:

Direct Examination ...............    V    2800–2809

SMITH, ALBERT E.:                              VOL.      PAGE

    Direct Examination ................ III   1690–1739
    Cross Examination ................        1739–1760
    Redirect Examination ..............        1760

SMITH, EDWARD M.:

    Direct Examination ................  V    2679–2683
    Cross Examination ................         2683–2685

SOLZ, REUBEN:

    Direct Examination ................ II   1112–1113
    Cross Examination ................        1113–1117
    Redirect Examination ..............        1117–1118

SPOOR, GEORGE K.:

    Direct Examination ................  V    2986–3007
    Cross Examination ................  VI   3052–3069
    Redirect Examination ..............        3069
    Recross Examination ..............         3069–3070

STEPHENS, THOMAS W.:

    Direct Examination ................ IV   2075–2079
    Cross Examination ................        2079–2080

STIEBEL, JOSEPH L.:

    Direct Examination ................  V    2786–2789

**Stipulations:**

STIPULATION as to Objections............    I      6

STIPULATION as to Return of Exhibits......  VI    3434

STIPULATION Waiving Signatures of Wit-
    nesses ..........................  VI    3435

STIPULATION as to Certification of Record...  VI  3435

STIPULATION *re* Defendants' Exhibit No. 164,
    being Docket Entries of Dyer & Dyer,
    etc. ................................  VI    3092

STIPULATIONS, Continued:        VOL.   PAGE

STIPULATION as to Custody of Defendants'
Exhibits Nos. 174 to 183, inclusive..... VI   3313

STIPULATION as to Letters Patent, Defendants' Exhibits Nos. 185 to 201, inclusive VI   3326

STREYCKMANS, HECTOR J.:

Direct Examination ................ II   961– 968
Direct Examination, Recalled......... VI  3347–3363
Cross Examination ................ II  1120–1125

STRUBLE, CORNELIUS D.:

Direct Examination ................ V  2789–2794

SUPER, EDWARD M.:

Direct Examination ................ IV  2107–2109
Cross Examination ................ 2109–2112
Redirect Examination .............. 2112

SURREBUTTAL, Defendants' .............. VI  3427–3434

SWAAB, LEWIS M.:

Direct Examination ................ II   800– 827
Direct Examination, Recalled........ VI  3363–3364
Cross Examination ................ II   877– 900
Cross Examination ................ 932– 961

SWANSON, WILLIAM H.:

Direct Examination ................ I   293– 323
Direct Examination ................ 342– 357
Direct Examination ................ 475– 478
Cross Examination ................ 479– 538
Cross Examination ................ II   647– 656
Cross Examination ................ 742– 768
Redirect Examination .............. 768– 769
Recross Examination .............. 769

TALMADGE, ARTHUR E.:

Direct Examination ................ VI  3250–3252
Cross Examination ................ 3252

THOMAS, HORACE M.:                          VOL.      PAGE

    Direct Examination ................  V    2745–2749
    Cross Examination .................       2749
    Redirect Examination ..............       2749–2750
    Recross Examination ...............       2750
    Redirect Examination ..............       2750

THORP, EDGAR A.:

    Direct Examination ................  II   1082–1087
    Cross Examination .................       1087–1089

TREDICK, ALTON:

    Direct Examination ................  IV   2254–2261
    Cross Examination .................       2261–2262
    Cross Examination .................       2401–2405
    Redirect Examination ..............       2405–2406
    Recross Examination ...............       2406–2407

VAN RONKEL, IKE:

    Direct Examination ................  IV   2228–2243
    Cross Examination .................       2243–2254
    Redirect Examination ..............       2254

**Vitagraph Company of America:**

    Agreement, Preliminary, for Assign-
        ment of Patents between the Pat-
        ents Co. and the Vitagraph Co.,
        dated Dec. 18, 1908; Petitioner's
        Exhibit 5 .....................  I      16

    License Agreement under Camera and
        Film Patents, Patents Co. and
        Vitagraph Co., Dec. 18, 1908, simi-
        lar to Exhibit 3 to Petition; Peti-
        tioner's Exhibit 6 .............  I      23

    Agreement between Edison Mfg. Co. and
        Vitagraph Company of America,
        dated Jan. 31, 1908; similar to Ex-
        hibit 1 to Answer of T. A. Edi-
        son, Inc.; Petitioner's Exhibit 92  I    356

VITAGRAPH CO. OF AMERICA, Continued: VOL. PAGE

License Agreement under the Projecting Machine Patents, between Patents Co. and Vitagraph Co., dated Jan. 7, 1909; similar to Exhibit 5 to Petition ............. I 244

Agreement between Vitagraph Company of America and General Film
Co., dated April 21, 1910; similar
to Exhibit 8 on page 116 of Petition ......................... I 552

Supplemental License Agreement, Patents Co. and Vitagraph Co., dated
on or about Jan. 26, 1909; similar
to Defendants' Exhibit 49 ...... III 1329

License Agreement between Patents
Co. and Vitagraph Co., dated
June 6, 1912; similar to Exhibit
3 to Answer of Patents Co.; Defendants' Exhibit 47 .............III 1309

License Agreement, dated June 20, 1913,
between Patents Co. and Vitagraph
Co.; similar to Defendants' Ex-
bibit 48 ...................... III 1310

Report of Special Master in the Matter
of Imperial Film Exchange, an alleged bankrupt, June 20, 1910;
Petitioner's Exhibit 157......... II 841

Order of District Judge Hough in the
Matter of Imperial Film Exchange,
alleged bankrupt, confirming the
above report and dismissing the petition of Vitagraph Company and
others to have said Exchange adjudged an involuntary bankrupt,
dated June 28, 1910; Petitioner's
Exhibit 158 ................... II 853

VITAGRAPH CO. OF AMERICA, Continued:     VOL.     PAGE

Opinion of the Circuit Court of Appeals, Second Circuit, dated May
  16, 1912, in the Matter of Imperial
  Film Exchange, alleged bankrupt,
  affirming Order of District Court
  dismissing Petition and reversing
  confirmation of Master's Report;
  Defendants' Exhibit 10a .......  II     997

Writ of Injunction dated Sept. 18, 1900,
  out of Circuit Court for Southern
  District of New York on the part
  of T. A. Edison directed to Vitagraph Co. and Walter Arthur, individually, on Letters Patent 589,-
  168; Defendants' Exhibit 114.....  IV     1985

WALES, HERBERT C.:

Direct Examination ................  IV     2286–2292
Cross Examination ................          2443–2445
Redirect Examination ..............         2445–2447
Recross Examination ..............          2447
Redirect Examination ..............         2447–2448
Recross Examination ..............          2448–2449
Redirect Examination ..............         2449

WARNER, JACOB:

Direct Examination ................  V     2777–2782

WATERS, PERCIVAL L.:

Direct Examination ................  V     2961–2974
Cross Examination ................   VI    3072–3080
Redirect Examination ..............         3080
Recross Examination ..............          3080–3081
Redirect Examination ..............         3081

WEISS, ALFRED:

Direct Examination ................  VI    3364–3368
Cross Examination ................          3379–3384
Redirect Examination ..............         3384–3385
Redirect Examination ..............         3386–3387
Recross Examination ..............          3385–3386
Recross Examination ..............          3387–3391

WILLIAMS, THEODORE W.:                    VOL.     PAGE

    Direct Examination ................ V    2951–2954
    Cross Examination ................       2954–2956

WORTHINGTON, CHARLES L.:

    Direct Examination ................ V    2956–2958
    Cross Examination ................       2958–2959

WRIGHT, WILLIAM:

    Direct Examination ................ VI   3427–3428
    Cross Examination ................       3428–3430
    Redirect Examination ..............       3430
    Redirect Examination ..............       3431
    Recross Examination ..............       3430–3431